NAKAMA 2

NAKAMA 2

INTERMEDIATE JAPANESE: *COMMUNICATION, CULTURE, CONTEXT*

Enhanced Third Edition

Yukiko Abe Hatasa
Hiroshima University

Kazumi Hatasa
Purdue University
School of Japanese, Middlebury College

Seiichi Makino
Princeton University

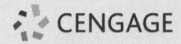

Australia • Brazil • Mexico • Singapore • United Kingdom • United States

Nakama 2: Intermediate Japanese: Communication, Culture, Context, Enhanced Third Edition
Yukiko Abe Hatasa, Kazumi Hatasa, Seiichi Makino

Product Director: Marta Lee-Perriard

Senior Product Team Manager:
Heather Bradley-Cole

Associate Product Manager: Melody Sorkhabi

Product Assistant: Samantha Caveny

Senior Content Manager: Isabelle Alouane

Learning Designer: Jarmila Sawicka

Senior Digital Delivery Lead: John Lambert

Marketing Manager: Mary Reynolds

Associate Market Development Manager:
Jessica Quila

IP Analyst: Christine M. Myaskovsky

Manufacturing Planner: Fola Orekoya

Senior Designer: Sarah B. Cole

Cover Designer: Brenda Carmichael

Cover Image: David Madison/The Image Bank/
Getty Images

For product information and technology assistance, contact us at
Cengage Customer & Sales Support, 1-800-354-9706
For permission to use material from this text or product,
submit all requests online at **www.cengage.com/permissions**.
Further permissions questions can be emailed to
permissionrequest@cengage.com.

Library of Congress Control Number: 2019950843

Student Edition:
ISBN: 978-0-357-14203-5

MindTap IAC:
ISBN: 978-0-357-14200-4

Loose-Leaf Edition:
ISBN: 978-0-357-14204-2

Annotated Instructor's Edition:
ISBN: 978-0-357-44170-1

Cengage
200 Pier 4 Boulevard
Boston, MA 02210
USA

Cengage is a leading provider of customized learning solutions with employees residing in nearly 40 different countries and sales in more than 125 countries around the world. Find your local representative at **cengage.com**.

Cengage products are represented in Canada by Nelson Education, Ltd.

To learn more about Cengage platforms and services, register or access online learning solutions, or purchase materials for your course, visit **cengage.com**.

Printed in Mexico
Print Number: 03   Print Year: 2020

ABOUT THE AUTHORS

Professor Yukiko Abe Hatasa received her Ph.D. in linguistics in 1992 from the University of Illinois at Urbana-Champaign. She is known nationwide as one of the premier Japanese methodologists in the United States and as an experienced coordinator of large teacher-training programs. She has served as the coordinator of the Japanese language program at the University of Iowa and is currently a professor of the Department of Teaching Japanese as a Second Language at Hiroshima University, where her primary responsibilities are teacher training and SLA research.

Professor Kazumi Hatasa received his Ph.D. in education in 1989 from the University of Illinois at Urbana-Champaign. He is currently a professor at Purdue University and Chair of Department of East Asian Languages. He was Director of the Japanese School at Middlebury College from 2005 to 2018. He is recognized internationally for his work in the integration of information technology in Japanese language instruction. He also works with traditional performing artists such as rakugo storytellers to integrate them in language instruction.

Professor Seiichi Makino is an emeritus Professor of Japanese and Linguistics at Princeton University. He received his Ph.D. in linguistics in 1968 from the University of Illinois at Urbana-Champaign. He is an internationally prominent Japanese linguist and scholar, recognized throughout the world for his scholarship and for his many publications. Before beginning his tenure at Princeton University in 1991, he taught Japanese language, linguistics and culture at the University of Illinois while training lower-division language coordinators. An experienced ACTFL oral proficiency trainer, he frequently works internationally to train Japanese instructors in proficiency-oriented instruction and in the administration of the Oral Proficiency Interview.

CONTENTS

CHAPTER 2: TRAVEL PLANS

CHAPTER 3: PREPARING FOR THE FUTURE

Chapter 4: Asking for Favors

Chapter 5: Asking for and Giving Directions

CHAPTER 6: GIFTS

CHAPTER 7: COOKING

TO THE STUDENT

Nakama 2 is based on the principle that learning another language means not just acquiring facts and information, but also acquiring skills that we learn by doing. To further this goal, the chapter materials continue the approach established in *Nakama 1* by systematically involving you in many activities that incorporate the language skills of listening, speaking, reading, and writing. We also believe that culture is an integral component of language. To help you become familiar with Japanese culture, your text includes high-interest culture readings and relevant communication strategies. Chapter dialogues, each featuring the Japanese-American exchange student and her friends introduced in *Nakama 1*, cover a range of real-world situations that you are likely to encounter in Japan. The enhanced edition is supported by the online platform, MindTap.

ORGANIZATION OF THE TEXTBOOK

Nakama 2 consists of a preliminary review chapter and eleven regular chapters. The review chapter covers the vocabulary and grammar presented in *Nakama 1*. Each of chapters 1–11 focuses on a common communicative situation and contains the following features:

- **Chapter Opener:** Each chapter opens with a theme-setting photograph and a list of chapter contents by section. Keeping in mind the objectives listed at the top of the opener will help you focus on achieving your learning goals.

- **Vocabulary:** The vocabulary is presented in thematic groups, each followed by a variety of communicative activities and activities in the context in which the vocabulary would normally be used. Supplemental vocabulary is also provided throughout the chapter for additional exposure to the Japanese language. All active vocabulary is listed by function at the beginning of each chapter.

- **Dialogue:** The lively dialogues center on Alice Ueda, a Japanese-American college student who is spending two years studying in Japan. Through the dialogue and accompanying audio, you will get to know a series of characters and follow them through typical events in their lives. Related activities will reinforce your understanding of the content, discourse organization, and use of formal and casual Japanese speech styles.

- **Japanese Culture:** Up-to-date culture readings in English explore social, economic, and historical aspects of Japanese life that are essential to effective communication.

- **Grammar:** Clear, easy-to-understand grammar explanations are accompanied by sample sentences and notes that help you understand how to use the grammar appropriately. In-class pair and group activities let you practice immediately what you've learned. As there is a high correlation between successful communication and grammar accuracy, this section is especially important. New grammar tutorial videos and printable worksheets are available in MindTap.

- **Listening:** Useful strategies and pre-listening activities for general comprehension precede the section's main listening practice. Post-listening activities concentrate on more detailed comprehension and apply what you have learned to other communicative purposes.

- **Communication:** This section will provide you with knowledge and practice of basic strategies to accelerate your ability to communicate in Japanese.

- **Kanji:** Chapters 1 through 11 introduce a total of 254 **kanji**. The section begins with useful information such as the composition of individual characters, word formation, and how to use Japanese dictionaries. The presentation of each character includes stroke order to help you master correct penmanship when writing in Japanese and to prepare you for the reading section. The MindTap platform features new stroke-order tutorials and printable **kanji** writing practice activities.

- **Reading:** Each reading passage begins with a reading strategy and includes pre- and post-reading activities. **Hiragana** subscripts (**furigana**) are provided for unfamiliar **kanji** throughout the textbook. The readings include a small number of unknown words to help you develop strategies for understanding authentic texts.

- **Integration:** Integrated practice wraps up every chapter using discussion, interviewing, and role-play activities that interweave all the skills you've learned in the current and previous chapters.

STUDENT COMPONENTS

- **Student Text:** Your student text contains all the information and activities you need for in-class use. Each chapter contains vocabulary presentations and activities, a thematic dialogue and practice, grammar presentations and activities, cultural information, reading selections, writing practice, and ample communicative practice. Valuable reference sections at the back of the book include a list of particles, a **kanji** list, and a Japanese-English and English-Japanese glossary.

- **MindTap:** MindTap for *Nakama 2* supports the core textbook and offers a media-enhanced eBook, easy access to program audio and video, asynchronous communication activities, flashcards, downloadable practice worksheets, and a mobile app for language learning on-the-go. MindTap also offers a course management system that enhances students' language-learning experience.

- **Text Audio Program:** The Text Audio Program contains recordings of all the listening activities in the text as well as all active chapter vocabulary. The audio activity clips and the vocabulary pronunciations are available in MindTap within the media-enabled eBook. These audio materials are designed to maximize your exposure to the sounds of natural spoken Japanese and to help you practice pronunciation.

- **Student Activities Manual (SAM):** The SAM includes out-of-class practice of the material presented in the textbook. Each chapter of the SAM includes a workbook section, which focuses on written vocabulary, grammar, **kanji** writing and reading practice, and a lab section, which focuses on pronunciation and listening comprehension, including Dict-a-Conversation dictation activities.

- **SAM Audio Program:** The SAM Audio Program corresponds to the audio portion of the SAM and reinforces your pronunciation and listening skills. The audio is available in MindTap.

- **Video Program:** The multi-tiered *Nakama 2* video program includes videos that bring to life topics and cultural segments tied to the theme of each chapter. In addition, new grammar tutorials and kanji stroke-order videos are available in MindTap.

ACKNOWLEDGMENTS

The authors and publishers would like to thank Satoru Ishikawa for his hard work on the new activities in the Student Activities Manual. They would also like to thank Shoko Asay and Takahisa Koide of Boise State University for their work in revising the testing program for this edition.

They are especially grateful to Yu Rim Kim for authoring new material, Minami Matsuo for editing, Ellen (Jihyun) Kulpa for her consulting, Lori Tyler, and Julie Scardiglia at Integra.

The authors are also grateful to the following people at Cengage for their valuable assistance during the development of this project: Melody Sorkhabi, Jarmila Sawicka, Isabelle Alouane, Elyssa Healy, John Lambert, and Macy Lawrence.

Review Chapter

序章（じょしょう）

101cats/iStockGetty Images

復習
ふくしゅう
Review

かんじのふくしゅう

Kanji Review

Activity 1   Circle the character that does not belong in the group.

1. 山　川　木　水　上
2. 五　八　円　千　百
3. 父　男　弟　母　妹
4. 曜　週　年　分　何
5. 買　好　話　食　見
6. 行　出　読　来　帰
7. 休　手　目　足　耳
8. 金　月　土　上　火
9. 入　寝　度　聞　書

Activity 2   How are the **kanji** in each pair different?

1. 木　休
2. 男　田
3. 読　話
4. 耳　目
5. 入　八

6. 上　土
7. 三　川
8. 姉　妹
9. 母　毎
10. 回　口

Activity 3   下のことばを読んで下さい。

1. 山川　田中　中田　小川　大川　川中　中川　山中　上田　本田　小山
　 下田　中本　山本　金田　高田　高山　古川　古山　古田　友田　川口

2. 大きい　小さい　高い　一番　新しい　古い　安い　大変（な）
　 大丈夫（な）　好き（な）　大好き（な）　親切（な）　寒い　暑い　多い
　 少ない　明るい　元気（な）上手（な）

3. 時　今　三十分　何時　一時　二時　三時　四時　五時　六時　七時
　 八時半　九時　十時　三時間　朝　毎朝　今朝　毎晩　今晩　午前　午後
　 毎日　今日　明日　昨日　二日前　三日後　何曜日　日曜日　月曜日
　 火曜日　水曜日　木曜日　金曜日　土曜日　週末　毎週　今週　来週
　 先週　二週間　毎月　今月　来月　先月　春　夏　秋　冬　毎年　今年
　 来年　去年　昨年　今度　休みの日　誕生日

4. 一本　二本　三本　四本　五本　六本　七本　八本　九本　十本　一つ
　　二つ　三つ　四つ　五つ　六つ　七つ　八つ　九つ　十　一人　二人
　　三人　何人　百円　千円　一万円　一回　二回　三回

5. 行く　来る　帰る　食べる　飲む　見る　聞く　読む　書く　話す　出る
　　会う　買う　起きる　寝る　作る　入る　晴れる　冷える　上がる　下がる
　　分かる　思う　上がって下さい　何をしますか　何ですか　一緒に
　　　　　　　　　　　　　　　　　　　　　　　　　　　　　　　しょ

6. 私　友達　先生　学生　留学生　大学院生　一年生　日本人　いい方
　　　だち　　　　　　　　りゅう　　　　いん
　　男の人　女の人　男の子　女の子　子供　家族　両親　兄弟　お子さん
　　父　お父さん　母　お母さん　姉　お姉さん　兄　お兄さん　妹さん
　　弟さん　ご主人　〜番目
　　　　　しゅ

7. 目　口　耳　足　手　人

8. 天気　雨　雪　風　温度　何度　東　西　南　北　南東　北東　北西
　　南西

9. 山　川　水　木　上　下　中　本　本棚　家　大学　学校　中学　高校
　　　　　　　　　　　　　　　　　だな
　　大学院　中国　〜学　学生会館　銀行　本屋　新聞　店　喫茶店　飲み物
　　　いん　　ごく　　　　　かん　　ぎん　　　や　　　　　　　きっさ　　　もの
　　和食　洋食　朝御飯　昼御飯　晩御飯　電話　日本語　生活　思い出
　　わ　　よう　　ごはん　　ごはん　　ごはん　でん　　　　　　かつ
　　図書館
　　と　かん

Activity 4　下のひらがなの文をかんじとひらがなで書いて下さい。
　　　　　　　　　　　　　ぶん

1. かねだ：　こんにちは。
　　おがわ：　こんにちは。あついですね。
　　かねだ：　ええ、そうですね。きょうは　どこかいくんですか。
　　おがわ：　ええ、いまから　ぎんこうにいって、そのあと
　　　　　　　デパートにかいものにいくんです。
　　かねだ：　そうですか。

2. 　　　こども：　ねえ、おかあさん。
　　おかあさん：　なに？
　　　　こども：　きょうのばんごはん、なに？
　　おかあさん：　そうね、こんばんはカレーよ。
　　　　こども：　え、またカレー？　カレーよりおすしがいいな。
　　おかあさん：　そうねえ。おすしもたべたいねえ。でも、きょうは、
　　　　　　　　　もうカレーつくったから、あした　おすしでどう？
　　　　こども：　うん、いいよ。

3. わたしは　ふるた　たかこです。こうこう　さんねんせいです。わたしのかぞくは　ごにんかぞくです。ちちと　ははと　あにと　おとうとがいます。ちちは　だいがくの　せんせいで　ははは　ほんやに　つとめています。ちちは　にほんじん　ですが、ははは　ちゅうごくじんです。あには　だいがくいんせいで、てとあしが　ながいです。　おとうとはちゅうがくせいです。　げんきで　いいこなんですが、いちばんしたなので、　あまえんぼう (spoiled child) です。あにも　おとうとも　だいすきですが、おんなの　きょうだいが　いないので、おねえさんか (or) いもうとが　ほしいです。

4. やまもと：　おそいね。

   なかがわ：　ごめん。きのうのばん、じゅうにじまで、バイトだったから。

   やまもと：　え、じゃあ、なんじごろ　うちにかえったの？

   なかがわ：　いちじごろだったとおもう。そのあと、しゅくだいして、さんじごろ　ねたんだ。

   やまもと：　じゃあ、あまりねてないの？

   なかがわ：　そうだね。はちじはんに　おきたから、ごじかんはんぐらいかな。

   やまもと：　そうだったんだ。それは、たいへんだね。

Chapter 1
The Japanese sound system and hiragana

Activity 1   Work with a partner and act out the following role plays.

1. It is a cold morning. You run into your teacher on your way to school.
2. Your class is over. Say goodbye to your teacher.
3. In the evening you decide to go out for a walk, and you run into a neighbor.
4. Your neighbor gives you a Japanese fruit. Thank him/her and ask him/her the name of the fruit.
5. Your neighbor tells you that he/she has just bought a スマホ. You don't know what it is. Ask him/her what スマホ means.
6. You are attending an orientation for international students at Joto University in Tokyo. You don't know the attendees sitting near you and would like to get to know them.
7. It is a sunny Sunday afternoon. You are walking in a park and run into your friend's mother.
8. You are in a teacher's office and are about to leave.

Activity 2   What kind of requests would you make in the following situations?

1. You didn't understand what your teacher just said.
2. You are talking with a salesperson on the phone, but you can't hear her/him well.
3. You are talking with a friend on the phone who is speaking too fast.
4. You want to know how your name is written in **kana**.
5. You are about to make an announcement to your class, so you need everybody's attention.
6. You want to know the reading of an unknown **kanji**.
7. You want to know the meaning of an unknown **kanji** (*meaning*=いみ).
8. You want your teacher to check to see whether you have written a particular **kanji** correctly.
9. You want to know the Japanese word for "numbers."

Activity 3   Convert the following polite expressions to their casual forms.

1. あれは日本語で何といいますか。
2. ゆっくり話して下さい。
3. このかんじのいみ (*meaning*) は何ですか。
4. このかんじを読んで下さい。
5. もう一度いって下さい。
6. *Library* は日本語で何といいますか。
7. このしゃしんを見て下さい。
8. 「らくご」って何ですか。

Activity 4   Go back to situations 1 through 5 in Activity 1. You are now talking with a friend. Change what you would say accordingly.

Activity 5   Look at the products below and try to figure out what each is. Ask your teacher or a classmate about any unfamiliar words or **kanji**. Ask questions in both polite and casual forms.

1

2

3

4

5

Chapter 2
あいさつとじこしょうかい

Activity 1 You are at a party and trying to get to know the other people there. First create a name tag by selecting one of the words from each of the following categories.

名前：　スミス　キム　チョー　シュミット　山中

大学：　ニューヨーク大学　シカゴ大学　シドニー大学　東京大学

学年：　大学院　一年生　二年生　三年生　四年生

せんこう：　アジアけんきゅう　文学　れきし　英語

くに (country)：　アメリカ　日本　かんこく　中国　オーストラリア　カナダ

Activity 2 Using the identity you have just created in Activity 1, greet and talk with as many people as you can. Remember them as you will later be asked to introduce them to others.

Example:　A:　はじめまして。私はスミスです。どうぞよろしく。

B:　はじめまして。シュミットです。こちらこそ、どうぞよろしく。

A:　シュミットさんのせんこうは何ですか。

B:　れきしです。

Activity 3 Using the names in Activity 1, ask others about the people across the room at the party. Find out their names, what they study, where they are from, etc. Remember that you are across the room from the people you are asking about.

Example:　A:　あの男の人はだれですか。

B:　ああ、あの人はキムさんですよ。

A:　キムさんの大学はどこですか。

B:　東京大学です。

A:　そうですか。キムさんはどこから来ましたか。

B:　かんこくから来ました。

Activity 4 You have just joined the Japan Student Association. Introduce yourself, providing appropriate information from the categories below.

名前：＿＿＿＿＿＿＿＿＿＿＿＿＿＿＿＿＿＿＿＿＿＿＿＿

〜年生：＿＿＿＿＿＿＿＿＿＿＿＿＿＿＿＿＿＿＿＿＿＿

大学の名前：＿＿＿＿＿＿＿＿＿＿＿＿＿＿＿＿＿＿＿＿

せんこう：＿＿＿＿＿＿＿＿＿＿＿＿＿＿＿＿＿＿＿＿＿

くに (country)：＿＿＿＿＿＿＿＿＿＿＿＿＿＿＿＿＿＿

しゅみ：＿＿＿＿＿＿＿＿＿＿＿＿＿＿＿＿＿＿＿＿＿＿

Activity 5 Work with a partner. Using the names of the cities in the box below, create a conversation in which one person asks the other what time it is in each city. Write the answer.

Example: A: 東京は今何時ですか。

B: 午前十一時ですよ。

A: そうですか。どうも。

B: いいえ。

> 東京、ニューヨーク、ロンドン、ホノルル、バンコク、シドニー、
> デリー、モスクワ、カイロ、バンクーバー

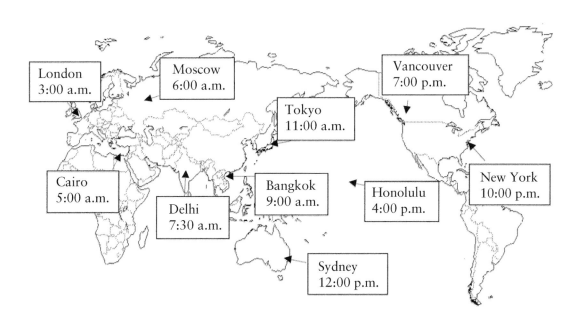

Chapter 3
毎日の生活
かつ

Activity 1   しつもんに日本語でこたえて下さい。

1. 毎朝何時ごろ起きますか。
2. 週末は何時ごろ寝ますか。
3. 朝御飯を食べますか。何を食べますか。
   ご はん
4. 日本語のじゅぎょうは何曜日にありますか。
5. たいてい何時ごろ家に帰りますか。
6. 毎日何時間ぐらいべんきょうしますか。
7. 毎日何時間ぐらい日本語のべんきょうをしますか。
8. テレビやえいがをよく見ますか。
9. お風呂に入りますか。シャワーをあびますか。
   ふ ろ
10. 週末よく何をしますか。

Activity 2   Ask each of your classmates the questions in Activity 1, and find out what the most common answers are for each question.

Activity 3   Form groups of four. Find out what your classmates do each day of the week. What classes do they have? Do they have a part-time job? Who has the most classes in a single day? What do they do over the weekend? Etc.

Example: A: ～さんは月曜日に何をしますか。

B: 私は九時と十時と三時にじゅぎょうがありますから、
大学に行きます。

A: そうですか。大変ですねえ。～さんはどうですか。
へん

C: 私は月曜日にはじゅぎょうはありません。

D: そうですか。じゃあ、月曜日には、いつも何をしていますか。

C: そうですね。家でゆっくりしています。

名前 (な)	月曜日	火曜日	水曜日	木曜日	金曜日	土曜日	日曜日
私							

Activity 4 Look at the train schedule and write down when the following trains depart from Shin-Osaka and arrive at Tokyo.

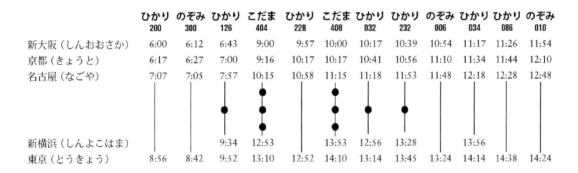

	ひかり 200	のぞみ 300	ひかり 126	こだま 404	ひかり 228	こだま 408	ひかり 032	ひかり 232	のぞみ 006	ひかり 034	ひかり 086	のぞみ 010
新大阪 (しんおおさか)	6:00	6:12	6:43	9:00	9:57	10:00	10:17	10:39	10:54	11:17	11:26	11:54
京都 (きょうと)	6:17	6:27	7:00	9:16	10:17	10:17	10:41	10:56	11:10	11:34	11:44	12:10
名古屋 (なごや)	7:07	7:05	7:57	10:15	10:58	11:15	11:18	11:53	11:48	12:18	12:28	12:48
新横浜 (しんよこはま)			9:34	12:53		13:53	12:56	13:28		13:56		
東京 (とうきょう)	8:56	8:42	9:52	13:10	12:52	14:10	13:14	13:45	13:24	14:14	14:38	14:24

Example: ひかり200ごう (No.) は六時に新大阪を出て、八時五十六分に
(しん　さか)
東京につきます (arrive)。
(きょう)

1. のぞみ 300
2. こだま 404
3. ひかり 126
4. のぞみ 006
5. ひかり 086
6. ひかり 232

Activity 5   Change the following into casual speech.

1. A: よくお風呂に入りますか。
    B: いいえ、あまり入りません。
2. A: 朝御飯を食べますか。
    B: いいえ、食べません。
3. A: 何を飲みますか。
    B: コーヒーを飲みます。
4. A: 今晩何をしますか。
    B: そうですね。テレビを見ます。
5. A: どこに行きますか。
    B: 図書館に行きます。

Activity 6   Act out the following role-plays.

1. You run into a friend whom you have not seen for a while. Greet him/her and ask what he/she is doing these days.
2. A Japanese student who has recently arrived in your country wants to know what college life is like. Explain what college students in the U.S. do on a typical day.

Chapter 4
日本のまち

Activity 1   Fill in the blanks with the appropriate words for buildings and places.

1. コーヒーを飲みに行くところは＿＿＿＿＿＿＿＿＿＿＿＿＿です。
2. 手紙を出しに行くところは＿＿＿＿＿＿＿＿＿＿＿です。
3. お金がたくさんあるところは＿＿＿＿＿＿＿＿＿＿＿です。
4. 日本のえきのちかくにある小さいたてものは、たいてい＿＿＿＿＿＿＿＿＿です。
5. 本やざっしを買うところは＿＿＿＿＿＿＿＿＿＿です。
6. 本やざっしや新聞を読みに行くところは＿＿＿＿＿です。

Activity 2   Define the following words in Japanese using the type of descriptive phrases that were used in Activity 1.

Example: カフェはコーヒーを飲みに行くところです。

1. こうえん   5. 図書館
2. デパート   6. コンビニ
3. えき   7. りょう
4. たいいくかん

👥 **Activity 3** Work with a partner. Imagine that you and your partner are at the police box. You are unfamiliar with this area, so you ask your partner, a police officer, for directions to the following places. Create a conversation using こそあど、〜は〜にあります／います and 〜に〜があります／います.

Example: A: あのう、すみません。

B: はい、何ですか。

A: 本屋はどこですか。

B: 本屋ですか。そこに銀行がありますね。

A: ええ。そのしろいたてものですね。

B: そうです。本屋はそのひだりですよ。

A: そうですか。どうも。

Activity 4　Work with a partner. Complete the following dialogue using こそあど words. The first one is done for you as an example.

スミス：　木村さん、＿＿それ＿＿、何の辞書？

木村：　英語の辞書よ。

スミス：　そうなんだ。

木村：　＿＿＿＿＿けしゴムは、どうしたの。

スミス：　＿＿＿＿＿？　つくえの下にあったんだよ。だれのかな。

木村：　さあ、分からない。あ、じゃあ、＿＿＿＿＿ノートもつくえの下にあったの？

スミス：　ううん。＿＿＿＿＿は　ぼくのだよ。

木村：　あ、そう。

スミス：　じゃ、＿＿＿＿＿えんぴつは　木村さんの？

木村：　ううん、＿＿＿＿＿は　私のじゃないけど。

スミス：　そうなんだ。じゃ、＿＿＿＿＿ハンドバッグは？

木村：　あ、＿＿＿＿＿は　私のよ。

スミス　　　　　　　　　　木村

Activity 5　Work with a partner. Think of food or items found at school or in a home that can be described in terms of type, color, shape, or size. Your partner will ask questions about the object's type, color, shape, size, etc., and try to figure out what the item is. Try to use the expressions in the box.

あかい	きいろい	あおい	ちゃいろい	しろい	くろい
大きい	小さい	古い	新しい	高い	ひくい　かたい　やわらかい
まるい	四角い	ながい	ほそながい	みじかい	あまい　にがい

Example: A: それは食べ物_{もの}ですか。

B: ええ、そうです。

A: それはしろいですか。

B: いいえ、しろくありませんよ。

A: じゃあ、あかいですか。

B: ええ、あかいです。

A: 大きいですか。

B: いいえ、大きくありません。

A: じゃあ、それは、トマトですか。

B: はい、そうです。

Activity 6   Work with a partner. Act out the following role-play. Use casual speech.

You are visiting your friend's college. Ask him/her about various facilities and their locations.

Chapter 5
日本の家

Activity 1   Which of the following items might you find in the rooms or buildings listed in 1–4 below? Use casual speech.

ベッド　いす　つくえ　本棚_{だな}　電話_{でん}　時計_{けい}　テレビ　コンピュータ
たんす　おしいれ　まど　ドア　いぬ　ねこ　ソファ　テーブル　ふとん
こくばん　ビデオ　しゃしん　え

Example: A: りょうのへやにはどんなものがある？

B: そう（だ）ね。ベッドがあるよ。それから、つくえもあるよ。

1. りょうのへや
2. きょうしつ
3. 日本の家
4. 子供のへや

Activity 2   Work with a partner. Describe the objects shown in one of the pictures below. Your partner's task is to determine which picture you are describing.

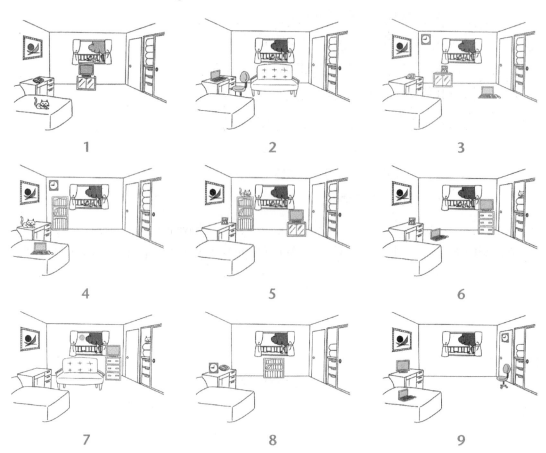

Activity 3   Work with a partner. Imagine that you are moving into a new room with your belongings and your partner is helping you. One partner should draw on the blank room where they would want to place their belongings. Then out loud they should describe their layout to their partner, who will draw the objects on the blank room as they are described. Compare the two pictures to see if they are identical. Use <location> に <object> をおいて (*put*) 下さい when telling your partner where to place the items.

ベッド　つくえ　コンピュータ　ソファ　テレビ　たんす　本棚　時計
　　　　　　　　　　　　　　　　　　　　　　　　だな　とけい

Example:　まどの前に、つくえをおいて下さい。

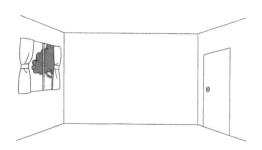

Activity 4   Change the following dialogues or statements into casual speech.

1. A: このへやのとなりに何がありますか。
   B: お手洗いがあります。
2. A: つくえの下に何がいますか。
   B: ねこがいます。かわいいですよ。
3. A: そこにだれがいますか。
   B: スミスさんがいます。インターネットをしていますよ。
4. あ、あそこにきれいなさかながいますよ。見て下さい。

Activity 5   Work with a partner. Act out the following role-plays.

1. You are visiting a Japanese friend's house, and you have just arrived at the door. Greet your friend.
2. You are looking for an apartment. First, fill out the types of features of the apartment you want. Your friend knows a person who wants to sublet an apartment. Ask your friend about the apartment.

Number of rooms	_____	Surrounding area	_____
Size of apartment	_____	Types of rooms	_____
Old or new apartment	_____		

Chapter 6
休みの日

Activity 1   Work with a partner. Ask what your partner did last weekend and circle the activities that he/she did. Use the て -form to connect activities.

Example: A: 週末は何をしましたか。

B: そうですね。土曜日は、朝せんたくとそうじをして、午後

出かけました。日曜日は友達を家によんで、ゲームをしました。

りょうりを作る	せんたくをする	そうじをする	しごとをする	新聞／ざっしを読む
買い物に行く	手紙／メールを書く	日本語で話す	電話をかける	おんがくを聞く
出かける	コンサートに行く	ピクニックに行く	うんどうする	テニスをする
プールでおよぐ	ジョギングをする	友達に会う	さんぽをする	あそびに行く
ゲームをする	家でゆっくりする	お風呂に入る	友達をよぶ	パーティをする

Activity 2   Work with a partner. Use the expressions below to ask your partner about his/her childhood classes and teachers. Find out why your partner thought that these classes or teachers were or were not good (interesting, difficult, etc).

Example: A: どのじゅぎょうがよかったですか／よくなかったですか。

B: アメリカのれきしのじゅぎょうがよかったですね。

A: どんなところがよかったですか。(*What did you like about it?*)

B: 先生がやさしくて、おもしろかったですね。

		どうして
いい／じゅぎょう	はい	
	いいえ	
好き／先生	はい	
	いいえ	
大変／クラス へん	はい	
	いいえ	

Activity 3   Change the style of the following exchanges into casual speech.

1. A: 昨日どこに行きましたか。

   B: 友達とデパートに行って、えいがを見ました。
   だち

2. A: 今日は文学のテストでしたね。テストはどうでしたか。
   ぶん

   B: とてもながくて、むずかしかったんです。

3. A: 昨日のジョンソンさんのパーティにはだれが来ましたか。

   B: 田中さんや山本さんやリーさんが来ました。

4. A: 今日、えきまで何で行きますか。

   B: くるまで行って、それから、でんしゃにのります。

5. A: 天気がよさそうですから、一緒にテニスをしませんか。
   しょ

   B: あの、したいんですけど、ちょっとつごうがわるくて。

6. A: あ、あそこに古川さんがいますよ。

   B: そうですね。あ、中山さんもいますよ。何をしているん
   でしょうか。

7. A: ちょっと図書館に行きますから、ここでまっていて下さい。
   と かん

   B: はい、分かりました。

Activity 4 Work with a partner. Ask your partner about his/her most memorable trip (good or bad). Use the following items to learn what your partner did on the trip and whether he/she enjoyed the activities. Use casual speech.

1. When, where, and with whom you went
2. What you did
3. How the trip was (why it was good/bad)

Activity 5 Work with a partner. Imagine you are giving a speech about the lifestyle of U.S. college students to a group of visiting Japanese students. With your partner, create a questionnaire asking about your classmates' lifestyles. Write questions about their daily lives, workload, how they spend weekends, etc. Then interview your classmates and write a speech draft with your partner using the questionnaire.

Chapter 7
好きなものと好きなこと

Activity 1 Work with a partner. First, write on your own as many words as you can that belong to and/or are associated with each category. Then ask your partner what he/she has written and circle the items that you and your partner have in common. Then write the words from your partner's list that you don't have.

Example:　A:　どんなやさいの名前を書きましたか。
　　　　　B:　私はレタスとにんじんを書きました。
　　　　　A:　私もレタスとにんじんを書きました。そして、トマトも
　　　　　　　書きました。

1. やさい　＿＿＿＿＿＿＿＿＿＿＿＿＿＿＿＿＿＿＿＿
2. にく　＿＿＿＿＿＿＿＿＿＿＿＿＿＿＿＿＿＿＿＿
3. くだもの　＿＿＿＿＿＿＿＿＿＿＿＿＿＿＿＿＿＿＿＿
4. 飲み物　＿＿＿＿＿＿＿＿＿＿＿＿＿＿＿＿＿＿＿＿
5. スポーツ　＿＿＿＿＿＿＿＿＿＿＿＿＿＿＿＿＿＿＿＿
6. おんがく　＿＿＿＿＿＿＿＿＿＿＿＿＿＿＿＿＿＿＿＿
7. レジャー (leisure)　＿＿＿＿＿＿＿＿＿＿＿＿＿＿＿＿

Activity 2 Work as a class. Ask your classmates what foods and beverages they like or dislike. Determine which ones are the most and least popular in your class.

Example: A: どんな食べ物が好きですか。
　　　　　 B: 〜や〜が好きです。
　　　　　 A: 〜はどうですか。
　　　　　 B: そうですね。〜は〜（な）ので、あまり好きじゃありません。

Activity 3 Work with a partner. Ask your partner what sports or music he/she likes or dislikes and why. Use casual speech.

Example: A: どんなスポーツが好き？
　　　　　 B: 〜が好きだよ。／〜が好き。
　　　　　 A: 〜は、どう？
　　　　　 B: 〜（だ）から、あまり好きじゃないんだ。

Activity 4 A very rich person wants to give away a large sum of cash, but only to the person whose tastes most closely mirror certain criteria. Select one of your classmates to be the donor, and ask him/her about his/her favorite things. Then interview your classmates and select the person who is closest to the donor in terms of taste.

Example: A: 〜さんはどんなスポーツが好きですか。
　　　　　 B: やきゅうが好きです。
　　　　　 A: そうですか。テニスはどうですか。
　　　　　 B: テニスも好きですよ。でも、あまり上手じゃないんです。
　　　　　 A: そうですか。じゃあ、おんがくは何が好きですか。

Activity 5 Work with a partner. Ask your partner what he/she likes best and least among the items in each of the following categories. Rank them.

やさい　にく　くだもの　飲み物　スポーツ　おんがく　レジャー (leisure)

Example: A: やさいの中で何が一番好きですか。
　　　　　 B: トマトが一番好きですね。
　　　　　 A: にんじんとレタスはどうですか。
　　　　　 B: にんじんもレタスも好きですが、にんじんの方がレタスより好きです／にんじんもレタスも好きじゃないですが、にんじんの方がレタスよりまし (tolerable) ですね。

Chapter 8
買い物
もの

Activity 1   Work with a partner. First, write the appropriate counter for each of the following objects. Then, your partner should write a number (not larger than 100) and call out one of the objects on the list. Say the correct number-counter expression for the number of that item. You get one point for each correct answer.

Example: Your partner writes 24 and says「T シャツ」You say
「にじゅうよんまい」

セーター	ベルト	えんぴつ	ネックレス	かばん
———	———	———	———	———
さかな	いぬ	本	ざっし	りんご
———	———	———	———	———
ねこ	パンツ	けしゴム	シャツ	ノート
———	———	———	———	———

Activity 2   Work in groups of four. First, guess how much the following items cost in Japan (in yen) and record your guess in the table below. Then ask the other group members for their guesses, and record them as well. Your instructor will provide actual prices. The person who makes the most accurate guesses is the winner.

Example: A: たまごはいくらだと思いますか。

B: 100 円ぐらいだと思います。〜さんはいくらぐらいだと
思いますか。

A: 200 円ぐらいだと思います。

	私			
たまご（12）				
テレビ（32 インチ)				
ガソリン (*gasoline*) 1 リットル＊				
おんがくの CD				
ジーンズ				

＊1 リットル＝ 0.264 ガロン

Activity 3 Work with a partner. Ask your partner what he/she would do under the following circumstances. A list of verbs is provided to assist you. 〜としたら means *suppose (that)* ~ or *if* ~.

行く　帰る　飲む　入る　読む　書く　聞く　買う　作る　話す　あそぶ
うたう　およぐ　とる　つつむ　あびる　起きる　食べる　寝る　見る
かける　出かける　入れる　見せる　来る

Example:　A: 大金持ち (*rich person*) だったとしたら、どんなことが
　　　　　　　　おおがね も
　　　　　　　　したいですか。

　　　　　B: そうですね。くるまをたくさん買いたいですね。

1. 大金持ちだったとしたら、
　　おおがね も
2. あと二か月でしぬ (*die in two months*) としたら、
3. 男／女になったとしたら、
4. 今よりかっこよくなったとしたら、

Activity 4 Work with the class. Ask your classmates what they want most right now, and report the most interesting desire to the class. Use casual speech.

Example:　A: 〜さん、今、何が一番ほしい？
　　　　　B: 日本に行くお金がほしいかな。
　　　　　　　　　　　かね
　　　　　A: どうして日本に行きたいの？
　　　　　B: 日本にかれし (*boyfriend*) がいるから会いたいの。
　　　　　A: ああ、そうなんだ。

　　　　　〜さんは、かれしに会いたいから、日本に行くお金を
　　　　　ほしがっています。

名前 な	ほしいもの

Activity 5   Work with a partner. Act out the following role-plays.

1. You are at a department store. You want to know on which floor kimonos are sold. Ask the person at the information desk.
2. You are in the accessories department and want to see a necklace in the case. Get the attention of a sales clerk and ask him/her to take it out for you.
3. You are in the woman's clothing department. You want to buy a present for your mother but cannot decide what to get. Your budget is 10,000 yen. Get the attention of a sales clerk and explain what you need help with. Respond to questions about the size, color preference, etc. Have the clerk show you some items.
4. A sales clerk has shown you a sweater. Ask the clerk how much it is. If it is too expensive, ask for a more affordable one. Ask for ones with different colors. Ask for a bigger (or smaller) size.
5. Select the items that you want. Ask the sales clerk to box them up and gift wrap it for you.

Chapter 9
レストランとしょうたい

Activity 1   しつもんに日本語でこたえて下さい。

1. 「和食」って何ですか。
2. 和食にはどんな食べ物がありますか。
3. ラーメンは何りょうりですか。
4. アメリカにはどんなりょうりがありますか。
5. メキシコりょうりにはどんな食べ物がありますか。
6. どんな飲み物が好きですか。どんな飲み物がきらいですか。

Activity 2   Work in groups of four. You are at a diner. Ask each other what you are going to order and fill out the chart. Use both formal and casual speech.

Example: A: ～さんは何にしますか。
           B: 私は～にします。

           A: ～さん、何にする？
           B: えっと、～にする。

名前 な	飲み物と食べ物 もの　　もの

Activity 3   Work with a partner who was not in your group in Activity 2. You are still in the restaurant and your partner is the server. Using the information from Activity 2, order for your group.

Example: Server: ごちゅうもんは？
           A: コーラを三つおねがいします。
           Server: はい、コーラを三つですね。
           A: それから、～

Activity 4   You are conducting a survey on breakfast habits. Ask your classmates if they had anything to eat or drink for breakfast today. If they have, find out what. Then determine how many people didn't eat breakfast at all, and find out what the most popular breakfast food for the class was.

Example: A: キムさん、今朝、何か食べましたか。
           B: いいえ、何も食べませんでした。
           A: 何か飲みましたか。
           B: ええ、コーヒーとオレンジジュースを飲みました。

名前 な	食べ物 もの	飲み物 もの
キム	-------	コーヒー、オレンジジュース

Activity 5　Work as a class. Look at the event calendar below. Choose three things you would like to see or do and invite your classmates to go with you.

Example:　A:　〜さん、来週の水曜日に大学のスタジアム (*stadium*) でコンサートがあるんだけど、一緒に行きませんか。
　　　　しょ

　　　　B:　水曜日ですか、いいですね。／

　　　　すみません、木曜日にテストがあるから、水曜日はちょっと。

月曜日　ジャズコンサート（Jay's Cafe、十時）

火曜日　「Cats」ミュージカル（大学のコンサートホール、七時半）

水曜日　ロックコンサート（大学のスタジアム、九時）

木曜日　バスケットボールのしあい (*game*)（大学のたいいくかん、六時）

金曜日　クラシックのコンサート（大学のコンサートホール、八時）

土曜日　ブックセール（まちの図書館、十二時）
　　　　　　　　　　と　かん

　　　　日本のえいが（スミスホール、四時と七時）

日曜日　バザー (*bazaar*)（キャンパス、一時〜五時）

Activity 6   Look at the following pictures and give your impressions of the nature of the items being depicted by using 〜そうです.

1

2

3

4

5

6

Activity 7   Work with a partner. Act out the following situations. You will ask your partner to join you in an activity, and then together you must plan the details. Use question word + か／〜ませんか／〜ましょうか／〜ましょう.

Example: You are with your partner and you are thirsty.

A: 〜さん、何か飲みませんか。

B: ええ、いいですよ。じゃあ、どこかカフェに行きましょうか。

A: ああ、いいですね。あそこはどうでしょうか。

B: いいですね。あそこにしましょう。

1.   You and your friend are walking on the street. You feel hungry.
2.   You are free this weekend and want to go somewhere fun.
3.   You are at your friend's house. You think you would like to see a movie. Check the website to see what is playing, and discuss which movie you would like to see, and when, with your partner.

Chapter 10
私の家族

Activity 1 Look at the figures labeled in the family tree below. You are Chris.
Identify each person using an appropriate kinship term and ordinal
number.

Example: キャシーは私の姉です。上から二番目です。

Activity 2   しつもんに日本語でこたえて下さい。

1. 〜さんのクラスには学生が何人いますか。
2. 〜さんの大学には学生が何人ぐらいいますか。先生は何人ぐらい
    いますか。
3. 〜さんは友達が何人ぐらいいますか。
4. このクラスで年が一番下の人は何さいですか。
5. 〜さんは兄弟が何人いますか。〜さんの家族は何人家族ですか。
6. 〜さんは何さいですか。〜さんは上から何番目ですか。下から何番目ですか。

Activity 3 Work with a partner. Ask your partner about his/her family members (their physical characteristics, occupations, their homes, etc.). Use ～ている and ～は～が.

Example: A: ～さんのご家族は何人家族ですか。

B: 五人家族です。

A: へえ、五人ですか。ご家族は、どこにすんでいますか。

B: ロサンゼルスにすんでいます。

A: いいですね。お父さんはどんな方ですか。

B: 目が大きくて、せが高いです。

A: めがねをかけていますか。

B: ええ、かけています。

A: おしごとは何ですか。

B: 大学の先生です。

A: そうですか。

Activity 4 Work with a new partner. Work with your partner to decide on the name of a fictional character, then discuss what you would consider this person's ideal boyfriend or girlfriend in terms of physical characteristics, personality, skills, occupation, etc. Take notes. Use ～ている, ～は～が, and the て-form of verbs.

Example: A: ～さんはどんな人が好きだと思いますか。

B: そうですね。～さんはせが高いから、せが高い人が好きだと思います。

A: そうですか。かおはどんなかおがいいと思いますか。

B: 目が大きくて、はなが高い人がいいと思います。

A: じゃあ、せいかくはどうですか。

B: そうですね。明るくて、やさしい人がいいと思います。

A: 何が上手な人がいいでしょうか。

B: ～さんはテニスが好きだから、テニスが上手な人がいいでしょう。

Activity 5 Restate the following exchanges in casual speech using the types of abbreviations shown in the example.

Example: A: リンダさんはいつもきれいなふくをきていますね。

B: あの人はモデルなんですよ。

A: リンダさん、いつもきれいなふく、きてるね。

B: あの人、モデルなんだ／なのよ。

1. A: お父さんはニューヨークにすんでいるんですか。
   B: いいえ、フィラデルフィアにすんでいます。
2. A: あの人はとてもやせていますね。
   B: ええ、それにとても足がながくて、かっこいいですね。
3. A: あそこで日本人の学生が話していますね。山本さんはどの人ですか。
   B: めがねをかけていて、かみがみじかい人ですよ。
4. A: 学食の前でスミスさんと話している人はだれですか。
   B: ああ、あれは高田さんの妹さんだと思いますよ。

Activity 6 Work with a partner. In his or her mind, your partner will select a celebrity. Quiz your partner about physical characteristics, job, place of residence, clothing, etc., to figure out the celebrity's identity.

Example A: その人、かみながい？

B: うん。

A: じゃあ、何をするのが上手？

B: うた、うたうの。

A: どこにすんでるの？

B: ハリウッドにすんでると思う。

A: ビヨンセ？

B: うん、そう。／ううん、ビヨンセじゃないよ。

Chapter 11
きせつと天気

Activity 1 Identify the following weather symbols in Japanese.

     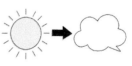

1　　　2　　　3　　　4　　　5　　　6

_____　_____　_____　_____　_____　_____

Activity 2   Work in groups of four. First, each person should choose five different verbs from the list below. He/She should write sentences using the selected verbs, and then act out what has been written in the sentences. The group will try to guess what the person is doing.

Example: B acts out doing laundry:

A: あそんでいますか。

B: いいえ、そうじゃありません。

C: せんたくをしていますか。

B: はい、そうです。

飲む　読む　書く　聞く　買う　作る　話す　あそぶ　べんきょうする
およぐ　とる　あびる　起きる　食べる　寝る　する　あるく　まつ
うたう　入れる　見せる　見る

Activity 3   Describe the following weather conditions using adverbial forms of adjectives and ている.

Example: 風がつよくふいています。

Example

1

2

3

4

5

6

Activity 4 The following chart shows the weather forecast for five locations around the world. Describe the weather in these locations.

Example: 東京は明日はくもりでしょう。気温は15度ぐらいで、あたた
かくなるでしょう。雨はふるかもしれませんが、ふらないかも
しれません。

	東京 （きょう）	アラスカ	ニューヨーク	シドニー	ロサンゼルス
天気	くもり	雪	くもりのち雨	晴れ	くもり時々晴れ （ときどき）
気温	59° F 15° C	-4° F -20° C	41° F 5° C	91.4° F 33° C	77° F 25° C
雨	50%	0%	80%	0%	30%
雪	0%	100%	15%	0%	0%

Activity 5 Describe the seasons in your area, using 〜は〜が and other appropriate phrases.

Example: 春はとてもあたたかくて、天気がいいです。六月と七月は
とても雨が多いです。夏は天気がいい日が多いですが、
とてもむし暑くなります。秋はすずしくて、雨は少ないです。
でも、朝と晩は寒いです。冬は雪がたくさんふって、とても
寒くなります。

Activity 6 Change the following conversations into casual speech.

Example: A: おはようございます。
B: おはようございます。

A: おはよう。
B: おはよう。

1. A: 今日は、朝からちょっと寒いですね。
   B: ええ、本当に寒いですね。北からふいている風もつよいですから。
   A: そうですね。くもっていますが、今晩、雪になるでしょうか。
   B: そうですね。この天気は、雪になるかもしれませんね。

2. A: だれか、ちょっと、ここに来てくれませんか。
   B: いいですよ。今、行きますよ。

3. A: 学生会館の前で電話で話している人はだれですか。
   　　　　 かん 　　 でん

   B: 小川さんですよ。金田さんをまっているんだと思います。

4. A: 今日は朝からいそがしそうですね。

   B: ええ、明日から出かけますから、今日はすることがたくさん
   あったんですよ。

Chapter 12
年中行事
ねんじゅうぎょう じ

Activity 1　　しつもんに日本語でこたえて下さい。

1. 夏休みは何月何日から何月何日までありますか。冬休みはどうですか。春休
   みは？

2. 今学期 (*this semester*) は何月何日にはじまって、何月何日におわりますか。
   　　 き
   来学期はどうですか。
   　　 き

3. 今日は何月何日ですか。昨日は何月何日でしたか。おとといは何月何日
   でしたか。

4. 明日は何月何日ですか。あさっては何月何日ですか。

5. ご家族の誕生日は何月何日ですか。
   　　　　 たん

6. 一か月前は何月何日でしたか。半年前は何月何日でしたか。

7. 一学期 (*one semester*) は何か月ありますか。夏休みは何か月ありますか。
   　 き

Activity 2　　Work in groups of four. Each person should take a guess about how
often or how long students in Japan do the following activities and
share it. Then check with your instructor to find out who made the most
accurate guesses. Use plain form + 〜と思います (*I think that . . .*).

Example:　A: 日本の高校生は一日に何時間ぐらいテレビを見ると思いますか。

　　　　　B: そうですね。一時間ぐらい見ると思います。

　　　　　C: 私は二時間ぐらい見ると思いますよ。

　　　　　D: そうですか。私は三時間ぐらい見ると思います。

	Your guess	＿＿さん	＿＿さん	＿＿さん
1. テレビを見る／一日／時間	＿＿＿＿＿	＿＿＿＿＿	＿＿＿＿＿	＿＿＿＿
2. べんきょうする／一日／時間	＿＿＿＿＿	＿＿＿＿＿	＿＿＿＿＿	＿＿＿＿
3. 寝る／一日／時間	＿＿＿＿＿	＿＿＿＿＿	＿＿＿＿＿	＿＿＿＿
4. アルバイトをする／一週間／日	＿＿＿＿＿	＿＿＿＿＿	＿＿＿＿＿	＿＿＿＿
5. 本を読む／一か月／さつ	＿＿＿＿＿	＿＿＿＿＿	＿＿＿＿＿	＿＿＿＿
6. えいがを見に行く／一か月／度	＿＿＿＿＿	＿＿＿＿＿	＿＿＿＿＿	＿＿＿＿

Activity 3 Work as a class. First, check off the experiences you have had in the past, and write your approximate age or the period in your life when you had the experience. Then ask your classmates whether they have had any of these experiences. If so, ask when. Use casual speech.

Example: A: 日本に行ったことがある？

B: うん、あるよ。

A: そう。いつ行ったの？

B: 高校三年生の時（かな）。／二か月前（くらい）。

	私		＿＿さん	＿＿さん	＿＿さん
	はい	いつ	いつ	いつ	いつ
日本に行く					
ミュージカルを見る					
きものをきる					
ハワイのうみでおよぐ					
ゆうえんちであそぶ					
キャンプをする					
飛行機にのる					
がいこくに行く					
おさしみを食べる					

Activity 4 Work in groups of three. One member should choose a place from the box below and define it using the 〜たり〜たりする form. The other members should try to figure out which place was selected. The person who guesses correctly gets a point. Take turns.

Example: A: 友達とべんきょうしたり、あそんだりするところです。
だち

B: 図書館ですか。
と　かん

A: いいえ。

高校　こうえん　カフェ　ゆうえんち　銀行　はくぶつかん　どうぶつえん
ぎん

うみ　びじゅつかん　水族館　スーパー　デパート　コンビニ　えき
かん

図書館　教会　山　川　びょういん　ゆうびんきょく　たいいくかん
と　かん　きょう

レストラン

Activity 5 Work with a partner. Ask your partner what he did or didn't do as a child.

Example: A: 子供の時どんなものをよく食べましたか。

B: ドーナツ (*donuts*) をよく食べました。

A: へえ、どうしてドーナツをよく食べたんですか。

B: 母がいつも買って来たんです／買って来たからです。

	＿＿＿＿＿さん
子供の時よく食べたもの	
子供の時あまり食べなかったもの	
子供の時よくしたこと	
子供の時あまりしなかったこと	
子供の時よく一緒にあそんだ人	
しょ	

Activity 6 Work with another partner. Report what your Activity 5 partner did or didn't do, using the 〜そうです (hearsay) form. Also, use noun modification.

Example: 〜さんが子供の時よく食べたものは、ドーナツだそうです。

Chapter 1

第一課
だい　か

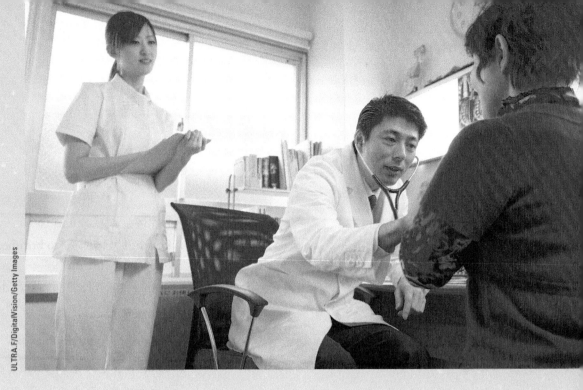

ULTRA.F/DigitalVision/Getty Images

健康
けんこう
Health

単語
たんご

Nouns

アレルギー		allergy
いき	息	breath, いきをする to breathe, いきができない to be out of breath
いしゃ	医者	medical doctor, お医者さん doctor
おなか		stomach
かおいろ	顔色	facial skin tone, complexion
かぜ	風邪	cold, かぜをひく to catch a cold, かぜ (wind) is written with the single character 風.
かた	肩	shoulders, かたがこる to have stiff shoulders
からだ	体	body
きぶん	気分	feeling, spirits, mood, きぶんがわるい to feel annoyed, feel sick/ill/unwell
きもち	気持ち	feeling, sensation, きもちがわるい to feel nausea, feel unpleasant, feel weird, feel revolted
くすり	薬	medicine, drug, ointment
くび	首	neck
けが	怪我	injury
こし	腰	lower back
しょうじょう	症状	symptom
ストレス		stress
せき	咳	cough
せなか	背中	back, upper back
ダイエット		diet
たばこ／タバコ	煙草	cigarette
ねつ	熱	fever, (high) temperature
のど	喉	throat
は	歯	tooth
びょうき	病気	sickness
マッサージ		massage
むね	胸	chest, breast

むり	無理	overwork, overstrain, むりをする to overwork, to overdo it
ゆび	指	finger

う -verbs

うごかす	動かす	to move (something) (transitive verb)
きる	切る	to cut
こる	凝る	to be stiff, かたがこる (to) have stiff shoulders
すう	吸う	to inhale, たばこをすう to smoke
だす	出す	to take out, to prescribe, to submit, くすりをだす to prescribe medicine, 学生がしゅくだいをだす students submit homework, 先生がしゅくだいをだす teachers assign homework
つまる	詰まる	to clog, はながつまる to have a stuffy nose
はかる	計る	to measure, ねつをはかる to check one's temperature
はく	吐く	to exhale, to throw up
はしる	走る	to run
ひく		to catch (a cold), かぜをひく to catch a cold
やすむ	休む	to rest, to be absent, じゅぎょうをやすむ to be absent from class

る -verbs

あける	開ける	to open
あげる	上げる	to raise (something) c.f. あがる to rise
さげる	下げる	to lower (something) c.f. さがる to go down
つける	付ける	to attach, apply (medicine), turn on, くすりをつける to apply an ointment, でんきをつける to turn on the lights
つかれる	疲れる	to grow tired, つかれている to be tired
でる	出る	to come out, せきがでる to cough, ねつがでる to run a fever
やめる	止める	to quit doing (something)
わすれる	忘れる	to forget

Irregular verbs

にゅういんする	入院する	to be hospitalized, 大学びょういんににゅういんする to be admitted to the university hospital

い -adjectives

いたい	痛い	hurt, painful
かゆい	痒い	itchy
ひどい		serious (injury), ひどいけが serious injury
わるい	悪い	bad, かおいろがわるい look pale

な -adjectives

いろいろ (な)	色々 (な)	various
けんこう (な)	健康 (な)	healthy, けんこうな人 healthy person
		can be used as a noun けんこうのため for the sake of health

Adverbs

すぐ		immediately, right away

Particles

を		from, じゅぎょうをやすむ be absent from a class, 大学をそつぎょうする to graduate from college

Expressions

ええっと／すみません、それはちょっと（こまるんですが）。		Well, uh, I'm sorry but . . . (that presents some problems.)
おだいじに。	お大事に。	Please take care of yourself.
～てもいいですか。		May I ～ ?, Is it OK to ～ ?
どうしましたか。／どうしたんですか。		What's wrong?
～たらいいですか。		Should I do ～ ?, どうしたらいいですか。What should I do, 飲んだらいいですか。Should I drink?
はい／ええ、かまいません。		I don't mind. (= yes, please)
はい／ええ、どうぞ。		Yes, please.
はい／ええ、もちろん。		Yes, of course, sure.
はじめてなんですが。	初めてなんですが。	This is my first time. . .
むりをする	無理をする	to push oneself too hard, to overwork
よこになる	横になる	to lie down
よるおそくまで	夜遅くまで	until late at night

単語の練習
たんご　れんしゅう

A. 体にいいことわるいこと、体にいいものわるいもの
からだ　　　　　　　　　　　　からだ

Things that are good for one's health and things that are bad for one's health

けんこうに気をつける	to pay attention to your health, take care of yourself
ダイエットをする	to go on a diet
マッサージをする	to (get a) massage
よく休む やす	to get a good rest
横になる よこ	to lie down
たばこをすう	to smoke (cigarettes)
よるおそくまで起きている	to stay up late at night
むりをする	to push oneself too hard
ストレスがある／ストレスが多い	to be stressed (out)
すぐ色々なことを忘れる いろいろ　　　わす	to be very forgetful, to forget things immediately

おぼえていますか。

アルバイト　散歩　しごと　ジョギング　生活　テニス　あそぶ　歩く　うんどうする
　　　　　　さんぽ　　　　　　　　　　かつ　　　　　　　　　　ある

およぐ　きゅうにやせる　シャワーをあびる　出かける　早く起きる　早く寝る　ふとる
　　　　　　　　　　　　　　　　　　　　　　　　はや　　　　はや

ゆっくりする　元気（な）　しずか（な）　大変（な）
　　　　　　　　　　　　　　　　　　　　へん

NOTE

元気 is sometimes confused with けんこう. Both can be nouns or な-adjectives. けんこう／けんこうな, however, refers to one's physical condition, as its core meaning is "health." On the other hand, 元気 means *spirit* or *energy*, so it can refer to both mental and physical conditions. For example, 元気だ means that a person is energetic and/or in good spirits, so even a sick person who is happy can be 元気. Conversely, 元気じゃない means that the person does not have any energy. He/she may be physically tired or unhappy. In addition, 元気がない means that someone is in low spirits or feeling down.

Supplementary Vocabulary: Common illnesses

インフルエンザ		flu
しょくちゅうどく	食中毒	food poisoning
かふんしょう	花粉症	hay fever
ねんざ	捻挫	sprain

Activity 1   Work with a partner. Classify the expressions on the previous page based on whether they are good or bad for one's health, and write them in the appropriate columns in the following chart.

体にいい	体にわるい

Activity 2   Work with a partner. Ask your partner whether any of the following statements applies to him or her, and if so how frequently. Then circle the correct response.

Example:　A:　〜さんはけんこうに気をつけています (*to take care of*) か。

　　　　　B:　ええ、いつも気をつけています。

　　　　　A:　そうですか。じゃあ、よく〜をしますか。

　　　　　B:　はい、よく／ときどきします。

　　　　　or いいえ、あまり／ぜんぜんしません。

	パートナーのこたえ			
けんこうに気をつけている	いつも	よく	あまり	ぜんぜん
うんどうをする	よく	ときどき	あまり	ぜんぜん
マッサージをする	よく	ときどき	あまり	ぜんぜん
週末はゆっくり休む	よく	ときどき	あまり	ぜんぜん
ごはんのあと (*after a meal*) すぐ横になる	よく	ときどき	あまり	ぜんぜん
たばこをすう	よく	ときどき	あまり	ぜんぜん
よるおそくまで起きている	たいてい	ときどき	あまり	ぜんぜん
むりをする	よく	ときどき	あまり	ぜんぜん
ストレスがある	よく	ときどき	あまり	ぜんぜん

B. 体　The body
かだ

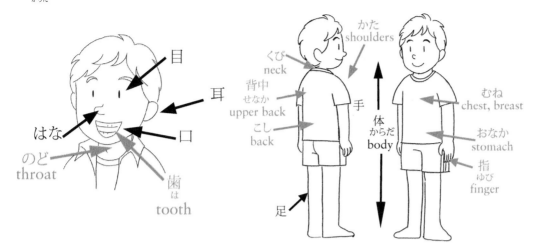

| | Activity 3 | Work with a partner. As soon as your partner calls out a part of the body, point to the corresponding part on your own body. Take turns. |
| | Activity 4 | Work with a partner. Clap your hands together twice, then play "rock-paper-scissors" in Japanese. The person who wins should name a part of the body. The other person points to the corresponding part on his/her own body. Then play it again as fast as you can. |

Supplementary Vocabulary: 体 Other parts of the body
からだ

あしくび	足首	ankle	ひざ	膝	knee
い	胃	stomach	つめ	爪	(finger) nail
うで	腕	arm	てくび	手首	wrist

C. 体のもんだいとしょうじょう Physical problems and symptoms
からだ

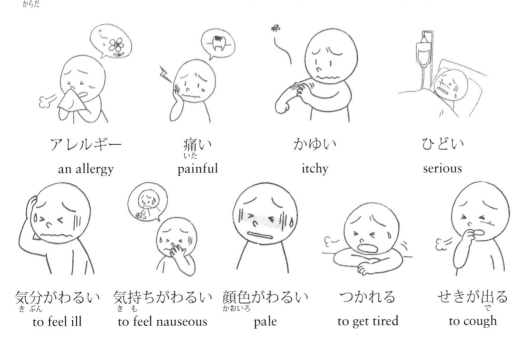

アレルギー	痛い	かゆい	ひどい
an allergy	いた painful	itchy	serious

気分がわるい	気持ちがわるい	顔色がわるい	つかれる	せきが出る
き ぶん to feel ill	き も to feel nauseous	かおいろ pale	to get tired	で to cough

熱がある／出る
<small>ねつ　　　で</small>
to have a fever

風邪をひく
<small>か　ぜ</small>
to catch a cold

けがをする
to be injured

指を切る
<small>ゆび　き</small>
to cut a finger

はく
to vomit

はながつまる
to have a stuffy nose

かたがこる
to have stiff shoulders

いきが出来ない
<small>で　き</small>
to have difficulty breathing
unable to breathe

おぼえていますか。

（熱が）上がる　（熱が）下がる　強い　よわい
<small>ねつ　　　　　　ねつ　　　　　　つよ</small>

Activity 5　しつもんに日本語でこたえて下さい。

1. 体は強い方ですか。よわい方ですか。
<small>　からだ　つよ</small>

2. アレルギーがありますか。何のアレルギーですか。

3. アレルギーのしょうじょうにはどんなものがありますか。

4. よく風邪をひきますか。
<small>　　か　ぜ</small>

5. 風邪のしょうじょうにはどんなものがありますか。
<small>か　ぜ</small>

6. むずかしいテストやアルバイトのあと (*after*)、よく体がどうなりますか。
<small>　　　　　　　　　　　　　　　　　　　　　　　からだ</small>

Activity 6　Work with a group. Students should take turns acting out the situations below and the rest of the group must identify which situation is being acted out. Complete all of these as fast as you can. The first group to finish wins.

頭が痛い　目がかゆい　指を切る　こしが痛い　背中がかゆい　かたがこる
<small>あたま　いた　　　　　　　　ゆび　き　　　　　　いた　　　せ なか</small>

せきが出る　くびがこる　熱がある　足が痛い　はながつまる
<small>　　　で　　　　　　　　　　　ねつ　　　あし　いた</small>

気持ちがわるい　おなかが痛い　風邪をひく　つかれる
<small>き も　　　　　　　　　　　いた　　か　ぜ</small>

Supplementary Vocabulary:
けがとしょうじょう Injuries and symptoms

あたまががんがんする	頭ががんがんする	to have a pounding headache
きりきりする		to have a sharp pain
げりをする	下痢をする	to have diarrhea
ずきずきする		to have a throbbing pain
はきけがする	吐き気がする	to feel nauseous
はなみずがでる	鼻水が出る	to have a runny nose
はれる	腫れる	to swell
ひりひりする		to have a stinging pain
ふるえる	震える	to tremble
ほねをおる	骨を折る	to break a bone
めまいがする		to feel dizzy

D.　病気の時にすることしないこと
Things you should and shouldn't do when you are sick

薬を飲む
to take(drink) medicine

薬をつける
to apply medicine

医者に行く
to go to a doctor

入院する
to be hospitalized

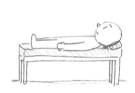

横になる
to lie down

口をあける
to open one's mouth

熱をはかる
to take one's
temperature

体をうごかす
to move one's body

いきをすう
to inhale

いきをはく
to exhale

おさけをやめる
to lay off drinking

足を上げる	足を下げる	学校を休む <small>やす</small>	走る <small>はし</small>
to raise one's legs	to lower one's legs	to stay home from school	to run

おぼえていますか。

しずかにする

Activity 7 Work with a partner. Choose one partner to be the doctor and the other to be the patient. The doctor should give commands for the following situations, and the patient should mimic the proper response.

1. You want to check his/her pulse.
2. You want to examine his/her throat.
3. You want to examine his/her stomach.
4. You want to check his/her lung capacity.
5. You want to check his/her temperature.
6. You want to see if he/she feels any pain when moving his/her arms and legs.

Activity 8 しつもんに日本語でこたえて下さい。

1. あなたはおなかが痛い時、何をしますか。あなたの国 (country) の人はどうですか。
   <small>いた</small>　　　　　　　　　　　　　　　　　　　<small>くに</small>

2. あなたは頭が痛い時、何をしますか。あなたの国 (country) の人はどうですか。
   <small>あたま</small>　<small>いた</small>　　　　　　　　　　　　　<small>くに</small>

3. 一年にどのぐらい医者に行きますか。どんな時、医者に行きますか。
   <small>い　しゃ</small>　　　　　　　　　　<small>い　しゃ</small>

4. 入院したことがありますか。いつ入院しましたか。どうして入院しましたか。
   <small>にゅういん</small>　　　　　　　　　<small>にゅういん</small>　　　　　　　　　<small>にゅういん</small>

Supplementary Vocabulary: Expressions doctors and nurses use

ここはどうですか。	Does this hurt?
大きく口をあけて下さい。	Please open your mouth wide.
上だけぬいで下さい。	Please take off your top (shirt, blouse, etc.).
後ろをむいて下さい。	Please turn around.
あおむけになって下さい。	Please lie on your back.
うつぶせになって下さい。	Please lie face down.
大きくいきをすって下さい。	Please take a deep breath.

ダイアローグ

はじめに

しつもんに日本語でこたえて下さい。

1. 病気の時、何をしますか。
2. 風邪の時、どんなしょうじょうがありますか。

熱があるんです。　*I have a fever.*

The order of the following **manga** frames is scrambled. Read the dialogue and unscramble the frames by writing the correct number in the box in each frame.

a

b

c

d

e

上田さんは石田さんに大学で会いました。

上田：　あ、石田さん、おはよう。

石田：　おはよう。

上田：　どうしたの、石田さん、ちょっと顔色がわるいけど。

石田：　ああ、昨日から気分がわるくて、何も食べられないんだ。

上田：　大変。病院行ったの？

石田：　ううん、まだ。

上田：　じゃあ、早く行った方がいいよ。

石田：　でも、今日はテストがあるから。

上田：　だけど、むりしすぎちゃだめよ。本当に早く行った方がいいよ。

石田：　そうかな。じゃあ、後で行くよ。

石田さんは病院に来ました。

医者：　どうしましたか。

石田：　昨日の朝から、気分がわるいんです。

医者：　そうですか。じゃあ、ちょっと熱をはかりましょう。

お医者さんは石田さんの熱をはかりました。

医者：　八度五分ありますね。じゃあ、口を大きくあけて下さい。

石田：　はい。

石田さんは口をあけます。

医者：　だいぶあかいですね。せきは出ますか。

石田：　いいえ、せきはないんですが、のどが痛くて、食べられないんです。

医者：　そうですか。じゃあ、薬を出しますから、それを飲んで二、三日家でよく休んで下さい。

石田：　あのう、先生、お風呂に入ってもいいですか。

医者：　お風呂ですか、入らない方がいいですね。シャワーはいいですよ。

石田：　はい、分かりました。どうもありがとうございました。

医者：　いいえ、それじゃあ、お大事に。

DIALOGUE PHRASE NOTES

- ううん、まだ means *no, not yet.*
- 八度五分 is 38.5°, which is 101.3°F.
- だいぶ means *fairly.*

ダイアローグの後で

A. しつもんに日本語でこたえて下さい。

1. 石田さんはどうして病院に行ったんですか。

2. どんなしょうじょうでしたか。

3. 石田さんの病気は何だと思いますか。

4. 石田さんはお風呂に入れますか。

5. 石田さんは何をしてもいいですか。

B. You are Alice Ueda. Complete the following entry in her diary by filling in the appropriate phrases.

今朝、石田さんに会った。石田さんは、＿＿＿＿＿＿＿＿わるくて、

＿＿＿＿＿＿＿＿そうだった。だから、石田さんは病院に＿＿＿＿＿＿＿＿

と思った。

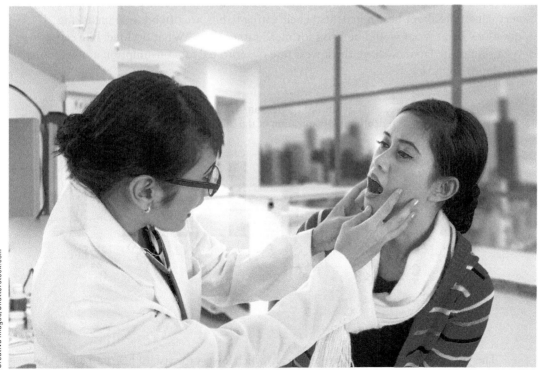

A Japanese doctor checks a patient's throat.

日本の文化
ぶん か

長生き   Longevity
なが い

The 2015 World Health Organization (WHO) report states that the Japanese have the longest lifespan in the world. According to 2014 statistics from the Ministry of Health and Labor, the average lifespan of Japanese men is 80.5 years and that of Japanese women is 86.8 years. This is considerably higher than the average life span of Americans (76.4 years for men and 81.2 years for women). In addition, Japan has one of the lowest infant mortality rates (2.8 infants per 1,000 infants) in the world. It is slightly higher than Singapore (2.6/1,000) but much lower than countries like the U.S. (5.4/1000), England (4.9/1,000), and France (3.8/1,000). Let's look at what's behind these numbers for Japan.

The Commonwealth Fund (2015) reported that Japan provides one of the best healthcare systems in the world. Virtually all residents of Japan are covered with one of many insurance programs, regardless of any pre-existing conditions they have or any actuarial risk of succumbing to illness. Premiums are affordable because they are based on income and ability to pay. The poorest can be supported by the national health insurance program offered by the government, which allows them to see the doctor without worrying about cost. National health insurance, which covers approximately 70 percent of all medical expenses, is available to both Japanese and foreigners who plan to stay in Japan for more than a year. Application forms are available at local ward or municipal offices. Those who plan to stay in Japan for less than a year can be easily covered by one of many private insurance programs. Japanese companies provide their employees with medical insurance regardless of nationality.

Another reason for the longevity is the Japanese diet. Japanese people are generally very conscious about health benefits. Their eating habits are often based on asking questions like "What would be good for me?" rather than "What do I feel like eating?" As a result, the Japanese have the lowest rate of saturated fat consumption among more developed countries.

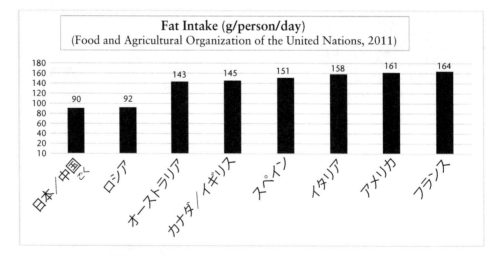

The Japanese eat more fish than red meat, which lowers the risk of heart attacks. Also, they consume a variety of soy products—a great source of protein that reduces heart disease and high blood pressure. In addition, Japanese green tea has numerous health benefits because it contains powerful antioxidants and inhibits the growth of cancer cells. Moreover, the Japanese eat small portions of food. Most Japanese portions are half the size of portions in the U.S. As a result, most Japanese men and women are thin, and it is rather uncommon to see overweight people.

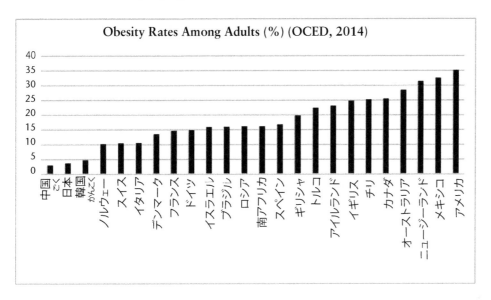

Obesity Rates Among Adults (%) (OCED, 2014)

日本の病院　Japanese hospitals
びょういん

There are two types of hospitals in Japan: general hospitals and private clinics. General hospitals handle a full range of medical problems and are equipped with the latest medical technology as well as complete hospitalization facilities. A patient, however, cannot choose a certain doctor or expect to see the same doctor each time. Also, general hospitals tend to be very crowded.

Private clinics are usually run by one or two doctors. Each doctor treats patients in his/her area of specialization and handles less complicated surgeries and routine illnesses. More complicated procedures are referred to specialists at general hospitals. With a smaller clientele, doctors at private clinics see patients on a long-term basis and are also available for informal consultations. These doctors play a role similar to that of a family doctor in the U.S.

Many Japanese doctors do not speak English, though some are able to understand it or write medical terms in English. Schools, embassies and consulates generally maintain lists of hospitals or clinics with personnel who speak English and other languages.

When a patient is diagnosed as having a terminal illness, the doctor often does not tell the patient before consulting the patient's family first. Traditionally, it has been considered cruel for a doctor to tell a patient the truth about a terminal illness, and it is left up to the family to decide whether or not to tell the patient.

In Japan, a medical doctor is addressed as 先生. The term 先生 can be used for any figure of authority whether he/she is a school teacher, master craftsman, religious leader, political leader, lawyer, or instructor in general. The term is not used within companies or business organizations. Instead, rank titles such as section head or department chief are used.

文法
ぶんぽう

I. Expressing capability using the potential form of verbs

The potential form of verbs expresses what a person can do or what is possible. The direct object particle を is replaced by が when the verb is in the potential form.

		Particle	Verb potential form (negative)
かたが痛くて いた	手	が	うごかせません。

My shoulder hurts and I cannot move my hand.

田中：どうしたんですか。		*What's wrong?*
友田：歯が痛くて寝られなかったんです。 　　　は　いた		*I had a toothache, so I couldn't sleep.*
田中：そうですか。それは大変ですね。 　　　　　　　　　　　へん		*Is that so? I'm sorry to hear that. (lit., That is awful/terrible, isn't it)*

医者： いしゃ	右手が上げられますか。 みぎ	*Can you raise your right hand?*
かんじゃ (patient)：	はい、上げられます。	*Yes, I can.*
医者： いしゃ	じゃあ、左手はどうですか。 　　　ひだり	*How about the left hand?*
かんじゃ (patient)：	痛くて、上げられません。 いた	*It's too painful to raise.*

る-verbs

The potential form of a る-verb is formed by replacing る with られる. In conversation, ら in られる can be omitted as in 起きれる instead of 起きられる, or つけれる instead of つけられる。

Dictionary form	Potential forms			
	Plain present		Polite present	
	Affirmative	Negative	Affirmative	Negative
忘れる (to forget) わす	忘れられる わす	忘れられない わす	忘れられます わす	忘れられません わす
起きる (to wake up)	起きられる	起きられない	起きられます	起きられません
つける (to put on)	つけられる	つけられない	つけられます	つけられません

う-verbs

The potential form of an う-verb is formed by changing /u/ sound in the dictionary form to /e/る.

Dictionary form	Potential forms			
	Plain present		Polite present	
	Affirmative	Negative	Affirmative	Negative
すう (*to inhale*)	すえる	すえない	すえます	すえません
走る (*to run*) はし	走れる はし	走れない はし	走れます はし	走れません はし
うごかす (*to move [something]*)	うごかせる	うごかせない	うごかせます	うごかせません
休む (*to rest*) やす	休める やす	休めない やす	休めます やす	休めません やす

Irregular verbs

Dictionary form	Potential forms			
	Plain present		Polite present	
	Affirmative	Negative	Affirmative	Negative
する (*to do*)	出来る でき	出来ない でき	出来ます でき	出来ません でき
来る (*to come*) く	来られる こ	来られない こ	来られます こ	来られません こ

Note: Potential forms of all verbs conjugate as る-verbs.

Verb types	Dictionary form	Potential forms				て -form
		Plain Present		Plain Past		
		Affirmative	Negative	Affirmative	Negative	
る -verb	寝る (*to sleep*)	寝られる	寝られない	寝られた	寝られなかった	寝られて
う -verb	飲む (*to drink*)	飲める	飲めない	飲めた	飲めなかった	飲めて
Irregular	する (*to do*)	出来る でき	出来ない でき	出来た でき	出来なかった でき	出来て でき

Note: there is no potential form for 分かる.

話してみましょう

Activity 1　Form a sentence describing what each person is able to do. Be sure to choose the correct verb from the box and use が to make the direct object.

Example:　ジョンソン　　　おすし
　　　　　ジョンソンさんは、おすしが食べられます。

┌─────────────┐
│ 食べる　　飲む │
└─────────────┘

1. ハモンド　　　　　　日本語で手紙
2. クラーク　　　　　　朝五時
3. 木村　　　　　　　　テニス
4. ジョーンズ　　　　　スペイン語
5. キム　　　　　　　　天ぷら
6. スペンサー　　　　　いやなこと

┌──────────────────────────────────┐
│ 起きる　する　書く　話す　忘れる　作る │
└──────────────────────────────────┘

Activity 2　Work in groups of three or four. Think of a place and describe what a person can or cannot do there. The other members of the group will try to guess what the place is. Use casual speech.

Example:　A:　ここでは安いコーヒーが飲めたり、安い食べ物も
　　　　　　　食べられたりするよ。
　　　　　B:　学食かな。
　　　　　A:　うん、そう。

Activity 3　Based on the reasons listed in the following sentences, make statements about what a person would not be able to do.

Example:　風邪をひきました。
　　　　　風邪をひいたから、学校に行けないんですね。

1. せきが出ます。　　　　　　5. 歯が痛いです。
2. 熱があります。　　　　　　6. 指を切りました。
3. アレルギーがあります。　　7. つかれています。
4. はながつまっています。　　8. ここまで走って来ました。

👥 **Activity 4**   Work with a partner. Using the cues below, create a conversation in which one person wonders why the other person has not performed a specified action, and the other person explains why.

Example: 食べる

A: あ、食べないんですか。

B: ええ、食べたいんですが、たまごはアレルギーで食べられないんです。

A: そうですか。ざんねんですね。

1. 朝早く起きる
2. 口を大きくあける
3. 薬をつける
4. やせる
5. 手をうごかす
6. うたう
7. 入院する
8. 横になる
9. 走る
10. じゅぎょうを休む

II. Expressing excessiveness using 〜すぎる

When すぎる is added after the stem of a verb, い-adjective, or な-adjective, it implies that something is excessive. The correct form for いい when used with すぎる is よすぎる.

薬をつけすぎました。	*I applied too much medicine.*
寝すぎました。	*I slept too much.*
山本さんは話しすぎる。	*Mr./Ms. Yamamoto talks too much.*
このけがはひどすぎる。	*This injury is incredibly serious.*
このレモンはすっぱすぎる。	*This lemon is too sour.*
あの人は元気すぎる。	*That person is too hyper.*
このしごとは大変すぎる。	*This job is too tough.*

すぎる itself is a る-verb and follows the conjugation pattern of る-verbs:

勉強をしすぎる	*does study too much*
勉強をしすぎない	*does not study too much*
勉強をしすぎます	*does study too much*
勉強をしすぎて	*does study too much and 〜*

リン：	どうしたんですか。	*What's wrong?*
山本：	歩きすぎて、足が痛いんです。	*I walked too much, so my feet hurt.*
リン：	大丈夫ですか。	*Are you OK?*
山本：	いや、痛すぎて、くつがはけません。	*No, it hurts too much to put on my shoes.*

話してみましょう

Activity 1   Excess in one's behaviors can cause problems. Describe what type of behavior could cause the following problems, using the verb stem + すぎる.

Example: よる、寝られない

<u>インターネットをしすぎて、よる、寝られないんです。</u>

1. 頭が痛い
   あたま　　いた
2. ストレスがある
3. つかれた
4. 朝早く起きられない
   はや
5. いきが出来ない
   　　　で き
6. 気分がわるい
   き ぶん
7. 足が痛い
   　　いた
8. かたがこっている

Activity 2   Work with a partner. Use the pictures as a basis for conversations between two friends. Use the example conversation below.

Example:

A: どうしたの？

B: 食べすぎて、おなかが痛いんだ／の。
   　　　　　　　　　　　　いた

A: 大丈夫？
   じょう ぶ

B: うん、まあ (so-so)。

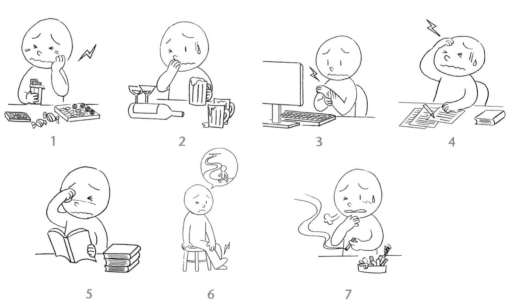

👥 **Activity 3**   Work with a partner. One person is a customer and the other person is a store clerk. Have a conversation based on the information provided about the items in the chart below. Be sure to talk about the size, length, and price of the items.

Example: セーター

店の人：　いかがですか。

おきゃくさん：　色 (color) は好きなんですけど、ちょっと大きすぎますね。
　　　　　　　　もう少し小さいのはありませんか。

店の人：　はい、ございます。こちらはいかがでしょうか。

おきゃくさん：　いいですね。これにします。

もの	色 (いろ)	大きさ・サイズ	ながさ (length)	ねだん (cost)
シャツ	OK	too small	OK	OK
パンツ	OK	OK	too long	OK
ジャケット	too bright	OK	too short	OK
かばん	OK	too big	OK	too expensive

III. Giving suggestions using 〜たらどうですか and 〜方がいいです

The expressions 〜たらどうですか and 〜方がいいです are used for making suggestions or giving advice. 〜方がいいです (*it's better to* 〜, *you should* 〜) is stronger than 〜たらどうですか (*How about doing* 〜, *why don't you* 〜).

A. 〜たらどうですか

The form 〜たらどうですか is made by adding ら to the plain past affirmative form of a verb. 〜たら is called the conditional form of the verb and has many functions which you will learn in later chapters. Using でしょうか instead of ですか softens the entire expression and makes it sound more polite.

横になったらどうですか。　*Maybe you should lie down?*
　　　　　　　　　　　　　　(*How about lying down?*)

アルバイトをやめたらどうですか。　*How about quitting your part time job?*

薬を飲んだらどう？　*How about taking some medicine?*

リー：どうしたの？　　　　　*What's wrong?*

山口：足が痛くて歩けないの。　*My feet hurt, so I can't walk.*

リー：少し休んだらどう？　　*Why don't you take a rest?*

B. 〜た方がいいです／〜ない方がいいです

The plain past affirmative or plain present negative of a verb with 方がいいです means *you should or should not do* 〜.

バスに<u>のった</u>方がいいです。　　*It's better to ride the bus. (You should ride).*

バスに<u>のらない</u>方がいいです。　*It's better not to ride the bus. (You shouldn't ride.)*

薬を<u>つけた</u>方がいいです。　　*It's better to apply some medicine.*

（く すり）　　　　　　　　　　　　*(You should apply some medicine.)*

薬を<u>つけない</u>方がいいです。　*It's better not to apply any medicine.*

（く すり）　　　　　　　　　　　　*(You should not apply any medicine.)*

パク：　どうしたの？

What's the matter?

東山：　足がすごくかゆいのよ。

My feet itch badly.

パク：　見せて。ああ、これは、ちょっとひどいね。薬をつけた方が
いいよ。

Show me. Oh, that looks really bad. You should put on some medicine.

東山：　今、持っていないの。

But I don't have any.

パク：　あそこにドラッグストア (drugstore) があるから、買いに行ったらどう？

There's a drugstore over there, so how about going to get some?

話してみましょう

Activity 1　Change each of the following into a suggestion using 〜たらどうですか and/or 〜た方がいいですよ.

Example:　早くしゅくだいを出す
早くしゅくだいを出したらどうですか。／早くしゅくだいを出した方がいいですよ。

1. マッサージに行く
2. 体をうごかす
3. はく
4. 薬をつける

5. 横になる
6. 熱をはかる
7. よく休む
8. 学校を休む

Activity 2   Work in pairs. Have conversations about the situations described in 1–6 below in which one person explains the problem and the other person makes suggestions for dealing with the problem. Make both positive and negative suggestions.

Example: おなかが痛いんです。

A: どうしたんですか。

B: おなかが痛いんです。

A: じゃあ、薬を飲んだらどうですか。それから、何も食べない方がいいですよ。

B: ありがとう。じゃあ、そうします。

1. むねが痛くて、いきが出来ません
2. こしが痛くて、歩けないんです。
3. ダイエットをしていますが、ぜんぜんやせません。
4. アレルギーで、目がかゆいんです。
5. 明日デートがありますが、熱が下がらないんです。
6. 明日テストがありますが、指を切って痛いんです。

Activity 3   Work with the class. Think of a physical condition such as having a cold or not being able to sleep. Get suggestions from your classmates in casual speech and report them in formal speech.

Example: A: どうしたの？

B: 風邪をひいて、熱があるんだ／の。

A: そう。じゃ、家に帰ってよく休んだ方がいいよ。

B: そう（だ）ね。じゃあ、そうする（ね）。

A: お大事に。

to class:

家に帰ってよく休んだ方がいいそうです。

IV. Making a negative request using 〜ないで下さい

The negative form of a verb + で下さい expresses a polite negative request. In casual speech 下さい is dropped.

風邪のしょうじょうがあるんですか。じゃあ、お風呂に入らないで下さい。
You have cold symptoms? In that case, don't take a bath.

アレルギーがあるなら、この薬は飲まないでください。
If you are allergic to this medicine, don't take it.

腰が痛いんですか。じゃあ、うごかないで下さい。
You have a backache? Then keep still and don't move around!

つかれているんだから、むりをしないで。
You're tired, so don't overdo things.

かさを持って行くのを忘れないで。
Don't forget to bring your umbrella.

話してみましょう

Activity 1   Look at the pictures of people suffering from certain physical ailments. You are a doctor. Tell the patients what not to do using 〜ないで下さい and 〜て下さい.

Example:

ひどいせきが出ていますね。じゃあ、今日はどこにも出かけないで下さい。薬を飲んで下さい。

1   2   3

4   5   6

Activity 2   Work with a partner. Create conversations between the pairs listed in 1–4 below in which one person makes positive and negative requests to the other person. Decide which of the two people in the pair should make the request. Pay attention to the level of formality.

Example: お父さん　お母さん

お母さんがお父さんにおねがいします。

お母さん：熱があるんだから、今日はゆっくり休んで。

お父さん：うん、だけど、しごとがあるから …。

お母さん：だめ、だめ (*No way*)。今日はどこにも行かないで。

お父さん：分かったよ。じゃあ、二階で横になるよ。

1. お母さん　子供
2. 男の人　女の人
3. 医者　かんじゃ (*patient*)
4. 先生　学生

V. Expressing unacceptable actions or situations using ～てはいけない; asking for and giving permission using ～てもいい

A. ～てはいけない

The て-form + はいけない／はだめ indicates that something is not allowed. This structure is commonly used to talk about rules. The colloquial form of ～てはいけない is ～ちゃ／じゃいけない or ～ちゃ／じゃだめ.

このへやに一人で入ってはいけません。	*You may not enter this room by yourself.*
学校を休んではいけません。	*You must not be absent from school.*
レポートを忘れたりおそく出したり　してはだめだよ。	*You must not forget your paper　or turn it in late.*
おそくまで起きていちゃだめです。	*You are not allowed to stay up late.*
だれともあそんじゃいけないよ。	*You may not play with anyone.*
今電気をつけちゃだめだよ。	*You are not allowed to turn on the lights now.*

健二：　ぼく、くるまで行くよ。

　　　I will go by car.

高子：　おさけ飲んでるから、うんてん (drive) しちゃだめよ。

　　　No, you shouldn't drive because you've been drinking alcohol.

〜てはいけない takes the て-form of verbs and adjectives.

	Plain Present Form	〜てはいけない／てはだめ 〜くちゃいけない／くちゃだめ		Meaning
る-verbs	いる	い	てはいけない／てはだめ ちゃいけない／ちゃだめ	*must not stay*
う-verbs	休む _{やす}	休ん _{やす}	ではいけない／ではだめ じゃいけない／じゃだめ	*must not rest/ take a day off*
Irregular verbs	来る	来	てはいけない／てはだめ ちゃいけない／ちゃだめ	*must not come*
	する	し	てはいけない／てはだめ ちゃいけない／ちゃだめ	*must not do*
い-adjectives	よわい	よわ	くてはいけない／くてはだめ くちゃいけない／くちゃだめ	*must not be weak*
な-adjectives	きらいだ	きらい	ではいけない／ではだめ じゃいけない／じゃだめ	*must not dislike*
Copula verb	この薬だ _{くすり}	この薬 _{くすり}	ではいけない／ではだめ じゃいけない／じゃだめ	*must not be this medicine*

NOTE

● When answering a question with the て-form + はいけませんか／だめ
ですか, use ええ、いけません／だめです to prohibit an action. Use い
いえ、いいです to permit the action.

田中：この薬を飲んではいけませんか。
_{くすり}
Can't I take this medicine?

医者：ええ、（飲んでは）いけません。
_{いしゃ}
No, you may not.

or いいえ、（飲んでも）いいですよ。
Yes, you may.

B. 〜てもいい It is OK to~, can, may

The て-form of verbs + もいいですか／もいいでしょうか／もかまいませんか is used to ask for permission. 〜てもいいでしょうか is more tentative and thus more polite than 〜てもいいですか, but it can also be used toward someone in one's peer group. 〜てもかまいませんか is as polite as 〜てもいいでしょうか. Although it ends in the negative, the way you answer is the same as 〜てもいいでしょうか.

走ってもいいですか／走ってもいい？	*Is it okay for me to run/jog?* (more casual)
走ってもいいでしょうか／走ってもいい？	*May I run/jog?*
走ってもかまいませんか／走ってもかまわない？	*May I run/jog?*

学生：先生、今日は早く帰ってもいいでしょうか。
> *Professor, may I go home early today?*

先生：え、どうしてですか。
> *Oh, why?*

学生：気持ちがわるくて、はきそうなんです。
> *I don't feel good; I feel like I'm going to vomit.*

先生：そうですか。じゃあ、今すぐ帰ってもいいですよ。
> *Oh, is that so? Well, you may go home right away, then.*

学生：ありがとうございます。
> *Thank you very much.*

先生：お大事に。
> *Take care.*

NOTES

- The following are common ways to respond positively to a request.

  はい／ええ、どうぞ。
  Yes, please go ahead.

  はい／ええ、かまいません／かまわない（よ）。
  That's fine. I don't mind.

  ええ、もちろん。
  Yes, of course.

  Although はい、いいです is grammatically correct, it would only be used when a superior is granting permission to a social inferior.

- Answering negatively can be awkward. Think of how you would deny a request in your own language. Using 〜てはいけない may be one way to respond, but it can also sound rude, unless you are in position of authority or you are explaining a rule. As in many other countries, the

Japanese tend to avoid direct statements of prohibition such as "No, you may not" and use instead phrases such as:

すみませんが、ちょっと。
I am sorry.

ええっと、それはちょっと。
Well, that would be a bit . . .

すみません、それはちょっとこまります。
I am sorry. That would be a little troublesome.

In such situations, the word ちょっと serves to deflect whatever tension may arise from withholding permission. It also saves the respondent from spelling out his/her reasons for denying permission.

話してみましょう

Activity 1 Change each sentence to a question asking for permission using 〜たい and 〜てもいいですか／てもいいでしょうか／てもかまいませんか. You will need to come up with the context for each request.

Example: 少し休む

つかれたので、少し休みたいんですが、ゆっくりしてもいいですか／てもいいでしょうか／てもかまいませんか。

1. 家に帰る
2. 足を上げる
3. 一緒に行く
4. 熱をはかる

5. じゅぎょうを休む
6. よるおそくまで起きている
7. えんぴつで書く
8. 横になる

Activity 2 State what is or is not acceptable in each of the following places, using the expressions provided and 〜てもいいです／〜てはいけない／〜ないで下さい.

Example: りょうのラウンジ (*lounge*) ではコーヒーを飲んでもいいですが、たばこをすってはいけません／たばこはすわないで下さい。

1. きょうしつ
2. 病院
3. 図書館

4. じんじゃやおてら
5. おばあさんの家
6. Create your own sentence.

Activity 3   Work with a partner. Think of three places and write them in the boxes labeled 1, 2, and 3. Your partner does the same. Now you and your partner will try to figure out what each of the three places is by asking questions using 〜てもいいですか／てもいいでしょうか／てもかまいませんか. You may ask only one question and make one guess at a time. The first one to reach ゴール (goal) wins.

Example: A:　ここでテレビを見てもいいですか。

B:　いいえ、見ない方がいいですよ。

A:　きょうしつですか。

B:　ありません。

パートナー | 1 | → | 2 | → | 3 | → ゴール！

聞く練習
れんしゅう

上手な聞き方

Using the setting as a clue

What you know about a setting gives you a lot of clues about the type of speech you hear. For example, the content of a conversation will be very different if you are in a doctor's office, at school, or in a restaurant. Also, you will use different phrases and words for the same topic depending on if you are at school or at home. The setting gives you clues about the content of a conversation, choice of words and phrases, and much more. The setting not only implies different locations, but also different times of the day. A conversation in the morning may be very different from one in the afternoon in context and in effectiveness, even if you are talking to the same person.

 練習
れんしゅう

いつどこで何がありましたか。

Listen to each conversation and try to identify where it took place. Circle the place name. Then write what happened in the blank.

1.　学校　　　病院　　　　　デパート　　　　家
　　　　　　びょういん

_____

2.　病院　　　デパート　　　学校　　　　　レストラン
　　びょういん

_____

3.　病院　　　レストラン　　学校　　　　　デパート
　　びょういん

_____

病院で
びょういん

聞く前に

A. 下のしつもんに日本語でこたえて下さい。

1. 病院のうけつけ (*reception desk*) でどんなことをいいますか。
びょういん

2. しんかん (*new patient*) の人は病院のうけつけ (*reception desk*) で何をしますか。
びょういん

3. かふんしょう (*hay fever*) にはどんなしょうじょうがありますか。

4. かふんしょう (*hay fever*) の人はどんなことをしてはいけませんか。

5. かふんしょう (*hay fever*) の人はどんなことをしたらいいでしょうか。

B. 下のえを見て、何が起きているのかいって下さい。(*Say what is happening*)

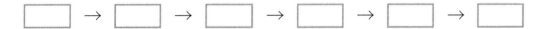

聞いた後で

A. Rearrange the pictures above based on the order in which the actions ocurred.

☐ → ☐ → ☐ → ☐ → ☐ → ☐

B. もう一度、会話 (*conversation*) の前半 (*first half*) を聞いて、しつもんに日本語で
かいわ　　　　　　　　　　　ぜんはん
こたえて下さい。

1. 女の人はパーカーさんです。パーカーさんはどうして病院に来ましたか。
びょういん

2. 「ようし」って何ですか。

3. パーカーさんは何が出来ないのですか。
で き

C. もう一度、会話 (*conversation*) の後半 (*last half*) を聞いて、しつもんに日本語でこたえて下さい。

1. 医者はパーカーさんにどんなしつもんをしましたか。
2. 医者によると、かふんしょう (*hay fever*) はどんな病気ですか。
3. パーカーさんは何をしてはいけませんか。

聞き上手話し上手

医者と話す

Going to a hospital can be nerve-wracking, especially when you are not familiar with the language. Even for native speakers, Japanese medical terms can be difficult to understand, so it is important to ask for clarification. Some useful phrases are:

はじめてなんですが。	I'm a new patient. (lit.: *this is my first time.*)
（日本語が）よく分からないんです。	I don't understand (Japanese) well.
もう少しやさしいことばでいって下さい。	Please say it with easier words.
これは何の薬ですか。	What is this medicine for?
一日に何回飲んだらいいですか。	How many times a day should I take it?

練習

A. Your instructor will be the doctor or a receptionist at a hospital and ask you questions or make requests. Respond accordingly.

B. Your instructor will be a nurse. Think about a physical problem you may want to discuss with a nurse; then tell the nurse about it and ask whether you can or cannot do various activities.

漢字
かんじ

Left-side component shapes of kanji

As mentioned in Chapter 7 of *Nakama 1*, component shapes appearing on the left side of **kanji** indicate a rough semantic category of **kanji**. The following chart shows some common left-side component shapes that you've seen so far. Examples in parentheses show the use of the component shape in a different location, or cases where a radical is used as a character by itself. If the component shape is a traditional radical, the name of the radical is listed. Component shapes that are not radicals do not have particular names. We use the concept of component shapes strictly as a pedagogical tool, and there might be discrepancies between the explanations in this book and those in traditional **kanji** dictionaries.

Names		Meaning	Examples	Related kanji
さんずい	氵	water	泳ぐ　海　湖　泊まる およ　うみ　みずうみ　と	川
つちへん	土	land, soil	地 ち	土
にんべん	亻	person	何　休　体　住む からだ　す	人
てへん	扌	hand	指　持つ　拾う *(to pick* ゆび　も　ひろ *up)*　払う *(to pay)* はら	手
にちへん・ひへん	日	day, sun	明るい　昨日　晩　時 晴　暗い　日曜日 くら	日　朝
しめすへん・ねへん	礻	god, shrine	お礼　神社　お祝い れい　じんじゃ　いわ	
きへん	木	tree	校　林 *(woods)*　机　橋 はやし　つくえ　はし 枚 まい	木　本　東　来 末　親
しょくへん	飠	eating	飲　ご飯　体育館 はん　たいいくかん	食
ゆみへん	弓	bow	引く　強い つよ	弱い　弟 よわ
かねへん	金	metal, gold	銀行　鉄 *(iron)*　鉱 ぎん　てつ　こう *(mineral)*	金
おんなへん	女	female	好き　姉　妹　結婚 けっこん	女
かたへん	方	direction	家族　旅行 りょ	方
ぎょうにんべん	彳	way	行く　後　待つ ま	
ごんべん	言	say, language	話　語	言う い
のぎへん	禾	crop	私　秋	

いとへん	糸	thread	紙 (paper)　予約　結婚	糸 (thread)
			かみ　　　　よやく　けっこん	いと
たへん	田	rice field	町	田　畑 (field)
			まち	はたけ
つきへん	月	moon	服	月　朝
			ふく	
にくづき	肉	meat	胸　脚　腹　脱ぐ	肉
			むね　あし　ふく　ぬ	にく
こへん	子	child	孫	子
			まご	

病病	sickness　やま(い)　ビョウ	病気になる。　病院に行く。 びょうき　　びょういん	丶　亠　广　广　疒　疒　病　病　病

院院	institution　イン	入院する。　大学院生 にゅういん　　　いん	了　阝　阝　阝ˊ　阝ˋ　阝ˊ　陀　陀　院

医医	medical　イ	医者になる。 いしゃ	一　厂　厂　三　歹　矢　医

者者	person　もの　シャ	今日は歯医者(dentist)に行きます。 は　いしゃ	一　十　土　耂　耂　者　者

体体	body　からだ　タイ・テイ	体が大きい。　体をうごかす。 からだ　　　　　からだ	ノ　イ　仁　什　休　休　体

歯歯	tooth　は　シ	歯が痛い。　歯医者(dentist)に行く。 は　いた　　は　いしゃ	丨　卜　止　止　歨　歨　歯　歯

変変	strange, to change　か(わる)　ヘン	大変です。 たいへん	丶　亠　亇　亣　亦　亦　亦　変

熱熱	heat, fever　あつ(い)　ネツ	熱がある。　熱いコーヒー ねつ　　　　あつ	十　土　夫　坴　坴　刲　執　執　熱

薬薬	medicine, chemical　くすり　ヤク	これはいい薬です。 くすり	一　艹　芍　芍　苩　渞　漢　薬

顔	顔	face	亠 亠 立 产 彦 彦 彦 顔 顔 顔
		かお　ガン　　顔色がわるい。 かおいろ	

色	色	color	ノ ク 名 名 色 色
		いろ　ショク・シキ　　顔の色がくろい。　色々な人 かお　いろ　　　　　いろいろ	

指	指	finger	一 扌 扌 扌 扚 指 指 指 指
		ゆび　シ　　指がながいですね。　親指は thumbです。 ゆび　　　　　　おやゆび	

切	切	to cut	一 七 七刀 切
		き（る）　セツ　　あっ、痛い、指を切った。　親切な人 いた　ゆび　き　　　しんせつ	

歩	歩	to walk	｜ ｜｜ ｜｜ 止 歩 歩 歩 歩
		ある（く）　ホ　　家まで歩いて帰る。　こうえんを散歩する。 ある　　　　　　　　　さんぽ	

走	走	to run	一 十 土 キ キ 走 走
		はし（る）　ソウ　　毎日10キロ走っています。 はし	

勉	勉	exertion	ノ ク 夕 兪 兪 免 免 免 勉
		つと（める）　ベン　　日本語を勉強する。 べんきょう	

強	強	strong	フ コ 弓 弓 弘 弘 強 強 強
		つよ（い）　キョウ　　この薬は強いです。　勉強はたのしい。 くすり　つよ　　　　　べんきょう	

忘	忘	to forget	丶 亠 亡 亡 忘 忘 忘
		わす（れる）　ボウ　　走って、ストレスを忘れます。 はし　　　　　　　わす	

早	早	early	丨 冂 日 日 旦 早
		はや（い）　ソウ　　朝早く起きる。 はや	

持	持	to hold, to have	一 扌 扌 扌 扗 扗 扦 持 持
		も（つ）　ジ　　指を切ったので、かばんが持てません。　気持ち ゆび　き　　　　　　　も　　　　きも	

痛 痛	to hurt; pain いた（い）　ツウ 昨日走りすぎて、足が痛い。 はし　　　　　いた	亠 广 疒 疒 疒 疒 病 痈 痛
頭 頭	head あたま　ズ　　頭が痛い。　山田さんは頭がいい。 　　　　　　　あたま　いた　　　　　　　　あたま	一 口 豆 豆 豆 頭 頭 頭 頭
横 横	side よこ　オウ　　テーブルの横 　　　　　　　　　　　よこ	木 朾 柑 桔 栉 栉 楮 横 横

読めるようになった漢字
　　　　　　　　　かんじ

病院　病気　入院する　大学院　大学院生　医者　体　体育館　歯　大変　熱
　　　　　　にゅう　　　　　　　　　　　　　　　　　　　　たいいくかん

熱い　薬　顔　顔色　黄色い　茶色い　指　指輪　切る　親切　歩く　散歩
　　　　　　　　　きいろ　ちゃいろ　　　　わ　　　　　　　　　　　　さんぽ

走る　勉強　強い　忘れる　早い　お大事に　風邪　気分　気持ち　背中
　　　　　　　　　　　　　　　　　じ　　かぜ　　　　　　　　せなか

休む　上げる　下げる　出る　出す　出来る　持つ　痛い　頭　横

日本人の名前：　健二
　　な　　　　　けんじ

練習
れんしゅう

Read the following sentences aloud.

1. 弟は熱が 38 度あって体も熱かったので、家ですぐ横になりました。
2. 気分がわるくて、顔色もよくなかったので、学校を休んで朝早く病院に行きました。
3. 私の父は一日に三回薬を飲みます。
4. 体がとてもつかれていて、歯も痛くなってきて、もう歩けません。
5. 母が去年から病気で入院しているから、私の家は大変です。
6. 指を切って、痛くてえんぴつが持てないので、医者に行った。
7. リンさんは、昨日、おそくまで勉強したけど、しゅくだいを家に忘れました。
8. 体が強くなるから、毎日えきまで歩いたり、こうえんを走ったりしています。
9. 姉は子供の時、高い熱が出て病院に行ったそうです。

読む練習
れんしゅう

上手な読み方

Using your knowledge of the real world

As mentioned earlier in the textbook, you should always look at the title, subtitles, pictures and captions to determine what a reading is about before you start. Then think about what you know about the particular topic. This chapter is about illnesses, so you should try to remember what you know or have experienced concerning illnesses and hospitals in your country and apply your knowledge.

練習
れんしゅう

Most Japanese clinics and hospitals have their own pharmacies. A prescription drug is usually put in a small packet with instructions. Now look at the pictures and try to guess which one is a pharmacy packet.

1

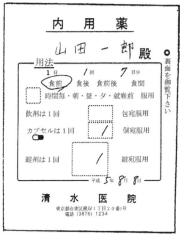

2

3

父の病気

読む前に

1. 日本のサラリーマン (*business man*) はどんな生活をしていると思いますか。

2. つかれた時は (*when you are very tired*)、どんなしょうじょうがありますか。

3. どんな時に、ごはんがあまり食べられませんか。

読んでみましょう

言葉のリスト
ことば

心配です　　　　worried
しんぱい

これはインターネットの人生相談 (*advice column*) の手紙です。
じんせいそうだん　　　　　　　　　　　　　　がみ

> 私の父はお酒が大好き、仕事でよくお酒を飲みに行きます。毎晩
> さけ　　　　しごと　　　さけ
>
> 遅くまで飲んでいるので、十二時ごろまで家に帰れません。家でも晩
> おそ
>
> 御飯の時にビールを二、三本飲みますから、飲みすぎだと思います。
> ごはん
>
> ですから、このごろとても顔色が悪くて、ごはんもあまり食べられな
> わる
>
> いんです。父は仕事が大好きで、家でゆっくりするのはあまり好きじ
> しごと
>
> やないので、病気で会社を休んだことはありません。でも、私も母も
> しゃ
>
> とても心配です。一週間ぐらい前に父と話しましたが、父はお酒をや
> しんぱい　　　　　　　　　　　　　　　　　　　　　　　さけ
>
> めたくないそうです。私と母は、どうしたらいいんでしょうか。

読んだ後で

1. お父さんはけんこうですか。

2. お父さんは何をするのが好きですか。

3. お父さんはどのぐらいお酒を飲みますか。
さけ

4. お父さんは何がきらいなんですか。

5. お父さんは仕事を休みたがっていますか。
しごと

6. この手紙を書いた人にアドバイス (*advice*) をして下さい。
がみ

総合練習
そうごうれんしゅう

Integration

けんこうですか。

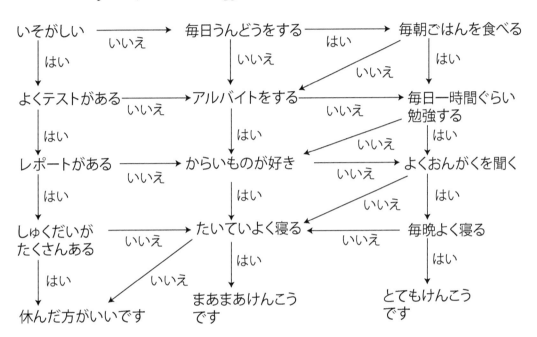 Work with a partner. Your partner should not look at the flow chart. Ask him/her about various habits and follow the flow chart according to the answers. If your partner's physical condition is not perfect, make some suggestions.

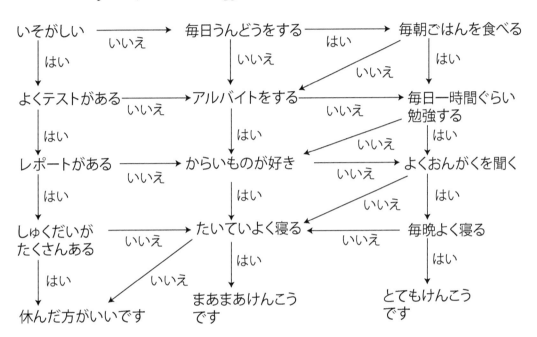

Example:　A:　いそがしいですか。

B:　いいえ。

A:　じゃあ、毎日うんどうをしますか。

B:　いいえ、うんどうはあまりしませんね。

[. . . . . the dialogue continues . . . . . .]

A:　しゅくだいがたくさんありますか。

B:　はい。

A:　～さんは、あまりけんこうじゃなさそうですね。

B:　そうですか。

A:　少しうんどうをした方がいいですよ。それからアルバイトはあまりしない方がいいですね。

👥 ロールプレイ

1. You are at a hospital. You are a new patient and have to tell the staff at the reception desk what kind of problem you have.
2. You started feeling sick in the middle of class. Ask your instructor if you can excuse yourself.
3. Your friend looks sick. Ask what's wrong and give several suggestions.
4. You are going on a trip tomorrow, but you feel sick. Tell a doctor what you want to do during the trip, and ask for advice.

Chapter 2

Photo courtesy of Yukiko Koguchi

第
二
課
だい
か

旅行の計画
りょ　　　けいかく
Travel Plans

単語
たんご

Nouns

（お）かね	お金	money
（お）みやげ	お土産	souvenir
おんせん	温泉	hot spring
かいがい	海外	overseas, かいがいりょこう overseas travel
ガイドブック		guidebook
かんこう	観光	sightseeing, かんこうする to go sightseeing, かんこうバス chartered bus for sightseeing, かんこうりょこう sightseeing trip
		かんこうち tourist attraction, sightseeing spot
きっぷ	切符	ticket, でんしゃのきっぷ train ticket
きゃく	客	customer, guest, おきゃくさん, かんこうきゃく tourist
くうこう	空港	airport
くに	国	country
クレジットカード		credit card
けいかく	計画	plan
こくない	国内	domestic, こくないりょこう domestic travel
ことば	言葉	language, words, expressions
じかん	時間	time, じかんがある to have time, じかんがない to not have time
じゅんび	準備	preparation, じゅんびする to prepare じゅんびができる preparations are complete
スーツケース		suitcase
ツアー		tour
デジカメ		digital camera, デジタルカメラ
でんしゃ	電車	train
にもつ	荷物	one's belongings, luggage
ばしょ	場所	location
パスポート		passport
ひがえり	日帰り	day trip

ふね	船	ship, boat
みずうみ	湖	lake
よてい	予定	schedule, plan, よていをたてる to make plans
よやく	予約	reservation, きっぷのよやくをする／きっぷをよやくする to reserve a ticket
りょかん	旅館	Japanese-style inn

な -adjective

| べんり（な） | 便利（な） | convenient |

う -verbs

さがす	探す／ 捜す	to look for. Use 捜す to look for something that has been lost. Otherwise, use 探す.
つかう	使う	to use
つく	着く	to arrive, (place) につく to arrive at (a place)
とまる	泊まる	to stay, (place) にとまる to stay in (a place)
ぬぐ	脱ぐ	to take off (shoes, clothes)
はらう	払う	to pay
もつ	持つ	to hold, もっている to be holding, to own
もっていく	持って行く	to take, to bring something
もどる	戻る	(for someone) to return

る -verbs

こたえる	答える	to answer, しつもんにこたえる to answer a question
きめる	決める	to decide, 〜に　きめる to decide on, 〜を　きめる to decide something
しっている	知っている	to know. Use しらない to express *do not know.* しる means come to know, and it is a う -verb.
しらべる	調べる	to check, investigate, explore
たてる	建てる／立てる	to build, establish, make. Use 建てる to build something. Otherwise, use 立てる.
でる	出る	to leave, うちをでる to leave home, ねつがでる to have a fever

Adverbs

とくに	特に	especially, in particular
もう		already, yet, any more
まだ		still, yet

Suffix

～はく（ぱく）	～泊	～ nights, ～はく（ぱく）～日 nights and days いっぱくふつか one night and two days

Conjunctions

けれども		however
そのあいだ（に）	その間に	during that time
そのあと（で）	その後で	after that
そのまえ（に）	その前に	before that
そのとき（に）	その時に	at that time
それで		then, so
だから		so
だけど		but
つぎに	次に	next
ですから		therefore, so
というのは		it's because
ところで		by the way
まずはじめに	まず始めに	first (of all)
また		also

Expressions

～について		about ～ , そのりょこうについて about the trip
もしもし		Hello (on the phone)
いいえ、ちがいます（よ）。	いいえ、違います（よ）。	No, you have the wrong number. (literally: No, it's not correct.)

単語の練習
たん ご　　れんしゅう

A. 旅行　Travel
りょ

Look at the illustration below. Your instructor will call out a number that corresponds to an object in the illustration, and you will respond by giving the name of the object in Japanese. As you go, match the numbers with their object in the vocabulary list below.

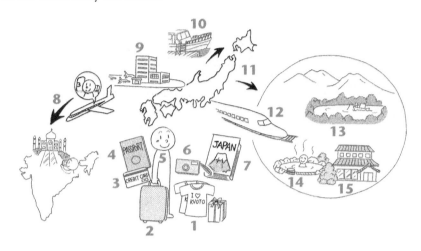

__	かんこう	sightseeing		__	乗り物 の　もの	transportation
__	海外 かいがい	overseas		__	でんしゃ	train
__	国内 こくない	domestic		__	ふね	ship
__	ツアー	tour		__	切符 きっ ぷ	ticket
__	ばしょ	location		__	パスポート	passport
__	ホテル	hotel		__	クレジットカード	credit card
__	旅館 りょかん	Japanese-style inn		__	ガイドブック	guidebook
__	温泉 おんせん	hot spring		__	荷物 に もつ	luggage
__	みずうみ	lake		__	スーツケース	suitcase
__	デジカメ	digital camera		__	空港 くうこう	airport
__	（お）土産 み やげ	souvenir		__	かんこうきゃく	tourist
__	ことば	word, language				

おぼえていますか。

海 おてら おまつり 思い出 外国 買い物 会社 家族 かばん かぶき
川 きせつ 教会 くるま けいたい電話 水族館 しごと しゃしん
じんじゃ 動物園 はくぶつかん 飛行機 ビジネス 美術館 ホテル 店
ゆうえんち レストラン アメリカ イギリス オーストラリア カナダ 韓国
スペイン たいわん 中国 フランス メキシコ

Supplementary Vocabulary: 旅行にかんすることば
Other travel-related expressions

あんない（する）	案内（する）	to guide, to show (someone) around
あんないじょ	案内所	information center
えはがき	絵葉書	picture postcard
がくわり	学割	student discount
ガイド		guide
クルーズ		cruise
じゆうこうどう	自由行動	free time, free activity
しゅうゆうけん	周遊券	(travel) pass
しゅくはくち	宿泊地	place to stay overnight
～つき	～付き	included, equipped with
	シャワーつき	equipped with shower,
	ちゅうしょくつき	lunch included
ビザ		visa
ペンション		western-style private guesthouse, B&B
ほけん	保険	insurance
もくてき	目的	purpose
もくてきち	目的地	destination
やど	宿	inn
ユースホステル		youth hostel

Activity 1 Work in pairs. Create conversations in which you attempt to guess the Japanese words for the following terms.

Example:　A: Domestic travel って日本語で何だと思う。

　　　　　B: そうだね。国内旅行かな。

Overseas travel ＿＿＿＿＿＿＿＿＿＿
Sightseeing trip ＿＿＿＿＿＿＿＿＿＿
Overseas tour ＿＿＿＿＿＿＿＿＿＿
Domestic tour ＿＿＿＿＿＿＿＿＿＿
Travel agency ＿＿＿＿＿＿＿＿＿＿
Airport limousine ＿＿＿＿＿＿＿＿＿＿

Activity 2　Work in pairs. Create conversations in which you attempt to guess the English (or Japanese) words for the following terms.

Example:　A: アメリカ旅行って何だと思う。
　　　　　　B: Traveling in America だと思う。

旅行ガイド　　　　＿＿＿＿＿＿＿＿＿＿＿＿

家族旅行　　　　　＿＿＿＿＿＿＿＿＿＿＿＿

温泉旅行　　　　　＿＿＿＿＿＿＿＿＿＿＿＿

温泉旅館　　　　　＿＿＿＿＿＿＿＿＿＿＿＿

かんこうバス　　　＿＿＿＿＿＿＿＿＿＿＿＿

かんこうきゃく　　＿＿＿＿＿＿＿＿＿＿＿＿

ビジネスホテル　　＿＿＿＿＿＿＿＿＿＿＿＿

Activity 3　Find a word that corresponds to the following descriptions. Some of the items have more than one answer.

1. 飛行機が出るところです。
2. バスや飛行機やふねやでんしゃのことです。
3. 旅行の時に読むものです。
4. 旅行の時に、ここで寝たりごはんを食べたりします。
5. 旅行の時に買うものです。
6. 「ところ」のことです。
7. 旅行の時に、これで色々な物が買えますが、お金じゃありません。
8. 外国人が持っている物です。
9. これを買って、でんしゃや飛行機に乗ります。
10. これでしゃしんがとれます。
11. ここでつりをしたり、およいだりします。

Activity 4　Complete the following sentences using the appropriate words.

1. でんしゃの＿＿＿＿＿を＿＿＿＿＿＿＿で、はらいます。
2. 海外旅行に行く人は、＿＿＿＿＿＿＿をとって下さい。
3. 海外では、＿＿＿＿＿＿が分からなくて、とても大変でした。
4. 日本では、＿＿＿＿＿＿ではなくて、＿＿＿＿＿に泊まりたいです。

B. じゅんびをする　Preparation

計画をたてる _{けいかく}	to make plans
有名なホテルに泊まる _{ゆうめい}　_と	to stay in a famous hotel
〜からホテルにもどる	to return to the hotel from 〜
じゅんびをする	to prepare
〜をつかう	to use
〜をしらべる	to check
〜を知っている／知らない 　　_し　　_し	to know / to not know
予約する _{よ やく}	to make a reservation
お金をはらう 　_{かね}	to pay money
〜を持って行く 　_も	to bring something
〜に着く 　_つ	to arrive at
時間がかかる	to take time
〜をさがす	to look for
〜に答える 　_{こた}	to answer, to respond

おぼえていますか。

しつもん　ところ　りょうり　会う　家を出る　出かける　話す　まつ　明るい
くらい　せまい　早い　ひろい　きれい（な）　有名（な）　それから
　　　　　　　　　　　　　　　　　　　　　　　　_{ゆうめい}

Activity 5　新しいことばをつかって、旅行の前にすること (things to do) を書い
　　　　　　　　　　　　　_{りょ}
て下さい。

Activity 6   Choose the appropriate words from the list on page 80 to complete the following sentences.

1. 旅行の計画を＿＿＿＿＿＿下さい。お金は私が＿＿＿＿＿＿。
   りょ　けいかく

2. 今からお土産を買いに行きますが、六時にはホテルに＿＿＿＿＿＿。
   みやげ

3. 乗り物についてガイドブックで＿＿＿＿＿＿。
   の　もの

4. 勉強しなかったけど、先生のしつもんに＿＿＿＿＿＿。

5. 夕方の六時に東京に＿＿＿＿＿＿から、その日は東京えきのちかくのホテル
   ゆう　きょう　きょう
   に＿＿＿＿＿＿。

6. ホテルを＿＿＿＿＿＿たいんですが、お金がないから、安いホテルを＿＿＿＿＿＿
   かね
   くれませんか。

7. 林田さんは大きいスーツケースを＿＿＿＿＿＿ので、えきまでタクシー (taxi)
   はやしだ
   を＿＿＿＿＿＿。

8. フランスりょうりは時間が＿＿＿＿＿＿から、今から＿＿＿＿＿＿しま
   しょう。

C. 〜泊〜日　Number of days and nights
はく

日帰り	ひがえり	day trip
一泊二日	いっぱくふつか	two days, one night
二泊三日	にはくみっか	three days, two nights
三泊四日	さんぱくよっか	four days, three nights
四泊五日	よんはく（ぱく）いつか	five days, four nights
五泊六日	ごはくむいか	six days, five nights

NOTE

● 〜泊〜日 is not commonly used when the stay is longer than one week. In that case, use 〜日（間）泊まる。（八日（間）泊まる）

おぼえていますか。

〜日

◆ **Activity 7**   Say the length of each trip using the number of days and nights that match the following expressions.

Example: 火曜日に行って、水曜日に帰ります。

一泊二日の旅行
いっぱく　　りょ

1. 月曜日に来て、金曜日に出ます。　　　　　　_____の旅行
りょ

2. 明日来て、明後日帰ります。　　　　　　　　_____の旅行
りょ

3. 一昨日来ました。明日帰ります。　　　　　　_____の旅行
りょ

4. 月曜日の午後から土曜日の朝までいます。　　_____の旅行
りょ

5. 今日行って、明後日帰ります。　　　　　　　_____の旅行
りょ

6. 明日行って、明日帰ります。　　　　　　　　_____の旅行
りょ

◆ **Activity 8**   Work with a partner. One person should come up with a sentence similar to those in activity 7, and the other should state the number of days and nights indicated.

Example: A: 水曜日に行って、金曜日に帰ります。

B: 二泊三日の旅行でしょう。
に　はく

D. せつぞくし　Conjunctions

だけど	but	その前（に）	before that
けれども	however	その時（に）	at that time
というのは	it's because	その間（に）あいだ	during that time
（まず）はじめに	first, first (of all)	それで	then, so
つぎに	next	ですから	therefore, so
ところで	by the way	だから	so
その後（で／に）	after that	また	also

おぼえていますか。

そして　それから　でも

Activity 9   Use the appropriate conjunctions to improve the flow between the following sentences.

Example: 高男くんは十五さいです。ビールは飲めません。
          たか お
          高男くんは十五さいです。だから／ですから、ビールは
          たか お
          飲めません。

1. 私はバレーボールをしました。山田さんは寝ていたそうです。

2. 旅行の計画をたてます。安い旅館をさがします。旅館の予約をしたいと思い
     りょ けいかく   りょかん   りょかん よやく
     ます。

3. 山本さんは病気です。今日は来られないそうです。

4. クレジットカードでお金をはらいました。お金がなくなったからです。
                        かね   かね

5. ふねの切符を買いました。時間をしらべました。
          きっぷ

6. 五泊六日でハワイに行きました。色々なばしょでしゃしんをとりました。
     ご はく   いろいろ

ダイアローグ

はじめに

しつもんに日本語で答えて下さい。
              こた

1. どんなところに旅行に行ったことがありますか。
                 りょ

2. 何日ぐらい行きましたか。(Use ~days~nights)

3. どんなことをしましたか。 (Use 〜たり〜たりする)

4. 旅行の前にどんなことをしますか。
     りょ

5. 旅行に行く時、どんなものを持って行ったらいいと思いますか。
     りょ   も

6. 海外旅行はどこへ行きたいですか。どうしてですか。
     かいがいりょ

7. 国内旅行はどこへ行きたいですか。どうしてですか。
     こくないりょ

今度の休み   *Upcoming vacation plans*

The order of the following **manga** frames is scrambled. Read the dialogue and unscramble the frames by writing the correct number in the box in each frame.

先生がリーさんと上田さんに今度の休みについて聞いています。

先生：　今度の休みはどうしますか。

上田：　北海道に行く予定です。

リー：　北海道？

上田：　うん、さっぽろで雪まつりがあるから、見に行こうと思ってるの。

リー：　雪まつり？　それ、おまつり？

上田：　ええ、雪で作った建物や動物がたくさん見られるの。

リー：　へえ、そうなんだ。おもしろそうだね。

先生：　でも、二月の北海道はまだ寒いから、あたたかくして行った方がいいですね。

上田：　ええ、ですから、今度買い物に行った時に、新しいコートを買うつもりです。

先生：　そうですか。ところで、リーくんの予定は？

リー：　ぼくは、たいわんへ帰るつもりです。

先生：　そうですか。いつ帰るんですか。

リー：　今学期がおわったら、すぐ出ようと思っています。

上田：　そう、じゃあ、もうすぐね。

リー：　うん。だから、今週の週末は、お<u>土産</u>とスーツケースを買いに
　　　　行こうと思ってるんだ。あ、先生、それで、レポートのことな
　　　　んですが。

先生：　はい、何ですか。

リー：　十五日に出るかもしれませんので、十四日に出してもよろしい
　　　　でしょうか。

先生：　ああ、もちろんいいですよ。

DIALOGUE PHRASE NOTES

- さっぽろ is the capital city of the northernmost major island,
  北海道.
- 今学期 means *this semester* or *this quarter*.
- よろしい is the polite form of いい.

ダイアローグの後で

A. 上田さんとリーさんの休みの計画を下のひょう (chart) に書いて下さい。

	上田さん	リーさん
行くばしょ		
行った時にすること		
行く時にすること		

B. しつもんに日本語で答えて下さい。

1. 上田さんは何をしに出かけますか。

2. 雪まつりはどんなおまつりですか。

3. リーさんはどうして十四日にレポートを出すつもりですか。

C. Identify whom each of the speeches is directed at in the dialogue. Pay attention to the level of formality used.

D. Identify the phrases that introduce a new topic.

日本の文化
ぶん か

国内旅行 Traveling in Japan
こくないりょ

Among domestic airlines, a highway system, and several types of rail systems, the best way to travel in the country is probably by train. Various discount tickets and railway passes are available for travelers, but some of them must be purchased before arriving in Japan. For example, Japan Railways Group (JR), a group of the nation's largest railroad companies, sells the Japan Rail Pass, which allows unlimited travel on its trains anywhere in Japan. The pass is available to travelers who stay in Japan for more than a week, and it must be purchased before arriving in Japan. JR trains include most local trains, the airport express, and the 新幹線 (bullet
しんかんせん

© Kenneth Hamm / Photo Japan

train). Some local stations are not equipped with an elevator or an escalator, though, so it is not a good idea to carry heavy luggage. There are, however, very good delivery services called 宅配便 available if you want to ship a large amount of luggage within Japan. You
たくはいびん
can even send luggage to and from the airport.

Iain Masterton/Photographer's Choice/Getty Images

A Japanese bento contains a variety of different selections.

One of the pleasures of traveling by train is the 駅弁,
えきべん
or station lunch box. These packaged lunches are sold in trains and stations all over Japan. They usually contain some regional specialty, making them popular with travelers. Most cost between 500 and 1,000 yen.

If you do not use a railway pass, you may want to check domestic airfares. Airline companies offer highly competitive prices for tickets purchased in advance. The two major airlines, ANA and JAL, also offer air passes (ANA Experience Japan Fare and Oneworld Yokoso Visit Japan Fare, respectively) for foreign visitors to Japan. These allow you to fly anywhere in Japan for 10,000 yen. Both the airline companies and JR offer inexpensive packages that include transportation and hotel accommodation. You may find packages that are cheaper than a round-trip air or train ticket.

There are all kinds of accommodations available in Japan. Western-style hotels (ホテル) are usually more expensive than others, though they are more likely to have staff who speak English. Also, they often have English newspapers, maps and other services. Business hotels (ビジネスホテル) are budget hotels for those who wish to travel affordably. The rooms are extremely small, but they are very inexpensive, provide essential amenities, and serve breakfast.

Another option is 旅館, Japanese-style inns. The cost of these can vary from very inexpensive to expensive. Although some 旅館 have western-style rooms, many have only Japanese-style rooms. Also, a Japanese-style breakfast and dinner are included in the price. Hotel personnel come to your room to lay out or put away ふとん and to serve meals, tea, and snacks. This may be one of the few instances in Japan where tipping is accepted. (Tips are not necessary for most services, such as in restaurants and taxis.) Some 旅館 have rooms with a bathroom, but many of them have communal baths and restrooms which are segregated by sex. They also provide casual summer kimonos called ゆかた to be used as bathrobes. It is perfectly acceptable for guests to walk around 旅館 wearing ゆかた.

Private guest houses such as 民宿 (Japanese-style inns) and ペンション (western-style bed and breakfast establishments) are usually less expensive than hotels or 旅館, and are popular among young people and students. Both 民宿 and ペンション serve breakfast and dinner in the dining area, but no special room service is provided, and the bathing areas and lavatories are communal.

John S Lander/Getty Images

文法
ぶんぽう

I. Expressing intention using the volitional form of the verb + と思う

There are various ways of expressing one's intention, depending on how strongly you feel. This chapter introduces three forms of intention. The first form, the volitional form of verbs + と思う, expresses a tentative intention.

温泉に　入ろうと思います。　　*I'm thinking of taking a bath at a hot spring.*
おんせん

ふねに　乗ろうと思います。　　*I'm thinking of taking a ship.*
の

今、じゅんびしようと思う。　　*I'm thinking of starting preparations now.*

Volitional form of verbs

Verb types	Dictionary form		Formation	Volitional form
る -verbs	答える こた	(to answer)	答え + よう こた	答えよう こた
	しらべる	(to check)	しらべ + よう	しらべよう
う -verbs	さがす	(to look for)	さが + そ + う	さがそう
	つかう	(to use)	つか + お + う	つかおう
Irregular Verbs	する	(to do)		しよう
	来る	(to come)		来よう こ

森山：　海外旅行に行こうと思うんだけど。
もりやま　かいがいりょ
I'm thinking of going on an overseas trip.

山本：　いいね。どこに行くの。
Sounds good. Where are you going?

森山：　まだ、分からないけど、ハワイかな。
もりやま
I don't know yet, but I am thinking of going to Hawaii.

山本：　じゃあ、パスポートをとった方がいいよ。
Then you should get a passport.

When the subject is the speaker, the use of 思っています indicates that the speaker has been thinking of doing something for some time, while 思います merely indicates the speaker's current thinking.

もうすぐ出かけようと思います。
I am thinking of going out soon.

夏休みに国に帰ろうと思ってるから、アルバイトをしてるんだ。
くに
I've been thinking of returning to my hometown/country next summer vacation, so I am working part-time.

NOTES

- When the subject is someone other than the speaker, 思っています must be used to express his/her current thinking as well as his/her thinking over time.

  妹はでんしゃの時間をしらべようと思っています。
  My younger sister is thinking of checking the train schedule.

  しほさんはクレジットカードでお金をはらおうと思っている。
  Shiho is thinking of paying with a credit card.

- The volitional form above indicates the speaker's willingness to do something. It is the plain form of ましよう, which means *Let's ~.*

  夏休みの計画をたてましょう。　　*Let's make plans for the summer.* (polite)

  夏休みの計画をたてよう。　　*Let's make plans for the summer.* (casual)

- The volitional form of the verb must be used before 〜かしら or 〜かな to express the speaker's ruminations about what he/she should do.

  明日出かけようかな。　　*I wonder if I should go out tomorrow.*

  今日は何をしようかな。　　*I wonder what I should do today.*

- The form 〜たいと思います is often used to express desire. This is less direct than 〜たいです, and thus, it sounds more formal and polite.

  いつか日本にもどりたいと思います。
  I would like to go back to Japan someday. (more polite and formal)

  いつか日本にもどりたいです。
  I want to go back to Japan someday. (direct)

話してみましょう

Activity 1   Work with a partner. Ask your partner what he/she is thinking of doing for his or her next vacation. Your partner will answer using the picture cue and 〜ようと思います.

Example:

A: 今度の休みに何をしようと思いますか。

B: 海外旅行をしようと思います。
かいがいりょ

1   2   3

4   5   6

Activity 2   Work as a class. Ask if your classmates have any plans tomorrow and what they will do. Use casual speech.

Example: A: 明日、何か予定ある?
よてい
B: うん、家でパーティしようと思ってるんだけど。

or いや、とくに何もないけど。

名前	明日の予定
な	よてい

Activity 3   Work as a class. First, each person should decide on one social activity for the weekend and write the time and location on the following schedule sheet. Then, each person should invite his/her classmates to this activity. If you decide to accept a classmate's invitation, add it to your schedule. If you decide not to accept an invitation due to a schedule conflict or lack of interest, politely refuse the invitation. Try to make your schedule as full as possible.

Example   A: 今週の土曜日はいそがしいですか。

B: 朝はいそがしいですけど、午後はひまですよ。

A: そうですか。テニスをしようと思ってるんですが、一緒にどうですか。

B: 何時からですか。

A: 一時から五時ごろまでです。

B: そうですか。いいですよ。

(write テニス from 1:00 p.m. to 5:00 p.m. under Saturday.)

or   すみません。三時からはちょっとようじがあって。

	土曜日	日曜日
8:00 a.m.		
9:00 a.m.		
10:00 a.m.		
11:00 a.m.		
12:00 p.m.		
1:00 p.m.		
2:00 p.m.		
3:00 p.m.		
4:00 p.m.		
5:00 p.m.		
6:00 p.m.		
7:00 p.m.		
8:00 p.m.		
9:00 p.m.		
10:00 p.m.		
11:00 p.m.		
12:00 a.m.		

II.　Expressing intention and plans using the plain present form of the verb + つもり or 予定

A. Expressing intention using つもり (*intend to ～*)

つもり also expresses the intention of the speaker or someone close to the speaker. Compared to the volitional form of verbs + と思う, つもり expresses a stronger intention.

明日、日曜日の予定をきめるつもりです。	*Tomorrow I intend to make plans for Sunday.*
母は日帰りツアーを予約するつもりです。	*My mother intends to make reservations for a day trip.*
お土産を買うつもりです。	*I intend to buy a souvenir.*
今度は国内旅行にするつもり（だ）。	*I intend to decide on domestic travel this time.*
三時にはもどるつもり（だ）。	*I intend to return at 3.*
あつ子：旅館に泊まるの？	*Are we staying in a Japanese-style inn?*
ウィル：うん、そのつもり。	*Yeah, that's our plan.*

NOTES

- つもり is a dependent noun and thus follows the plain present form of verbs. It can also follow the demonstrative word その, as in そのつもり, which means to intend to do so.

明日きめるつもりです。	*I intend to decide tomorrow.*
明日はきめないつもりです。	*I do not intend to decide tomorrow.*
私の一番上の姉もそのつもりです。	*My oldest sister intends to do so, too.*

- Use the copula verb です／だ after つもり to indicate the presence of intention or a plan or just end the sentence with つもり.　Use ～つもりはありません／ない to indicate a lack of intention or plan.

  ガイドブックを持って行くつもりです。
  I intend to take a guidebook. (polite)

  ガイドブックを持って行くつもり（<u>だ</u>）。
  I intend to take a guidebook. (casual)

  ガイドブックを持って行くつもり<u>はありません</u>。
  I don't intend to take a guidebook. (polite)

  ガイドブックを持って行くつもり<u>はない</u>。
  I don't intend to take a guidebook. (casual)

B. Expressing plans using 予定 (*plan to* 〜)

Used without a modifier, 予定 is a noun meaning *plan*.

今日の予定は何ですか。　　　　　　*What is the plan for today?*

今日は予定がありません。　　　　　*I don't have any plans today.*

予定 follows the plain present form of a verb when it is used with a modifier to indicate a specific plan. 予定 is followed by the copula verb です／だ. The subject of a statement with 予定 can be any person.

六時の飛行機で出る予定です。　　　　*I plan to leave here on the 6 o'clock plane.*

ホテルには泊まらない予定だ。　　　　*I plan to not stay in hotels.*

リーさんは今年の冬に中国に帰る予定です。　*Mr. Li plans to go back to China this winter.*

スミス：　今度の休みに何か予定がありますか。
　　　　　Do you have some kind of plan for your next day off?

森：　ええ、上野の美術館に行く予定です。スミスさんは？
　　　　Yes, I plan to go to the art museum in Ueno. How about you, Mr. Smith?

スミス：　とくに予定はありませんが、どこかへ出かけようと思っています。
　　　　　I don't have any particular plans, but I am thinking of going somewhere.

NOTE:

● Use 〜予定はありません／ない to indicate the lack of a plan.

かんこうする予定はありません。　　　　*I don't plan to go sightseeing.*

みずうみに行く予定はないよ。　　　　　*We don't plan to go to the lake.*

話してみましょう

Activity 1　　You are a tour guide, taking a group of tourists to Lake Yamanaka, near Mt. Fuji. The following is the tour schedule. Explain your plans to the tour participants, using 予定.

© Kenneth Hamm / Photo Japan

一日目	8:00 a.m.	バスが出る
	10:30 a.m.	山中湖 (Lake Yamanaka) に着く
	10:30 a.m. 〜 12:00 p.m.	自由行動 (free time)
	12:00 p.m.	ランチ　（ホテル　マウントふじ）
	1:30 p.m.	文学の森公園ツアー
	3:00 p.m.	山中湖プラザホテル
	3:00 p.m.	自由行動 (free time)
	6:00 p.m.	夕食 (Dinner)
二日目	9:00 a.m.	朝食 (Breakfast)
	11:00 a.m.	バスで東京へ
	1:30 p.m.	東京にもどる

Example: 八時にバスが出る予定です。

Activity 2 The following chart shows Ms. Ueda and her family's plans for this summer. A double circle (◎) indicates a definite plan, and a single circle (○) indicates an intention. A question mark (？) indicates a tentative plan. You are Ms. Ueda. Describe each family member's plans and intentions using the volitional form of verb + と思う, the plain present form of verb + つもり or 予定, and appropriate transition devices.

Example: 父は友達とふねで旅行する予定です。色々な国に行くつもりです。そして、かんこうしようと思っています。

お父さん	お母さん	パム（妹）	私（アリス）
○ 色々な国に行きます。	◎ 日本に来ます。	◎ フランスに行きます。	○ 国内旅行をします。
？ かんこうをします。	？ ガイドブックを買います。	○ フランス人の友達を作ります。	◎ 日本語を勉強します。
◎ 友達とふねで旅行します。	○ 旅館に泊まります。	？ フランスでアルバイトをします。	？ でんしゃとバスをつかいます。

Activity 3   Work with a partner. Write down your plans for this week, including both plans that are fixed and things that you intend to do. Then ask your partner about his/her plans. Decide which of you is busier. Use casual speech.

Example: A: 月曜日と火曜日の予定はどうなってるの？

B: えっと、月曜日は九時から十二時までじゅぎょうに出る予定（だ）よ。火曜日は九時から五時までバイトする予定なんだ。

A: いそがしそう（だ）ね。週末もいそがしいの？

B: あ、土曜日は日帰りで温泉に行くつもり（だ）よ。

A: そう。それはいいね。

例	予定	月曜日　（九時から十二時）じゅぎょう 火曜日　（九時から五時まで）バイト
	つもり	土曜日　友達と日帰り旅行（温泉）
私	予定	
	つもり	
パートナー	予定	
	つもり	

Activity 4   Work with a partner. Each partner should decide on his/her next vacation. Ask your partner about his/her vacation plans and take notes, using the table below. Your partner should respond using 予定、つもり、or 〜ようと思っている depending on how firm his/her plans are. Use casual speech. Then report to the class using polite speech.

Example   A: 今度の休みはどうするの？

B: 家族でオレゴンに旅行に行く予定なんだ。

A: いいね。何日ぐらい行くの？

B: 三泊四日の予定だけど。

A: どこに泊まるの？

B:　まだ、分からないけれど、べんりなばしょにするつもりなんだ。

A:　そう。それで、オレゴンではどんなことしようと思ってるの?

B:　そうだね。つりをしたり、キャンプしたりしようと思って
　　るんだ。

A:　そうなんだ。それはたのしそうだね。

私は〜さんと話しました。〜さんは三泊四日でオレゴンに行く予
定です。〜さんはべんりなところに泊まるつもりだそうです。オ
レゴンでは、つりをしたりキャンプをしたりしようと思っている
そうです。

	＿＿＿＿＿＿さんの旅行の計画 りょ　　　けいかく
行くばしょ	
〜泊〜日 はく	
泊まるところ と	
すること	

III. Expressing occasion and time using 時

In Chapter 12 of *Nakama 1*, 時 is used with nouns and adjectives as in 病気の時、
小さい時 and 元気な時. 時 can be combined with verbs, but the relationship between the
main clause and the 時 clause is different depending on the verb tense in the 時 clause.

A. Plain present form + 時 (uncompleted action)

When 時 is combined with an action verb, the tense in the 時 clause indicates whether the
action in this clause was completed by the time the action in the main clause takes place.
Thus, the present form indicates that the action in the 時 clause had not been not completed
when the action in the main clause took place.

家を	出る時、電話して下さい。 でん	*Please call me when you leave home.*
本を	読む時、めがねをかける。	*I put on glasses when I read a book.*
空港に くうこう	行く時、バスで行く予定です。 よてい	*I plan to take the bus when I go to the airport.*
お金を かね	はらう時、クレジットカードをつかった。	*I used a credit card when I made the payment.*

B.   Plain past form + 時 (completed action)

Use of the past tense in the 時 clause indicates that the event in this clause has been completed by the time the event in the main clause takes place.

そのさかなを　　食べた時、　おなかが痛くなりました。

I got a stomachache when/after I ate the fish.

ホテルに　もどった時、　電話して下さい。
　　　　　　　　　　　　でん

Call me when/after you get back to the hotel.

切符を　予約した時、　お金をはらいませんでした。
きっぷ　　よやく　　　　かね

I didn't pay when I reserved the ticket.

これはハワイに　　行った時に、買った。

I bought it when I went to Hawaii.

Note that regardless of the tense in the 時 clause, the tense in the main clause indicates when the entire event took place.

家を　出る時、友達に電話します。 　　　　　　　だち　でん	*I will call my friend when/before I leave home.*
家を　出た時、友達に電話します。 　　　　　　だち　でん	*I will call my friend when/after I have left home.*
家を　出る時、友達に電話しました。 　　　　　　だち　でん	*I called my friend when/before I left home.*
家を　出た時、友達に電話しました。 　　　　　　だち　でん	*I called my friend when/after I had left home.*

NOTES

- The form of adjectives, verbs and nouns before 時 is the same as it is for noun modification. The use of 時 with nouns and adjectives was introduced in Chapter 12 of *Nakama 1*. It is not necessary to use the past tense when pairing 時 with nouns, adjectives, and verbal expressions which express a state such as ある, いる, 〜ている, or 〜ない.

  日帰りの時は、たいてい飛行機をつかいます。
  ひがえ　　　　　　　　ひき

  I tend to go by plane for day trips.

  日帰りじゃない時は、でんしゃで行きます。
  ひがえ

  I go by train when it is not just a day trip.

  ひまな時は、かんこうをしました。

  I went sightseeing when I had free time.

  ひまじゃない時は、あまりかんこうは出来ませんでした。

  I could not do much sightseeing when I didn't have any free time.

  いそがしい時は、あまり出かけられませんでした。

  I couldn't go out much when I was busy.

いそがしくない時、よく映画を見ました。
I often watched movies when I wasn't busy.

旅館に泊まっている時、パスポートがなくなった。
I lost my passport when I was staying at the inn.

お金がある時、よくおいしいりょうりを食べに行った。
I often went out for good food when I had money.

ことばが分からない時は、辞書でしらべる。
When I don't understand a word, I look it up in the dictionary.

● The particle に is optional when expressing time and 〜時 can appear in the forms 〜時に、〜時は、〜時には.

ホテルをさがす時には、よくインターネットをつかいます。
I often use the Internet to look for a hotel.

知っている時は答えられるけど、知らない時は答えられない。
I can answer your question when I know the answer, but not when I don't know it.

● Use が to mark the subject of the 時 clause if it is different from that of the main clause.

林さんが来た時、川口さんも来ました。
When Mr. Hayashi was here, Ms. Kawaguchi came as well.

でんしゃが東京に着いた時、外はもうくらかったです。
When the train arrived in Tokyo, it was already dark outside.

雨がふった時、かさを持っていませんでした。
I didn't have an umbrella when it rained.

話してみましょう

Activity 1   Choose the correct main clause for each of the 時 clauses.

Example: おなかが痛くなった時、薬を飲みました。

1. おなかが痛くなった時	a. いぬとあそびました。
2. 家に帰る時	b. 友達があそびに来ていました。
3. 旅行に行く時	c. バスで帰りました。
4. 旅行に行った時	d. 時間がかかりました。
5. 計画をたてる時	e. 薬を飲みました。
6. 家に帰った時	f. お土産を買いました。
7. こうえんに行った時	g. ホテルの予約をしました。
8. こうえんに行く時	h. サンドイッチを持って行きました。

Activity 2　Complete the following sentences by supplying the 時 clause.

Example:　<u>海外旅行に行った時</u>、お土産を買いました。
　　　　　　かいがいりょ　　　　　　　みやげ

1. ＿＿＿＿＿＿＿＿＿＿＿＿＿＿、おもしろいツアーをさがそうと思います。

2. ＿＿＿＿＿＿＿＿＿＿＿＿＿＿、りっぱな旅館に泊まりたいです。
　　　　　　　　　　　　　　　　　　りょかん　と

3. ＿＿＿＿＿＿＿＿＿＿＿＿＿＿、デジカメでとりました。

4. ＿＿＿＿＿＿＿＿＿＿＿＿＿＿、ガイドブックとインターネットで色々
　　　　　　　　　　　　　　　　　　　　　　　　　　　　　　いろいろ
　　しらべました。

5. ＿＿＿＿＿＿＿＿＿＿＿＿＿＿、くつをぬいで下さい。

6. ＿＿＿＿＿＿＿＿＿＿＿＿＿＿、温泉に入るつもりです。
　　　　　　　　　　　　　　　　　　おんせん

7. ＿＿＿＿＿＿＿＿＿＿＿＿＿＿、ばしょが分かりませんでした。

8. ＿＿＿＿＿＿＿＿＿＿＿＿＿＿、みずうみでふねに乗りました。
　　　　　　　　　　　　　　　　　　　　　　　　　　の

Activity 3　Work with a partner. Discuss what you would do in the following situation using 時.

Example:　A: 旅館に泊まる時、どうしますか。
　　　　　　　りょかん　と
　　　　　　B: そうですね。英語を話す人がいる旅館をさがします。
　　　　　　　　　　　　　えい　　　　　　　　りょかん
　　　　　　A: じゃあ、旅館に泊まった時、どうしますか。
　　　　　　　　　　りょかん　と
　　　　　　B: ゆかたを着ようと思います。(ゆかた = *an informal cotton kimono*.)
　　　　　　　　　　き

1. ホテル／旅館に泊まる
　　　　　りょかん　と
2. 温泉に入る
　おんせん
3. レストランに行く
4. しごとをきめる
5. ハイキングをする
6. 山登りをする
　のぼ

Activity 4　Work with a partner. Using 時, describe to your partner an interesting incident you or someone you know once experienced.

Example:　ハワイに行った時、バスに乗ったんです。そのバスに乗った時、私は
　　　　　　　　　　　　　　　　　　　の　　　　　　　　　　　　の
　　　　　　お金を持っていませんでしたが、そのことを忘れていました。
　　　　　　　　　も
　　　　　　大変だと思って、下を見た時、目の前にお金がありました。

IV. Using もう and まだ

The words もう and まだ are adverbs that are often used to indicate the progress or lack of progress of an activity. The English equivalents of もう or まだ are *already, yet, now, still,* and *(not) yet,* depending on the verbal endings. This chapter introduces how these adverbs are used in Japanese.

A.   Using もう

The adverb もう indicates that a situation which existed some time ago no longer exists. For example, 山田さんはもう出かけました (*Ms. Yamada has already left*) implies that Ms. Yamada was here some time ago, but she is not here now. Similarly, もう食べられません (*I can no longer eat*) implies that I was able to eat some time ago, but this state no longer exists. In English, もう corresponds to *already* or *now* in affirmative declarative sentences, to *yet* or *already* in affirmative interrogative sentences, and to *(not) anymore* or *(not) any longer* in negative sentences.

じゅんびは<u>もう</u>しました。	*I've already finished the preparations.*
予定、<u>もう</u>知ってる。	*I already know the plan.*
乗り物は<u>もう</u>きめましたか。	*Have you decided on transportation yet?*
りかちゃん、<u>もう</u>空港に着いた？	*Has Rika arrived at the airport yet?*
<u>もう</u>計画はたてたくありません。	*I don't want to make any more plans.*
<u>もう</u>食べられません。	*I can't eat any more.*

お母さん：	お土産はもう買ったの？	*Have you bought souvenirs yet?*
子供：	うん、もう買ったよ。	*Yeah, I already did.*
お母さん：	じゃあ、荷物はもうかばんに入れた？	*Well, have you put your things in the bag?*
子供：	あ、忘れてた。	*Oh, I forgot.*

B.   Using まだ

The adverb まだ indicates that a state that existed some time ago still remains. For example, 子供はまだ寝ています (*The child is still sleeping*) implies that the child was sleeping some time ago and this state still exists now. Also, 山田さんはまだ来ていません (*Ms. Yamada has not come here yet*) implies that Ms. Yamada was not here some time ago and is not here now. In English, まだ means *still* in affirmative sentences, and *yet* or *still* in negative sentences.

まだ計画をたてています。	*I am still planning.*
まだばしょをしらべてない。	*I have not yet looked for a place.*
あいちゃん、まだ、ねこ、さがしてる？	*Is Ai still looking for her cat?*
まだつかっていませんか。	*Are you not using it yet?*

When まだ is followed by an action verb + ていません, it expresses *have not done ~ yet*. If まだ is used with the simple negative form of an action verb, it means *won't do ～for a while.*

その計画はまだ見ていません。 <small>けいかく</small>	*I haven't seen the plan yet.*
その計画はまだ見ません。 <small>けいかく</small>	*I won't see the plan for a while.*
林 さんはまだもどっていません。 <small>はやし</small>	*Ms. Hayashi has not come back yet.*
林 さんはまだもどりません。 <small>はやし</small>	*Ms. Hayashi won't come back for a while.*
c.f. まだ知りません。	*I don't know yet.*

NOTES

● まだです can be used to mean *not yet.*

早川：　じゅぎょうはもうはじまりましたか。
<small>はやかわ</small>
Has the class started yet?

ブラウン：　いいえ、まだです。
No, not yet.

森 山：　旅館はもうきめたの？
<small>もりやま　りょかん</small>
Have you chosen an inn yet?

山本：　いいえ、まだきめてないよ。
No, I haven't decided yet.

先生：　まだしゅくだいを出していませんね。
You haven't turned in your homework yet.

学生：　すみません。今度のしゅくだいはむずかしいので、
　　　　まだしらべているんです。
I am sorry but this homework is difficult, so I'm still doing research.

話してみましょう

Activity 1   The chart below contains today's schedules for Mr. Miller, Ms. Hayashi, and Ms. Cheng. The time now is 12 p.m. Answer the questions using もう or まだ.

Example: 林さんはもう学校に行きましたか。
いいえ、まだ、行っていません。

	ミラー	林	チェン
6:00 a.m.	家に帰る		
7:00 a.m.	寝る		起きる
8:00 a.m.		起きる	朝御飯を食べる
9:00 a.m.		朝御飯を食べる	学校に行く
10:00 a.m.			
12:00 p.m.			
1:00 p.m.		学校に行く	
4:00 p.m.	起きる		家に帰る
5:00 p.m.	食事をする		勉強する
6:00 p.m.			
8:00 p.m.	しごとに出かける	家に帰る	

1. ミラーさんは、もう朝御飯を食べましたか。
2. 林さんは、もう起きましたか。
3. ミラーさんは、もう起きましたか。
4. チェンさんは、もう学校に行きましたか。
5. ミラーさんは、もう家に帰りましたか。
6. チェンさんは、もう家に帰りましたか。
7. 林さんは、まだ寝ていますか。

👥 **Activity 2** Work with a partner. Imagine that you and your partner are going on a trip, and you're dividing the tasks needed to prepare for the trip. The following is a checklist for each of you. Put a checkmark next to some of the items to indicate that you have completed them, and randomly leave some of them blank. Ask each other which preparations are done and which are not done. Use casual speech.

Example: A: もうホテルの予約をした？
　　　　　　　　　　 よやく
　　　　　 B: うん、もう、したよ。or ごめん (sorry)。まだ、してない。

私		パートナー	
	ホテルの予約をする 　　よやく		でんしゃの時間をしらべる
	デジカメを買う		でんしゃの切符を買う 　　　きっぷ
	おもしろいツアーをさがす		あつまるばしょをきめる
	レストランをきめる		パスポートをとる
	お金をじゅんびする 　かね		荷物をかばんに入れる 　にもつ

👥 **Activity 3** Work with a partner. Ask your partner if there is anything that he/she did when young and is still doing now, or anything that he/she did when young but is not doing now and doesn't want to do any longer. Ask for reasons why.

Example: A: 子供の時、よく何をしましたか。
　　　　　 B: やきゅうをしました。
　　　　　 A: 今もまだしているんですか。
　　　　　 B: ええ、好きだからしていますよ。
　　　　　　　 or いいえ、下手だからもうしていません。／やきゅうは、
　　　　　　　　　　もうしたくないですね。

V. Expressing conditions and sequence using 〜たら

There are several types of conditional sentences in Japanese. The conditional たら is formed with the plain past form of a verb/adjective + ら.

雨が　ふったら、	*If it rains,*
雨が　ふらなかったら、	*If it does not rain,*
計画が　よかったら、 けいかく	*If the plan is good,*
計画が　よくなかったら、 けいかく	*If the plan is not good,*
べんりだったら、	*If it is convenient,*
べんりじゃなかったら、	*If it isn't convenient,*
かんこうきゃく　だったら、	*If (a person) is a tourist,*
かんこうきゃく　じゃなかったら、	*If (a person) is not a tourist,*

The condition expressed in the たら clause must be completed (or satisfied) before the action/event in the main clause can take place. Therefore, you can say 手紙を書いたら、ゆうびんきょくに持って行って下さい , (*After you write the letter, please take it to the post office*) but you cannot say ~~手紙を書いたら、えんぴつで書きます。~~ (*After I write a letter, I write it with a pencil*). This is because the use of たら here implies that one act is completed before the other takes place.

寒くなかったら、プールに行きましょう。	*If it is not cold, let's go to a pool.*
日本に行ったら、富士山が見たいです。	*If I go to Japan, I want to see Mt. Fuji.*
もっと勉強したら、上手になります。	*If you study harder, you will improve.*
私が山田さんだったら、先生に話すでしょう。	*If I were Mr. Yamada, I would talk to the teacher.*
お金がなかったら、日本へは行きません。	*If I didn't have the money, I wouldn't go to Japan.*
明日天気がよかったらいいですね。	*It would be great if the weather were nice tomorrow.*

The たら clause can also express an actual sequence of events without introducing a condition. In this case, the event/action in the たら clause takes place before the event/action in the main clause.

家に帰ったら、電話します。	*I'll call after I get home.*
旅館に着いたら、温泉に入ります。	*I will soak in the hot spring when I get to the inn.*
ごはんを食べたら、出かけます。	*I will leave after I eat.*

If the main clause is in the present tense, it can be used to express the speaker's intention, request, obligation, etc. However, it cannot express an event that has already transpired.

しつもんを読んだら、すぐ答えて下さい。	*Please answer the question as soon as you have finished reading it.*
じゅんびが出来たら、よぶつもりです。	*I intend to call for you when the preparations are completed.*
お金があつまったら、持って行きます。	*I'll bring the money over when it has been collected.*

When the main clause is in the past tense, the event in the main clause expresses a situation which is uncontrollable to the speaker. Thus, the main clause tends to express surprise or a realization. (an unexpected event)

おさけを飲んだら、気分がわるくなった。	*I didn't feel well after I drank the sake.*
家に帰ったら、ねこがへやにいた。	*When I got home, there was a cat in my room* (and it surprised me).
アパートにもどったら、ウィルはいなかった。	*When I went back to his apartment, Will was not there.*

話してみましょう

Activity 1   Complete the following sentences.

Example　日本に行ったら、富士山に行きたいですね。

1. でんしゃの方がべんりだったら、＿＿＿＿＿＿＿＿＿＿＿＿＿＿。

2. お金をはらったら、＿＿＿＿＿＿＿＿＿＿＿＿＿＿。

3. 知っていたら、＿＿＿＿＿＿＿＿＿＿＿＿＿。

4. 時間がかかったら、＿＿＿＿＿＿＿＿＿＿＿＿＿。

5. その映画がよかったら、＿＿＿＿＿＿＿＿＿＿＿＿。

6. ＿＿＿＿＿＿＿＿＿＿＿＿＿＿、答えて下さい。

7. ＿＿＿＿＿＿＿＿＿＿＿＿＿＿、三泊四日ぐらいがいいですね。

8. ＿＿＿＿＿＿＿＿＿＿＿＿＿＿、スーツケースを持って行きましょうか。

9. ＿＿＿＿＿＿＿＿＿＿＿＿＿＿、でんしゃの切符をさがして下さい。

Activity 2

Describe the following sequence of events using 〜たら.

Example: 家を出たら、雨がふっていました。

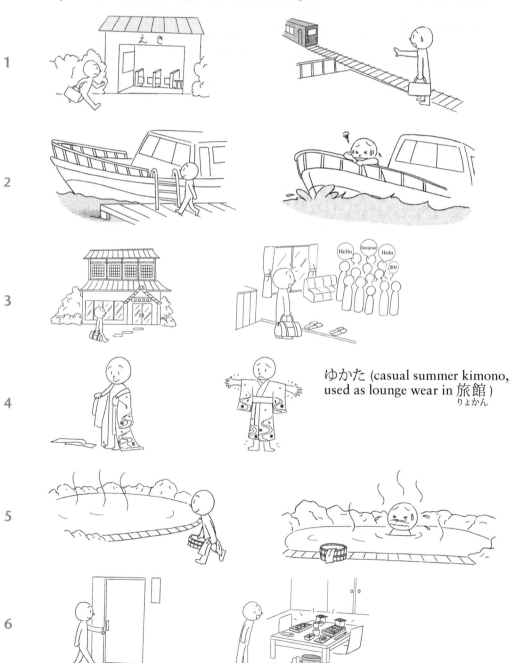

ゆかた (casual summer kimono, used as lounge wear in 旅館)
りょかん

Activity 3   Work with a partner. Ask your partner what he/she would want to do in the following situations:

Example: 日本へ行く

A: 日本へ行ったら、何をしようと思いますか。

B: おいしいすしを食べようと思います。

しゅくだいを忘れる

A: しゅくだいを忘れたら、どうしようと思いますか。

B: つぎのじゅぎょうの時に出そうと思います。

1. スペインに行ける

2. 日本語が上手

3. クレジットカードがつかえなくなる

4. 先生のしつもんに答えられない

5. 外国の文学についてよく知っている

6. 有名なホテルに泊まる

Activity 4   Work with the class. Ask your classmates where they would want to go if they had a lot of money, and what they would want to do there.

Example: A: <u>お金がたくさんあったら、</u>どこへ行きたいですか。

B: 日本に行こうと思います。

A: 日本で何をしようと思いますか。

B: <u>日本に行ったら、</u>秋葉原でデジカメを買おうと思います。

名前	ばしょ	したいこと

聞く練習
れんしゅう

上手な聞き方

Using transition devices, and the difference between the そ -series and the あ -series

As with written material, conversation is full of transitions. Transition devices are used to cooperatively form a cohesive discourse among two or more speakers. In particular, the speaker often uses そ-words (for example, それ, in comments like それはよかったですね) to refer to what is being said. Occasionally, the speaker chooses あ -series instead of そ-words. The difference between the two is that そ-series words are used when either the speaker or the listener is unfamiliar with what is being discussed, and あ -series words are used to refer to matters which both the speaker and the listener are familiar with and share knowledge about. For example, その in the following dialogue indicates that 大木さん does not know much about the 旅館, but あそこ implies that 木村さん has previously stayed in, worked at, or checked up on the 旅館, and 木村 さん is expressing the fact that he shares the knowledge about it with 山田さん.

山田：森下旅館に泊まったんですよ。
　　　もりしたりょかん　　と
大木：その旅館はどこにあるんですか。
　　　　　りょかん
木村：京都にあるんですよ。あそこはとてもいい旅館ですね。
むら　きょうと　　　　　　　　　　　　　　　　　　りょかん

練習
れんしゅう

　　　どの「こそあど」言葉
　　　　　　　　　　ことば

Listen to the dialogues, circle the demonstrative words used in the conversation, and write what each refers to. Then explain why these particular demonstrative words are used, and why the speaker chose そ or あ.

Example:　それ/⨀その/そこ/あれ/あの/あそこ　　　<u>黒田さん</u>
　　　　　　　　　　　　　　　　　　　　　　　　　　　　くろだ
　　　　　　<u>男の人は黒田さんを知らないからです。</u>
　　　　　　　　　くろだ　　　　し

1. それ/その/そこ/あれ/あの/あそこ　　　_____
　　_____

2. それ/その/そこ/あれ/あの/あそこ　　　_____
　　_____

3. それ/その/そこ/あれ/あの/あそこ　　　_____
　　_____

どのツアーにしようと思いますか。

聞く前に

下のツアーのスケジュールを読んで、しつもんに答^{こた}えてください。Note the kanji words 大阪_{おおさか} and 名古屋_{なごや}.

1. 一番安いツアーはどれですか。

2. スケジュールが大変なツアーはどれですか。

3. 夏休みに行くツアーはどれがいいですか。

ニューヨーク 6日間　149,000円より		
スケジュール（6日間）		
1	夕刻：大阪発 → ニューヨークへ 夜：ニューヨーク着　ホテルへ	ニューヨーク泊
2	終日：ニューヨーク市内観光	ニューヨーク泊
3・4	終日：自由行動	ニューヨーク泊
5	午後：ニューヨーク発　帰国の途へ	機中泊
6	夕刻：大阪着	

ケアンズ 5・6日間　169,000円より			
スケジュール（5・6日間）			
1		午後：大阪→名古屋→ケアンズへ	機中泊
2		早朝：ケアンズ着 着後：ホテルへ	ケアンズ泊
3		終日：自由行動	ケアンズ泊
4	4	終日：自由行動	ケアンズ泊
	5	終日：自由行動	ケアンズ泊
5	6	午後：ケアンズ発→名古屋へ 夜：名古屋→大阪着	

イタリアの休日 9日間　253,000円より		
スケジュール（9日間）		
1	午前：大阪発→夜：ローマ着	ローマ泊
2・3	終日：自由行動	ローマ泊
4	午前：自由行動 午後：ローマ→フィレンツェ	フィレンツェ泊
5	午前：フィレンツェ市内観光 午後：自由行動	フィレンツェ泊
6	午前：自由行動 午後：フィレンツェ→ミラノ	ミラノ泊
7	終日：自由行動	ミラノ泊
8	午前：ミラノ発→帰国の途へ	機中泊
9	午後：大阪着	

ロンドンとローマとパリ 10日間　178,000円より		
スケジュール（10日間）		
1	夜：大阪発→ローマへ	機中泊
2	午前：ローマ着 着後：自由行動	ローマ泊
3	終日：自由行動	ローマ泊
4	午前：ローマ→パリへ 午後：パリ着→着後：自由行動	パリ泊
5・6	終日：自由行動	パリ泊
7	午前：パリ→ロンドンへ 着後：自由行動	ロンドン泊
8	終日：自由行動	ロンドン泊
9	午後：ロンドン発→帰国の途へ	機中泊
10	午後：（東京乗継ぎ）大阪着	

シドニーとゴールドコースト 6・7・8日間 199,000円より				
スケジュール（6・7・8日間）				
1			夕刻：大阪発→ブリスベンへ	機中泊
2			午前：（シドニー乗継ぎ）→ブリスベンへ 着後：ドリームワールドへ	ゴールドコースト泊
3	3・4		終日：自由行動	ゴールドコースト泊
4	5		午前：ブリスベン発→シドニーへ 着後：シドニー市内観光	シドニー泊
5	6	7・8	終日：自由行動	シドニー泊
6	7	8	午前：シドニー発→帰国の途へ 午後：大阪着	

サンフランシスコとロサンゼルス 6日間　135,000円より		
スケジュール（6日間）		
1	夕刻：大阪発→サンフランシスコへ 午後：サンフランシスコ市内観光	サンフランシスコ泊
2	終日：自由行動	サンフランシスコ泊
3	午前：サンフランシスコ発→ロサンゼルスへ 着後：ロサンゼルス市内観光	ロサンゼルス泊
4	終日：自由行動	ロサンゼルス泊
5	午前：ロサンゼルス発→帰国の途へ	機中泊
6	夕刻：大阪着	

🔊 聞いてみましょう

A. ダイアローグを聞いて、女の人が行くツアーの名前を書いて下さい。それから、
行くきかん (*duration*) も書いて下さい。Ignore other details in the conversation.

	ツアーの名前 な	～泊（～日） はく／ぱく
1		
2		
3		

B. Now answer the following questions about the people who appear in the dialogues.

1. 1の女の人が行くツアーについて、しつもんに答えて下さい。
   1. この女の人はいつツアーに行きますか。
   2. どうしてそのツアーにしましたか。
   3. この女の人と男の人のかんけい (*relationship*) は何ですか。

2. 2の人のツアーについてしつもんに答えて下さい。
   1. 女の人はいくらぐらいお金がありますか。
   2. どうしてそのツアーにしましたか。
   3. この女の人と男の人のかんけい (*relationship*) は何ですか。

3. 3の人についてしつもんに答えて下さい。
   1. きせつはいつですか。
   2. 女の人はどうしてそのツアーにしましたか。

👥 聞いた後で

A. Work with a partner. One person is a student living in Japan and thinking about going on a trip during summer or winter break. The other person is a travel agent. The traveler should decide on the budget and length of the trip and explain these travel preferences to the agent. The travel agent should make suggestions.

B. Work with a partner. Imagine that both of you work for a travel agency in Japan. Plan a trip to your own country for Japanese college students during their summer or winter break.

聞き上手話し上手

電話をかけたりうけたりする。
でん

In every language there are specific ways to make and answer phone calls and to initiate a conversation. Cell phones and e-mail are the most common methods of communication. In Japan, cell phones are so common that it is difficult to find a public phone in many places. So it is a good idea to rent a cell phone in Japan if you plan to visit.

In cell phone conversations the caller can assume that the receiver is the one who answers the call, and the receiver sometimes knows who the caller is. This chapter introduces basic cell-phone manners. In Conversation A, もしもし functions very much like *hello* or *excuse me* in English. It is used to start a phone conversation, or to address a stranger on the street, as in "Excuse me, but isn't this your wallet?" However, もしもし is not allowed in business conversation. When you call a company, a store or a school, the person who answers normally identifies his/her workplace or department as in Conversation B. In Conversation B, Mr. Smith calls a restaurant to make a reservation.

Conversation A: How to make a call to a mobile phone

スミス： もしもし。

森田： はい。
もりた

スミス： あのう、スミスです。森田さん、こんにちは。
　　　　　　　　　　　　もりた

Conversation B: How to call a business

Situation: You are calling Restaurant Ogawa to make a reservation.

店の人： はい、レストラン小川です。

スミス： あのう、明日の七時に予約したいんですが、大丈夫でしょうか。
　　　　　　　　　　　　　　　よやく　　　　　　　　じょうぶ

店の人： はい、何人さまですか。

スミス： 三人です。

Japanese people tend to say ええ and はい more often than speakers of English say *Uh-huh* or *OK*. This often affects phone conversations between a Japanese person and an English speaker in two ways. One is that English speakers may begin to feel pressured when they hear ええ or はい too often. The other is that a Japanese person speaking with a native speaker of English may start feeling unsure about whether the other party is still on the line, because the Japanese person is not receiving enough listening feedback. The Japanese person may start saying もしもし, which, in this case, is equivalent to *Are you there?*

練習
れんしゅう

Work with a partner. Practice making a phone call in the following situation: you call Ms. Hiroko Suzuki (or Mr. Hiroshi Suzuki). Your partner answers the phone as Ms./Mr. Suzuki.

漢字
かん じ

Right-side components of kanji

Component shapes appearing on the right side of **kanji** often indicate their pronunciation. In this case, "pronunciation" refers to the pronunciation of the character in Chinese at the time the character was adapted for use in Japan. Those pronunciations are still reflected in the Japanese **on-reading**. For example, the component 工 gives a **kanji** the **on-reading** コウ. 江, 紅, 虹, 釭, and 舡 all have the **on-reading** コウ, but they are not necessarily related in meaning. The component 青 gives a **kanji** the **on-reading** セイ. The characters 晴, 情, 清, 精, and 請 all share the same **on-reading**, セイ. The component 青 by itself has the meaning of *blue*, but these **kanji** do not necessarily share this meaning. Even if the phonetic component of a compound has a meaning, it is the pronunciation and not the meaning of the component that has significance in the character. The historical background of **kanji** is another tool to organize your knowledge of **kanji**. Possessing this knowledge makes it possible, to some extent, to guess the meaning.

Try the following:
1. Group the **kanji** you know by looking for common component shapes.
2. Find some shared properties in their meanings and pronunciations.

Name	🔲	Pronunciation	Meaning	Examples	Related kanji
りっとう	刂		cut	刈 刊 列 判 別 利 刻 制 到	
おおがい	頁		face	頭 顔 願 題	
おおざと	阝		community	部 郵 郊 郎 郡 郭 郷 都	
ぼくづくり・のぶん	攵		to hit	散 改 放 敗	
ちから	力		power	助 動 効 勉	力
あくび	欠		open mouth wide	歌 欲	欠
ふるとり	隹		bird	雄 雅 雑 雌 難 離	
みる	見		see	親 規 視 観	見
また	又		hand movement	取 収 双	又
ほこづくり	戈		fight	戦 戯	
おのづくり	斤		cut into two pieces	新 断	
つき	月		date	朝 期 朗 明	月
てら	寺	ジ	temple	時 待 持	寺
	青	セイ	blue	請 晴 清 情	青
	工	コウ	factory	江 紅	工
	冓	コウ	assemble	溝 講	
まじわる	交	コウ	intersection	校 効	交

| 海 | 海 | sea, ocean | ` ` シ シ 汀 汇 海 海 海 | | | | |
| | | うみ　カイ | 海が好きです。　海外旅行　北海道
うみ　　　かいがいりょ　ほっかいどう | | | | |

| 外 | 外 | outside, other | ノ ク タ 列 外 | | | | |
| | | そと　ガイ | 家の外　外国人
そと　がいこくじん | | | | |

| 国 | 国 | country, nation | 丨 冂 冂 冃 囯 国 国 国 | | | | |
| | | くに　コク・ゴク | 小さい国　中国　国内　韓国
くに　ちゅうごく　こくない　かんこく | | | | |

| 旅 | 旅 | travel, trip | ㇐ 亠 方 方 扩 扩 旅 旅 旅 | | | | |
| | | たび　リョ | 旅行が好きです。
りょ | | | | |

| 館 | 館 | (large) building, hall | 人 今 今 食 食 飣 飣 節 館 | | | | |
| | | カン | 旅館　図書館　学生会館
りょかん　と　かん　かいかん | | | | |

| 予 | 予 | in advance | ㇇ マ 予 予 | | | | |
| | | あらかじ(め)　ヨ | 予定があります。　ホテルの予約
よてい　よやく | | | | |

| 定 | 定 | decide, determine | ` ` 宀 宀 宁 宇 定 定 | | | | |
| | | さだ(める)　テイ | 明日は病院に行く予定です。
よてい | | | | |

| 約 | 約 | promise, approximately | ㇗ 幺 幺 糸 糸 糸 約 約 | | | | |
| | | ヤク | 旅館を予約した。
りょかん　よやく | | | | |

| 計 | 計 | measuring, plan | ` 亠 ニ 言 言 言 言 計 計 | | | | |
| | | はか(る)　ケイ | 旅行の計画をたてる。　高い時計ですね。
りょ　けいかく　とけい | | | | |

| 画 | 画 | picture, painting | 一 丆 丙 丙 丙 面 画 画 | | | | |
| | | カク・ガ | 来年の計画はまだありません。　映画
けいかく　えいが | | | | |

| 荷 | 荷 | load, cargo, baggage | 一 卄 艹 艹 花 荷 荷 荷 | | | | |
| | | ニ・カ | 大きい荷物を持って行く。
にもつ　も | | | | |

| 物 | 物 | object, thing | ノ | ㇒ | 牛 | 牛 | 牛 | 牞 | 物 | 物 | |
| | | もの　ブツ・モツ | 荷物
にもつ | 食べ物
もの | 飲み物
もの | 動物園
どうぶつえん | 買い物
もの | | | |

| 答 | 答 | to answer, an answer | ノ | ㇒ | ケ | ㇒ケ | 竺 | 筌 | 答 | 答 | 答 |
| | | こた（える）　トウ | しつもんに答える。
こた | | | | | | | |

| 知 | 知 | to know | ノ | ㇒ | ㇗ | ㇏ | 矢 | 知 | 知 | 知 | |
| | | し（る）　チ | 名前を知っています。　知らない人
な　　し　　　　　　　　　　　し | | | | | | | |

| 泊 | 泊 | to stay overnight | ヽ | ㇉ | ㇒ | 氵 | 汁 | 泊 | 泊 | 泊 | |
| | | と（まる）　ハク・パク | 二泊三日の旅行　ホテルに泊まる。
にはく　　りょ　　　　　　　　　と | | | | | | | |

| 乗 | 乗 | to ride, get on | ノ | 二 | 三 | 千 | 乒 | 乒 | 垂 | 乗 | 乗 |
| | | の（る）　ジョウ | でんしゃに乗る。　ふねに乗る。
の　　　　　　　　の | | | | | | | |

| 着 | 着 | to arrive, to put on | ヽ | ㇒ | ㇒ | 羊 | 羊 | 羊 | 着 | 着 | |
| | | つ（く）・き（る）　チャク | 日本に着く。　シャツを着る。
つ　　　　　　　き | | | | | | | |

| 名 | 名 | name | ノ | ク | タ | タ | 名 | 名 | | | |
| | | な　メイ・ミョウ | お名前は何ですか。　有名なばしょ
な　　　　　　　　ゆうめい | | | | | | | |

| 空 | 空 | sky | ヽ | ㇒ | 宀 | 宀 | 穴 | 空 | 空 | 空 | |
| | | そら　クウ | 成田空港に行きます。　空(sky)がきれいです。
なりた　くうこう　　　　　　そら | | | | | | | |

| 港 | 港 | harbor | シ | 氵 | ㇒ | 㳇 | 洪 | 洪 | 港 | 港 | |
| | | みなと　コウ | 羽田空港はべんりです。　港 (harbor) に着く。
はねだ　くうこう　　　　　みなと | | | | | | | |

森	森	forest	一	十	才	木	木	森			
							木	森			
		もり　シン	これは森田先生の荷物です。 もりた　　　　にもつ							

| 林 | 林 | woods | 一 | 十 | 才 | 木 | 林 | | | | |
| | | はやし　リン | 林さんは旅館に泊まりました。
はやし　　りょかん　と | | | | | | | |

| 々 | 々 | kanji for repetition | ノ | ク | 々 | | | | | | |
| | | N/A | 色々な人　時々
いろいろ　ときどき | | | | | | | |

読めるようになった漢字
かんじ

海　海外　外　外国　国　中国　国内　韓国　旅館　映画館　旅行　予定　予約
　　　　　　　　　　　　　　　　　かん　　　　　　えい

天気予報　計画　計る　映画　時計　荷物　食べ物　飲み物　買い物　建物
ほう　　　　　　　　えい　　　　　　　　　　　　　　　　　　　　　　たて

動物　動物園　図書館　博物館　美術館　学生会館　答える　知る　持っていく
どう　どう　えん　　と　　　　はく　　　びじゅつ

泊まる　二泊　日帰り　お金　乗る　着く　着る　着物　名前　有名　温泉
　　　　　　　　　　　　　　　　　　　　　　　　　　　　　　ゆう　　せん

切符　空港　色々　時々
ぷ

日本人の名前：黒田　森　森下　森田　森山　林　林田　高男　早川
　　　　　くろ

練習
れんしゅう

Read the following sentences aloud.

1. 森田先生は来月、四泊五日の海外旅行に出かける予定です。 色々な国に行きます。

2. その海の近くの温泉旅館に泊まりたいので、今から予約をしようと思います。
　　　　　　せん

3. 林さん、荷物はもうスーツケースに入れましたか。

4. 雨がふって、計画していた日帰り旅行はだめになりました。

5. その高そうなシャツを着ている男の人の名前を知らなかったから、となりの人に聞いた。

6. 切符を持って行かなかったので、ふねに乗れませんでした。
　　ぷ

7. ホテルに着いたら、少し休みたいと思っています。

8. 東京からアジアの国に行く時は、羽田空港がべんりです。
　　きょう　　　　　　　　　　　　　　はね　だ

読む練習
れんしゅう

上手な読み方

Using transition devices

Transition devices, such as conjunctions and clause connectors, help clarify the relationships among sentences and paragraphs. Paying attention to these connectors will help you understand how a text is organized and will provide clues for finding important information. There are many expressions that use そ-series of demonstrative expressions such as そこ, その後, その前, その時, and その人. When they are used to refer to something that the speaker cannot physically see, they refer to something previously mentioned. In this sense, they are similar to *the* or *that* in English.

昨日、レストランに行きました。そこはとても大きい . . .

昨日、レストランに行きました。その後で、. . .

A. Fill in the blanks with the appropriate transition devices.

そして　それから　その後で　その前に　それに　それで　その間（に）

つぎに　まずはじめに　というのは　ですから　でも　ところが

---

1. 昨日、こうえんへ行きました。＿＿＿＿＿＿森山さんの家に行きました。
   ＿＿＿＿＿＿森山さんはいませんでした。＿＿＿＿＿＿家へ帰りました。

2. 日本に行く時には、行きたいところがすぐに分かるようにガイドブックを買って
   読んだ方がいい。＿＿＿＿＿＿いい旅行会社をさがした方がいい。
   しゃ
   ＿＿＿＿＿安い飛行機の切符を買った方がいい。＿＿＿＿＿＿二か月ぐらい前
   ひ　き　ぶ
   に予約をした方がいい。

3. 昨日は学校に行けませんでした。＿＿＿＿＿＿ルームメートが病気になったの
   で、一緒に病院へ行ったのです。
   しょ

ハワイ旅行 (Trip to Hawaii)

読む前に

1. ハワイに行ったことがありますか。

2. ハワイは何月がいいと思いますか。

3. ハワイではどんなことが出来ると思いますか。

4. ハワイではどんなお土産が買えると思いますか。

5. Skim the following text and tour information. そして、この人に一番いいツアーを下の旅行計画からさがして下さい。

読んでみましょう

言葉のリスト

〜島	island
ポリネシア文化センター	Polynesian Cultural Center
内容	contents
宿泊地	accommodation
自由行動	free activity

今年の冬は大阪からハワイに遊びに行くつもりです。休みは十二月十九日から一月八日までなので、その間に五泊六日ぐらいの旅行に行こうと思います。ハワイ島には行ったことがありますが、オアフ島とマウイ島にはまだ行ったことがないので、そこに行きたいと思っています。それから、ポリネシア文化センターはおもしろいそうなので、ハワイに行ったら、そこにも行きたいと思います。お金があまりないから、安いツアーをさがしています。

旅行日数			内容・宿泊地
5	6	7	
1-2	1-2	1-2	夜：大阪発→ホノルルへ（日付変更線通過） 午前：ホノルル着（レイ・グリーティングはありません。） 着後：バスにてワイキキへ。トラベル BOX にて滞在中の説明会（昼食は各自でお取り下さい。） 午後：ホノルル市内・近郊観光 ホテルチェックインは観光後になります。　　　　ワイキキ
3	3-4	3-5	終日：自由行動（各種オプショナルツアー）　　　　ワイキキ
4	5	6	朝：バスにて空港へ 午前：ホノルル発→大阪へ（日付変更線通過）　　　　機中
5	6	7	午後：大阪着

オプショナルツアー
OPTIONAL TOURS

マウイ島日帰り観光 コース
No. 3097-1
約 11 時間。毎日 06:30 前後発。昼食付き
最少催行人員 1 名 . 大人 28,000 円、子供 22,000 円
＜主催：トラベルプラザ＞

カウアイ島日帰り観光コース
No. 3097-2
約 11 時間。毎日 7:40 前後発。昼食付き
最少催行人員 1 名　大人 28,000 円、子供 22,000 円
＜主催：トラベルプラザ＞

ハワイ島日帰り観光コース
No.3097-3
約 11 時間。毎日 7:40 前後発　昼食付き
最少催行人員 1~2 名・大人 28,000 円、
子供 22,000 円
＜主催：トラベルプラザ＞

旅行代金　　おとな・こども同額

	ブーゲンビリアコース		
	5日コース	6日コース	7日コース
	食事なし	食事なし	食事なし
出発日	3110-0 MC	3105-0 MC	3115-0 MC
11/21, 22, 23, 25, 26, 27, 28, 29, 30	95,000	99,000	105,000
12/21	108,000	111,000	115,000
12/19, 20, 22, 23	114,000	116,000	120,000
1/5, 6, 7, 8, 9, 10, 12, 13, 14, 15, 16	139,000	143,000	149,000
2/1, 2, 3, 4, 5, 6, 7, 8, 9, 10, 11, 12	150,000	154,000	160,000
3/16, 17, 18, 19, 20, 22, 23, 24, 25	161,000	165,000	171,000
1/11, 2/15	178,000	182,000	188,000
3/15, 21	202,000	206,000	212,000

```
デラックス・ポリネシア文化
センターコース
No. 1098-1
約 9 時間半  日曜日を除く
毎日 8:45 前後発
夕食付き・最少催行人員 1 名
大人 15,000 円、子供 13,000 円
＜主催：トラベルプラザ＞

シーライフ・パーク・ツアー
No. 1077-2

約 4 時間半   毎日 11:00 発
最少催行 人員 1 名
大人 5,000 円、子供 4,000 円
＜主催：トラベルプラザ＞
```

読んだ後で

A. 下のしつもんに日本語で答えて下さい。そして、せつぞくし (conjunction)
   をつかって、旅行計画を書いて下さい。

1. 何日に大阪を出たらいいと思いますか。

2. 何日にホノルルを出たらいいでしょうか。

3. ポリネシア文化センターにはいつ行けますか。

4. マウイ島へはいつ行ったらいいと思いますか。

5. お金はいくらぐらいかかると思いますか。

B. 下の旅行計画を読んで下さい。Underline the conjunctions in the text.
   Then see what the differences are between your plan and this plan.

　一月一日の晩に大阪を出て、一日の朝、ホノルルに着く予定です。その後、ホノルルのまちをバスで観光して、ホテルに行きます。昼御飯はホテルに着いた時に食べて下さい。二日は朝十一時半にホノルルを出て、ポリネシア文化センターに行く予定です。ポリネシア文化センターでは、自由行動ですが、午後八時から十時まで、ショーがありますから、七時半までにセンターの入口にあつまって下さい。ショーが終わったら、バスでホテルへ帰ります。三日目と四日目は自由行動です。五日の晩、ホノルルを出て、つぎの日に大阪に着く予定です。

総合練習
そうごうれんしゅう

ツアーの計画

Work in groups of four. You are travel agents who want to attract young Japanese tourists. Choose some travel destinations within your country and make a tour plan. Then present your travel plan.

Example:　A:　日本からどこへ行ったらいいかな。

B:　ニューヨークとボストンはどう？

C:　いいね。何泊ぐらいしようかな。

D:　そうだね。日本からニューヨークまで何時間ぐらいかかるかな？

C:　東京から十六時間ぐらいだと思うけど。

ロールプレイ

1. You are in Tokyo and thinking of going to Hiroshima. Tell a travel agent where you want to go and what you want to see there. Then ask what is the best way to get there.
2. You want to make a hotel reservation in Kyoto. Call the hotel, tell the clerk that you need to make a reservation, and find out if there is a room available. Ask the clerk to speak in easy Japanese rather than using the very polite forms. (Most hotel clerks use very polite speech.) You need to specify the type of room (シングル、ダブル), and your arrival and departure dates.
3. You are talking to a Japanese friend. Tell your friend about the most memorable trip you have taken. Describe where you went, what you did, and what happened.
4. You are talking to a Japanese friend who is thinking of going to the United States this summer. Tell your friend what to do before, during, and after visiting the United States.

Chapter 3

第三課
_{だい さん か}

Fast&Slow/PIXTA

将来のために
_{しょうらい}
Preparing for the Future

Objectives   Expressing future plans and current states; expressing what to do to achieve future objectives.

Vocabulary   Lifestyles and one's future life, parties and ceremonies, vocations, intransitive verbs and transitive verbs

Dialogue   本田先生のけんきゅうしつで *At Professor Honda's office*

Japanese Culture   Changes in family structure, the Japanese economy and employment trends

Grammar   I.   Expressing chronological order using 前 and 後
_{あと}

   II.   Talking about preparations using ～ておく; expressing completion, regret, or the realization that a mistake was made using ～てしまう

   III.   Using transitive and intransitive verbs; expressing results of intentional actions using ～てある

   IV.   Expressing purpose, using the plain form of the verb/noun の + ため, in order to ~, for ~

   V.   Expressing obligation using ～なければ/なくては + ならない、～なければ/なくては + いけない; expressing a lack of obligation using ～なくてもいい

Listening   Paying attention to speech styles, 将来の計画
_{しょうらい}

Communication   Making confirmations and checking comprehension

Kanji   Top component shapes of **kanji**

言 葉 漢 字 質 問 卒 業 授 仕 事

結 婚 式 社 同 違 留 達 電 英 客 残

Reading   Using prefixes and suffixes, 日本人と結婚
_{けっこん}

単語
たん ご

Nouns

エンジニア		engineer (as in electrical engineer)
かいしゃ	会社	company, かいしゃいん businessman, ぼうえきがいしゃ trading company
がくしゃ	学者	scholar
けんきゅう	研究	research, けんきゅう（を）する to do research
さいふ	財布	wallet, purse
しき	式	ceremony
じぶん	自分	self, oneself, I
しゃちょう	社長	company president
じゆう	自由	freedom, じゆう（な）is a な -adjective meaning *free*
しゅうしょく	就職	getting a job, 〜にしゅうしょくする to get a job at 〜
しょうたい	招待	invitation, 〜を〜にしょうたいする to invite
しょうらい	将来	future
そうべつかい	送別会	farewell party
そつぎょう	卒業	graduation, 〜をそつぎょうする graduate from 〜
でんき	電気	electricity, electric light
どうそうかい	同窓会	reunion party
とし	年	year, age, 年をとる to grow old, 年が上 older
にゅうがく	入学	entering a school, 〜ににゅうがくする to enter 〜
ひっこし	引っ越し	moving (house, residence, etc.), ひっこし（を）する to move (house, residence)
ふつう	普通	ordinary, regular
べんごし	弁護士	lawyer
へんじ	返事	response, reply へんじをする to respond.
ぼうえき	貿易	trading, ぼうえきがいしゃ trading company
ゆ	湯	warm water, hot water (see わかす and わく)
りゅうがく	留学	study abroad, りゅうがく（を）する to study abroad, りゅうがくせい international student

う -verbs

あく	開く	(for something) to open
あつまる	集まる	to get together, to gather, (place) にあつまる
おこす	起こす	to wake up (someone)
おとす	落とす	to drop (something)

おわる	終わる	(for something) to end
かかる		(for a telephone) to ring
かわる	変わる／替わる	(for something) to change
がんばる	頑張る	to try to do one's best, to hang on
きまる	決まる	(for something) to be decided
けす	消す	to turn off
しまる	閉まる	(for something) to close
しぬ	死ぬ	to die
ちがう	違う	to be different, A とBはちがう A and B are different. A はBとちがう A is different from B.
つく	付く／点く	(for something) to turn on
なおす	治す／直す	to cure; to fix; to repair (something)
なおる	治る／直る	(for something) to heal, to be fixed
なくなる	亡くなる／無くなる	to pass away, to die; to disappear, to get lost, to run out of, さいふがなくなる a wallet is missing, お金がなくなる I run out of money.
のこす	残す	to leave (something)
のこる	残る	(for something) to be left, to remain
はじまる	始まる	(for something) to begin
はたらく	働く	to work
ひっこす	引っ越す	to move (house, etc.), to relocate
ひやす	冷やす	to chill, to let (something) cool down
まちがう	間違う	(for someone) to be mistaken, commonly used as まちがえている
よごす	汚す	to make (something) dirty
わかす	沸かす	to bring (water, bath) to boil, （お）ゆをわかす bring water to boil, （お）ふろをわかす prepare a bath
わく	沸く	(for water, bath) to be boiled, （お）ゆがわく water is boiling

る -verbs

あける	開ける	to open (something)
あつめる	集める	to collect, to gather together (something/someone)
うまれる	生まれる	(for someone/something) to be born
おえる	終える	to end (something), to finish (something)
おちる	落ちる	(for something) to fall
かえる	変える	to change (something)
かんがえる	考える	to think intellectually, to take (something) into consideration
きえる	消える	(for something) to go out, to go off

しめる	閉める	to close (something)
つづける	続ける	to continue (something)
でる	出る	to attend, しきにでる to attend a ceremony
のせる	乗せる	to give a ride (to someone) 〜を〜にのせる
はじめる	始める	to begin (something)
ひえる	冷える	(for something) to cool down
まちがえる	間違える	to miss (something), to make a mistake
よごれる	汚れる	(for something) to become dirty

い -adjective

| わかい | 若い | young. わかい is used to describe teenagers and young people older than teenagers, but not small children. |

な -adjectives

おなじ	同じ	same, A とBはおなじ A and B are the same A はBとおなじ A is the same as B. な must be deleted before a noun, as in おなじ人
じゆう（な）	自由（な）	free, じゆうな生活 free (independent) lifestyle
だいじ（な）	大事（な）	important

Particles

| か | | or, either or, 晴れか雨 rain or shine |
| までに | | by, 五時までに帰る I will come back by 5 o'clock |

Suffixes

〜いん	〜員	member, 会社員 businessman, 銀行員 banker, 店員 store clerk, 会員 membership, member (of an association, a society), ゆうびんきょくいん postal employee
〜かい	〜会	party, 同窓会 reunion, 送別会 farewell party, 誕生日会 birthday party
〜しき	〜式	ceremony, 卒業式 graduation ceremony, 入学式 matriculation ceremony, 結婚式 wedding
〜しゃ	〜者	person of, 学者 scholar, 研究者 researcher, 医者 doctor
〜じょう	〜状	letter of, しょうたいじょう letter of invitation
〜や	〜屋	retail store, さかなや fish market, にくや meat store, はなや flower shop, 本屋 bookstore. These could also indicate the owners of the stores.

単語の練習
たん ご　れんしゅう

A. ライフスタイルと将来の生活　Lifestyle and one's future life
しょうらい　かつ

自分 じぶん self, I	ふつう ordinary, average	人と同じ おな same as other people	人と違う ちが to be different from others
じゆう（の／な） freedom, free	わかい young	かんがえる to think	がんばる to hold on, to do one's best
生まれる う to be born	入学する にゅうがく to enter a school	卒業する そつぎょう to graduate	留学する りゅうがく to study abroad
けんきゅうする to do research	ひっこす to relocate, move	ひっこし moving, relocation	会社にしゅうしょくする かいしゃ to get a job at a company
店を持つ to own a store	はたらく to work	年をとる とし to age	しぬ to die

おぼえていますか。

アルバイト　仕事　生活　留学生　家を買う　外国にすむ　結婚する　さがす　大学に入る
　　　　　　し ごと　かつ　りゅう　　　　　　　　　　　　　　　　　けっこん

つとめる　やめる

> **Activity 1**　State the words and expressions that correspond to the following pictures.

Example:

年をとる
とし

1　　2　　3　　4

5　　6　　7　　8

Activity 2   Work in groups. Find out who identifies with the categories in the chart below. Write their names in the chart.

Example: A: ～さんは、自分はふつうの人だと思いますか。
　　　　　　　　　じぶん

　　　　　　　B: ええ、たぶんそう思います。

　　　　　　　　or いいえ、自分はちょっとふつうの人とは違うと思います。
　　　　　　　　　　　　　じぶん　　　　　　　　　　　　ちが

自分は～と思う じぶん	名前
ふつうの人	
人と違うより同じ方が好き 　ちが　　　おな	
じゆうなライフスタイルが 好き	
何でも (everything) よく がんばる方	

B. パーティと式   Parties and ceremonies
　　　　　　しき

入学式　　　　　卒業式　　　　　結婚式　　　　同窓会　　　誕生日会
にゅうがくしき　そつぎょうしき　けっこんしき　どうそうかい　たん　　かい
entrance　　　　graduation　　　wedding　　　reunion　　　birthday
ceremony　　　　ceremony　　　　ceremony　　　　　　　　　party

送別会　　　　　会場　　　　　　しょうたいする　しょうたいじょう
そうべつかい　　かいじょう
farewell party　meeting place　to invite　　　　invitation (letter)

おぼえていますか。

教会　ばしょ　計画をたてる　しらべる　電話をかける　よぶ　予約する
きょう　　　　　　　　　　　　　　　　　　でん

Supplementary Vocabulary: 色々なあつまり   Various gatherings

かんげいかい	歓迎会	welcome party
こんしんかい	懇親会	social gathering
しんねんかい	新年会	beginning-of-the-year party
（お）そうしき	（お）葬式	funeral
ぼうねんかい	忘年会	year-end party

新年会 is a party held sometime during the first two weeks of the new year.

Activity 3   質問に日本語で答えて下さい。
しつもん

1. どんな時にしょうたいじょうを出しますか。

2. 今までどんな式やパーティに出たことがありますか。
　　　　　　しき

3. 自分の結婚式にだれをしょうたいしたいですか。誕生日会はどうですか。
　じぶん　けっこんしき　　　　　　　　　　　　　たん　　かい

4. どの式に両親をよびたいと思っていますか。
　　　しき

C. 仕事　Vocations
　　　しごと

エンジニア　　　　べんごし　　　学者／けんきゅうしゃ　　社長
　　　　　　　　　　　　　　　　がくしゃ　　　　　　　　　しゃちょう

engineer　　　　　lawyer　　　scholar/researcher　company president

おぼえていますか。

会社員　　　　　　　先生　　　　　　　医者
かいしゃいん

さかなや　　　　　　本屋　　　　　旅行会社
　　　　　　　　　　　や　　　　　　　　がいしゃ

Supplementary Vocabulary: しょくぎょう   Occupations

アーティスト		artist, performing artist
かいけいし	会計士	accountant
きょうし	教師	teacher, instructor (more formal than 先生)
きょうじゅ	教授	professor
ぐんかんけい	軍関係	military-related (field)
けいさつかん	警察官	police officer
こうむいん	公務員	public officer, civil servant
コンサルタント		consultant
サラリーマン		businessman
じえいぎょう	自営業	self-employment
しょうぼうし	消防士	firefighter
しゅふ	主婦	housewife
じむいん	事務員	business clerk
せいじか	政治家	politician
とうしか	投資家	investor
のうか	農家	farmer

Activity 4   下の言葉のいみ (meaning) は何だと思いますか。

飲み屋　くつ屋　食べ物屋　とうふ屋　ケーキ屋　じてんしゃ屋　店員
銀行員　けんきゅういん　歯医者

Activtity 5   質問に日本語で答えて下さい。

1. ご両親は、どんな仕事をしていますか。
2. 将来、お父さんやお母さんと同じ仕事をしたいですか。違う仕事の方がいいですか。
3. どんなところにしゅうしょくしたいと思いますか。
4. 自分が出来る仕事は、どんな仕事だと思いますか。
5. わかい時はどんな仕事がいいですか。年をとったら、どんな仕事がいいですか。
6. 何さいぐらいまで、はたらきたいと思いますか。

Activity 6   Match the phrases in column A with the words in column B.

Column A	Column B
1. 十二さいから三十さいぐらいまでの人	a. エンジニア
2. 六十さいぐらいの人	b. はたらく
3. 私のこと	c. けんきゅうしゃ
4. こまった時 (*when you have a problem*) に話しに行く人	d. 年をとった人
5. くるまやコンピュータや電気についてよく知っている人 でん き	e. 自分 じ ぶん
6. 違わないこと ちが	f. 社長 しゃちょう
7. 大学の先生がすること	g. けんきゅう
8. 新しいことを勉強する人	h. わかい人
9. 仕事をすること し ごと	i. べんごし
10. 会社の中で一番お金をもらう人 かいしゃ	j. 同じ おな

D. じどうしとたどうし　Intransitive verbs and transitive verbs

Transitive verbs		Intransitive verbs	
まどをあける	to open the window	まどがあく	the window opens
ドアをしめる	to close the door	ドアがしまる	the door closes
電気をつける *	to turn on the light	電気がつく	the light is on
電気をけす	to turn off the light	電気がきえる	the light is off
電話をかける *	to make a phone call	電話がかかる	the phone rings
時間をかける *	to take time	時間がかかる	it takes time
映画をはじめる	to begin the movie	映画がはじまる	the movie begins
授業をおえる	to finish the class	授業がおわる	the class ends
ねこをかばんに入れる *	to put the cat in the bag	ねこがかばんに入る *	the cat goes into the bag
子供を起こす	to wake up the child	子供が起きる *	the child wakes up
子供をくるまに乗せる	to put the child in the car	子供がくるまに乗る *	the child gets in the car
お金を出す	to pay (literally, to take out money)	お金が出る *	it will be paid (literally, the money comes out)
おゆをわかす	to bring the water to boil	おゆがわく	the water boils/is boiled
ジュースを冷やす	to chill juice	ジュースが冷える	the juice is chilled
仕事をつづける	to continue the work	仕事がつづく *	the work continues
人をあつめる	to gather people	人があつまる	people get together
時間をきめる *	to decide on a time	時間がきまる	the time is decided
ばしょを変える	to change the place	ばしょが変わる	the place changes
病気をなおす	to cure an illness	病気がなおる	the illness is cured
さいふをおとす	to drop a wallet	さいふがおちる	the wallet is dropped
食べ物を残す	to leave some food	食べ物が残る	the food remains
漢字を間違える	to make a **kanji** mistake	漢字が間違っている	the **kanji** is wrong
ふくをよごす	to soil the clothes	ふくがよごれる	the clothes become dirty

Notes

● Words with asterisks (*) have been introduced in previous chapters.
● The commonly used form of 間違う is 間違っている.

おぼえていますか。

上がる　上げる　入れる　起きる　帰る　きめる　下がる　下げる　出る
電話をかける　乗る　入る
でん

Activity 7　下線 (underline) に、てきとうな (appropriate) 言葉を書いて下さい。
かせん　　　　　　　　　　　　　　　　　　　　ことば

1. 子供をお風呂に_____、私もお風呂に_____。
   ふろ　　　　　　　　　　　　　　　　　ふろ
2. ケーキが少し_____から、食べませんか。
3. さいふをどこかで_____ので、今、お金がありません。
4. この漢字は違うから、_____方がいいですね。
   かん じ　 ちが
5. けんたろうくんはまだ寝ています。授業におくれるから、_____方が
   　　　　　　　　　　　　　　　じゅぎょう
   いいですね。
6. せいせき (grade) を_____んですか。じゃあ、もっと勉強した方が
   いいですね。
7. リーさんが時間を_____ので、さとみさんはえきでリーさんを一時間
   まっていました。
8. いい仕事がないから、今の仕事を_____つもりです。
   し ごと　　　　　　　　　　し ごと
9. 昨日は朝まであつ子さんのへやの電気が_____、朝まで勉強してい
   　　　　　　　　　　　　　　　 でん き
   たんでしょう。
10. 午後九時ですが、さやかさんのへやの電気が_____から、さやかさ
    　　　　　　　　　　　　　　　　　　 でん き
    んは今晩はどこかに出かけているんでしょう。
11. 仕事が_____ので、家を新しいところに_____。
    し ごと
12. 風でまどが_____て、雨が家の中に入って来ました。だから、まど
    を_____下さい。
13. 学生が_____ら、映画を_____。
    　　　　　　　　　　えい
14. このへやはちょっとくらいから、電気を_____下さい。それに、暑
    　　　　　　　　　　　　　　　でん き
    いから、まどを_____くれませんか。
15. 私の予定はもう_____から、高山さんの予定を_____下
    さい。

Activity 8   Work with a partner. One person should select a verb pair from the chart on page 130 and create a phrase using either the transitive or intransitive verb from the pair. The other partner should then create a corresponding phrase with the remaining verb.

Example: A: まどをあけます。
            B: まどがあきます。

Activity 9   Work with a partner. One person makes a set of cards with transitive verbs. The other person makes a set of cards with intransitive verbs. Combine the cards and mix them up. One person picks up a card and reads the verb on the card. The other person tries to say the transitive or intransitive verb that would pair with the one on the card. If the person can say the verb correctly, he/she gets the card.

Example: A: picks up a card with あく written on it and reads it.
            B: あける

ダイアローグ

はじめに

A. 質問に日本語で答えて下さい。

1. 今、何のために日本語を勉強していますか。

2. 大学を卒業したら、どんな仕事をしたいと思いますか。

3. そのために、どんなことをしようと思いますか。

B. 下のことをするためには、どんなじゅんびをしておかなければなりませんか。

1. 卒業式のパーティをします。

2. 冬休みにクラスで日本に行きます。

3. 高校の同窓会をします。

本田先生のけんきゅうしつで   *At Professor Honda's office*

The order of the following **manga** frames is scrambled. Read the dialogue and unscramble the frames by writing the correct number in the box in each frame.

a

b

c

d

e

f

上田さんは、けんきゅうしつでゼミ (*seminar*) の先生の本田先生と話しています。

先生：　上田さんは日本に来てどのくらいになりますか。

上田：　一年半になります。来年の八月にはアメリカに帰ります。

先生：　早いですね。もう一年半ですか。で、アメリカに帰ったら、どうするんですか。

上田：　卒業までにまだ一年ありますから、大学にもどります。
　　　　そつぎょう

先生：　そうですか。じゃあ、その後は？
　　　　　　　　　　　　あと

上田：　まだよく分かりませんが、卒業した後は、また日本にもどって、日本
　　　　　　　　　　　　　　　そつぎょう　あと
　　　　語がつかえる仕事をさがしたいと思います。
　　　　　　　　しごと

先生：　そうですか。がんばって下さいね。

上田：　どうもありがとうございます。

上田さんは本田先生のけんきゅうしつの外で石田さんに会いました。
　　　　　　　　　　　　　　　　　　　いし

石田：　あ、上田さん、ちょうどよかった。今度のゼミの懇親会のこと、本田
いし　　　　　　　　　　　　　　　　　　　　　　　　こんしんかい
　　　　先生に話した？

上田：　あ、ごめん。忘れちゃった。

石田：　じゃ、まだ話してないんだね。じゃ、いいよ。ぼくも、後で先生に会
いし　　　　　　　　　　　　　　　　　　　　　　　　　あと
　　　　うから、話しとくよ。

上田：　ありがとう。それで、もうじゅんびはおわったの？

石田：　うん。レストランの予約とりょうりのちゅうもんは、もうしてあるよ。
いし

上田：　じゃあ、みんなにメールは？

石田：　うん、先週出しといたから、そろそろ返事が来ると思うけど。
いし　　　　　　　　　　　　　　　　　　へんじ

上田：　すごい、石田さん。何から何までありがとう。
　　　　　　いし

DIALOGUE PHRASE NOTES

- ゼミ is short for "seminar." It refers to a class taken by college seniors with their advisors.
- 懇親会 is a type of social gathering at which participants get to know
  こんしんかい
  each other and strengthen relationships among themselves. It often involves a sit-down dinner and drinking.
- そろそろ means *pretty soon*.
- 何から何までありがとう means *thank you for everything*.

ダイアローグの後で

A. Complete the following paragraph based on the dialogue.

上田さんは＿＿＿＿＿＿＿＿＿＿＿にアメリカに帰る予定です。そして、

＿＿＿＿＿＿＿＿＿ために、大学にもどって勉強するつもりです。大学を卒
業した後、＿＿＿＿＿＿＿、日本語をつかえる仕事をさがそうと思ってい
ます。

B. ゼミの懇親会について下の質問に日本語で答えて下さい。

1. 懇親会のために、どんなことがしてありますか。

2. まだ、何がしてありませんか。

3. しょうたいのメールが来た人は何をしておかなければならないと思いますか。

C. Underline the sentences or phrases in the dialogue where the speaker is confirming what has been said.

D. Change the conversation between Ms. Ueda and Professor Honda by substituting Mr. Ishida for Professor Honda and by using casual speech for those dialogue lines.

日本の文化
ぶん か

人口と家族構成の変化
じんこう　　こうせい　へんか

Population change and changes in family structure

Japan's population increased dramatically after World War II, going from 93.4 million in 1960 to more than 128 million in 2010, an increase of 37% in 50 years. Since 2010, however, it has been decreasing rapidly. The number of children under 15 years old started declining in 1980, while the number of people over 65 years old has increased. In 2015, 12.8 % of Japanese are under 15 years old and 33.3% are more than 65. According to a government's projection made in 2012, Japan's total population will go down to 87 million by 2060: a decline of 32%.

This declining population is a combination of a rapidly aging population and a low birth rate. As the world's healthiest nation, the number of elderly people in Japan is on the rise. This number is projected to jump to 40% of the population in 2060. Additionally, a large number of baby boomers have begun to retire and even more expect to be out of the workforce in the next ten years. The birthrate declined from 4.54 in 1947 to 2.05 in 1974, and down to 1.25 in 2005. It has recovered slightly (1.42 in 2014), but not enough to reverse the population shrinkage. The low birthrate is the result of the fact that more people postpone marriage until their late twenties and consequently have fewer children. The average age for marriage is 30.9 for males and 29.3 for females.

A Japanese wedding ceremony

Eric Kotara / Alamy Stock Photo

Traditionally, the Japanese have considered young people to be fully independent adults only after they get married, but this idea no longer holds much credibility. Instead, a growing number of young adults view marriage as constraining. As a result, three-generation families declined from 15.3% in 1986 to 6.9% in 2014. The average size of a Japanese family declined from 5.97 in 1955 to 2.49 in 2014, and the proportion of households without children grew from 32.6% in 1986 to 50.4 % in 2014.

日本の経済と採用傾向
けいざい　　さいようけいこう

The Japanese economy and employment trends

Japan has suffered from a severe economic slow-down since the "bubble economy" (バブル経済) burst in the late 1980s. This bubble economy was based largely on
けいざい

overpriced real estate. As a small country with a large population, Japan placed a high value on real estate, and the price of real estate and stocks surged during the 1980s. People started investing in real estate as well as stocks for short-term profits. This resulted in unreasonably high prices for real estate, hence the term "bubble economy." During this period, banks made a number of loans taking overvalued real estate as collateral. The abrupt plunge in the price of real estate resulted in an economic slump.

This was referred to as バブルがはじ
ける (The bubble bursts.). Banks still
have a large number of bad loans
that cannot be recovered.

amana images inc./Alamy Stock Photo

The bursting of the bubble
economy resulted in many businesses
going through organizational
restructuring (リストラ). Japan's
employment system has been in
transition since. Although it was
once popular to identify the practice
of lifetime employment (終身雇用) as a major characteristic of Japanese employment,
しゅうしん こ よう
this practice has become less prevalent. And the emphasis placed on the life-long
employment system was always suspect, because this system was never the only or even
the most prominent employment system in Japan. In reality, employees of large
corporations (大企業) are the only people who enjoyed a high level of job security.
だい き ぎょう
Workers at smaller businesses (中小企業、零細企業) have never had this type of job
ちゅうしょう き ぎょう　れいさい き ぎょう
security.

Seniority (年功序列), traditionally the main determining factor for job promotions
ねんこうじょれつ
in Japan, is now sometimes abandoned in favor of merit-based promotions. This shift
has made it more acceptable for people to change jobs on their own initiative and has
also made it more economically viable. People now have the chance to be hired at
positions equivalent to the ones they have given up at their old companies, instead of at
entry-level positions, as was once the case.

The bursting of the bubble economy also resulted in a significant increase in the
number of businesses using temporary workers instead of regular employees. The
proportion of temporary workers grew from 26.0% in 2000 to 37.4 % in 2014.
Temporary workers are employed on an hourly basis, and depending on the workplace,
their contracts are renewed every three months to annually. Even those temporary
workers who remain with the same company for a long time are not eligible for the
benefit packages given to permanent employees.

Due to the fact that the rapidly aging population will negatively affect the economy,
the government has been trying to help more temporary and female workers obtain
regular employment. In 2014, 77.8% of males and 43.0% of females had regular
employment. In 2013, 70.8% of women between 15 and 55 years of age held a job. This
number, however, ranks 23rd of the 34 countries surveyed (OECD, 2014) because of the
large proportion of temporary workers, lower wages, and lack of promotion among
female workers. The government has been promoting equal employment and passed a law
mandating that large cooperations increase their percentage of full-time female employees
and female executives in 2015. In addition, the government plans to further increase the
percentage of married women who hold jobs outside of the home and has set a goal of
70% employment for the year 2017.

文法
ぶんぽう

I. Expressing chronological order using 前 and 後
あと

In Chapter 5 of *Nakama 1*, 前 and 後ろ are introduced to indicate spacial relationships, such as つくえの前 (*in front of the desk*) and つくえの後ろ (*behind the desk*). In Chapter 12 of *Nakama 1*, duration of time + 前 and 後 are used to indicate time, such as 三年前 (*three years ago*) and 四年後 (*four years later, four years from now*). This chapter introduces expanded usage of 前 and 後 to indicate chronology. Both 前 and 後 are nouns that can be used with nouns and verbs. Be careful to pronounce 後 in this usage as あと.

A. Noun の前 (に) ／ the dictionary form of verbs + 前 (に), *before* 〜

The particle に to express time is optional with 〜前. As it can be used as a topic, 前 can be combined with は as in 前は or 前には.

授業の前に、	話があります。	*I have to talk to you before class.*
ひっこしの前に、	くるまをなおします。	*I will fix the car before moving.*
しけんの前は、	あまり寝られない。	*I cannot sleep well before an exam.*
旅行に行く前には、	計画をたてた方がいいですよ。	*You should make plans before you go on a trip.*
店がしまる前に、	買いに行こう。	*Let's go shopping before the stores close.*
卒業する前に、	やりたいことがある。	*I have something that I want to do before graduation.*

The form should be noun + の + 前 or the dictionary form of verb + 前. The use of the dictionary form in a subordinate clause such as 前 indicates that the event in the subordinate clause was not completed before the performance of the event in the main clause. Since the event in the 前 clause cannot be completed until after the event in the main clause, the verb preceding 前 must be in the present form regardless of the tense used in the main clause.

結婚する前に、家を買いたいです。	*I want to buy a house before getting married.*
結婚する前に、家を買いました。	*I bought a house before getting married.*
南：　もう帰るの？	*Are you going home?*
大川：　うん。	*Yeah.*
南：　じゃあ、帰る前にこれ見て。	*Well, look at this before you go.*

NOTES

- If the subject of the 前 clause is different from the main clause, it must be marked with the particle が.

  母が来る前に、へやをそうじしました。

  I cleaned my room before my mother came.

- 前に can also be used as an independent expression.

  この会場には、前に来たことがあります。

  I have come to this meeting place before.

  あのみずうみは、前はとてもきれいだった。

  That lake was once very clean.

B. Noun の後（で）／ the plain past affirmative form of verbs ＋ 後（で）, after ～

The particle で to express time is optional with ～後. Because it can be used as a topic, 後 can be combined with は as in 後は or 後では.

送別会の後で、ひっこした。	*I moved after the farewell party.*
卒業式の後で、友達と写真をとった。	*I took a picture with my friend after the graduation ceremony.*
日本に留学した後で、その人と会った。	*I met the person after I went to Japan on a study abroad program.*
しゅうしょくした後で、結婚したい。	*I want to get married after I get a job.*

Use of the plain past form in a subordinate clause indicates that the event in the subordinate clause was completed before the event in the main clause. The completion of the event in the 後 clause is necessary for the performance of the event in the main clause, and the verb in the 後 clause must be in the past tense regardless of the tense of the main clause.

木山：小山さんの送別会、行った？

　　　Did you go to Ms. Koyama's farewell party?

キム：うん、バイトがおわった後で行ったから、少しおそくなったけど。

　　　Yeah, but I was a bit late because I went after I got off work from my part-time job.

お母さん：いつそうじするの？	*When are you going to clean* (your room?)
子供：学校から帰った後でするよ。	*I will do it after I come back from school.*

If the subject of the 後で clause is different from that of the main clause, it must be marked with the particle が.

田中さんは、子供が生まれた後で、仕事をはじめた。	*Mr. Tanaka started working after his child was born.*
はたらいた後で飲むビールはとてもおいしい。	*Beer after work is delicious.*

後 can be used independently, with no clause.

後で来て下さい。	*Please come later.*

話してみましょう

Activity 1   Describe the following schedule for the day of the birthday party, using 前（に）and 後（で）.
あと

Example: 五時まではたらいた後で、家に帰ります。
あと
家に帰る前に、はたらきます。

午後五時	はたらきます。
	家に帰ります。
	少し休みます。
六時	買い物に行きます。
六時半	パーティのじゅんびをします。
七時	友達が来ます。 だち
七時半	誕生日会をはじめます。 たん　　　かい
十時	誕生日会がおわります。 たん　　　かい
十時半	部屋のそうじをします。 へ や

Activity 2   Answer the questions using 前 and 後.
あと

Example: いつしゅくだいをしますか。

家に帰った後します。
あと
寝る前にします。

1. いつ勉強しますか。

2. いつご両親に電話しますか。
でん

3. いつ海外旅行に行きたいですか。

4. いつしゅうしょくするつもりですか。

5. いつごろ、結婚しようと思いますか。
けっこん

6. いつ、今すんでいるところから、ひっこしをしたいですか。

👥 **Activity 3** Work with a partner. Each partner should ask the other what he/she wants to do before or after the following occasions. Then both should report their partner's response to the class.

Example: A: 卒業する前にどんなことがしたいですか。
そつぎょう

B: そうですね。日本に留学したいですね。
りゅうがく

〜さんは卒業する前に日本に留学したいそうです。
そつぎょう　　　　　りゅうがく

	〜前にすること	〜後ですること あと
卒業します そつぎょう		
しゅうしょくします		
結婚します けっこん		

> ## II. Talking about preparations using 〜ておく; expressing completion, regret, or the realization that a mistake was made using 〜てしまう

The て-form of verbs can be combined with many types of auxiliary verbs to express different nuances. For example, you have learned that ている expresses ongoing action, continued existence of a result of an action, and habitual action. There are many other types, such as ておく (*do ~in advance*), てしまう (*finish doing ~*), てある (*has been done*), てみる (*try doing ~*), てもいい (*can do~*), てはいけない (*must not do*) and so on. This chapter introduces three of them: 〜ておく, 〜てしまう, and 〜てある. In this section, the first two of these constructions are introduced.

A. Talking about preparations using 〜ておく, do 〜 in advance

The て-form of the verb + おく is used when someone does something for a future purpose or leaves the current state as is for a future purpose. In the following sentence, for example, making plans for the future is done as a preparation to getting a job.

しゅうしょくする前に、将来の計画をたてておいた方がいいですよ。
しょうらい
You should make plans for your future before you start looking for a job.

ひっこしのじゅんびをしておきます。
I will make preparations for moving.

〜ておく／〜でおく becomes 〜とく／〜どく in casual speech.

Formal speech	Casual speech	Meaning
食べ物を残しておきます のこ	食べ物、残しとく のこ	*to leave some food for someone*
おゆをわかしておきます	おゆ、わかしとく	*to boil water in advance*
薬を飲んでおきます	薬、飲んどく	*to take medication in advance*

今晩友達が来るから、ワインを冷やしときましょう。

I will chill wine (in advance) since my friends are coming over tonight.

しゅくだいをはじめる前に、ゲームであそんどこう。

Let's play some more games before I start doing homework.

大学院生： 先生、ドア、しめましょうか。

        Shall I close the door?

   先生： いや、学生が来ますから、あけておいて下さい。

        No, a student's coming, so please leave it open.

お父さん： げんかんの電気、けそうか。

        Shall I turn off the light in the entrance?

お母さん： あ、つけといて。まだ、大輔が帰ってきてないから。

        Leave it on. Daisuke's not home yet.

NOTES

- 〜ておく conjugates as an う-verb.

書いておかない	書いとかない
書いておきます	書いときます
書いておく	書いとく
書いておこう	書いとこう
書いておいて	書いといて

B. Expressing completion, regret, and the realization that a mistake was made using 〜てしまう

The て-form of the verb + しまう can have two interpretations. The first emphasizes the completion of an action. In this interpretation, 〜てしまう indicates that the speaker has finished doing something more clearly than the simple verb form does. For example, ごはんを食べてしまった emphasizes the idea that the speaker has finished the meal, as opposed to ごはんを食べた, which merely reports that the speaker performed the act of eating a meal.

明日までに履歴書を書いてしまいます。

I will finish up writing the resume by tomorrow.

古くなったらおいしくないから、今食べてしまった方がいいよ。

It won't taste good if it gets old, so you should finish it up now.

その DVD はもう見てしまいました。

I have already seen that DVD.

〜てしまう／でしまう becomes 〜ちゃう／じゃう in casual speech.

Formal speech	Casual speech	Meaning
テストで間違えてしまいました	テストで間違えちゃった	*I made a mistake on the exam.*
その本はもう読んでしまいました	その本もう読んじゃった	*I already finished reading the book.*

今日は、もうジョギングをしてしまった。 　*I have already gone jogging today.*

リーさんへのプレゼント、もうつつんじゃったよ。 　*I have already wrapped Mr. Li's gift.*

お母さん： しゅくだいはおわったの。 　*Is your homework finished?*

　　子供： うん、もうしちゃったよ。 　*Yes it's finished. (lit.: I've finished it.)*

The second usage of 〜てしまう indicates that something that should not have happened took place, or that someone did something that he or she should not have done. In this case, the て-form of the verb + しまう often conveys regret. Whether the て-form of the verb + しまう indicates completion or regret depends on the context.

大事なレポートをおとしてしまった。 　*I accidentally lost an important report.*

いぬがしんでしまった。 　*My dog has died.*

あ！ 教科書忘れちゃった！ 　*Oh! I forgot my textbook.*

田中： どうしたんですか、その足。 　*What's wrong with your foot?*

上田： かいだんからおちちゃったんです。 　*I fell down the stairs.*

すみません、田中さんのケーキは私が食べてしまったんです。
I'm sorry, but I ate Mr. Tanaka's cake.

NOTES

- 〜てしまう conjugates as an う-verb.

食べてしまわない	食べちゃわない
食べてしまいます	食べちゃいます
食べてしまう	食べちゃう
食べてしまおう	食べちゃおう
食べてしまって	食べちゃって
食べてしまった	食べちゃった

話してみましょう

Activity 1 Answer the following questions using the て-form of verbs + おく and the expressions in the box.

Example: 結婚式の前に何をしますか。
けっこんしき
友達にしょうたいじょうを出しておきます。
だち

友達にしょうたいじょう を出す	お金をあつめる	お風呂をわかす ふ ろ	後のことをよくかん あと がえる
先生に電話をかける でん	色々なことをする	まどをしめる	ホテルの予約をする
新しい仕事をさがす し ごと	風邪をなおす か ぜ	飲み物を冷やす ひ	電気をけす でん き

1. 友達があそびに来る前に、何をしておきますか。
   だち
2. 授業を休む前に、どうしますか。
   じゅぎょう
3. 出かける時、どうしますか。
4. 今の仕事をやめる前に、何をしておいた方がいいですか。
   し ごと
5. 旅行に行く前に、何をしておいた方がいいですか。
6. 寝る前に、何をしておきますか。
7. 家を買う前に、何をしておきますか。
8. 送別会の前に、どんなじゅんびをしておきますか。
   そうべつかい
9. しぬ前に、どんなことをしておきたいと思いますか。

Activity 2 Work with a partner. Think about three activities for which some preparations are necessary. Then write as many specific preparations as needed for each activity.

Example: 日本語のテスト
漢字を勉強しておく。友達と話すれんしゅうをしておく。
かん じ　　　　　　　　　だち
CDをよく聞いておく。教科書をよく読んでおく。
　　　　　　　　　　　　きょう か

Main activities	じゅんび
1	
2	
3	

Activity 3   Make a sentence by choosing a main clause (a–g) for each subordinate clause (1–7), then changing the appropriate verb in the main clause to 〜 てしまう.

Example: 1.   ケーキが少し残っているから、／   b. 食べましょう。
　　　　　　　　　　のこ
　　　　　　ケーキが少し残っているから、食べてしまいましょう。
　　　　　　　　　　のこ

1. ケーキが少し残っているから、
　　　　　　　のこ

　　a.　旅行の計画について考えた方が
　　　　いいです。

2. 旅館の予約がむずかしくなる前に、

　　b.　食べましょう。

3. 五時にお客さんが来るから、
　　　　　　きゃく

　　c.　社長に話したらどうでしょうか。
　　　　しゃちょう

4. 二十五さいになる前に、

　　d.　今のアパートから大きい家に
　　　　ひっこします。

5. 子供が生まれる前に、
　　　　　　う

　　e.　早くばしょをきめましょう。

6. 今度の同窓会は人がたくさん来るから、
　　　　どうそうかい

　　f.　大事な仕事をおえましょう。
　　　　だいじ　しごと

7. 社長が知る前に、
　　しゃちょう

　　g.　大学を卒業したいです。
　　　　　　そつぎょう

Activity 4   You inadvertently did the things listed in 1–6 below and need to apologize. Apologize using the phrases in 1–6 and 〜てしまう.

Example: マクレーさんのコンピュータをおとす。

　　　　　　すみません。マクレーさんのコンピュータをおとしてしまったんです。

1. 昨日メールを出したけど、メールアドレスを間違えていた。
　　　　　　　　　　　　　　　　　　　　　まちが

2. （友達）の大事な本をよごした。
　　だち　　だいじ

3. バスの時間を間違えて、授業におくれた。
　　　　　　　まちが　　じゅぎょう

4. さいふを家に忘れた。

5. （友達）と話す前に、一人できめた。
　　だち

6. 山田さんのプレゼントを私のだと思って、あけた。

Activity 5   Work with a partner. Create dialogues in which you must tell someone that you have done something unfortunate, then ask that person for help. Use the following situations and 〜てしまう. Share your dialogues with the class by acting them out.

Example:　パスポートがなくなる。

　　　A:　あ、キムさん。どうしたの？

　　　B:　パスポートがなくなってしまったんだ。

　　　A:　それは大変！ じゃあ、一緒にさがそうよ。

1.　電車の中で寝ていて、かばんを忘れた。

2.　200ドル入っているさいふをおとした。

3.　はたらきたくなかったから、仕事をやめた。

4.　ノートに書いていたけれども、テストの日を間違えた。

5.　コンピュータをつかいすぎて、手が痛くなった。

6.　友達のふくをよごした。

III. Using transitive and intransitive verbs; expressing results of intentional actions using 〜てある

A. Using transitive and intransitive verbs

Transitive verbs are verbs that express action directed by someone toward a specific object. The object, known as a *direct object*, is marked with the particle を in Japanese: 私はドアをあけた (*I opened the door*).

Intransitive verbs do not take a direct object, but rather are used in situations where the object acts on its own. An example would be ドアがあいた (*The door opened* [on its own]). English has similar verb pairs such as *to raise* and *to rise* (*Bob raised the flag* vs. *the flag rose*). However, native English speakers are often unaware of the differences between transitive and intransitive verbs, partly because the same verb can often be used in both transitive and intransitive constructions. The verb *to open* in the example above is one such verb. Japanese verbs, on the other hand, often come in transitive/ intransitive pairs, such as あける／あく, and the same verb cannot be used for both functions in Japanese.

ドアを　あけた。
I opened the door.

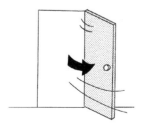

ドアが　あいた。
The door opened (on its own).

お母さんは子供を八時に起こします。　　　子供は八時に起きます。
The mother wakes the child up at eight o'clock.　　*The child wakes up at eight o'clock*

Use a transitive verb when the focus is on the person who performs the action. Use an intransitive verb when the focus is on the event/action itself.

私は　電話を　かけています。　　　　*I am making a phone call.*
　　　電話が　かかりました。　　　　*The phone is ringing.*

Except for some verbs like 入る, which can take an animate subject, as in 私はお風呂に入る, many intransitive verbs of transitive/intransitive verb pairs take an inanimate subject and do not express the speaker's intentional action. When they are used with the て-form of verbs + いる structure, they express a resultant state as introduced in Chapter 9 of *Nakama 1*.

電気がついています。　　　*The light is on.*

まどがしまっています。　*The window is closed.*

山本：このくつ、よごれていますね。　　　　　*These shoes are dirty.*

時田：ええ、子供がよごしてしまったんですよ。　*Yes, my child got them dirty.*

先生：スミスさんのしゅくだいが出ていませんね。
　　　Mr. Smith, you haven't turned in your homework. (lit.: Mr. Smith's homework has not been turned in.)

スミス：すみません。まだしていないんです。明日出します。
　　　I am sorry. I have not done it yet. I will turn it in tomorrow.

大川：まだケーキが残っていますよ。だれか食べませんか。
　　　Some cake is still left. Would anybody like to eat it?

リー：あ、それはキムさんのケーキですから、残しておいたんです。
　　　Ah, since that is Ms. Kim's cake, I left it for her.

山田：この漢字、間違ってるよ。
　　　This kanji is wrong.

上田：あ、本当だ。この漢字はむずかしいから、よく間違えるんだ。
　　　Oh, you're right. This kanji is difficult, so I often get it wrong.

B. Expressing results of intentional action using 〜てある

〜てある expresses a state that results from someone's intentional action. It is usually used to express a situation where someone has done something for some purpose and the speaker wants to talk about the state resulting from that action. Therefore, 晩御飯が作ってある in the following sentence indicates that the dinner has been cooked for a purpose and is ready.

晩御飯が作ってありますから、後で食べて下さい。
I made dinner for you, so please eat it later. (lit.: Dinner has been made, so please eat it later.)

The verb in the 〜てある construction can be transitive or intransitive, but it must express an intentional action.

雨がふりそうだから、まどがしめてあります。
Since it looks as if it will rain, the windows have been closed.

たくさんトレーニングはしてあるから、マラソンでいいタイムが出せるでしょう。
Since I trained a lot, my time for the marathon should be good.

When the main verb is transitive, the direct object can be marked with either が or を. The particle を tends to be chosen when the action was performed by the speaker.

たくさん食べ物<u>が</u>　買ってあります。　*A lot of food has been purchased. (by me or others)*

たくさん食べ物<u>を</u>　買ってあります。　*A lot of food has been purchased (by me).*

In the case of transitive and intransitive verb pairs, transitive verbs indicate an intentional action. So the て-form of transitive verbs + ある is used to express a state resulting from an intentional action. In contrast, intransitive verbs in the transitive/intransitive verb pairs usually express non-intentional action. Use of the particle を in the second and third examples below indicate that the agent causing the resultant state was probably the speaker. However, some verbs, such as 入る and 乗る, are not used in 〜てある constructions. Instead, they are used in 〜いる constructions to express a resultant state, as in the first two examples below.

ねこがかばんの中に入っています。	*The cat has gone into the bag.*
バスに乗っています。	*I am on the bus.*
ビールを冷やしてあります。	*The beer has been chilled. (I chilled it)*
ビールが冷えています。	*The beer is cold.*
おゆをわかしてあります。	*The water has been boiled. (I boiled it)*
おゆがわいています。	*The water is boiling.*

トム：	どうしてまどがあいているの？	*Why is the window open?*
かおり：	暑いから、あけてあるの。	*Since it's hot, I left it open.*

川口：　来週のじゅんびはもうおわりましたか。
　　　　Are you ready for the trip? (lit.: Have preparations been finished?)

北山：　ええ、ホテルの予約もしてあるし、飛行機の切符も買ってありますよ。
　　　　Yes, the hotel reservation has been made, and plane ticket has been purchased.

タクシーをよんであるから、もうすぐ来ます。
I've called a cab already, so it should be here soon. (lit.: Since a cab has been called, it should be here soon.)

そのことについては私から先生に少し話してあるから、そうだんしてみたらどうですか。
I've spoken to the teacher a little bit about it, so why don't you talk with him?

高山：　朝早かったから大変でしょう。
Since you had to get up early this morning, it might be tough, won't it?

石田：　いいえ、よく寝てありますから、大丈夫ですよ。
No, since I (have) slept well (since I got a good sleep), I'll be OK.

話してみましょう

> **Activity 1** Make sentences using the following noun/verb pairs.

Example:　水／出る
　　　　　水が出ます。

1. 水／出す
2. 仕事／変わる
3. 電気／つく
4. くるま／乗せる
5. バイト／つづく
6. 時間／間違える
7. さいふ／おとす
8. へや／よごれている
9. お金／あつまる
10. 電気／きえる
11. ジュース／残る
12. 電話／かかる
13. 病気／なおす
14. 卒業式の日／きまる
15. 授業／おえる

> **Activity 2** Work in groups of four. Make a pile of cards with a transitive or intransitive verb written on each. One person selects a card and creates a phrase using the verb written on it. The other three should try to make a phrase using the verb's corresponding transitive or intransitive form. The first person to correctly construct a phrase wins the round.

Example:　A:　(The card has あく written on it.) まどがあきます。
　　　　　B:　まどをあけます。

> **Activity 3** Look at the picture of Mr. Ishida's room. Describe his room using intransitive verbs.

Example:　電気がついています。

Activity 4   Mr. Ishida's parents are visiting him today, so he cleaned his room. It is a very hot day today. Describe his room in the following picture using the て-form of verbs + ある. Note that はな means *flower*.

Example: まどがあけてあります。

Activity 5   Work with a partner. What kind of preparations should you complete before the following events? Create a dialogue using the phrases in 1–5 below with ~てしまう and ~てある. Use casual speech.

Example: 誕生日会／お母さんに話す／お父さんに言う

    A:　今度の誕生日会のことなんだけど。

    B:　お母さんに話してあるの？

    A:　うん。もう話しちゃったよ。

    B:　あ、そう。じゃあ、お父さんにも言ってあるの？

    A:　それはまだ。明日言うつもり。

1. 旅行／切符を買う／旅館の予約をする

2. 卒業式／ガウン (*gown*) を買う／先生をよぶ

3. 母の日／カードを書く／カーネーション (*carnation*) を買う

4. 同窓会／会場をきめる／しょうたいじょうを出す

5. 入学式／両親に言う／新しいふくを買う

IV. Expressing purpose, using the plain form of the verb/ noun の + ため, in order to ~, for ~

The ます stem of the verb + に (*Nakama 1*, Chapter 6,) expresses purpose, but this construction is limited to cases where the main verb is a motion verb such as 行く, 来る, and 帰る. This chapter introduces the dependent noun ため, which expresses a purpose and can be used with a wider variety of verbs. In addition, ため can be used to express reason. Whether ため describes a purpose or a reason depends on the type of verb used with ため and the type of main verb.

When the dictionary form of verb + ため indicates a purpose, the main clause expresses an action or event that is controlled by the speaker. Also, ため is often preceded by a noun + の or a plain present affirmative form of a verb which expresses an action or event that can be controlled by the speaker. For example, in order to express the idea of someone standing up in order to open a door, ドアをあける, which is controlled by the speaker, is used rather than ドアがあく, which is not controlled by the speaker. Therefore, the sentence should be ドアをあけるためにたった.

エンジニアになるために、勉強しています。	*I am studying in order to become an engineer.*
けんきゅうするために、来ました。	*I have come to do research.*
自分のためになる仕事がしたい。	*I want to do work that will be good for my own development.*
何のために、その会社にしゅうしょくするんですか。	*Why are you taking a job at that company?*
留学するために、アルバイトをする。	*I work part-time to study abroad.*
将来のために、わかい時は色々なことをした方がいい。	*For the sake of your future, you should experience a variety of things while you're young.*

Notes

- When ため is used with a motion verb such as 行く, 来る, and 帰る, ため expresses a rather important purpose. On the other hand, the ます-stem of verbs + に can be used without a directional phrase, and the purpose does not have to be important.

しけんの勉強をするために図書館に行きました。

I went to the library in order to study for the exam.

しけんの勉強をしに図書館に行きました。

I went to the library to study for the exam.

コーヒーを飲むために来ました。　*I came in order to have some coffee.*

コーヒーを飲みに来ました。　*I came to have some coffee.*

- Also, ため can be followed by the particle に (when it modifies a verbal phrase) or の when it modifies a noun. The particle に can be optionally deleted.

日本に留学するため（に）アルバイトをしているんです。
りゅうがく
I'm working part-time in order to go to Japan to study.

これは、新しいくるまを買うためのお金です。
This is the money to buy a new car.

体育館は、うんどうするための建物です。
いくかん　　　　　　　　　　　たて
A gym is the place where people exercise.

- ため indicates a reason or cause (1) when ため is preceded by an adjective or the past plain form of a verb and adjective, or (2) when the main clause expresses an action or event that cannot be controlled by the speaker.

祖父がなくなったため、学校に来られませんでした。
そ
I couldn't come to school because my grandfather died.

博物館はここからとおいため、くるまで行った方がいいでしょう。
はく
You should probably go to the museum by car because it's far away from here.

しゅうしょくがきまらないため（に）、毎晩寝られない。
I cannot sleep at all at night because I have not gotten a job.

雪のため、電車がおそく来た。
でんしゃ
The train arrived late because of the snow.

話してみましょう

Activity 1   Define each of the following objects using the dictionary form of the verb + ための 〜 .

Example: はし
　　　　　食べるためのものです。／食べるためのもの（だ）よ。

1. 薬
2. コート
3. えんぴつ
4. コンピュータ
5. たんす
6. タブレット PC (tablet PC)
7. くるま
8. さいふ

Activity 2   Work with a partner. Create a dialogue in which one preson selects one of the purposes listed in 1-5 and the other person suggests how this goal can be achieved.

Example: べんごしになる

A:　将来べんごしになりたいんです。
　　　　しょうらい

B:　べんごしになるためには、（むずかしいしけんがあるから）たくさん勉強した方がいいですね。

1.　日本に留学する
　　　　　りゅうがく
2.　大学院でけんきゅうする
3.　自分の店を持つ
4.　50 さいで仕事をやめる
　　　　　　　しごと
5.　大きい家にすむ

Activity 3   Work as a class. Ask your classmates what they want to do in the future and what they are doing to achieve their goal, using 〜ために. Also, ask why they study Japanese. Use casual speech.

Example: A:　将来どんなことがしたいの。
　　　　　　　しょうらい

B:　そうだね。自分の会社を作りたいんだ。
　　　　　　じ ぶん　かいしゃ

A:　すごいね (impressive)。じゃあ、会社を作るためにどんなこと
　　　　　　　　　　　　　　　　　　かいしゃ
してるの。

B:　けいえい学を勉強してるんだ。

A:　そうなんだ。じゃあ、日本語も社長になるために勉強してるの？
　　　　　　　　　　　　　　　しゃちょう

B:　いや、日本語は仕事のためじゃないよ。自分の勉強のため
　　　　　　　　しごと　　　　　　　　じ ぶん
（だ）よ。

名前	何のため	今していること

> ## V. Expressing obligation using 〜なければ／なくては + ならない, 〜なければ／なくては + いけない; expressing a lack of obligation using 〜なくてもいい

In Japanese, verbs and adjectives can be combined with other phrases to express new meanings. You have already learned that the て-forms of verbs are used extensively in this regard. Similarly, the stem of the negative form (the part preceding ない) can be used with other phrases to express new meanings. This chapter shows how negative stems are used to express obligation or lack thereof.

A. 〜なければ／なくては + ならない, 〜なければ／なくては + いけない, *must* ~

The negative form with 〜なければ／なくては + ならない, 〜なければ／なくては + いけない expresses obligation and ~なくてもいい expresses a lack of obligation. Study the following four sentences.

明日、入学式に出なければならない。	*I/You must attend the entrance ceremony tomorrow.*
明日、入学式に出なくてはならない。	*I/You must attend the entrance ceremony tomorrow.*
明日、入学式に出なければいけない。	*I/You must attend the entrance ceremony tomorrow.*
明日、入学式に出なくてはいけない。	*I/You must attend the entrance ceremony tomorrow.*

Although the above four sentences are are virtually interchangeable, いけない carries a stronger sense of obligation than ならない. When one talks about obligations or necessities that are general in nature, 〜なければならない or 〜なくてはならない tends to be used. For more specific cases, 〜なければいけない or 〜なくてはいけない tends to be used.

〜なければ／なくては + ならない, 〜なければ／なくては + いけない can be used with the negative stem of verbs and adjectives. The combination of any of these forms and a verb indicates one must or has to do something. When they are combined with an adjective or the copular verb, the sentence indicates one is expected to be a certain way.

もっと勉強しなければならない。	*I/You have to study harder.*
卒業式を休まなくてはいけない。	*I/You must excuse my/yourself from the graduation ceremony.*
ここにいなければいけません。	*I/You must stay here.*
二十一さいじゃなければならない。	*I/You must be 21 years old.*
子供は元気じゃなければならない。	*Children are expected to be healthy.*
ゆうえんちは、たのしくなければならない。	*Amusement parks ought to be fun.*

なければ／なくては is derived from the negative ending 〜ない.

	Dictionary	**Negative form**	**negative stem + なければ／なくては**
る -verb	つづける (to continue)	つづけない	つづけなければ／つづけなくては
う -verb	ぬぐ (to take off)	ぬがない	ぬがなければ／ぬがなくては
Irregular verbs	来る (to come)	来ない	来なければ／来なくては
	する (to do)	しない	しなければ／しなくては
い -adjectives	やさしい (kind)	やさしくない	やさしくなければ／やさしくなくては
な -adjectives	しずかだ (quiet)	しずかじゃない	しずかじゃなければ／しずかじゃなくては
Copula verbs	医者だ (doctors)	医者じゃない	医者じゃなければ／医者じゃなくては

In casual speech, the following contracted forms are used. Also, ならない／いけない can be omitted or replaced by だめ.

Formal speech	**Casual speech**
～なければならない／いけない	～なきゃ（なんない／いけない／だめ）
～なくてはならない／いけない	～なくちゃ（なんない／いけない／だめ）
知らなければなりません／いけません	知らなきゃ（なんない／いけない ／だめ）
知らなくてはなりません／いけません	知らなくちゃ（なんない／いけない ／だめ）

送別会に出るためには、今、もどらなければなりません。
そうべつかい
I must go back now in order to attend the farewell party.

同窓会のお金をあつめなければならない。   *I have to collect money for the reunion.*
どうそうかい

その子をくるまに乗せなくちゃならない。   *I have to give a ride to the child.*

西川：　もう帰るんですか。
にしかわ
　　　　Are you going home already?

山本：　ええ、明日は東京に行かなければならないんです。
　　　　　　　　きょう
　　　　Yes, I must go to Tokyo tomorrow.

かおる：　どこ行くの？
　　　　　Where are you going?

健一：　ゆうびんきょく。この手紙、出さなきゃならないんだ。
けん　　　　　　　　　　　がみ
　　　　The post office. I must mail this letter.

お母さん：　つかった後は、トイレのドアはしめなきゃだめよ。
　　　　　　　　　　あと
　　　　　　After using the toilet, you must close the door.

子供：　はい。
　　　　OK.

NOTES

- Because the negative form of the verb ある is ない, 〜なければ／なくては + ならない, 〜なければ／なくては + いけない by themselves mean *something must exist* or *one must have something*.

ここに先生のサインがなければいけない。
You must have a teacher's signature here.

学生証がなければいけませんよ。
You must have a student ID.

- To answer questions with 〜なければ／なくては + なりませんか, 〜なければ／なくては + いけませんか, use ええ、〜なければ／なくては + いけません to express an obligation. Use いいえ、〜なくてもいいです to express the lack of an obligation.

B. Expressing the acceptability of an action or state using the negative stem + なくてもいい

The negative stem of verbs and adjectives + なくてもいい means that one does not have to do something or something does not have to be in a certain way. It is the opposite of the negative stem + 〜なければ／なくては + ならない, 〜なければ／なくては + いけない. The negative stem + なくてもいい is also derived from the negative ending 〜ない.

やめなくてもいいです。	*You don't have to stop.*
違わなくてもいいです。	*It does not have to be different.*
同じじゃなくてもいいです。	*It does not have to be the same.*
わかくなくてもいいです。	*He/She does not have to be young.*

スミス：	会場を変えなければなりませんか。	*Do we have to change the meeting place?*
山本：	いいえ、変えなくてもいいですよ。	*No, you don't have to change it.*
明：	ネクタイしなきゃいけないの？	*Do I have to wear a tie?*
ケイト：	いや、しなくてもいいよ。	*No, you don't have to wear one.*
学生：	同じのでなければなりませんか？	*Does it have to be the same one?*
先生：	いや、同じのじゃなくてもいいよ。	*No it does not have to be the same one.*
	違うのでもいいよ。	*You can use a different one.*

Notes

- The negative stem + なくてもいい by itself means something does not have to exist or one does not have to have something.

パスポートがなくてもいいですよ。
You don't have to have your passport.

- Instead of the negative stem + なくてもいい, the negative stem + なくてもけっこうです and the negative stem + なくてもかまいません are used in polite speech. Store clerks, bank tellers and post office clerks commonly use this more polite version.

学生証は、なくてもけっこうです。
しょう
You don't have to have your student ID.

しょうたいじょうは、なくてもかまいませんよ。
You don't have to have an invitation letter.

話してみましょう

Activity 1   A student asks you about the rules and regulations of your university. Answer the questions using the following academic calender. Use polite speech.

Example: 科目とうろく (*class registration*) はいつまでに (*by*) しなければ
か もく
なりませんか。

八月三十日までにしなければなりません／いけません。

八月三十日までにしなくてはなりません／いけません。

August 25–August 30	On-campus registration
September 1	Instruction begins
September 14	Last day to add a course or to change sections
September 20	Last day to pay tuition without penalty
October 30	Last day to drop a course
November 30	Last day to submit a graduation request
December 5	Instruction ends
December 8–14	Final examination

1. セクションは、いつまでに変えなければなりませんか。
か

2. 卒業する人は、いつまでに卒業申込書 (*application*) を出さなくてはいけませんか。
そつぎょう   そつぎょうもうしこみしょ

3. 授業料 (*tuition*) は、いつまでにはらわなくてはいけませんか。
じゅぎょうりょう

4. コースをおとしたい時は、いつまでにおとさなければなりませんか。

5. 期末 (*final*) しけんは、いつまでにうけなければなりませんか。
き まつ

Activity 2 Work with a partner. Ask each other the course requirements for your Japanese class.

Example:　毎日漢字を勉強する
かん　じ

　　　A:　日本語の授業では毎日漢字を勉強しなければなりませんか。
じゅぎょう　　　　　　　　　かん　じ

　　　B:　はい、しなければなりません。

　　　or いいえ、しなくてもいいです。

1.　毎日、日本語で話す。

2.　日本人にインタビューする。

3.　毎日、漢字テストをうける。
　　　　　かん　じ

4.　毎週、先生のけんきゅうしつに行く。

5.　日本語でブログを書く。

6.　日本語のウェブページを読む。

Activity 3 Respond to the following questions, requests, or invitations using 〜なければ／なくては + ならない , 〜なければ／なくては + いけない and the appropriate phrase. Use casual speech. ごめん is the casual expression for an apology.

Example:　映画を見に行く／アルバイトをする。
えい

　　　A:　今日の午後、映画、見に行かない?
えい

　　　B:　行きたいんだけど、今日の午後はバイトに行かなくちゃなんないから、ごめん。

1.　テニスをする／病院に行く。

2.　ゲームをしに来る／レポートのデータをあつめる。

3.　あそびに来る／今日は早く家に帰る。

4.　食事に行く／会社に残って仕事をする。
　　じ　　　　　　かいしゃ　の　こ　　し ごと

5.　今晩、家に泊まる／明日までにレポートをおえる。

Activity 4   State as many things as you can do in advance to achieve the following goals, using the て-form of verbs + おく.

Example: 学者になります。
　　　　　　がくしゃ
　　　　　　学者になるためには、勉強とけんきゅうをつづけておかなければ
　　　　　　がくしゃ
　　　　　　なりません。

1.　卒業した後も日本語の勉強をつづけます。
　　そつぎょう　　あと

2.　五十さいぐらいで仕事をやめます。
　　　　　　　　　　　しごと

3.　日本に留学します。
　　　　　りゅうがく

4.　社長になります。
　　しゃちょう

5.　将来、自分のレストランを持ちます。
　　しょうらい　じ　ぶん

6.　ハワイで結婚式をします。
　　　　　　けっこんしき

Activity 5   Work with a partner. One person plays the role of a student and the other person should be his/her Japanese instructor. The student asks the instructor what he/she is or is not required to do in the Japanese course or other related situations, and the instructor answers the questions. Create a dialogue for the following situations. Use the course syllabus of your Japanese class if necessary. Use polite speech.

Example: A: 先生、あのう。日本語のレベル３の授業をとりたいんですが。
　　　　　　　　　　　　　　　　　　　　　　　　　じゅぎょう
　　　　　　　　B: はい。
　　　　　　　　A: どんなことをしなければならないでしょうか。／
　　　　　　　　　　何をしたらいいでしょうか。
　　　　　　　　B: そうですね。しけんをうけなければなりませんね。
　　　　　　　　A: じゃあ、どんなじゅんびをしたらいいでしょうか。
　　　　　　　　B: 何もしなくてもいいですよ。

1.　来年の夏に日本に留学する。
　　　　　　　　　　りゅうがく

2.　日本語のけんきゅうについて知りたい。

3.　病気で一週間休んだので、授業が分からない。
　　　　　　　　　　　　　　じゅぎょう

4.　おもしろい日本語の言葉をあつめたい。
　　　　　　　　　　　ことば

5.　日本の会社ではたらきたい。
　　　　かいしゃ

聞く練習
れんしゅう

上手な聞き方

Paying attention to speech styles

The use of appropriate speech style is very important in one's career in Japan. In many cases, language skills are considered a type of competence, so Japanese college students are often explicitly taught how to use polite language before they start looking for a job. If a job candidate cannot use polite language he/she will not be considered for the job regardless of how competent he/she is. For this reason, paying attention to how people use polite and casual speech styles depending on the context of a conversation is essential to understanding how communication works.

練習
れんしゅう

A company is looking for a person who can do the following.

> 月曜日から金曜日、午前朝九時から十二時まではたらける人
> 土曜日も仕事に来られる人
> しごと
> ひょうけいさんソフト (*spreadsheet software*) がつかえる人

Listen to three job interviews and decide who is the best candidate for the job. Explain your choice.

名前：＿＿＿＿＿＿＿＿＿＿＿＿＿＿＿

どうして：＿＿＿＿＿＿＿＿＿＿＿＿＿＿＿＿＿＿＿

将来の計画
しょうらい

聞く前に

Work with a partner. Look at the chart of four college students and discuss what kinds of careers and lifestyles they may have.

名前	山田 友美 ともみ	北川 高子 きたがわ	安田 春子 やすだ はるこ	高田 友輝 たかだ ゆうき
年	18 さい	23 さい	19 さい	21 さい
せんこう	文学 ぶん	れきし	びじゅつ (*art*)	きょういく (*education*)
アルバイト	ウェイトレス	家庭教師 かていきょうし (*tutor*)	デパートの店員 てんいん (*clerk*)	日本語学校の先生
しゅみ	本を読む	旅行	テニス	おんがく

聞いた後で

A. Listen to the three college students in the above chart talk about their future plans and current lifestyles. They do not reveal their names in the conversation. Then do the following:

1. Write the future plans of each and what, if anything, each is doing to achieve that plan.

学生	将来の計画 しょうらい	しておくこと／してあること
A		
B		
C		

2. Work with a partner. Try to identify the students names by comparing the description you have just listened to and the descriptions in the chart in 聞く前に.

Aさんの名前 _____

Bさんの名前 _____

Cさんの名前 _____

B. 質問に日本語で答えて下さい。
　　しつもん

1. Aさんは、卒業したら、好きなことが出来ると思っていますか。
　　　　　　そつぎょう

2. Aさんは結婚したいと思っていますか。
　　　　　けっこん

3. Aさんはしゅうしょくしたいと思っていますか。

4. Bさんは来年何をするつもりですか。どうしてですか。

5. Bさんはどこでアルバイトをしていますか。

6. Bさんは結婚したいと思っているでしょうか。
　　　　　けっこん

7. Cさんは卒業したらすぐしゅうしょくするつもりですか。
　　　　　そつぎょう

8. Cさんは英語が上手ですか。
　　　　えい

9. Cさんは英語の勉強をするために外国に行くのですか。
　　　　えい

C. パートナーと下の質問について話して下さい。
　　　　　　　　しつもん

1. Aさん、Bさん、Cさんの中で、自分はどの人に一番ちかいと思いますか。ど
　うしてそう思いますか。　　　　じぶん

2. Aさん、Bさん、Cさんの中で、自分はどの人と一番違うと思いますか。どう
　してそう思いますか。　　　　　じぶん　　　ちが

3. Aさん、Bさん、Cさんはどんな人だと思いますか。どの人と友達になりたい
　と思いますか。　　　　　　　　　　　　　　　　　　だち

🔊 D. Listen to the conversation between two people. One of the two people is either student A, B, or C. Using listening strategies such as key word search, your knowledge about the students, and speech style, try to guess which student is talking, where and with whom the conversation takes place, and what the conversation is about. Then summarize the content of the conversation.

学生の名前 _____

学生が話している人 _____

話しているところ _____

トピック_____

ないよう (contents) _____

_____

_____

👥 E. Work with a partner. Each of you should write a short description of your future plans on a piece of paper. Include your age, interests, what you want to do in the future, and what you are doing or must do to achieve your goal. The description should not include your name. Then, exchange your description and proofread your partner's description.

👥 F. Work in groups of six, making sure your partner in Activity E is not in your group. One person collects the descriptions written in activity A from each member and then gives them to the other members so that nobody has his/her own paper. Each person reads a description, and the rest of the group figures out the name of the person who wrote it.

聞き上手話し上手

Making confirmations and checking comprehension

Communication strategies such as asking for repetition or paraphrases, checking the other person's comprehension, and confirming what is said, are very important in sustaining conversation and preventing a breakdown in communication. Chapter 6 of *Nakama 1* introduced how to ask for repetition and paraphrase. (あのう、すみません、もう一度言って下さい and ゆっくり言って下さい) You can also use もう一度おねがいします or ゆっくりおねがいします, which is more polite than 言って下さい.

This chapter focuses on making confirmation and checking comprehension. To check someone's comprehension, you can use わかりますか (*Are you following me?* or *Do you understand what I am saying?*), or わかりましたか (*Did you understand what I meant?*). If your conversation partner does not understand you, don't immediately give up or change the subject. Try your best to paraphrase what you are trying to say. Making such an effort gives you more opportunity to try out a variety of structures and expressions. It helps you to increase your knowledge and retention as well as fluency.

Conversely, if you are not sure about your understanding of the other person's speech, you should confirm what has been said. This will help you get important information and prevent you from running into a major misunderstanding.

There are several ways of confirming information in Japanese.

1. Repeating a word or expression with rising or falling intonation.

川田：	あのう、銀行はどこですか。／ねえ、銀行どこ？	*Where is the bank?*
山本：	そのケーキ屋の後ろです。／そのケーキ屋の後ろだよ。	*It's behind that cake shop.*
川田：	ケーキ屋の後ろですか。／ケーキ屋の後ろ？	*Behind the cake shop?*
山本：	ええ。／うん。	*Yes.*

Another strategy is to use a brief pause (which may be as long as five seconds or so), but a pause can also indicate a lack of comprehension or communication difficulty.

2. Repeat a word or expression and add ですか with a rising intonation. In casual speech, simply repeat with a rising intonation.

川田：	電車は何時に出ますか。／電車、何時に出るの？	*What time does the train leave?*
山本：	朝六時半に出ますよ。／朝六時半に出るよ。	*It leaves at 6:30 a.m.*
川田：	六時半 (に) ですか。／六時半（に）？	*6:30 a.m.?*
山本：	ええ。／うん。	*Yes.*

A short rising intonation not only helps confirm information but also expresses surprise.

3. Repeat a word or expression and add ですね or ね (casual speech) with a short rising intonation. The intonation does not indicate any surprise. The use of ね, instead of か, indicates that you are convinced, or at least satisfied, with the information given to you.

川田： どこでおとしたんですか／おとしたの？
Where did you drop it?

山本： あのこうえんのちかくの高校の前で。
In front of the high school near that park.

川田： ああ、分かりました／分かった。東高校の前ですね／だね。
Oh, I see. It's in front of Higashi High School.

山本： はい、そうです。／うん、そうだよ。
Yes, it is.

4. Repeat a sentence or verb phrase using 〜んですね／〜んだね.

川田： ビールとワインは、ありますか。／ビールとワイン、ある？
Do you have beer and wine?

山本： ええ、買ってありますよ。／うん、買ってあるよ。
Yes, I've got them.

川田： ビールもワインも買ってあるんですね／だね。
You've got beer and wine, right?

山本： ええ。／うん。
Yes.

練習
れんしゅう

A. Complete the following conversations by writing confirming remarks on the blank lines.

1. A: あのう、すみません。トイレはどこにありますか。

   B: 一階のエレベータの横にありますよ。
      かい

   A: _____

2. A: ねえ、今週、日本の映画があるそうだけど、いつ、どこであるの？

   B: 金曜日の午後八時から、図書館の二階のラウンジであるそうだよ。
                      と   かい

   A: _____

3. A: あの、来年の夏、日本で勉強したいと思うんですけど。

   B: じゃあ、三階にある留学生センターのじむしつ (office) に行ったらどう？
                 がい   りゅう

   A: _____

4. A: ビールとワインはもう買ってあるから、ジュース買っといてくれる？

   B: _____

B. Listen to a series of short statements. Confirm what has been said.

1. _____   5. _____

2. _____   6. _____

3. _____   7. _____

4. _____   8. _____

C. Listen to a series of announcements about your Japanese class. Confirm what has been said, and write down the content of the announcements in Japanese.

1. _____

2. _____

3. _____

D. Work with a partner. Imagine one of you is a reporter and the other is a celebrity. The reporter should interview the celebrity, take notes, and confirm what was written. The celebrity should make sure the reporter understands by checking his/her comprehension.

漢字
かん じ

Top component shapes of kanji

Like the left component, many of the top components indicate a semantic category to which the meaning of a **kanji** belongs. Some of them, such as くさかんむり, うかんむり, and たけかんむり, appear in a large number of **kanji** while others are more limited in their use.

Name		Meaning	Examples
くさかんむり	⺿	grass	英 茶 荷 菜 葉 落 薬 花 草
うかんむり	⼧	housing	安 家 客 室 定 宿 寒 寝
たけかんむり	⺮	bamboo	笑 符 第 答 等 節 箱
あめかんむり	⻗	rain	雪 雲 電 雷 震 霜
ひとやね	⼈	person	全 今 会 合 令 企 余 舎 倉 傘
あみがしら / よつがしら / よこめ	⺲	net	罪 署 置 罰
あなかんむり	⽳	hole	空 究 突 窃 窓
やまかんむり	⼭	mountain	岸 岩 崇 崩 嵐
おいかんむり / おいがしら	⺹	elderly, aged	考 老 者
なべぶた	⼇	pot lid	亡 交 京 享 亭
わかんむり	⼆	cover	冗 写 冠
はつがしら	⼎	two legs split apart	発 登

言 言	to say, to speak	` 一 亠 言 言 言 言	
	い(う)・こと　ゲン・ゴン	もう一度言って下さい。 言葉 い　　　　　　　　　　　ことば	

葉 葉	leaf	一 ⺿ 芏 苹 苹 苹 苹 葉 葉	
	は　ヨウ	韓国の言葉は日本語と違います。 かん　ことば　　　　　　ちが	

漢 漢	Chinese	シ シ 氵 汁 洪 洪 漢 漢 漢	
	カン	中西さんは漢字がたくさん書けます。 かんじ	

字 字	letter	` 宀 宁 字 字	
	ジ	漢字を読むのは大変です。 かんじ	

質	質	quality, matter	丶	ｲ	斤	斤	竹	竹	竹	笧	笪	質
		シツ・シチ・チ			旅行の計画について質問する。							
						しつもん						

問	問	question	丨	冂	⺆	門	門	門	門	問	問	
		と(う)・と(い)　モン			漢字の質問はありますか。							
					かんじ　しつもん							

卒	卒	to graduate	丶	亠	广	亠	卒	卒	卒	卒		
		ソツ	大学を来年の五月に卒業する予定です。									
			そつぎょう									

業	業	work, industry	丨	丷	⺌	业	丵	単	業	業		
		わざ　ギョウ・ゴウ	大学の卒業式　日本語の授業									
			そつぎょうしき　　じゅぎょう									

授	授	to confer, to give	一	扌	扌	护	护	护	护	授	授	
		さず(ける)　ジュ	授業を三つとっています。									
			じゅぎょう									

仕	仕	to serve, to do	丿	イ	イ一	什	仕					
		つか(える)　シ・ジ	新しい仕事を中国ではじめる。									
			しごと									

事	事	abstract thing, affair	一	一	戸	戸	亐	写	写	事		
		こと　ジ	来年の仕事　大事なテストがある。　食事に行く。									
			しごと　だいじ　　　　　　じ									

結	結	to tie, to bind	⼡	⼅	幺	幺	糸	紅	結	結	結	
		むす(ぶ)　ケツ・ケッ	来年、結婚する。									
			けっこん									

婚	婚	marriage	⼡	女	女	女	女	妒	妖	婚	婚	
		コン	結婚式の予約をとりました。									
			けっこんしき									

式	式	style, ceremony	一	二	三	王	式	式				
		シキ	友達の卒業式に行く。									
			だち　そつぎょうしき									

社	社	company, society	丶	⼆	ネ	ネ	ネ一	礻	社			
		やしろ　シャ	会社の社長の仕事は大変です。会社員　神社									
			かいしゃ　しゃちょう　しごと　　　　かいしゃいん　じんじゃ									

| 同 | 同 | same
おな(じ)　ドウ | 丨 冂 冂 冋 同 同 |
| | | | 同じ本を読んだ。　高校の同窓会がある。
おな　　　　　　　　　どうそうかい |

| 違 | 違 | to differ, to violate
ちが(う)・ちが(い)　イ | ノ ヵ 五 吾 查 查 查 韋 違 |
| | | | 答えが間違っている。　毎日天気が違う。
まちが　　　　　　　　ちが |

| 留 | 留 | to keep, to stay
と(める)・と(まる)　リュウ・ル | ノ ㇄ 厶 厽 幻 幻 留 留 留 |
| | | | 留学生センター　日本に留学する。
りゅう　　　　　　　　りゅうがく |

| 達 | 達 | to attain
タツ・ダチ | 一 十 土 キ 幸 幸 幸 達 達 |
| | | | 昨日、子供の時の友達と会った。
だち |

| 電 | 電 | electric
デン | 一 冖 冖 雨 雨 雫 雫 雷 電 |
| | | | 携帯電話の番号を知りません。電気をつける。電車
けいたいでん　　ごう　　　　　でんき　　でんしゃ |

| 英 | 英 | distinguished, England
エイ | 一 十 艹 芢 苉 苫 英 英 |
| | | | 会社の仕事は英語でしています。
かいしゃ　しごと　えい |

| 客 | 客 | guest
キャク | ﾞ ﾞ 宀 宀 宀 客 客 客 |
| | | | お客さんがたくさん来ました。
きゃく |

| 残 | 残 | to be left, to leave
のこ(る)・のこ(す)　ザン | 一 ㇆ 歹 歹 殊 残 残 残 |
| | | | 仕事が残っています。　残念
のこ　　　　　ざんねん |

読めるようになった漢字

言葉　言う　漢字　質問　卒業　授業　仕事　食事　大事　卒業式　結婚する
結婚式　会社　同じ　違う　留学生　友達　電気　電話　英語　客　生まれる
年　入学　起こす　同窓会　社長　神社　自分　変わる　将来　残る　残す
　　　　　　　　　　　　そう　　ちょう　じん　じ　　　　　しょう
残念　返事
ねん　へん
日本人の名前：南　木山　北山　時田　安田　西川　北川　明　大輔　友美
　　　　　　　　　　　　　　　　　　　　　　　　　　　　　すけ
友輝　春子　あつ子
き

Read the following sentences aloud.

1. 言葉は少し話せます。でも、残念ですが、漢字は知りません。
2. 弟の入学式と兄の卒業式には同じスーツを着て行くつもりです。
3. 質問に英語ではなくて、日本語で答えて下さい。
4. 山本さんは来年留学するので、今、会社でバイトをしています。
5. 授業で分からないことがあったので、友達に電話をかけて、質問をした。
6. 会社は同じだけど、違う仕事をする予定です。
7. 社長は会社に残って、新しいお客さんと話しました。
8. 今年の秋に結婚するので、早くホテルの予約をしなければなりません。

読む練習

上手な読み方

Using prefixes and suffixes

The size of a person's vocabulary is strongly correlated to his/her reading proficiency. In order to understand a text completely, a reader needs to know over 90 percent of the vocabulary in the text. For this reason, it is important to acquire vocabulary through reading. One way to achieve this is to use prefixes and suffixes to guess the meaning of a word. In this book, many suffixes and prefixes have already been introduced and practiced. Try using them to guess the meanings of new words as you encounter them.

Guess the meanings of the following expressions using your knowledge of prefixes and suffixes.

研究会　学会　大会　研究員　教員　映画館　毎回　毎度　大会社　子会社

日本人と結婚

読む前に

A. In Japanese, genre, rather than formality, determines whether to use plain or polite forms in writing. For example, compositions, diaries, and newspaper articles are usually written in plain form while letters and post cards are written using polite forms. Check the writing styles of the reading materials in the previous chapters as well as other authentic materials. Determine which types of writing use the plain form and which use the polite form.

B. 結婚について、下の質問に日本語で答えて下さい。

1. あなたの国では、男の人は何さいぐらいで結婚しますか。女の人はどうですか。

2. 結婚した後、だれが家の外ではたらきますか。

3. 結婚した後、家事 (*household work*) や子供の世話 (*care*) はだれがしますか。

4. あなたは結婚したいと思いますか。したくありませんか。どうしてそう思いますか。

C. Work as a class. You are going to conduct a survey (アンケート) about how your classmates think about marriage.

1. First, look at the following survey form, a summary sheet, and the expressions below. (The expressions in this activity will appear in the reading materials for this chapter.) Identify the types of information that you need to complete the summary sheet. Then conduct the survey and complete the survey form by classifying responses according to the gender of the interviewee.

平均 へいきん	average	家事 かじ	household work
年齢 ねんれい	age (formal expression)	世話 せわ	(child) care
男性 だんせい	formal word for 男の人	養う やしな	to support (financially)
女性 じょせい	formal word for 女の人		

Example:　A:　何さいぐらいで結婚したいと思いますか。

B:　三十さいぐらいで結婚したいと思います。

質問	女性 じょせい	男性 だんせい
何さいぐらいで 結婚したい		
家事はだれが かじ した方がいい		
子供の世話は せわ だれがした方が いい		
結婚したら、 だれが家族を 養った方がいい やし		
結婚したら、 じゆうな生活が 出来ない かつ		

2. Now complete the following summary sheet based on the results of your survey.

	男性 だんせい	女性 じょせい
結婚したい 平均年齢 ねんれい	＿＿＿＿＿さい	＿＿＿＿＿さい
家事 かじ	ご主人＿＿＿＿＿％ しゅ	ご主人＿＿＿＿＿％ しゅ
	おくさん＿＿＿＿＿％	おくさん＿＿＿＿＿％
	ご主人とおくさん＿＿＿＿＿％ しゅ	ご主人とおくさん＿＿＿＿＿％ しゅ
子供の世話 せわ	ご主人＿＿＿＿＿％ しゅ	ご主人＿＿＿＿＿％ しゅ
	おくさん＿＿＿＿＿％	おくさん＿＿＿＿＿％
	ご主人とおくさん＿＿＿＿＿％ しゅ	ご主人とおくさん＿＿＿＿＿％ しゅ
家族を養う やしな 人	ご主人＿＿＿＿＿％ しゅ	ご主人＿＿＿＿＿％ しゅ
	おくさん＿＿＿＿＿％	おくさん＿＿＿＿＿％
	ご主人とおくさん＿＿＿＿＿％ しゅ	ご主人とおくさん＿＿＿＿＿％ しゅ
じゆうな 生活 かつ	出来る＿＿＿＿＿％	出来る＿＿＿＿＿％
	出来ない＿＿＿＿＿％	出来ない＿＿＿＿＿％

読んでみましょう

　　日本人の平均結婚年齢は毎年少しずつ上がっている。三十年前の平均結婚年齢は男性が 25.4 歳、女性が 24 歳だったが、今は男性が 30.9 歳、女性も 29.3 歳になっている。
　　これはどうしてだろうか。2015 年のアンケートでは、まだ結婚していない人で、将来結婚したくないと答えた人は、女性が 31％、男性が 16％だった。結婚したくない理由は、男女ともに「一人でいるのが好きだから」と答えた人が一番多かった。また、男性は「給料が安いから」とも答えた。つまり、男性は、結婚したら、家族のために働かなければならないから、好きなことが出来ないと考えているのだ。それに、三十年前より今の方が生活にお金がかかるので、わかい時に結婚したら大変だと思っているのだ。
　　また、同じアンケートでは、多くの女性が「一人でも生活できるし、結婚したら自由な生活が出来ないから、あまり結婚したくない」と答えていた。日本では働く女性も、結婚した後も仕事を続ける人が多い。けれども、女性は、子供が生まれたら、家事や子供の世話をしなければならないという考えはまだ残っている。だから、結婚するより、就職して好きなことをしたい、結婚したくない人はしなくてもいいと考えるのかもしれない。

読んだ後で

A. Choose the statement that best summarizes the passage above.

1. この文章 (text) は日本の男性と女性の平均結婚年齢について書いてあります。
2. この文章 (text) はどうして日本人の女性が結婚しないかについて書いてあります。
3. この文章 (text) はどうして日本人がはやく結婚したがらないかについて書いてあります。

B. Circle はい if the statement is consistent with the passage and いいえ if it isn't.

1. 日本人は男性も女性もはやく結婚したいと思っている。　　はい　　いいえ
2. 働く女性は多くなった。　　はい　　いいえ
3. 仕事を持つ女性が家事をすることが多い。　　はい　　いいえ
4. 日本の男性は結婚した後、自分が家族を養わなければならないと思っている。　　はい　　いいえ

C. 下の質問に日本語で答えて下さい。

1. What does これ (underlined) refer to in the second paragraph of the reading?
2. What are the subjects of the following sentences?

    a. Fourth sentence of the second paragraph:

三十年前より今の方が生活にお金がかかるので、わかい時に結婚したら大変だと思っているのだ。

    b. Third sentence of the third paragraph:

結婚するより、就職して好きなことをしたい、結婚したくない人はしなくてもいいと考えるのかもしれない。

総合練習
そうごうれんしゅう

そうだんしたいことがあります

Work with a group of four. Imagine that you are consultants for people with various kinds of problems. Read the following statements about the worries these people have and discuss suggestions as to what steps they should take to solve them.

Example: マクドナルドさん

私は 18 さいで、スーパーではたらいていますが、仕事がおもしろくないので、仕事を変えたいと思います。高校はきらいだったので、一年前にやめたんです。でも、卒業しておいた方がよかったのかもしれません。どうしたらいいですか。

A: 高校を卒業していないから、いい仕事がないんだと思います。高校にもどった方がいいですね。

B: 大学に入るためのしけん (examination) をうけたら、どうでしょうか。

C: そうですね。そして、新しい仕事をさがす前に、大学も卒業しておいた方がいいですね。

1. ホンさん

私は今大学二年生ですが、大学をやめた方がいいかもしれません。高校の時は何でもよく出来ましたが、大学に入った後は、あまりいい成績がとれていません。Dをたくさんとってしまったんです。両親は大学を卒業した方が将来のためにいいからやめてはいけないと言いますが、私には分かりません。

2. ジョンソンさん

日本人のガールフレンドがいるんですが、春に大学を卒業して、日本に帰ってしまったんです。ぼくはまだ学生ですが、将来はその人と結婚したいと思っています。でも、彼女 (girlfriend) の両親は外国人はきらいだそうです。どうして外国人がきらいなのか、よく分かりません。今度の冬には日本へ行くつもりですが、その時彼女の両親に会おうと思っています。今から何をしておいたらいいでしょうか。

ロールプレイ

 1. You broke your friend's computer. Tell him/her what you have done, apologize, and offer some compensation.

2. You are an organizer of a workshop. You want to make sure that everything is ready. You are talking to a Japanese assistant. Confirm with the assistant that the following things are ready:
   a. speaker's hotel reservation
   b. conference site reservation
   c. preparation for coffee and snacks
   d. name tags (バッジ)
   e. staff at the registration desk (うけつけ)

3. A Japanese friend of yours has invited you for a weekend trip, but you're not sure if you can go because you have to study for final exams and finish your final papers. Tell your friend about your situation.

4. You lost your bag on the train in Japan. Important things such as your wallet, keys, and textbooks are in the bag. Go to the lost-and-found department and explain the situation. Describe what is inside the bag and ask for help. Also, leave your telephone number and ask to be called if the bag is found.

Chapter 4

第四課

ABSODELS/Getty Images

おねがい
Asking for Favors

単語
たんご

Nouns

ATM（エーティーエム）		automatic teller machine
いみ	意味	meaning
うんてんめんきょしょう	運転免許証	driver's license
かいわ	会話	conversation
カード		card
きって	切手	postage stamp
こうざ	口座	bank account, こうざをひらく to open a bank account
こづつみ	小包	parcel post
ざいりゅうカード	在留カード	residence card
サイン		signature, サインをする to sign
さくぶん	作文	composition
しけん	試験	examination, test
じゅぎょうりょう	授業料	tuition
じゅうしょ	住所	address
すいせん	推薦	recommendation, すいせんする to recommend, すいせんじょう recommendation (letter)
せつめい	説明	explanation, せつめいする to explain
たくはいびん	宅配便	parcel delivery service. Also called 宅急便, a registered company trademark commonly used instead of 宅配便
たんご	単語	vocabulary
ドル		dollar
はがき	葉書	postcard
はんこ	判子	seal
ふうとう	封筒	envelope
ふつうよきん	普通預金	regular bank account
ぶんぽう	文法	grammar
ポスト		public mail collection box
ゆうびんうけ	郵便受け	mailbox, to receive mail
ゆうびんばんごう	郵便番号	postal code
ようし	用紙	form

よきん	預金	bank account, よきんする to deposit money, よきんがある to have money in the bank
レポート		report, term paper, term project
れんしゅう	練習	practice, れんしゅうする to practice

う-verbs

いる	要る	to need, お金がいる to need money. The verb いる (*to need*) is an う-verb and written with the **kanji** 要る. It is different from いる (*to exist*) which is a る-verb and can be expressed in **kanji** as 居る.
おくる	送る	to send
かえす	返す	to return something
かす	貸す	to lend
つれていく	連れて行く	to take (someone somewhere)
てつだう	手伝う	to assist, help
とどく	届く	(for something) to arrive, to be delivered
ひきだす	引き出す	to withdraw (money)
ひらく	開く	to open, こうざをひらく to open an account
もうしこむ	申し込む	to apply, もうしこみようし application form

る-verbs

うける	受ける	to receive, to get, しけんをうける to take an exam
おしえる	教える	to tell, to teach
おぼえる	覚える	to memorize, おぼえている to remember, to recall
かえる	替える／変える	to change, セクションをかえる to change a section
かりる	借りる	to borrow, to rent (a house, apartment)
ためる	貯める	to save (money)
とどける	届ける	to deliver, send

Irregular verbs

もってくる	持って来る	to bring (something)
つれてくる	連れて来る	to bring (someone)

い-adjective

すごい	凄い	amazing, awesome, terrible, すごい先生 amazing teacher, すごい雨 terrible rain

な-adjective

だめ（な）	駄目（な）	no good, impossible, hopeless, not useful, not acceptable

Prefix

らい〜	来〜	来学期 next semester/quarter/term, 来週 next week, 来月 next month, 来週 next week, 来年 next year

Suffixes

〜かた	〜方	how to, way of 〜 ing
〜しょう	〜証	card (for identification), 学生証 student identification

Expressions

ありがとう。たすかります。	有り難う。助かります。	Thank you. That helps me a lot.
ごめん（なさい）	ご免（なさい）	I'm sorry. (used only for an apology, more colloquial than すみません）
じつは	実は	Actually
たすかります。	助かります。	That will be helpful.
ちょっとおねがいがあるんですけど	ちょっとお願いがあるんですけど	I have a small favor to ask.
ほんとうにいいんですか。	本当にいいんですか。	Are you sure you are OK with it?

単語の練習
たんご　れんしゅう

A. 身分証明書　Personal identification
みぶんしょうめいしょ

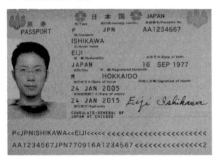

パスポート
passport

うんてんめんきょしょう
driver's license

学生証
しょう
student ID

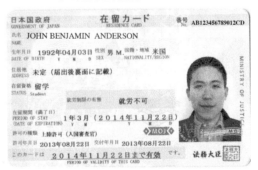

在留カード
ざいりゅう
residence card

Activity 1 Work with the class. Ask your classmates whether they have the following IDs and find out how many people have them.

Example: A: ～さんはパスポートを持っていますか。

B: ええ、持っていますよ。～さんもパスポートを持っていますか。

or いいえ、持っていません。～さんは持っていますか。

A: ええ、持っています。or いいえ、持っていません。

ID	持っている人
パスポート	
うんてんめんきょしょう	
学生証 しょう	
在留カード ざいりゅう	

B. 学校で勉強する

会話 かい わ	conversation	文法 ぶんぽう	grammar	作文 さくぶん	composition
レポート	report, paper	練習 れんしゅう	exercise	意味 い み	meaning
試験 し けん	examination	授業料 りょう	tuition	単語 たん ご	vocabulary
作り方 かた	how to make	話し方 かた	how to talk, manner of talking	すいせんする	to recommend

すいせんじょう letter of recommentation　　　教える to tell, to teach
　　　　　　　　　　　　　　　　　　　　　　　　おし

説明する せつめい	to explain	手伝う て つだ	to assist	試験を受ける し けん う	to take an exam
単語をおぼえる たん ご	to memorize vocabulary			授業を取る と	to take a course

授業を受ける to attend a class　　今学期 this semester　　来学期 next semester
う　　　　　　　　　　　　　　き　　　　　　　　　　　　　　き

おぼえていますか。

アジアけんきゅう　英語　おんがく　工学　経営学　文学　れきし　学食　学生会館　学期
　　　　　　　　　　　　　　　こう　けいえい　ぶん　　　　　　　　　　　　　　　　　き
漢字　教科書　教室　研究者　高校　こくばん　授業　宿題　じゅんび　せんこう　大学
　　　きょうか　　　けんきゅう　　　　　　　　　　しゅくだい
大学院　大学院生　テスト　同窓会　図書館　留学生　けんきゅうする　答える　質問する
　　　　　　　　　　　　　そう　　と
卒業する　留学する

Activity 2   質問に日本語で答えて下さい。

1. 日本語の授業ではどんな宿題がよく出ますか。

2. 日本語の何がむずかしいですか。何がやさしいと思いますか。

3. 漢字をおぼえるために、どんなことをしていますか。どんなことをしたらいい
   と思いますか。

4. 単語をおぼえるのがはやいと思いますか。

5. どうやって、単語をおぼえていますか。

6. 英語を教えたことがありますか。

7. 英語の文法が説明できますか。

8. 先生の仕事を手伝ったことがありますか。

9. 今学期はどんな授業を取っていますか。来学期はどうですか。

10. 先生にすいせんじょうをおねがいしたことがありますか。

Activity 3   Work with the class. Ask your classmates whether they know how to perform the actions listed in the following table and write the name of one person who knows how to do each.

Example: おすしを食べる

   A: おすしの食べ方を知っていますか。

   B: ええ、知っています。

Activity	クラスメートの名前
おすしを食べる	
日本語のメールを書く	
国際電話 (*international call*) をかける	
ちずを見る	
天ぷらを作る	

C. 郵便局と宅配便   Post Office and parcel delivery services

宅配便	Parcel delivery service	切手	postage stamp	ふうとう	envelope
小包	parcel	葉書	postcard	カード	card
住所	address	郵便番号	postal code	送る	to send
荷物をとどける	to deliver a package		荷物がとどく	a package is delivered	
郵便受け	post box to receive mail		ポスト	public mailbox	

おぼえていますか。

手紙 荷物 場所 はらう
(がみ)　　　(ばしょ)

Supplementary Vocabulary: 郵便局や宅配便でつかう言葉
　　　　　　　　　　　　　　　(ゆうびんきょく)　(たくはいびん)

EMS		international express mail
あてさき	宛先	recipient's address
うけとりにんばらい	受取人払い	fee paid by the recipient, COD
おくりじょう	送り状	sender's bill/shipping manifest
かきとめ	書留	insured mail
そくたつ	速達	express mail
ほけん	保険	insurance
りょうきん	料金	fee

Activity 4 下に説明してある単語は何ですか。
　　　　　　(せつめい)　　　(たんご)

1. 手紙を入れる物です。
   (がみ)
2. クリスマスやバレンタインデーにとどける物です。
3. ふうとうにはる (to affix) 物です。
4. 旅行している時、友達や家族によく送る物で、カードや手紙より安いです。
   　　　　　　　　　　　　　　(おく)　　　　　　　　(がみ)
5. 小包やスーツケースをとどけるサービス (service) です。
   (こづつみ)
6. これが書いていない荷物はとどきません。

D. 銀行
　　(ぎん)

ATM	automatic teller machine	ふつう預金 (よきん)	regular bank account
判子 (はんこ)	seal	サイン　signature サインをする to sign	
ドル	dollar	口座をしめる (こうざ)	to close an account
口座をひらく (こうざ)	to open a bank account	預金する (よきん)	to deposit money
預金がある (よきん)	to have money in the bank	お金を引き出す (ひ)(だ)	to withdraw money
お金をかえす	to repay money	お金をかす	to lend money
お金をかりる	to borrow money	お金をためる	to save money

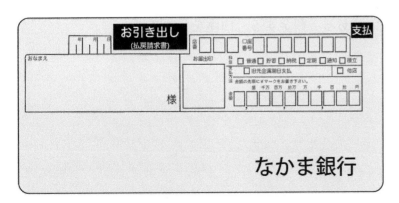

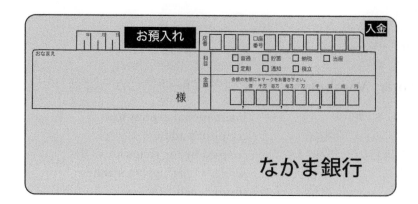

Supplementary Vocabulary: 銀行でつかう言葉

がいこくかわせ	外国為替	foreign currency exchange
キャッシュカード		ATM card
ぎんこうふりこみ	銀行振込	wire transfer of funds
げんきん	現金	cash
じどう	自動	automatic
じどうひきおとし	自動引き落とし	automatic payment of bills (from a bank account)
そうきん	送金	sending money
てすうりょう	手数料	transaction fee
つうちょう	通帳	account book
まどぐち	窓口	window (bank teller, municipal office, etc.)

Activity 5　質問に日本語で答えて下さい。

1. アメリカの銀行で口座をひらく時、どんな物がいりますか。

2. ATM でどんなことが出来ますか。

3. 銀行の口座を持っていますか。どんな口座を持っていますか。

4. キャッシュカードとクレジットカードは何が違いますか。

Activity 6　下の言葉を日本語で説明して下さい。

判子　ドル　預金がある　預金する　口座をしめる

ダイアローグ

はじめに

質問に日本語で答えて下さい。

1. 銀行口座をひらく時、何がいりますか。

2. あなたの国には、判子がありますか。どんな判子がありますか。

3. パスポートを持っていますか。

4. アメリカに住んでいる外国人は、在留カードを持っていなければ
なりませんか。

🔊 銀行口座をひらく　*Opening a bank account*

The following manga frames are scrambled, so they are not in the correct order. Read the dialogue and unscramble the frames by writing the correct number in the box in each frame.

a

b

c

d

e

f

g

リー：　石田くん、ちょっと聞きたいことあるんだけど。

石田：　何？

リー：　判子作りたいんだけど、どこで作ってもらえるのかな？

石田：　判子は判子屋に行った方がいいよ。

リー：　そう、判子屋ってどこにあるか知ってる？

石田：　ああ、駅前のスーパーのとなりにあるよ。一緒に行こうか？

リー：　ありがとう。でも、大丈夫。今から、行ってくるよ。

リーさんは判子屋へ行きました。
<ruby>判子屋<rt>はんこや</rt></ruby>

　リー：あのう、すみません。判子を作ってほしいんですが。
<ruby>判子<rt>はんこ</rt></ruby>

判子屋：色々ありますけど、どんなのがいいですか。
<ruby>判子屋<rt>はんこや</rt></ruby>

　リー：銀行口座をひらくための物なんですが。
<ruby>銀行口座<rt>ぎんこうざ</rt></ruby>

判子屋：じゃあ、こんなのはどうですか。
<ruby>判子屋<rt>はんこや</rt></ruby>

　リー：ああ、いいですね。じゃあ、これでおねがいします。

判子屋：名前はどうしますか。
<ruby>判子屋<rt>はんこや</rt></ruby>

　リー：漢字で「李」と書いて下さい。
<ruby>李<rt>り</rt></ruby>

判子屋：分かりました。
<ruby>判子屋<rt>はんこや</rt></ruby>

　リー：いつ、取りに来たらいいですか。
<ruby>取<rt>と</rt></ruby>

判子屋：そうですね。来週の木曜日までには出来ますよ。
<ruby>判子屋<rt>はんこや</rt></ruby>

　リー：そうですか。じゃ、木曜日の午後、取りに来ます。よろしくおねがい
<ruby>取<rt>と</rt></ruby>

　　　　します。

次の週の木曜日にリーさんは銀行に行きました。
<ruby>銀<rt>ぎん</rt></ruby>

　リー：あのう、ふつう預金の口座をひらきたいんですが。
<ruby>預金<rt>よきん</rt></ruby> <ruby>口座<rt>こうざ</rt></ruby>

銀行員：外国の方ですか。
<ruby>銀行員<rt>ぎんいん</rt></ruby>

　リー：はい、そうです。

銀行員：では、パスポートと在留カードをお持ちですか。
<ruby>銀行員<rt>ぎんいん</rt></ruby> <ruby>在留<rt>ざいりゅう</rt></ruby>

　リー：はい、持ってます。

銀行員：では、あちらで、このもうしこみ用紙にご記入下さい。
<ruby>銀行員<rt>ぎんいん</rt></ruby> <ruby>用紙<rt>ようし</rt></ruby> <ruby>記入<rt>きにゅう</rt></ruby>

　リー：はい、分かりました。

Dialogue Phrase Notes

- 銀行員 means a *banker* or a *bank teller*.
<ruby>銀行員<rt>ぎんいん</rt></ruby>
- 「李」と書く means to *write with the kanji* 「李」.
<ruby>李<rt>り</rt></ruby> <ruby>李<rt>り</rt></ruby>
- 記入 means to *fill out*.

ダイアローグの後で

A. Complete the following paragraph based on the dialogue.

リーさんは＿＿＿＿＿＿を作りたいと思いましたが、＿＿＿＿＿＿を
持っていませんでした。でも、どこで作ったらいいか分からなかったので、
＿＿＿＿＿＿に場所を聞きました。そして、スーパーの＿＿＿＿＿＿
にある＿＿＿＿＿＿に、判子を＿＿＿＿＿＿に行きました。一週間後
　　　　　　　　　 はんこ
に＿＿＿＿＿＿が出来たので、＿＿＿＿＿＿に行って、＿＿＿＿＿＿
を作ってもらいました。

B. Identify the phrases in the dialogue that Mr. Li uses to start a conversation and those
he uses to introduce the topic of a conversation.

A row of ATM machines

日本の文化
ぶん か

日本郵便と郵便局   Japan Post and post offices
ゆうびん　ゆうびんきょく

Japan's postal service is very efficient. Regular postcards and letters usually reach their destinations within two days. The Japan Post (JP) offers a range of postal services including the shipping of post cards, letters, and parcels. Mail is delivered once a day except Sunday. Outgoing mail must be dropped into a public mailbox (郵便ポスト or ポスト)
ゆうびん
since private mailboxes (郵便受け) are intended
ゆうびん う
only for receiving mail. Japan Post also offers pick-up services although it is more common for people to go to the post offices.

cowardlion/Shutterstock.com

There are two types of postal facilities in Japan: standard post offices (郵便局) and
ゆうびんきょく
distribution centers (集配局). Most are 郵便
しゅうはいきょく　　　　　　ゆうびん
局 , which are open Monday to Friday from
きょく
9 a.m. to 5 p.m. and are closed on weekends and national holidays. 集配局 are large and
しゅうはいきょく
they are open on weekdays until 7 p.m. They may also be open on Saturdays and Sundays. They offer a wider range of services for businesses than normal post offices. JP Bank (ゆうちょ銀行) and JP Insurance (かんぽ保険) are often located within or next to the 郵便局 . This is because Japan Post also
ほ けん　　　　　　　　　　　　　　　　　　ゆうびんきょく
handled life insurance and banking services until it was privatized and divided into four separate companies in 2007.

The post office symbol is 〒. It can be seen both at post offices and on post boxes. It also precedes postal codes in written addresses.

宅配便   Parcel delivery services
たくはいびん

宅配便 is a convenient door-to-door delivery service for regular parcels, oversized
たくはいびん
boxes, fresh or frozen foods, computers, ski and golf bags, clothing that should not be wrinkled, furniture, luggage, and various other types of goods. Delivery costs are moderate, deliveries are usually made within a day or two, and desired drop-off times can be specified. Most companies also offer express options at a surcharge, which ensures expedited delivery.

Goods can be sent from and delivered to almost any address in Japan, including private homes, offices, hotels, airports, and 宅配便 service centers. Pickup times
たくはいびん
may be scheduled with the nearest service center to send goods from a private home. Additionally, goods may be dropped off for shipment at most convenience stores, as well as a variety of other stores that display a 宅配便 sign, and at 宅配便 service centers.
たくはいびん　　　　　　　たくはいびん
Some stores, such as souvenir shops, can arrange for purchased merchandise to be sent directly to a designated recipient. In addition, Japanese people often use 宅配便 to send
たくはいびん
their luggage from an airport to a hotel or between hotels, in order to avoid hauling

heavy luggage onto crowded trains and up and down stairways. Several 宅配便 counters
can be found in the arrival lobbies of airports.

日本の住所 **Japanese addresses**

With the exception of major roads, Japanese streets are not named. Instead, cities and
towns are subdivided into areas, subareas and blocks, and houses within each subarea are
in the temporal order in which they are constructed. If addresses are written in Japanese,
they start with the postal code, followed by the prefecture, city and subarea(s), and end
with the recipient's name. As with all Japanese text, addresses may be written vertically
from right to left instead of horizontally. If addresses are written in English, they start
with the recipient's name and end with the prefecture and postal code. A typical Japanese
address looks like this:

〒 100-0001 東京都千代田区内幸町 1 丁目 1-1

1-1, Uchisaiwai-cho 1-chome, Chiyoda-ku, Tokyo 100-0001

銀行

Cash cards and credit cards (クレジットカード) are the most prevalent methods of
personal financial transactions in Japan, and banks do not have checking accounts for

DAJ/Getty Images

private use. Most business transactions, including
payroll disbursements, are made via bank transfers
(銀行振込) or クレジットカード. Other services
offered by banks include direct debit payment for
utility bills (自動引き落とし), travelers checks (ト
ラベラーズチェック) issuance, and bank-to-bank
money transfers. Bank transfers are used to make a
variety of payments such as tuition and mail order
charges.

It is difficult for a short-term visitor to Japan
to open a bank account because this transaction is
highly restricted in order to prevent crimes, such as
money laundering and the use of fictitious names
for bank accounts. To open a bank account, non-
Japanese need to present both an ID, such as a
パスポート or driver's license (運転免許証), and a
residence card (在留カード). It is also necessary to
bring an initial deposit and a personal seal or stamp
(判子 or 印鑑). Some banks, especially those with

a foreign currency exchange service, will accept a handwritten signature to open an
account, but since personal seals are so widely used in Japanese society, it's a good idea
to have an inexpensive one made at a local stamp shop. Personal stamps usually have
one's last name. Most bank accounts for foreigners are registered in either **katakana** or
roman letters. It's also possible to use a **kanji** combination that approximates the sound
of a non-Japanese last name. Banks have special teller windows for regular savings
accounts, and foreign customers can transact business using personal stamps with their
names transcribed in **katakana**.

文法
ぶんぽう

> ## I. Expressing and inquiring about one's factual knowledge using the clause か（どうか）

To express or inquire about someone's knowledge of an event, situation, or fact, a question is embedded within another sentence in English and Japanese. For example, the statement, *I don't know when John is coming* contains a question, *When is John coming.* This type of question is called an indirect question. Two types of questions, yes-no questions and information questions, can be embedded. In English, an embedded yes-no question is preceded by "whether (or not)" or "if," and an embedded information question is preceded by a question word. This chapter explains the formation of embedded questions in Japanese.

A. Indirect information question (*when, what, where,* etc.)

In Japanese, an embedded information question ends with a plain form followed by か. The only exceptions are noun + the copula verb だ and な-adjectives. In these cases, だ is deleted. Thus, the formation of the construction is the same as かもしれません and でしょう.

Indirect questions can be followed by a range of main verbs, including 知っている, 見る, 聞く, 分かる, かんがえる, 教える, 忘れる, きめる, and おぼえている.

小包がいつとどくか知りません。 こづつみ	*I don't know when the package is arriving.* (will arrive)
どの銀行がいいか聞きました。 ぎん	*I asked which bank is a good one.*
住所はどこか教えて下さい。 じゅうしょ　　　　おし	*Please tell me where the address is.* (what the address is)
どこでその人に会ったか忘れました。	*I forgot where I met that person.*
いくらお金をかりたかおぼえていますか。	*Do you remember how much money you borrowed?*

田中： 英語の試験はいつか知ってる？
　　　　　　　しけん
　　　Do you know when the English exam will be?

川上： あ、来週の火曜日だよ。
　　　Oh, that will be next Tuesday.

田中： じゃあ、どこ勉強したらいいか分かる？
　　　Well, then do you know which part I should study?

川上： ううん、知らない。でも、先生が今日授業で話すと思うよ。
　　　No, I don't know. But I think the teacher will talk about it in class today.

NOTE

● The subject of the question clause is often, but not always, marked by が, when it refers to something or someone other than the speaker. This makes it clear that the subject of the question is different from the speaker.

教室はどこですか。
きょうしつ
Where is the classroom?

教室がどこか知りません。
きょうしつ
I don't know where the classroom is.

B. Indirect yes-no questions, whether or not ~; if ~

In order to embed a yes-no question, use かどうか instead of か.

銀行からお金をかりるかどうかまだきめていません。
ぎん
I have not decided whether I will borrow money from the bank.

今、ドルを円にかえた方がいいかどうか教えて下さい。
おし
Please tell me whether I should exchange dollars for yen now.

川田：　アメリカの銀行でふつう預金の口座をひらく時、パスポートがいるか
　　　　ぎん　　　　　よきん　こうざ
　　　　どうか知っていますか。
　　　　Do you know if I need my passport when I open a regular bank account in the US?

タン：　すみません、分かりません。
　　　　Sorry, I don't know.

話してみましょう

Activity 1   Work with a partner. One partner should use indirect questions to ask the other whether he or she knows the answer to the following. The partner should answer the question, then ask his or her own question.

Example: 日本では、何時まで銀行があいていますか。

A: 何時まで銀行があいているか知っていますか／分かりますか。

B: ええ，知っていますよ／分かりますよ。３時まであいています。

or   さあ、知りません／分かりません。

1. 日本では、宅配便でどんな物が送れますか。
2. 宅配便と郵便局は何が違いますか。
3. 日本では、郵便局と宅配便とどちらの方が安いですか。
4. 日本の郵便局は何時にしまりますか。
5. 日本では、ATM でいくらまでお金が引き出せますか。
6. 今、一ドルは何円ですか。
7. ATM で日本から海外にお金が送れますか。
8. 日本では、銀行口座をひらく時、サインがつかえますか。
9. 日本では、宅配便は日曜日に荷物を取りに来ますか。
10. 日本では、家の郵便受けから手紙を出すことが出来ますか。
11. 日本では、コンビニで切手が買えますか。

Activity 2   Work with a partner. Each partner should ask the other whether he/she remembers something that the questioner has forgotten.

Example: A: 今度の漢字のテストが<u>いつあるか</u>忘れちゃったんですが、

〜さんは<u>いつか</u>おぼえていますか。

B: さあ、おぼえていません。先生に<u>いつあるか</u>聞いた方がいいですね。

Activity 3   Work with the class. Think of four interesting facts that you know about Japan and create a quiz. Then quiz your classmates to find out if they know the answers. Write the name of each classmate under 知っている人 or 知らない人, depending on whether they know. Write the answers if you have been able to discover them. Use casual speech. The first three quiz questions are provided for you as practice.

Example: A: はじめてアメリカ人が日本に来た年はいつか知ってる？

B: いや、知らない。

or   うん、知ってるよ。1791 年だよ。

A: そのとおり (*That's right*)。すごいね！

クイズ	知らない人	知っている人	答え
Ex. はじめてアメリカ人が日本に来た年はいつですか。			
1. 日本で一番古い建物はきょうとにありますか。			
2. 東京からホノルルまで飛行機で何時間かかりますか。			
3.			
4.			
5.			
6.			

II. Expressing movement away from or toward the speaker through space using 〜ていく and 〜てくる

The て-form of verbs + いく and くる indicates an action or event which moves away or towards the speaker. For example, 持っていく, which consists of the verb 持つ (*to hold*) and 行く (*to go*) means *to take*, but 持ってくる means *to bring*.

A. 〜ていく

〜ていく is used when the direction is away from the current location of the speaker. It can be used when the speaker does something and leaves his/her current location, as in the following example.

朝御飯を食べていきましょう。　　*Let's eat breakfast before we go.*
　　　　　　　　　　　　　　　　(lit.: *Let's eat breakfast and go/leave.*)

宿題をしていきます。　　*I will do my homework before I go.*

ここで少し休んでいきましょう。　*Let's take a little break here before we go.*

単語をおぼえていきます。　　*I will memorize the vocabulary before I go.*

In the above situations, the speaker finishes something (e.g., eating, doing homework, and resting) and then goes out, so the meaning of the sentence is the same as 〜て (*and*).

In addition, 〜ていく is used when the speaker does something in a direction away from where he/she starts.

銀行にうんてんめんきょしょうを持って行きました。
I took my driver's license to the bank.

郵便局までくるまに乗って行きます。
ゆうびんきょく

I will go to the post office by car.

子供を学校につれて行きました。

I took my child to school.

In these situations, the act of holding (持つ), riding (乗る), or accompanying (つれる) takes place in the direction away from where the speaker is. Thus, it expresses taking something *to*.

お父さん：じゃあ、行ってくるよ。

       I'm leaving.

お母さん：じゃあ、この葉書、ポストに入れていってくれない？
         は がき

       Well, can you put this postcard into a mailbox on your way (to your office)?

NOTES

- The verbs いく and くる do not necessarily correspond to the English "to come" and "to go." For example, when called, an English speaker might respond by saying "I'm coming." In Japanese, however, the corresponding response would be すぐ行くよ. This is because the speaker's position is considered the center point. So いく is used when the speaker or someone or something else moves away from the speaker's current position. This is true when いく is used as an auxiliary verb in the て-form of the verb + いく form. Therefore, the て-form of the verb + いく indicates an action or event which moves away from the speaker's current location.

- In casual speech, the sound い in ～ていく may be dropped.

  ごはんを作っていきますよ。
  ごはん、作ってくよ。
  I will cook a meal and go.

  山田さんのところに持って行って下さい。

  山田さんのところに持ってって。
  Take (it) *to Mr. Yamada.*

  晩御飯を食べていったらどうですか。
  ご はん
  晩御飯を食べてったらどう？
  ご はん
  How about eating supper before leaving?

B. 〜てくる

The て-form of verbs + くる is the exact opposite of the て-form of verbs + いく. While the use of いく implies a direction away from the current location of the speaker, くる indicates a movement toward the location of the speaker.

ふうとうを買って来ました。	*I bought some envelopes before I came* (here). (lit.: *I bought some envelopes and came.*)
作文を書いてきましたか。 さくぶん	*Have you written a composition before coming* (here)?
単語の意味をしらべてきましたか。 たんご　　いみ	*Have you checked the vocabulary meaning before coming* (to class)?
会話の練習をしてきましたか。 かいわ　　れんしゅう	*Did you practice speaking before coming* (to class)?
判子を作ってきて下さい。 はんこ	*Please have your seal made and bring it.*
学生証を持って来て下さい。 　　しょう	*Please bring your student ID.*
友達が電話をかけてきた。	*My friend phoned before coming* (over).
弟をここまでつれて来ました。	*I brought my brother here.*

ジョン： 文法の宿題、してきた？
　　　　ぶんぽう　しゅくだい
Did you bring your grammar homework?

さなえ： え、今日宿題あったの？
　　　　　　　しゅくだい
What? Did we have an assignment for today?

NOTES

- Because the spatial point of reference is the current location of the speaker, 今ジュースを買ってきます and 明日ジュースを買ってきます imply slightly different situations. 今ジュースを買ってきます would mean that the person will go to the store, buy some juice, and come back. On the other hand, 明日ジュースを買ってきます means that the person will buy the juice before coming to this location.
- When verbs like いく or くる are used as auxiliary verbs, they are usually written in **hiragana**. However, in this usage the original verb meanings are retained, so you may see spellings such as 持って行く and 持って来る.

話してみましょう

Activity 1 The following diagram illustrates actions directed toward certain people or places, or actions that ocurred before the subject moved toward a certain place. Make sentences which express actions and directionality using 〜ていく／〜てくる.

Example: スミスさんは私に本をかえしてきました。

私はスミスさんの家にふうとうと切手を買っていきました。

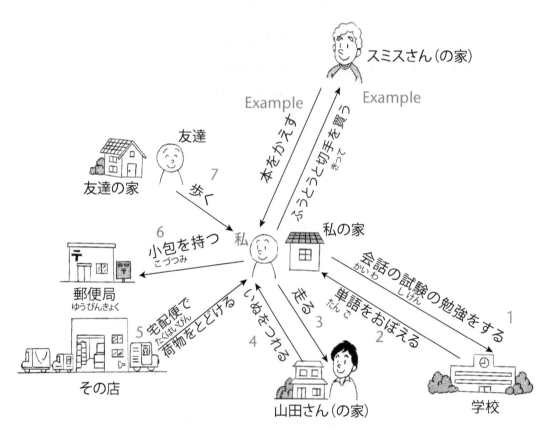

Activity 2 Work as a class. Ask your classmates what they did before coming to school or have brought to school.

Example: A: 学校に来る前に、どんなことをしてきましたか。

B: 会話の練習をしてきました。

👥   **Activity 3**   Work with a partner. Imagine that you are roommates and that you each have a blind date this evening. Ask each other what you will do before going out using 〜ていく.

Example: A: 今日のデート、何、着ていく？

B: そうだね。新しいジーンズはいていこうかな。〜さんは？

A: 私は白いワンピースを着ていこうと思う。

III. Expressing one's desire for someone to do something using 〜てもらう／いただく and 〜てほしい

In Chapter 6 of *Nakama 1*, you learned request forms such as 〜て下さい／〜て下さいませんか／〜てくれませんか, and that the て-form of verbs can be used for casual requests. This chapter introduces expressions that convey the speaker's desire for someone to do something. They are often used to make requests as well.

A. 〜てもらう and 〜ていただく

The combination of the て-form of verbs and もらう／いただく, which means *to receive* and たい (*want*) are used to express the speaker's desire to have someone do something. いただく is a polite version of もらう and used toward a superior and/or in a formal situation.

この荷物を	とどけてもらいたい。	*I want you to deliver this package.*
弟を	すいせんしてもらいたい。	*I want you to recommend my younger brother.*
お金を	かしていただきたい。	*I would like you to lend me some money.*
ふつう預金の口座を	ひらいていただきたい。	*I would like you to open a regular bank account (for me).*

うんてんめんきょしょうのもうしこみ方を　教えていただきたい。

I would like for you to tell me how to apply for a drivers license.

Adding phrases like 〜と思います makes the expression less direct and more polite while the speaker's intention is still very clear. Adding 〜んです can be used to introduce a topic as shown throughout this text.

その本をかえしてもらいたいと思います。	*I would like to have my book back.*
その本かえしてもらいたいんだけど、いい？	*I would like to have my book back, OK?*
住所を教えていただきたいと思います。	*I would like to know your address.*
住所を教えていただきたいんですが。	*I would like to know your address . . .*

In addition, the potential form of もらう／いただく with forms such as ませんか is used to make a request.

その本をかえしてもらえませんか。	*Can I have my book back?* (lit.: *Can I receive the favor of getting my book back?*)
住所を教えていただけませんか。	*Could you tell me the address?* (lit.: *Could I receive the favor of being taught your address?*)

スミス： あのう、高山さん。
Umm, Ms. Takayama?

高山： え、何？
What?

スミス： この漢字の書き方が分からないんだけど、書いてもらえないかな？
I don't know how to write this kanji, so can you write it for me?

高山： ああ、いいよ。
Oh, sure.

田中： すみませんが、しゃしん、とっていただけませんか。
Excuse me, could you take a picture of us?

通行人： ああ、いいですよ。
(Passerby) Sure.

田中： ありがとうございます。
Thank you.

Notes

- If the potential form is used with the main verb, the speaker is simply asking the listener whether he/she is capable of doing something. Therefore it does not indicate a request.

  その本を<u>かえせますか</u>。
  Are you physically capable of returning that book?

  その本を<u>かえせませんか</u>。
  Are you physically incapable of returning that book?

  その本をかえして<u>もらえませんか</u>。
  Can I have that book back?

- The level of politeness between 〜てくれませんか and 〜てもらえませんか is roughly the same. Similarly, 〜てくださいませんか and 〜ていただけませんか have a similar level of politeness. The choice between くれる and もらえる or くださる and いただく tends to depend on personal preferences, regional differences, stylistic variations, and generation.

B. Expressing a desire to have someone do something, using 〜てほしい

In Chapter 8 of *Nakama 1*, the adjective ほしい as in いぬがほしい (*I want a dog*) is introduced to express one's desire for something. The combination of the て-form of the verb + ほしい is used to express the speaker's desire to have someone do something as well. The speaker, 私, and the person who actually performs the act is marked by the particle に but is usually omitted if understood from context. The て-form of the verb + ほしい cannot be used to express the speaker's desire to have a socially superior person do something. Use 〜ていただきたい instead.

この荷物、ちょっと持ってほしいんだけど、いい？
I'd like you to hold this luggage, is that OK?

明日レポートを持って来てほしいんだけど、いい？
I'd like you to bring the report, is that OK?

To express a desire to have someone not do something, use 〜ほしくない, 〜もらいたくない, or 〜ないでほしい.

この葉書は<u>つかってほしくない</u>んですけど。 <small>はがき</small>	*I don't want you to use this postcard.*
この葉書は<u>つかわないでほしい</u>んですけど。 <small>はがき</small>	*I don't want you to use this postcard. (lit.: I want you to not use this postcard.)*
この葉書は<u>つかってもらいたくない</u>んですけど。 <small>はがき</small>	*I don't want you to use this postcard. (lit.: I don't want to have you use this postcard.)*

NOTES

- To express a desire for a specific person other than the listener to do something, use the particle に.

山田さん<u>に</u>　行ってほしい。	*I want Mr. Yamada to go.*
山田さん<u>に</u>　行ってもらいたい。	*I want Mr. Yamada to go. (lit.: I want to have Mr. Yamada go.)*
山田さん<u>に</u>　行っていただきたい。	*I want Mr. Yamada to go. (lit.: I want Mr. Yamada to do me the favor of going.)*

話してみましょう

Activity 1   Make polite requests to your instructor using 〜ていただけませんか and 〜て下さいませんか.

Example:　もう一度言う
　　　　　先生、もう一度言っていただけませんか。
　　　　　先生、もう一度言って下さいませんか。

1. 宿題を明日までまつ
   <small>しゅくだい</small>
2. すいせんじょうを書く
3. この文法を説明する
   <small>ぶんぽう　　せつめい</small>
4. DVD をかす
5. アニメのれきしについて話す
6. 漢字のおぼえ方を教える
   <small>　　　　かた　おし</small>
7. 作文の下書き (*draft*) を読む
   <small>さくぶん　したが</small>

Activity 2   Work with a partner. You are roommates. Based on the pictures below, ask each other for favors using 〜てほしい and 〜もらいたい.

Example: A: あのう、〜さん、暑いから、まどをあけてほしいんだけど。

B: ああ、いいよ。

A: ありがとう。

1   2   3

4   5   6

Activity 3   Work with a partner. One of you visits various stores and needs to ask for help. In each of the following situations, make requests using 〜てもらえませんか, 〜てもらいたいんですが and 〜てくれませんか. The other partner is a store employee, and he/she needs to respond to the requests appropriately.

Example: デパートにいます。ほしいかばんがありますが、とても高い所にあります。

A: すみませんが、あのかばんを取ってもらえませんか／取ってもらいたいんですが／取ってくれませんか。

B: はい、あれですね。

A: ええ、おねがいします。

1. 銀行にいます。ATM のつかい方が分かりません。

2. 銀行にいます。円をドルにかえたいです。

3. 郵便局にいます。アメリカまで手紙を送りたいんですが、切手がいくらか知りたいです。

4. 電話で宅配便の会社と話しています。明日の晩、荷物を送りたいです。

5. レストランにいます。30 分まちましたが、注文したりょうりがまだ来ません。

6. さかなやにいます。お金がないので、少し安い方がいいと思っています。

Activity 4 Work with a partner. One person plays the role of A and the other of B. In each case, B has a problem and asks A for help. A has the option of helping or refusing. If A decides not to help B, A should make sure to state the reason.

Example: B: あのう、山田さん、おねがいがあるんですけど。
　　　　　A: 何ですか。
　　　　　B: 明日、日本語の試験があるんだけど。
　　　　　A: ええ。
　　　　　B: 分からない文法があるので、説明してもらいたいんですけど。
　　　　　A: ああ、いいですよ。

パートナー	私	問題 (problem)
Ex. 山田さん（友達）	日本語の学生	試験があるけど、分からない文法がある。
1. 日本人の友達	外国人学生	病院に行きたいけど、くるまがない。
2. 先生	学生	来学期に先生の授業があるかどうか知りたい。
3. 客	宅配便の人	住所と電話番号が知りたい。
4. 兄／姉	弟／妹	デートするので、兄／姉のくるまを一日つかいたい。
5. 先生	学生	もうしこみ用紙に先生のサインがいる。
6. お母さん／お父さん	子供	コンピュータを買いたいけど、お金がない。

IV. Expressing willingness using ～ましょう／ましょうか

In Chapter 9 of *Nakama 1*, ましょうか (*shall we ~*) and ましょう (*let's ~*) are used to make suggestions. The same structure can also be used to express the speaker's willingness to do something for someone else. In casual speech, you can use the plain forms of the volitional ～ましょう, such as 行こう or 食べよう. Add 私が／ぼくが to emphasize the speaker's willingness to do something.

荷物をとどけましょうか。	*Shall I deliver the luggage?*
おばあちゃんに何を送りましょうか。	*What shall I send to my grandmother?*
私がかえしておきましょう。	*I will return it.*
お金はぼくが銀行へ行って、引き出してこよう。	*I'll go to the bank and withdraw the money.*
田中： 寒いですね。	*It's cold, isn't it?*
川口： じゃあ、まどをしめましょうか。	*Shall I close the windows?*

田中： 大変ですね。手伝いましょう。　*It looks tough* (too much for you). *I will help you.*

山本： ありがとう。　*Thank you.*

健一： どうしたの。　*What's wrong?*

道子： 雨がふってるの。　*It's raining!*

健一： じゃあ、かさかりてこようか。　*Well, then, shall I go borrow an umbrella?*

NOTE

- To explicitly offer help, rather than simply show willingness to do something, use the て-form of the verb + あげましょう(か)／あげよう(か). The auxiliary verb forms あげる and あげましょう／あげよう indicate that the speaker is doing a favor for the listener. This form should not be used with a social superior, because offering a favor to a superior sounds arrogant in Japanese.

  上田： あ、ペン、忘れちゃった。
  Oh, I forgot my pen.

  石田： じゃあ、ぼくのをかしてあげようか。
  I can lend you mine.

  上田： ありがとう。
  Thank you.

話してみましょう

Activity 1　Your friend is having a problem in each of the following pictures. Offer to help or provide a solution for each of the following situations using ましょう／ましょうか. Use formal speech.

Example:　私がはらいましょう／私がはらいましょうか。

1   2   3

4   5   6

Activity 2   Work as a class. In the following chart, write three things you would like help with. Tell a classmate about one of your problems. Your classmate may or may not offer to help you. Write down the names of anyone who offers help. If someone else asks you for help, offer assistance if you can.

Example: A: どうしたんですか。

B: このペン、書けなくて。

A: じゃあ、私のをかしてあげましょうか／かしましょうか。

or こまりましたね。私、今、ペン持ってないので、すみません。

	友達の名前

Activity 3   Work in groups of four. Each group should plan a party and invite classmates. Decide what to buy, what to make, etc. Then decide on volunteers to do the various tasks. Write down who will do what.

Example: A: パーティ、いつ、どこで、しようか。

B: 土曜日の晩はどう？ ぼくの家でしようよ。

C: ありがとう。じゃ、時間は七時からはどう？

D: いいね。じゃあ、食べ物はどうしようか。

A: じゃあ、私はサラダを作ろうかな。

C: じゃあ、ぼくは、飲み物を持って行こう。

V. Expressing time limits using までに (*by ~, by the time ~*)

The particle までに specifies a time limit within which an action or event must be completed. If までに is used, the action in the main clause must be completed.

明日までに授業料をはらわなければならない。 *I must pay my tuition by tomorrow.*

十二時までに作文を出して下さい。 *Please turn in your composition by 12 o'clock.*

今度の誕生日までに 10 キロやせたい。 *I want to lose 10 kilograms (22 pounds) by my next birthday.*

までに can be used with a clause that ends with the plain present form.

夏休みがおわるまでに、レポートを書かなければならない。
I must write a paper by the end of the summer break.

小包がとどくまでに、何日ぐらいかかりますか。
How long will it take for the package to arrive?

卒業するまでに、日本語能力試験の N1 を取りたい。
I want to pass N1 of the Japanese Language Proficiency Test by the time I graduate.

NOTES

- までに and 前に overlap in usage. While 前に merely indicates chronological sequence, までに indicates a time limit or deadline by which something must be completed. For this reason, までに often occurs with phrases such as なければならない (*must*). For example, 日本に留学する前に、100万円ためなければならない means *I must save one million yen before going to Japan.* 日本に留学するまでに、100万円ためなければならない also conveys the same action, but in this case, the speaker's trip to Japan is the definitive deadline to save up one million yen. This sense of a definitive deadline is not conveyed with 前に.

- Another similar expression is まで (*until*). Like までに, まで can be used with a clause ending in the plain present from as in 先生がいらっしゃるまで (*until the teacher comes*). However, there are two major differences between まで and までに. First, まで can be used with time expressions and space expressions but までに can be used only with time expressions. Second, まで indicates that the action or event must continue until the specified time. On the other hand, までに indicates that the action or event must be completed by the specified time.

  四時までまちました。 *I waited <u>until</u> four o'clock .*

  明日の昼までにかえして下さい。 *Please return it <u>by</u> noon tomorrow.*

  新しいテレビがとどくまで、家でまっています。
  I will wait at home <u>until</u> the new TV arrives.

  新しいテレビがとどくまでに、へやのそうじをしてしまいましょう。
  Let's clean up the room <u>before</u> the new TV arrives.

話してみましょう

Activity 1   Work with a partner. You have just arrived in Japan to study at Joto University and need to get settled quickly. But you still have a lot to do. The calendar below indicates upcoming events. Discuss things that you need to get done before each event on the calendar.

Example: A: まだ住む所がきまっていないんですよ。

B: じゃあ、留学生オリエンテーションまでに／8日までに、アパートをさがさなければなりませんね。

1. まだ銀行の口座がありません。
2. まだ日本語の試験を受けていません。
3. まだどの授業を取るか先生と話していません。
4. まだ学生証がありません。
5. まだ在留カードを持っていません。

日	月	火	水	木	金	土
	1	2	3	4	5	6
7	8 留学生オリエンテーション	9	10 学部 (under-graduate) オリエンテーション	11	12	13
14	15 Class begins	16	17	18	19	20 Parents' visit
21	22	23	24 Last day for registration	25	26	27
28	29	30 Last day to pay tuition				

Activity 2   Work with a partner. Using the calendar below, mark the day by which you will need to have completed five different tasks. Ask each other about your schedules, and each partner should add their partner's schedule to their calendar. Use a different color for each partner.

Example: A: 今週、何かしなければならないことある？

B: うん、火曜日までに作文を書かなければならないんだ。
さくぶん

A: あ、私もそう。

日	月	火	水	木	金	土
		Example: 作文を出す さくぶん				

Activity 3   Work with a partner. Ask each other what you need to get done before the following events take place. Also, each person should ask the other what he/she would like to do by the time that these events take place.

Example: A: 卒業するまでに何をしておきたいと思いますか。

B: そうですね、日本語能力試験 (*Japanese Language Proficiency Test*)
のうりょく し けん
の N1 を取っておきたいですね。
と

A: そうですか。いいですね。じゃあ、卒業するまで、どんなことを
していたいですか。

B: そうですね。たくさんあそんでいたいですね。

1.   卒業します。
2.   30 さいになります。
3.   結婚します。
4.   子供が出来ます。
5.   50 さいになります。
6.   仕事をやめます。
7.   しにます。

聞く練習
れんしゅう

上手な聞き方
かた

Knowing how to use varied request forms appropriately

A request is a type of imposition from the speaker to the listener, because it normally benefits the speaker and not the listener. Depending on the context of the conversation and the relationship between the speaker and the listener, the tone, directness, and politeness of a request varies. For example, an athletic coach may make a strong request to an athlete during training. On the other hand, a business executive may make a very polite request to a representative of another company. English has a variety of expressions for making requests, such as *please ~*, *can you ~*, *could you*, *do you mind ~*, as well as the simple imperative form. Also, requests may be implied such as in the examples *Do you have an extra pen?* and *I can't find my pen.* Japanese also has a variety of ways to make a request, as you have been seen throughout this book. Knowing how to use them properly is extremely important for maintaining good social relationships, so it is essential to be aware of when and with whom to use each kind of request form.

練習
れんしゅう

    1. Complete the following table.

Expressions	Situations Casual/ Formal	Listener types Social superior/ Equal/ Social inferior	Social relationship Close/ Average/ Distant	Directness of request Implied/ Overt & indirect/ Overt & direct
寒いね。	Casual	Equal, inferior	Close /average	Implied
あ、まどがあいてる。				
まど、しめてくれない？				
まど、しめて。				
まど、しめてくれませんか。				
まど、しめてもらえませんか。				
まど、しめてほしいんですけど。				
まど、しめてもらいたいんですけど。				
まど、しめて下さいませんか。				
まど、しめていただけませんか。				
まど、しめていただきたいんですが。				

2. Listen to the following requests and circle the person being spoken to. There may be more than one answer.

Example: ね、早く起きて。

子供   客   いい友達   先生

1. クラスメート   先生   友達   客

2. お母さん   同じアパートにすんでいる人   妹   いい友達

3. 学生   よく知らない学生   日本語の先生   先輩 (*a person is senior to you in a school or business organization*)
せんぱい

三つのおねがい

聞く前に

There are many occasions for which you want to ask for favors in your daily life. Given the following situations and relationships, write the kind of request you might make in Japanese.

学校で   友達_____

              先生_____

家で   両親_____

              兄弟_____

              近所の人 (*person in the neighborhood*) _____
              きんじょ

みち (*street*) で 知らない人 _____

              友達_____

聞いてみましょう

Listen to the three dialogues and complete the table below by writing the name or title of the person who has made the request, the content of the request, and the name or title of the person to whom the request is being made. Circle はい if the request is accepted. Circle いいえ if it is denied.

Example: A: 行ってきます。

B: あっ、まもる、今日はおばあちゃんが来るから、早く帰ってきてよ。

A: ああ、分かったよ。

	だれが	何を	だれが	はい・いいえ
Example	お母さん	家に早く帰ってくる	子供 or まもる	(はい)・いいえ
1.				はい・いいえ
2.				はい・いいえ
3.				はい・いいえ

聞いた後で

Based on the chart you have just completed in 聞いてみましょう, write a brief summary of each conversation.

聞き上手話し上手

Making a request and turning down a request or an invitation

A. Making a request

Making a request has a relatively fixed conversational structure. First, use a conversation opener such as あのう or あのう、すみません to get the attention of the listener. You then have the option of following that with an expression that implies that a request is on its way, such as じつは、ちょっとおねがいがあるんですけど (*Actually, I have a small favor to ask*).

スミス：あのう。

山本：何、スミスさん？

スミス：じつは、ちょっとおねがいがあるんですけど。

山本：あ、何ですか。

Then express a desire, problem, or fact that will lead to a request, such as 明日、会話の試験があるんですけど. Finally, make the request itself, like 一緒に練習してくれませんか. If a request is a difficult one, show your concern for the listener by adding a phrase such as よかったら (*if it's OK with you*) or 時間があったら (*if you have time*).

スミス：　明日、会話の試験があるんですけど、（時間があったら、）一緒に練習
　　　　　してくれませんか。

Then express gratitude and appreciation. In addition to ありがとう, you may want to add
本当に、いいんですか or たすかります (*That will be helpful*). If a request could be seen to
be an imposing one, you may want to use すみません instead of ありがとう.

　山本：　あ、今、ちょっといそがしいけど、昼御飯の後だったら、いいですよ。
スミス：　ありがとう。たすかります。

B. Refusing a request or an invitation

Although there are a number of situations where you might need to turn down a request or
invitation, a typical refusal will begin with an expression of regret such as 残念ですが or an
apology such as すみません or ごめん（なさい）. Then state a reason. When stating a
reason, it is very common not to finish the sentence. Leaving the sentence incomplete makes
your refusal sound less assertive and more hesitant, which in turn makes it sounds more
considerate. Avoid the use of 〜たくありません (*don't want to do~*), since it is considered
impolite in this situation. You can suggest an alternative. It is also a good strategy to indicate
your willingness to offer help on another occasion or to do something with the person at
another time.

まもる：　あの、今ちょっといい？
さやか：　あ、いいけど。何？
まもる：　あの、英語の作文の宿題してるんだけど、ちょっと手伝って
　　　　　もらえないかな。
さやか：　あ、わるいけど、英語の宿題はちょっと。
まもる：　そう、だめ？
さやか：　う〜ん。ごめん。英語はちょっと。あ、上田さんに聞いたらどう？
まもる：　あ、そうだね。そうするよ。

練習

A. Work with a partner. Practice making requests in the following situations.

1. You want to try on a pair of pants in the display case at a department store. Make a request for help to a store clerk.
2. You want to buy something to drink, but don't have money. Make a request to a close friend.
3. You want to use your friend's car for a date. Ask your friend if you can borrow his/her car.
4. You want your doctor to write you a note so your absence will be excused.

B. Work with a partner. Your partner will ask you to do one of the following things. Politely turn down the request.

1. to lend him/her some money
2. to explain to him/her how to do something
3. to teach him/her how to use e-mail
4. to teach him/her how to cook _____ (choose a dish)

C. Work with a partner. Your partner invites you to one of the following events. Politely turn down the invitation.

> 誕生日会　　　コンサート　　　映画　　　食事
> たん　　　　　　　　　　　　　えい

漢字

Bottom and enclosing component shapes of kanji

There are not as many bottom components as side components, but they tend to indicate rough meanings of **kanji**, just like the left components. For example, 心, which means *heart*, indicates that the **kanji** with this component has something to do with human emotion and thought, as in 忘 (*forget*), 思 (*think*), 悪 (*bad*), and 悲 (*sad*).

Name	▯	Meaning	Examples
こころ	心	heart	忘 思 急 悪 忠 念 応 怠 怒 恐 恵 息 恋 患 悲 惑 意 感
れんが・れっか	灬	fire	熱 点 烈 煮 焦 然 無 照 熟 為
ひとあし	儿	walking	元 兄 光 充 先 克 児 免 党
こがい	貝	money	買 貞 負 貢 貨 貫 責 貧 賀 貴 貸 費 貿 資 賃 賛 質 賞 賓 賢
いわく	曰	say	書 曹 替
ころも	衣	cloth, clothing	袋 装 裂 製 襲
はち	八	eight	六 共 兵 具 典

There are three types of enclosing components. One is called たれ and covers the left side and the top. The second one, にょう, covers the left side and bottom. And the last one, かまえ, encloses three sides or all four sides. These shapes do not provide any clues to the pronunciation of a character.

Name たれ (left and top)		Meaning	Examples
やまいだれ	疒	sickness	病　痛
まだれ	广	slanting roof	店　度　広
がんだれ	厂	cliff	原　厚　歴

Name にょう (left and bottom)		Meaning	Examples
しんにょう	辶	road	週　送　近　遠　道　運　通
えんにょう	廴	progress, extend	建　延
そうにょう	走	run	起　超

Name かまえ (three or four sides)		Meaning	Examples
くにがまえ	囗	enclosure	四　国　回　園　図
もんがまえ	門	gate	門　問　聞　開　閉
けいがまえ	冂	N/A	円　再　冊
はこがまえ・かくしがまえ	匚	box	匠　医　区　匹
うけばこ	凵	receiving box	出　凶　凹
つつみがまえ	勹	wrap	包　勺　匁

郵　郵　mail
ユウ　この葉書に郵便番号を書いて下さい。
　　　はがき　　ゆうびんばんごう
ノ　ニ　弁　弃　垂　垂　垂　郵　郵　郵

便　便　post, convenient
たよ(り)　ベン・ビン　郵便ポスト　宅配便　便利な
　　　　　　　　　　　　ゆうびん　　　たくはいびん　　べんり
ノ　イ　仁　仨　何　何　何　便　便

局　局　bureau, limited part
キョク　郵便局に行きます。
　　　　ゆうびんきょく
⁊　コ　尸　月　局　局　局

銀　銀　silver
ギン　銀行に行きます。　きれいな銀のネックレスですね。
　　　ぎん　　　　　　　　　　ぎん
ハ　△　牟　釒　金　釒　釕　銀　銀

送　送　to send
おく(る)　ソウ　メールを送る。　送別会
　　　　　　　　　おく　　　　そうべつ
丶　丷　丷　业　关　关　送　送

紙	紙	paper かみ　シ	＜　幺　幺　糸　糸　紀　紅　紅　紙 手紙を書きます。　コピー用紙を下さい。 がみ　　　　　　　　　ようし
住	住	to reside, to live す(む)　ジュウ	ノ　イ　イ`　仁　住　住　住 東京に住んでいます。　住所が分かりません。 きょう　す　　　　　　　じゅうしょ
所	所	place ところ　ショ	`　ﾗ　ﾗ　ﾞ　戸`　所　所　所 住む所がない人をホームレスといいます。 す　ところ
引	引	to pull ひ(く)　イン	フ　ヲ　弓　引 銀行からお金を引き出す。 ぎん　　　　　ひ　だ
練	練	to train, practice ね(る)　レン	幺　幺　糸　糸　糾　紅　絧　紳　練 会話の練習をする。 れんしゅう
習	習	to learn, custom なら(う)　シュウ	フ　ヲ　ヲ`　ヲフ　ヲヲ　ヲヲ　習　習　習 テニスを練習する。 れんしゅう
宿	宿	lodge, inn やど　シュク	`　宀　宀　宀　宀　宿　宿　宿 宿題を出すのを忘れてしまった。 しゅくだい
題	題	title, topic, problem ダイ	日　早　早　是　是　是　題　題　題 今晩、宿題をしなければなりませんか。 しゅくだい
試	試	to try こころ(みる)・ため(す)　シ	宀　言　言　訂　訂　訂　詁　試　試 日本の入学試験は二月にあります。 しけん
験	験	test ケン	丨　丅　馬　馬　馬`　馬`　馬`　験　験 明日の日本語の会話試験は大変です。 かいわ　しけん
受	受	to receive う(ける)　ジュ	ﾉ　ﾜ　ﾜ　ﾜ　ﾜ　ﾜﾜ　学　受 試験を受ける。　受験する。(*take an entrance exam*) しけん　う　　　　じゅけん

教教	to teach おし(える)　キョウ	十　土　尹　考　孝　孝　孝　教　教 作り方を教えて下さい。　　教科書　教室 　つく　かた　　おし　　　　　きょうか　　きょうしつ
文文	sentence, letter, writing ふみ　ブン・モン	、　一　ナ　文 作文　文法　文房具　文学 さくぶん　ぶんぽう　ぶんぼうぐ　ぶん
法法	law, method ホウ	、　、、　氵　氵　氵　氵土　法　法 この文法の使い方を教えて下さい。 　　　ぶんぽう　　　　　　おし
意意	mind, attention イ	一　ウ　立　产　音　音　音　意　意 言葉の意味が分かりません。 　　　　いみ
味味	taste あじ　ミ	丨　口　口　口一　口二　叶　味　味 この文の意味を説明して下さい。 　　　　いみ　せつめい
取取	to take と(る)　シュ	一　丁　FF　丨三　耳　取　取 日本語の授業を取りたいと思っています。 　　　　　　　と
用用	business, to use もち(いる)　ヨウ	ノ　刀　月　月　用 用事があります。　用紙 ようじ　　　　　ようし

読めるようになった漢字

郵便局　郵便番号　銀行　送る　手紙　用紙　用事　住む　所　住所　引き出す
　　　　　　　ごう
練習　受ける　宿題　入学試験　教える　教科書　教室　文法　作文　文学
　　　　　　　　　　　　　　　　　　　か
文房具　意味　葉書　会話　切手　口座　小包　説明　判子　預金　手伝う
　ぼうぐ　　　　　　　　　　　ざ　つみ　せつ　はん　よ　　つだ
作り方　行き方　来学期
　　　　　　　　き

練習

1. 来月英語の試験を受けるので、会話の練習をしておきます。
2. 住所と郵便番号を この用紙に書いて下さい。
　　　　　　　ごう
3. 銀行でお金を引き出して、郵便局で手紙と小包を送ってしまいましょう。
　　　　　　　　　　　　　　　　　　　　つみ
4. 漢字がむずかしすぎて宿題ができないので、読み方と意味を教えてくれません
　か。
5. 文学の宿題が出たので、今日の午後にするつもりです。

6. 卒業した後、ニューヨークに住んだら、お金がためられるかどうか分からない。

7. この文法が分からないので、答え方も分かりません。

8. 来学期どの授業を取るかまだきめていません。

<h2 align="center">読む練習</h2>

上手な読み方

Filling out forms

Forms such as applications forms, bank transfer forms, and delivery request forms often contain a lot of **kanji** words, but the information needed to fill out the form is restricted depending on the purpose of a given form. Therefore, consider the purpose of the form and think about what sort of information you would normally need to supply. Then look at any examples. Note the **kanji** that you've already learned, and guess the meanings of words that include them.

練習

A. 質問に答えて下さい。

1. 口座をひらく時、どんな物をじゅんびしなければなりませんか。

2. お金を引き出す時、どんな物がいりますか。何がなくてもいいですか。

3. 預金する時、どんなことについて知っていなければなりませんか。 どんな物がいりますか。何がなくてもいいですか。

B. 下の言葉の意味は何だと思いますか。日本語で言って下さい。

入金　口座番号　郵送　本人　日付（〜年〜月〜日）　お届け予定日
おところ

C. Fill out the following forms.

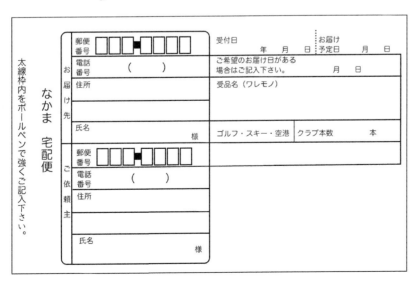

1. Parcel service

2. Seal registration for a bank

3. Application to open a bank account

ホストファミリー

読む前に

1. アメリカのホストファミリーは外国人にどんなことをしてほしいと思うでしょうか。クラスで話して下さい。
2. 日本のホストファミリーはアメリカの大学から来た留学生に何をしてほしいと思っていると思いますか。日本人に聞いて下さい。

読んでみましょう

言葉のリスト

困る　to be in trouble 　　頼む　to ask, to request
こま　　　　　　　　　　　たの

> 　私は今ホストファミリーと住んでいます。私は掃除や洗濯が好きなので、自分の服の洗濯や部屋の掃除をよくしています。それに料理も好きですから、よくホストファミリーのために料理をします。でも、最近ちょっと困っているのです。
>
> 　私のホストファミリーのお母さんはとてもいい人ですが、よく色々なことを私に頼んできます。それで、私はよくリビングルームの掃除をしたり、子供達と遊んだりします。時々洗濯もします。私も出来るだけ手伝おうと思うのですが、手伝わなければならないことが多くて、勉強したり友達と遊んだりする時間が取れません。ホストファミリーのお母さんと話をしたいのですが、どう言ったらいいかよく分かりません。

読んだ後で

A. 質問に日本語で答えて下さい。

1. この人はだれと住んでいますか。
2. この人はどんなことをするのが好きですか。
3. この人はどんなことをしたいと思っていますか。
4. この人はどうしてこまっているのですか。

B. この人にアドバイス (advice) をして下さい。

C. 日本でホストファミリーと住む時のマナー (manners) について、日本人や日本に行ったことがある友達に聞いて、作文を書いて下さい。

総合練習
そうごう

日本に留学する

1. Work in groups of four. Obtain catalogues or brochures for a few exchange programs or study abroad programs in Japan, and describe the programs as thoroughly as you can.

   Example: このプログラムは東京の大学に留学するプログラムです。
   きょう
   ホストファミリーもりょうもありませんから、アパートを
   さがさなければなりません。

2. Compare the programs and decide on one you like.

3. Write an e-mail in Japanese asking your Japanese instructor to write you a letter of recommendation. State why you want to study abroad and why you have chosen this particular program.

4. Design your own personal stamp. You can use English, **katakana**, or create your own **kanji** name, as you can see from the examples below.

ロールプレイ

1. You want to buy a present for a friend but don't have enough money because it is the end of the month. You should receive some money in a week or so. Ask another friend to lend you the money to buy the gift.

2. You are travelling with a friend. Your luggage was stolen, so you've lost everything, including your passport, cash, and laptop. Ask for help.

3. You are travelling with a friend. Your friend's luggage got stolen, so everything is lost, including his/her passport, cash, and laptop. Offer some help.

4. You are graduating in a few months and have been looking for a job but haven't gotten one yet. You are getting worried about not having a full-time job after graduation. Ask your instructor for some advice and help.

Chapter 5

第五課
だい か

Kenneth Hamm/Photo Japan

道の聞き方と教え方
みち
Asking for and Giving Directions

単語
たん

Nouns

いりぐち	入り口／入口	entrance
えいがかん	映画館	movie theater
おうだんほどう	横断歩道	pedestrian crossing
かいさつ（ぐち）	改札（口）	ticket gate
かいだん	階段	stairs
かくえきていしゃ	各駅停車	local train (literally: train that stops at every station)
ガソリンスタンド		gas station
かど	角	corner
きゅうこう（れっしゃ）	急行（列車）	express train
こうさてん	交差点	intersection
ＪＲ		Japan Railway, pronounced as ジェイアール. Formerly government owned but now privatized railway system
しやくしょ	市役所	city hall
しんごう	信号	traffic signal
たいしかん	大使館	embassy, 大使 ambassador たいし
タクシー		taxi
ターミナル		terminal, バスターミナル bus depot
ちかてつ	地下鉄	subway
ちず	地図	map
ちゅうしゃじょう	駐車場	parking lot
つぎ	次	next
つきあたり	突き当たり	at the end of the street, T-road
でぐち	出口	exit
でんしゃ	電車	train
どうろ	道路	road, street
とっきゅう（れっしゃ）	特急（列車）	limited express train
はし	橋	bridge
バスてい	バス停	bus stop
ふつう（れっしゃ）	普通（列車）	local train, same as かくえきていしゃ
へん	辺	area, このへん this area

みち	道	road, street, way
あいだ	間	between
こちらがわ	こちら側	this side
さき	先	beyond, further ahead
てまえ	手前	just before
むかいがわ	向かい側	the other side, the opposite side

い -adjectives

| ちかい | 近い | close to, near, こうえんにちかい close to the park |
| とおい | 遠い | far from, こうえんからとおい far away from the park |

う -verbs

こむ	混む	to become crowded
とおる	通る	to go through, to pass
とまる	止まる	(for someone or something) to stop [intransitive verb]
まがる	曲がる	(for someone or something) to turn [intransitive verb]
よる	寄る	to drop by
わたる	渡る	to cross (bridge, road, etc.)

る -verbs

おりる	降りる	to get off
とめる	止める	to stop (something) [transitive verb]
のりかえる	乗り換える	to transfer, to change transportation
みえる	見える	can see ~ (literally: something is visible)

Adverbs

| まっすぐ | 真っ直ぐ | straight |
| すぐ | | soon, shortly |

Particles

で		limit
を		place in which movement occurs
を		out of ~, from ~

Suffixes

| ～いき | ～行き | bound for ~, 東京行き bound for Tokyo, 京都行き bound for Kyoto |

～がわ	～側	side, こちらがわ this side, むかいがわ the other side, the opposite side, みぎがわ right-hand side, ひだりがわ left-hand side
～かん	～館	mansion, building, 図書館 library, 体育館 gym, 水族館 aquarium, 博物館 museum, 美術館 art museum, 旅館 Japanese style inn, 映画館 movie theater, 大使館 embassy
～ぐち	～口	~ entrance/exit, 西口 west exit
～せん	～線	~ line (train line), 山手線 the Yamanote Line, 中央線 the Chuo Line
～つめ	～つ目	ordinal numbers, 一つ目 first
～ばんせん	～番線	track number (train), 三番線 Track 3
～メートル		meter (distance measurement), 10 メートル ten meters

Expressions

～という		called ~
～のをたのしみにしています	～のを楽しみにしています	to be looking forward to ~, お会い出来るのをたのしみにしています I am looking forward to seeing you.
みちなりに	道なりに	following the road

単語の練習
たん

A. X というY   *Y called X*

大江戸線という地下鉄	a subway called the Ooedo line
おおえどせん　　　ちかてつ	
ローソンというコンビニ	a convenience store called Lawson
三越というデパート	a department store called Mitsukoshi
みつこし	
スタバ（スターバックス）というカフェ	a café called Starbucks

In the expression XというY, the noun Y indicates a general category such as person, place, school, and name, and the noun X indicates a specific instance of Y. In this usage, という is usually written in **hiragana** instead of **kanji**.

Activity 1   日本語で質問に答えて下さい。

Example: 家の近くにどんな店がありますか。
　　　　　　　ちか
　　　　　　　ファミリーマートというコンビニがあります。

1. 家の近くにどんな店がありますか。
　　ちか

2. 何というレストランによく行きますか。

3. よくどこでふくを買いますか。

4. どんなうたが好きですか。

5. どんなテレビ番組 (*TV program*) をよく見ますか。
   ばんぐみ

Activity 2   Use the form 〜という to ask whether someone knows about the following places and things. Use both casual and polite speech.

Example: 山田さん

山田さんという人を知っていますか。／山田さんって人、知ってる？

1. デニーズ
2. SONY
3. カーネーション
4. ペプシ

5. シーズー (*Shih Tzu*)
6. ブラジル
7. ハイアット
8. ラッコ (*sea otter*)

B. 道しるべ   Landmarks
　　みち

Using the words below, identify the numbered objects in the illustration.

行き方	way of going
映画館 えい	movie theater
横断歩道 おうだん ほ どう	crosswalk
ガソリンスタンド	gas station
かど	corner
こうさてん	intersection
市役所 し やくしょ	city hall
しんごう	traffic signal
大使館 たい し	embassy
地図 ち ず	map
駐車場 ちゅうしゃじょう	parking lot
道路 どう ろ	road
橋 はし	bridge
バスターミナル	bus terminal
バスてい	bus stop
道 みち	street

おぼえていますか。

アパート　駅<ruby>えき</ruby>　〜かい　学生会館　カフェ　川　喫茶店<ruby>きっさ</ruby>　銀行　空港　公園<ruby>こうえん</ruby>
交番<ruby>こう</ruby>　このへん　コンビニ　住所　スーパー　体育館<ruby>いく</ruby>　建物<ruby>たて</ruby>　デパート　動物園<ruby>どう　えん</ruby>
所　博物館<ruby>はく</ruby>　場所<ruby>ば</ruby>　美術館<ruby>びじゅつ</ruby>　病院　ビル　ホテル　本屋<ruby>や</ruby>　町<ruby>まち</ruby>　みずうみ　山
郵便局　りょう　旅館　レストラン

Supplementary Vocabulary: ほかの道<ruby>みち</ruby>しるべ   **Other landmarks**

こうみんかん	公民館	public hall, a community center
じゅうたくがい	住宅街	residential district
しょうてんがい	商店街	shopping district
ショッピングセンター		shopping mall
みなと	港	port
りょうじかん	領事館	counsulate

Activity 3   下の質問に日本語で答えて下さい。

1. この町<ruby>まち</ruby>にどんな建物<ruby>たて</ruby>がありますか。
2. 道<ruby>みち</ruby>という漢字をつかっている言葉はどれですか。
3. 館という漢字をつかっている言葉はどれですか。
4. 車<ruby>くるま</ruby>のためにあるものはどれですか。
5. 道<ruby>みち</ruby>にあるものはどれですか。

Activity 4   Supply the words that match the following descriptions.

1. 川をわたるためにある物　＿＿＿＿＿＿＿＿＿＿＿＿＿＿＿

2. バスが来る所　＿＿＿＿＿＿＿＿＿＿＿＿＿＿＿

3. 二つの道<ruby>みち</ruby>がまじわる (intersect) 所　＿＿＿＿＿＿＿＿＿＿＿＿＿＿＿

4. 車<ruby>くるま</ruby>にガソリンを入れる所　＿＿＿＿＿＿＿＿＿＿＿＿＿＿＿

5. パスポートがなくなった時に行く所　＿＿＿＿＿＿＿＿＿＿＿＿＿＿＿

6. 道<ruby>みち</ruby>をしらべる時につかう便利な物<ruby>り</ruby>　＿＿＿＿＿＿＿＿＿＿＿＿＿＿＿

C. 場所と方向　Locations and directions

道の右側
みち　みぎがわ

道の左側
みち　ひだりがわ

まっすぐ

銀行のむかい
（がわ）

道のこちら
みち　　がわ

right side
of the street

left side
of the street

straight

across the street
from the bank

this side of the
street

道と道の間
みち　みち

こうさてんの手前
てまえ

こうさてんの先
さき

between the streets

just before the intersection

past the intersection

銀行のすぐ先
さき

つきあたり

道なりに行く
みち

right after the bank

at the end of the street

follow the road

おぼえていますか。

上　下　前　後ろ　中　外　近く　となり　横　右　左　東　西　南　北
　　　　　　　　　　　　　　ちか

北東　北西　南東　南西

Activity 5   Look at the following map. Two people, A and B, are at the gas station walking toward the park. Complete the following sentences, using words that indicate direction.

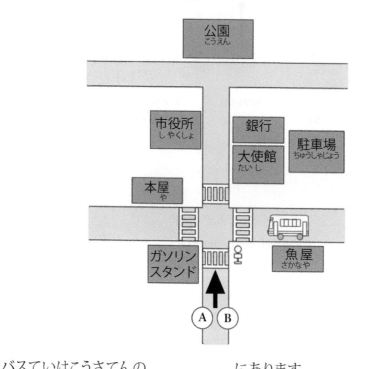

1. バスていはこうさてんの＿＿＿＿＿＿にあります。

2. 公園は＿＿＿＿＿行って、＿＿＿＿＿＿にあります。
   こうえん

3. 市役所は一つ目のかどと二つ目のかどの＿＿＿＿＿で、道路の左側にあり
   しやくしょ　　め　　　　　　め　　　　　　　　　　　　　　どうろ　ひだりがわ
   ます。銀行の＿＿＿＿＿です。

4. 大きい道の＿＿＿＿＿にはガソリンスタンドやバスていやさかな屋があります。
   みち　　　　　　　　　　　　　　　　　　　　　　　　　　　　　や

5. ガソリンスタンドの＿＿＿＿＿には本屋があります。
   や

6. 大使館と銀行はこうさてんの＿＿＿＿＿にあります。
   たいし

7. 大使館のすぐ＿＿＿＿＿に銀行があります。大使館のすぐ＿＿＿＿＿に
   たいし　　　　　　　　　　　　　　　　　　たいし
   駐車場があります。
   ちゅうしゃじょう

8. この道の＿＿＿＿＿に銀行があって、＿＿＿＿＿に市役所があります。
   みち　　　　　　　　　　　　　　　　　　　　　　　　しやくしょ

Activity 6   Work with a partner. Imagine that you are in front of the building where you are studying right now. Tell each other what buildings and facilities are around your building, using the location and direction expressions above as well as other expressions you know. Verify the information you receive.

D. 行き方を教える時につかう言葉   Expressions used in giving directions

～をわたる	to cross ~
～を通る	to go through/pass ~
～がとまる	(for something) to stop ~
～をとめる	to stop something ~
～をおりる	to get off ~
～を右 / 左にまがる	to turn right/left at ~
～で～から～に乗りかえる	to transfer from ~ to ~ at ~
～が見える	can see ~
～に近い	close to ~
～から遠い	far from ~
～メートル	~ meters
～つ目	the ~th (一つ目のかど the first corner)

～つ目 is not used for large numbers. The larger the number, the less likely it is to be used.

Use ～番目 (Chapter 10 of *Nakama 1*) for numbers larger than nine.

おぼえていますか。

歩く　行く　来る　変える　（時間が）かかる　乗せる　乗る

Activity 7   Say the following expressions.

何メートル	一メートル	二メートル	三メートル	四メートル	五メートル
	六メートル	七メートル	八メートル	九メートル	十メートル
いくつ目	一つ目	二つ目	三つ目	四つ目	五つ目
	六つ目	七つ目	八つ目	九つ目	

Activity 8   Match the phrases in the box with the pictures.

かどを右にまがる	しんごうでとまる	駅から遠い	バスをおりる
中央線に乗りかえる	公園を通る	山が見える	駅に近い
バスに乗る	橋をわたる	かいだんをおりる	公園に近い
かどを左にまがる	道なりに歩く		

1　　　　　2　　　　　3　　　　　4

| 5 | 6 | 7 | 8 |

Activity 9   Draw the following directions on the street map below.

1. 一つ目のこうさてんを右にまがる。
2. しんごうを右にまがって、左にある。
3. 三つ目のかどを左にまがって、まっすぐ行く。
4. まっすぐ行って、二つ目のかどの手前。
5. 50メートルぐらいまっすぐ行く。
6. 一つ目のかどを左にまがる。
7. 公園を通って橋をわたる。

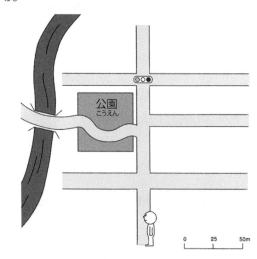

E. 駅と乗り物　Stations and transportation

出口	exit	各駅停車	local train
入口	entrance	普通（列車）	local train
〜口（北口、西口、南口）	〜 exit/entrance	急行（列車）	express train
かいさつ（口）	ticket gate	特急（列車）	limited express train
地下鉄	subway	〜線	〜 line (山手線 Yamanote line)
タクシー	taxi	〜行き	bound for 〜 (京都行き bound for Kyoto)
JR	Japan Railway	〜番線	track number

Supplementary Vocabulary: 駅でつかう言葉 Other expressions used in stations

かいすうけん	回数券	a coupon book for train/bus tickets
がくわり	学割	student discount (shortened form of がくせいわりびき [学生割引])
きっぷうりば	切符売り場	ticket booth
していせき	指定席	reserved seat
じゆうせき	自由席	unreserved seat
しゅうゆうけん	周遊券	(travel) pass
ていきけん	定期券	train/bus commuter pass
わりびき（けん）	割引（券）	discount (ticket)

Activity 10   下の質問に答えて下さい。

1. よく電車をつかいますか。どこに行く時、電車をつかいますか。

2. あなたの町のバスは便利ですか。バスはいくらぐらいかかりますか。

3. 一番近くの空港から家までタクシーでどのくらいかかりますか。

4. あなたの国に地下鉄がありますか。どの町に地下鉄がありますか。

5. 地下鉄に乗ったことがありますか。どこで乗りましたか。

Activity 11   下のえは上野駅から成田空港までの路線図 (train map) です。路線図を見て、日本語で質問に答えて下さい。

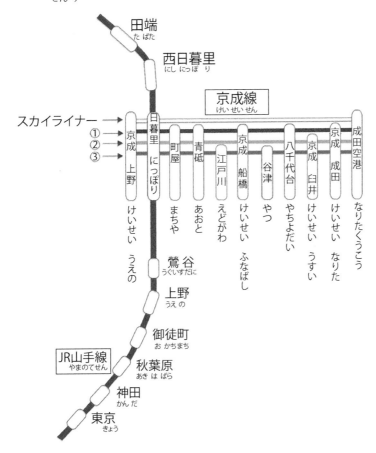

1. どれが各駅停車ですか。
   _{かくえきていしゃ}

2. どれが急行ですか。とっきゅうですか。
   _{きゅうこう}

3. 急行やとっきゅうがあるのは何線ですか。
   _{きゅうこう}　　　　　　　_{せん}

4. 山手線はどの駅にとまりますか。
   _{やまのてせん}　　_{えき}

5. 京成上野駅から成田空港 (*Narita Airport*) までどの電車が一番はやいですか。
   _{けいせいうえのえき}　　_{なりた}　　　　　　　　　　　　　　_{しゃ}

6. その電車で日暮里のつぎの駅はどこですか。
   _{しゃ}　_{にっぽり}　　　_{えき}

Activity 12　下のえは、東京駅のターミナル (*terminal*) です。えを見て質問に答え
　　　　　　　　　　　_{きょうえき}
　　　　　　て下さい。

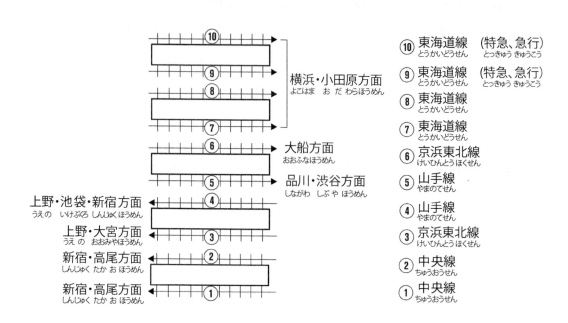

1. 横浜に行く時は何番線の電車に乗りますか。 はやいのは何番線ですか。
   _{よこはま}　　　　_{ばんせん}　_{しゃ}　　　　　　　　　　　　　_{ばんせん}

2. 新宿に行きたい人は何線に乗りますか。
   _{しんじゅく}　　　　　　_{せん}

3. いけぶくろに行く人は何番線の電車に乗りますか。何線ですか。
   　　　　　　　　　　_{ばんせん}　_{しゃ}　　　　　　_{せん}

4. しぶやに行く人は何線に乗らなくてはいけませんか。何番線ですか。
   　　　　　　　　_{せん}　　　　　　　　　　　　　　_{ばんせん}

ダイアローグ

はじめに

質問に日本語で答えて下さい。

1. 東京は電車の方が車より便利です。あなたの町ではどうですか。

2. 電車でどこかへ行く時、どんな言葉をつかいますか。

3. あなたの国では道を教える時、どんな建物や物の名前をよくつかいますか。

4. 道を聞く時は、どんな言葉がつかえると思いますか。

ヒルトンホテルへの行き方 *Directions to the Hilton Hotel*

The following **manga** frames are scrambled, so they are not in the order described in the dialogue. Read the dialogue and unscramble the frames by writing the correct number in the box located in the upper right corner of each frame.

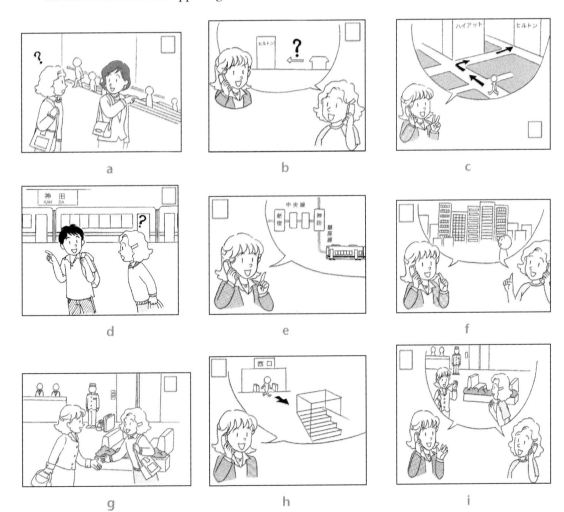

ブラウンさんはあさくさに住んでいます。明日ヒルトンホテルで道子さんと会う予定ですが、行き方が分からないので、電話で道子さんに行き方を聞いています。

ブラウン：ここからヒルトンホテルまで、どう行ったらいいの？

道子：新宿までは、行き方分かる？

ブラウン：ごめん。分からない。

道子：そう、じゃあ、まず、地下鉄の銀座線で、神田まで行くの。

ブラウン：銀座線で神田まで行って、それから？

道子：神田で中央線に乗りかえて、三つ目の駅が新宿だから、そこでおりるの。

ブラウン：OK。中央線で新宿まで行くのね。で、新宿で電車をおりてから、どこへ行くの？

道子：西口のかいさつを出て。出たら、すぐ目の前に地下道があるから、その道をまっすぐ行って。

ブラウン：西口を出て地下道をまっすぐ行くのね。

道子：うん、そう。十分か十五分ぐらい歩くと、高いビルがたくさん見えてくるはずよ。

ブラウン：ああ、あのビルがたくさんある所？

道子：そう。二つ目のかどにハイアットホテルがあるから、その手前を右にまがるの。

ブラウン：ハイアットは道の右側、左側？

道子：右側だよ。

ブラウン：分かった。じゃあ、で、ハイアットの手前を右ね。

道子：うん。で、右にまがってから、まっすぐ行くと、つきあたりにヒルトンが見えるはず。

ブラウン：分かった。で、時間はどれくらいかかるの？

道子：新宿の駅までは、十五分から二十分ぐらい、ホテルまでは歩いて二十分ぐらいだから、四十分ぐらいかかると思うけど。

ブラウン：ありがとう。じゃあ、明日一時にヒルトンのロビー (lobby) でね。

道子：じゃあ、明日ね。

つぎの日、ブラウンさんは神田駅にいます。

ブラウン：あのう、すみません。中央線の新宿行きは何番線ですか。

　男の人：一番線ですよ。

ブラウン：あ、どうもありがとうございました。

ブラウンさんは新宿駅にいます。

ブラウン：　あのう、西口はどこですか。

　女の人：　ああ、西口なら、あそこのかいだんをおりたところですよ。

ブラウン：　どうも。

ブラウンさんはホテルに着きました。

　道子：　あ、ブラウンさん。ここ、ここ。　道、分かった？

ブラウン：　道子さん。うん、すぐ分かった。

　道子：　ああ、よかった。

DIALOGUE PHRASE NOTES

- ごめん is a casual form of ごめんなさい, which means *I'm sorry*.
- 地下道 is an underground street or underground passageway.

ダイアローグの後で

A. Circle the stations where Ms. Brown gets on or off trains, then follow her route on the map.

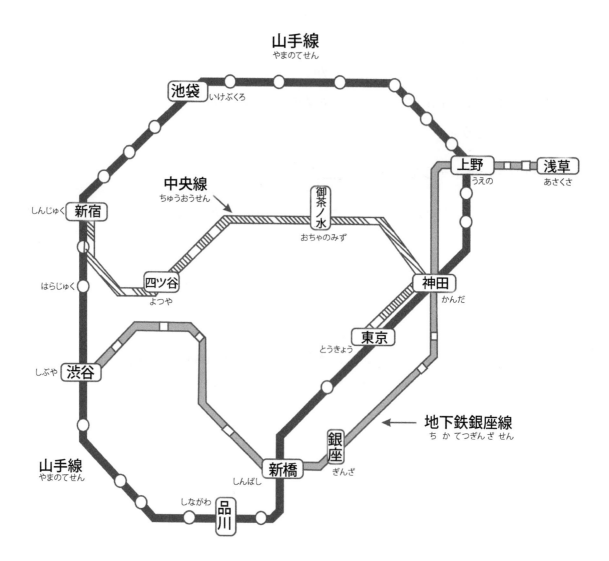

B. Follow Michiko's directions after Ms. Brown gets off the train at Shinjuku. The Hilton Hotel is either building A, B, C, D, or E. Which is it?

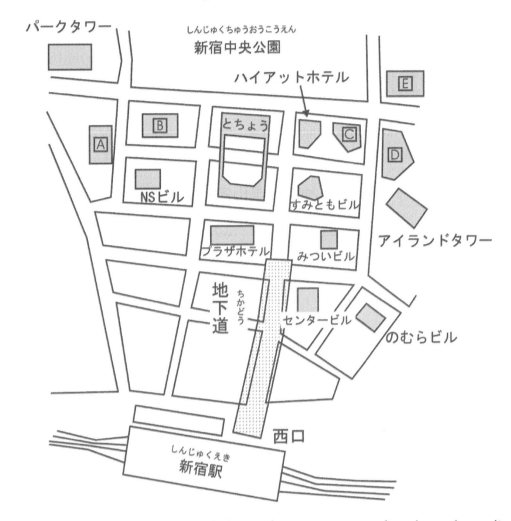

C. Identify the expressions in the dialogue where Ms. Brown confirms her understanding.

D. Suppose Ms. Brown is asking directions of her Japanese instructor. Rewrite the dialogue and make Michiko the **sensei**.

E. Explain how to go to パークタワー and the NS ビル from Shinjuku Station, using the map of Shinjuku in Exercise B.

日本の文化
ぶん か

日本の道と住所 Streets and addresses in Japanese cities
みち

The Japanese address system is considerably different from the one used in the United States. Because not all streets have names, it is not always possible to specify a location with a number and a street name. In Japan, addresses are expressed in terms of a sub-area within a larger area (as shown in the map below). For example, 「神奈川県山田市本町 2-4-8」 indicates house number 8 in neighborhood 4 of sub-area 2 in Honmachi district, Yamada-city, Kanagawa prefecture. (Yamada-city is fictitious.)
か な がわけん
し まち

神奈川県山田市
か な がわけん し

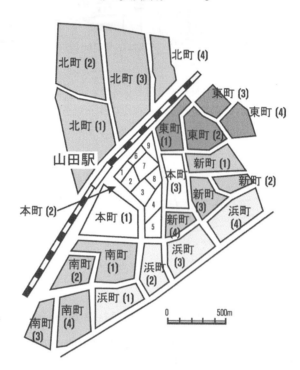

Sub-areas are organized by number, but the order of these numbers is not consistent from one area to another. It would not be uncommon for residents of sub-area 1 to not know where sub-area 2 is. Also, house numbers are somewhat arbitrary. That is, house numbers 2 and 3 are likely to be adjacent, but house 2 could be either to the right or the left of house 3. Neighborhood maps are posted in each neighborhood to help non-residents find numbers. It can be difficult even for a Japanese person to find a given house address. For this reason, some mobile phones are equipped with a GPS or navigation system just like those in cars. When in doubt, ask a local resident or an officer at a nearby police box for assistance.

日本の鉄道 The Japanese train system
てつどう

The Japanese train system, including subways, is well developed and very reliable. If a train is scheduled to arrive at 12:58, it nearly always comes at 12:58. There are many different transportation companies, all of them now private. The largest one is the JR Group, derived from Japan Railways and pronounced as ジェイアール. This is the former

National Railway, now divided into six regional companies (ＪＲ東日本, ＪＲ東海, ＪＲ西日本, ＪＲ九州, ＪＲ四国, ＪＲ北海道). Other private lines run in different directions and serve commuters in surrounding areas. The lines mentioned in this book are in Tokyo. 山手線, 中央線, and 新幹線 are JR lines; 京成線 is a private line; and 銀座線 and 丸ノ内線 are subway lines. The 山手線 loops around the Tokyo metro area and carries the largest number of passengers a day.

Trains in Japan do not use tokens. Instead, they use tickets and turnstiles. Passengers must retain their tickets throughout the ride because they need to reinsert them in the turnstile when exiting the station at their destination. Fares increase with distance. Because you must purchase the ticket for your specific destination, you need to figure out the fare by using a fare table or by asking others. The minimum fare is about 130 yen. Electronic train passes (IC cards) such as Suica (スイカ) and Pasmo (パスモ) are convenient alternatives to tickets in the Tokyo area. Other parts of Japan offer similar types of passes, though スイカ can be used in other areas of Japan. These passes are smart cards that can be used as rechargeable debit cards for train or subway fares as well as for purchases at stores and kiosks in Japan. They can be purchased in stations at ticket vending machines. Japanese smartphones and cell phones offer similar technology and can be converted into electronic train passes or debit cards, although these features do not apply to rental phones used by tourists.

JR offers a range of discount tickets for foreign travelers. One pass offers unlimited rides in a certain area for a fixed number of days (e.g., one week) such as ジャパン・レール・パス or the JR East Pass. If you are planning a trip to visit a series of different places, this type of ticket will save you money. There is also a special IC card for foreign travelers. You can obtain detailed information from the JR Group's website.

JR also offers a 20% student discount (学生割引 or 学割) for one-way fares for distances of more than 100km. Travel agents (旅行会社) and びゅうプラザ (JR's own travel service, found in major stations) are a good source of information about the different types of discounts available.

文法

> ## I. Expressing a route using the particle を; expressing a point of departure using the particle を; expressing scope or limit using the particle で

So far you have learned that the particle を indicates the direct object. The particle で indicates a place of action or events as well as a means or instrument for an action. This chapter introduces two other uses of を and another use of the particle で.

A. Expressing a route, using the particle を

The particle を indicates a location in cases where movement occurs. It takes a verb of motion such as 行く, 来る, 帰る, 歩く, 通る, 走る, or およぐ.

大使館はこの道をまっすぐ行った所にあります。
The embassy is straight ahead on this road.

第三コースをおよぎます。　　(I) *swim in lane 3.*

毎日公園を走る。　　*I run (jog) in the park every day.*

ゆみ：　ここから学校までは遠いから、歩きたくない。
　　　　I don't want to walk because the school is far away from here.

まもる：　そんなことないよ。あの駐車場を通って行くと近いよ。
　　　　It's not far. It's close if you go through that parking lot.

B. Expressing a point of departure using the particle を (*out of ~, from ~*)

The particle を here indicates a place or vehicle from which one gets off or leaves. A noun preceding で indicates an enclosed space such as vehicles, buildings, elevators, etc.

バスをおりて、電車に乗りかえる。　*I got off the bus and transferred to a train.*

駅を出たら、すぐ右にまがります。　*When you leave the station, you immediately turn right.*

去年大学を卒業しました。　　　　*I graduated from college last year.*

つぎの駅で地下鉄をおりる。　　　*I get off the subway at the next station.*

C. Expressing scope or limit using で

When the particle で is preceded by an expression for quantity, time, or amount, it indicates an extent or limit.

十分でもどります。　　　　　　　*I will return in 10 minutes.*

あと一週間で休みです。　　　　　*Vacation starts in another week.*

そのみかんは五つで三百円です。　*Those oranges are 300 yen for five.*

このシャツはセールだったから、　*This shirt was on sale, so I bought it for 500 yen.*
　五百円で買ったよ。

話してみましょう

Activity 1　Complete the following sentences by supplying the particles を (*route*), を (*out of; from*), で (*location*),で (*limit*), に (*goal*), or から (*from*).

Example:　市役所の前／通る
しゃくしょ　　　とお
市役所の前を通る。
しやくしょ　　　　とお

1. こうさてん／とまる

2. とっきゅう／乗る

3. 東京駅／電車／おりる
きょうえき　　しゃ

4. 四つ目のかど／左／まがる
め　　　　　　ひだり

5. 公園／歩く
こうえん

6. 橋／わたる
はし

7. 三十分ぐらい／着く

8. 横断歩道／わたる
おうだん ほ どう

9. 東京駅／山手線／中央線／乗りかえる
きょうえき　　やまのてせん　　ちゅうおうせん

10. 川／あそぶ

11. 急行／各駅停車／乗りかえる
きゅうこう　　かくえきていしゃ

12. バスていの前／通る
とお

13. 市役所／よる
し やくしょ

14. かいだん／おりる

Activity 2　Work in groups of four. First, fill in the blanks with the appropriate particles. Then one person should choose an expression from the box and act it out. The other members should try to guess which expression was chosen.

横断歩道＿＿＿わたる おうだん ほ どう	橋＿＿＿わたる はし	左＿＿＿まがる ひだり	タクシー＿＿＿乗る
しんごう＿＿＿車＿＿＿とめる くるま	大きい道路＿＿＿まっすぐ行く どう ろ	せまい道＿＿＿歩く みち	
先生の後ろ＿＿＿通る とお	かど＿＿＿右＿＿＿まがる みぎ	橋の手前＿＿＿道＿＿＿入る はし て まえ　みち	

Example:　横断歩道
おうだん ほ どう
A:　横断歩道をわたるんですか。
おうだん ほ どう
B:　いいえ、違います。
A:　じゃ、橋をわたるんですか。
はし
B:　ええ、そうですよ。

Activity 3   Work with a partner. Choose a place in your town that your partner knows. Explain how to get there from the building you are in. Use the expressions in Activity 2 as well as other expressions when necessary, but do not use the name of the place you have in mind. Your partner may ask questions except for the name of the place. He or she should try to guess the place on the basis of your directions. Use polite speech.

Example: A: この建物を出て、横断歩道をわたります。すぐ右にまがって、
たて　　　　　　　　　おうだんほどう　　　　　　　　　みぎ
10 メートルぐらい歩きます。その建物は右側にあります。
　　　　　　　　　　　　　　　　　　たて　みぎがわ

B: 大学の本屋ですか。
や

A: はい、そうです。

II. Expressing conditions leading to set consequences using the plain form + と

The conditional と can be translated as *if*, *when*, or *whenever*, although the interpretation of a sentence with と depends on the tense of the main clause.

If the sentence ends in the present tense, と indicates a condition for which the event in the main clause is the natural or automatic consequence. Therefore, this usage tends to be for facts or statements of habit. *When* or *whenever* is the closest in meaning.

左にまがると、公園がすぐ先に見えます。　　　*If you turn to your left, you can see the*
ひだり　　　　こうえん　　　さき　　　　　　　　　　*park just ahead.*

冬になると、このへんはとても寒くなる。　　　*When the winter comes, it gets very cold*
　　　　　　　　　　　　　　　　　　　　　　　around here.

駅を出ると、目の前にかいだんがあります。　　*When you leave the station, there will be*
えき　　　　　　　　　　　　　　　　　　　　　*stairs in front of you.*

と is preceded by the plain present form of verbs, adjectives, and the copula verb.

	Verb	い -adjective	な -adjective	Noun
Dictionary form	よる (to drop by)	遠い とお (far from)	しずか (quiet)	山手線 やまのてせん (Yamanote line)
Affirmative	よると	遠いと とお	しずかだと	山手線だと やまのてせん
Negative	よらないと	遠くないと とお	しずかじゃないと	山手線じゃないと やまのてせん

A sequence of two events connected by と expresses an inevitable or habitual cause-and-effect relationship. On the other hand, a sentence with たら conditional expresses a temporal, accidental cause-and-effect relationship. In this sense, と conditional conveys a general statement of a fact rather than any specific event. For example, in the case of 冬になると、スキーに行きます (*I go skiing when the winter comes*), the speaker always goes skiing in winter. In contrast, 冬になったら、スキーに行きます means the speaker plans to go skiing this winter. The other difference between と and たら is that the main clause in sentences containing the と conditional cannot express intention, desire, or a request, invitation, or command made by the speaker.

橋をわたると、左側に学校が見えます。 はし　　　　　ひだりがわ	*You will see the school on your left immediately after you cross the bridge.*
橋をわたったら、左側に学校が見えます。 はし　　　　　　ひだりがわ	*Upon crossing the bridge, the school can be seen on your left.*
地下鉄をおりたら、電話して下さい。 ち　か　てつ	*Please call me when you get off the subway.*
~~地下鉄をおりると、電話して下さい。~~ ち　か　てつ	*Please call me as a result of getting off the subway.*
山田さんが来たら、行きましょう	*Let's go as soon as Yamada-san comes.*
~~山田さんが来ると、行きましょう。~~	*Let's go as a result of Yamada-san's arrival.*

When the main clause is in the past tense, と expresses an unexpected or surprising event resulting from the condition described. In these cases, と and たら are interchangeable.

家に帰ると、母が来ていた。	*When I went home, [I found that] my mother had arrived.*
家に帰ったら、母が来ていた。	*When I went home, [I found that] my mother had arrived.*

話してみましょう

Activity 1   Match the statements in columns A and B and connect them using と, たら, or both.

Example: 1 と f

梅雨になると、三日に二日雨がふります。
つ　ゆ

Column A

1. 梅雨になります。
   つ　ゆ
2. 好きな人が出来ます。
3. うんどうをします。
4. 友達の家によりました。
5. 時間がかかりそうです。
6. 道なりに歩いて行きます。
   みち
7. 各駅停車に乗ります。
   かくえきていしゃ

Column B

a. シャワーをあびて下さい。
b. おそくなってしまいました。
c. とっきゅうで行きませんか。
d. 勉強が出来なくなります。
e. 時間がかかると思います。
f. 三日に二日雨がふります。
g. つきあたりに映画館があります。
   えい

Activity 2 Look at the map below and describe what will be visible right after you perform the following activities.

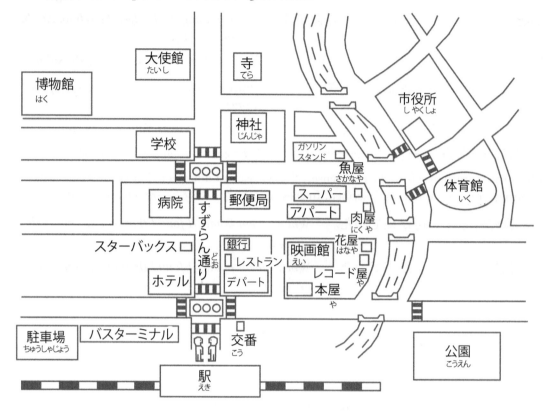

Example: 駅を出る
えき
駅を出ると前にしんごうと横断歩道が見えます。
えき　　　　　　　　おうだん ほ どう

1. 駅を出て、右にまがります。
   えき　　　　みぎ

2. 駅を出て、横断歩道をわたります。
   えき　　　おうだん ほ どう

3. 駅を出て、左にまがって、まっすぐ行きます。
   えき　　　ひだり

4. 駅を出て、すずらん通りを三つ目のかどまでまっすぐ行きます。
   えき　　　　　　どお　　　　め

5. 映画館の前の道を右にまっすぐ行きます。
   えい　　　みち みぎ

6. 公園の前の横断歩道をわたって、まっすぐ行きます。
   こうえん　　　おうだん ほ どう

7. デパートと本屋の間の道を通って、つきあたりまで行きます。
   ほん や　　みち とお

Activity 3 Work with a partner. Look at the map in Activity 2. You are at the station. Ask your partner where the following landmarks are. Your partner will answer using 〜と. Take turns.

Example: 交番
こう
A: 交番はどこですか。
こう
B: 駅を出ると、右側にありますよ。
えき　　　みぎがわ

1. 駐車場　2. 公園　3. ホテル　4. 神社　5. 博物館
ちゅうしゃじょう　こうえん　　　　　　　　じんじゃ　　はく

Activity 4   Work with a partner. You are at the intersection at the bottom of the map below. You would like to know where the following are: bus stop, subway station, public phone, gas station, and parking lot. Ask your partner, who is a passerby, the locations of these objects and places. Your partner will have randomly assigned the 5 locations to the spots designated by the numbers on the map and will use 〜と to describe how to get to the location you ask about. Based on these directions, tell your partner the number he/she assigned to the location.

バスてい

地下鉄の駅
ちかてつ　えき
電話

ガソリンスタンド

駐車場
ちゅうしゃじょう

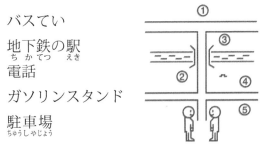

Example: B has chosen location 1 for the public phone.

A:　このへんに電話がありますか。

B:　ええ、まっすぐ行くと、橋がありますから、橋をわたって下さい。
　　はし　　　　　　　　　　　　はし
　　わたると、目の前にあります。

A:　じゃあ、この地図だと、一番ですか。
　　　　　　　　ちず

B:　ええ、そうです。

Passengers ready to board bus from Narita Airport in Chiba Prefecture.

III. Expressing chronology using the て -form of the verb + から

The て-form of the verb + から means *after doing ~*. Because から originates in the particle から (from), the event in the てから clause tends to signal the beginning point at which the action in the main clause starts.

地図で道をしらべてから、行ったらどう？	*How about if we checked the street on a map and then went?*
見てから、買うかどうかきめるつもりだ。	*I plan to decide whether to buy it after seeing it.*
一月になってから、寒い日がつづいている。	*It's been continuously cold since the beginning of January.*
家に帰ってから、どうしたんですか。	*What did you do after you got home?*

～てから is similar to ～後で, so they can be used interchangeably in some cases, but not all the time. Here are some major differences between the two. First, as mentioned before, ～てから indicates when the action in the main clause begins. On the other hand, ～後で merely indicates the sequence of two events. For example, 八月から日本語を勉強する means the speaker will start studying Japanese in August. Similarly, 日本に行ってから日本語を勉強する indicates the speaker will start studying Japanese once he/she arrives in Japan. 日本に行った後で日本語を勉強する merely indicates that the act of going to Japan precedes the act of studying Japanese. For this reason, if someone asks when you would start studying Japanese, it would be appropriate to use ～てから, but answering with ～後で is somewhat awkward.

八月から、日本語を勉強する。	*I will start studying Japanese in August.*
日本に行ってから、日本語を勉強する。	*I will start studying Japanese after going to Japan.*
日本に行った後で、日本語を勉強する。	*I will study Japanese after I go to Japan.*

This also means that ～てから tends to imply that two events must be sequenced in that order, while 後で does not imply any inevitability about the order of two events. Therefore, it is more natural to use ～てから when the order is an important factor. For example, one must take off one's shoes before entering the house in Japan. To describe this situation, ～てから is more appropriate than 後で.

くつをぬいでから、入って下さい。	*Please enter after taking off your shoes.*
~~くつをぬいだ後で、入って下さい。~~	~~*Please enter (sometime) after you take off your shoes.*~~

On the other hand, if the order is not important, and you merely want to indicate that two events take place in a sequence, use 〜後で. For example, if you met Mr. Tanaka after you went to the movie, it would be more natural to use 〜後で. Using 〜てから in this case imply that the meeting with Mr. Tanaka after watching a movie was a planned event.

映画を見た後で、田中くんに会った。 *I met Mr. Tanaka after seeing a movie.*
映画を見てから、田中くんに会った。 *I met Mr. Tanaka after seeing a movie*
(and it was planned beforehand).

The final difference is that 〜てから can be used when the event in the main clause continues after the event in the 〜てから clause has taken place. 〜後で cannot be used in this case because it does not indicate continuity.

祖父がしんでから、三年になる。 *It has been three years since my grandfather died.*
祖父がしんだ後で、三年になる。 *It has been three years since my grandfather died.*

大学に入ってから、ずっと一人で住んでいる。 *I have lived alone since entering college.*
大学に入った後で、ずっと一人で住んでいる。 *I have lived alone since entering college.*

NOTE

- Like other subordinate clauses, the subject of clauses with てから must be marked by the particle が if it is different from the subject of the main clause.

しんごうが青になってから、道路をわたった方がいいですよ。
It's best to cross the road after the signal turns green.

そのこうさてんで一度とまってから、左にまがって下さい。
Stop at the intersection, and then turn left.

話してみましょう

Activity 1 Complete the following sentences using 〜てから, 後で, or both.

Example: ガソリンスタンドによる。家に帰ろう。
ガソリンスタンドによってから、家に帰ろう。

1. 家に帰りました。母から電話がありました。
2. 大使館に着きました。もう三時間です。
3. 結婚します。家を買います。
4. 切符を買います。地下鉄に乗ります。
5. しんごうが青になります。横断歩道をわたって下さい。
6. 山手線で東京に行きます。成田行きの急行に乗りかえます。
7. お土産を買います。空港に行った方がいいですよ。

Activity 2   Look at the map below. Using てから, describe what you have to do to go from place to place as specified.

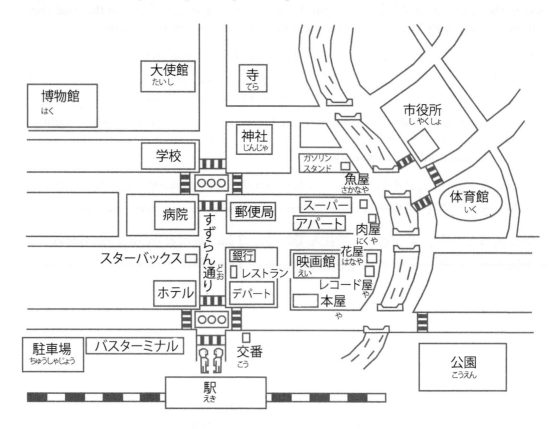

Example: 公園から体育館まで行く
　　　　　　　　公園を出て、横断歩道をわたってから、道なりに行くと、右側にあります。

1. 駅からデパートに行く

2. スターバックスから郵便局に行く

3. 本屋から公園に行く

4. デパートから郵便局に行く

5. 肉屋から市役所に行く

Activity 3   Work as a class. Think of one thing you habitually do before going to bed, and make up a sentence about it using 〜てから、寝ます. Interview your classmates about their habits and record in the chart what your classmates do.

Example: A: 〜さんは、寝る前に何をしますか。

B: 私は〜てから、寝ます。

A: そうですか。

名前	〜てから、寝ます。

IV. Expressing presuppositions using the plain form + はず

はず indicates the speaker's judgment about the likelihood of an action or event happening and can be translated as *I expect that ~*, *it is expected that ~*, *ought to ~*, or *~is supposed to*. The judgment is based on some objective information or knowledge. That is, the speaker thinks that the event or action ought to take place if his or her interpretation of the information or knowledge is correct. In this sense, はず is very different from だろう, which expresses a subjective speculation.

この電車は新宿駅にとまるはずだ。	*This train is supposed to stop at Shinjuku Station.*
昨日は休みじゃなかったはずです。	(According to my expectations/as far as I know) *Yesterday was not a holiday. The day off was not supposed to have been yesterday.*
あの人はまだ学生のはずです。	*That person should (as far as I know) still be a student.*

はず is grammatically a noun but it never stands on its own. The preceding verb and adjective forms must be identical to those in other instances where verbs and adjectives are used to modify nouns.

	Verb	**い -adjective**	**な -adjective**	**Copula verbs**
Dictionary form	こむ (to become crowded)	近い (close)	だめ (no good)	こちらがわ + だ (to be this side)
Present affirmative	こむはず	近いはず	だめなはず	こちらがわのはず
Present negative	こまないはず	近くないはず	だめじゃないはず	こちらがわじゃ ないはず
Past affirmative	こんだはず	近かったはず	だめだったはず	こちらがわだった はず
Past negative	こまなかった はず	近くなかった はず	だめじゃなかった はず	こちらがわじゃ なかったはず

The subject of a sentence containing はず cannot be the speaker. Although it is possible to say *I'm supposed to do ~* in English, はず cannot be used in this sense. Use 〜なければなら ない/なくてはいけない instead.

私は明日東京に行かなければなりません。	*I must/am supposed to go to Tokyo tomorrow.*
~~私は明日東京に行くはずです。~~	*~~I am supposed to go to Tokyo tomorrow.~~*
田中さんは明日東京に行かなければなりません。	*Mr. Tanaka must go to Tokyo tomorrow.*
田中さんは明日東京に行くはずです。	*Mr. Tanaka is supposed to go to Tokyo tomorrow.*

キム：　韓国大使館はこのへんでしょうか。	*Is the Korean embassy around here?*
半田：　ええ、この先にあるはずですよ。	*Yes, it should be just ahead.*
キム：　そうですか。どうもありがとう。	*I see. Thanks a lot.*
川上：　つぎのとっきゅうはいつ出ますか。	*What time will the next limited express leave?*
イー：　五時二十五分に出るはずですが。	*It is supposed to leave at 5:25.*
川上：　じゃあ、まだ乗れます。	*Then we can still catch it.*

話してみましょう

Activity 1   Look at the following train and subway map. Answer the questions using はず.

Example: 山手線で上野に行けますか。
やまのてせん うえの
　　　　　ええ、行けるはずです。

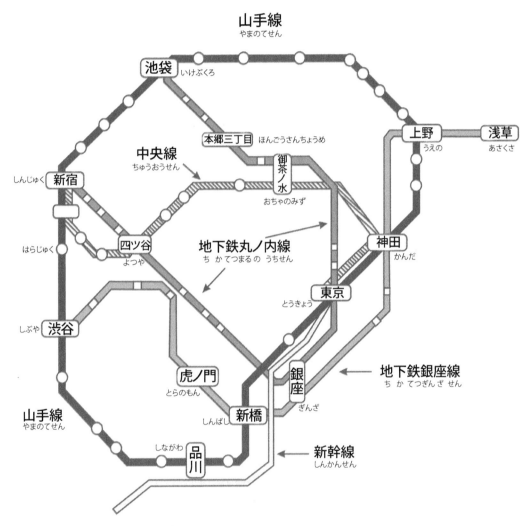

1. 山手線であさくさに行けますか。
やまのてせん
2. 中央線で神田のつぎの駅は何ですか。
ちゅうおうせん かんだ えき
3. まるのうち線は銀座を通りますか。
せん ぎんざ とお
4. 新宿でまるのうち線に乗れますか。
しんじゅく せん
5. 新宿で銀座線に乗れますか。
しんじゅく ぎんざせん
6. 上野で山手線から地下鉄に乗りかえられますか。
うえの やまのてせん ちかてつ
7. 上野で山手線から中央線に乗りかえられますか。
うえの やまのてせん ちゅうおうせん

◆ **Activity 2**　Using はず, make up sentences based on the following information that express an inference or judgment.

Example:　天気予報を見たら明日は晴れだと書いてありました。
　　　　　　ほう
　　　　　　明日は晴れのはずです。

1. 山田さんは昨日病気で入院しました。
2. スミスさんは日本に十年住んでいました。
3. キムさんは毎日午後九時に寝ます。
4. 京都は日本で一番古い町の一つです。
　　きょうと　　　　　　　　　　　まち
5. 東京には有名な人がたくさん住んでいます。
　　きょう　ゆう
6. ハワイは一年中気候がよくて、きれいです。
　　　　　　　　こう

◆ **Activity 3**　Work as a class. Ask your classmates what time they leave school and how long it takes to get from school to home. Then confirm the approximate time of arrival and complete the chart.

Example:　A:　今日は何時ごろ家へ帰るの？

　　　　　　B:　五時ごろ帰るつもり。

　　　　　　A:　家までどのくらいかかるの？

　　　　　　B:　歩いて、十五分か二十分ぐらいかな。

　　　　　　A:　じゃあ、五時二十分ごろには家に着くはずだね。

クラスメートの名前	学校を出る時間	かかる時間	家に着く時間

V.　Expressing conditions originated by others using ～（の）なら

なら is used when the speaker uses something from a previous context as a condition, and it is translated as *if it is the case that ~*. Inserting the optional の or ん before なら emphasizes the sense of condition and is translated as *if it is indeed the case that*.

キム：　このへんに駐車場はなさそうですね。
　　　　　　　　　ちゅうしゃじょう
　　　　It does not look like there is a parking lot around here.

白川：　駐車場がない（の）なら、あそこに車をとめたらどうですか。
しらかわ　ちゅうしゃじょう　　　　　　　　　　　くるま
　　　　If there is no parking lot, how about parking over there?

イー： 朝は道がこんでいるから、時間がかかりそうです。

It will probably take time because the traffic is heavy in the morning.

木村： 道がこんでいる（の）なら、地下鉄で行きましょう。

If the roads are crowded, we can take the subway.

町田： 急行は、この駅にとまりませんね。

Express trains do not stop at this station.

川口： 急行に乗る（の）なら、つぎの駅で乗りかえた方がいいでしょう。

If we are to take an express train, we should transfer at the next station.

ミラー： このへんにアメリカ大使館がありますか。

Is the U.S. Embassy around here?

通行人： アメリカ大使館なら、この道をまっすぐ行くと、右側にありますよ。

Passerby: *If it's the U.S. Embassy you want, go straight and you will see it on the right.*

Like ～でしょう, なら must be preceded by a clause ending with an adjective or verb in the plain form. The copula だ (for nouns and な -adjectives) is omitted from clauses followed by なら. Hence, one says 寒い（の）なら (include い), but 電車（なの）なら (omit だ).

Verbs

とめる (to stop)	とめる（の）なら	*if it is the case that you stop*
	とめない（の）なら	*if it is the case that you do not stop*
	とめた（の）なら	*if it is the case that you stopped*
	とめなかった（の）なら	*if it is the case that you did not stop*

い -adjectives

はやい (fast)	はやい（の）なら	*if it is the case that it is fast*
	はやくない（の）なら	*if it is the case that it is not fast*
	はやかった（の）なら	*if it is the case that it was fast*
	はやくなかった（の）なら	*if it is the case that it was not fast*

な -adjectives

便利だ (convenient)	便利（なの／なん）なら	*if it is the case that it is convenient*
	便利じゃない（の）なら	*if it is the case that it is not convenient*
	便利だった（の）なら	*if it is the case that it was convenient*
	便利じゃなかった（の）なら	*if it is the case that it was not convenient*

Copula verb

出口だ (exit)	出口（なの／なん）なら	*if it is the case that it is an exit*
	出口じゃない（の）なら	*if it is the case that it is not an exit*
	出口だった（の）なら	*if it is the case that it was an exit*
	出口じゃなかった（の）なら	*if it is the case that it was not an exit*

なら is different from たら in the following ways:
(1) なら uses something from the previous context as a condition. In this sense, the condition usually originates from a source other than the speaker. On the other hand, たら can be used without previous context and when the condition originates with the speaker. For example, when someone says 今週の土曜日、いそがしくなかったら、家に来ませんか (*If you are not busy this Saturday, would you like to come to my house?*), the speaker does not have any information as to whether you are busy this Saturday. So the speaker can just create the condition that you aren't busy on his/her own and use it as a condition for invitation. On the other hand, the speaker must have some reason to assume that you are not busy this Saturday in order to say 今週の土曜日、いそがしくないなら、家に来ませんか (*If it is indeed the case that you are not busy this Saturday, would you like to come to my house?*). Such reason is provided by a prior context usually provided by someone other than the speaker.

(2) The condition in the たら clause must be satisfied or completed before the event in the main clause takes place. For example, おさけを飲んだら、うんてんしない (*I don't drive if I've drunk alcohol*) indicates the act of drinking must occur first in order for the speaker to decide not to drive. On the other hand, in the sentence, おさけを飲むなら、うんてんしてはいけない (*If you are going to drink alcohol, you should not drive*), the speaker does not have to drink alcohol before deciding not to drive—just the intention of drinking is enough for him/her to avoid driving. In this sense, the condition expressed in the なら clause does not have to take place before the event in the main clause takes place.

話してみましょう

Activity 1   A new student asks you the locations of various facilities on campus. The student and you are at the bottom of the picture (at the spot marked ここ). Respond to the following questions using なら.

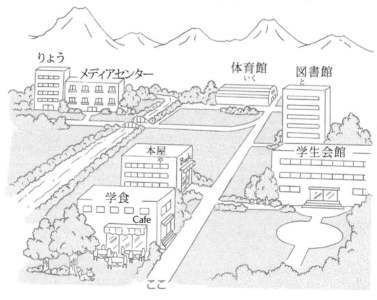

Example: 体育館はどこにありますか。
            体育館なら、この道をまっすぐ行って、つきあたりにあります。

1. 体育館   2. 学食   3. 学生会館

4. 図書館   5. メディアセンター   6. りょう

Activity 2 Work with a partner. One person asks a question using the phrases given. The other person makes recommendations using 〜なら.

Example: けいたい電話がほしいです。どれがいいか分かりません。

  A: けいたい電話がほしいんだけど、どれがいいか分からないんだ。

  B: けいたいなら、日本のがいいよ。

1. はじめての (first) デートです。どこに行ったらいいか分かりません。
2. お金がありません。どうしたらいいか分かりません。
3. 道が分からなくなりました。どうしたらいいか分かりません。
4. 大使館に行きたいです。行き方が分かりません。
5. いそいでいます。バスに乗れるかどうか分かりません。
6. 車をとめなければなりません。どこにとめたらいいか分かりません。

Activity 3 Work as a class. Write one thing about which you would like some advice. Then ask four or five classmates for suggestions and write them down. Report the best advice.

Example: A: あのう、ちょっと今いい?

  B: うん、何?

  A: 日本語がつかえる仕事をしたいんだけど、どうしたらいいかな。

  B: 日本語がつかえる仕事をするなら、図書館でアルバイトしたらどう?

聞く練習

上手な聞き方

Announcements at stations and on trains

What you know about the setting gives you a lot of clues about the type of speech you hear. For example, announcements in a train station would be different from those within a train because the purpose of each announcement is different. Being aware of purpose in these settings allows you to determine key words to listen for.

練習

A. 日本語で質問に答えて下さい。

1. 駅でどんなアナウンス (announcements) を聞いたことがありますか。
2. どんなアナウンスがあったらいいと思いますか。
3. 電車の中でどんなアナウンスを聞いたことがありますか。

B. In the following chart, write down the possible reasons for an announcement on the platform and on the train, and then write possible key words.

	目的 （Purpose） もくてき	キーワード
プラットフォーム (platform) ／駅 えき	Example: delay	おくれる　〜時〜分
電車の中 しゃ		

駅と電車のアナウンス　Announcements at stations and on trains
えき　　しゃ

聞く前に

Look at the photos below of the platform area of a train station. Say what kind of signs you see in the picture. Usually you will see yellow lines on the platform. Guess why they are there.

Kenneth Hamm / Photo Japan

聞いてみましょう

A. 日本の駅や電車の中でも色々なアナウンスがあります。つぎのアナウンスを
えき　　しゃ
聞いて、何のためのアナウンスかかんがえて下さい。

Example:　You hear:　二番線に電車がまいります。あぶないですから、黄色い線
　　　　　　　　　　　ばんせん　　しゃ　　　　　　　　　　　　　　　　　　きいろ　せん
　　　　　　　　　　　の後ろに下がっておまち下さい。

　　　　　　You say:　二番線に電車が来ます。
　　　　　　　　　　　ばんせん　　しゃ

1. _____　　2. _____

3. _____　　4. _____

B. もう一度アナウンスを聞いて、下の質問に答えて下さい。

1. どんな電車が来ますか。

2. この電車はこの駅にとまりますか。

3. この電車はどこ行きですか。

4. この電車がとまる駅はどれですか。

Circle all that apply:　四ツ谷　しなのまち　千駄ケ谷　代々木　新宿

この電車がとまらない駅でおりたい人はどうしますか。

聞いた後で

Mr. Chan has not understood the announcements in 聞いてみましょう, so he asks for your help. Complete the following dialogues with Mr. Chan.

Example:　チャン：　あのう今のアナウンスよく分からなかったんですが。

あなた：　ああ、二番線に電車が来るそうですよ。

チャン：　ああ、そうですか。どうもありがとうございます。

1. チャン：　あのう、今のアナウンス、よく分からなかったんですか。

あなた：　＿＿＿＿＿＿＿＿＿＿＿＿＿＿＿＿＿＿＿＿＿＿＿

チャン：　あ、そうですか。どうも。

2. チャン：　あのう、どこに行く電車ですか。

あなた：　＿＿＿＿＿＿＿＿＿＿＿＿＿＿＿＿＿＿＿＿＿＿＿

チャン：　電車は東京駅にとまりますか。

あなた：　＿＿＿＿＿＿＿＿＿＿＿＿＿＿＿＿＿＿＿＿＿＿＿

3. チャン：　あのう、今のアナウンス、よく分からなかったんですが、
　　　　　　ひかり十三号はいつ出るんでしょうか。

あなた：　＿＿＿＿＿＿＿＿＿＿＿＿＿＿＿＿＿＿＿＿＿＿＿

チャン：　そうですか。どうも。

4. チャン：　あのう、今のアナウンスよく分からなかったんですけど、代々木は
　　　　　　この電車で行けますか。

あなた：　＿＿＿＿＿＿＿＿＿＿＿＿＿＿＿＿＿＿＿＿＿＿＿

チャン：　そうですか。じゃあ、つぎの駅でおりなきゃならないんですね。
　　　　　　どうもありがとうございます。

聞き上手話し上手

道の聞き方と教え方　Asking for and giving directions
<small>みち</small>

Japanese people do not use street names or terms like north and south when they give directions. Except for a few cities such as Kyoto, streets in Japanese cities run in various directions, so it is often difficult to orient oneself in terms of north, south, east, or west. Also, most streets do not have names. Japanese people thus use relative locational terms such as right and left, number of blocks, public facilities, large buildings, and other noticeable landmarks. Many people use trains and subways where available. It is very common to give directions that start from a train station. When it is necessary to transfer to different lines or a different means of transportation, it is also necessary to explain where the new mode of transportation is going, where to get off, or where to transfer, as shown in the following example:

東京駅で三鷹行きの中央線に乗って、四つ目の駅が新宿ですから、そこでおりて下さい。新宿で中野行きのバスに乗りかえて、一つ目のバスていでおりて下さい。

Take the Chuo Line bound for Mitaka at Tokyo Station and get off at Shinjuku Station, which is the fourth station from Tokyo Station. Then, at Shinjuku, transfer to the bus bound for Nakano, and get off at the first stop.

Common expressions used in asking for directions:

あのう、すみません。アメリカ大使館に行きたいんですけど。
<small>たいし</small>

Excuse me, but I want to go to the U.S. Embassy.

あのう、すみません。このへんにガソリンスタンドはありますか。

Excuse me, but is there a gas station around here?

あのう、すみません。郵便局はどこですか。

Excuse me, but where is the post office?

あのう、すみません。新宿まで行きたいんですが、どう行ったらいいでしょうか。
<small>しんじゅく</small>

Excuse me. I want to go to Shinjuku. How can I get there?

Use the following expressions to ask how long it takes to get to a specified place:

東京駅から新宿まで、バスで何分ぐらい／どのぐらいかかりますか。
<small>きょうえき　　しんじゅく</small>

How many minutes/How long does it take to go from Tokyo Station to Shinjuku by bus?

歩いてどのぐらいかかりますか。

How long does it take on foot?

大阪から東京まで新幹線で何時間ぐらい／どのぐらいかかりますか。
<small>さか　　　きょう　　　しんかんせん</small>

How many hours/How long does it take from Osaka to Tokyo by the Shinkansen Express?

To ask for specific buses, lines, tracks, or terminals, use:

新宿行きの電車は何番線ですか。
<small>しんじゅくい　　しゃ　　ばんせん</small>

Which track does the Shinjuku train leave from?

中央線の新宿行きは何番線ですか。
<small>ちゅうおうせん　しんじゅくい　　ばんせん</small>

Which track is the Chuo Line train bound for Shinjuku?

新宿行きのバスはどれですか。
しんじゅく い
Which bus goes to Shinjuku?

新宿行きのバスはそのターミナルから出ますか。
しんじゅく い
Does the Shinjuku bus leave from that terminal?

Finally, it is very important to confirm your understanding using the confirmatory expressions introduced in Chapter 5 as well as the あいづち in Chapters 2 and 3 in *Nakama* 1.

練習

A. 下の地図を見て下さい。地図には建物の名前が書いてありません。会話を
ちず　　　　　　ちず　　　　たて
聞いて、建物の名前を地図に書いて下さい。
たて　　　　　　ちず

Example:　A:　あのう、このへんにそば屋がありますか。

B:　駅を出るとすぐに大きい道路があります。
えき　　　　　　　　　や　　どうろ
そば屋は道路をわたったところの右側のかどにありますよ。
や　どうろ　　　　　　　　　　　みぎがわ

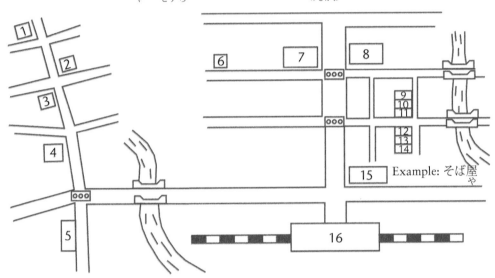

B. Listen to this series of six answers to questions. On a separate sheet of paper, write appropriate questions asking for directions that would have led to these answers.

C. Work with a partner. Ask your partner how to get from one place on the map on page 237 to another place. (Decide where to start first.) Take notes on what your partner says, but don't look at the map. Make sure to confirm your understanding. Then look at the map and verify the locations.

D. Work with a partner. Ask your partner how to get from the station to various places on the map used with Exercise C. Take notes on what your partner says, but don't look at the map. Make sure to confirm your understanding using あいづち and other confirmatory expressions. Then use your notes to trace a route on the map to verify what you have understood.

漢字

Importance of pronunciation in letter identification and kanji words

Native speakers are implicitly aware of the sound and spelling correspondence in their language, though how the spelling and sound correspond to each other may be different depending on the language. For example, native speakers of English know the presence of the letter "e" at the end of a word may affect the vowel sound in a one-syllable words like the following:

cap cape   mat mate   hat hate   pin pine   kit kite
win wine   sit site   not note   pet Pete   cut cute

Native speakers of alphabetic languages such as English rely heavily on sound information when processing written letters and words. For example, it takes more time to identify pronounceable non-words than unpronounceable non-words because native speakers try to process sound information if the word is pronounceable. Similarly, word identification time correlates with the number of syllables in English.

When reading **kanji**, native English speakers tend to process them in terms of sound. This is reasonable because native Japanese speakers use sound information as well, although they rely on other sources of information such as graphic and semantic information.

In order to use sound information, readers must be sensitive to the phonetic radicals. Also, they should remember how a **kanji** is read in other words, especially those words consisting of more than one **kanji**.

Try the following:

1. Try to write the phonetic component of a kanji you know.
2. Try to guess the pronunciation of the following words:

話題　会計　英会話　朝会　親族　作家　半人前　語学　学友　親友
晴天　毎回　出番　間食　海上　漢語　医学　休日　休館　学習　英文
住人　薬局　式場　変人　英国　年度　名人　達人　留年

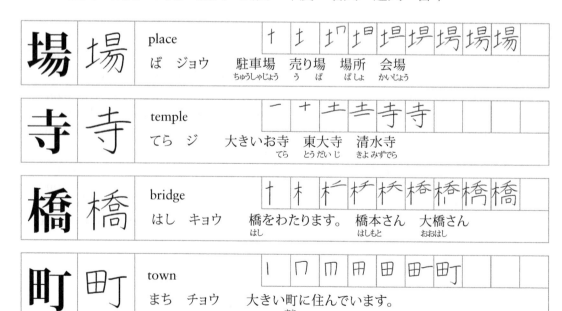

		place									
場　場　ば　ジョウ
駐車場　売り場　場所　会場
ちゅうしゃじょう　うば　ばしょ　かいじょう

寺　寺　temple　てら　ジ
大きいお寺　東大寺　清水寺
てら　とうだいじ　きよみずでら

橋　橋　bridge　はし　キョウ
橋をわたります。　橋本さん　大橋さん
はし　はしもと　おおはし

町　町　town　まち　チョウ
大きい町に住んでいます。
まち

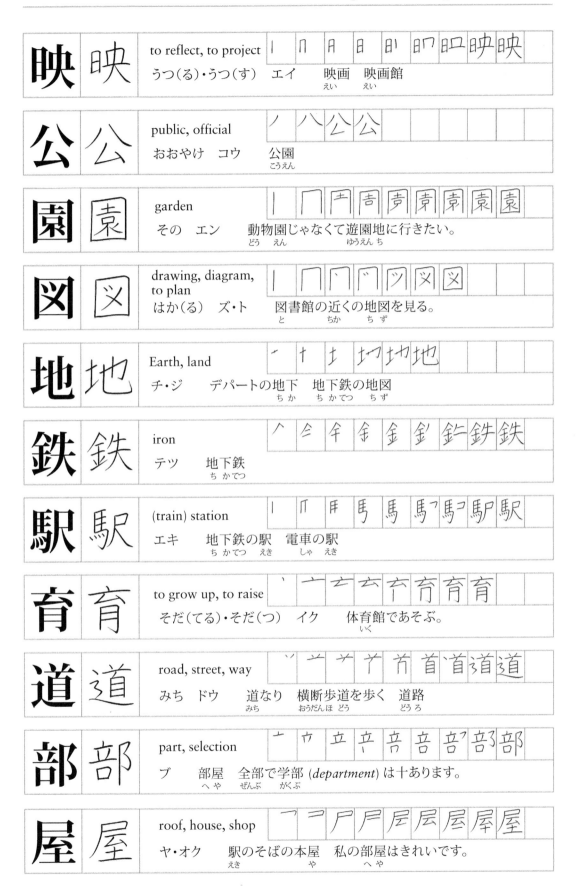

| 映 | 映 | to reflect, to project | 丨 | 冂 | 日 | 日 | 旫 | 町 | 肌 | 映 | 映 |
| | | うつ(る)・うつ(す)　エイ　　映画　映画館 えい　えい | | | | | | | | | |

| 公 | 公 | public, official | ノ | 八 | 公 | 公 | | | | | |
| | | おおやけ　コウ　　公園 こうえん | | | | | | | | | |

| 園 | 園 | garden | 丨 | 冂 | 圭 | 吉 | 声 | 京 | 南 | 園 | |
| | | その　エン　　動物園じゃなくて遊園地に行きたい。 どう　えん　　　ゆうえん ち | | | | | | | | | |

| 図 | 図 | drawing, diagram, to plan | 丨 | 冂 | 冂 | 冈 | 汉 | 図 | | | |
| | | はか(る)　ズ・ト　　図書館の近くの地図を見る。 と　　ちか　ちず | | | | | | | | | |

| 地 | 地 | Earth, land | ˊ | 十 | 土 | 圫 | 地 | 地 | | | |
| | | チ・ジ　　デパートの地下　地下鉄の地図 ちか　ちかてつ　ちず | | | | | | | | | |

| 鉄 | 鉄 | iron | 𠆢 | 全 | 全 | 金 | 金 | 釒 | 針 | 鈇 | 鉄 |
| | | テツ　　地下鉄 ち か てつ | | | | | | | | | |

| 駅 | 駅 | (train) station | 丨 | 冂 | 馬 | 馬 | 馬 | 馬 | 馬 | 駅 | 駅 |
| | | エキ　　地下鉄の駅　電車の駅 ちかてつ　えき　　しゃ　えき | | | | | | | | | |

| 育 | 育 | to grow up, to raise | ˋ | 亠 | 云 | 产 | 产 | 育 | 育 | | |
| | | そだ(てる)・そだ(つ)　イク　　体育館であそぶ。 いく | | | | | | | | | |

| 道 | 道 | road, street, way | ˋ | 丷 | 丷 | 产 | 首 | 首 | 首 | 道 | 道 |
| | | みち　ドウ　　道なり　横断歩道を歩く　道路 みち　おうだんほ どう　どうろ | | | | | | | | | |

| 部 | 部 | part, selection | 亠 | 立 | 立 | 立 | 音 | 音 | 音 | 部 | 部 |
| | | ブ　　部屋　全部で学部(department)は十あります。 へ や　ぜんぶ　がくぶ | | | | | | | | | |

| 屋 | 屋 | roof, house, shop | 丁 | 丆 | 尸 | 尸 | 层 | 层 | 层 | 屋 | 屋 |
| | | ヤ・オク　　駅のそばの本屋　私の部屋はきれいです。 えき　　や　　へ や | | | | | | | | | |

読めるようになった漢字

売り場　駐車場　場所　寺　橋　町　映画　映画館　公園　図書館　地図　地下
う　　　ちゅう

地下鉄　遊園地　駅　体育館　道　横断歩道　道路　部屋　全部で　本屋　車
　　　　ゆう　　　　　　　　だん　　　　　ろ　　　　ぜん

電車　各駅停車　右側　右手　左側　左足　近い　近く　最近　遠い　普通　通る
　　　かく　　てい　　がわ　　　　　　がわ　　　　　　　　さい　　　　　　　ふ

大使館　東京　京都　京成線
　し　　　　　　　と　　せいせん

日本人の名前：半田　川上　白川　町田　道子
　　　　　　　　　　　　　しら

練習

Read the following sentences aloud.

1. A: この映画館のチケット売り場はどこですか。

   B: このビルの前を通って、左にまがった所にあります。

2. A: この近くに地下鉄の駅はありませんか。

   B: この道路をまっすぐ歩いていって、横断歩道をわたった、右側にあります。

3. この町には大きい公園と新しい図書館があります。そして、古いお寺がたくさんあります。川が多いので、橋もたくさんあります。

4. 明日は遊園地と動物園に友達と行くつもりです。

5. 本屋で南アメリカの地図を買いました。

6. 体育館の予約をとりました。

7. 私が泊まっているホテルの部屋は出口から遠いです。

読む練習

上手な読み方

Reading maps

As mentioned in the Culture Readings, Japanese streets and towns are not well organized and directions like north, south, east, and west make little sense when following directions or identifying a location. For this reason, it is important for you to be able to read maps in Japan. In fact, many people, including taxi drivers, use car navigation systems or GPS. Cell phones with navigation systems are also common.

練習

1. Go to the English version of the MapFan web site to get a map of the area around Tokyo Station.
2. There are several symbols on the map. Surf the web to find out what these symbols mean.
3. Go to the corresponding Japanese map. Find out the names of some of the buildings and facilities marked by the symbols and identify the differences between the English and Japanese versions.

東京大学へ行く

読む前に

A. 下の新幹線の時刻表 (timetable) を見て質問に答えて下さい。

	ひかり 200	のぞみ 300	ひかり 126	こだま 404	ひかり 228	こだま 408	ひかり 032	ひかり 232	のぞみ 006	ひかり 034	ひかり 086	のぞみ 010
新大阪	6:00	6:12	6:43	9:00	9:57	10:00	10:17	10:39	10:54	11:17	11:26	11:54
京都	6:17	6:27	7:00	9:16	10:17	10:17	10:41	10:56	11:10	11:34	11:44	12:10
名古屋	7:07	7:05	7:57	!0:15	10:58	11:15	11:18	11:53	11:48	12:18	12:28	12:48
	⊠	⊠	⊠	○	⊠	○	⊠	⊠	⊠	⊠	⊠	⊠
	⊠	⊠	○	○	⊠	○	○	○	⊠	⊠	⊠	⊠
	⊠	⊠	○	○	⊠	○	⊠	⊠	⊠	⊠	⊠	⊠
品川	⊠	⊠	9:47	13:05	⊠	14:05	13:09	13:40	⊠	14:09	⊠	⊠
東京	8:56	8:42	9:52	13:10	12:52	14:10	13:14	13:45	13:24	14:14	14:38	14:24

1. 新大阪から東京まで行く一番はやい新幹線はどれですか。
2. 京都と品川にとまる新幹線はどれですか。
3. 一時ごろ東京に着くためには、何時の新幹線に乗らなければなりませんか。

B. 下の文章 (text) を読んで、日本語で質問に答えて下さい。

　　パークさんは大阪大学の大学院で勉強している留学生です。明後日、研究のために東京大学の大山先生に会いに行く予定です。大山先生は三時ごろ研究室にいらっしゃるはずですから、パークさんは三時少し前に東京大学に着いていなければなりません。

1. パークさんは今どこに住んでいますか。

2. パークさんはいつ東京に行く予定ですか。

3. パークさんは何時にどこに行かなければなりませんか。

読んでみましょう

下の手紙は大山先生の助手 (assistant) の本田さんがパークさんへ送ったメールです。

パークさんへ

　明後日の三時に大山先生が研究室でお待ちですから、東京駅から大学までの行き方を書いておきます。何か分からないことがあったら、私（本田）に電話して下さい。電話番号は 080-1234-5678 です。それでは明後日お会いしましょう。

　東京駅で地下鉄丸ノ内線の池袋行きに乗り換えます。そして、本郷三丁目の駅で降りて下さい。四つ目の駅ですから十分ぐらいで着くはずです。電車を降りたら、本郷通りの方に出る改札に行って下さい。本郷通りはとても大きいので、すぐ分かるはずです。

　本郷通りを左の方に行くと、大きい交差点があります。その交差点を通って、まっすぐ行くと、右側に赤い門が見えます。門の前に横断歩道がありますから、道路を渡って下さい。中に入ったら、すぐ左に曲がって下さい。大山先生の研究室は、二番目の建物です。三階の305号室です。本郷三丁目の駅から大学までは歩いて十分ぐらいかかります。

読んだ後で

A. 下の路線図 (train map) を見て、パークさんが乗る電車と駅に○をつけて
下さい。おりる駅もさがして下さい。

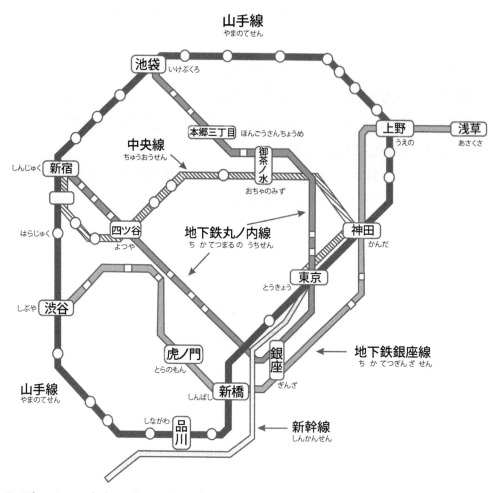

B. The picture below shows the subway station and Hongodori. Draw a line from the
station to the approximate location of Professor Oyama's office.

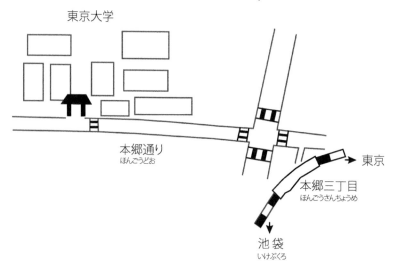

C. 地下鉄では一つの駅からつぎの駅まで3分ぐらいかかります。東京駅から東京大学までどのくらいかかるか言って下さい。

D. 三時に大山先生の研究室に行くためには、パークさんは何時の新幹線に乗らなければなりませんか。260ページの新幹線の時刻表 (timetable) をつかって言って下さい。

E. Mr. Park needs to send an email to Mr. Honda to thank him for the directions and to confirm his visit. Write an email, being sure to include the following information:

1. Date
2. Expression of thanks
3. Departure time of train from Osaka
4. Arrival time in Tokyo
5. Estimated arrival time at Tokyo University
6. What Mr. Park will do if he cannot get there on time
7. Say that he is looking forwarded to meeting them. （お会い出来るのをたのしみにしております。）

総合練習
そうごう

A. 私の家

1. Work with a partner. Invite your partner for dinner and give him or her directions to your home. First, decide on a starting point. Draw a map and give directions as though you were in Japan, without using street names or expressions such as north, south, east, or west. Your partner should take notes while confirming the directions. Then he or she should also draw a map. Compare the two maps to verify how accurately you have given the directions.
2. Repeat the above activity, using another local place as a destination (parent's house, grandparent's house, friend's house, etc.).

B. 成田空港で (At Narita Airport)
なりた

1. Ms. Brown and Mr. Jones have just arrived at Narita Airport. Mr. Jones calls up his Japanese friend. Listen to the conversation between Mr. Jones and the friend and identify the friend's name and why Mr. Jones called her.

名前：＿＿＿＿＿＿＿＿＿＿＿＿＿＿＿＿＿＿＿＿＿＿＿＿＿＿＿＿

理由：＿＿＿＿＿＿＿＿＿＿＿＿＿＿＿＿＿＿＿＿＿＿＿＿＿＿＿＿
りゆう

2. Listen to the conversation again and answer the following questions.

   a. ジョーンズさんは何で（どうやって）行くつもりですか。
   b. ジョーンズさんの友達によると京成線とJR線とどちらのほうが便利ですか。どちらの方がはやいですか。
      せいせん　　　せん　　　　　　　　　　　　　　　　　　　　　り
   c. ジョーンズさんは、新宿で何をしますか。
      しんじゅく

3.　Work with a partner. Imagine you and your partner have just arrived at Narita Airport. You are staying at the Plaza Hotel in Shinjuku (see the map on page 233). Look at the following information about the transportation services from Narita to downtown Tokyo. Discuss with your partner how you would go to Shinjuku.

成田空港　————————————　日暮里　————————————　新宿
なりた　　　京成アクセス特急（66分, 1240円）　にっぽり　JR（20分, 200円）　しんじゅく
　　　　　せい　　　　　とっきゅう

成田空港　————————————　日暮里　————————————　新宿
なりた　　　成田スカイライナー（36分, 2470円）　にっぽり　JR（20分, 200円）　しんじゅく
　　　　　なりた

成田空港　————————————　東京　————————————　新宿
なりた　　　JR 成田エクスプレス（58分, 3020円）　JR（15分, 200円）　しんじゅく
　　　　　　　なりた

成田空港　————————————————————————————　新宿
なりた　　　　　　　リムジンバス（115分, 3,100円）　しんじゅく

ロールプレイ

1. You are looking for a mailbox. Ask a passerby where you can find one.
2. A Japanese student wants to go to the student union and a bookstore. Give him or her directions.
3. You are new to town. Ask your friends about good restaurants, shops, etc. Ask how to get to each place and how long it takes.
4. You are in Tokyo Station. You want to go to Asakusa. Ask a passerby which train to take, whether you need to transfer, and how long it takes to get there. Use the diagram showing the Tokyo Station terminal on page 228.

Chapter 6

第六課
だい・か

KPG Payless2/Shutterstock.com

贈り物
おく もの
Gifts

単語
たん

Nouns

えさ	餌	food (for animals, fish)
おいわい	お祝い	congratulatory gift
おかし	お菓子	confectionary, sweets
おかえし	お返し	thank-you gift
おきもの	置物	ornament placed in an alcove, desk, cabinet, etc., such as figurines, clocks, pottery, and other art pieces
おくりもの	贈り物	gift
おじさん		middle-aged man, someone else's uncle, also used when speaking to one's own uncle
おじいさん		elderly man
おせいぼ	お歳暮	end-of-year gift exchange
おちゅうげん	お中元	mid-year gift exchange
おばさん		middle-aged woman, someone else's aunt, also used when speaking to one's own aunt
おばあさん		elderly woman
おみまい	お見舞い	sympathy gift
おもちゃ		toy
おれい	お礼	thank-you gift
カーネーション		carnation
キャンディ		candy
きんじょ	近所	neighborhood, 近所の人 きんじょ neighbor
けしょうひん	化粧品	cosmetics, also use コスメ cosmetics
こうはい	後輩	one's junior at a school, university, office, etc.
コーヒーカップ		coffee cup, mug
じょうし	上司	boss, workplace superior
しょうせつ	小説	novel
しょっき	食器	dishes
スイーツ		sweets
せっけん	石鹸	soap
せんぱい	先輩	one's senior at a school, university, office, etc.
タオル		towel
タブレット		tablet computer
チケット		ticket for entertainment such as movies, theaters, and concerts

ちちのひ	父の日	Father's Day
どうりょう	同僚	co-worker, colleague
どうぶつ	動物	animal
DVD ディーブイディー		DVD
にんぎょう	人形	doll
ぬいぐるみ		stuffed animal
パソコン		personal computer
はちうえ	鉢植え	potted plant, house plant
はな	花	flower
ははのひ	母の日	Mother's Day
ばら／バラ	薔薇	rose
バレンタインデー		Valentine's Day
ぶか	部下	junior employee, subordinate
ペット		pet
フルーツ		fruit
ボール		ball
ようふく	洋服	Western clothes (not traditional Japanese attire)
リボン		ribbon, リボンをかける to put on a ribbon
ワイングラス		wine glass

い-adjectives

| おもい | 重い | heavy |
| かるい | 軽い | light |

な-adjectives

| たいせつ（な） | 大切（な） | precious, important |

う-verbs

いただく	頂く／戴く	to receive
えらぶ	選ぶ	to choose
かう	飼う	to raise, keep (an animal)
くださる	下さる	to give (from a social superior to me or a person in my in-group)
つつむ	包む	to wrap
やる		to give (to a socially subordinate person)
よろこぶ	喜ぶ	to be pleased

る-verbs

| あげる | | to give (to a socially equal person) |

| くれる | | to give (to a socially equal or subordinate in-group person) |
| さしあげる | 差し上げる | to give (to a socially superior out-group person) |

Particles

| に | | from 〜にもらう（〜からもらう）to receive something from 〜 |

Prefixes

| こ〜 | 子〜 | baby 〜, 子犬 puppy, 子猫 kitten |

Suffixes

| 〜いわい | 祝い | congratulatory gift, 結婚祝い wedding gift, 就職祝い gift for getting a new job, 卒業祝い graduation gift |
| 〜さ | | suffix to convert an adjective to a noun for measurement 大きさ (size) 高さ (height) ながさ (length) おもさ (weight) |

Expressions

あまりきをつかわないでください。 あまり気を遣／使わないで下さい。		Please don't put yourself out for me.
おきをつかわせてしまいまして。 お気を遣／使わせてしまいまして。		You shouldn't have gone to so much trouble for me/us.
（そんな）おきをつかわないでください。 （そんな）お気を遣／使わないで下さい。		Please don't go to so much trouble.
おすきだとよろしいのですが。 お好きだとよろしいのですが。		I hope this will be to your liking.
おれいにとおもいまして。 お礼にと思いまして。		I thought I would make this a token of my appreciation.
おめでとうございます。		Congratulations!
（そんな）しんぱいしないでください。 （そんな）心配しないで下さい。		Please don't go to so much trouble.
せわになる・（お）せわになる（お）世話になる		to be cared for or helped by somebody
たいしたものじゃありませんから たいした物じゃありませんから		It is of little value.
ほんのきもちですから	ほんの気持ちですから	Just a token of my appreciation.
ほんのすこしですから	ほんの少しですから	It's not such a big deal, just a little bit . . .
やくにたつ	役に立つ	useful

単語の練習
たん

A. 贈り物　Gifts
おく　もの

お菓子／スイーツ か し sweets	キャンディ candy	けしょうひん cosmetics	フルーツ fruit	はちうえ potted plant
花 はな flowers	カーネーション carnation	ばら／バラ rose	動物 どうぶつ animal	ペット pet	子犬 こ いぬ puppy
子ねこ こ kitten	えさ food (for pets)	置物 おきもの ornament	おもちゃ toy	人形 にんぎょう doll	ぬいぐるみ stuffed animal
ボール ball	パソコン PC	タブレット tablet PC	小説 しょうせつ novel	DVD DVD	チケット ticket	洋服 ようふく Western clothes
食器 しょっき dishes	コーヒーカップ coffee cup	ワイングラス wine glass	石鹸 せっけん soap	タオル towel

Supplementary Vocabulary: ほかのプレゼント Other gifts

おさら	お皿	plates
かんづめ	缶詰	canned food
クッキー		cookies
グローブ		baseball glove or boxing gloves
こうすい	香水	perfume
シーツ		sheets, linens
しょうひんけん	商品券	gift certificate
スカーフ		scarf
スニーカー		sneakers
ゼリー		Jello
せんざい	洗剤	detergent
（お）せんべい	（お）煎餅	rice crackers
てぶくろ	手袋	gloves
バット		(baseball) bat
ハム		ham
ハンドソープ		hand soap
ハンドクリーム		hand cream
ふうせん	風船	balloon
ボディソープ		body soap
ポテトチップ		potato chips
ユニフォーム		uniform
ようがし	洋菓子	Western-style sweets
マフラー		scarf, muffler
（お）まんじゅう	（お）饅頭	steamed buns
もうふ	毛布	blanket
ひもちするもの	日持ちする物	nonperishable items
ひもちしないもの	日持ちしない物	perishable items

おぼえていますか。

アイスクリーム　アクセサリー　あぶら　犬　イヤリング　腕時計　絵
えんぴつ　おちゃ　お土産　オレンジ　カード　かさ　（お）金　かばん
カレーライス　切符　着物　薬　果物　くつ　クッキー　靴下　車　携帯電話
ケーキ　ゲーム　けしゴム　こうちゃ　コート　コーヒー　コーラ　ゴルフ
さいふ　さかな　（お）さけ　さしみ　雑誌　サラダ　サンドイッチ　ジーンズ
辞書　自転車　ジャケット　写真　シャツ　ジュース　趣味　しょうたいじょう
食品　新聞　スーツ　スーツケース　スープ　スカート　スキー　（お）すし
ステーキ　ストッキング　スパゲティ　スマホ　セーター　そば　ソファ
食べ物　たまご　たんす　チーズ　チキン　地図　チャーハン　チョコレート
つくえ　Tシャツ　テーブル　手紙　デザート　デジカメ　テレビ　天ぷら
電話　時計　トマト　ドレス　にく　人参　ネクタイ　ねこ　ネックレス
バスケットボール　バナナ　パン　パンツ　ハンバーガー　ビール　ピザ
ビデオ　服　ふとん　フライドチキン　ブラウス　プレゼント　文房具　ベッド

ベルト　ペン　帽子　ボールペン　本　本棚　マッサージ　水　ミルク　メール
物　やさい　指輪　ラーメン　ランチ　りんご　レタス　ワイン　ワンピース

Activity 1　下の場所にはどんな物があるか、何をよく見るか言って下さい。

Example:　リビングルームにはたいていソファやテーブルがあります。

場所	よくある物や見る物
リビングルーム	
ベッドルーム	
お風呂 (ふろ)	
キッチン	
げんかん (entrance) (to house or building)	
子供の部屋	
体育館	
教室 (しつ)	
公園	
遊園地 (ゆう)	
動物園 (どうぶつ)	
博物館 (はく)	
美術館 (びじゅつ)	

Activity 2　List the words that fit in the following categories.

カテゴリー	物の名前
食べ物	
飲み物	
服 ふく	
アクセサリー	
動物 どうぶつ	
植物 (plants) しょくぶつ	
きかい (machines)	
文房具 ぼうぐ	
読み物 (reading matter)	
おもちゃ	

B. 贈り物をあげる人、もらう人　Gift givers and recipients
おく　もの

おばさん	middle-aged woman, someone else's aunt
おじさん	middle-aged man, someone else's uncle
おばあさん	elderly woman
おじいさん	elderly man
近所の人 きんじょ	neighbor
（お）世話になった人 せ わ	someone who has helped me
上司 じょう し	boss
同僚 どうりょう	co-worker, colleague
部下 ぶ か	junior employee, subordinate
先輩 せんぱい	one's senior at a school, university, or office
後輩 こうはい	one's junior at a school, university, or office

おぼえていますか。

家族　社長　先生　友達　祖父　祖母　父　お父さん　母　お母さん　（ご）主人
　　ちょう　　　　　　　　 そ ふ　そ ぼ　　　　　　　　　　　　　　　　　　　　　　しゅ
つま　おくさん　姉　お姉さん　兄　お兄さん　弟　弟さん　妹　妹さん

Activity 3　下にてきとうな (appropriate) 言葉を書いて下さい。

1. 一緒に仕事をしている人を＿＿＿＿＿＿と言います。
2. 八十さいぐらいの女の人を＿＿＿＿＿＿と言って、同じ年ぐらいの男の人を＿＿＿＿＿＿と言います。
3. 会社で自分より上の人を＿＿＿＿＿＿と言います。
4. 自分より後に大学に入学した人を＿＿＿＿＿＿と言います。
5. 高校の先生や、お医者さんを＿＿＿＿＿＿と言います。
6. 会社の同じ課 (section) で自分より下の人を＿＿＿＿＿＿と言います。
7. 自分の家の近くに住んでいる人を＿＿＿＿＿＿と言います。
8. 自分より前に大学に入学した人を＿＿＿＿＿＿と言います。
9. 四十さいぐらいの女の人を＿＿＿＿＿＿と言って、同じ年ぐらいの男の人を＿＿＿＿＿＿と言います。

Activity 4　日本語で質問に答えて下さい。

1. どんな人にお世話になったことがありますか。
2. 何さいぐらいになると、「おじさん」と言いますか。
3. 何さいぐらいになると、「おばあさん」と言いますか。
4. どんな後輩や先輩がいますか。
5. 自分はどんな先輩だと思いますか。
6. 近所にどんな人が住んでいますか。

C. 贈り物をする時に使う言葉　Gift-giving vocabulary

えらぶ　to select　リボンをかける　to put a ribbon on　つつむ　to wrap　よろこぶ　to be pleased

大切な　precious, important
やくにたつ　useful
おめでとう（ございます）　Congratulations

おぼえていますか。

あおい　あかい　明るい　温かい　新しい　あまい　いい　うれしい　おいしい
大きい　おもしろい　かっこいい　かなしい　からい　かわいい　黄色い
くろい　しろい　高い　楽しい　小さい　茶色い　つまらない　冷たい　ながい
古い　みじかい　安い　わかい　きらいな　きれいな　しずかな　好きな
大事な　便利な　有名な　りっぱな　送る　買う　かえす　（お金が）かかる
書く　きまる　きめる　さがす　知っている　作る　つける　取る

Activity 5　日本語で質問に答えて下さい。

1. 何か大切にしている物がありますか。どんな物を大切にしていますか。
2. 日本語の勉強にはどんな物がやくにたちますか。
3. 父の日のプレゼントにどんな物をえらびましたか。
4. 日本ではお祝いをする時、「おめでとうございます」とよく言います。あなたの国では何と言いますか。
5. 何をしたら、ご両親はよろこぶと思いますか。

Activity 6　下にてきとうな (appropriate) 言葉を書いて下さい。

1. 誕生日プレゼントはタブレットにしました。このタブレットは小さくて、とても
   _____。
2. 誕生日プレゼントにリボンを_____。
3. 誕生日ケーキに_____と書いた。
4. その男の子は誕生日ケーキを見て、とても_____。
5. 母は私にとって一番_____人です。

D. 贈り物をする場面　Gift-giving occasions

お中元	mid-year gift exchange	お見舞い	sympathy gift
おせいぼ	end-of-the-year gift exchange	おかえし	reciprocal gift
母の日	Mother's Day	お祝い	congratulatory gift
父の日	Father's Day	お礼	thank you gift

〜祝い　congratulatory gift for 〜

結婚祝い wedding gift, しゅうしょく祝い gift for new job, 卒業祝い graduation gift,
誕生日祝い birthday present, 入学祝い gift for entering school

おぼえていますか。

お土産　クリスマス　結婚　しゅうしょく　しょうたいじょう　送別会　卒業
みやげ　　　　　　　　　　　　　　　　　　　　　　　　　　べつ
誕生日　誕生日会　デート　同窓会　入学　バレンタインデー　ハロウィン
たん　　たん　　　　　　　　　そう

Activity 7　　Work as a class. Ask your classmates what kinds of gifts they tend to give in the following cases and determine the three most popular gifts for each situation.

Example:　A:　母の日の贈り物には何がいいと思いますか。
　　　　　　　　　　おく　もの
　　　　　　B:　あかいカーネーションがいいと思います。

Occasion	一番	二番	三番
母の日			
父の日			
結婚祝い いわ			
病気の人のお見舞い みま			
お世話になった先生 せわ にするお礼 れい			
バレンタインデー			
クリスマス			

Activity 8　　下にてきとうな (appropriate) 言葉を書いて下さい。

1. 日本ではお世話になった人に一年に二度贈り物をします。＿＿＿＿＿＿＿＿は
   せわ　　　　　　　　　　　おく　もの
   七月にします。＿＿＿＿＿＿＿＿は十二月にします。

2. 十二月二十五日は＿＿＿＿＿＿＿＿です。二月十四日は＿＿＿＿＿＿＿＿です。

3. ＿＿＿＿＿＿＿＿は五月の二週目の日曜日ですが、＿＿＿＿＿＿＿＿はいつですか。

4. だれかがしゅうしょくした時にする贈り物を＿＿＿＿＿＿＿＿＿と言います。
   　　　　　　　　　　　　　　おく　もの
   大学を卒業した時にする贈り物を＿＿＿＿＿＿＿＿と言います。
   　　　　　　　　　おく　もの

5. 友達が入院したので、＿＿＿＿＿＿＿＿にフルーツを持って行きます。

6. 入学祝いをもらったので、＿＿＿＿＿＿＿＿のカードを書きました。
   　　いわ

7. 旅行に行ったので、会社の同僚に＿＿＿＿＿＿＿＿を買いました。
   　　　　　　　　　　　どうりょう

8. 日本ではお見舞いをもらったら、＿＿＿＿＿＿＿＿をします。
   　　　みま

E. Nouns derived from い -adjectives

In the case of a pair of adjectives representing the opposite ends on the same scale, such as 大きい and 小さい, when combined with さ, the adjective on the higher end of the scale expresses the measurement of that attribute. When the adjective on the lower end of the scale is combined with さ, however, the resulting noun is limited in meaning to the attribute of the adjective from which it is derived.

High end of scale		Low end of scale	
い -adjectives	～さ	い -adjectives	～さ
明るい	明るさ (brightness)	くらい	くらさ (darkness)
暑い	暑さ (heat)	寒い	寒さ (coldness)
大きい	大きさ (size)	小さい	小ささ (smallness)
おもい (heavy)	おもさ (weight)	かるい (light)	かるさ (lightness)
高い	高さ (height)	ひくい	ひくさ (lowness)
強い	強さ (strength)	よわい	よわさ (weakness)
はやい	はやさ (speed)	おそい (slow, late)	おそさ (lateness)
ひろい	ひろさ (space)	せまい	せまさ (narrowness)
ふかい (deep)	ふかさ (depth)	あさい (shallow)	あささ (shallowness)
むずかしい	むずかしさ (difficulty)	やさしい	やさしさ (easiness)

Activity 9   質問に答えて下さい。

1. 「さ」の前の言葉はどんな言葉ですか。
2. 「さ」の前の言葉はどんなかたち (form) を使いますか。
3. 下の言葉の意味は何だと思いますか。

   よさ　ひろさ　しろさ　安さ　はやさ　むし暑さ　すずしさ　冷たさ
   かっこよさ　わかさ　古さ　やさしさ　おもしろさ　いそがしさ
   おいしさ　痛さ　ひどさ　かゆさ　やわらかさ　すっぱさ　にがさ
   しょっぱさ　あまさ　からさ　楽しさ　さびしさ　かなしさ　うれしさ

Activity 10   Give the antonyms of the words below.

大きい　新しい　高い　ながい　ひろい　しろい　いい　明るい　はやい
多い　楽しい　暑い　あたたかい　あまい
たの

ダイアローグ

はじめに

日本語で質問に答えて下さい。

1. どんな時に友達に贈り物をしますか。
おく　もの

2. 女の人にはどんなプレゼントがいいと思いますか。男の人にはどうですか。

3. おじいさんやおばあさんにはどんなプレゼントがいいと思いますか。子供には
どうですか。

4. 友達の誕生日プレゼントを買う時、いくらぐらいの物を買いますか。
たん

5. 家族の誕生日プレゼントを買う時、いくらぐらい使いますか。
たん　　　　　　　　　　　　　　　　　　つか

上田さんの誕生日プレゼント　*A birthday present for Alice*
たん

The order of the following **manga** frames is scrambled. Read the dialogue and unscramble
the frames by writing the correct number in the box in each frame.

a

b

c

d

e

f

石田さんは道子さんとキャンパスで話しています。

石田：　あのう、道子さん、もうすぐ上田さんの誕生日だよね。

道子：　ええ、そうよ。

石田：　もうプレゼント買った？

道子：　ううん、まだ。

石田：　ぼくも、まだなんだ。自分でえらんでみようかと思ったんだけど、何を
　　　　あげたらよろこぶか、ぜんぜん分からないんだ。

道子：　じゃあ、一緒に買い物に行こうか。

石田：　いいの？　ありがとう。

道子：　じゃあ、明後日の午後でもいい？

石田：　もちろん、いいよ。

石田さんと道子さんはデパートにいます。

道子：　予算はいくらぐらい？

石田：　そうだね、五千円ぐらいかな。

道子：　じゃあ、おさいふはどう？　アリスが今持ってるのは古いから、新しい
　　　　のがほしいって言ってたし。

石田：　どんなのがいいかな。

道子：　かわいくて、使いやすいのがいいと思うよ。

石田：　じゃあ、これはどう？

道子：　これは、色もきれいだし、かわいいけど、ちょっと大きすぎるかもしれ
　　　　ない。

石田：　じゃあ、これはどう？　大きさ、大丈夫？

道子：　ああ、これなら、使いやすそう。

店員：　はい、いらっしゃいませ。

石田：　あのう、このあかいさいふ、いくらですか。

店員：　五千円でございます。

石田：　じゃあ、これ下さい。

店員：　はい、かしこまりました。リボンはおかけしますか。

石田：　はい、おねがいします。誕生日プレゼントなので。

店員：　はい、かしこまりました。

DIALOGUE PHRASE NOTES

- もちろん means *of course*.
- 予算 means *budget*.
  よさん
- 店員 means a *store clerk*.
  てんいん
- でございます is an extremely polite form of です.
- かしこまりました is an extremely polite form of 分かりました.
- おかけします is a humble form of かけます.

ダイアローグの後で

A. 日本語で質問に答えて下さい。

1. 石田さんは道子さんに何をしてほしかったのですか。
   いし
2. 道子さんと石田さんはどこに行きましたか。何のためにそこへ行きましたか。
   いし
3. 道子さんによると (*according to*)、上田さん（アリス）は何をほしがっている
   そうですか。それはどうしてですか。
4. 石田さんは何を買いましたか。
   いし
5. 石田さんはどんなのを買いましたか。どうしてそれにしましたか。
   いし

B. Suppose that Ishida is not a close friend of Michiko. Michiko and Ishida would then speak a little more politely than they do in the dialogue. Modify the conversation by using polite speech.

C. Suppose Michiko wants to buy a Christmas present for Mr. Li, but does not know what he likes. She asks Ishida to help her choose an appropriate present. Create a dialogue for this situation based on the dialogue above.

日本の文化
ぶん か

贈り物の習慣　Gift exchanges
おく もの しゅうかん

While exchanging gifts is an intricate part of many cultures, each culture develops different social norms and expectations around it. In Japanese culture, the gift exchange is a highly ritualized social practice. The chart on the following page shows some of the major gift-giving occasions and special terms used for these occasions.

　Among these, お中元 and お歳暮 are considered the two major gift-giving
ちゅうげん せい ぼ
seasons. People give gifts to those to whom they feel indebted such as 上司 (company
じょう し
bosses) and 恩師 (former teachers and mentors). During the お中元 and お歳暮
おん し ちゅうげん せい ぼ
seasons, department stores put gift packs on sale, distribute gift catalogs, and set up special sections and websites to take orders and send out gifts. The customer fills out a form with his or her name and address and the recipient's name and address, and the department stores take care of the rest. Having gifts delivered is quite acceptable in Japan, but it is a nice gesture to deliver gifts personally to close acquaintances or friends. It is considered good manners when you receive a gift to call the sender soon afterwards.

　Money is commonly given at weddings, funerals, as New Year's gifts for children and to mark the birth of a new baby, but it must be put in a special envelope. There are a variety of special envelopes, specific to the different gift-giving occasions.

Setsuko Suzuki / HAGA / The Image Works

　Christmas in Japan is by and large a commercial event. Parents give their children special Christmas presents but there is no tradition of exchanging gifts among friends or other relatives. At the New Year holiday, parents, relatives, and friends of the family give children pocket money called お年玉. On a personal level, the Japanese usually take a gift
としだま
when visiting others' homes or when they come back from trips. It is a nice gesture to bring a small gift if you have been invited to a Japanese family's home for dinner or a visit. When sending a personal gift, the Japanese often write a short message or letter congratulating the recipient on his or her wedding, birthday, or employment. Usually the letter starts with a congratulatory message such as お誕生日おめでとうございます (*Happy birthday*) or ご結婚お
たん
めでとうございます (*Congratulations on your wedding*). This is followed by the appropriate wish for the recipient's happiness and health, such as すばらしい一年であることをおいのりします (*I hope you have a wonderful year*), お二人のおしあわせをおいのりします (*I wish happiness for you both*), or ごかつやくをおいのりします (*Wishing you success*). The writer may then include some news about him or herself and a message about the gift.

おかえし　Reciprocation

Reciprocation is also an important aspect of gift giving in Japan. It is customary to reciprocate by spending about one half of the original amount of the gift received. This custom is called 半返し. In the case of お中元 or お歳暮, however, it is not necessary
はんがえ ちゅうげん せい ぼ
to give anything in return, though a thank-you note or phone call is important.

Occasion	Recipient	Timing	Gift
Mid-season gift お中元 ちゅうげん	to neighbors, friends, someone you owe a favor, boss, relatives	July 1–5 (Kanto region) July 15–August 10 (others)	Practical gift worth ¥3,000–10,000
End-of-the year gift お歳暮 せいぼ	to neighbors, friends, someone whom you owe a favor, boss, relatives, etc.	Dec. 1–31 (Kanto region) Dec. 13–31	Practical gift worth ¥3,000–10,000
New Year's お年玉 としだま	to children who visit you	Jan 1–3	¥1,000–20,000 (money)
Visiting someone's home 訪問のごあいさつ ほうもん	to your host	during the visit	A gift worth ¥1,000–5,000 (usually food)
Returning from a trip お土産 みやげ	to family, coworkers	after the trip	Something your family will enjoy; inexpensive gift or local food to co-workers
Birthday 誕生祝い たん いわ	to a birthday boy or girl (usually children or an adult who is close to you.)	birthday	Something that the recipient will enjoy
Valentine's Day (from female to male) バレンタインデー	to male coworkers; to a romantic interest	2/14	Small inexpensive chocolate (ぎりチョコ) for friends, and specialty or homemade chocolate (ほんめいチョコ) for someone special.
White Day (from male to female) ホワイトデー	to a woman who has given you chocolate on Valentines' Day and to a romantic interest	3/14	Marshmallows, cookies, candies, etc.
Christmas クリスマス	to family members, boyfriend/girlfriend, etc.	12/24–25	toys, clothing, hand made items, etc., jewelry
Hospitalization 病気見舞い みま	to a sick person	during a hospital visit	Practical gifts (pajamas, sheets, towels, money), fruit (but make sure the patient can eat it), flowers (avoid potted plants and white flowers)
Wedding 結婚祝い いわ	to the couple	before the wedding ceremony or at the reception	¥20,000–100,000. Avoid using the numbers 4 and 9; 8 is considered a good number
Getting a Job しゅうしょく祝い いわ	to someone who has just gotten a new job	when informed about the new job	Practical gift that can be used at the job (pen, tie, etc)
Graduation 卒業祝い いわ	to the graduate	around the time of graduation	Practical gift for future use (worth ¥3,000–10,000); if graduate is getting a job or going to another school you do not need to give a graduation gift.

<h1 style="text-align:center">文法</h1>

I. Using verbs of giving and receiving

Japanese has two sets of verbs for giving, 下さる／くれる and 差し上げる／あげる／やる,
and one set for receiving, いただく／もらう. Each set contains two or more verbs. The usage
of these verbs is determined by the social relationships among giver, recipient, and speaker.

A. Using the verbs of giving 下さる and くれる

The first group of verbs of giving, 下さる and くれる, is used when the recipient is the
speaker or a member of the speaker's in-group (someone close to the speaker such as a family
member or close friend). The giver can be anyone except the speaker. The honorific verb
下さる should be used when the giver is a member of the speaker's out-group and is socially
superior to the speaker. Otherwise, use くれる. くれる is normally used among family
members. The social relationships involved are depicted by the following diagram:

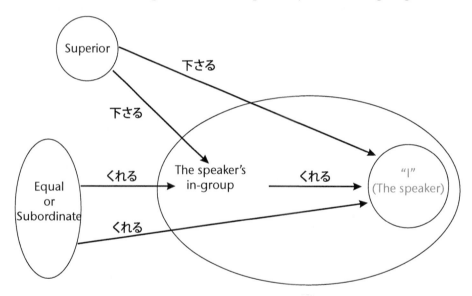

The recipient of a gift is the indirect object and is marked by the particle に, so the sentence
structure is "Gift giver は recipient に Xを 下さる／くれる."

橋本先生は	私に	辞書を下さいました。	*Professor Hashimoto gave me a dictionary.*
そのおじいさんは	弟に	お菓子を下さいました。	*The elderly man gave my younger brother some sweets.*
上田さんのお父さんが	私に	人形を下さいました。	*Ms. Ueda's father gave me a doll.*
その子は	私に	フルーツをくれた。	*The child gave me some fruit.*
花子さんは	妹に	おもちゃをくれました。	*Hanako gave my younger sister a toy.*
母は	私に	洋服をくれました。	*My mother gave me clothes.*

くれる is a る-verb and 下さる is an う-verb. The polite present form of 下さる is 下さいます, not 下さります.

Dictionary form	Plain negative form	Polite affirmative form	Conditional form	Volitional form	て -form
下さる	下さらない	下さいます	下されば	下さろう	下さって
くれる	くれない	くれます	くれれば	くれよう	くれて

近所の人：かわいいぬいぐるみね。   *What a cute stuffed animal!*
きんじょ

子供：おばあちゃんがくれたの。   *My grandmother gave her to me.*

花田：いい腕時計ですね。   *That's a nice watch.*
はな だ　　うで

寺山：先輩が結婚祝いに下さったんです。   *My senior at college gave it to me as a*
てらやま　せんぱい　　いわ   *wedding gift.*

NOTE

- The polite request 〜を下さい (*please give me~*) is an extension of the use of 下さる.

B. Using verbs of giving 差し上げる／あげる／やる
　　　　　　　　　　　　　　さ

The second group of verbs of giving, 差し上げる, あげる, and やる, is used when the
　　　　　　　　　　　　さ
recipient is not a member of the speaker's in-group. The giver can be anyone. The verbs
差し上げる, あげる, and やる are used when the giver is the speaker. The humble verb,
さ
差し上げる, is used if the recipient is socially above to the speaker and is a member of the
さ
recipient's out-group. This might include professors, bosses, or older acquaintances. The verb
やる is used if the recipient is socially below the speaker. It is used mainly when recipients
are animals, plants, or one's family members. あげる can be used for both social equals and
social subordinates. The diagram below shows these relationships.

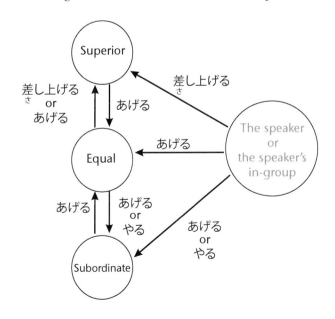

私は 高校の時の先生に お見舞いを 差し上げた。		*I respectfully gave an* **omimai** *gift to my high school teacher.*

母は 父の会社の 上司に おせいぼを 差し上げました。　　*My mother gave my father's boss an* **oseibo**.

私は　　　山田さんに　　子犬を　あげた。　　*I gave a puppy to Mr. Yamada.*

姉は 近所のおばさんに はちうえの花を あげました。　　*My sister gave a neighbor a flowering potted plant.*

キムさんは　　　後輩に　ＤＶＤを　あげました。　　*Ms. Kim gave her junior a DVD.*

私は　　　　花に　　水を　やった。　　*I watered a flower. (literally: I gave water to a flower.)*

母は　　　子ねこに　えさを　やった。　　*My mother gave some food to the kitten.*

差し上げる and あげる are る -verbs, and やる is an う -verb. They conjugate as follows:

Dictionary form	Plain negative form	Polite affirmative form	Conditional form	Volitional form	て -form
差し上げる	差し上げない	差し上げます	差し上げれば	差し上げよう	差し上げて
あげる	あげない	あげます	あげれば	あげよう	あげて
やる	やらない	やります	やれば	やろう	やって

けんじ：　ねえ、母の日にお母さんに何かあげる？
Hey, are you going to give something to your mother on Mother's Day?

アリス：　そうね。私はいつもカーネーションをあげるんだけど。けんじはどうする？
Well, I always give her carnations. What about you, Kenji?

けんじ：　そうだなあ。花より、あまい物か洋服かな。
Well, I might give (my mother) some sweets or clothes instead of flowers.

山本：　お中元はもう送りましたか。　　*Have you sent* **ochuugen** *yet?*
石川：　ええ、橋本先生に送りました。　　*Yes, I sent one to Professor Hashimoto.*
山本：　何にしたんですか。　　*What did you send?*
石川：　ワイングラスを差し上げました。　　*I gave him wine glasses.*

NOTES

- If both the giver and the recipient are members of the speaker's in-group, あげる or やる can be used more or less interchangeably with くれる. The use of くれる implies that the speaker feels closer to the recipient than to the giver and thus presents the recipient's point of view, while the use of あげる or やる implies that the speaker feels closer to the giver than to the recipient or is at a neutral distance between them.

母が弟にお土産<ruby>土産<rt>みやげ</rt></ruby>をくれた。

My mother gave my brother some souvenirs. (The speaker identifies with his brother.)

母が弟にお<ruby>土産<rt>みやげ</rt></ruby>をあげた。

My mother gave my brother some souvenirs. (The speaker is neutral or identifies with his mother.)

● The diagram below shows these relationships.

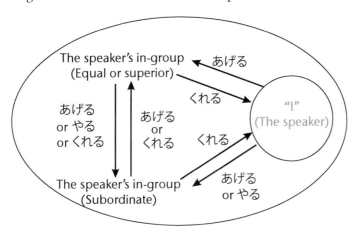

C. Using the verbs of receiving いただく and もらう

Both いただく and もらう mean *to receive*. They are used when the recipient is the subject of the sentence. It is important to remember that the giver cannot be the speaker, but the recipient can be anyone. The choice between いただく and もらう depends on the social relationships among the giver, recipient, and speaker. If the giver is socially above both speaker and recipient, use いただく. Otherwise, use もらう. The giver is marked by the particle に or から. The particle に indicates the source from which the gift originates.

兄は	先生に／から	カードを	いただいた。	*My older brother received a card from his teacher.*
私は	上司<rt>じょうし</rt>に／から	結婚祝<rt>いわ</rt>いを	いただきました。	*I received a wedding gift from my boss.*
私は	同僚<rt>どうりょう</rt>に／から	結婚祝<rt>いわ</rt>いを	もらいました。	*I received a wedding gift from my coworker.*
私は	部下<rt>ぶか</rt>に／から	結婚祝<rt>いわ</rt>いを	もらいました。	*I received a wedding gift from my subordinate.*
田中さんは	かれに	バラの花<rt>はな</rt>を	もらいました。	*Ms. Tanaka received a rose from her boyfriend.*
妹は	父に	人形<rt>にんぎょう</rt>を	もらいました。	*My younger sister received a doll from our father.*

In cases where the giver is an institution, such as a 大学, rather than a human being, the particle から must be used; the use of に implies that the speaker feels close to the giver.

上田さんは	大学から	メールをもらった。	*Ms. Ueda received an e-mail from the university.*
上田さんは	お母さんに	メールをもらった。	*Ms. Ueda received an e-mail from her mother.*

Both いただく and もらう are う-verbs and are conjugated as shown below. Before beginning to eat, Japanese people say いただきます (*I humbly receive*). This expression comes from the verb いただく.

Dictionary form	Plain negative form	Polite affirmative form	Conditional form	Volitional form	て -form
いただく	いただかない	いただきます	いただけば	いただこう	いただいて
もらう	もらわない	もらいます	もらえば	もらおう	もらって

話してみましょう

Activity 1   The following chart shows several gift exchanges between different people. You are the speaker. Describe each exchange using 下さる or くれる.

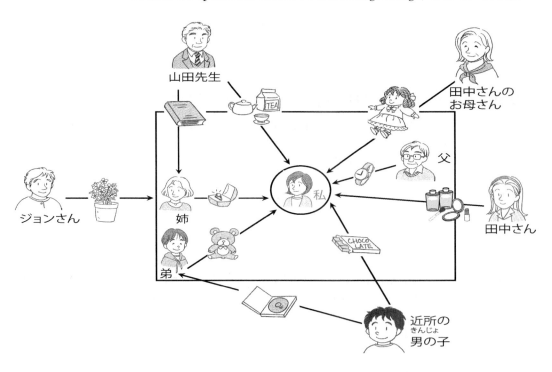

Example: 姉は私に指輪をくれました。
　　　　　　　 わ

Activity 2   Express the same gift exchanges using the verbs of receiving いただく or もらう.

Example: 私は姉に指輪をもらいました。
　　　　　　　 わ

Activity 3   The following chart illustrates gift exchanges among people. You are the speaker. Describe each exchange using 差し上げる, あげる, or やる.

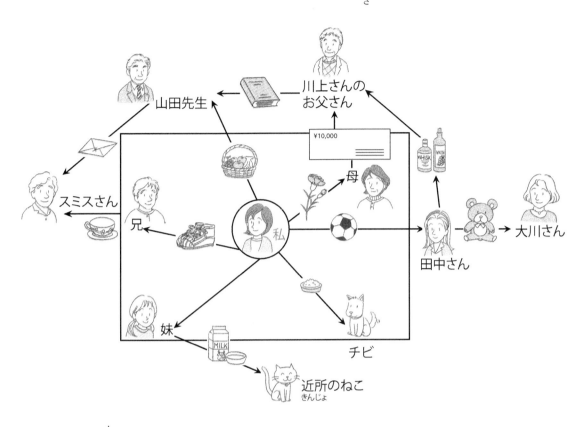

Example: 私は田中さんにサッカーボールをあげました。

Activity 4   Express the same gift exchanges as in Activity 3 using the verbs of receiving. Identify which exchanges cannot be expressed with a verb of receiving.

Example: 田中さんは大川さんにぬいぐるみをあげました。

大川さんは田中さんにぬいぐるみをもらいました。

Activity 5   Work with a partner. The two of you want to jointly give a gift on the occasions in the following table. Discuss what to give and why it will be an appropriate gift. Use casual speech.

Example:　A:　病気のお見舞いに何あげたらいいと思う？

　　　　　B:　そうね。スイーツはどう？

　　　　　A:　でも、食べられなかったら、どうする？

　　　　　B:　そうだね。じゃあ、雑誌はどう？　病院の生活、つまらないと思うから。

　　　　　A:　いいね。そうしよう。

Occasion	贈り物
病気のお見舞い	
先生の誕生日	
近所の子供の入学祝い	
大切な友達の卒業祝い	
母の日	
父の日	
バレンタインデー	

Activity 6   Work with a partner. Ask your partner what kinds of gifts he or she has received on the occasions noted in the table, and from whom. Use verbs of receiving and casual speech.

Example:　A:　誕生日にだれかにプレゼントもらった？

　　　　　B:　うん、父に自転車をもらった。それから、友達に置物をもらったよ。

　　　　　A:　それはよかったね。

	くれた人	くれた物
誕生日		
クリスマス		
バレンタインデー		

II. Expressing the fact that something is easy or hard to do using the stem of the verb + やすい／にくい

やすい and にくい are い-adjectives that are combined with verbs to indicate that an act is easy or hard to perform. Both やすい and にくい immediately follow the polite stem of the verb. For example, the stem of 食べます is 食べ, so 食べやすい means *easy to eat* and 食べにくい means *hard to eat*. Similarly, the stem of 飲みます is 飲み, so 飲みやすい means *easy to drink* and 飲みにくい means *hard to drink*. The subject of the sentence is the item or person that the speaker feels is easy or hard to deal with.

この腕時計は	見やすいです。	*This wristwatch is easy to read.*
このおさけは	飲みやすいです。	*This sake is easy to drink.*
このくつは	歩きやすいね。	*These shoes are easy to walk in.*
橋本先生は	話しやすい先生です。	*Professor Hashimoto is an easy teacher to talk with.*
この大きさは	持ちやすいです。	*This size is easy to hold.*
この明るさは	見やすいですね。	*It is easy to see with this level of light* (brightness).
このコーヒーカップは	持ちにくいですね。	*This coffee cup is hard to hold.*
このいすの高さは	すわりにくいです。	*The height of this chair makes it difficult to sit in.*
日本では大きい動物は	かいにくいですね。	*Large animals are hard to raise* (as pets) *in Japan.*
この食器は	使いにくいと思います。	*I think this dish is difficult to use.*

話してみましょう

Activity 1   Look at the pictures and describe the objects using 〜やすい and 〜にくい.

Example: このハンバーガーは食べにくいです。

Example   1   2   3

4   5   6

Activity 2   Work with a partner. Choose a word from the box below and explain in what way it can be easy or hard, but do not use the word itself. Your partner will try to guess which word you selected. Take turns. Once each word has been identified, see if you can make a sentence contrasting the item with an opposite, as in the example. Work through as many words as you can in five minutes.

Example: A: これは食べやすいです。

B: サンドイッチですか。

A: ええ、そうです。

<u>サンドイッチは食べやすいですが、とうふは食べにくいです。</u>

サンドイッチ　うどん　冷たいスープ　熱いスープ　やきゅうのボール

りょうのベッド　日本語の文法　先生の話　日本の車　子ねこ　英語の辞書

着物　Ｔシャツ　携帯電話　バラの花　日本語の小説

スタバ（スターバックス）のコーヒーカップ

Activity 3   Work with a partner. Following the example, create a conversation between a customer and a store clerk, based on the pictures numbered 1-4 below. Use 〜すぎる and 〜やすい／にくい.

Example   1

2   3   4

Example: A: いかがでしょうか。

B: ちょっと大きすぎて、歩きにくいですね。もっと小さいのは
ありませんか。

A: では、こちらはいかがでしょう。

B: あ、この大きさだと、歩きやすいですね。

Activity 4 Work with a partner. Look at the list of words below and ask your partner what, if he or she were to receive one of these objects, would be the most desirable quality it could have. Your partner should respond using 〜やすい.

Example: A: パソコンをもらうなら、どんなのがいい？

B: 使いやすくて、持ちやすいのがいいね。

1. タブレット
2. タオル
3. ワイングラス
4. おもちゃ
5. ペット
6. ぬいぐるみ
7. お菓子／スイーツ
　　か　し
8. 置物
　おきもの

Activity 5 Work with a partner. You want to buy gifts for the following occasions. Ask your partner for suggestions. He or she will make suggestions based on the ease or difficulty of doing something.

Example: A: 友達の結婚祝いに何かあげようと思うんですが、何がいいと
　　　　　　思いますか。
　　　　　　　　　いわ

B: 使いやすい物がいいですね。
　　つか

A: じゃあ、食器はどうですか。
　　　　しょっき

B: ああ、それはいいですね。

1. 友達／結婚祝い
　　　　いわ
2. 先生／お中元
　　　　ちゅうげん
3. 会社の同僚／お土産
　　　どうりょう　みやげ
4. 近所の子供／クリスマス
　きんじょ

5. 会社の上司／お見舞い
　　　じょうし　み ま
6. お父さん／父の日
7. 友達／結婚祝いのおかえし
　　　　いわ

III. Listing actions and states, and implying a reason, using the plain form + し

The connective particle し lists two or more mutually compatible states or facts. It can be used to list characteristics or factors that lead to a result or conclusion. The use of し is similar in some respects to the て-form, but し conveys more of a sense of making a list than て. The て-form can be used to connect states, and also to express a chronological sequence leading to a conclusion. On the other hand, the use of し suggests states that are being listed in no particular order.

A. Listing actions and states

スミスさんはやさしいし、きれいだし、親切です。

Ms. Smith is gentle, pretty, and kind as well.

この石鹸は安いし、使いやすいです。
　せっけん　　　　つか

This soap is inexpensive and easy to use.

この子ねこは元気がないし、いつも寝ています。　*This kitten is not energetic and is always sleeping.*

ねこもかっているし、犬もかっている。　*I keep both a cat and dog.*

私はおさけも飲まないし、たばこもすいません。　*I don't drink, nor do I smoke.*

お見舞いに上司から花をいただいたし、同僚からフルーツももらった。
When I was sick, I received flowers from my boss and fruit from my colleagues.

映画のチケットは買えなかったし、電車にもおくれたし、いやな一日だった。
It was a bad day because I couldn't buy a ticket for the movie, and I was late for the train.

し is preceded by the plain form of verbs and adjectives, which may be in the affirmative, negative, present tense, or past tense form.

		Present		Past	
		Affirmative	**Negative**	**Affirmative**	**Negative**
Verbs	つつむ (*to wrap*)	つつむし	つつまないし	つつんだし	つつまなかったし
い-adjectives	いい	いいし	よくないし	よかったし	よくなかったし
な-adjectives	大切な (*precious*)	大切だし	大切じゃないし	大切だったし	大切じゃなかったし
Copula verbs	お礼だ (*thank-you gift*)	お礼だし	お礼じゃないし	お礼だったし	お礼じゃなかったし

し can be used to imply a reason instead of explicitly stating one.

母の日だし、今日は家でごはんを食べます。　*It's Mother's Day, so I'll eat at home today.* (indirect)

母の日だから、今日家でごはんを食べます。　*Because it's Mother's Day, I'll eat at home today.* (direct)

ペットもかいたいし、プライバシーも大事だし、アパートより家の方がいいよ。
I want to have a pet, and privacy is important, so I prefer a house to an apartment.

トム：　この絵、好きなんでしょ。どうして買わないの？

　　　Why don't you buy this picture? You like it, right?

キム：　でも、今あまりお金がないし。

　　　But I don't have much money, so . . . (usage is more indirect than から *or* ので).

NOTE

- The particle も often appears with し to reinforce the meaning of し. It does not change the essential meaning.

  雨もふっているし、今日は家にいます。
  It's raining, so I'll stay home today. (stronger)

話してみましょう

Activity 1   Combine the following sentences using 〜し.

Example: スミスさんは明るいです。それに、スミスさんは親切です。
ですから、スミスさんはたくさん友達がいます。

スミスさんは明るいし、親切だから、たくさん友達がいます。

1. キムさんが好きです。キムさんはバレンタインデーにチョコレートをくれました。ホワイトデー (*White Day*) にケーキをあげようと思います。
2. そのおじいさんと話したことがありません。いつも一人でさびしそうです。今度会ったら、話そうと思います。
3. 先生があまり好きじゃありません。授業もおもしろくありません。ですから、もう授業に行かないつもりです。
4. プレゼントをつつみました。リボンもかけました。カードを書いたらあげられます。
5. まどはしめました。テレビもけしました。ですから、もう出かけられます。
6. 大学の時、先生にとてもお世話になりました。今も時々先生に会いに行きます。結婚式に先生をよぶつもりです。
7. 道子さんは動物が好きです。犬をかいたがっています。子犬をあげたらいいと思います。
8. 父は、誕生日に何もくれませんでした。いつもあまりやさしくありません。好きじゃありません。

Activity 2   Work with a partner. Below there are three choices each for apartments, tours, and restaurants. Select one choice from each group. Your partner will ask what you have chosen and why. Respond to him or her using 〜し.

Example: A: どうしてアパートAをえらんだんですか。

B: このアパートは安いし、あまり古くないからです。

アパートA	駅から歩いて 20 分	1 DK	30,000 円	築三年
アパートB	駅から歩いて 10 分	2 LDK	78,000 円	築一年
アパートC	駅から歩いて 15 分	2 LDK	50,000 円	築十年

築〜年 indicates how old the building is.

ツアーA	一泊二日	京都	食事あり	六万五千円
ツアーB	四泊五日	京都と大阪	食事なし	十万円
ツアーC	五泊六日	京都となら	食事なし	七万円

Note that あり means ある and なし means ない.

レストランA	イタリアりょうり	4,000円から	ライブあり	バイキング (buffet) なし
レストランB	メキシコりょうり	2,000円から	ライブなし	ランチバイキングあり
レストランC	スペインりょうり	5,000円から	ライブなし	日曜日バイキングあり

Note that ライブ means *live music*.

Activity 3 Work with the class. Ask your classmates what they want to receive from their parents for their birthdays and why. Then report the results to the class.

Example: A: お誕生日にご両親からどんな物をもらいたいですか。
たん

B: そうですね。動物が好きだし、アパートもひろいので、
どうぶつ

子犬をもらいたいです。
こいぬ

A: そうですか。いいですね。

名前	もらいたい物	どうして

IV. Trying something using 〜てみる

The て-form of the verb + みる is used to indicate that the speaker has done something on a trial basis (or experimentally) to see what the result would be. In this usage, みる is written in **hiragana**.

いただいたワイングラスを使ってみました。 つか	*I tried using the wine glass that I received as a gift.* (lit.: *I used the wine glass to see what it was like.*)
この小説読んでみたらどう？ しょうせつ	*How about trying this novel?*
日本の着物を着てみたいです。	*I want to try wearing a Japanese kimono.*

山田：	このお菓子、おいしそうね。食べてみてもいい？ かし	*These sweets look good. Can I try some?*
キム：	いいよ。どうぞ。	*Sure. Here you go.*

山本：	動物をかってみたいんだ。 どうぶつ	*I'd like to keep an animal* (to see what it's like).
パク：	ぼくもかってみたいね。	*I would like to keep one, too.*

話してみましょう

Activity 1   Respond to the following questions by indicating that you have not done the action in question but would like to try it. Use 〜てみたい.

Example: A:　日本へ行ったことがありますか。

B:　いいえ、行ってみたいけど、行ったことはありません。

1.　おすしを作ったことがありますか。

2.　日本人形をもらったことがありますか。
　　にんぎょう

3.　日本に手紙を送ったことがありますか。

4.　ライオン (*lion*) にえさをやったことがありますか。

5.　日本から贈り物をもらったことがありますか。
　　　　　おく　もの

6.　温泉に入ったことがありますか。
　　せん

7.　日本のお菓子を食べたことがありますか。
　　　　　か　し

Activity 2   Work as a class. Ask your classmates what they want to learn or try to do and why. Then determine the most common interests among your classmates and record them in the table below.

Example: A:　〜さんはどんなことがしてみたいですか。

B:　そうですね。外国に住んだことがないし、外国語も勉強したいから留学してみたいですね。

A:　そうですか。

B:　〜さんは、どんなことがしてみたいですか。

A:　私は〜てみたいです。

名前	してみたいこと

Activity 3   Work with a partner. Ask your partner what he or she would like to do if he or she were one of the people or things listed in the chart below, then complete the chart.

Example: A: お金持ち (*rich person*) だったら、どんなことがしてみたいですか。
かね も
           B: そうですね。うちゅう (*outer space*) に行ってみたいですね。

～たら	してみたいこと
お金持ち (*rich person*) かね	
先生の上司 じょう し	
犬 いぬ	
スーパーマン	

Activity 4   Work as a class. Ask your classmates whether they have ever done the things described in the following chart. Write the name of any person who has performed one of these actions on the line under the act in the chart below. If the person you are interviewing has not performed the act in question, ask whether he or she is interested in trying it. Question each classmate until you receive an affirmative response, then move to the next action with a different classmate. This is a bingo game, so the first person to complete an entire row, an entire column, or a diagonal line with names is the winner.

Example: A: 日本の会社で仕事したことある？
           B: いや、ないよ。
           A: してみたいと思う？
           B: うん、してみたいね。 or いや、してみたくないね。

日本の会社で 仕事をする _____	日本のスイーツ を食べる _____	飛行機に乗る き _____	子ねこをかう _____	自分の音楽の じ ぶん おんがく ＤＶＤを作る _____
日本人と住む _____	たばこをすう _____	日本の学校に 行く _____	スペイン語を 勉強する _____	ゴルフをする _____
先生の仕事を 手伝う つだ _____	ハワイに行く _____	バラの花を もらう _____	日本で勉強する _____	先輩の家に行く せんぱい _____
おすしを作る _____	小説を書く しょうせつ _____	父の日にお父 さんと旅行する _____	大学院に行く _____	日本のおさけを 飲む _____
英語を教える _____	日本語でノート をとる _____	日本人形を買う にんぎょう _____	日本のうたを うたう _____	かぶきを見に 行く _____

V. Quoting speech and words, using 〜と言う

In Chapter 12 of *Nakama 1* you learned that the plain form of verbs + そうだ expresses hearsay, as in 本屋はこの先にあるそうです。 (*I hear that the bookstore is straight ahead*). This chapter introduces another form of reported speech using the quotation marker と. The particle と indicates that the preceding clause is a quoted clause or phrase. There are four usages of と言う, some of which have already been introduced.

A. Using direct quotes with と言う , ~ *say "~"*

In direct quotes, what was actually said is quoted without modification and placed inside the Japanese quotation marks, which are "「" and "」".

スミスさんは「すみません。」と言いました。	*Mr. Smith said, "I'm sorry."*
キムさんは「自分でえらんだんだ。」と言った。	*Mr. Kim said, "I chose it myself."*
アリス：山田さんは鈴木さんに何て言ったの？	*What did Mr. Yamada say to Ms. Suzuki?*
道子：「好きだ。」って言ったのよ。	*He said, "I love you."*
アリス：それで、鈴木さんは何て言ったの？	*Then, what did Ms. Suzuki say?*
道子：「ごめんなさい。」って言ったのよ。	*She said, "I'm sorry." (This is a polite way of saying no in this situation.)*

B. Using indirect quote X は (Y に) Clause (plain form) と言う , *X says (tells Y) that ~*

With indirect quotes, what is quoted is expressed in the clause preceding と, which ends with a plain form, and the typical final particles such as よ and ね are deleted at the end of the sentence. In colloquial speech, the particle と is often replaced by って. In a question, 何て is pronounced なんて.

スミスさんは　　　　すまないと言いました。	*Mr. Smith said that he was sorry.*
キムさんは　　自分でえらんだと言った。	*Mr. Kim said he chose it himself.*
山田さんは鈴木さんに　好きだと言った。	*Mr. Yamada told Ms. Suzuki that he loves her.*

上司は部下に部下が書いたレポートはやくにたったと言ったが、同僚はやくにたたなかったと言った。

The boss told his subordinate that his report was useful, but the subordinate's co-worker said that it wasn't.

To quote a question in an indirect quote, use 聞く instead of 言う. Either 答える or 言う can be used to quote an answer. The plain present affirmative form of the copula verb だ must be deleted before the question particle か.

その写真は大切なのかと聞きました。	*I asked if the photograph is important.*
そのけしょうひんは安いと答えました。	*I answered that the cosmetics are inexpensive.*

その雑誌はおもしろかったと答えました。 *I answered that the magazine was interesting.*

その音楽はきれいだと答えました。 *I answered that the music is beautiful.*

川口：絵美さんは、田中さんは明日来るかどうか聞いていました。
Emi was asking me whether you (Mr. Tanaka) are coming tomorrow.

田中：ああ、明日は来ないと言って下さい。
Oh, yeah, tell her that I am not coming tomorrow.

田中：絵美さんは、あの人はだれかと聞きました。 *Emi asked who that person is.*

川口：石田さんはキムさんだと言いました。 *Mr. Ishida said it was Mr. Kim.*

キム：田中さんに上司のお中元は何にしたのって聞いたの。
I asked Ms. Tanaka what she got for a mid-season gift for the boss.

サム：そう。で、田中さん何て答えた？
I see. Then what did she say?

キム：タオルと石鹸のセットをえらんだって言ってたよ。
She said that she chose a towel-and-soap set.

Notes

- 〜か（どうか）, introduced in Chapter 4 of *Nakama 2*, is a type of indirect quote because a question is embedded in the structure.
- The use of 言いました merely reports the fact that something was said, while 言っていました tends to emphasize the content of what was said. The form 言っています also focuses on the content, but it implies that the original statement has not been recognized by the listener or it has not been realized. The form 言います is used to quote words spoken habitually, or to indicate a future action. The tenses of the quoted clause and the main clause do not have to agree.

スミスさんは、パソコンは使わないと<u>言いました</u>。
Ms. Smith <u>said</u> she would not use a personal computer.

スミスさんは、パソコンは使わないと<u>言っていました</u>。
Ms. Smith <u>was saying</u> she would not use a personal computer.

スミスさんは、パソコンは使わなかったと<u>言っています</u>。
Ms. Smith <u>says</u> she did not use a personal computer.

日本人はよく贈り物をすると<u>言います</u>。
It <u>is said</u> that the Japanese often exchange gifts.

明日近所のおばあさんに電話をかけて、その子ねこを下さいと<u>言います</u>。
I'll call the elderly woman in the neighborhood tomorrow and <u>say</u> that I want her to give me the kitten.

- When the particle と is replaced by って in colloquial speech, the verb 言う can be deleted if the subject of 言う is not used.

川口さんは、おさけは飲まないって。

I heard that Mr. Kawaguchi does not drink sake. (lit.: Someone said that Mr. Kawaguchi does not drink sake.)

C. X を Y と言う, *call X Y*

This usage was introduced in Chapter 1 of *Nakama 1* in the phrase 〜は日本語で〜と言います, but it can be used in a variety of sentences as shown below.

Personal computer は日本語でパソコンと言います。   *A personal computer is called* pasokon *in Japanese.*

日本人は personal computer をパソコンと言います。   *The Japanese call a personal computer* pasokon.

日本語ではこれをパソコンと言いますが、英語では personal computer と言います。
This is called pasokon *in Japanese, but it is called a* personal computer *in English.*

山田さんの名前はさとしと言います。   *Yamada-san's first name is Satoshi.*

(Looking at Japanese quotation marks, 「　」)

チェ：これを／は何と言いますか。   *What are these called?*

大木：かぎかっこと言います。   *We call these* kagikakko.

Notes

- Use とよぶ when you state the name of something you have named, such as a dog's name.

  鈴木さんはその子犬をラッキーとよんでいる。

  Mr. Suzuki calls the puppy "Lucky."

  アリスはこの子ねこをミッキーってよんでるんだ。

  Alice calls this kitten "Mickey."

- To ask a question about how to pronounce unknown characters, use 読む instead of 言う.

  (Mr. Brown is asking about the **kanji** compound 自転車.)

  ブラウン：この漢字は何と読みますか。   *How do you read these* kanji?

  　　山田：「じてんしゃ」と読みます。   *They are read as* jitensha.

  (A girl is asking her elder sister about a label in the box witten as お中元.)

  妹：お姉ちゃん、これ何て読むの？

  　　How do you read this?

  姉：ああ、これ、「おちゅうげん」って読むの。

  　　This is read as ochuugen.

- The expression X という Y, which was introduced in Chapter 5, is derived from this structure. X indicates a specific instance of Y, and いうin this expression is usually written in **hiragana** instead of **kanji**.

話してみましょう

Activity 1　Work as a class. When you travel overseas, knowing some basic phrases in the language of the country can come in handy. Choose three expressions from the box and ask how they are said in other languages.

こんにちは　さようなら　はじめまして　すみません　お元気ですか　ありがとう

Example:　A:　～さんはフランス語が分かりますか。

　　　　　B:　ええ、分かりますよ。　　or　B:　いいえ、分かりません。

　　　　　A:　フランス語では「こんに　　　　A:　そうですか。失礼しました。
　　　　　　　ちは」って何と言いますか。　　　　　　　　しつれい
　　　　　　　　　　　　　　　　　　　　　　　　　　　(Excuse me)

　　　　　B:　「Bonjour」と言います。

日本語			
中国語			
スペイン語			
フランス語			

Activity 2　You are thinking of going on a trip to Japan for two weeks and are gathering some information. Your friends say the following. Confirm the information using indirect quotes. Use both casual and polite speech.

Example:　飛行機は ANA がいいよ。(ANA refers to *All Nippon Airways*.)
　　　　　　　き

　　　　　　飛行機は ANA がいいと聞きましたが、本当ですか。
　　　　　　　き　　　　　　　　　　　　　　　　　とう

1.　お中元は七月に送ります。
　　ちゅうげん

2.　日本では、結婚祝いにナイフ (knife) を送ってはいけません。
　　　　　　　　　いわ

3.　病気のお見舞いにお金をあげてもいいです。
　　　　　　み　ま

4.　日本の携帯電話の方がアメリカの携帯電話より便利です。
　　　　けいたい　　　　　　　　　　けいたい　　　　り

5.　東京にはドルが使える店があります。
　　　　　　　　つか

6.　日本のペットショップはとても高いです。

7.　入学祝いをもらったら、おかえしに何かあげなければなりません。
　　　　いわ

Activity 3 Work with a partner. The following street signs are used in Japan. Guess the meanings of the signs, using the example conversation as a model.

Example: A: 一番はどんな意味だと思う？

B: 郵便局って意味だと思うけど、どう？

A: うん、私もそう思う。

1 2 3 4 5 6 7

Activity 4 Work with a partner. Formulate four questions about your partner's gift exchanging experience. Then ask the questions and have your partner restate them to you for confirmation. Your partner should then answer each question, and you should restate the answer for confirmation. Use both casual and polite speech.

Example: A: 先生にお見舞いをあげたことがありますか。

B: 先生にお見舞いをあげたことがあるかって聞きましたか。

A: ええ、聞きました。

B: ありますよ。

A: あると答えましたね。

B: ええ、答えました。

聞く練習

上手な聞き方

Shadowing and concentrating

Listening requires a lot of concentration. If you don't pay attention to what you are hearing, you can lose information very quickly. One way to improve your listening ability is to engage in shadowing. Shadowing is a technique used to train simultaneous interpreters. This technique is found to improve both speaking and listening skills among foreign language learners because it helps them to process information faster. Shadowing also requires a lot of concentration, so it helps learners to sustain their attention to speech.

To practice shadowing, you need a relatively easy audio-recorded story. As soon as you hear the sentence, start repeating it without waiting to hear the end of the sentence. Repeat this process two or three times. You will have to pay attention to incoming words while processing the meaning of the sentence. This sounds rather difficult, and it is indeed difficult for someone who has never practiced shadowing or someone with relatively low proficiency. So, it is easier to practice shadowing with a transcript. As you become more accustomed to the practice, try to do the shadowing without a transcript. The text should be relatively short and easy to minimize frustration.

🔊 練習

Listen to the following stories to practice shadowing. If you would like a transcript, request one from your instructor.

1. Text 1
2. Text 2

いつどこで何がありましたか。

🔊 聞く前に

A. Listen to each short statement and write the name of the giver, receiver, and the gift.

Example: You hear: 父は私にお金をくれた。

Giver <u>父</u>　　Receiver　<u>私</u>　　Gift <u>お金</u>

1. Giver _____ Receiver _____ Gift _____
2. Giver _____ Receiver _____ Gift _____
3. Giver _____ Receiver _____ Gift _____
4. Giver _____ Receiver _____ Gift _____
5. Giver _____ Receiver _____ Gift _____
6. Giver _____ Receiver _____ Gift _____
7. Giver _____ Receiver _____ Gift _____

B. Describe what people in your country do on Christmas Day.

🔊 聞いた後で

A. 上田さんと石田さんがクリスマスについて話しています。 会話をよく聞いて何について話しているか、分かったことを書いてみて下さい。

B. もう一度会話を聞いて、質問に答えて下さい。

1. 石田さんによると、日本ではクリスマスにはどんなことをしますか。
2. アリスさんの家族はクリスマスによくどんなことをしますか。
3. 石田さんは今年のクリスマスに何をしましたか。アリスさんはどうですか。
4. アリスさんはだれから何をもらいましたか。
5. アリスさんはだれかに何かをあげましたか。石田さんはどうですか。

C. Write a description of the most important holiday season for your family, explaining the activities that you and your family enjoy, the guests you often invite (if any), and what kinds of gifts you exchange.

D. Work with a partner. Ask your partner about the most important holiday season for his or her family. Ask him or her what his or her family does together, whether they invite friends and relatives (親戚 しんせき), whether they exchange any gifts with each other, and what kinds of gifts have been exchanged in the past.

聞き上手話し上手

贈り物をあげたりもらったりする時に使う言葉
おく　　もの　　　　　　　　　　　　　　　つか

Phrases used when giving or receiving gifts

When a Japanese person offers a gift, he or she often uses a set phrase. In formal situations, the most common phrase is これ、つまらないものですが、どうぞ. つまらない means *worthless* or *uninteresting* and the entire phrase means *this is a thing of little worth, but please* (accept it). This expression is used even if the gift is a very valuable one. Some people choose to use other expressions, such as お好きだとよろしいのですが (*I hope this will be to your liking*), and お礼にと思いまして (*I thought I would make this a token of my appreciation*), even in formal situations. In casual situations, a simple phrase like これ、～です。どうぞ is used.

Casual　　　これ、お土産／お祝いです。どうぞ。

これ、ケーキです。みなさんでどうぞ。

これ、母が送ってきたんです。少しですが、どうぞ。

Very casual　これ、お土産／お祝い。どうぞ。

これ、ケーキ。みんなで食べて。

これ、母が送ってきたの。少しだけど、どうぞ。

It is very common for the recipient of a gift to show hesitation when accepting it. This does not mean that he or she does not want the gift. Instead, hesitation indicates modesty on the part of the recipient. For example, in the following exchange, Tanaka-san says そんなしんぱいしないで下さい (*Don't go to so much trouble*) to show his hesitation.

スミス：これ、ハワイからのお土産です。どうぞ。

田中：そんなしんぱいしないで下さい。

スミス：いいえ、ほんの気持ちですから。 *This is a token of my appreciation.*

田中：そうですか。じゃあ、すみません。

Other phrases used to express hesitation are:

Very formal	お気を使わせてしまいまして、もうしわけありません。	
	Oh, you shouldn't have gone to so much trouble for us. That's really good of you.	
	そんなお気を使わないで下さい。	*Please don't go to so much trouble.*
Formal	あまり気を使わないで下さい。	*Please don't put yourself out for me.*
	しんぱいしないで下さい。	*Please don't worry about it.*
Casual	そんな気を使わないで。	
	そんなしんぱいしないで。	

After the recipient shows hesitation, the giver can use phrases such as the following:

Very formal	ほんの気持ちですから。	*Just a token of my appreciation*
	本当につまらないものですから。	*This really is a thing of little worth.*
Formal	ほんの気持ちですから。	
	たいしたものじゃありませんから。	*It is of little value.*
	ほんの少しですから。	*It's not such a big deal.*
Casual	気持ちだから。	
	たいしたものじゃないし。	

Then the recipient will usually accept the gift by saying そうですか。じゃあ、いたただきます (*Is that so? Then I will humbly receive it*) , すみませんね。 ありがとう（ございます） (*Thank you so much for your trouble*).

練習

A. Act out the following gift exchanges.

1. A: あのう、これつまらないものですが、どうぞ。お礼にと思いまして。
   B: そんな、お気を使わないで下さい。
   A: いいえ、ほんの気持ちですから。
   B: そうですか。じゃあ、いただきます。

2. A: あのう、これ、クッキーです。みなさんでどうぞ。
   B: すみませんね。でも、しんぱいしないで下さい。
   A: いいえ、たいしたものじゃありませんから。
   B: そうですか。じゃあ、ありがとうございます。

B. Act out the above conversations using casual speech.

C. Work with a partner. Role-play various gift-giving situations with your partner.

漢字

送りがな   Okurigana

Okurigana was introduced briefly in Chapter 9 of *Nakama 1*. **Okurigana** allows for many semantically related words with different pronunciation to be distinguished from one another. It also indicates that some words are derived from others.

The rules for **okurigana** are complex and there are many exceptions. The following are the basic guidelines set by the Japanese Ministry of Education in 1973.

Principle 1	Use **okurigana** for inflected forms of words that conjugate, such as verbs and adjectives Examples: 書く　話す　高い　and 大切な
1-1.	If the stem of an い -adjective ends with し, begin okurigana with し. Examples: 新しい and 楽しい.
1-2.	If the stem of a な -adjective contains か, やか, or らか, begin okurigana with か, やか, or らか, respectively. Examples: 静かだ　穏やかだ (*calm*)　明らかだ (*obvious*)
1-3.	The following are some of the exceptions: 味わう (*to taste*)　悲しむ　(*to feel sad*)　異なる (*to differ*)　明るい　危ない (*dangerous*)　大きい　少ない　小さい　冷たい　同じだ　幸せだ (*happy*)
Principle 2	Use the same **okurigana** for verbs and adjectives, with contrasting or related words, and with words containing a noun.
2-1.	Transitive and intransitive verbs Examples: 動かす・動く　起こす・起きる　上がる・上げる
2-2.	Adjectives and adverbs that contain the stem of the shortest words Examples: 重たい・重い (*heavy*)　柔らかい・柔らかだ (*soft*)　古めかしい・(*old-fashioned*)・古い
2-3.	Words that contain a noun Examples: 汗ばむ (*to sweat*)・汗 (*sweat*)　男らしい (*manly*)・男
Principle 3	Do not use **okurigana** for nouns unless they are derived from verbs and adjectives or from the Japanese number series. Examples: 花　山　川　vs. 大きさ　高さ and 一つ　二つ
Principle 4	If a noun is derived from a verb or an adjective, use the same **okurigana** convention for the original word. Examples: ～行き　近く　晴れ　大きさ
Principle 5	Use **okurigana** for the last morae for adverbs and connectives. Examples: 必ず (*for sure*)　少し　全く (*not at all*)

Principle 6   In the case of compound words, follow the rule for each of the combined words.

     6-1.   Compound verbs and adjectives.

         Examples: 申し込む 書き直す (*to rewrite*) 女々しい (*wimpy*)
                  もう こ   なお   めめ

     6-2.   Compound nouns.

         Examples: 落書き (*graffiti*) 押し入れ (*closet*) 教え子 (*pupil*) 生き物
                  らくが   お   ご   い もの

         (*living being*) 行き帰り 長生き (*longevity*) 早起き (*early riser*)
                                  ながい   はやお

Principle 7   Do not use **okurigana** for the following types of compound words.

     7-1.   Conventionally used without **furigana** in certain fields such as occupations, job titles, postal terms.

         Examples: 関取 (*sumo wrestler*) 頭取 (*bank president*) 切手 小包
                せきとり   とうどり   づつみ

         切符
          ぷ

     7-2.   Idiomatic compounds

         Examples: 日付 (*date*) 物置 (*storage*) 建物 受付
                ひづけ   ものおき   たて   うけつけ

犬 犬	dog	一 ナ 大 犬
	いぬ　ケン	家に犬がいます。　かわいい子犬です。 （いぬ）　　　　　　　　（こいぬ）

花 花	flower	一 十 サ サ 艾 花 花
	はな　カ	母の日の花はカーネーションです。　生け花 （はな）　　　　　　　　　　　　　（い ばな）

形 形	shape, form	一 二 チ 开 开 形 形
	かたち　ケイ・ギョウ	日本人形 　　　（にんぎょう）

服 服	clothes, dress	ノ 刀 月 月 肟 肟 服 服
	フク	洋服　紳士服　婦人服 （ようふく）（しんしふく）（ふじんふく）

辞 辞	word, to resign	ニ 千 舌 舌 舌 舌 舌 舌 辞
	や(める)　ジ	お礼に辞書をあげました。 （れい）（じ）

礼 礼	courtesy	ヽ ヲ ネ ネ 礼
	レイ	お礼にと思いまして。 （れい）

祝 祝	to celebrate, congratulate	ヽ ヲ ネ ネ ネ 初 初 初 祝
	いわ(う)　シュク	これはお祝いです。 （いわ）

誕 誕	birth	言 言 言 言 言 言 証 誕 誕
	タン	誕生日のお祝い （たん）　（いわ）

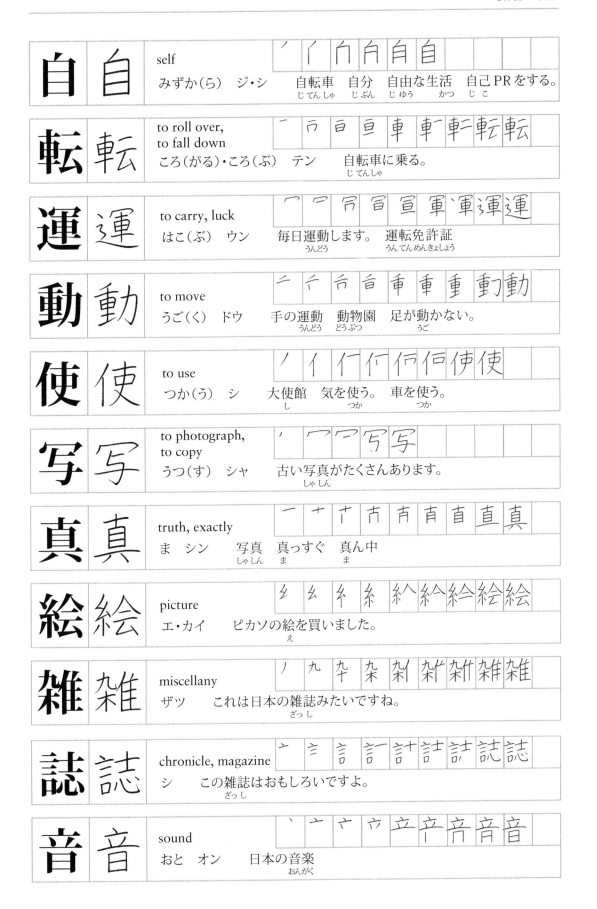

自	自	self みずか（ら）　ジ・シ	′ 个 冂 白 白 自
			自転車　自分　自由な生活　自己PRをする。 じてんしゃ　じぶん　じゆう　かつ じこ

転	転	to roll over, to fall down ころ（がる）・ころ（ぶ）　テン	一 ┌ 白 亘 車 軒 転 転 転
			自転車に乗る。 じてんしゃ

運	運	to carry, luck はこ（ぶ）　ウン	宀 冖 冃 冒 宣 軍 軍 運 運
			毎日運動します。　運転免許証 うんどう　うんてんめんきょしょう

動	動	to move うご（く）　ドウ	一 千 斤 白 車 重 重 動 動
			手の運動　動物園　足が動かない。 うんどう　どうぶつ　うご

使	使	to use つか（う）　シ	′ 亻 仁 行 仴 佢 使 使
			大使館　気を使う。　車を使う。 し　つか　つか

写	写	to photograph, to copy うつ（す）　シャ	′ 冖 宀 写 写
			古い写真がたくさんあります。 しゃしん

真	真	truth, exactly ま　シン	一 十 忄 古 古 有 直 直 真
			写真　真っすぐ　真ん中 しゃしん　ま　ま

絵	絵	picture エ・カイ	⺰ 幺 糸 糸 紣 紣 絵 絵 絵
			ピカソの絵を買いました。 え

雑	雑	miscellany ザツ	ノ 九 杂 杂 剁 剁 剁 雑 雑
			これは日本の雑誌みたいですね。 ざっし

誌	誌	chronicle, magazine シ	⺀ 言 言 訁 計 計 誌 誌
			この雑誌はおもしろいですよ。 ざっし

音	音	sound おと　オン	ゝ 一 宀 立 立 音 音 音
			日本の音楽 おんがく

楽	楽	music, to enjoy たの（しむ）　ガク・ラク	´ 个 冂 白 泊 泊 渔 楽 楽

音楽は楽しいです。
おんがく　　たの

世	世	world, reign, age セ・セイ	一 十 丗 丗 世

お世話になります
せ　わ

石	石	stone いし　セキ	一 ア イ 石 石

石田さん　　石川さん　　川の石
いし　　　いしかわ　　　かわ　いし

説	説	theory, explanation セツ	` 亠 言 言 訁 訁 訬 説 説

小説　　説明する
しょうせつ　せつ

読めるようになった漢字

犬　子犬　花　人形　洋服　婦人服　紳士服　辞書　お礼　失礼　お祝い
　　　　　　　　　　　よう　　ふ　　　　しん　し　　　　　　　　　　　　　　いわ

誕生日　自転車　自分　運動　運転　動物園　動く　使う　大使館　写真　絵

雑誌　音楽　楽しい　世話　お中元　大切な　小説　説明する　近所　部下

日本人の名前：石田　石川　石山　花田　寺山　橋本　絵美
　　　　　　　　　　　　　　　　　　　　　　　　　　み

練習

Read the following sentences aloud.
1. 誕生日のお祝いに、辞書と自転車をもらいましたから、お礼を言いました。
2. 動物園には犬はいません。
3. 石田さんはどんな音楽が好きですか。
4. この雑誌は絵や写真が多いですね。
5. 動物の世話は大変ですが、花の世話も大変です。
6. そのかわいい洋服を取って下さい。
　　　　　　　　　　よう
7. これは中国にある日本大使館の写真です。
8. 女の子は楽しそうに人形であそんでいます。
9. 村上春樹の小説について説明して下さいませんか。
　むらかみはる　き

読む練習

上手な読み方

Making strategic inferences

Vocabulary knowledge is known to be the most significant factor for reading development, and language learners tend to learn vocabulary from reading. It is not beneficial to look up every unknown word you encounter while reading because it can disrupt the flow of reading. So, when you encounter an unknown word, the first thing to do is ignore it and keep reading. If the word is important, it will likely show up again. You may then be able to guess the meaning of the word from the context. If that doesn't work, figure out whether the unknown word is a noun, verb, adjective, etc. Then try to determine the general type or meaning of the word (e.g., an action) from the immediate context. Think about a possible word meaning and see if it works in context. If the sentence makes sense, continue reading. Alternatively, if you wish to confirm the meaning at this point, look it up in a dictionary to see how well you have guessed.

練習

> Read the following text and underline the unknown words. Try to guess the meaning of each word, using the strategies described above. Then check the meanings in a dictionary.

日本ではフォーマルな場面で、人の家を訪ねる時、色々なマナーがあります。まず、冬の寒い日はコートを着ていてもいいですが、そうではない時は、ドアのチャイムを押す前にコートは脱がなければなりません。チャイムがない家では、ドアの前で「ごめん下さい」と言います。ドアが開いたら中に入って、後ろを向かないでドアを閉めます。そして、靴を脱ぐ前に、あいさつをします。「上がって下さい」と言われたら、靴を脱いで、完全に後ろを向かないようにすわります。そして、靴の先をドアの方に向けて、端の方におきます。

贈り物のマナー   The etiquette of giving and receiving gifts

読む前に

下の質問に答えて下さい。

1. あなたの国ではどんな時に贈り物をしますか。
2. 結婚祝いやしゅうしょく祝いにはどんな物をあげますか。
3. あげてはいけない物はありますか。
4. 贈り物をする時、何と言いますか。
5. 贈り物をもらう時、何と言いますか。
6. 贈り物をもらった後で、よく何をしますか。

言葉のリスト

お返し（かえ）	reciprocation, return gift	お葬式（そうしき）	funeral
宗教（しゅうきょう）	religion	仲（なか）	relationship, terms
〜によって	depending on 〜	値段（ねだん）	price
包丁（ほうちょう）	kitchen knife		

読んでみましょう

Read the following passage and write, on a separate sheet of paper, the things you have to be careful about when you give or receive gifts in Japan.

　日本では、贈り物をあげる時には、いろいろなマナーがあります。まず、贈り物の目的によって、あげてもいい物とあげてはいけない物があります。例えば、包丁は何かを切る物なので、結婚する二人の仲を切るという意味になりますから、結婚のお祝いにあげてはいけません。

　つぎに、贈り物をもらう人がどんな人かよく知っていなければなりません。例えば、お葬式に花を贈る時にはもらう人の宗教によって、贈ってもいい花と贈ってはいけない花があります。それから、子供が多い人に何かあげる時は、たくさんある物がいいのです。

　また、贈り物によってはいつあげるか決まっているものがあります。例えば、お中元は七月初めから八月十五日までに、お歳暮は十二月十日ごろから十二月三十一日までにあげなければなりません。

　そしてよくお中元やお歳暮はデパートから送りますが、果物や肉など悪くなりやすい食べ物をあげる時は、いつごろ着くか電話しておきます。

　それから、贈り物をもらう時にも色々なマナーがあります。まず、贈り物をくれた人がよく知っている人でなければ、その人の前で贈り物を開けてはいけません。そして、贈り物をもらったらすぐ電話か手紙でお礼を言います。最後に、お祝いをもらったら、お返しをしなければなりません。お返しのためには、たいていもらった物の半分ぐらいの値段の物をあげます。日本では色々な時に贈り物をしますが、マナーがとても難しいので、よく分からない時は日本人の友達に聞いた方がいいでしょう。

読んだ後で

A. Circle はい if the statement is true and いいえ if it isn't.

1. はい　いいえ　結婚式にあげてはいけない物はない。

2. はい　いいえ　お葬式には花をおくってはいけない。
そうしき

3. はい　いいえ　子供がいる人にはたくさんある物をあげた方がいい。

4. はい　いいえ　あまり知らない人からプレゼントをもらったら、その人の
　　　　　　　　前でプレゼントをあけない方がいい。

B. 質問に答えて下さい。

1. 包丁にはどんな意味がありますか。
ほうちょう

2. 食べ物をデパートから送る時、だれに電話をした方がいいのですか。

3. お返しをする時、どんな物をあげるといいですか。
かえ

C. The reading on page 310 can be divided into two major parts. Where is the division between them?

D. The first part identified in Activity C consists of more than one paragraph, and several transition words are used to signal the organization of paragraphs or sentences. Underline the words and write an outline for this part.

E. Work in groups of four. Discuss the similarities and differences in the etiquette of gift giving and receiving between your country and Japan.

F. When you receive a gift, it's a good idea to write a thank-you note. As with other letters, a thank-you note starts with a brief greeting. This is followed by an expression of thanks and a comment about the gift. Read the following letter, and identify (1) the initial greeting, (2) the expression of thanks, (3) the gift that the writer has received and her comments about it, and (4) the final closing phrase.

毎日寒いですが、お元気ですか。昨日はとてもかわいいクリスマスプレゼントをどうもありがとうございました。私はぬいぐるみが大好きなので、とてもうれしかったです。大切にします。それでは、よいお年をおむかえ下さい。みなさんによろしく。
十二月二十六日

スーザン・ハリス

G. Imagine that you received a new Japanese dictionary from your Japanese host family. Use the letter format in Activity F to write a thank-you note.

総合練習
そうごう

どんなプレゼントがいいですか。

Work in groups of four. Discuss what kinds of gifts would be appropriate for each situation described below. Think of as many possibilities as you can.

Case 1: 来年一年間日本に留学します。日本ではホストファミリーの所に住む予定です。ホストファミリーにはまだ会ったことがありませんが、四十五さいのお父さんと四十二さいのお母さんと中学生の女の子と十さいの男の子と七十さいのおばあさんがいます。ホストファミリーにどんな物をあげたらいいでしょうか。

Case 2: 私は今、日本の会社ではたらいています。今度の休みには二週間ぐらいアメリカに帰るつもりです。日本人は旅行に行くと、会社の人や近所の人にお土産をよく買うそうですね。でも、私は会社の人や近所の人にお土産を買ったことがないので、何をあげたらいいかよく分かりません。
みやげ

Case 3: 今までお世話になった先生が、学校をやめるそうです。クラスで何か先生にお礼をしたいと思いますが、どんなものを差し上げたらいいでしょうか。
さ

ロールプレイ

1. You are in Japan. You want to give an **oseibo** gift to your professor, but you don't know what is appropriate. Ask a friend for suggestions.
2. Your friend took care of you when you were sick, so you want to express your gratitude by doing something for him or her. Thank him or her and offer some help or a gift.
3. You invited a Japanese friend home to spend winter vacation with your family. Your friend wants to bring a gift. Talk about your family and their favorite things and offer some suggestions.
4. You teach English to a Japanese child. Her mother has given you a rather expensive gift in addition to the tutoring fee. You feel a little uneasy about it but don't want to be rude to the mother. Ask your friend what you should do.
5. You are at a department store. You want to give a shirt to your Japanese friend on her birthday, but she is very petite and you cannot find anything small enough to fit her. Ask a clerk for help.

Chapter 7

第七課
だい か

Robert Przybysz/Shutterstock.com

料理
りょう り
Cooking

Objectives	Explaining procedures, explaining important points
Vocabulary	Ingredients for cooking, cooking expressions, kitchen equipment
Dialogue	まきずしの作り方 *How to make sushi rolls*
Japanese Culture	Food culture in Japan, convenience stores, vending machines
Grammar	I. Expressing the performance of two actions simultaneously using 〜ながら
	II. Expressing the idea of *without doing* ~ using 〜ないで
	III. Expressing an open or hypothetical condition using the ば conditional form
	IV. Expressing possibility and capability using the dictionary form of the verb + ことが出来る
	V. Using question word + でも〜 affirmative form
Listening	Understanding signaling devices used in instructions, cooking programs
Communication	Giving instructions
Kanji	Statistical facts about **kanji** and learning tips
	料 理 飯 野 菜 果 魚 鳥 肉 油 止
	始 終 洗 悪 黒 白 青 赤 茶 短 長 焼
Reading	Understanding the characteristics of written instructions, えびだんご shrimp dumplings

単語
たん

Nouns

あじ	味	taste, あじをみる check the taste
いちご	苺	strawberry
おおさじ	大さじ	tablespoon
オーブン		oven
えび／エビ	海老	shrimp, えびだんご shrimp dumplings
カップ		cup, けいりょうカップ measuring cup
かに／カニ	蟹	crab
キャベツ		cabbage
ぎゅうにく	牛肉	beef
きゅうり		cucumber
グラム		gram
こさじ	小さじ	teaspoon
こしょう		pepper (spice)
こめ／おこめ	（お）米	uncooked rice
コーンスターチ		cornstarch
こむぎこ	小麦粉	flour
ざいりょう	材料	material(s), ingredient(s)
さとう	砂糖	sugar
さら／おさら	お皿	plate
サラダゆ／サラダあぶら	サラダ油	vegetable oil (lit. salad oil)
しお	塩	salt
じゃがいも		potato
ジャム		jam
しょうゆ	しょう油	soy sauce
す	酢	vinegar
すいはんき	炊飯器	rice cooker
スプーン		spoon
ソース		sauce
だし	出汁	broth
たまねぎ	玉ねぎ	onion
ちゃわん	茶碗	rice bowl, （お）ちゃわん rice bowl (polite)

でんしレンジ	電子レンジ	microwave oven
とりにく	鶏肉／鳥肉	chicken (meat)
ドレッシング		(salad) dressing
ナイフ		knife
ねぎ		green onion
のり	海苔	seaweed
なべ	鍋	pot
（お）はし	箸	chopstick(s)
バター		butter
ひ	火	fire
フォーク		fork
ぶたにく	豚肉	pork
フライパン		frying pan, skillet
ボウル		mixing bowl
ほうちょう	包丁	butcher knife, kitchen knife
ほうれんそう	ほうれん草	spinach
マヨネーズ		mayonnaise
ミキサー		(electric) mixer
みそ	味噌	soybean paste

う -verbs

あらう	洗う	to wash
さます	冷ます	to let something cool down, おゆを冷ます to let hot water cool down
たく	炊く	to cook, ごはんをたく to cook rice
たす	足す	to add, to make up (for a deficit)
やく	焼く	to bake, to fry, to grill
やる		to do
むす	蒸す	to steam

る -verbs

あげる	揚げる	to deep-fry
あたためる	温める	to heat up
いためる	炒める	to stir-fry, to sauté (cooking)
かける		to pour
くわえる	加える	to add (an ingredient)
つける	漬ける／浸ける	to dip, to soak, to pickle
にる	煮る	to boil, to stew

のせる		to put on, ごはんにのりをのせる to put seaweed on rice
まぜる	混ぜる	to mix
ゆでる	茹でる	to boil, to poach

い -adjectives

うすい	薄い	thin, あじがうすい to have little taste
こい	濃い	thick, あじがこい to have a strong taste

な -adjectives

てきとう（な）	適当（な）	appropriate

Adverbs

すこしずつ	少しずつ	little by little

Conjunctions

さいごに	最後に	lastly, at last, finally

Expressions

みずをきる	水を切る	to drain

単語の練習
たん

A. 料理の材料　**Ingredients for cooking**
りょう り　　ざいりょう

鶏肉／鳥肉
とりにく　とりにく
chicken

豚肉
ぶたにく
pork

牛肉
ぎゅうにく
beef

海老
え び
shrimp

かに
crab

のり
seaweed

きゅうり
cucumber

たまねぎ
onion

ねぎ
green onion

ほうれんそう
spinach

出汁
だし
broth, stock

いちご
strawberry

じゃがいも
potato

キャベツ
cabbage

（お）こめ
uncooked rice

ジャム
jam

バター
butter

マヨネーズ
mayonnaise

さとう
sugar

しお
salt

こしょう
black pepper

しょう油
soy sauce

す
vinegar

味噌
soybean paste

ソース
sauce

ドレッシング
dressing

サラダ油
vegetable oil

小麦粉
flour

コーンスターチ
cornstarch

おぼえていますか。

アイスクリーム　油　イタリア料理　うどん　お茶　オレンジ　カレーライス　果物
クッキー　ケーキ　コーラ　魚　さしみ　サラダ　サンドイッチ　ジュース　スープ
すし　ステーキ　スパゲティ　そば　たまご　チーズ　チキン　チャーハン　中華料理
チョコレート　定食　デザート　天ぷら　トースト　トマト　肉　人参　バナナ　パン
ハンバーガー　ビーフ　ビール　フライドチキン　ポーク　水　ミルク　野菜　ゆ　洋食
ラーメン　ライス　ランチセット　りんご　レタス　ワイン　和食

温かい　あつい　あまい　かたい　からい　しょっぱい／しおからい　すっぱい
冷たい　にがい　やわらかい

▶ **Activity 1**   Guess the meaning of the following words.

トマトソース　チーズソース　チーズケーキ　クリームソース　りんごす

フレンチドレッシング　しょう油ドレッシング　赤ワイン　白ワイン

強火　　中火　　弱火
つよび　ちゅうび　よわび

▶ **Activity 2**   質問に日本語で答えて下さい。

1. 316–317 ページの料理の材料の言葉の中で野菜はどれですか。肉はどれですか。果物はどれですか。

2. 日本料理ではどんな材料をよく使いますか。中華料理ではどうですか。アメリカの料理はどうですか。

3. 体にいいものはどれですか。体によくないものはどれですか。

4. 日本人がよく食べている物は何だと思いますか。

5. 下の料理の材料を言って下さい。知らない言葉は先生に聞いて下さい。

   カレー　　サラダ　　ハンバーガー　　ピザ　　トースト　　サンドイッチ
   チーズケーキ　　バナナケーキ　　バーベキュー (*barbecue*)

Supplementary Vocabulary: 料理の材料　**Other ingredients**

いか		squid, calamari
たい	鯛	red snapper
たこ		octopus
はまぐり	蛤	clam
まぐろ	鮪	tuna
ひきにく	挽肉	ground meat, ぎゅうひき肉, ground beef
むねにく	胸肉	breast meat
ももにく	もも肉	(chicken) thigh
カリフラワー		cauliflower
さやえんどう		snow peas
しいたけ	椎茸	shiitake mushrooms
だいこん	大根	daikon radishes
とうもろこし		corn
パイナップル		pineapples
パセリ		parsley
ブロッコリー		broccoli
まめ	豆	beans
ようなし	洋梨	pears (Asian pears are called なし)
かんづめ	缶詰	canned goods
きょうりきこ	強力粉	bread flour

はくりきこ	薄力粉	cake flour
パンこ	パン粉	bread crumbs
ベーキングパウダー		baking powder
ウスターソース		Worchestershire sauce
オリーブオイル		olive oil
ケチャップ		ketchup
スパイス		spice
なまクリーム	生クリーム	whipping cream
バルサミコす	バルサミコ酢	balsamic vinegar
みりん	味醂	sweet rice wine for cooking

B. 料理をする時の言葉
りょう り

味がうすい あじ	weak taste	味がこい あじ	strong taste
ご飯をたく はん	to cook rice	洗う あら	to wash
焼く や	to bake, to fry, to grill	水を切る	to drain
あげる	to deep-fry	いためる	to stir-fry, sauté
にる	to stew, to boil, to simmer	ゆでる	to poach, to boil
まぜる	to mix	むす	to steam
かける	to pour over	温める あたた	to warm up, to reheat
くわえる	to add (an ingredient)	足す た	to adjust (seasoning)
つける	to dip, to soak	冷ます さ	to let something cool

NOTES

- ゆでる means to boil eggs, vegetables, or meat in water, but にる means to boil or stew in a broth, sauce, or soup.

- くわえる merely means to add something to something, but 足す means
た
to add something to make up for a deficiency. For example, if you have put salt in a soup but still don't think it is salty enough and need to add more, use しおを足す. On the other hand, if you are boiling meat to
た
make a stew and then add vegetables, use 野菜をくわえる.
やさい

- Both 料理をする and 料理を作る refer to cooking, but they are not used
りょうり りょうり
in the the same way. 料理をする is usually used to express the action of
りょうり
cooking in general. On the other hand, 料理を作る is used to talk about
りょうり
cooking specific type of dishes. For example, use 料理をする to ask
りょうり
whether a person cooks at all, as in 料理をしますか. Use 料理を作る to
りょうり りょうり
ask what kind of dish a person makes, (どんな料理を作りますか。) and
りょうり
whether a person makes a specific type of dish (フランス料理を作ります
りょうり
か。).

おぼえていますか。

教える　切る　つける　取る　わかす　わく

Activity 3　Complete the following recipes by using the appropriate verb forms.

1. サラダを作る時は、野菜をよく＿＿＿＿＿＿＿＿＿＿ら、水を
   ＿＿＿＿＿＿＿＿＿＿ボウルに入れます。そして、ドレッシングを
   ＿＿＿＿＿＿＿＿＿、よく＿＿＿＿＿＿＿下さい。

2. ステーキはよく＿＿＿＿＿＿＿＿＿＿方が好きだ。

3. スープの味が＿＿＿＿＿時は、出汁を＿＿＿＿＿＿＿＿と、おいしくなる。

4. カレーライスを作る時は、牛肉とたまねぎを＿＿＿＿＿＿＿＿＿。そして、
   水を＿＿＿＿＿＿＿＿＿、一時間ぐらい＿＿＿＿＿＿＿＿＿＿。その
   後、カレーこ (curry powder) を＿＿＿＿＿＿＿＿＿＿。

5. 野菜はいためるより＿＿＿＿＿＿＿＿＿方が体にいいです。

6. このスープは冷たいから、＿＿＿＿＿＿＿＿＿方がいいですね。

7. バーベキュー (barbecue) をする時は、肉をソースに1時間ぐらい
   ＿＿＿＿＿＿＿＿＿とおいしいですよ。

8. このおゆは熱すぎるから、少し＿＿＿＿＿＿＿＿＿方がいいよ。

Activity 4　Work with a group. One person in the group should act out one of the verbs in vocabulary B (p. 319), and the rest of the group should try to guess which verb is being acted out. As soon as someone guesses the correct verb, the next person should act out another verb. Repeat this process as fast as you can until the group completes all the verbs.

Supplementary Vocabulary:　料理をする時に使うほかの言葉
Expressions used to talk about cooking

つよび	強火	high heat
ちゅうび	中火	medium heat
よわび	弱火	low heat
あえる	和える	to mix, to dress something with a sauce, dressing, etc.
あわだてる	泡立てる	to whip
いる	煎る	to roast
うつす	移す	to transfer
かきまぜる	かき混ぜる	to mix thoroughly, to beat
こねる		to knead
スイッチをいれる	スイッチを入れる	to turn on an electrical switch
とかす	溶かす	to (let something) thaw
とける	溶ける	(for something) to melt
ぬる	塗る	to spread, to paint
はかる	量る／計る	to measure, りょう (quantity) をはかる
はさむ	挟む	to pinch

ひからおろす	火から下ろす	to remove from heat
ひにかける	火にかける	to heat, to cook over heat
ひをおとす	火を落とす	to lower the heat
ふる	振る	to shake, しおをふる to salt
ふりかける	振りかける	to sprinkle
まく	巻く	to roll (as with sushi in a roll)
まぶす		to coat, to dust
むく	剥く	to peel, かわ (skin) をむく

C. 料理する時に使う物　Kitchen equipment
りょう り

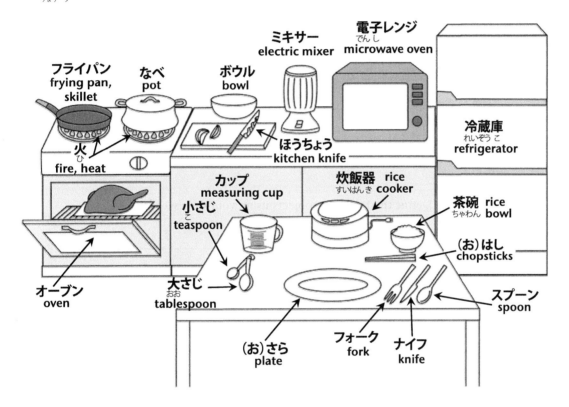

フライパン frying pan, skillet
なべ pot
ボウル bowl
ミキサー electric mixer
電子レンジ でんし microwave oven
冷蔵庫 れいぞうこ refrigerator
火 ひ fire, heat
ほうちょう kitchen knife
炊飯器 すいはんき rice cooker
茶碗 ちゃわん rice bowl
カップ measuring cup
小さじ こ teaspoon
大さじ おお tablespoon
オーブン oven
(お)はし chopsticks
(お)さら plate
フォーク fork
ナイフ knife
スプーン spoon

> **Activity 5**   Based on the examples below, guess the reading and meaning of the following expressions.

Examples:　1カップ　　　いちカップ　　　one cup

1／2カップ　　にぶんのいちカップ　　half a cup

2／3カップ　　さんぶんのにカップ　　two thirds of a cup

1.　1／3カップ　＿＿＿＿＿＿＿＿＿　＿＿＿＿＿＿＿＿＿

2.　1／4カップ　＿＿＿＿＿＿＿＿＿　＿＿＿＿＿＿＿＿＿

3.　3／4カップ　＿＿＿＿＿＿＿＿＿　＿＿＿＿＿＿＿＿＿

Activity 6   Name the items that fit the following descriptions.

1. 肉を焼く時に使う物です。
2. サラダをまぜる時に使う物です。
3. 和食を食べる時に使う物です。
4. ステーキを食べる時に使う物ですが、ナイフではありません。
5. ご飯をたく時に使うものです。
6. ケーキやサンドイッチをのせる物です。
7. 冷たい食べ物や飲み物を入れておく所です。
8. ご飯を食べる時にご飯を入れる物です。
9. 料理をする時に使う物です。これをつけたら、焼いたり、いためたり、にたり出来ます。
10. 料理をする時に使う小さいスプーンで、大きいのと小さいのがあります。

Activity 7   Define the following objects using your own words.

1. ほうちょう   _____

2. なべ   _____

3. フライパン   _____

4. スプーン   _____

5. 炊飯器   _____

6. ミキサー   _____

7. オーブン   _____

8. 電子レンジ   _____

Supplementary Vocabulary: 料理する時に使うほかの物
Additional kitchen equipment

おたま	お玉	ladle
キッチンばさみ		kitchen scissors
さいばし	菜箸	long chopsticks (used in cooking, or in serving food at the table)
タイマー		timer
はかり	秤	scale
フライがえし	フライ返し	spatula
まないた	まな板	cutting board
やかん／ケトル		kettle

ダイアローグ

はじめに

A. 質問に日本語で答えて下さい。

1. 和食のレストランに行ったことがありますか。
   わ
2. どんな日本料理を知っていますか。
   りょう り
3. どんな料理の作り方を知っていますか。
   りょう り

B. Look at the pictures below and do the following:

1. Identify the Japanese words for the cookware and kitchen utensils pictured. If you don't know the word, ask your teacher or look it up in the dialogue phrase notes.
2. Describe each picture.

1   2   3

4   5   6

まきずしの作り方 *How to make sushi rolls*

まきずし (*rolled sushi*) is a combination of the stem of the verb まく and the noun すし.
上田さんはまきずしを作りたいと思っていますが、作り方を知りませんから、これから道子さんに聞きます。

上田：　ねえ、道子さん、まきずし、作れる？

道子：　もちろん。

上田：　今度、留学生センターでパーティがあるから、まきずしを作ってみたいんだけど、作り方が分からないの。教えてくれない？

道子：　いいよ。じゃあ、明日、一緒に作ってみようか。

上田：　ありがとう。たすかる。

つぎの日、アリスと道子さんはキッチンにいます。

道子：　えーっと、ご飯のたき方は知ってる？

上田：　うん。おこめを洗って、炊飯器でたくんでしょ。

道子：　そうなんだけど、おすしの時は、少し水を少なくするのよ。後ですをくわえるから、少しかたい方がいいの。水が多いと、やわらかくなりすぎて、おいしくないから。

上田：　そうなんだ。

道子：　それから、おすしのぐを細長く切っておくの。

上田：　えっ、ぐって、何？

道子：　あ、ぐはね、おすしの中に入れる物よ。たまごとか、きゅうりとか。

上田：　あ、そう。分かった。

道子：　今日はカリフォルニアまきを作るから、きゅうりとアボカド、切って。

上田：　分かった。で、おすしのすはどうやって作るの？

道子： すしずね。かんたんよ。す大さじ６、さとう大さじ４、しお小さじ２を
まぜるのよ。

上田： どんなすでもいいの？

道子： ううん。こめずって言うんだけど、おこめのすを使うの。

上田： リンゴすやバルサミコすで作ることは出来ないの？

道子： 作ったことないから、おいしいかどうかよく分からない。今度作ってみ
ればいいよ。

上田： そうだね。

道子： ご飯がたけたら、すしおけにご飯を入れるの。そして、うちわや扇風機
でごはんを冷ましながら、すしずを少しずつまぜていくのよ。ほら、
出来た。

上田： じゃあ、どうやってまくの？

道子： まず、まきすの上にのりをのせて、

上田： まきすって何？

道子： このたけのシートよ。

上田： あ、そうなんだ。

道子： のりの上にすし飯をひらたくのせるんだけど、むこうのはしまで、ご飯
をのせないで、のりを少し残しておくの。

上田： どうして？

道子： ご飯が先まであると、まけないのよ。ご飯の上にかにとアボカドときゅ
うりをのせて、こうやってまくの。

上田： 上手ね、道子さん。

道子： アリスもやってみる？

上田： うん、あ、でも、むずかしい！

道子： 少しおしながらまけば、きれいにまけるよ。

上田： 本当だ。あ、出来た。

道子： 出来たら、後は、てきとうな大きさに切るの。

上田： 分かった。どうもありがとう。

Dialogue Phrase Notes

- まき means rolled. まきずし means *rolled sushi*, and カリフォルニアまき means *California roll*.
- かんたん means *easy* or *simple*.
- ご飯がたける means *the rice is cooked*.
- ぐ means *ingredient*.
- たまごとかきゅうりとか means *eggs, cucumbers, etc.*
- リンゴす is apple cider vinegar, バルサミコす is balsamic vinegar.
- すしおけ is a special wooden bucket used to make sushi rice.
- すし飯 is *sushi rice*.
- うちわ is a *Japanese fan*, and a 扇風機 is an *electric fan*.
- 出来た means *finished* or *it's done*.
- たけ is *bamboo*. たけのシート is a *bamboo sheet*.
- ひらたくのせる means *to spread*.
- のせる means *to put on*.
- はし is an *edge* or *end*.
- おす means to *press, push*. おしながらまく means *to roll while applying some pressure*.

ダイアローグの後で

A. 日本語で質問に答えて下さい。

1. すしずって何ですか。

2. こめずは何から作られますか。

3. まきすは何のために使いますか。どんな物ですか。

4. すしご飯（すし飯）をたく時、どんなことが大事ですか。

5. おすしをまく時、どうすれば上手にまくことが出来ますか。

6. ぐって何ですか。

7. ご飯にすをまぜる時、どんなことが大事ですか。

B. Look at the pictures at the beginning of the dialogue section, which show the steps for making rolled sushi. Unscramble the pictures so that the steps are correctly shown by writing the sequence number in the box.

☐ → ☐ → ☐ → ☐ → ☐ → ☐

C. Working as a class, use these directions to try making まきずし.

A sushi chef prepares ingredients.

日本の文化
ぶん か

日本の食文化　Food culture in Japan
ぶん か

Food has a special place in Japanese culture. The government officially recognized the importance of food culture through its *Shoku ni Kansuru Shorai Bijion* (Global Food Value Strategy) adopted in 2009. Under this plan, the government promoted regional agricultural and fishing and facilitated the development of tourism and local industries. They also promoted Japanese cuisine, *washoku*, internationally, and it was added to UNESCO's Cultural Heritage List in 2013.

TungCheung/Shutterstock.com

In addition, food education is conducted not only in primary and secondary schools but also in adult education programs in order to promote, or disseminate information about, the importance of food safety for the welfare of the people. As a result, the Japanese people are health conscious. According to a 2014 report by the Organization for Economic Cooperation and Development (OECD) only 3.5 percent of Japanese are obese, although obesity rates are increasing and it is considered a serious health problem. Partly for this reason, the amount of food served in Japanese restaurants is much less than that served in restaurants in the United States, a fact which may surprise some American visitors.

The Japanese demand variety and quality over quantity, and they don't mind paying a high price for good food. For example, the tire company Michelin publishes gourmet restaurant guides for more than 30 major cities including Paris, New York, San Francisco, and Hong Kong. Their Tokyo Guide has listed more restaurants than any other city in the world, with the largest number of starred restaurants for eight consecutive years since 2007 (*Japan Times*, 2015).

Another characteristic of Japanese food culture is that restaurants and retail shops offer seasonal items. In the spring, many stores carry food items related to cherry blossoms, the national flower of Japan. These include cherry cookies, cherry buns, and cherry pastries. A variety of cold sweets and noodles are sold in the summer, and in the autumn, sweet items made from chestnuts and persimmons are very common. These items disappear as soon as the season is over.

The term デパ地下 is used for the basement floor of department stores and refers to the stores' food departments. The デパ地下 is considered crucial to attract a large number of shoppers, so some department stores devote more than one floor to food. One floor may be filled with gourmet sweets, snacks, expensive liquors, wines, or gourmet foods from around the world, while another may offer prepared food, side dishes and fruits, vegetables, and so on. In addition, department stores often offer food tastings and sales events which featire a certain country, or city or region of Japan. This is another way to attract a large number of customers.

コンビニ   Convenience stores

Food items are usually delivered to convenience stores two to five times a day from factories, and items may change depending on the time of day. Because variety is important, these items may be sold for a couple of months and then replaced with new products. This is true even for bottled items, such as water, tea, coffee and juice. So even if you find a drink you like, there is no guarantee that it will be available for more than a year.

自動販売機   Vending machines
じ どうはんばい き

Many different items are sold in vending machines in Japan. These include soda, beer, cigarettes, magazines, rice, and hot noodles, to name a few. There are large numbers of these machines in service 24 hours a day on street corners and in front of stores, and you can expect every one of them to be in good working order.

Kyodo News/Getty Images

A convenience store clerk arranges remedies for hay fever.

文法

I. Expressing the performance of two actions simultaneously using 〜ながら

The ます-stem of verbs + ながら describes an action occurring simultaneously with another action. The actions in the ながら clause and in the main clause must be performed by the same person.

音楽を聞きながら、さらを洗います。　　*I wash dishes while listening to music.*

ソースをかけながら、まぜて下さい。　　*Stir well while pouring the sauce.*

テレビを見ながら、ご飯を食べてはいけません。
　　You shouldn't watch TV while eating.

ワインをくわえながら、肉を焼く。　　*Fry the meat while adding wine.*

ゆみ：こんな所で何してるの？　　*What are you doing here?*

さとる：田中さん、まってるんだ。　　*Waiting for Mr. Tanaka.*

ゆみ：あ、そう。それで本、読んでるの？　　*Oh, I see. So, you're reading a book?*

さとる：うん。ちょっと早く着いたから、本、読みながら、まってるんだ。
　　Yes, I arrived a bit early, so I'm waiting while reading.

	Dictionary form	ます -stem	〜ながら
る -verb	にる (*to stew, to simmer*)	にます	にながら
	あげる (*to deep-fry*)	あげます	あげながら
う -verb	洗う (*to wash*)	洗います	洗いながら
	足す (*to add*)	足します	足しながら
Irregular verb	する	します	しながら

来る is not normally used with ながら.

NOTE

- In this structure, the action expressed in the main clause is the main action, and it is accompanied by the secondary action described in the ながら clause. Thus, in the sentence コーヒーを飲みながら、話しましょう (*Let's talk over a cup of coffee*), the main action is talking, and the act of talking is done while the speaker is drinking coffee. The closest equivalent of ながら in English is *while ~ ing*, but in English the main action may be expressed in either the while clause or the main clause. For example, コーヒーを飲みながら、話しましょう can be translated as *Let's talk while drinking a cup of coffee.* (The main action is expressed in the main clause, and the secondary action is expressed in the while clause.) It could also be translated as *Let's have a cup of coffee while we talk,* where the main action appears in the while clause and the secondary action in the main clause.

話してみましょう

Activity 1   Complete the following sentences by choosing an appropriate phrase from the table below and using it with 〜ながら.

Example: 出来たらすぐ食べたいから、<u>魚をむしながら</u>、ソースを作りましょう。
さかな

なく	魚をむす	携帯電話で話す	本を読む	ノートをとる	下を見る
足す	人に聞く	私の目を見る	地図を見る	タバコをすう	まぜる

（足す＝た、魚をむす＝さかな、携帯電話で話す＝けいたい）

1. マヨネーズを作る時は、＿＿＿＿＿＿＿＿＿＿＿＿油をくわえます。
あぶら

2. ＿＿＿＿＿＿＿＿＿＿＿＿歩いていたら、お金を見つけた。(find)

3. 行ったことがなかったので、＿＿＿＿＿＿＿＿＿＿＿＿その店まで行った。

4. ＿＿＿＿＿＿＿＿＿＿＿授業を受けた。

5. その人は＿＿＿＿＿＿＿＿＿＿＿＿＿好きだと言った。

6. ソースを＿＿＿＿＿＿＿＿＿＿＿＿肉を焼きました。
にく　や

7. ＿＿＿＿＿＿＿＿＿＿＿＿＿歩いていたら、道を間違えた。

8. 少しずつさとうを＿＿＿＿＿＿＿＿＿＿＿＿＿、味を見ました。
あじ

Activity 2   Describe what the people are doing in the following pictures.

1   2   3

4   5   6   7

Activity 3　Work with a partner. Think of three sets of actions you can perform simultaneously. Act out each set for your partner to have him/her guess what you are doing.

Example:　テレビを見ながら、キャベツを切る。

A:　(Acts out a scene of chopping vegetables while watching TV.)

B:　テレビを見ながら、キャベツを切っているんですか。

A:　はい、そうです。

Activity 4　Work as a class. Ask your classmates what kind of things they do while they are studying, eating dinner, etc., using 〜ながら. Discover what habits your classmates have in common.

Example:　A:　勉強する時、よく何かしますか。

B:　ええ、お菓子を食べながら、勉強します。〜さんは？

A:　そうですね。私はよく音楽を聞きながら、勉強しますね。

クラスメートの名前	〜ながら、勉強する	〜ながら、ご飯を食べる

II. Expressing the idea of *without doing* ~ using 〜ないで

The negative verb form で下さい, as in 見ないで下さい, was introduced in Chapter 1 in its use of indicating a negative request. When this negative form is used alone, it means *without ~ing.*

野菜は洗わないで、ゆでてもいいです。 — *It's OK to boil the vegetables without washing them.*

鶏肉に小麦粉をつけないで、あげた。 — *I deep fried chicken without dipping it into flour.*

炊飯器を使わないで、ご飯をたいた。 — *I cooked rice without using a rice cooker.*

練習しないで、上手になる人はいない。 — *There is no one who can become good at anything without practicing it.*

キム：　　おはしもナイフもフォークも使わないでご飯を食べるの？
　　　　　Do you eat your meals without using a knife, a fork or chopsticks?

ラジュ：　うん、南インドでは、手で食べるんだ。
　　　　　Yeah, we eat with our hands in southern India.

話してみましょう

Activity 1　　Mr. Smith and Mr. Tanaka have different habits. Describe their habits using 〜て and 〜ないで .

Example:　田中さんはコーヒーにさとうを入れないで飲みますが、
　　　　　スミスさんはさとうを入れて飲みます。

👥 **Activity 2** Work with a partner. Ask your partner a choice question using the following statement. Your partner will answer the question.

Example: 毎朝、ご飯を食べて出かけます。
　　　　　毎朝、ご飯を食べて出かけますか、食べないで出かけますか。

1. パンにバターをつけて食べます。

2. コーヒーにさとうを入れて飲みます。

3. 鶏肉はよく焼いて食べます。

4. ほうれんそうはゆでて食べます。

5. 魚はむして食べます。

6. ヨーグルトにジャムをまぜて食べます。

👥 **Activity 3** Work with a partner. Check the はい column for things in the following chart that you do, and check the いいえ column for things that you don't do. Then ask your partner whether or not he/she does these things. Use both the casual and polite styles of speech.

Example: A: 朝御飯を食べて学校に行きますか。
　　　　　B: いいえ、たいてい食べないで行きます。〜さんは？
　　　　　A: 私も食べないで行きます。

	私		パートナー	
	はい	いいえ	はい	いいえ
朝御飯を食べて学校に行く				
人参をゆでて食べる				
じゃがいもにバターををつけて食べる				
豚肉はよく焼く				
ほうれんそうは、むして食べる				
いちごはミルクをかけて食べる				
コーヒーにさとうを入れて飲む				

👥 **Activity 4** Work with a partner. The following items make our lives easier. Name some things we can do or don't have to do because of each of them.

インターネット　電子レンジ　ミキサー　携帯電話　炊飯器　パソコン　冷蔵庫
DVD プレイヤー　E メール　ボウル　フライパン

Example: インターネット
　　　　　これを使うと、新聞を買わないで、ニュースが読めます。

III. Expressing an open or hypothetical condition using the ば conditional form

The ば conditional clause indicates a condition necessary for the event or action in the main clause to take place. In this sense, it can be translated as *if* or *only if*. It can refer to a future condition that has not yet been realized or to a hypothetical condition that cannot be realized. This chapter introduces both types of condition.

A. Expressing an open condition using the ば conditional form

If the ば conditional refers an event that may or may not be realized in the future, it expresses the condition necessary for the event in the main clause to become true.

じゃがいもと豚肉を一緒ににれば、おいしくなると思う。
I think it will taste even better if you stew the potatoes and pork together.

味噌とさとうとサラダ油とすをまぜれば、おいしいドレッシングが作れるよ。
You can make a delicious dressing if you mix miso, sugar, salad oil, and vinegar.

この魚はあげれば、おいしくなるよ。
This fish will be delicious if you deep fry it.

古いレタスは、10分水につけて、よく水を切れば、おいしくなるよ。
Lettuce that is beginning to wilt is tasty if you soak it into water for ten minutes then drain it well.

The ば conditional form is made as follows:
1. る-verbs and irregular verbs:
    Replace る with れば
2. う-verbs:
    Same as the potential form except that ば is used instead of る at the end of the phrase. (e.g. 歩ける→歩けば)
3. い-adjectives and the negative ending ない:
    Replace い with ければ. The negative form of the ば conditional is 〜なければ which is the same as the 〜なければ found in 〜なければならない. All negative forms use 〜なければ, regardless of what part of speech they are.
4. な-adjectives and nouns:
    Replace だ with なら (ば) or であれば. The ば in 〜なら (ば) is optional.

	Dictionary form	Affirmative conditional (if ~)		Negative conditional (if ~not)	
		Formal	**Colloquial**	**Formal**	**Colloquial**
る -verbs	温める あたた (*to heat up*)	温めれば あたた	温めりゃ あたた	温めなければ あたた	温めなきゃ あたた
	にる (*to stew*)	にれば	にりゃ	になければ	になきゃ
う -verbs	むす (*to steam*)	むせば	むしゃ	むさなければ	むさなきゃ
	やる (*to do*)	やれば	やりゃ	やらなければ	やらなきゃ
Irregular verbs	来る	来れば く	来りゃ く	来なければ こ	来なきゃ こ
	する	すれば	すりゃ	しなければ	しなきゃ
い -adjectives	こい (*thick*)	こければ	こけりゃ	こくなければ	こくなきゃ
	いい	よければ	よけりゃ	よくなければ	よくなきゃ
な -adjectives	しずかだ (*quiet*)	しずかなら （ば）／しず かであれば	N/A	しずかじゃ なければ	しずかじゃ なきゃ
Copula verbs	材料だ ざいりょう (*ingredient*)	材料なら ざいりょう （ば）／材料 ざいりょう であれば	N/A	材料じゃ ざいりょう なければ	材料じゃ ざいりょう なきゃ

キム： ボウルとなべはどこ？
Where are the bowls and pots?

まもる： 分からないけど、アリスさんに聞けば分かると思うよ。
I don't know, but you should be able to find out if you ask Alice.

Note that 〜ばいい can express suggestions or the speaker's hope:

道子：ちょっと味がこいね。
あじ
Oh, it's seasoned too much.

健一：じゃあ、水を足せばいいよ。
けん   た
It'll be fine if you add some water.

黒田：まだ野菜がかたいね。
くろだ   やさい
The vegetables are not cooked enough. (lit.: still hard)

青山：少しいためれば、やわらかくなるよ。
あおやま
They should get tender if you stir fry them a bit.

NOTE

- The colloquial form of the ば construction is made by replacing 〜れば, which becomes 〜りゃ for い-adjectives, for the negative form ない, and for る-verbs. For う-verbs, the /-eba/ becomes /-ya/. (The dash indicates a consonant sound, such as /k-eba/ for /k-ya/.) There is no colloquial form for 〜なら(ば).

B. Expressing a hypothetical condition using the ば conditional form

In this usage, the condition in the ば clause may express a counter-factual situation or a hypothetical condition.

味噌があれば、味噌汁を作ったんですが。	*If there were some soybean paste, I would have made some miso soup.*
かにがあれば、もっとおいしかったはずです。	*It would have tasted better if we had had some crab.*
その鶏肉、かたくなければ食べられた。	*I could have eaten that chicken if it weren't so tough.*

〜ばよかった is used to express the speaker's regret about something that the speaker wished he or she had done, or something that he or she wished had happened.

こしょうをかけすぎなければよかった。	*I wish I hadn't put in so much pepper.*
電子レンジがあればよかった。	*I wish I had had a microwave oven.*
電話しておけばよかったんです。	*I wish I had called in advance.*
マヨネーズを使えばよかった。	*I wish I had used mayonnaise.*

The expressions 〜ばいいのに／〜ばいいんだけど／〜ばいいんですが are often used when the speaker wishes for something that does not or will not take place in reality.

あの人まだいるの？　早く帰ればいいのに。	*Is that person still here? I wish he'd go home soon.*

石田：　ケーキ作れる？
Can you bake a cake? (lit. *make*)

上田：　もちろん。でも、この家オーブンないんだ。オーブンがあればいいんだけど。
Of course. But we have no oven here. I wish we had one.

白鳥：山田さん、今日は仕事でおそくなるから、来られないって。
Mr. Yamada says he can't come today because he has to work late.

黒木：そう、残念ね！　来られればいいのに。
That's too bad. I wish he could come.

話してみましょう

Activity 1   Change each phrase in Column A using 〜ば, and choose the appropriate result from Column B.

Example:　天気がいい
　　　　　天気がよければ、歩いて行きます。

	Column A		Column B
1.	たまねぎです	a.	ご飯が上手にたけます。
2.	炊飯器を使う	b.	チャーハンが出来ません。
3.	牛肉がかたい	c.	ケーキが作れます。
4.	いためない	d.	マウイ・オニオンがおいしいですよ。
5.	お茶碗がない	e.	味がこくなりますよ。
6.	フォークがない	f.	コーンスターチにつければ、やわらかくなります。
7.	ソースをまぜる	g.	おさらを使ったらどうですか。
8.	赤いいちごがある	h.	木のスプーンが使いやすいですよ。

Activity 2   Work with a partner. Think about what kinds of things you could do if you were in the following situations. Tell your partner what you would do.

Example:　百万ドルあれば、新しい家が買えます。

1. 百万ドルある
2. 冬休みになる
3. 日本に住んでいる
4. 結婚する
5. 大学を卒業する

Activity 3   Work with a group of four. Choose one word from the list below and tell your group what would be possible or impossible if that item was or wasn't present. The rest of the group will try to guess what word you selected.

小麦粉　さとう　パンこ　コーンスターチ　ほうれんそう　出汁　豚肉　のり　す
火　茶碗　（お）はし　スプーン　フライパン　冷蔵庫　なべ　味噌　鶏肉　油

Example:　A:　これがあれば、ケーキやクッキーが焼けます。
　　　　　　　これがなければ、作れません。
　　　　　B:　小麦粉ですか。
　　　　　A:　はい、そうです。

◆ **Activity 4**   Work with the class. Ask a classmate if there have been incidents which he/she regrets, and report to the class about what you have learned. Use the 〜ばよかった form.

Example: A: 〜さん。〜さんは、こうすればよかったと思ったことがありますか。

B: ええ、ありますよ。先週、新しいドレッシングを買ったんですが。

A: ええ。

B: おいしくなかったので、買わなければよかったと思いました。

A: そうですか。それは残念でしたね。

クラスメートの名前	すれば・しなければよかったこと

IV. Expressing possibility and capability using the dictionary form of the verb + ことが出来る

The dictionary form of the verb + ことが出来る means *can* or *be able to do* in English. It is similar to the potential form, indicating possibility or capability depending on the context, but it is usually a little more formal than the potential form and tends to be used to make objective statements about whether doing something is possible or not.

さとうやぎゅうにゅうを使わないでおいしいお菓子を作ることが出来る。
It is possible to make delicious sweets without using sugar or milk.

フライパンで鶏肉をあげることが出来ます。   *It is possible to deep-fry chicken with a frying pan.*

オーブンで温めることが出来る。   *You can reheat it in the oven.*

川本： 電子レンジでケーキを焼くことが出来ますか。
Is it possible to bake a cake using a microwave oven?

上田： もちろん、出来ますよ。
Of course it is.

話してみましょう

| **Activity 1** | Answer the questions using the dictionary form of the verb + ことが出来る. |

Example: アメリカでは日本のテレビ番組が見られますか。
（テレビ番組 = *TV program*）
ええ、大きい町なら見ることが出来ますよ。

1. アメリカでは何さいから車の運転が出来ますか。
2. だれでもアメリカの大統領 (*president*) になれますか。
3. 安いチケットはどこで買えますか。
4. アメリカでは何さいからおさけが飲めますか。
5. このしゅう (*state*) では何さいから結婚出来ますか。

| **Activity 2** | Work with a partner. Select an object from the list below and explain what can be done with that object, and have your partner guess which object you are talking about. |

Example: A: これは、色々な物を焼くことが出来る物です。
B: フライパンですか?
A: はい、そうです。

冷蔵庫　車　飛行機　ほうちょう　フォーク　たまご　のり　コーンスターチ
サラダ 油　ソース　ボウル　ミキサー　オーブン　しょう油　小麦粉　味噌
ねぎ　（お）さら

Activity 3   Work as a class. The following are traffic signs used in Japan. Find people who know the meanings of the signs in the chart, and write their names and the meanings of the signs.

Example:　A:　あのう、このひょうしき (*traffic sign*) の意味は何ですか。

　　　　　　B:　ここでタクシーに乗ることが出来るんですよ。

　　　　　　A:　ああ、そうですか。

標識 (*traffic sign*) ひょうしき	名前	標識 (*traffic sign*) の意味 ひょうしき

V. Using question word + でも ～ affirmative form

In *Nakama 1*, Chapter 9, you learned that using a question word + か indicates an indefinite something, someone, etc., and that a question word + も followed by a negative form means *not ~any*. This chapter introduces another combination of question word and particle: question word + でも. This form can be used only in sentences ending in an affirmative form, and it means *any*, *all*, or *whatever/whenever/wherever*, etc.

木村さんは何でも食べられます。	*Kimura-san can eat anything.*
川本：だれをしょうたいしようか。	*Whom shall we invite?*
木村：だれでもいいよ。	*Anybody is fine.*
ジェフ：いつがいいですか。	*When should we go/do it?*
さなえ：明日ならいつでもいいです。	*Anytime tomorrow will be fine.*
ジェフ：どこに行きましょうか。	*Where shall we go?*
さなえ：おいしい店ならどこでもいいです。	*Anywhere will be fine as long as it serves good food.*

The following chart summarizes phrases that can be created with a question word and the particles か, も, and でも.

Question word	+ か ～ affirmative	+ も ～ negative	+ でも ～ affirmative
何	何か (*something*)	何も (*nothing, not at all*)	何でも (*anything, whatever*)
だれ	だれか (*someone*)	だれも (*no one*)	だれでも (*anybody, whoever*)
いつ	いつか (*sometime*)	*いつも (*never*)	いつでも (*anytime*)
どこ	どこか (*somewhere*)	どこも (*nowhere*)	どこでも (*anywhere*)

NOTE

● * When いつも is used in an affirmative sentence, it means *always*. For example, いつも朝御飯を食べる means *I always eat breakfast*.

The particles が and を are not used with the question word + も or でも. However, other particles such as に and と can be inserted between the question word and ～も or でも.

昨日はだれにも会いませんでした。	*I didn't meet anybody yesterday.*
こしょうはどこにもありません。	*There is no pepper anywhere.*
このソースは何とでもあいます。	*This sauce works with anything.*
仕事はいつからでも始められます。	*I can start the job anytime.*
サラダ油はどこででも買えます。	*You can buy vegetable oil anywhere.*

話してみましょう

Activity 1   Answer the questions, using the question word + も 〜 negative or the question word + でも 〜 affirmative.

Example 1:   朝、何か食べますか。

いいえ、朝は何も食べません。

Example 2:   何を作りましょうか。

何でもいいですよ。

1. 朝、何か飲みましたか。
2. だれかと一緒に食事に行きますか。
3. 日本のしょう油はどこかにありますか。
4. キャベツとえびをいためてくれる人はいませんか。
5. いつステーキを焼いたらいいですか。
6. いくらお金をあつめたらいいでしょうか。
7. だれをパーティによんだらいいでしょうか。
8. どこで材料を買いましょうか。
9. だれがたまねぎと人参を切りますか。

Activity 2   Work as a class. Ask your classmates about their likes and dislikes regarding food.

Example: A: 〜 さんはどんな食べ物が好きですか。

B: そうですね。野菜が好きですね。

A: 野菜なら、何でも食べられますか。

B: ええ、食べられます。／いいえ、ねぎはあまり好きじゃありません。

Activity 3   Work with a partner. Imagine you and your partner are roommates and you have decided to make dinner together. Decide what to make and what kind of ingredients you will need to prepare. Create a dialogue using the example as a model.

Example: A: 〜さん、今晩、何にしようか？

B: 何が食べたい？

A: 何でもいいよ。

B: じゃあ、天ぷらはどう？

A: いいね。じゃあ、何を買ったらいい？

B: 野菜なら、何でもいいと思うけど。

A: じゃあ、魚は？

聞く練習

上手な聞き方

Understanding signaling devices used in instructions

Nakama 2, Chapter 2 introduced transition devices, such as そして, その間（に）, その後（で）, その時（に）, その前（に）, それで, だから, だけど, つぎに, ですから, というのは, ところで, まず始めに, and また. Some of these expressions—for example, まず始めに, つぎに, それから, and そして —are commonly used to indicate sequence. Another commonly used expression is 最後に (*lastly, finally*), which indicates the last step. It is important to pay attention to these devices because what follows them is the most important information in the instructions.

練習

　　A. Listen to the following two dialogues, then identify the number of steps in each set of directions.

　　1. ほうれんそうのおひたし (*boiled*) の作り方　＿＿＿＿＿＿＿

　　2. 天ぷらの作り方　　　　　　　　　＿＿＿＿＿＿＿

　　B. Now listen to the dialogues again. This time, try to write down each step.

　　1. ほうれんそうのおひたし (*boiled*) の作り方

　　　　＿＿＿＿＿＿＿＿＿＿＿＿＿＿＿＿＿＿＿＿＿＿＿＿＿＿＿

　　2. 天ぷらの作り方

　　　　＿＿＿＿＿＿＿＿＿＿＿＿＿＿＿＿＿＿＿＿＿＿＿＿＿＿＿

料理番組　Cooking programs

聞く前に

下の質問に答えて下さい。

　　1. テレビで料理の番組を見たことがありますか。

　　2. 料理番組にはだれが出てきますか。

　　3. 料理番組のキッチンにはどんな物がありますか。

新しい言葉

ひらたく	同じように	ぬる	まぶす
flat	in the same way	to spread over	to sprinkle

🔊 聞いてみましょう

A. 下の材料のリストを見て、使わない材料に×をつけて下さい。
　　ざいりょう　　　　　　　　　　　　　　　　　　ざいりょう

セロリ (celery)	_____	たまねぎ	_____
さやえんどう (snow peas)	_____	す	_____
チェダーチーズ	_____	マヨネーズ	_____
ピーマン (green peppers)	_____	レタス	_____
ベーコン (bacon)	_____	さとう	_____
たまご	_____	しお	_____

B. Write the quantity necessary for each ingredient in the blanks in A.

聞いた後で

料理のステップを書いて下さい。そして、クラスメートと答えをチェックして
りょうり
下さい。

聞き上手話し上手

Giving instructions

Verbal instructions in English tend to be presented in the imperative form such as do this or do that, but in Japanese they are presented in statement form, using both 〜ます and plain forms. 〜ます is often used in giving instructions because it tends to express the speaker's awareness of a public audience. Therefore, when the speaker wants to convey a message, 〜ます tends to appear even in rather casual conversations. Since the plain form alone does not imply such awareness, it is often used with expression such as 〜の (だ) and 〜んだ, which convey the nuance that the preceding sentence is an explanation/instruction. You can use the request form 〜下さい as well, but the frequent use of 下さい sounds rather strange in instructions. It is better to use a combination of ます and 下さい.

練習

1. Explain how to make green salad (グリーンサラダ) in Japanese.
2. Explain how to make scrambled eggs (スクランブルエッグ) in Japanese.

漢字

Statistical facts about kanji

You have learned more than 250 **kanji** so far, and you may be wondering how many more you have to learn. Here are some statistical facts about the **kanji** used in Japan that should help you build an overall perspective.

1. There are about 50,000 characters listed in one comprehensive **kanji** dictionary, but most of these are not commonly used. The National Institute of Japanese Language Research conducted a study of the use of **kanji** in newspapers and magazines and found that the 200 most frequently used **kanji** accounted for about 50 percent of all **kanji** appearing in the text. The 500 most frequently used **kanji** accounted for over 80 percent of all **kanji**, and 1,000 **kanji** accounted for 90 percent of the total. The 2,000 most frequently used **kanji** accounted for about 99 percent of all **kanji** used in newspapers. Having learned 250 **kanji**, you should be able to recognize about one-half of the **kanji** appearing, for example, in a Japanese magazine. Once you learn 500, you will know 80 percent of the **kanji** you will encounter in most publications.
2. Japanese children learn about 150 to 200 **kanji** each year in elementary school. By the time they reach the sixth grade, they know about 1,000 **kanji**.
3. The most frequently read **kanji** are visually simpler (contain fewer strokes) than the less frequently used ones.
4. There are many **kanji** compounds, so it is important to build your vocabulary knowledge to improve your reading skills even if you know basic **kanji**.

Learning tips

As the number of **kanji** you have learned begins to grow, you will face the inevitable problem of retaining everything. To keep from forgetting characters, it is a good idea to create different groupings of **kanji**. One such grouping may be done according to meaning categories, while another grouping could be based on component parts. Different ways of organizing your knowledge of **kanji** should provide you with multiple ways of remembering them.

It is also a good idea to write **kanji** when you try to remember them. Writing in this case can also be done by moving your arm through the air. Research has shown that involving different parts of your body will activate more regions in your brain, resulting in a higher degree of cognitive activity, which, in turn, leads to better retention.

Flashcards can be used to practice recognition, writing, and the grouping of **kanji**. You can make flashcards with the kanji on one side and the meaning, the **on-reading** (in **katakana**), and the **kun**-reading (in **hiragana**) on the other side. Then you can practice reading by looking at the **kanji** on the front of the card and practice writing by looking at the readings and meaning on the back. You can spread your **kanji** cards out on the floor and group them according to meaning, component shape, and pronunciation.

料 料	material, ingredient	` ´ ⌐ ⼗ ⽶ 米 ⽶ 料 料
	リョウ　日本料理を作る。　料理の材料　授業料	
	りょうり　　　りょうり ざいりょう　りょう	

理 理	logic	⼀ 丁 王 玎 珇 珇 理 理
	リ　フランス料理が好きです。　無理です。	
	りょうり　　　　　　むり	

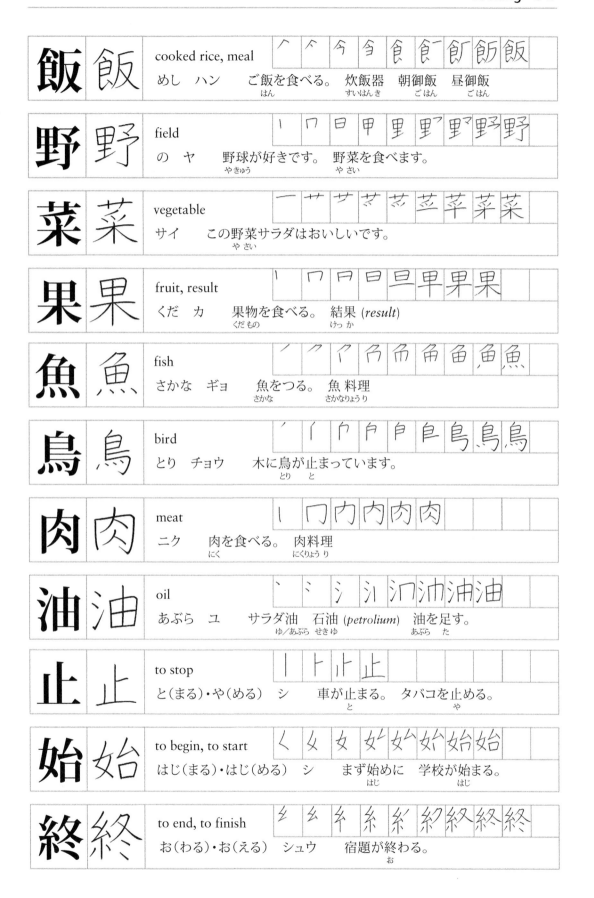

| 飯 | 飯 | cooked rice, meal | ノ | ㇏ | 今 | 今 | 食 | 食 | 飣 | 飯 | 飯 |
| | | めし ハン　ご飯を食べる。 炊飯器 朝御飯 昼御飯 | | | | | | | | | |

| 野 | 野 | field | 丨 | 口 | 日 | 甲 | 里 | 里 | 野 | 野 | 野 |
| | | の ヤ　野球が好きです。 野菜を食べます。 | | | | | | | | | |

| 菜 | 菜 | vegetable | 一 | 艹 | 艹 | 芷 | 苎 | 茓 | 茶 | 苹 | 菜 |
| | | サイ　この野菜サラダはおいしいです。 | | | | | | | | | |

| 果 | 果 | fruit, result | 丨 | 口 | 日 | 日 | 旦 | 早 | 果 | 果 | |
| | | くだ カ　果物を食べる。 結果 (result) | | | | | | | | | |

| 魚 | 魚 | fish | ⺈ | ⺈ | 冎 | 舟 | 帘 | 角 | 角 | 魚 | 魚 |
| | | さかな ギョ　魚をつる。 魚料理 | | | | | | | | | |

| 鳥 | 鳥 | bird | ′ | ⺈ | 宀 | 户 | 自 | 鸟 | 鳥 | 鳥 | 鳥 |
| | | とり チョウ　木に鳥が止まっています。 | | | | | | | | | |

| 肉 | 肉 | meat | 丨 | 冂 | 内 | 内 | 肉 | 肉 | | | |
| | | ニク　肉を食べる。 肉料理 | | | | | | | | | |

| 油 | 油 | oil | ㇔ | ⺀ | 氵 | 汁 | 汀 | 沺 | 油 | 油 | |
| | | あぶら ユ　サラダ油 石油 (petrolium) 油を足す。 | | | | | | | | | |

| 止 | 止 | to stop | 丨 | 卜 | 止 | 止 | | | | | |
| | | と(まる)・や(める) シ　車が止まる。 タバコを止める。 | | | | | | | | | |

| 始 | 始 | to begin, to start | く | 女 | 女 | 女´ | 如 | 始 | 始 | 始 | |
| | | はじ(まる)・はじ(める) シ　まず始めに 学校が始まる。 | | | | | | | | | |

| 終 | 終 | to end, to finish | 幺 | 幺 | 糸 | 糸 | 約 | 紁 | 終 | 終 | |
| | | お(わる)・お(える) シュウ　宿題が終わる。 | | | | | | | | | |

洗 洗	to wash あら(う)　セン	手を洗う。　洗濯をする。 あら　　　せんたく
悪 悪	bad わる(い)　アク	つごうが悪い。 わる
黒 黒	black くろ(い)　コク	黒い犬がいます。　黒板に書いて下さい。 くろ　　　　　　こくばん
白 白	white しろ(い)　ハク	白いねこ　雪は白いです。 しろ　　　ゆき しろ
青 青	blue あお(い)　セイ	青い海　空が青い。 あお　　　　あお
赤 赤	red あか(い)　セキ	赤いりんご あか
茶 茶	brown, tea チャ・サ	茶色いかばん　お茶を飲む。　喫茶店 ちゃ　　　　　ちゃ　　　きっさ
短 短	short みじか(い)　タン	このスカートは短いです。 みじか
長 長	long なが(い)　チョウ	長い　会社の社長 なが　　　　　ちょう
焼 焼	to burn, to bake や(く)・や(ける)　ショウ	ケーキを焼く。　火事(fire)で家が焼ける。 や　　　かじ　　　　や

読めるようになった漢字

料理　材料　授業料　朝御飯　昼御飯　晩御飯　炊飯器　電子レンジ　野球　野菜
　　　ざい　　　　　　ご　　　　ご　　　　ご　　すい き　　　　　　　　きゅう
魚　魚料理　肉料理　鳥肉　鶏肉　止まる　車を止める　タバコを止める
　　　　　　　　　　　　とり
始まる　始める　まず始めに　終わる　洗う　洗濯　悪い　黒い　黒板　白い
　　　　　　　　　　　　　　　　　　　　　たく　　　　　　　　　ばん

赤い　茶色い　お茶　紅茶　茶碗　喫茶店　短い　長い　社長　味　焼ける
冷ます　温める　果物　油　サラダ油　醤油　最後

日本人の名前：　黒田　黒木　白鳥　青山

練習

下の文を読んで下さい。

1. 結婚式の肉料理は油が少なくてよかったです。
2. この魚料理の材料と作り方を教えてくれませんか。
3. 肉より野菜や果物の方が好きです。
4. これは少し長いので、短くして下さい。
5. 雪は白くて、空は青い。
6. あの茶色いセーターを着ている人はだれですか。
7. 映画は八時に始まって、十時に終わりますから、歩いて帰ります。
8. 車が銀行の前に止まりました。
9. 野菜を洗って、小さく切ったら、ここに持って来て。つぎに、肉を焼いて。

読む練習

上手な読み方

Understanding the characteristics of written instructions

People read written materials for various purposes. For example, you may skim newspapers to get an overall idea of what is gong on that day, or you may search for a particular type of house in housing ads. You may also read novels, short stories, or manga for entertainment. Furthermore, you may have to read a textbook for a test. Depending on the purpose of reading, you may scan, skim, engage in a very detailed reading, or read while taking notes. Therefore, you should be aware of why you are going to read a given text and what you want to do with it, and then think about what information you should get out of the material and the most efficient way of reading it.

Written instructions are among the easiest writing styles to understand. Each step is usually separated, numbered, and often accompanied by illustrations. You can use visual cues and format to help you understand the text. Written instructions are also grammatically simple in Japanese. They are written in the present tense, and the text can be either in plain form or the formal form. The difficulty of written instructions is usually due to context-specific vocabulary and the **kanji** associated with this vocabulary. It is important to have a good idea of what vocabulary will be used before you begin reading.

練習

A. Think about when you might read a set of instructions and what you would do after reading it.

B. Suppose you are to read manuals or recipes for the following items. Identify what kind of nouns and verbs you will need to know.

炊飯器　携帯電話　ピザ
すい　き　けいたい

C. The following is a typical recipe in Japanese. Identify similarities and differences in format between recipes in Japanese and recipes in English.

ひき肉のパン揚げ（1人分）
あ　　　ぶん

材料
ざい

食パン (*sliced bread*)　2枚
しょく　　　　　　　　　まい
牛ひき肉 (*ground beef*)　50g
ぎゅう
スライスチーズ　1枚
まい
塩、こしょう　少々
しお
バター　少々

作り方

1　肉に塩、こしょうをふって、味をつけます。
しお

2　食パンと食パンの間にバターをぬって、肉とチーズをはさみます。
しょく　　しょく

3　油を160度ぐらいに温めて、ゆっくり揚げます。
あ

4　四つに切ります。

海老団子   Shrimp dumplings
えびだんご

読む前に

A. 日本とアメリカでは材料のはかり方 (*unit of measurement*) が違います。
ざい

アメリカ		日本	
パウンド (*pound*)	オンス (*ounce*)	キログラム (*kilogram*)	グラム (*gram*)
2.2 lb	35 oz	1 kg	1,000 g
ガロン (*gallon*)	パイント (*pint*)	リットル (*liter*)	
1 gal	8 pt	3.8 L	
パイント (*pint*)	カップ（アメリカ）	cc	カップ（日本）
1 pt	2 c	473 cc	2.4 カップ
オンス (*ounce*)	大さじ	グラム (*gram*)	大さじ
0.5 oz	1 tbl	15 g	大さじ 1

1. 500 グラムは、何パウンドぐらいになりますか。
2. 1リットルは、何ガロンですか。
3. アメリカの1カップは、何パイントですか。何 cc ですか。
4. 日本の1カップはアメリカの何カップですか。
5. 日本では、大さじ1は 15g で、小さじ1は 5g です。アメリカではどうですか。

B. 写真を見て、海老団子の作り方を言ってみて下さい。知らない言葉が
えびだんご
あったら先生に聞いて下さい。

1　　　　　2　　　　　3

4　　　　　5　　　　　6

C. 下の材料を読んで、分からない言葉があったら、先生に聞いて下さい。AとB
　　は何のことですか。

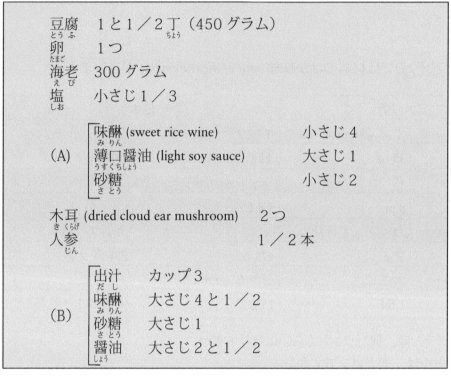

豆腐	1と1／2丁（450グラム）	
卵	1つ	
海老	300グラム	
塩	小さじ1／3	
(A)	味醂 (sweet rice wine)	小さじ4
	薄口醤油 (light soy sauce)	大さじ1
	砂糖	小さじ2
木耳 (dried cloud ear mushroom)		2つ
人参		1／2本
(B)	出汁	カップ3
	味醂	大さじ4と1／2
	砂糖	大さじ1
	醤油	大さじ2と1／2

D. The following steps are out of order. Match each step with the picture.

__1__ 豆腐の上におもい (heavy) 物をのせて、水を切る (drain)。

___ 人参と木耳を小さく切って、2と混ぜる。

___ 揚げた団子に熱いお湯をかける。

___ 3で小さい団子を作って、油で揚げる。

___ 5をBの出汁で15分ぐらい煮る。

___ 海老を包丁で小さくなるまでたたいて (pound)、豆腐と海老と卵の黄身 (yolk)
　　とAをよく混ぜる。

読んだ後で

A. 日本語で質問に答えて下さい。

1. どんな料理が好きですか。
2. どんな料理を作ったことがありますか。
3. お母さんはどんな料理が上手ですか。お父さんはどうですか。
4. どんな料理を作ってみたいと思いますか。

B. 下の質問に答えて、好きな料理の作り方を日本語で書いて下さい。

1. どんな材料を使いますか。
2. フライパンやなべを使いますか。
3. ステップはいくつぐらいありますか。
4. まず始めに何をしますか。
5. つぎに何をしますか。
6. その後、何をしますか。
7. 最後に何をしますか。

総合練習
そうごう

料理を作ろう

Choose a dish that you can make and prepare a presentation on how to make it. Make a list of ingredients you will need and write the directions below the list. Then deliver your presentation. You can use PowerPoint, draw pictures, or bring the actual dishes if your instructor allows you to do so.

材料
ざい

作り方

1.

2.

3.

4.

5.

👤👤 ロールプレイ

1. You are showing a friend how to make rolled sushi. Your friend will ask you questions about its preparation and you will tell him/her how it is prepared.
2. Ask a Japanese friend to teach you an easy-to-make Japanese dish and write a recipe for it.
3. You cannot cook and have started taking cooking classes. Tell your instructor some mistakes you have made while trying to cook and your instructor will try to tell you how to avoid those mistakes in the future.

Chapter 8

第八課(だいはっか)

MICHAEL S. YAMASHITA/National Geographic Creative

うわさ
Rumors

Objectives	Describing events, making small talk, and expressing one's conjectures and opinions
Vocabulary	Disasters and accidents, crimes and unpleasant experiences, expressions that describe feelings and emotional states, animals used as metaphor
Dialogue	東京に地震(じしん)が来るみたいです。*It appears that Tokyo will have an earthquake.*
Japanese Culture	Natural disasters, earthquakes, crimes
Grammar	I. Expressing problems and events using the passive form
	II. Expressing conjecture based on indirect evidence using 〜らしい; expressing conjecture based on direct evidence using 〜ようだ／みたいだ
	III. Nのような／みたいな (*like ~*); NらしいN (*typical*)
	IV. Expressing limited degree using だけ〜 affirmative and しか〜 negative
	V. Expressing opinions indirectly using 〜んじゃない (かと思う)
Listening	Expressions in oral narrative; ブタの話
Communication	Telling a story well and listening to a story well
Kanji	Using a **kanji** dictionary
	心 配 困 難 弱 招 待 呼 遊 泳 建 経 売
	交 落 暗 洪 利 全 急 故 台 不
Reading	Understanding the structure of Japanese narrative texts, global warming

単語
たん

Nouns

あんしん	安心	a sense of relief, あんしんする to feel relieved.
いじめ		bullying, いじめにあう being bullied
うさぎ	兎	rabbit
うそ	嘘	lie, falsehood, うそをつく to tell a lie
うわさ	噂	rumor
かじ	火事	a fire
かのじょ	彼女	girlfriend, she
かみなり	雷	lightning, かみなりがおちる lightning strikes
かめ	亀	turtle, tortoise
かれ（し）	彼（氏）	boyfriend, he
クジラ	鯨	whale
くま	熊	bear
けいけん	経験	experience, けいけんする to have an experience
けんか	喧嘩	a fight
こうずい	洪水	flood
こうつう	交通	traffic, こうつうじこ traffic accident
さいがい	災害	disaster, calamity
さる	猿	monkey
じこ	事故	accident, こうつうじこ traffic accident
じしん	地震	earthquake
しんぱい	心配	anxiety, anxious, しんぱいする to be worried
ぞう	象	elephant
たつまき	竜巻	tornado
とり	鳥	bird
どろぼう	泥棒	thief
はっけん	発見	discovery, はっけんする to discover
はんざい	犯罪	crime
ひがい	被害	damage, loss
へび	蛇	snake
ライオン		lion
わるくち	悪口	bad-mouthing, speaking ill of a person

う -verbs

あう	遭う／遇う	to encounter
うる	売る	to sell
おこす	起こす	to cause (something) to happen
おそう	襲う	to attack
おどろく	驚く	to be surprised, 〜におどろく to be surprised at 〜
こまる	困る	to be in trouble
こわす	壊す	to destroy
しかる	叱る	to scold
だます	騙す	to deceive
ぬすむ	盗む	to steal
ふむ	踏む	to step on, 足をふむ to step on somebody's foot

る -verbs

いじめる	苛める	to bully
おきる	起きる	to happen, to take place
すてる	捨てる	to throw away, to discard
にげる	逃げる	to run away, to escape
ふえる	増える	to increase
ぶつける		to hit (as with a car), to crash into
ほめる	誉める	to praise
やける	焼ける	to burn
ゆれる	揺れる	to shake
わかれる	別れる	to leave, to break up

い -adjectives

こわい	怖い	frightening, scary

な -adjectives

あんぜん（な）	安全（な）	safe
ふべん（な）	不便（な）	inconvenient
むだ（な）	無駄（な）	wasteful

Prefixes

おお〜	大〜	heavy, big, 大雨 heavy rain, 大雪 heavy snow 大かじ big fire, 大じしん big earthquake

Expressions

ええ、ええ	uh huh
へえ、そうですか。	Oh, I see.
それで…そのあと、どうなったんですか。　それで…その後、どうなったんですか。	
	Well then . . . what happened after that?
それはおきのどくでしたね。　　　　それはお気の毒でしたね。	I am sorry to hear that.
まさか。	You're kidding.
うっそー	No way! (very casual)
まじー	Are you serious? (very casual)

単語の練習
たん

A. さいがいと事故　**Disasters and accidents**
じ こ

地震が起きる じ しん earthquake	たつまきが起きる tornados	建物がゆれる たて a building shakes	洪水になる こうずい flood
かみなりが落ちる お lightning / thunder	火事になる か じ fire breaks out	家が焼ける や a house burns	大雨 おおあめ heavy rain
大雪 おおゆき heavy snow	交通事故にあう to be in a traffic accident	火事からにげる か じ to flee from a fire	ひがい damage

> **Activity 1**　下の絵は、どんなさいがいや事故の絵か言って下さい。
> じ こ

1　　　　2　　　　3　　　　4

5　　　　6　　　　7　　　　8

おぼえていますか。

台風
たい

Supplementary Vocabulary: 自然のさいがい   **Natural disasters**
                               し ぜん

あらし	嵐	storm
かんばつ	干ばつ	drought
じすべり	地すべり	landslide
たかなみ	高波	high tide
つなみ	津波	tsunami
ふぶき	吹雪	snow storm, blizzard
ふんか	噴火	volcanic eruption
きゅうきゅうしゃ	救急車	ambulance
けいさつ	警察	police
しょうぼうしゃ	消防車	fire truck
パトカー		police car

Activity 2   つぎの言葉の意味は何だと思いますか。

大　地震　山火事　飛行機事故　自転車事故
だい/おおじしん　やまかじ　　き じ こ　　　じ こ

Activity 3   List the disasters, accidents, and crimes you have heard about.

	さいがい	事故 じ こ
テレビや新聞で見たことがある		

Activity 4   Fill in the blanks.

1. 2008年に中国で起きた地震の＿＿＿＿＿＿＿はとても大きかったです。
                        じ しん

2. 家や建物が焼けることを＿＿＿＿＿＿＿と言います。
     たて　　や

3. 4月から7月ごろまで、テキサスやオクラホマではよく＿＿＿＿＿＿＿が＿＿＿＿＿＿＿。

4. ゴルフ場 (golf course) で＿＿＿＿＿＿＿が＿＿＿＿＿＿、ゴルフをしていた人がなくなったそうです。
     じょう

5. ＿＿＿＿＿＿＿がふると、川が近いところでは、よく＿＿＿＿＿＿＿になります。

6. アメリカの東の方は、冬になると、＿＿＿＿＿＿＿のひがいがあります。

7. 昨日、横断歩道で＿＿＿＿＿＿＿＿＿＿にあいました。
            だん

8. お父さんは、車を＿＿＿＿＿＿＿＿＿、けがをした。

B. はんざいといやな経験 Crimes and unpleasant experiences
けいけん

どろぼうがお金をぬすむ	人をおそう	人をだます
a thief steals money	to attack somebody	to cheat somebody

事故を起こす	車をぶつける	いじめにあう
じ こ		
to cause an accident	to hit with a car	to be bullied

いじめる	悪口を言う	うわさをする
	わるくち	
to bully	to bad-mouth somebody	to start a rumor

うそをつく	しかる	物をこわす	服をよごす
to lie	to scold	to break something	to get clothes dirty

足をふむ	友達とけんかする	彼女／かれしとわかれる
		かのじょ
to step on someone's toes	to have a fight with a friend	to break up with a girl/boyfriend

おぼえていますか。

きらい（な）　けがをする　仕事をやめる　しぬ　入院する　人がなくなる

Supplementary Vocabulary: はんざい Crimes

あきす	空き巣	breaking into an empty house to steal something
ごうとう	強盗	robbery
さぎ	詐欺	fraud, swindling
スリ		pickpocketing
ちかん	痴漢	a molester
ひきにげ	ひき逃げ	hit and run
ゆすり	強請	extortion, blackmailing
わいろをおくる	賄賂を贈る	to bribe someone
さつじん	殺人	murder

Activity 5 Use the words above to describe what is happening in the illustrations.

1 2 3 4

おぼえていますか。

きらい（な）　好き（な）　結婚する　仕事をやめる　入院する　留学する

Activity 6　Work with a partner. Ask your partner whether he/she knows anyone who has had the following experiences. Circle his/her answers.

Example:　だれかの大事な物をこわしたことがある人

A:　だれかの大事な物をこわしたことがある人を知っていますか。

B:　ええ、知っています。私の父です。

or　いいえ、知りません。

経験がある人 けいけん	Circle 知っています or 知りません	その人の名前
Example: だれかの大事な物をこわしたことが ある人	(知っています)・知りません	父
かれしか彼女とわかれた友達 かのじょ	知っています・知りません	
人の悪口を言ったことがある人 わるくち	知っています・知りません	
最近友達とけんかした人 さい	知っています・知りません	
両親をだましたことがある人	知っています・知りません	
いじめにあったことがある人	知っています・知りません	
先生にうそをついたことがある人	知っています・知りません	
先生の足をふんだ人	知っています・知りません	
だれかの服をよごした人	知っています・知りません	

Activity 7   Work with a partner. List typical rumor topics for the following age groups. Note that 〜代 means *generation*, so 30 代 and 50 代 refer to people in their thirties and fifties, respectively.

うわさのトピック	
小学生	
高校生	
大学生	
30 代 だい	
50 代 だい	
70 代 だい	

C. 気持ちをあらわす言葉
Expressions that describe feelings and emotional states

こわい	むだ	不便 ふべん	ひどい	
scary	wasteful	inconvenient	serious	

困る こま	心配する しんぱい	おどろく	安全 あんぜん	安心する あんしん
to be in trouble, to be perplexed	to worry	to be surprised	to be safe	to be relieved

Activity 8   Use the words above to describe what is happening in the illustrations.

1   2   3   4   5

おぼえていますか。

うれしい　かなしい　かわいい　さびしい　楽しい　つまらない　ひどい
いや（な）　きらい（な）　残念（な）　すき（な）　大丈夫（な）　大変（な）
　　　　　　　　　　　　ねん　　　　　　　　　　　　　じょうぶ
だめ（な）

Activity 9   下の質問に日本語で答えて下さい。

1. どんなこわい経験をしたことがありますか。その経験について話して下さい。
　　　　　　　　けいけん　　　　　　　　　　　　　　けいけん

2. 何かこわいものはありますか。

3. 何がないと不便だと思いますか。
　　　　　　ふべん

4. どんなことがむだだと思いますか。

5. 今困っていることがありますか。どんなことで困っていますか。
　　こま　　　　　　　　　　　　　　　　　　　こま

6. どんな時に、心配しますか。今までで一番心配した経験について話して
　　　　　　しんぱい　　　　　　　　　しんぱい　けいけん
　下さい。

7. 最近何かにおどろいたことがありますか。どんなことにおどろきましたか。
　さい

8. たつまきが多い所では、何があると安心できますか。洪水が多い所ではどう
　　　　　　　　　　　　　　　あんしん　　　　こうずい
　ですか。

D. 動物にたとえる   Animals used as metaphor

鳥 とり bird	くま bear	さる monkey	かめ turtle, tortoise	へび snake
うさぎ rabbit	ライオン lion	ぞう elephant	クジラ whale	うま horse

おぼえていますか。

犬　魚　ねこ

Supplementary Vocabulary: ほかの動物   Other animals

イルカ		dolphin
カバ		hippopotamus
カンガルー		kangaroo
キリン		giraffe
コアラ		koala
ゴリラ		gorilla
サイ		rhinoceros
さめ	鮫	shark
しか	鹿	deer
ジャガー		jaguar
チーター		cheetah
とら	虎	tiger
パンダ		panda
りす		squirrel

Activity 10   What animal would you associate with each of the following types of people?

1. やさしい人
2. こわい人
3. 大きい人
4. 足がおそい人
5. 頭がいい人
6. かわいい人
7. 強い人
8. 弱い人
   よわ
9. いやな人

Activity 11   Think of an animal that characterizes you. Ask your classmates what animals they think of themselves as being like.

ダイアローグ

はじめに

日本語で質問に答えて下さい。

1. 地震を経験したことがありますか。どこでしたか。
   じしん　　けいけん

2. 地震はこわいですか。
   じしん

3. どんなさいがいがこわいですか。

🔊 **東京に地震が来るみたいです。**　*It appears that Tokyo will have an*
じしん
earthquake.

The order of the following **manga** frames is scrambled. Read the dialogue and unscramble
the frames by writing the correct number in the box in each frame.

a   b   c

d   e   f

教室で。
しつ

ブラウン：あれ、こんなところにさいふがある。

　リー：あ、それ、ぼくの。

ブラウン：だめだよ。こんなところにおいてたら、取られちゃうよ。

　リー：あ、そうだよね。

小さい地震が起きる。
じしん

ブラウン：何、これ？

リー：　あっ、地震だ。

ブラウン：　えーっ、こわい。

リー：　大丈夫。あまり大きくないから。まだ少しゆれてるけど、すぐ終わるから、安心して。

ゆれが止まる。

リー：　ああ、止まったよ。ブラウンさん、大丈夫？

ブラウン：　ああ、こわかった。日本は地震が多いって聞いてたけど、本当だったんですね。

上田さんが教室に入ってくる。

上田：　今、地震があったけど、大丈夫だった？

リー：　うん、ぼくは大丈夫。でもブラウンさんは、ちょっとこわかったんじゃないかな。

ブラウン：　ええ、とてもこわかったです。上田さんは、こわくないんですか。

上田：　ええ、私はカリフォルニアにいる時に、何度か経験したから、大丈夫です。

本田先生が入ってくる。

リー：　あっ、先生、今地震がありましたね。

本田先生：　ええ、新潟で地震があったらしいですよ。かなりゆれたみたいです。

リー：　え、新潟なんですか。もっと近い所かと思いました。

上田：　ええ、そうなんですよ。でも東京にも大きい地震が来るらしいですよ。

ブラウン：　えっ、そうですか。うわさじゃないんですか。

上田：　いいえ、うわさだけじゃないようですよ。東京では70年に一度ぐらい大きい地震が起きているんですよ。だけど、1923年に関東大震災という 大 地震があってから、まだ地震らしい地震が起きてないそうなんです。だから、そろそろ…。

ブラウン：　えー、そうなんですか。

本田先生：　まあ、その時はその時で、何とかなるんじゃないかと思うよ。

リー：　そうですよね。

ダイアローグの後で

A. 日本語で質問に答えて下さい。

1. どうしてブラウンさんはリーさんにだめだと言ったのですか。

2. ブラウンさんは地震を経験したことがありましたか。

3. リーさんは地震を経験したことがありましたか。

4. 上田さんは地震を経験したことがありましたか。

5. いつ東京で大きな地震がありましたか。

6. 東京では何年ぐらいに一度大きい地震がありますか。

7. 将来、東京に地震は来ますか。

B. Suppose Ms. Brown had experienced an earthquake before and was able to stay calm. How would you change what she says?

DIALOGUE PHRASE NOTES

- そろそろ means *it's about time* (for something to happen) . . .
- その時はその時で、何とかなる means *when that happens, we will manage.*
- Responding to a negative question like うわさじゃないんですか is a little tricky in Japanese because the use of はい／ええ is not the same as *yes/no* in English. Use はい／ええ if you agree with the content of question (うわさじゃない), and use いいえ if you disagree with it and the opposite, うわさだ, is true.

日本の文化
ぶん か

自然の災害   Natural disasters
し ぜん さいがい

Japan is prone to different types of natural disasters due to its location, geographical features, geological characteristics, and climate. Japan is mountainous and rivers flow rapidly. Heavy rain causes flooding and landslides. In recent years, due to housing development, landslides have accounted for a significant portion of the damage caused by natural disasters. Natural disasters in Japan include earthquakes, typhoons, heavy rain, heavy snow, floods, landslides, tsunami, and volcanic eruptions.

地震   Earthquakes
じ しん

Japan lies on the edge of a continental plate and an ocean plate. Thus, it has more than 100 active volcanoes (7 percent of all active volcanoes in the world) and a higher than average share of earthquakes. About 20 percent of all earthquakes with a magnitude 6 or higher happen in Japan. Additionally, 7 percent of the active volcanoes in the world are in Japan. Since Japan occupies only 0.25 percent of the world land mass, its share of natural disasters is high. In 2007, there were more than 2,000 earthquakes powerful enough for people to feel.

Earthquake-damaged road in Kumamoto Prefecture

KAZUHIRO NOGI/AFP/Getty Images

In the Great East Japan Earthquake (東日本大震災) of 2011, more than 18,000
ひがし に ほんだいしん さい
people were killed and 400,000 houses were completely or partially destroyed. The massive tsunami reached the East coast of Japan (Tohoku region) causing extensive damage. Due to the total loss of electricity for the cooling system caused by the fourteen-meter-high tsunami, a nuclear power plant in Fukushima experienced meltdown and hydrogen explosions. The plant is being prepared for a permanent shut down. This accident caused the shut down of all nuclear power plants in Japan, and the very use of nuclear power is being debated. As long as three years after the disaster, more than 280,000 people were still living in temporary housing. There has been a much higher level of awareness in preparing for emergencies. Many local municipalities have begun to play more active roles.

犯罪   Crimes
はんざい

Japan is considered one of the safest countries in the world (Global Peace Index 2015 by the Institute for Economics & Peace, 2015), and a UN report in 2015 shows that its murder rate for 2015 was only 0.28 per 100,000 people. This compares to a rate of 3.82 in the United States. As to the types of crime found in Japan, a government report from 2014 found that 74 percent of crimes in Japan are theft, and 20 percent are non-violent crimes such as scams, embezzlements, bribery, and prostitution. Only about 6%

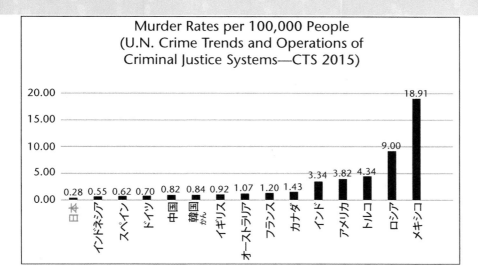

Murder Rates per 100,000 People
(U.N. Crime Trends and Operations of
Criminal Justice Systems—CTS 2015)

of crimes are violent crimes such as robbery, arson, rape, sexual assault, and extortion. Japan has strict gun control laws, strict laws against drunk driving, and strict laws against controlled substances such as marijuana and cocaine. The use of guns is generally limited to members of organized crime gangs.

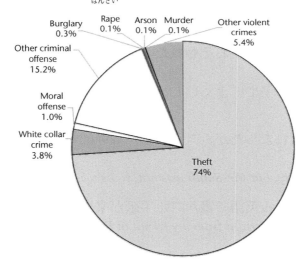

日本の犯罪のタイプ (MPO, 2014)
はんざい

The arrest rates for violent crimes, with the exception of theft, are generally very high. As a result, Japan's arrest rate has been around 30 percent though the overall crime rate has been declining.

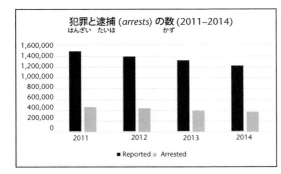

犯罪と逮捕 (arrests) の数 (2011–2014)
はんざい　たいほ　　　　かず

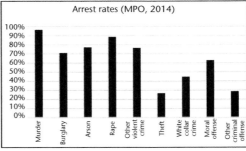

Arrest rates (MPO, 2014)

文法

I. Expressing problems and events using the passive form

A. Direct passive

The direct passive in Japanese is the equivalent to the passive construction in English. When someone does something that affects another person, the situation can be expressed from two different points of view. One is the viewpoint of the performer of the action, and the other is the viewpoint of the person affected by the action. In English, the former is expressed in active sentences such as, "Tom hit Jim," and the latter is expressed in passive sentences such as "Jim was hit by Tom." Similarly, in Japanese, an active sentence expresses the performer's point of view, and a passive sentence expresses the viewpoint of the receiving end of the action:

先生はメアリーをほめた。　　メアリーは先生にほめられた。
The teacher praised Mary.　　*Mary was praised by the teacher.*

A passive sentence takes the pattern: Subject は／が + agent に + passive verb form.

私は	先生に	しかられた。	*I was scolded by the teacher.*
ペットの鳥が	へびに	おそわれた。	*My pet bird was attacked by a snake.*
小さい時、私は	女の子に	よくいじめられました。	*I was often bullied by girls when I was little.*

私はパーティに呼ばれましたが、スミスさんは呼ばれなかったので、心配していました。
I was invited to the party, but Mr. Smith was not, so he was worried about it.

イギリスにいる友達から英語で書かれた手紙が来ました。
A letter written in English arrived from my friend in England.

Verb types	Meaning	Dictionary form	Passive form		Formation
る -verbs	to discard to see	すてる 見る	すて＋られる 見＋られる	すてられる 見られる	Add られる to the stem
う -verbs	to deceive to invite to steal	だます 呼ぶ ぬすむ	だま<u>さ</u>ない 呼<u>ば</u>ない ぬす<u>ま</u>ない	だまされる 呼ばれる ぬすまれる	Add れる to the plain negative stem; replace ない with れる
Irregular verbs	to come to do	来る する		来られる される	

The particle に marks the agent (performer of the action), and the subject indicates the person who is affected by the action. (に can be replaced with から when the agent is considered as a source from which something is coming.)

私は友達に／から日本の大学について聞かれた。
I was questioned by a friend about Japanese universities.

The passive form （ら）れる conjugates as a る-verb.

negative form	いじめられない	こわされない
polite form	いじめられます	こわされます
dictionary form	いじめられる	こわされる
conditional form	いじめられれば	こわされれば
て -form	いじめられて	こわされて

The verb of a direct passive sentence must be a transitive verb. An agent is sometimes marked with によって instead of に.

村上春樹の新しい本は色々な人に読まれている。
Haruki Murakami's new book is being read by many people.

マチュピチュはハイラム・ビンガム３世によって発見された。
Machu Picchu was discovered by Hiram Bingham III.

The agent in a direct passive sentence can be deleted if it is understood from the context, unknown, or of no particular interest.

こんな所にごみがすてられている。　　　*Garbage is discarded in places like this.*

このお寺は 1200 年に建てられました。　　*This temple was built in 1200.*

あの先生は日本でもよく知られている。　　*That professor is well known even in Japan.*

B. Indirect passive

Unlike English, Japanese has a second type of passive construction called the indirect passive. In an indirect passive sentence, someone does something or something happens, and the subject is adversely affected by it or troubled by the action or event. The subject has no direct involvement in the actual act or occurrence. For example, in the following sentence, the subject's TV was stolen by a burglar. In this case, the subject 私 is not directly involved in the action of stealing, but the TV was. As a consequence, however, the subject is adversely affected. The indirect passive sentence allows the subject to express negative feelings caused by the event. Direct translations of such sentences can seem very strange in English.

私はどろぼうにテレビをぬすまれた。
My TV was stolen by a thief. (lit.: *I got my TV stolen by a thief.*)

電車の中でだれかに足をふまれた。
Someone stepped on my foot in the train. (lit.: *(I) had my foot stepped on by someone in the train.*)

The action may be a natural occurrence or an accident, and the verbs in indirect passive sentences can either be intransitive or transitive verbs. English grammar does not allow intransitive verbs to be used in passive sentences.

私はスミスさんに悪口を言われた。   *Smith-san spoke ill of me .*

   (lit.: I was bad-mouthed by Smith-san.)

雨にふられた。   *(I) got rained on.*

となりの人に服をよごされた。   *I got my clothes dirtied by the person next to me.*

だれかに車をぶつけられて、困っている。

I am annoyed because my car was hit by someone. (lit.: I am annoyed because my car got hit by someone.)

飛行機の中で、子供になかれて、困りました。

My child cried in the airplane, and I was embarrassed. (Lit.: I was embarrassed because I was cried on by my baby.)

リー：　昨日、家にどろぼうに入られちゃったんだ。
   A thief broke into my house yesterday. (lit.: Yesterday (I had) my house broken into by a thief.)

山田：　何か取られたの？
   Was anything stolen?

リー：　うん。パソコンをぬすまれちゃったんだ。
   Yes, my PC was stolen. (lit.: (I had) my PC stolen.)

Notes

- Unlike the direct passive, the subject of an indirect passive is always animate; that is, the subject must be capable of having feeling. Also, the agent of an indirect passive sentence is usually specific and is rarely omitted.
- One crucial difference between the direct and indirect passive is that the indirect passive tends to have a negative connotation, but the direct passive can have either a negative or a positive connotation.
- Many passive sentences in English are not necessarily expressed in passive in Japanese. For example, the verbs "to understand" and "to need" can be used in passive sentences such as "the message was understood" and "more efforts are needed." But, there is no passive form for 分かる or いる (to need).
- The passive forms of る-verbs and 来る are identical to their potential forms. Sentence patterns, however, are very different between passive and potential sentences.

  あの動物園のさるは、フォークを使って物が食べられる。 (potential form)

  The monkey at that zoo can eat things using a fork.

  さるに私のりんごを食べられた。 (passive form)

  My apple was eaten by the monkey.

- The indirect passive is unique to Japanese and it is used quite often. Mastery of this construction will make your Japanese sound significantly more fluent.

話してみましょう

Activity 1　The following statements express what happened but do not express the speaker's feeling. Change the sentences to express speaker's viewpoint more clearly by using the passive form and adding a phrase that expresses the speaker's feeling.

Example:　　友達が私をだましました。

　　　　　　友達にだまされて、とてもかなしかったです。

1.　先生が私をほめました。
2.　台風が日本をおそいました。
　　　たい
3.　友達が私をパーティに招待しました。
　　　　　　　　　　　しょうたい
4.　友達が私をいじめました。
5.　母が私をしかりました。
6.　かみなりが私の家をこわしました。
7.　どろぼうが私の家に入りました。
8.　女の人が私の足をふみました。
9.　妹が私の車をぶつけました。
10.　大雨がふりました。
　　　おおあめ
11.　どろぼうがにげました。

Activity 2　Work with a partner. Look at the following pictures and, using the passive construction, create a short dialogue to describe what has happened.

Example:　A:　どうしたんですか。

　　　　　B:　雨にふられちゃったんです。

　　　　　　　雨にふられました。／雨にふられてしまいました。

Example　　　　　1　　　　　2　　　　　3

4　　　　　5　　　　　6　　　　　7

Activity 3   Work with the class. Use the passive construction to ask your classmates what they would prefer that others not do. Write their names and responses.

Example: A: 人にどんなことをされたら、いやですか。

B: そうですね。うそをつかれたら、いやですね。

名前	人にされたらいやなこと

Activity 4   Work with the class. Using the passive construction, ask your classmates about things and people who fit into the following categories. Ask as many classmates as you can to find the most common answers.

Example: A: 世界 (*the world*) で一番よく知られているアメリカ人はだれだと思いますか。

B: レディー・ガガだと思います。

世界 (*the world*) で一番〜	クラスメートの答え
Well-known American	
Well-known Japanese	
Well-read book	
Frequently visited place	
Frequently spoken language	
Frequently consumed drink	
Frequently eaten food	

II. Expressing conjecture based on indirect evidence using 〜らしい ; expressing conjecture based on direct evidence using 〜ようだ／みたいだ

A. Expressing conjecture based on indirect evidence using 〜らしい
(I understand that 〜 ; I hear that 〜 ; the general belief is that 〜)

The auxiliary adjective 〜らしい is used to express conjectures made by the speaker on the basis of information obtained indirectly, such as through print or word of mouth. This expression can also be used with conjectures based on visual observations, but unlike the form involving the verb or adjective stem + そうだ (*it looks like ~*), which implies a guess based on what the speaker has seen, らしい implies that the conjecture has been based on a more careful observation.

台風の後、まだ電気がつかなくて、不便らしい。
I understand that it's inconvenient because the electricity has not yet been restored since the typhoon.

気候が変わって、たつまきがふえているらしい。
It's my understanding that the climate has changed and there are more tornados.

洪水のひがいはあまりひどくなかったらしい。
It's my understanding that the damage from the flood was not very serious.

The word 〜らしい can be combined with both adjectives and verbs. The formation is the same as for 〜でしょう (*probably*) or かもしれない (*may*). That is, use a noun or な-adjective stem + らしい for the plain present affirmative form. Otherwise use the plain form + らしい.

NOTES

- If the speaker's conjecture is not strong, らしい is almost the same as the hearsay expression plain form + そうだ (*I heard ~*).

  ニュースによると、中国で大きい地震があったらしい。
  According to the news, there was a big earthquake in China.

  ニュースによると、中国で大きい地震があったそうだ。
  According to the news, there was a big earthquake in China.

- A negative conjecture is expressed by 〜ない／なかったらしい.

  あれは事故じゃないらしい。
  The general belief is that it was not an accident.

  洪水のひがいは大きくなかったらしい。
  The word is that the damage from the flood wasn't serious.

B. Expressing conjecture based on direct evidence using 〜ようだ／みたいだ (it appears that ~)

The auxiliary adjective 〜ようだ expresses a conjecture based on first hand, reliable information (usually visual information) and the reasonable knowledge of the speaker. This expression is thus used when the likelihood of a specific action or event happening or not happening is the greatest in the speaker's mind. On the other hand, the use of verb / adjective stem + そうだ (it looks like ~) indicates that the speaker is making a guess based on the his or her sensory input (what the speaker sees or feels), so in this case the reliability of the speaker's guess will vary.

昨日あの店にどろぼうが入ったようだ。　　*It appears that a thief broke into the store yesterday.*

The form 〜ようだ is different from 〜らしい in that 〜らしい usually expresses a conjecture based on second-hand information obtained from reading or hearsay, while 〜ようだ implies that the conjecture has come from first-hand information and the speaker's knowledge. Finally, it is different from 〜でしょう／だろう, which is used when the speaker's conjecture is not necessarily based on any information and he or she is merely guessing.

　　〜みたいだ is a colloquial version of 〜ようだ. The degree of the speaker's confidence in his or her conjecture is less with 〜みたいだ than with 〜ようだ.

山本：　清水先生は有名な先生のようだよ。
　　　　Apparently, Professor Shimizu is a famous professor.

高木：　そうなの？　あの先生、小さくてかわいくて、学生みたいだけど。
　　　　Really? She's so small and cute; she looks like a student.

A negative conjecture is expressed by 〜ないようだ／〜ないみたいだ／なかったようだ／なかったみたいだ.

彼女とはけんかしたけど、わかれなかったようだ。
It appears that he had a fight with his girlfriend but did not break up with her.

このへん冬になるとくまがよく出てくるが、今年はまだだれも見ていないみたいだ。
There are often bears here in the winter, but apparently this year no one has seen one.

あの火事で建物のひがいは大きかったけど、なくなった人はいなかったようだ。
The structural damage from the fire was severe, but no one seems to have died.

NOTES

- Both 〜ようだ and 〜みたいだ can be combined with adjectives and verbs. The formation of 〜みたいだ is the same as 〜らしい. That is, nouns and な-adjectives are followed by な before 〜みたいだ in the plain present affirmative form, but the plain forms of adjectives and verbs are used for other forms. Adjectives and verbs are combined with 〜ようだ in the same way that they are with 時—nouns are followed by the particle の and な-adjectives take な before 〜ようだ for the plain present affirmative form, but the plain form of adjectives and verbs are used for other forms.
- The following table shows the conjugation, source of evidence, and reliability of conjecture of らしい, ようだ, and みたいだ, as well as そうだ (it looks like) and でしょう.

Term of conjecture	Formation		Source of evidence and reliability of conjecture
	Verbs　　　　　焼ける (*to burn*) い -adjective　　こわい (*scary*) な -adjective　　不便（な）(*inconvenient*) Noun　　　　　　うそ (*lie*)		
	Affirmative	**Negative**	
Plain form + ようだ・みたいだ (*it appears that, it seems*)	焼けるようだ 焼けたようだ こわいようだ こわかったようだ 不便なようだ 不便だったようだ うそのようだ うそだったようだ	焼けないようだ 焼けなかったようだ こわくないようだ こわくなかったようだ 不便じゃないようだ 不便じゃなかったようだ うそじゃないようだ うそじゃなかったようだ	• First hand, reliable information • Most reliable
	焼けるみたいだ 焼けたみたいだ こわいみたいだ こわかったみたいだ 不便みたいだ 不便だったみたいだ うそみたいだ うそだったみたいだ	焼けないみたいだ 焼けなかったみたいだ こわくないみたいだ こわくなかったみたいだ 不便じゃないみたいだ 不便じゃなかったみたいだ うそじゃないみたいだ うそじゃなかったみたいだ	
Plain form + らしい (*I understand that*)	焼けるらしい 焼けたらしい こわいらしい こわかったらしい 不便らしい 不便だったらしい うそらしい うそだったらしい	焼けないらしい 焼けなかったらしい こわくないらしい こわくなかったらしい 不便じゃないらしい 不便じゃなかったらしい うそじゃないらしい うそじゃなかったらしい	• Indirect evidence or direct observation • More reliable than stem+ そうだ
Plain form + でしょう (*Probably*)	焼けるでしょう 焼けたでしょう こわいでしょう こわかったでしょう 不便でしょう 不便だったでしょう うそでしょう うそだったでしょう	焼けないでしょう 焼けなかったでしょう こわくないでしょう こわくなかったでしょう 不便じゃないでしょう 不便じゃなかったでしょう うそじゃないでしょう うそじゃなかったでしょう	• Evidence is not required, • Reliability varies from almost none to 100%
Adjective & verb stem + そうだ (*It looks like*)	焼けそうだ こわそうだ 不便そうだ	焼けなさそうだ／焼けそうにない こわくなさそうだ 不便じゃなさそうだ	• Direct (often visual) impression • May or may not be reliable

Plain form +
そうだ
(*I heard*)
	焼けたそうだ
	こわいそうだ
	こわかったそうだ
	不便だそうだ
	不便だったそうだ
	うそだそうだ
	うそだったそうだ
		焼けなかったそうだ
		こわくないそうだ
		こわくなかったそうだ
		不便じゃないそうだ
		不便じゃなかったそうだ
		うそじゃないそうだ
		うそじゃなかったそうだ
			· Hearsay,
			· No conjecture,
			  because it
			  is reported
			  speech

話してみましょう

Activity 1　You have overheard the following conversations between A and B. Based on what you have heard, tell your conjectures to your classmates, using 〜らしい.

Example:　A: 昨日どろぼうに入られたんですって？

B: ええ、家に帰ってきたら、パソコンがなくなっていたんですよ。

Your conjecture:　パソコンをぬすまれたらしいです。

1. A: 田中さん、結婚指輪を売るんだそうですよ。
   B: え、どうして？
   A: ご主人とわかれるそうですよ。
2. A: 山田さんの家の近くで火事があったそうですね。
   B: ああ、火事はあったけど家からはちょっと遠かったですよ。
3. A: 先生、どうしたんですか、その足？
   B: 昨日、交通事故にあってね。
4. A: 木村さん、このごろ暗いよね。
   B: うん、かれとけんかしたって言っていた。
5. A: 山田さん、休みなの？
   B: うん、昨日かいだんから落ちて、ケガしたんだって。
   A: え、それは大変。

Activity 2　Using the data presented in the culture section of this chapter, express your conjectures with 〜ようだ.

Example:　日本はほか (*other*) の国よりはんざいが少なくて安全なようだ。

Activity 3　Work with a partner. Think about a rumor that you've recently encountered and the source of information, and then have a conversation about it.

Example:　A: 東京で大きい地震が起きるかもしれないらしいよ。

B: え、そうなの？　どうして？

A: 東京では70年に一度大きい地震があるけど、1923年から大きい地震が起きていないんだって。

III. N のような／みたいな (*like ~*); N らしい N (*typical*)

The conjectural expressions 〜よう, 〜みたい, and らしい can be used to modify a noun to express its characteristics, and when preceded by another noun, such as "Noun 1 のような／みたいな Noun 2," means *Noun 2 that is just like Noun 1*. However, "Noun 1 らしい Noun 2" expresses quite a different meaning. This section deals with the usage of these expressions when they are preceded by another noun.

A. N のような／みたいな (*like ~*)

Both Nのような and Nみたいな describe something or someone based on resemblance to something else. The resemblance tends to be visual, but not necessarily limited to that. みたい is the colloquial form of ような.

pandara / Shutterstock.com

日本でアヒルのような電車を見ました。	*In Japan I saw a train that looks like a duck.*
日本でアヒルみたいな電車を見ました。	*In Japan I saw a train that looks like a duck.*
へびのようなせいかくの人	*a person who has the personality of a snake*
くまのようなおじさん	*a middle-aged man who looks like a bear*
うさぎのようなくも	*a cloud which looks like a bunny*
たつまきのような風	*a wind like a tornado*
ぞうの目のようなやさしい目をした人	*a person with eyes that are so gentle that they look like an elephant's eyes.*

ように and みたいに are adverbial forms of ような and みたい.

レディー・ガガのように有名（ゆう）になりたい。	*I would like to become famous like Lady Gaga.*
ぼくの彼女（かのじょ）は、さくらの花のようにかわいい人です。	*My girlfriend is just as cute as a cherry blossom.*
ライオンのように強くなりたい。	*I want to become strong like a lion.*

B. Noun + らしい (typical)

In this usage らしい means *having typical characteristics of* ~. Grammatically, it is an adjective. Thus, 男らしい人 is interpreted as *manly person*. In Japanese this expression does not have the negative connotation found in words such as *chauvinistic*, but anyone described in this way has to be male. If the person is female, the correct Japanese is 男のような人 (*a person who acts like a man*).

子供らしい子供　　*a typical child*

女らしい人　　　　*a ladylike person (female)*

男らしい人　　　　*a manly person (male)*

女らしい女　　　　*a ladylike woman*　　　　女のような男　*a man who acts like a woman*

男らしい男　　　　*a manly man*　　　　　　男のような女　*a woman who acts like a man*

話してみましょう

Activity 1　　Describe the following items using 〜のような.

Example:　ハンバーガーのようないす

Example　　　　　　1　　　　　　　　2　　　　　　　　3　　　　　　　　4

ちょきんばこ　　　はいざら
piggy bank　　　*ash tray*

5　　　　　　　　6　　　　　　　　7　　　　　　　　8

えんぴつけずり
pencil sharpener

Activity 2   Work with a classmate. Ask what kind of person he/she wants to become in the future and write down this wish in the table. Your classmates will answer using 〜のような or 〜のように.

Example: A: 将来どんな人になりたいですか。
しょう

B: 私は父のような人になりたいです。

or 父のように、強くてやさしい人になりたいです。

名前	〜のような・〜のように〜人

Activity 3   Work with a partner. Ask your partner what he/she considers typical about the following types of people or things.

Example: 冬らしい日

A: 冬らしい日って、どんな日ですか。

B: 雪がたくさんふって、寒い日です。

〜らしい人／物	パートナーの答え
1. アメリカ人らしいアメリカ人	
2. フランス人らしいフランス人	
3. 先生らしい先生	
4. 学生らしい学生	
5. 日本の車らしい車	
6. イタリアらしいデザイン	
7. 休みらしい休み	

◆ **Activity 4**   Work with the class. Ask your classmates on what occasions they think people might exhibit the characteristics listed in the table below.

Example: 男らしい

A: どんな時、男の人を男らしいと思いますか？

B: スポーツをしている時、男らしいと思います。

〜らしい	クラスメートの名前	クラスメートの答え
男らしい		
女らしい		
日本人らしい		
アメリカ人らしい		

ちょっとトリビア：The origin of the name Godzilla

One day in the Toho Studio, Mr. Tsuburaya (a special effects expert) saw a staff member who looked like a gorilla (ゴリラ) eating lunch like a whale (クジラ). ゴリラのような男がクジラのように昼御飯を食べていた。 He combined the two words—hence, ゴジラ.

IV. Expressing limited degree using だけ〜 affirmative and しか〜 negative

The suffixes だけ and しか follow a noun or quantity expression and both of them mean *only*. However, だけ is used only with an affirmative ending, and しか is used only with a negative ending.

A. Using だけ〜 affirmative (*just; only*)

だけ follows a noun or a quantity expression to express the meaning of *only*.

山田さんだけが来ました。	*Only Mr. Yamada came.*
友子：まだ歩くの？	*Do we still have to walk?*
まもる：もう少しだけ。あと百メートルだけだから。	*Just a little farther. Only another hundred meters.*
高子：その話、だれかにしたの？	*Have you told the story to anyone?*
ボブ：うん、彼女にだけ話した。	*Yeah, only to my girlfriend.*
山本：この駅には各駅停車だけが止まります。	*Only local trains stop at this station.*
鈴木：そうですか。つぎの駅は？	*I see. How about the next station?*
山本：つぎの駅には急行も止まります。	*Express trains also stop at the next station.*

昨日はつかれていたので、宿題だけしてすぐ寝ました。
Since I was tired yesterday, I just did my homework and went to bed immediately after.

When だけ is used with a noun, particles such as で and に may be placed either before or after だけ Exceptions are the particles が and を. These two particles must be placed after だけ or not used at all.

動物園だけ[で]見ることが出来ます。　　or　　動物園[で]だけ見ることが出来ます。
You can see it only in the zoo.

日本だけ[に]あります。　　　　　　or　　日本[に]だけあります。
It is only in Japan.

かれしだけ[を]招待しました。　　　or　　かれしだけ招待しました。
　　　　しょうたい　　　　　　　　　　　　　　　　しょうたい
I invited only my boyfriend.

山田さんだけ[が]来ました。　　　　or　　山田さんだけ来ました。
Only Yamada-san came.

B. Using しか〜 negative (only)

Like だけ, しか also means *only*, but it must be used in a sentence with a negative ending. しか is used with nouns and quantity expressions. しか implies *only 〜 and nothing else*, and sounds more exclusive than だけ. Therefore, しか is often used when the speaker expects more but finds less.

高橋さんしか来ませんでした。　　*Only Mr. Takahashi came.* (Other people should have
たかはし　　　　　　　　　　　　　　come.)

一万円しかありません。　　　　　*I only have 10,000 yen, and that is all.* (I should have
　　　　　　　　　　　　　　　　　more.)

一万円だけあります。　　　　　　*I have only 10,000 yen.*

去年、台風は三つしか来ませんでした。
　　　　たい
Only three typhoons came last year. (implies more typhoons usually come)

私は小さい地震しか経験したことがありません。
　　　　　じしん　　けいけん
I have only experienced a small earthquake.

どろぼうは家の中に５分ぐらいしかいなかったようだ。
It appears that the thief was in the house for only about five minutes.

When しか is used with a noun, the particle associated with it must precede しか. The particles が and を are omitted, but other particles remain except for the に of location, which may be deleted.

高橋さんしか知りません。　　　　　　*Only Mr. Takahashi knows.*
たかはし
肉しか食べません。　　　　　　　　　*I eat only meat.*

ここ（に）しかありません。　　　　　*It exists only here.*

私は山田さんに大学でしか会いません。　*I meet Yamada-san only on campus.*

話してみましょう

Activity 1 Answer the questions using the expressions in the parentheses and だけ or しか.

Example:　昨日たくさん人が来ていた？（高田さん）

いいえ、高田さんだけが来ていたよ。

いいえ、高田さんしか来ていなかったよ。

1. だれが知っていますか。（鈴木さん）
2. どろぼうは何人いましたか。（一人）
3. 交通事故にあったことがありますか。（一度）
4. その本はどこで売っていますか。（大学の本屋）
5. 今週はずっと休みなの？（金曜日）
6. 昨日たくさん電話があった？（田中さん）
7. 何をぬすまれたんですか。（さいふ）

Activity 2 Work as a class. First write the number of each of the items below that you have in your bag or backpack. Exchange information with your classmates to find out who has more or fewer items than others. Use だけ or しか if the number of items is small.

Example:　A：私はえんぴつを三本持っています。〜さんは何本持っていますか。

B：私は十本持っています。

C：たくさんありますね。ぼくは二本しか持っていません。

	私	クラスメート
えんぴつ		
黒か青のボールペン		
赤のボールペン		
マーカー (*marker*)		
ノート		
かぎ (*key*)		
本		
other (　　　)		
other (　　　)		

Activity 3 Work in a group of three to write as many sentences as possible with the words below, using both だけ and しか with each word. Each group should read its sentences to the class to see which has come up with the most sentences. Also, determine which sentence is the most creative and unique.

Example: ライオンは肉しか食べません。／肉だけ食べます。

1. 動物園のさる
2. かめ
3. 大きいさいがい
4. たつまき
5. 海外旅行
6. 日本語
7. 学生

 Activity 4 Work with a partner. Think of a relative, friend, or other person who habitually does only one particular thing under certain circumstances. Then tell your partner about that person. Your partner should show an interest in what you are saying.

Example: 田中先生は昼にカレーライスしか食べません。

A: ねえ、聞いて下さいよ。

B: 何？

A: 田中先生って、昼にカレーライスだけ食べるんですよ。／ カレーライスしか食べないんですよ。

B: へえ、本当<ruby>当<rt>とう</rt></ruby>！

V. Expressing opinions indirectly using 〜んじゃない （かと思う）

〜じゃないかと思う expresses the speaker's opinion but indicates some uncertainty.

かみなりが落<ruby>お<rt></rt></ruby>ちるんじゃないかと思う。　*I think lightning might strike.*
新しいインフルエンザじゃないかと思う。 *I think this might be the new flu.*

It is similar to 〜だろうと思う but is less certain.

Certain	ニュースは本当<ruby>当<rt>とう</rt></ruby>だと思う。	*I think the news is true.*
Less certain	ニュースは本当<ruby>当<rt>とう</rt></ruby>だろうと思う。	*I think the news is probably true.*
Least certain	ニュースは本当<ruby>当<rt>とう</rt></ruby>なんじゃないかと思う。	*I think the news might be true.*

～んじゃないか does of itself not indicate a negative, but merely emphasizes the uncertainty of the opinion. Use of the negative form before ～んじゃないか shows that the speaker's uncertain opinion is leaning toward the negative.

たつまきは起きないんじゃないかと思う。   *I think that a tornado will not form.*

大雨はふらないんじゃないかと思う。   *I think it won't rain heavily.*
<small>おおあめ</small>

いそがしいんじゃないかと思って、電話しなかったんだ。
I thought you'd be busy, so I didn't call you.

あの火事で田中さんの家も焼けたんじゃないかと思って、心配していたんだ。
<small>か じ</small>　　　　　　　　　　　　　　　　　　<small>や</small>　　　　　　　　　　　　　<small>しんぱい</small>
I thought Tanaka-san's house might have been destroyed by the fire, so I was worried.

The expressions ～んじゃないですか／でしょうか, ～んじゃないかな and ～んじゃない? can be used instead of ～んじゃないかと思う to indicate that something is the speaker's opinion or that the speaker is uncertain about it.

どろぼうはにげたんじゃない？   *I think the thief has already escaped.*
どろぼうはにげたんじゃないかな。   *I think the thief has already escaped.*

変なうわさがあるんじゃないですか。   *I think there is a strange rumor.*
変なうわさがあるんじゃないでしょうか。   *I think there is a strange rumor.*

話してみましょう

Activity 1   Answer the questions using ～んじゃないかと思う.

Example: 今日雪がふるでしょうか。

　　　　　さあ、よく分かりませんが、ふるんじゃないかと思います。

　　　　　さあ、よく分かりませんが、ふらないんじゃないかと思います。

1. 地震が起きた時、この建物は安全だと思いますか。
<small>じ しん</small>　　　　　　　<small>たて</small>　　<small>あんぜん</small>
2. 火事の方が台風よりこわいと思いますか。
<small>か じ</small>　　　<small>たい</small>
3. 犬は頭がいいと思いますか。
4. クジラは魚だと思いますか。
5. 日本にもくまがいると思いますか。
6. へびはライオンを食べられると思いますか。

Activity 2　Work with the class. First, write the names of the animals that you think fit the descriptions in the chart in the 私 column. Then ask three classmates about what animals they think fit the descriptions, and complete the chart.

さる　くま　クジラ　へび　かめ　ぞう
ライオン　犬　ねこ　ぶた　パンダ

Example:　A:　中国にいないのはどの動物だと思う？
　　　　　B:　そうだね。クジラじゃないかと思うけど。

	私	＿＿＿さん	＿＿＿さん	＿＿＿さん
中国にいない動物				
オーストラリアにいない動物				
動物園では見られない動物				
多すぎる動物				
少なくなっている動物				

Activity 3　Work with a partner. Ask your partner whether he or she agrees with statements 1 through 5, and why or why not.

Example:　さいがいの中では台風が一番こわいです。
　　　　　A:　さいがいの中では、台風が一番こわいと思う？
　　　　　B:　ううん、台風より火事の方がこわいんじゃない？
　　　　　A:　どうしてそう思うの？
　　　　　B:　だって ('Cause)、台風はいつ来るか分かるけど、
　　　　　　　火事は分からないからね。

1. 生きる (to live) ためなら、人は動物を食べてもいいです。
2. いじめははんざいです。
3. 人の悪口を言ってはいけません。
4. アメリカははんざいが多すぎます。
5. 勉強はむだです。

聞く練習

上手な聞き方

Expressions in oral narrative

Oral narratives are very common in interpersonal communication in any language. It is a part of human nature to share stories with others when something happens, whether it is good or bad. Being able to tell a story well is an important skill to have in learning a new language. The process of storytelling involves different kinds of information. For example, before you start the main plot of the story, you will need to get the attention of your listeners. Verb-past tense + んです is used frequently as an attention-getting phrase. (e.g. 「ねえ、聞いて（下さいよ）。〜があったんですよ。」) This helps to orient the audience by providing a setting and context. The main plot usually progresses chronologically. Conjunctions, such as そして, それから, それで, and the like, are used to string a chain of events. Other common expressions found in storytelling are reported speech (e.g. 「〜と言う」), and 「〜てしまう」.

練習

Listen to the following conversation between two people. Try to identify the common expressions used in story telling as explained above.

ブタの話

聞く前に

日本語で答えて下さい。

1. アメリカの学校では動物をかいますか。どんな動物をかいますか。
2. ブタはどんな動物だと思いますか。

聞いてみましょう

Listen to this conversation between a man and a woman, and answer the following questions..

1. 男の人と女の人のどちらが「話」をしていますか。
2. 何について話していますか。
3. 映画のタイトルは何ですか。
4. どんな映画ですか。
5. ブタは最後にどうなったと思いますか。

聞き上手話し上手

上手に話をする　上手に話を聞く
Telling a story well and listening to a story well

As explained in the previous section, when you want to tell a story you must first get the listeners' attention. Some typical opening phrases are listed below, but there are many others as well. As you can see, ねえ (or ねえねえ) is very common in casual speech.

ねえねえ、聞いて（よ）。

ねえ、昨日、おもしろいことがあったんだ。

あのう、昨日、ちょっとおもしろいことがあったんですけど。

おもしろいこと can be changed to ひどいこと, うれしいこと, かなしいこと, etc.

The listener plays a very important role in the successful telling of a story. It is important for the listener to remain attentive and provide feedback to help the speaker tell the story. You learned あいづち in *Nakama 1*, Chapters 3 and 4 such as ええ, うん, あ, and そう to indicate that you are listening. You can go a step further to become a good listener. Some common phrases are listed below.

1. Indicating an interest in a conversation and maintaining the flow
   ええ、ええ。　へえ、そうですか。

2. Eliciting more information
   それで…　その後、どうなったんですか。

3. Offering a reaction
   それは大変でしたね。　それはお気のどくでしたね。　それはよかったですね。　それはうれしかったでしょうね。　それはおどろいたでしょうね。
   それは心配ですね。

4. Showing a spontaneous reaction such as surprise
   まさか。　えーっ、本当ですか。　うっそー。 (very casual)
   まじー。 (very casual)

As you can see, the listener is not a passive participant. However, keep in mind your initial task is to have the other person tell the entire story, and not to engage in a conversation while the story is in progress.

練習

Try to remember incidents that made you angry, happy, sad, concerned, or surprised. Relate these to your partner as stories. Your partner should provide feedback to encourage the storytelling, as in the two examples below.

A: ねえ、ねえ、聞いて。「おくりびと」ってアカデミーしょう (*Academy Award*) を取った映画らしいよ。

B: えっ、「おくりびと」って何？

A: 知らないの？　何年か前の日本の映画で、なくなった人の体をきれいにしたりする人のお話よ。とてもいい映画だった。

B: そうなんだ、ぜんぜん知らなかった。かなしい映画？

A: ううん、なけるところはあるけど、かなしい映画じゃないと思う。

A: この間、かれとデートしたの。

B: うんうん。よかったじゃない。

A: でも、30分、おくれて来たの。

B: ええ、ひどい。

A: しかも (*moreover*)、「ごめん」って言わないの。

B: うっそー。

A: うん、でも、食事も映画も、全部おごってくれたから、いいの。（おごる = *to treat someone*）

B: なんだ、ばかばかしい。(*What! That's ridiculous!*)

漢字

Using a kanji dictionary

As you begin reading more advanced materials, you will need to be able to use some sort of comprehensive **kanji** dictionary. There are several kanji dictionaries for learners of Japanese available, and most of them use variations of the traditional method to look up characters. (If you want to purchase one, you should compare them and consult with your instructor.)

Characters in a **kanji** dictionary are always grouped according to traditional radicals (部首) and ordered according to residual stroke counts within each radical group. Residual stroke counts are the number of strokes required to write a character exclusive of those needed to write the radical. Radicals themselves are ordered from the simplest to most complex in stroke counts. Thus, in order to look up a character, you must first identify its traditional radical. Then, go to the section of the dictionary that contains that radical. Lastly, count the residual strokes and look through the pages until you find the character you are looking for.

As was described in *Nakama 1*, Chapter 11, identifying a traditional radical is at times difficult, yet it is the crucial first step in using a traditional **kanji** dictionary. For example, the radical of 家 is 宀, but the radical of 字 is 子. For another example, the radical of 勝

(meaning *to win*) is 力, and not 月. This difficulty comes from the fact that the traditional radical system was created more than 1,000 years ago for the purpose of classifying characters, and the most salient component of the **kanji** was not necessarily assigned as the radical.

Most of the **kanji** dictionaries for learners of Japanese overcome this problem by rearranging radical groupings from traditional radicals to the most salient component shapes. In these dictionaries, you will find 家 and 字 in the same group, namely under 宀. 勝 is found in the 月 group instead of the 力 group. Once you become familiar with the idea of component shapes, it is fairly easy to identify the correct grouping in these dictionaries. The component shapes are ordered according to the number of strokes, so you need to be able to count the number of strokes correctly. The shape 宀 requires three strokes and 月 is four strokes. Some dictionaries may have a table like the one below on the inside of the front cover.

Simplified table of component shapes
(or radicals)

2 亻 ハ 冫 儿 匚 凵 冂
3 木 土 女 艹 宀 口
4 彳 月 心 辶
5 禾 罒 疒
6 糸
7 言
8 門 雨 金

Once you identify the most salient component shape and its stroke count, the second step is to count the residual strokes. Since there are no short cuts for this step, you must be able to count them correctly. Within each group, there might be several characters that share the same number of residual strokes. Since they are not listed in any particular order, you will need to go through them to find the one you are looking for.

Dictionaries also have a pronunciation index for kanji at the end, so if you know or can guess either the **kun** or the **on** reading of a character, you can look it up there, also. But remember that there are many **kanji** which share the same **on** reading. Readings such as こう and せい, for example, are particularly common. Thus, if you have a choice between **on** and **kun** readings, it is better to use the **kun** reading. If an index uses Romanization for pronunciation, **on** readings are usually written in upper-case letters and **kun** readings are in lower-case letters.

Electronic dictionaries（電子辞書）

In addition to the traditional printed kanji dictionaries, many electronic dictionaries（電子辞書）are available on the market. These electronic dictionaries contain a large number of dictionaries such as English-Japanese, Japanese-English, Japanese-Japanese, encyclopedia, **kanji** dictionaries, and the like. With a **kanji** dictionary in an electronic format, you can search for a **kanji** by selecting its component shapes（部品検索）rather than its traditional radical（部首検索）. Thus, an important skill is to break down a kanji into different component shapes. You can certainly search a **kanji** through **on** or **kun** reading as well.

Some models let you use a stylus to input **kanji** by hand（手書き入力）. This type of handwriting input system is sensitive to the correct stroke order although it allows minor deviations. This is a good reason to learn the correct stroke order for the **kanji** you study.

The significant advantage of an electronic dictionary over paper dictionary is the ability to jump from one dictionary to another. Thus, you can easily go from a single **kanji** to a series of compounds, and then to a Japanese-English dictionary to find meanings.

There is dictionary software available for some game consoles. One can purchase dictionary software to use the game console as a 電子辞書.

1. Practice counting the strokes of the following components. The correct answers are provided.

> **a.** 匚 **d.** 广 **g.** 囗 **j.** 火 **m.** 冊 **p.** 頁 **s.** 券 **u.** 灬
> **b.** 糸 **e.** 川 **h.** 月 **k.** 廴 **n.** 生 **q.** 己 **t.** 門 **v.** 聿
> **c.** 日 **f.** 勹 **l.** 艹 **i.** 乂 **o.** 付 **r.** 井

(a. 2, b. 6, c. 4, d. 3, e. 3, f. 2, g. 3, h. 4, i. 3, j. 4, k. 3, l. 2, m. 5, n. 5, o. 5, p. 9, q. 3, r. 4, s. 8, t. 8, u. 4, v. 6)

2. Now, use a **kanji** dictionary to look up the following **kanji** and the **kanji** appearing in this chapter.

   1. 勝   2. 区   3. 囲   4. 細   5. 建   6. 順   7. 府   8. 包   9. 簡   10 燃
   11. 星

3. Using the same **kanji** dictionary, find the following characters by looking them up under their **kun** and **on** readings. Compare how fast you can find them.

   1. 近 (**on:** KIN, **kun:** chikai)   5. 高 (**on:** KO , **kun:** takai)   9. 静 (**on:** SEI **kun:** shizuka)

   2. 習 (**on:** SYU, **kun:** narau)   6. 兄 (**on:** KYO, **kun:** ani)   10. 時 (**on:** JI, **kun:** toki)

   3. 会 (**on:** KAI, **kun:** au)   7. 校 (**on:** KO)

   4. 雪 (**on:** SETSU, **kun:** yuki)   8. 究 (**on:** KYU, **kun:** kiwa)

4. Write as many of the component shapes of the following **kanji** as you can.

   1. 試   3. 遊   5. 泳   7. 売   9. 困
   2. 験   4. 地   6. 払   8. 落   10. 急

心 心	mind, heart こころ　シン	ノ 心 心 心		

母の病気のことが心配です。
しんぱい

配 配	to deliver くば(る)　ハイ・パイ	一 丆 両 两 西 酉 酉 酉 配		

心配しないで下さい。
しんぱい

困 困	to be in trouble こま(る)　コン	丨 冂 冂 団 困 困 困		

となりの人がうるさくて困っています。
こま

難 難	difficult むずか(しい)　ナン	艹 苫 苣 茣 茣 菓 斳 斳 難		

説明が難しかった。
むずか

弱　弱　weak　よわ（い）　ジャク　体が弱い。
　　　　　　　　　　　　　　　　　　　よわ

招　招　to invite　まね（く）　ショウ　食事に招待されました。
　　　　　　　　　　　　　　　　　　　　しょうたい

待　待　to wait　ま（つ）　タイ　パーティに招待されました。　待って下さい。
　　　　　　　　　　　　　　　　　　　しょうたい　　　　　　　ま

呼　呼　to call　よ（ぶ）　コ　タクシーを呼んで下さい。
　　　　　　　　　　　　　　　　　よ

遊　遊　to play, idle　あそ（ぶ）　ユウ　友達と遊園地で遊びました。
　　　　　　　　　　　　　　　　　　　　ゆう　　あそ

泳　泳　to swim　およ（ぐ）　エイ　魚みたいに泳ぎます。
　　　　　　　　　　　　　　　　　　　　およ

建　建　to build　たて（る）・た（つ）　ケン・コン　建物　建設
　　　　　　　　　　　　　　　　　　　　　　　　　たて　けんせつ

経　経　passage of time　ケイ・キョウ　日本の経済　経済学　経験
　　　　　　　　　　　　　　　　　　　けいざい　けいざいがく　けいけん

売　売　to sell　う（る）　バイ　ネットでギターを売りました。
　　　　　　　　　　　　　　　　　　　　　　　　　　う

交　交　to intersect, to mix　まじ（わる）　コウ　交通事故にあう。
　　　　　　　　　　　　　　　　　　　　　　　こうつうじ こ

落　落　to fall, to drop　お（ちる）・お（とす）　ラク　試験に落ちました。
　　　　　　　　　　　　　　　　　　　　　　　　　　　お

暗	暗	dark くら(い)　アン	暗いから気をつけて下さい。 　くら	l ｜ 冂 ｜ 日 ｜ 日⌐ ｜ 日ヴ ｜ 日立 ｜ 日产 ｜ 日音 ｜ 暗
洪	洪	flood コウ　洪水 　　こうずい	丶 ｜ 氵 ｜ 氵 ｜ 氵一 ｜ 氵十 ｜ 氵世 ｜ 洪 ｜ 洪
利	利	advantage リ　電車を利用する。　便利 　　　　りよう　　　　り	ノ ｜ 二 ｜ 千 ｜ 千 ｜ 禾 ｜ 利 ｜ 利
全	全	whole, entirely まった(く)　ゼン　全然悪くありません。　全部　安全 　　　　　　　　　　ぜんぜん　　　　　　ぜんぶ　あんぜん	ノ ｜ 人 ｜ 仝 ｜ 今 ｜ 仝 ｜ 全
急	急	sudden, steep, hurry いそ(ぐ)　キュウ　急に家に帰った。　急行　特急 　　　　　　　　　　きゅう　　　　きゅう　とっきゅう	ノ ｜ ク ｜ ㇖ ｜ 刍 ｜ 刍 ｜ 刍 ｜ 急 ｜ 急 ｜ 急
故	故	deceased, old コ　交通事故 　こうつうじこ	一 ｜ 十 ｜ 古 ｜ 古 ｜ 古 ｜ 古 ｜ 故 ｜ 故
台	台	pedestal, platform counter for machines ダイ・タイ　車が三台ある　台風 　　　　　　　　だい　　　たい	㇄ ｜ ㇖ ｜ 台 ｜ 台 ｜ 台
不	不	not, un- (prefix) フ　ここは不便です。 　　　ふべん	一 ｜ ㇇ ｜ 不 ｜ 不

読めるようになった漢字

泳ぐ　売る　売り場　落ちる　落とす　待つ　遊ぶ　遊園地　呼ぶ　招待する

暗い　心配　困る　経験　経営学　火事　事故　交通事故　変わる　洪水　便利
　　　　　　　　えい

不便　難しい　弱い　安全　安心　急な　急行　特急　建物　台風　全部
　　　　　　　　　　　　　　　　　　　　　　　　とっ

日本人の名前：清水　高木　高橋　友子
　　　　　　　し

練習

下の文を読んで下さい。

1. この試験は受けた経験がないし、難しそうなので心配しています。試験に落ちるかもしれません。
2. 私の会社は、駅から遠くて不便な所にありましたが、先月駅に近くて便利な建物に引っ越しました。
3. 友達を待っていたら、急に空が暗くなった。台風が来るらしい。
4. A: 今度の週末に遊園地に行きませんか。
   B: すみません、急な仕事が入って、今週末はちょっとだめなんです。
5. 好きな人を映画に招待しようとかんがえています。
6. 大きい店なのに、パソコン売り場がないので、困った。
7. 体が弱いので、泳がない方がいいと思います。
8. 友達を呼んで、パソコンで遊んだ。
9. このへんは交通事故が多くて、あまり安全じゃありません。
10. 大雨がふっているから、洪水になるかもしれない。

読む練習

上手な読み方

Understanding the structure of Japanese narrative texts

When narrating a story, an English writer often organizes the story in terms of how events are sequenced. For example,

Tomoko did not do well on the test, so her mother scolded her.

This is also the case in Japanese. However, the story also needs to be organized in terms of a single person's perspective in Japanese. Therefore, a literal translation of an English story, such as the following example, sounds awkward in Japanese. In this example, the two sentences express different perspectives: Tomoko in the first sentence and the mother in the second sentence.

友子さんはテストが出来なかった。だから、お母さんはおこった。

In order to maintain a consisent viewpoint throughout the story, the topic of the sentence should be kept constant across sentences.

友子さんはテストが出来なかった。だから、お母さんにおこられた。

Tomoko did not do well on the test. So she was scolded by her mother.

Another difference between English and Japanese narrative is the use of tense. In English, a writer normally stays in a single tense (i.e. present or past), but tenses can be mixed in Japanese. Writers can use the past tense to describe the foreground, or main events in a sequence. At the same time the writer can also use the present tense to express background information or to express events in a vivid, imaginative way.

Compare the following example in Japanese and in its literal translation in English.

あやかは朝起きて、空を見た。今日はとてもいい天気だ。かずおはまだ寝ている。あやかはコーヒーをいれて、かずおを起こしに行った。

Ayaka woke up in the morning and looked at the sky. It is a fine day today. Kazuo is still sleeping. Ayaka made coffee and went to wake Kazuo up.

練習

Text A and B describe the same story, but one of them flows better than the other. Compare the texts, decide which one is better, and explain why it is better.

Text A
この間、父は、おなかが痛くなって、病院に行った。そしたら、手術 (*surgery*) をしなければならないと言われた。父は医者も病院もきらいだ。だから、手術はしたくない。でも、手術の予約をするために病院に電話したら、「明日入院して下さい。」と言われた。突然だったので、父は思わず、「今、ちょっと気分が悪いので、来週にしてもらえませんか。」と言ってしまった。

Text B
父はこの間おなかが痛くなって、病院に行った。そしたら、医者が手術をしなければならないと言った。父は医者も病院もきらいだった。だから、手術はしたくなかった。でも、手術の予約をするために病院に電話したら、病院が「明日入院して下さい。」と言った。突然だったので、父は思わず、「今、ちょっと気分が悪いので、来週にしてもらえませんか。」と言ってしまった。

地球の温暖化　Global warming
ち きゅう　 おんだん か

読む前に

A. 下の文を読んで、下線 (*underline*) の言葉の意味は何かかんがえて下さい。
か せん

1. 地球は今私たちや動物が住んでいる所で、外から見ると、青くてきれいだそう
ち きゅう
です。

2. 地球が暖かくなることを温暖化といいます。
ち きゅう　あたた　　　　　　おんだん か

3. 小さい子供のおもちゃはたいていプラスチックで作られています。赤ちゃんの
食べ物の入れ物もたいていプラスチックで作られています。

4. 色々な国の人が会ってする大きいミーティングを国際会議と言います。
こくさいかい ぎ

5. トースターやオーブンやドライヤーのことを電気製品と言います。
せいひん

6. 人や動物は二酸化炭素を出します。車も二酸化炭素を出します。
に さん か たん そ　　　　　　　　　　　　 に さん か たん そ

B. 質問に答えて下さい。

1. 地球は毎年暖かくなっていると言われていますが、それについてどう思いますか。
ち きゅう　　　あたた

2. どうして地球は暖かくなっているのだと思いますか。
ち きゅう　あたた

3. 地球の気温が上がるとどうして困るのですか。
ち きゅう

4. ～さんの国ではこの問題について、どんなことをしていますか。

5. ～さんはどんなことをしたらいいと思いますか。

読んでみましょう

つぎの文章 (*text*) には知らない言葉がたくさんありますが、気にしないで (*without*
ぶんしょう
worrying) 読んで、概要 (*gist*) だけ取って下さい。
がいよう

言葉のリスト

沈む しず	to sink	砂漠 さ ばく	desert
二酸化炭素 に さん か たん そ	CO$_2$	世界 せ かい	world

1850年頃まで、地球の温度はあまり変わらなかったそうだ。しかし、1850年から地球の温度は少しずつ上がっているそうだ。そして、1970年頃から気温の上がり方が急に高くなっていると言われていて、1900年から2100年までに地球の温度は2℃から6℃ぐらい上がるそうだ。これを地球温暖化という。

温暖化が進むと、海面水位は60cmから1mぐらい上がってしまうらしい。そうなると、海の中に沈んでしまう国もあるようだ。例えば、オーストラリアの北東にあるツバルという国や、ダイビングで有名なモルディブは沈んでしまうと言われている。

温暖化の被害は他にもある。例えば、アメリカではハリケーンが、日本では台風や洪水が多くなるし、中国の北の方は砂漠が増えていくようだ。そこで、この問題について、1992年から色々な国で国際会議が開かれているようだ。

温暖化を起こすものは色々あるが、そのうち64%は二酸化炭素である。1994年の調べでは、日本は世界で四番目に二酸化炭素を多く出していた。また、日本では、1992年から1994年までに、二酸化炭素が7%も増えていた。

二酸化炭素が急に増えたのは、人のライフスタイルが変わったからである。毎年、森は少しずつなくなり、畑や町になった。そして、歩く人は少なくなり、車に乗る人が増えた。テレビや冷蔵庫は大きくなり、オーブンやエアコンなどの電気製品を使う人も多くなった。それに、スーパーやデパートでは野菜も果物も肉もプラスチックの入れ物に入れられているし、スプーン、フォーク、お皿など色々な物がプラスチックで作られ、捨てられている。実際、私達が毎日出す二酸化炭素は全体の45%にもなるらしい。

温暖化を防ぐために、国や工場や大会社がしなければならないことはたくさんあるが、一人一人が自分のライフスタイルを変えなければならないのではないだろうか。便利だから、楽だからといって、自動車や電気製品を使いすぎないように今からしていかなければ、この地球を守ることは出来ない。

読んだ後で

A. 下の質問に日本語で答えて下さい。

1. 地球温暖化って何ですか。

2. この文章 (*text*) を書いた人は何が言いたいのですか。

3. 2100 年までにはどんなことが起きるかもしれませんか。それはどうしてですか。

4. この文章を書いた人は、どうして二酸化炭素は多くなっていると言っていますか。

B. Read the following statements about global warming. Circle はい if the statement is true according to what you read, and いいえ if it isn't.

1. はい　いいえ　温暖化のげんいん (*cause*) は二酸化炭素だけだ。

2. はい　いいえ　電気を使うと二酸化炭素が多くなる。

3. はい　いいえ　温暖化になると、中国で洪水が増える。

4. はい　いいえ　日本では二年間で二酸化炭素が7パーセントふえた。

5. はい　いいえ　温暖化をふせぐためには、公害を起こさないようにする
　　　　　　　　ことが一番大事だ。

C. 下のグラフは二酸化炭素をたくさん出している国のデータです。グラフを見て、質問に答えて下さい。

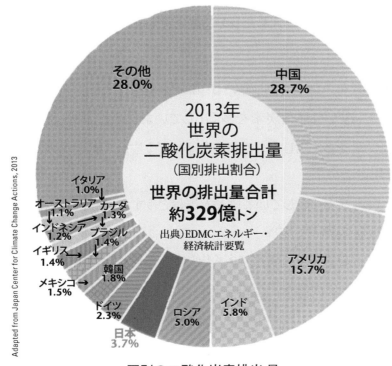

国別の二酸化炭素排出量

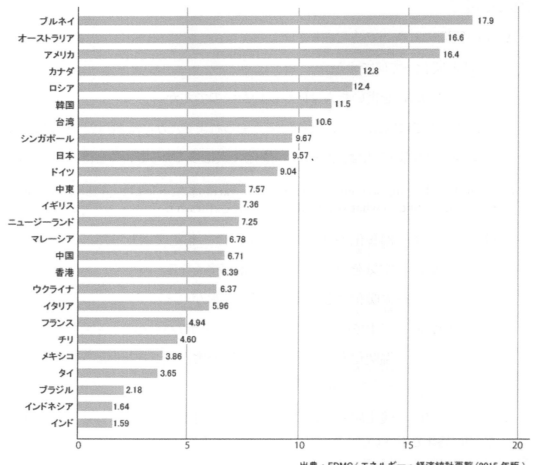

出典：EDMC/ エネルギー・経済統計要覧（2015 年版）

一人あたりの二酸化炭素排出量
に さん か たん そ はいしゅつりょう

1. 二酸化炭素を一番多く出している国はどの国ですか。
   に さん か たん そ

2. どの国の人達が二酸化炭素を多く出していますか。
   に さん か たん そ

3. 二酸化炭素を多く出している国や人達はどうして二酸化炭素を多く出している
   に さん か たん そ　　　　　　　　　　　　　　　　　　　　に さん か たん そ
   のだと思いますか。

4. 二酸化炭素を多く出している国や人達はどうすれば二酸化炭素を少なくするこ
   に さん か たん そ　　　　　　　　　　　　　　　　　　　　に さん か たん そ
   とが出来ると思いますか。

5. 二酸化炭素を世界で二番目に多く出している国はどの国ですか。
   に さん か たん そ

6. この国が二酸化炭素を出しているのはどうしてだと思いますか。
   に さん か たん そ

総合練習
そうごう

A. うわさ話 *(rumors)* をしてみよう
ばなし

Work in groups of three or four. Gossip about the topics below.

うわさ話1：　えりかです。ボーイフレンドがほしいんですが、今はいません。
ばなし
　　　　　　　好きなタイプはキムタクみたいな男の人です。せが高くて、イケ
　　　　　　　メンが好きです。

うわさ話2：　高橋です。来年、アメリカに行って、日本のレストランではたら
ばなし
　　　　　　　こうと思っています。でも、英語がぜんぜん出来ないので、心配
　　　　　　　です。レストランのオーナーになりたいんです。

うわさ話3：　さいとうです。この間、おさけを飲みすぎてしまいました。パー
ばなし
　　　　　　　ティでうたをうたったり、さわいだりしたのですが、おぼえてい
　　　　　　　ません。朝起きたら自分のアパートで寝ていて、おどろきました。
　　　　　　　でも、どうやって帰って来たのか分かりませんでした。

B. さいがいの経験 Experiences with natural disasters

1. When you talk about your or someone else's experiences with accidents, natural disasters, etc., what sorts of details do you think are important to include?
2. If you are listening to people describing their experience about accidents, natural disasters, etc., what sorts of questions would you ask?
3. When listening to such stories, what kinds of expressions do you use to show your emotional support, interest, and understanding?
4. Work with a partner. Recall a personal experience with a natural disaster. (If you have never experienced one, relate the experience of a family member or friend.) Try to recall all the details so you can describe them to your partner. Ask questions to each other. Then write about what you have heard and tell the story to the class.

Example:　A:　〜さんはさいがいを経験したことがありますか。

　　　　　B:　ええ、あります。私は小学校三年生の時、日本に住んでいたん
　　　　　　　ですが、その時、大きい地震がありました。
　　　　　　　　　　　　　　　　　　　　じしん

　　　　　A:　そうですか。日本のどこに住んでいたんですか。

　　　　　B:　東京です。

　　　　　A:　そうですか。じゃあ、その時のことをもう少し話してくれませんか。

　　　　　B:　ええ、いいですよ。その日は日曜日で、私は家にいたんです。

C. 日本のニュースについてしらべてみよう
Let's check out the Japanese news

Look through some Japanese websites and find a piece of recent news in Japanese that you can understand. Print it out and then summarize it in Japanese. Show and tell your news to your class.

👬 ロールプレイ

1. You heard a rumor that an earthquake is likely to happen in Tokyo in the near future. Ask your friend what to do when an earthquake happens.

2. You heard about a severe earthquake in a town where some of your Japanese friends live. You tried to call your friends, but the phone lines were jammed. You would like to know more about the situation. Tell another Japanese friend about it and ask what you should do.

3. You suspect that the nearby factory is polluting your town and causing a health problem. Tell your neighbor about your suspicion and explain why you think this. Express your anger and concern.

4. You think that you are being discriminated against by your boss because of your race (or gender). Describe your situation to your friend and ask for suggestions.

5. You have a roommate who is irresponsible. The roommate does many irresponsible things, such as staying up late, bringing friends over, not cleaning up, etc. Complain to your friend about your roommate.

6. You had your apartment broken into and some things are missing. Report the incident to a police officer.

7. You heard a rumor that a new type of influenza is spreading in the United States. In a few days you are supposed to meet a friend at Narita Airport who is coming from the United States to Japan. Ask someone for advice.

Chapter 9

第九課
だいきゅうか

Photo courtesy authors

文化と習慣
ぶんか　しゅうかん
Culture and Customs

Objectives	Describing customs and regulations and expressing appreciation, and asking for permission to do something
Vocabulary	Culture and customs, world religions, socializing, leave taking
Dialogue	日本で困ったこと *Problems Alice faced in Japan*
Japanese Culture	An outline of Japanese history; religion and customs in Japan
Grammar	I. Expressing the performance of a favor using てあげる／くれる／もらう
	II. Making or letting someone do something using the causative form
	III. Requesting permission to do something using the causative て-form and expressions of requests
	IV. Expressing the immediate future using 〜る + ところ; the current situation using 〜ている + ところ; and the immediate past using 〜た + ところ
	V. Expressing time durations using 間 and 間に; tense in subordinate clauses
Listening	Monitoring and evaluating your understanding, きせきの口紅 *Miracle lipstick* くちべに
Communication	Leave taking
Kanji	Guessing the meanings of unfamiliar **kanji**
	笑　泣　助　考　払　化　調　集　的　失
	当　期　和　重　界　正　由　宗　治　次　有　最　興
Reading	Monitoring and evaluating your understanding, マンガ

単語
たん

Nouns

あいさつ	挨拶	a greeting, 〜にあいさつ（を）する to greet ~
アドバイス		advice, アドバイスをする to advise
アニメ		animation
いけばな	生け花	flower arranging
イスラムきょう	イスラム教	Islam
いのり	祈り	prayer, おいのりをする to offer a prayer
インターネット		Internet, it can be abbreviated as ネット
おじぎ	お辞儀	bowing, おじぎをする to bow
キス		kiss, キスをする to kiss
きょういく	教育	education
きょうみ	興味	interest, 〜にきょうみがある interested in ~
キリストきょう	キリスト教	Christianity
げいじゅつ	芸術	art
けいざい	経済	economy
さどう	茶道	tea ceremony
し	詩	poetry
しゃかい	社会	society
しゅうかん	習慣	custom
しゅうきょう	宗教	religion
しゅうじ	習字	calligraphy
しんとう	神道	Shinto religion
せいざ	正座	formal Japanese-style sitting posture, せいざをする to sit in a formal Japanese style
せいじ	政治	politics
せかい	世界	world
たのみ	頼み	request
チップ		tip, gratuity
つきあい		keeping company with someone, associating with someone
はいく	俳句	a Japanese verse form that consists of three lines, containing five, seven, and five syllables respectively
ハグ		hug, ハグをする to hug
ぶっきょう	仏教	Buddhism

ブログ		blog
ぶんか	文化	culture
ほか	他	other, ほかの人 other people, ほかの学生 other students
マンガ	漫画	cartoon, graphic novel, manga
みおくり	見送り	farewell, leave taking
み（ん）な	皆	all, everyone, みなさん everyone
むかえ	迎え	meeting, greeting むかえに行く／来る to go/come to pick up (someone)
もんだい	問題	problem
ゆか	床	floor
ユダヤきょう	ユダヤ教	Judaism
らくご	落語	rakugo, a traditional storytelling performance
りゆう	理由	reason (for doing something)

う -verbs

あやまる	謝る	to apologize
いわう	祝う	to celebrate
ことわる	断る	to refuse, to decline, たのみをことわる to decline a request 招待をことわる to decline an invitation
すわる	座る	to sit down
つきあう	つき合う	to go out with, to keep company with, to have a steady relationship
ならう	習う	to learn

る -verbs

しんじる	信じる	to believe
たすける	助ける	to save, to help

い -adjectives

こころぼそい	心細い	lonely, helpless

な -adjectives

しつれい（な）	失礼（な）	rude
ていねい（な）	丁寧（な）	polite
でんとうてき（な）	伝統的（な）	traditional

Adverbs

ぜったい（に）	絶対（に）	definitely
はっきり		explicitly

Suffixes

〜てき（な）	〜的（な）	suffix that converts kanji compound nouns to な -adjectives meaning "pertaining to ~", e.g., でんとうてき traditional, せいじてき political, けいざいてき economical or pertaining to economics, しゃかいてき social, ぶんかてき cultural

Expressions

いろいろおせわになりました。	色々お世話になりました。	You've taken very good care of me. Thank you for everything.
おかげ（さま）で	お陰（様）で	thanks to 〜
これからもどうぞよろしく（おねがいします）。	これからもどうぞよろしく（お願いします）。	Please stay in touch (with me) in the future, too.
そろそろしつれいします。	そろそろ失礼します。	I should be going.
たのみ／ねがいをきく	頼み／願いを聞く	to grant a request
どうもごちそうさま（でした）。	どうもご馳走様（でした）。	Thank you very much for the meal/drinks.
なんのおかまいもしませんで。	何のおかまいもしませんで。	We did not offer much (by way of treats).

単語の練習
たん

A. 文化と習慣　Culture and customs
ぶん か　しゅうかん

政治	教育	経済	社会	げいじゅつ
せいじ	きょういく	けいざい	しゃかい	
politics	education	economy	society	art

生け花	茶道	習字	はいく	落語
い　ばな	さ どう	しゅう じ		らく ご
flower arranging	tea ceremony	calligraphy	haiku poetry	Japanese storytelling

し	マンガ	アニメ	インターネット	ブログ
poetry	cartoon, graphic novel	anime	Internet	blog

お辞儀をする	キスをする	ハグする	正座する
じ ぎ			せい ざ
to bow	to kiss	to hug	to sit in formal Japanese style

ゆかにすわる	習字を習う	チップをはらう	〜に興味がある
	しゅう じ　なら		きょう み
to sit on the floor	to learn calligraphy	to tip (a waiter/waitress, etc.)	to be interested in

伝統的（な）	文化的（な）
でんとうてき	ぶん か てき
traditional	cultural

Activity 1　Use the words on page 406 to identify what is happening in the illustrations.

1　　2　　3　　4

5　　6　　7　　8

おぼえていますか。

お寺　思い出　おまつり　かぶき　カラオケ　きせつ　教会　神社　博物館　美術館
ミュージカル　れきし　和食

Activity 2　日本語で質問に答えて下さい。

1. どれが伝統的な文化ですか。どれが文化的に新しいですか。

2. 日本の文化のどんなものに興味がありますか。

3. 落語を見に行ったことがありますか。かぶきはどうですか。

4. 生け花や茶道や習字をしたことがありますか。してみたいものがありますか。

5. 最近のアメリカの経済はどうですか。

6. いい社会って、どんな社会だと思いますか。

7. 日本の政治や経済に興味がありますか。ほかに、日本の何に興味がありますか。

8. 教育と経済とどちらの方が大事だと思いますか。

9. アメリカにある習慣はどれですか。ない習慣はどれですか。

10. 日本にある習慣はどれだと思いますか。ない習慣はどれだと思いますか。

伝統文化　Traditional culture
でんとうぶんか

うきよえ	浮世絵	traditional Japanese woodblock prints
おどり	踊り	traditional dance
げいじゅつ	芸術	art
げいのう	芸能	entertainment, show
こと	琴	Japanese harp, koto
しゃみせん	三味線	Japanese three-string guitar, shamisen
とうげい	陶芸	ceramic art
のう	能	Noh Play
にんぎょうじょうるり	人形浄瑠璃	puppet theater
やきもの	焼き物	ceramics, ceramic ware, pottery

げんだい文化　Modern culture
ぶんか

あぶらえ	油絵	oil painting
えんげき	演劇	drama, play
かいが	絵画	painting
クラフト		crafts
ダンス		western style dance
バレエ		ballet

B. 世界の宗教　World Religions
せ かい　しゅうきょう

キリスト教 きょう	イスラム教 きょう	仏教 ぶっきょう	神道 しんとう	ユダヤ教 きょう
Christianity	Islam	Buddhism	Shinto	Judaism

しんじる	おいのりをする	祝う いわ
to believe	to offer a prayer	to celebrate

NOTE

- おいのりをする means literally *to do a prayer*. The noun いのり
  (*prayer*) is derived from the ます-stem of the verb いのる.

Activity 3　質問に答えて下さい。

1. 世界で一番しんじられている宗教はどれですか。二番目はどれですか。
   せ かい　　　　　　　　　しゅうきょう

2. ほかに、世界にはどんな宗教がありますか。
   せ かい　　　　しゅうきょう

3. どの宗教についてよく知っていますか。どの宗教のことはあまり知りませんか。
   しゅうきょう　　　　　　　　　　　　　　しゅうきょう

4. 日本でよくしんじられている宗教は、どの宗教だと思いますか。
   しゅうきょう　　　　しゅうきょう

Activity 4   Work with a partner. Identify three different countries that have a significant number of followers of each of the religions on the list below. When you are done compare your list with those of the other pairs.

Example: A: キリスト教をしんじている人はどの国が一番多いと思う？
B: アメリカだと思う。〜さんは？

宗教 しゅうきょう	国
キリスト教 きょう	
イスラム教 きょう	
仏教 ぶっきょう	
ユダヤ教 きょう	

Activity 5   Work with the class. Ask your classmates what customs are associated with each of the religions below.

Example: A: キリスト教にはどんな習慣がありますか。
きょう   しゅうかん
B: 日曜日に教会へ行っておいのりをする習慣があります。
しゅうかん

宗教 しゅうきょう	習慣 しゅうかん
キリスト教 きょう	
イスラム教 きょう	
仏教 ぶっきょう	
ユダヤ教 きょう	

C. おつきあい   Socializing

〜とつきあう／〜につきあう   あいさつ（を）する   ことわる
to associate with someone,   to greet   to refuse, to decline
to keep someone's company

あやまる   助ける   アドバイスをする   たのみ／ねがいを聞く
to apologize   たす   to advise   to grant a request
              to save, to help

見送りに行く   むかえに来る   はっきり   理由を言う
み おく   り ゆう
to go to see someone off   to go/come to pick up (someone)   explicitly   to say the reason

みんな   ほかの人   ていねい（な）   失礼（な）
                                                              しつ
all people, everyone   other people   polite   rude

NOTE

- 助ける means *to help someone out of a difficult situation*, such as
  rescuing a person, saving someone's life, saving someone from shame, or
  lending someone money. On the other hand 手伝う (*Nakama 2*, Chapter
  4) means to *provide assistance*, such as helping someone with moving
  furniture or helping someone do homework.

おぼえていますか。

いじめる　お礼を言う　かす　かりる　招待する　たのむ　つれていく
つれてくる　手伝う　なれる　よろこぶ　あげる　いただく　差し上げる
下さる　くれる　もらう　家族　ご家族　近所の人　心配

Activity 6   Compare the Japanese customs below with customs from your own
country.

Example: 日本では、バレンタインデーに女の人から男の人にチョコレートをあげる
習慣があります。
アメリカでは、女の人にも男の人にもプレゼントをあげる習慣があります。

1. 日本では、クリスマスにデートをする習慣があります。

2. 日本では、お正月に子供にお金をあげたり、神社やお寺に行ったりする習慣
があります。

3. 日本では、食事の前に「いただきます」という習慣があります。

4. 日本では、ご飯を食べたら、「ご馳走様でした」という習慣があります。

5. 日本では、部屋のドアをいつもしめておく習慣があります。

6. 日本的な家では、ゆかにすわる習慣があります。

7. 日本では、あやまる時、理由をあまり言わない習慣があります。

8. 日本では、何かをたのまれた時、はっきりことわらない習慣があります。

Activity 7   Complete the following sentences by inserting the appropriate
expressions in the blanks.

1. キムさんはパクさんとつきあっていましたが、＿＿＿＿＿＿＿＿そうです。

2. 小学校の時の友達と＿＿＿＿＿＿＿＿時、キスをしますか。

3. 車が止まって困っている人を＿＿＿＿＿＿＿＿あげた。

4. 友達がガールフレンドのことで困っていたので、＿＿＿＿＿＿＿＿をしました。

5. スミスさんがアメリカに帰るので、空港まで＿＿＿＿＿＿＿＿に行きました。

6. 今日新しい先生が来るので、みんなで先生を＿＿＿＿＿＿＿＿に行きました。

7. 私のたのみを＿＿＿＿＿＿＿＿下さい。

D. わかれる時のあいさつ

色々お世話になりました。	Thanks for all the hospitality you've shown me.
これからもどうぞよろしく（おねがいします）。	Please stay in touch in the future.
（どうも）ご馳走様（でした）。	Thank you for the meal.
たいしたおかまいもしませんで。	We did not offer much (by way of treats).
そろそろ、失礼します。	I should be going; it's about time for me to leave.
おかげ（さま）で	thanks to 〜

おぼえていますか。

おめでとうございます　さようなら

◆ **Activity 8**　次の会話を練習して下さい。

1. 空港で
   A: 今まで色々お世話になりました。どうも有り難うございました。
   B: いえ、これからもがんばって下さいね。
   A: はい、これからもどうぞよろしくおねがいします。

2. 送別会で
   A: みなさんのおかげで、とても楽しい一年でした。どうも有り難うございました。
   B: 元気でね。

3. 友達のご両親の家で
   A: 今日はどうもご馳走様でした。とてもおいしかったです。
   B: いいえ。何のおかまいもしませんで。
   A: じゃあ、そろそろ失礼します。

ダイアローグ

はじめに

質問に日本語で答えて下さい。

1. どんな所に旅行に行ったことがありますか。
2. 何日ぐらい行きましたか。

🔊 日本で困ったこと　*Problems Alice faced in Japan*

The following **manga** frames are scrambled, so they are not in the order described by the dialogue. Read the dialogue and unscramble the frames by writing the correct number in the box in each frame.

石田さんと上田さんと鈴木道子さんが話しています。
　　　　　　　　　　すず

石田：　アリス、日本に来てもう二年かな？

上田：　うん、そうね。

石田：　早いね。

上田：　ええ、でも日本に来たばかりの時は、日本の文化や習慣が分からなくて
　　　　　　　　　　　　　　　　　　　　　　　　ぶんか　しゅうかん
　　　　大変だった。

石田：　そうなんだ。

上田：　うん、お風呂やおはしについては、アメリカの学校でも教えてもらった
　　　　　　　ふろ
　　　　んだけど、判子をいつ使うか分からなかったから、よく判子を忘れたり、
　　　　　　　　　はん　　　　　　　　　　　　　　　　　　　　　　　はん
　　　　ATM の日本語が読めなくて使えなかったり。

鈴木：　ほんと、はじめは大変そうだったよね。
すず

上田：　それにね、道が分からなくて、ホストファミリーを心配させちゃったこ
　　　　ともある。

石田：　え、何があったの？

上田：　電車を間違えて、千葉の方に行っちゃったの。でも、電車をおりた
　　　　ところで、帰りの電車がなくなっちゃったって分かって。

石田：　で、どうしたの？

上田：　で、どうしようかと思ってるところで、親切な人がけいたいをかしてく
　　　　れたの。それで、その電話で家に電話をかけさせてもらったの。

石田：　え、けいたい持ってなかったの？

上田：　まだ買ってなかったの。で、お父さんがむかえに来てくれたんだけど、
　　　　待ってる間、寒くて心細かった。

石田：　そりゃ、そうだよね。

上田：　だから、お父さんの顔を見た時、本当にうれしかった。

鈴木：　その後、すぐけいたい買わされたよね。

上田：　うん、でもけいたいはぜったいいるなあって、あの時つくづく思った。

石田：　たしかにそうだね。日本は公衆電話が少ないし、さがすのも大変だから、
　　　　けいたいのない生活なんて、考えられないね。

DIALOGUE PHRASE NOTES

- 来たばかり means *have just come.*
- あの時 means *at that time.* あの is used when both the speaker and the hearer are assumed to be familiar with an event, as in this context. その is used when the speaker does not assume that the listener is familiar with the event.
- つくづくmeans *deeply* or *sincerely.*
- 公衆電話 means *public phone.*

ダイアローグの後で

A. 日本語で質問に答えて下さい。

1. 上田さんは日本に何年いますか。
2. 上田さんはホストファミリーをどんなことで困らせましたか。
3. 上田さんが電車を間違えた時、だれが何を上田さんにしてくれましたか。
4. お父さんが車でむかえに来る間、上田さんはどこで何をしていましたか。
5. ホストファミリーのお父さんは上田さんに何をさせましたか。
6. 上田さんは、日本では何がいると思っていますか。
7. 石田さんは上田さんと同じ考えですか。どうしてそう思いますか。

B. Assume that Ms. Ueda and Ms. Suzuki are talking with Professor Tanaka instead of Mr. Ishida. Re-create the conversational styles in the dialogue using more polite expressions.

日本の文化
ぶんか

日本の歴史 An outline of Japanese history
れきし

The Japanese islands separated from the mainland Asian continent about 10,000 years ago. Ancient Japan was mainly agricultural. Many small states existed in Japan, but by the eighth century Japan had become united under a ruling family based in Yamato (Nara). During this period the Japanese imported a good deal of culture and advanced knowledge from China, including Buddhism, Confucianism, political systems, and orthography, and this borrowing continued throughout early Japanese history. In 710, the Imperial family established Nara as the first capital of Japan. In 794, a new capital, modeled after the Chinese capital city, was created in Kyoto. During this time Japanese society was dominated by aristocrats. Life in the capital was marked by elegance and refinement, but all the

A *haniwa* figure from ancient Japan.

while military families were gaining power in the outlying areas. Between 1167 and 1185, the warrior clan Heike established the first government run by members of the warrior class. Although the Heike maintained a close relationship with the aristocrats and adopted many of their customs, many scholars consider this the beginning of the Japanese feudal period, characterized by the rule of the 武士, or 侍 (*warriors*). In
ぶし　　　　　　　　　　　　さむらい
1185, the Minamoto, also a warrior clan, took over the government and established a military government called 幕府 in Kamakura (near present-day Tokyo). During the
ばくふ
15th century, feudal lords fought among themselves for dominance, and in 1603 the Tokugawa family reunited the country, establishing the 江戸幕府. Edo (present-day
えどばくふ
Tokyo) became the country's political center. The Tokugawa family adopted a policy called 鎖国 (*national isolation*), closing Japan to the outside world except for China
さこく
and Holland (whose representatives were allowed contact with the country through the port of Nagasaki only). For the next 280 years, Japan was relatively peaceful. During this period, Japanese culture matured. 歌舞伎 theater, 人形浄瑠璃 (*puppet theater*),
かぶき　　　　　　　　　じょうるり
浮世絵 (*wood prints*), やきもの (*pottery*), and 俳句 are well known products of the
うきよえ　　　　　　　　　　　　　　　　　　　はいく
Edo culture. Although agriculture and transportation made some advancements, technologically Japan was well behind Europe and America. In the mid-nineteenth century European and American ships started appearing off the coast of Japan. The Tokugawa government eventually was forced to open the country, and political authority was restored to the Emperor in 1868. During the Meiji Era (1868–1911), Japan tried to catch up with the West by modernizing society. The government's goals were economic prosperity and a strong military, with the Emperor standing as the absolute symbol of Japan. As the military gained power, Japan began a military invasion of Asia. This led to conflict with other countries in the world. Japan launched hostilities in 1941, which led to its involvement in World War II. Japan was defeated in 1945 after the bombing of Hiroshima and Nagasaki. Under the U.S. occupation, Japan adopted a new constitution which renounced war. Japan started down the road toward economic recovery after the war and became one of the world's leading economic

powers by 1980. Most of the current stereotypes of the Japanese as hard workers are derived from the image of businessmen and workers during the 1950s and 1960s.

宗教と慣習　Religion and customs in Japan
しゅうきょう　　かんしゅう

The Japanese constitution guarantees freedom of religion. The country's two major religions are 神道 (Shinto) and 仏教 (Buddhism). Shinto, which is based on belief in
しんとう　　　　　　　ぶっきょう
animistic deities known as 神, is the indigenous religion of Japan. Buddhism was
かみ
introduced to Japan from China in the 6th century. Although Buddhism soon became predominant, it was always able to coexist with Shinto. This arrangement is still intact, and many Japanese claim adherence to both Shinto and Buddhism.

Christianity was brought to Japan in 1549 by Jesuit missionaries. The 16th century was a period of political unrest, and Christianity spread rapidly at first among people

Courtesy of the author

looking for a new spiritual symbol. It was banned in 1639 after the unification of Japan was completed, and this ban remained until the Meiji Restoration in the middle of the 19th century. About 1 percent of the Japanese population is currently Christian.

Many Japanese people visit a Shinto shrine when a baby is born and when they get married. They also go to shrines to pray for good luck before school entrance examinations. The same people often turn to Buddhism during times of bereavement, such as deaths. Visiting

shrines and Buddhist temples during the New Year season is an old tradition, and about 70–80 percent of the entire population visit shrines and temples during the first three days of the year. The influence of Shinto and Buddhist beliefs is present in many rituals, festivals, and events throughout Japan year round.

There are many traditions related to both Shinto and Buddhism, and both of these religions have played crucial roles in the history of the country and its social customs, but evidence suggests that the Japanese do not view these two traditions in the same sense that religion is viewed in the West. A survey conducted by *Yomiuri Newspaper* in 2005 found that 75 percent of the people who responded said they do not believe in religion, while only 23 percent said they do believe. About 60 percent of people think that religion is not important for a happy life, and only 30 percent think that it is. Even so, 81 percent of people go to shrines, temples, or churches.

日本人が考える日本のよさ
かんが

In 2013, the internet company NIFTY asked 5,264 Japanese people what made them feel lucky to have been born in Japan. The results of this survey show that the Japanese have a number of reasons for feeling good about their country. That it is a safe place to live and has four distinct seasons tied for first (78 percent of respondents), and having clean water, punctuality (for both people and public transportation), and good infrastructure all tied for third (66 percent). These were followed by clean toilets (63 percent), food quality and variety (51 percent), an extensive public transportation system (48 percent), the quality of commercial goods (48 percent), and advanced technology (47 percent).

文法

I. Expressing the performance of a favor using てあげる／くれる／もらう

Chapter 6 introduced two giving verbs—あげる and くれる—and a receiving verb, もらう. These verbs can be used to express the speaker's appreciation or gratitude. That is, in Japanese, an action done for the benefit of someone else can be expressed by using the て-form with a verb of giving or receiving.

A. Expressing appreciation for a favor done for you or a member of your in-group using 〜てくれる／下さる

Like くれる and 下さる in Chapter 6, the recipient of the favor is the speaker or a member of the speaker's in-group when 〜てくれる／下さる is used. The giver can be anyone but the speaker. 下さる is used when the giver is an out-group person who is socially superior to the speaker. The recipient of a favor can be marked by the particle に, but it does not have to be overtly marked if it is obvious.

先生は私にはいくを教えて下さいました。
My teacher taught me haiku (for my benefit).

先生がていねいな説明とアドバイスをして下さいました。
The professor gave me a detailed explanation and advice.

上司が私のねがいを聞いて下さった。	*My boss kindly did me a favor.*
姉がマンガをかしてくれた。	*My older sister loaned me a manga.*
同僚が妹を落語につれて行ってくれました。	*My co-worker took my younger sister to a rakugo performance.*
父はいつも私をしんじてくれている。	*My father always believes me.*

学校で一番かっこいい男の子が私とつきあってくれた。
The cutest guy in school went out with me.

私には、困った時に、いつも助けてくれる友達がいる。
I have a friend who always helps me out when I'm having problems.

道子：あ、早かったね。	*Oh, you're early.*
友子：うん、アリスが車でむかえに来てくれたから。	*Yeah, Alice came for me by car.*

荷物が重くて困っていた時、知らない人が持ってくれました。
When I was struggling with heavy luggage, a stranger carried it for me.

The in-group/out-group distinction can be applied in social contexts other than family. For example, employees of the speaker's company comprise an in-group, while non-employees comprise an out-group. In this case, use 〜て下さる when a customer (who is regarded as a social superior to company members in a business context) does something for any member of the company, including the speaker's boss or even the company president (who would be considered the speaker's superior in a strictly in-company relationship).

お客さまが社長にお祝いを持って来て下さいました。
The customer kindly brought a congratulatory gift to the president.

NOTE

● Request forms such as 〜て下さい, 〜てくれませんか, and 〜て下さいませんか (*Nakama 1*, Chapter 6) are derived from this structure.

B. Expressing willingness to help using 〜てあげる／やる

As is the case with the verbs あげる and やる discussed in Chapter 6, the recipient of any action expressed by 〜てあげる／やる is usually in the speaker's out-group. If both giver and recipient are in the speaker's in-group, it is okay to use 〜てくれる／あげる／やる, but the use of くれる implies identification with the recipient and the use of あげる or やる indicates neutrality or identification with the giver.

　　〜てあげる／やる must be used if the giver is the speaker. Use やる if the recipient is socially inferior to the speaker. Social inferiors mainly include animals, plants, and one's family members. あげる can be used for both social equals and inferiors.

私は	友達に	生け花を	教えてあげた。	*I taught my friend flower arrangement* (for her benefit).
私は	かれしに	しを	書いてあげた。	*I wrote a poem for my boyfriend.*
ぼくは		犬に	ボールを　買ってやった／あげた。	*I bought a ball for my dog.*

The recipient can be marked by the particle に, but the recipient is not mentioned if it is obvious from the context.

私は	黒田さんを	見送りに行ってあげた。	*I went to see Ms. Kuroda off* (for her benefit).
私は		犬と　遊んでやった／あげた。	*I played with the dog* (for the benefit of the dog).
母は	子ねこを	お風呂に入れてやりました／あげました。	

My mother gave the kitten a bath (for the benefit of the kitten).

困った時は、私が助けてあげるから、心配しないで。
Don't worry, I'll help you if you're having problems.

道子：五時までに駅に行かなきゃいけないんだけど、おくれそうなの。
　　　I have to be at the station by five o'clock, but it looks like I'm going to be late.

石田：じゃあ、ぼくが車で送ってあげるよ。
　　　Well, I can drive you (to the station).

弟が心細そうだったので，一緒に行ってあげた／やった。
Since my brother looked lonely, I went with him (for him).

Although it is theoretically possible to use 差し上げる in this structure, in reality 〜て差し上げる is rarely used. 差し上げる explicitly indicates that the giver is doing a favor for a superior, and such explicit remarks are considered condescending. In such cases use either a humble expression (Grammar section II of chapter 11) or the simple ます form.

私は先生のかばんを持って差し上げました。　*I carried the professor's bag (for his benefit).*

私は先生のかばんを持ちました。　*I carried the professor's bag.*

私は先生のかばんをお持ちしました。　*I humbly carried the professor's bag. (humble form of 持つ)*

C. Expressing that someone has benefited from someone else's action using 〜てもらう／いただく

As is the case when もらう or いただく is used as the sentence's main verb, the recipient of the favor is the grammatical subject and the giver of the favor is the source in the 〜てもらう／いただく construction.

私は　道子さんに　たのみを聞いてもらった。
　　　　　　　　　　　　　　　　　　I got Michiko to do a favor for me.
妹は　　その人に　ハグをしてもらった。　*My sister got the person to hug her.*
その子は　近所の人に　　ほめてもらった。　*The child got his neighbor to praise him.*
弟は　　先生に　　助けていただいた。　*My younger brother got the teacher to help him.*

The giver is marked by 〜に or by から, but the use of から is limited to cases such as 送る, where the main verb indicates the transfer of an object.

友達に／から　本を　送ってもらった。　*I had my friend send a book.*
友達に　　　本を　読んでもらった。　*I had my friend read a book.*
(The particle から cannot be used in the sentence above.)

Sentences with 〜てもらう may imply that the recipient is asking the giver for a favor. This is especially true when the verb is used in the future tense.

弟は父に理由を説明してもらうつもりです。
My younger brother intends to get my father to explain the reasons to him.

鈴木さんに見てもらいたいと思っています。
I've been thinking of having Mr. Suzuki look at it.

Requests made with 〜ていただける (*Nakama 2*, Chapter 4) are derived from this structure. いただける is the potential form of いただく. The expression 〜ていただけませんか means *could I humbly receive the favor of your doing (this)*. The potential form of もらう, もらえる, can be used instead of いただける to express a less formal request. 〜てもらえませんか means *can I receive the favor of your doing ~*, and is interchangeable with 〜てくれませんか.

来週のパーティはことわってもらえませんか。／来週のパーティはことわってくれませんか。
Could you decline the invitation to next week's party for me?

ねえ、今日ちょっとつきあってもらえる？／ねえ、今日ちょっとつきあってくれる？
Hey, could you spend a little time with me today?

Use 〜ていただきたい to express a desire directed toward a superior. 〜ていただきたい is a combination of いただく and たい. 〜てもらいたい (a combination of もらう and たい) also expresses the speaker's desire and can be used interchangeably with 〜てほしい. Finally, 〜てほしい／もらいたい／いただきたい can be used for indirect requests, which are less forceful than 〜ていただけませんか／もらえませんか／下さいませんか／くれませんか.

今の日本の経済について話していただきたいんですが。
けいざい
Could I ask you to talk about the current Japanese economy?

もう少していねいに教えてくれませんか。
Could you teach me with more care (in greater detail)?

ゴルフバッグが重いから、宅配便で送ってもらえませんか。
おも　　　　　　　　たく
Since the golf bag is heavy, could you send it by a parcel service?

山田： ブログを見てもらいたいんだけど。／ブログを見てほしいんだけど。
　　　　Can I get you to look at my blog? (lit.: I want to get you to read my blog.)

山本： あ、ごめん。今ちょっといそがしいから、後でいい？
　　　　Oh, I'm sorry. I'm a bit tied up now—can I look at it later?

話してみましょう

Activity 1 The following chart illustrates favors done for the speaker or members of the speaker's in-group. You are the speaker. Describe each exchange using the て-form of the verb + 下さる／くれる.

Example: 弟は私にあやまってくれました。

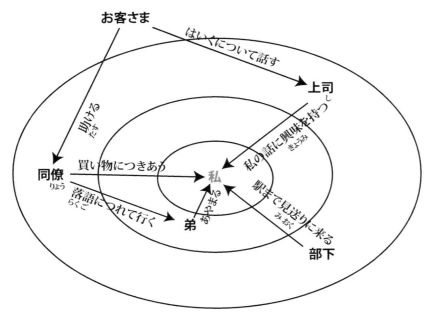

Activity 2   Express the same favors described in Activity 1, this time using the
て -form of the verb + いただく／もらう.

Example: 私は弟にあやまってもらいました。

Activity 3   The following chart illustrates favors done by and for different people.
Describe the exchanges using the て -form of the verb + あげる／やる.

Example: 私は川口さんに生け花を教えてあげました。

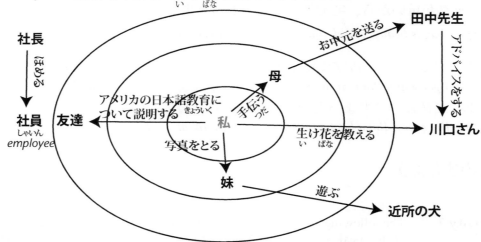

Activity 4   Express the same favors described in Activity 3, this time using the
て -form of the verb + いただく／もらう. Note that not every exchange
can be expressed with いただく or もらう.

Example: 川口さんは田中先生にアドバイスをしていただきました。

Activity 5   Work as a class. Write down three things that you wouldn't mind doing for your classmates. Also, write three things that you would like to ask your classmates to do for you. Ask your classmates to do one of the favors you hope to receive, and write the name of the first person who agrees to do it for you. When you have found someone to do the first favor proceed to the next, and so on. Your classmates will also ask you for favors. You are allowed to agree to do something for someone only if it is something you have written down that you wouldn't mind doing for your classmates. Find a different person to do each favor for you. Give a reason for not doing a favor if you have not marked it in the 私がしてあげること column. Use casual speech.

Example: A: あのう、10 ドルかしてくれない？

B: ごめん。かしてあげたいけど、持ってないんだ。

or いいよ。かしてあげるよ。

してもらいたいこと	してくれる人の名前	私がしてあげること

Activity 6   Use the results from Activity 5 to tell the class who helped you.

Example: ～さんに 10 ドルかしてもらいました。

～さんにノートを見せてもらいました。

II. Making or letting someone do something using the causative form

The causative construction in English is used when someone (causer) either forces or allows someone else (causee) to do something. If the causer forces the causee, the verb "make" is used, but the verb "let" is used if the causer gives the causee permission to do something, as in:

The teacher let everyone write a blog.
The teacher made everyone write a blog.

Japanese has two types of causatives as well. In both cases, the causer is the subject of the sentence just like in English, but the distinction between the make-causative and the let-causative is not always clear from the verb forms alone.

父は　妹にいい教育を受けさせた。   *My father made/let my sister get a good education.*

上司はみんなを集めて、その問題について考えさせた。   *The boss called all of us and made us think about the problem.*

先生は　子供たちにていねいなあいさつをさせた。　　*The teacher had the children greet each other politely.*

The formation of causative forms is similar to the formation of passive verbs. Instead of the passive endings れる／られる, the endings せる／す／させる／さす are used.

Verb type	Dictionary form	Causative form
る -verbs		Replace る with させる or さす
	見る (*to see*) 食べる (*to eat*)	見る + させる／さす ⇨ 見させる／見さす 食べる + させる／さす ⇨ 食べさせる／食べさす
う -verbs		Replace the negative ending ない with せる or す
	すわる (*to sit*) 話す (*to talk*)	すわらない + せる／す ⇨ すわらせる／すわらす 話さない + せる／す ⇨ 話させる／話さす
Irregular verbs	する (*to do*) 来る (*to come*)	させる or さす 来させる or 来さす

The causative construction is slightly different between transitive and intransitive verbs.

A. Intransitive verbs

When an intransitive verb is used, the causee can be marked by the particle を or に. Although both of these particles can be used in the let- and make-causative constructions, に tends to be used for the let-causative construction.

社長は　ほかの人を　あいさつに　行かせた。　*The president made* (let) *another person go to greet* (someone).

社長は　ほかの人に　あいさつに　行かせた。　*The president let another person go to greet* (someone).

　母は　　　　　私を　買い物に つきあわせた。　*My mother made* (let) *me go shopping with her.*

　　　　彼女を　笑わせたかったのに、泣かせてしまった。
　　　　　　　　I wanted to make my girlfriend smile, but made her cry instead.

In order to explicitly mark the let-causative, combine the causative form with a verb of giving, which implies that the causer is doing the causee a favor by allowing him or her to do the action in question. In this case it makes no difference whether the particle used is に or を.

上司は　　　　部下を／に　出張に　行かせてやった。
　　　　　　　　　　　　　　　　The boss let his subordinate go on assignment.

先輩は　　　　後輩を／に　すわらせてあげた。
　　　　　　　　　　　　　　　　The older student let the younger student sit down.

　母は　　　　私を／に　買い物に　　つきあわせてくれた。
　　　　　　　　　　　　　　　　My mother let me go shopping with her.

B. Transitive verbs

When the verb is a transitive verb, the causee is usually marked by the particle に. In this case, it is not possible to tell the difference between make- and let-causative constructions without context or giving/receiving verbs.

先生は	みんなに	ブログを書かせた。	*The teacher made/let everyone write a blog.*
先生は	ほかの学生に	発音の練習をさせた。	*The teacher made/let other students practice pronunciation.*
先輩は	ぼくに	チップを払わせた。	*The older student made/let me pay the tip.*
父は	私に	正座をさせた。	*My father made me sit on the floor in formal Japanese style.*
先生は	真理さんに	しを書かせてあげた。	*The teacher let Mari write a poem.*

先生は日本人の学生に神道と仏教の習慣について、留学生にキリスト教とユダヤ教とイスラム教の習慣について話をさせた。

The teacher made/let the Japanese students talk about Shinto and Buddhist customs, and made/let international students talk about Christian, Jewish, and Islamic customs.

話してみましょう

Activity 1   Say whether you think Japanese parents tend to make children under 12 do the following activities. Then say what American parents would tend to do.

Example: 毎日勉強する

日本人は子供に毎日勉強させると思います。

or   日本人は子供に毎日勉強させないと思います。

1. 九時までに寝る
2. テレビを見る
3. 習字を習う
4. 生け花を習う
5. いすにすわる
6. 一人で家にいる
7. お正月に和食を食べる
8. アルバイトをする
9. 携帯電話を持つ
10. 正座をする

Activity 2   Describe the following situations using the causative form.

Example: 男の子が女の子にけがをさせました。

| Example | 1 | 2 | 3 |

| 4 | 5 | 6 | 7 |

III. Requesting permission to do something using the causative て-form and expressions of requests

The て-form of a causative verb can be combined with a variety of endings, such as verbs of giving and receiving, to indicate requests. The general meaning of these varieties is *please allow me to do~* or *please let me do ~*.

日本の政治の問題について説明させてくれませんか。
せい じ　　もんだい
Please let me explain Japanese political problems.

日本の政治の問題について説明させていただけませんか。
せい じ　　もんだい
Please allow me to explain Japanese political problelms.

日本の政治の問題について説明させてほしいんですが。
せい じ　　もんだい
I'd like you to let me explain Japanese political problems.

理由について少し考えさせて下さい。　　　　*Please let me think about the reason.*
り ゆう　　　　　　 かんが

そのマンガ、読ませて。　　　　　　　　　*Please let me read that manga.*

帰る前にあいさつをさせて下さい。　　　　*Please let me say hello before I go home.*

私にむかえに行かせていだだけませんか。　*Would you let me go pick (him/her) up?*

私にお礼を言わせてくれませんか。　　　　*Could you let me express my appreciation?*

見送りに行かせてほしいんですけど。　　　*I would like to come to see you off.*
み おく

Chapter 1 introduced a similar expression, 〜てもいいですか. Although 〜てもいいですか can be used in a very general and non-specific manner, the て-form of the causative form + request expression is used specifically for personal favors only.

ゆかにすわってもいいですか。　*Is it OK if I sit on the floor /Is sitting on the floor allowed here?*

ゆかにすわらせてくれませんか。　*Would you mind if I sat on the floor?*

話してみましょう

Activity 1　Suppose you would like to do the following things but need to get permission. Make a request using the causative form.

Example:　授業中にトイレに行きたいので、先生におねがいする。
　　　　　　<u>先生、トイレに行かせていただけませんか。</u>

1. 気分が悪くて、家に帰りたいので、先生におねがいする。
2. 宿題が出来なかった理由を先生に説明したいので、おねがいする。
3. 友達がおいしそうに食べているケーキを、少し食べたいので、おねがいする。
4. 日本人のホストファミリーのお母さんをハグしてもいいかどうか分からないので、聞いてみる。
5. お客さんをむかえに行きたいので、上司におねがいする。
6. 友達のたのみをことわった理由を説明したいので、友達におねがいする。

Activity 2　Work with a partner. Ask your partner what he/she was permitted and not permitted to do as a child. Make sure to insert some comments to make your conversation lively.

Example:　A: 小さい時、ご両親はどんなことをさせてくれましたか。
　　　　　　B: そうですね。色々な運動をさせてくれましたよ。
　　　　　　A: いいですね。だから、〜さんは、色々なスポーツが出来るんですね。
　　　　　　　　じゃあ、どんなことはさせてくれませんでしたか。
　　　　　　B: そうですね。テレビはあまり見させてくれませんでした。
　　　　　　A: そうですか。私もテレビは見させてもらえませんでした。

👥   **Activity 3**   Work with a partner. Ask each other what you would like your parents and your school to let you do and why.

Example: A: ご両親に何をさせてもらいたいと思いますか。

B: そうですね。日本に留学させてもらいたいと思っています。

A: そうですか。日本ではどんなことがしたいんですか。

B: 日本の伝統的な文化について勉強したいんです。
でんとうてき　ぶんか

A: いいですね。

私	させてもらいたいこと／させていただきたいこと	理由 り ゆう
両親		
先生		
パートナー	させてもらいたいこと／させていただきたいこと	理由 り ゆう
ご両親		
先生		

👥   **Activity 4**   Work with a partner. Using the information in Activity 3, create dialogues in which you make requests to your parents and and to your teacher. Make sure that the conversation is natural and appropriate in terms of the sequence of topics to be introduced and the level of politeness.

Example: A: お父さん、お母さん、ちょっといい？

B: ああ、いいけど、何？

A: あのう、...。

IV. Expressing the immediate future using 〜る + ところ; the current situation using 〜ている + ところ; and the immediate past using 〜た + ところ

Plain affirmative verb form + ところ

ところ literally means *place*, and by extension it also means *point in time* or *moment*. It is preceded by a plain affirmative verb, but depending on the form of the verb preceding it, ところ can describe matters or events that are just about to happen, are just happening, or have just happened. When ところ is preceded by the dictionary form of a verb it means *about to do* 〜. When ところ is preceded by 〜ている, it means *to be in the middle of doing* 〜. Finally, when the plain past precedes ところ, it means *have just finished doing* 〜.

チップを	払う はら	ところです。	*I am about to leave a gratuity.*
チップを	払っている はら	ところです。	*I am leaving a gratuity.*
チップを	払った はら	ところです。	*I have just left a gratuity.*

今出かけるところですから、後で電話して下さい。
I am just going out, so please call back later.

今、ぼくの好きなアニメが始まるところなんだよ。
My favorite anime is about to start.

習字のレッスンが終わるところです。
The calligraphy lesson is about to finish.

もう少しで、あの人の話をしんじるところだった。
I was almost ready to believe what he said.

今、生け花の練習をしているところです。
I am in the middle of practicing flower arranging.

今、この問題について考えているところだから、ちょっと待って。
I am in the middle of thinking about this problem, so please wait a moment.

その話は今ことわったところだ。　　　　　*I've just declined the offer* (lit.: story).

今すわったところだから、少し休ませて下さい。　*I've just sat down, so let me rest for a moment.*

和子：あっ、いたの？　　　　　*Oh, so you're here after all.*

正男：うん。今帰ってきたところ。　*Yes, I've just come back.*

NOTES

Note the following differences between 〜ている and 〜ているところ:

● Verbs in the 〜ている construction can be any action verb, but verbs in the 〜ているところ constructions are usually action verbs whose 〜ている form suggests action in progress. For example, 勉強する can be used in both constructions because its 〜ている form 勉強している (someone is studying) suggests ongoing action. On the other hand, しぬ cannot be used in the 〜ているところ construction because しんでいる suggests a resultant state (someone is dead).

● 〜ている can have different interpretations such as a resultant state, a progressive action, or a habitual action, but 〜ているところ does not.

● While 〜ている can denote a long-term on-going process, 〜ているところ only indicates an action that is taking place at this particular moment. For example, in the first sentence below, 習っている can be used when the speaker has begun taking lessons but 習っているところだ in the second sentence can mean only that the speaker is actually practicing at this moment. Therefore, the former sentence can use an adverb such as 最近, but the second sentence cannot.

最近生け花を習っている。　　*I'm learning flower arrangement nowadays.*

生け花を習っているところだ。　*I'm learning flower arrangement (right at this moment).*

話してみましょう

| Activity 1 | The following pictures illustrate scenes in which a person is about to do something, is doing something, or has just done something. Describe each picture using 〜ところ. |

Example: Picture A   お辞儀をするところです。

Picture B   お辞儀をしているところです。

Picture C   お辞儀をしたところです。

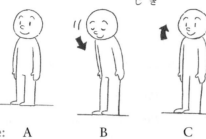

Example: A   B   C

1   A   B   C

2   A   B   C

3   A   B   C

4   A   B   C

5   A   B   C

6   A   B   C

Activity 2   Work with a partner. Assume that the person in Column A of the chart has asked the person in Column B to do something. First, complete the chart by writing a few requests. Then play the role of the person in Column A, and ask a favor of your partner, who will be the person in Column B. Your partner will refuse, using ～ところ to say the timing is not convenient. If you are not satisfied with your partner's reason, ask him/her for the favor again.

Example: **Column A**   **Column B**

　　　　　お父さん／お母さん　　　　子供

　　A: ちょっと、犬の散歩(さん)に行ってきて。

　　B: あ、だめ。今テレビ見ているところだから。

　　A: テレビは後で見ればいいでしょ。

	Column A	**Column B**
1.	お父さん／お母さん	子供
2.	ルームメート	ルームメート
3.	先生	学生
4.	上司(し)	私
5.	主人(しゅ)	つま

V. Expressing time durations using 間 and 間に; tense in subordinate clauses

間 is a noun that means *space between*, *period*, or *duration*. The phrase 〜間 means *while ~* or *during ~*. The usage of 間 differs depending on whether it is being used alone, as in 間, or with the time particle に, as in 間に.

A. Expressing the continuation of an action or event during a specified time span using 間

When 間 is used without the time particle に, the action or state described in the main clause must continue for as long as the state described in the 間 clause is in effect. In the following sentence, for example, the act of reading continues during the entire time the baby is sleeping. The tense of the 間 clause is normally present, regardless of the tense of the main clause. Like other subordinate clauses, the subject of the 間 clause is marked by the particle が if it is different from that of the main clause.

子供が寝ている間、本を読む。   *I read books while the child is sleeping*

子供が寝ている間、本を読んだ。   *I read a book while the child was sleeping*

To form an 間 clause use the ている form for action verbs. Use the dictionary form for stative verbs that indicate a state or situation, such as いる, ある, or わかる.

	Dictionary form		〜間
Verb (action verb)	ことわる (*to refuse*)	Verb ている + 間	ことわっている間
Verb (stative verb)	いる (*to exist*)	Dictionary form + 間	いる間
い -adjective	わかい (*young*)	Stem + い + 間	わかい間
な -adjective	不便な (*inconvenient*)	Stem + な + 間	不便な間
Noun	休み (*holiday*)	Noun + の + 間	休みの間

夏休みの間、何もしませんでした。
I didn't do anything during summer vacation.

父が元気な間は、東京ではたらくつもりです。
I plan to work in Tokyo as long as my father is healthy.

スミスさんは東京にいる間、茶道を習っていました。
Mr. Smith studied tea ceremony while he was in Tokyo.

話を聞いている間、ずっと正座をしていました。
I sat in formal Japanese style the whole time I listened to the story.

子供が小さい間は、あまりほかの人とつきあわなかった。
When my child was small, I didn't have a chance to associate with people outside my family.

The negative form ない + 間 can be used in this structure, but it is not as common as the affirmative form.

先生がいない間、みんなで遊んだ。   *We goofed off while the teacher was not here.*

B. Expressing the completion of an action or event in a specified time span using 間に

When 間 is followed by the particle に, which indicates a specific point in time, the action or event in the main clause must be completed within the time specified in the 間に clause. Therefore the following sentence indicates that the act of doing laundry is completed within the time in which the baby is sleeping.

子供が寝ている間に洗濯をする。
たく

I do laundry while my child is sleeping.

日本にいる間に、日本のげいじゅつについて勉強した。

I learned about Japanese arts while I was in Japan.

安い間に、買った方がいいかもしれない。

It may be better to buy it while it's still cheap.

アメリカに留学している間に、宗教と政治の勉強を始めた。
しゅうきょう　せいじ

I began my studies of religion and politics while studying in the United States.

Summary of tense in the subordinate clause

The time expressions introduced in this text are listed below. When the past tense is used in time adverbial clauses such as 時, 〜たら, or 後, the action, event, or condition of the subordinate clause must have been completed or satisfied before the action or event of the main clause can take place. On the other hand, when the present tense is used in time adverbial clauses such as 間, 間に, 前, and 時, the action, event, or condition of the subordinate clause must not have been completed or satisfied before the action or event in the main clause takes place. That is, the event in the main clause may take place before the event in the subordinate clause, or the two events may take place concurrently.

1. Present tense + 間に
   日本にいる間に、落語を見に行きたいです。
   I want to go to see Japanese storytelling while I am in Japan.

2. Present tense + 前に
   日本に来る前に、日本の文化について勉強しました。
   I studied Japanese culture before I came to Japan.

3. Present tense + 間
   日本にいる間、日本の伝統的なげいじゅつについて勉強しました。
   I studied Japanese traditional art throughout the time I was in Japan.

4. Present tense + 時
   アメリカに帰る時、友達が見送りに来てくれました。
   My friend came to say goodbye when I went back to the United States.

5. Past tense + 時
   アメリカに帰った時、両親がむかえに来てくれました。
   My parents came to pick me up when I came back to the United States.

6. Past tense + ら
   アメリカに帰ったら、高校の時の友達が会いに来てくれました。
   My high school friends came to see me after I came back to the United States.

7. Past tense + 後で
   アメリカに帰った後で、結婚しました。
   I got married after I came back to the United States.

話してみましょう

Activity 1 The following chart illustrates how Mrs. Kawano and her son spent yesterday afternoon. Describe Mrs. Kawano's activities with reference to times when her son was doing something else, using 〜間 (に).

Example: 川野くんが寝ている間に、お母さんは起きて朝御飯を作ります。
川野くんが朝御飯を食べている間、お母さんも朝御飯を食べます。

時間	川野くん	時間	お母さん
	寝ている	6:00	起きる
		↓	朝御飯を作る
7:00	起きる	7:00	川野くんを起こす
7:30	朝御飯を食べる	7:30	朝御飯を食べる
↓		↓	
8:00	学校に行く	8:00	そうじをする
			洗濯をする
		2:30	茶道を習う
			買い物に行く
3:00	家に帰る		
	マンガを読む		
↓		3:30	家に帰る
4:00	経済学の宿題をする	4:00	晩御飯を作る
↓			
5:00		↓	
6:00	晩御飯を食べる	6:00	晩御飯を食べる
↓		↓	
7:00	お風呂に入る	7:00	テレビを見る
↓		↓	
8:00	インターネットで遊ぶ		
		9:00	お風呂に入る
		↓	
		10:00	日記をつける
↓		↓	
11:00	しを書く	11:00	寝る
↓			
12:00	寝る		

Activity 2   Work with the class. Survey what college students do during the following periods or seasons, using 〜間（に）. Write down the number of people who do each of the following activities. Report the results to the class.

Example: A: 夏休みの間に家に帰りますか。

B: ええ、帰ります。休みの間はずっと家にいます。

A: 学校にいる間に宿題をしますか。

B: ええ、たいてい学校で宿題をします。

夏休み	学校にいる	期末 (final) 試験
家に帰る	宿題をする	パーティをする
はいくを書く	寝る	天気がいい
旅行に行く	テレビを見る	大学がひま
おいのりをする	誕生日を祝う	友達と遊ぶ

Activity 3   Work with a group of four. Using 〜間, debate on the following two topics: is it better to be a student or have a full-time job, and is it better to be single or married. Two people should take each side. Fill out the following charts with the pros and cons of each position. Try to persuade your opponents, and tell your instructor which pair has won.

Example: A: 学生をつづけるのと仕事をするのとどちらがいいと思う？

B: 学生をつづけている間は、お金がないから、仕事をしている方がいいと思う。

C: そう？　でも、学生でいる間は、好きなことがたくさん出来ると思うけど。

	いいこと	悪いこと
学生をつづける		
仕事をする		

	いいこと	悪いこと
一人でいる		
結婚する		

👥 Activity 4   Work with a partner. Compare customs in Japan and your home country in terms of what is or is not considered good manners when you do the following activities. Use subordinate clauses, etc.

Example:　ご飯を食べる

A:　私の国／家ではご飯を食べる前においのりをします。

B:　日本ではご飯を食べる前に「いただきます」と言います。

A:　じゃあ、日本ではご飯を食べている間に、してはいけないことやしてもいいことがありますか。

B:　ええ、ありますよ。口の中に食べ物が入っている間は、話してはいけないんです。

1.　ご飯を食べる
2.　お風呂(ふろ)に入る
3.　結婚する
4.　おいのりをする
5.　電車に乗っている

THE ます-STEM OF VERBS

In Japanese nouns are often derived from the ます stem of the verbs. Some common expressions are:

遊び	play, game, pastime	遊ぶ
行き	(on) the way, bound for ～	行く
いじめ	bullying	いじめる
いのり	prayer	いのる *to pray*
動き	movement	動く
（お）祝い	congratulatory gift	祝(いわ)う
思い出	memory, recollection	思う＋出る
泳ぎ	swimming	泳ぐ
終わり	ending	終わる
帰り	a return	帰る
くもり	cloudy weather	くもる
答え	answer	答える
違い	difference	違う
知り合い	acquaintance	知り合う *to become acquainted with*
つかれ	fatigue	つかれる
作り	structure, construction	作る
つづき	sequel	つづく
つり	fishing	つる *to fish*
手伝(つだ)い	help, helper	手伝(つだ)う
ぬすみ	theft	ぬすむ
残り	leftover	残る
乗りかえ	transfer point	乗りかえる
はかり	scale	はかる
話	story	話す
晴れ	sunny weather	晴れる

間違い	mistake, error	間違う
見送り (みおく)	seeing someone off	見送る (みおく)
休み	holiday, day-off	休む
ゆれ	turbulence	ゆれる
よごれ	dirt, stain	よごれる
よろこび	joy	よろこぶ *to be pleased*

In addition the ます-stem can be combined with other nouns or suffixes to form a more complex noun.

売り場	sales point	売る + 場
おしいれ	Japanese-style closet; storage space	おす (*to push*) ＋入れる
買い物	shopping	買う＋物
着物	kimono	着る＋物
小包 (こづつみ)	package, parcel	小＋包む (つつ)
つき当たり (あ)	at the end of the street, T-intersection	つく (*to prick, to push*) ＋当たる (あ) (*to hit*)
出口	exit	出る＋口
飲み物	drinks	飲む＋物
乗り物	transportation	乗る＋物
むかいがわ	the other side, the opposite side	むかう (*to face*) ＋がわ (*side*)
申込書 (もうしこみ)	application form	申し込む (もう こ) ＋書

聞く練習

上手な聞き方

Monitoring and evaluating your understanding

As you listen, it is important to monitor your understanding and form tentative hypotheses. Successful listeners are capable of revising hypotheses as they encounter information that doesn't match their hypothesis and when they notice errors or inaccurate guesses they might have made. They are also capable of setting up alternative interpretations and making selections as they continue listening. In his *Teaching Listening and Speaking: From Theory to Practice* (Cambridge University Press, 2008), Jack Richards suggests that students should work on the following self-monitoring:

General listening development	Consider your progress against a set of criteria you have specified. Check and see if you continue to make the same mistakes. Determine how close you are to achieving short-term or long-term goals.
Specific listening tasks	Check understanding during listening. Identify the source of any difficulties you are having. Check the appropriateness and the accuracy of what is understood and compare it with new information.

In addition, successful listeners self-evaluate their overall comprehension progress and assess how well they have done. This enables them to make a realistic evaluation of their comprehension, while poor listeners sometimes develop a false level of confidence in their ability.

General listening development	Assess listening progress against a set of predetermined criteria. Assess the effectiveness of learning and practice strategies. Assess the appropriateness of learning goals and objectives set.
Specific listening tasks	Check the appropriateness and the accuracy of what has been understood. Determine the effectiveness of strategies used in the task. Assess overall comprehension of the text.

練習

Courtesy of the Author

落語 (らくご) is a Japanese traditional art of comedic story telling, and 小話 (こばなし) are very short stories which **rakugo** performers use at the beginning of their act to warm up the audience. Work with a partner. Listen to the following three 小話 (こばなし), then do the following:

1. Write the story.
2. Underline any parts you are not sure you understand.
3. Rate your confidence level in having understood the story. (100 percent = fully confident; 0 percent = no understanding)
4. Listen to the story again and check the accuracy of your understanding.
5. Evaluate how well you understood the story in your first listening and in your second listening.

A. **かみさま**   God

1. _____

    _____

    _____

    _____

    _____

    _____

3. _____ %

5. 1st listening _____ %   2nd listening _____ %

B. **文房具屋で**　At a stationary store
   ぶんぼう ぐ や

1. _____
   _____
   _____
   _____
   _____
   _____

3. _____ %

5. 1st listening _____ %　　　　2nd listening _____ %

C. **登校拒否**　Refusing to go to school
   とうこうきょ ひ

1. _____
   _____
   _____
   _____
   _____

3. _____ %

5. 1st listening _____ %　　　　2nd listening _____ %

きせきの口紅　Miracle lipstick
　　　くちべに

聞く前に

質問に日本語で答えて下さい。

1. 化粧 (*makeup*) をしたことがありますか。
   け しょう

2. 友達によく化粧をする人がいますか。その人はいつもどこで化粧をしますか。
   　　　　　　け しょう　　　　　　　　　　　　　　　　　　け しょう

3. どんな色の口紅 (*lipstick*) が好きですか。
   　　　　くちべに

言葉のリスト

鼻の穴 (はな あな)	a nostril
おれる	to break off
飛び出す (と)	to spring out
競馬新聞 (けい ば)	newspaper for horseracing
あたる	to hit (as in a jackpot)
馬券 (ば けん)	a betting ticket
万馬券 (まん ば けん)	a big winning ticket (on a horse)

🔊 **聞いてみましょう**

👥 Work with a partner. View the video of the **kobanashi** entitled きせきの口紅 (*Miracle lipstick*) in class or in MindTap. This **kobanashi** is longer and more complicated than the stories you listened to in the 上手な聞き方 section above. As you listen, pay attention to the performer's gestures and form a hypothesis about the possible story line. Then verbally summarize the story to your partner and check the parts you are sure or not sure about. Listen to the story again. This time, monitor your understanding, form a hypothesis, and check what you have and have not understood. Repeat this process one more time if necessary. When you feel reasonably confident, write down the story.

聞いた後で

👥 Work with a partner. Compare your written story with the version your partner has produced. Highlight the parts where you agree and disagree in different colors. Listen to the story again and revise if necessary.

Compare with the original text that your instructor will give you and evaluate how well you understood. Check the parts you did not understand and find out why.

聞き上手話し上手

おわかれを言う

At the beginning of *Nakama 1*, you learned expressions used in daily leave taking such as じゃあ、また, 失礼します, and さようなら. There are other cases when you have to say good-bye, such as when you are visiting someone's house, or when you are moving away.

When you visit someone's house and are ready to leave, you can use the expression （もう）そろそろ (literally, *well, it's almost time*) to indicate that you must be leaving. The host or hostess may ask you to stay longer by saying something like まだ、いいじゃない？／まだ、いいじゃないですか。／まだ、いいじゃありませんか (*It is still early, isn't it?*) or もうちょっといいでしょう (*Stay for a while longer, OK?*). You can then give the reason you need to leave.

川口：じゃあ、もうそろそろ失礼します。
　　　Well, I must be leaving now.

山本：まだ、いいじゃないですか。
　　　It's still early. Can't you stay a little longer?

川口：ええ、でも、これからちょっと行く所がありますので。
　　　Thank you, but I have to go somewhere now.

山本：そうですか。
　　　I see.

You then thank them for their hospitality. The following are used to express thanks:

今日は本当に有り難うございました。／今日は本当に有り難う。
Thank you very much for your hospitality.

どうもご馳走様でした。／どうもご馳走様。
Thank you very much for the meal/drinks.

今日はとても楽しかったです。／今日はとても楽しかったよ。
I had a very good time.

The host/hostess will usually respond by saying いいえ、何のおかまいもしませんで／何もなくて (*Oh, no, it was nothing*) when you thank them for a meal.

川口：　どうもご馳走様でした。
　　　　Thank you very much for the meal.

山本：　いいえ、何のおかまいもしませんで。
　　　　Oh, no, it was nothing.

川口：　いいえ、本当に楽しかったです。じゃあ、失礼します。
　　　　I've had a wonderful time. Well, I must be going now.

It is customary to express your appreciation again the next time you meet the host/hostess or talk with him/her on the phone. You should write a short thank you letter if you don't think you will have a chance to thank them again.

川口：　先日は／この間はどうも有り難うございました。とても楽しかったです。
　　　　Thanks very much for the invitation the other day. I had a good time.

山本：　いいえ、どういたしまして。また来て下さいね。
　　　　Not at all. Please come again.

Another occasion for leave taking is when you move away. The following expressions are frequently used to express thanks to friends, colleagues, and neighbors when you move away:

色々お世話になりまして、本当に有り難うございました。／

色々お世話になって、どうも有り難う。
Thank you very much for your help and hospitality.

これからもどうぞよろしくおねがいします。／これからもどうぞよろしく。
Please stay in touch.

 練習

A. Work with a partner. Listen to the conversation between Kawaguchi and Yamamoto in the explanation and practice the dialogue. Then listen to a more casual version of the same conversation and practice the dialogue.

B. Work with a partner. One person plays the role of a host/hostess and the other person is the guest. It is five o'clock now and the guest is thinking of leaving because it is dinnertime, and he/she doesn't want to inconvenience the host/hostess. The guest should think of a reason and start taking his or her leave.

C. Work with a partner. One person should be a student and the other a professor. The student is graduating. The student has come to the office to express thanks to the professor and invite the professor to the graduation ceremony.

D. Work with a partner. You are in Japan and going back to your own country in a few weeks. Your partner is a neighbor who has been very nice to you. Tell the neighbor you are leaving, leave him or her your new address, and ask him/her to forward any important messages you might receive after leaving.

漢字

Guessing the meanings of unfamiliar kanji

In general, most vocabulary is learned incidentally through reading and listening, rather than by consciously memorizing it. Studies show that good vocabulary learners combine multiple strategies to guess meanings of unknown **kanji** and **kanji** compounds in texts. Two common strategies are to guess the meaning using the structure of **kanji** compounds and to guess from context. This chapter deals with guessing from context and the next chapter discusses the structure of **kanji** compounds.

It is not advisable to attempt to guess the meaning of **kanji** from context in cases where the text is hard to understand. It is very difficult to take advantage of your guessing ability when you don't understand the gist of what you are reading. Therefore, to develop this skill, choose a text that is slightly difficult, containing unknown words here and there, but easy enough for you to get the general idea. Guessing from context means not only guessing from what you have already read, but also using grammatical structure and **okurigana**. For example, determine the position of an unknown word in the sentence, the particle that follows it, and so on. This will give you an idea about what part of speech it is. Also, verbs often restrict the types of noun that can be used as the subject or direct object of a sentence. Finally, **okurigana** might give you a clue for a word you already know but don't know how it is written in **kanji**. Needless to say, it is also important to know the meaning of surrounding words, because grammar information alone will not tell the meaning of words. Finally, don't forget the overall context of what you have already read, the purpose of the text, and any pertinent real-world information, as these provide important clues for guessing the meaning of text, which in turn helps you to guess the meaning of unknown words.

笑	笑	to laugh わら(う) ショウ	ノ ト ト ⺮⺮ ⺮⺮ ⺮⺮ 竺 竺 笑
			友達に笑われました。 わら
泣	泣	to cry な(く) キュウ	丶 冫 氵 氵 汁 汁 泣 泣
			子供に泣かれて、困りました。 な こま
助	助	to help, assist たす(かる)・たす(ける) ジョ	｜ 冂 月 月 目 助 助
			とても助かります。 たす
考	考	to think かんが(える) コウ	一 十 土 耂 耂 考
			よく考えてから、話す。 かんが
払	払	to pay はら(う) フツ	一 扌 扌 払 払
			レストランでお金を払わなかった。 はら

| 化 | 化 | to turn (oneself) into | ノ イ イ´ 化 | | | | |
| | | ば（ける）　カ　　日本の文化　インド文化
　　　　　　　　　　　ぶんか　　　　ぶんか | | | | | |

| 調 | 調 | to check, investigate | 宀 訁 言 訂 訓 訊 調 調 調 |
| | | しら（べる）　チョウ　　図書館で調べる。
　　　　　　　　　　　　　　　しら | |

| 集 | 集 | to collect, to gather | ノ イ イ´ 宀 什 隹 隹 隼 集 |
| | | あつ（める）・あつ（まる）　シュウ　　九時に集まって下さい。
　　　　　　　　　　　　　　　　　　　　　あつ | |

| 的 | 的 | having attribute of, target | ノ イ 白 白 白 白´ 的 的 |
| | | まと　テキ　　日本的な建物
　　　　　　　　てき | |

| 失 | 失 | to lose, to miss | ノ ノ￢ 二 失 失 |
| | | シツ　　失礼します。
　　　　　しつ | |

| 当 | 当 | hit, target | 丶 丷 丷 当 当 当 |
| | | あ（たる）　トウ　　本当ですか。
　　　　　　　　とう | |

| 期 | 期 | period, term, time | 一 廿 甘 其 其 期 期 期 期 |
| | | キ　　秋学期と春学期　期末試験
　　　がっき　　がっき　きまつ | |

| 和 | 和 | Japanese, peace | ノ 二 千 千 禾 禾 和 和 |
| | | ワ　　和食　平和 (peace)　和風 (Japanese style)
　　　わしょく　へいわ　　　　わふう | |

| 重 | 重 | heavy, weight | ノ 一 一 台 台 台 重 重 重 |
| | | おも（い）　ジュウ　　重い荷物
　　　　　　　　　おも | |

| 界 | 界 | world | 丨 冂 冂 用 田 男 界 界 界 |
| | | カイ　　世界で一番高い山　世界旅行
　　　せかい　　　　　　　せかい | |

| 正 | 正 | correct, right | 一 丁 下 正 正 |
| | | ただ（しい）　セイ・ショウ　　正しい答えは何ですか。　正座　正月
　　　　　　　　　　　　　　ただ　　　　　　　　　せいざ　しょうがつ | |

| 由 | 由 | reason, significance
ユウ | 丨 冂 冉 由 由 | | | |
| | | | 理由がわかりません。　自由
　り ゆう　　　　　　　　じ ゆう | | | |

| 宗 | 宗 | religion, sect
シュウ・ソウ | 丶 丷 宀 宁 宇 宇 宗 | | | |
| | | | 宗教
しゅうきょう | | | |

| 治 | 治 | government, healing
おさ(める)・なお(す)　ジ・チ | 丶 冫 氵 氵 氻 治 治 治 | | | |
| | | | 病気を治す。　政治
　　なお　　　せいじ | | | |

| 次 | 次 | next
つぎ　ジ | 丶 冫 冫 次 次 次 | | | |
| | | | 次の問題は難しいです。
つぎ | | | |

| 有 | 有 | to exist, to have
あ(る)　ユウ | 丿 ナ 冇 有 有 有 | | | |
| | | | 有名な先生です。　有り難う
ゆうめい　　　　　　あ　がと | | | |

| 最 | 最 | most
もっと(も)　サイ | 冂 日 旦 早 冐 冐 冐 最 最 | | | |
| | | | 最近
さいきん | | | |

| 興 | 興 | interest
おこす　キョウ・コウ | 丿 亻 臼 臼 𦥑 舆 舆 興 興 | | | |
| | | | 日本の文化に興味があります。
ぶんか　きょうみ | | | |

読めるようになった漢字

文化　政治　病気を治す　調べる　集める　集まる　日本的　失礼　本当　学期
　せい
期末　試験　和食　重い　世界　正しい　正月　理由　自由　生け花　〜教
教育　茶道　社会　習慣　宗教　習字　正座　落語　心細い　最近　泣く　笑う
　　　　　　　　　　かん　　　　　　　　ざ　　　　　ぼそ
助ける　考える　払う　有名な　有り難う　興味　お辞儀　祝う　習う
　　　　　　　　　　　　　　　　　　　　　　　ぎ
日本人の名前：川野　和子　正男　真理
　　　　　　　　　　　　　　　　ま

練習

1. 和食をたくさん食べる生活で病気が治りました。
2. 東京の文化と京都の文化は少し違うので、時々失礼になることがあります。
3. 生け花と茶道に興味があります。
4. 今学期の期末試験は難しかったので、答えを説明して下さい。
5. 最近日本は経済的に強くなった。しかし、理由はよく分からないが、政治的には世界的にまだ弱い。
6. その先生はよく笑って、よく泣くので、学生の間で有名です。
7. テニスの練習をしますから、九時に集まって下さい。
8. 荷物が重くなったので、私がお金を払いますから、タクシーで帰りましょう。
9. 色々考えたけれど、本当に答えが分からないんです。助けて下さい。
10. 長い間、正座をしていたので、足が痛くなりました。
11. 次の授業までに日本の宗教について調べなければいけません。

読む練習

上手な読み方

Monitoring and evaluating your understanding

As is the case with listening, the effective use of monitoring and evaluation strategies should help you improve your reading skills. One way to do this is to engage in reciprocal reading.

First, focus on the purpose and title of the text you are reading. Then try to skim through the text and identify the part that is relevant for your purpose. Ignore supplementary information or any parts you don't understand. Once you get a general idea, go back to the text again, check your comprehension, and determine how well you have understood the text. Then underline any parts you have problems with and try to guess possible meanings from the surrounding context. You may have more than one possible interpretation for some sections.

Once this is done, work with another student or a group of students. In reciprocal reading, students take turns reading the text. When you read a line of text aloud, try to read it so that pauses occur at natural break points rather than in the middle of a word or inflection. If you are unable to read a text or are having trouble reading aloud, get help from a listener. When you are listening to a text being read aloud, try to predict what will come next in the text. Then check your prediction and see if your guess is correct. This helps you improve your monitoring skills. If you don't understand what is being read, ask questions about it or provide feedback about your comprehension problem. Active discussion like this is beneficial for you and other students to resolve problems and to learn to monitor your own learning and thinking. After going through the text once, do the same thing again, while checking the level of your understanding in this session compared to the first session. If necessary, you should repeat this process again, because continuous practice is essential to acquire successful reading strategies. Once you feel you have understood the text sufficiently, summarize it by yourself or with other students.

練習

Work by yourself at first and then as a pair or in a group. Read the following text using the steps described above, and summarize the main point of the text in your own words.

　大衆文化は、ポピュラーカルチャー、ポップカルチャー、マスカルチャーとも呼ばれ、文学や芸術、美術などのハイカルチャーに対して、一般大衆が広く愛好する文化のことである。これとは別に、サブカルチャーという言葉があるが、これは大衆文化やハイカルチャーと違い、一部の人たちに愛されるマニアックな分野を指すものである。

　しかし、時代の変化によってこれらのカルチャーの区分も変わっていくことがあるので、境界線を引くのは難しい。例えば、かつてサブカルチャーであったようなフィギュアやオタク文化が、現在では大衆文化として受け入れられているのもその一例である。

マンガ

読む前に

1. 日本のマンガを読んだり見たりしたことがありますか。
2. どんなマンガでしたか。
3. アメリカのマンガやアニメと日本のマンガやアニメはどう違いますか。
4. 日本語を勉強するために、マンガを読んだらいいと思いますか。どうしてそう思いますか。

読んでみましょう

言葉のリスト

かかわる	教養	大衆	〜倍	貢献する
to be relevant to	education	public, the masses	~times	to contribute

　日本の文化というと、歌舞伎や茶道、生け花、着物と思う人も多いだろう。確かに、これらの伝統的な文化は今でも日本人の生活に深くかかわっている。例えば、日本には社会人が趣味や教養や健康のために色々なことを習えるカルチャーセンターと呼ばれる教室があるが、どのカルチャーセンターにもたいてい茶道教室や生け花教室がある。でも、日本の文化には伝統的なものだけではなく、今の日本の社会でよく見られる大衆文化もある。

　その中でもよく知られているのはマンガである。マンガは、アメリカでは子供が読むものというイメージが強かったが、日本のアニメやマンガがアメリカでも見られるようになって少しイメージが変わってきたようだ。一方、日本では、マンガは昔から子供も大人もみんなが楽しめるものである。マンガは、1950年代に子供を中心としてよく読まれるようになったが、その後、学生、大人のためのマンガが描かれるようになった。現在ではファンタジー、コミックはもちろん、スポーツ物、スパイ物、SF、ラブストーリー、ファミリードラマ、経済、社会問題をテーマにしたもの、料理などの趣味をテーマにしたものなど色々なものがある。そういう意味では、今のマンガは絵がついた小説のようなものだとも言えるだろう。長さも、4コママンガから、何十冊にもなる長いものまで色々で、普通の雑誌や新聞だけではなく、マンガ雑誌と呼ばれる雑誌や、マンガ本と言われるものまである。1995年のマンガ雑誌の売り上げは3,357億円、25億ドルにもなる。同じように、アニメも人気が集まり、今では日本だけではなく世界中にアニメクラブがあると言われている。今や日本は世界一の「マンガ大国」なのである。

　マンガは文学小説と違って、芸術的なイメージはないし、人前では読まないようにしているという人もいるようだ。けれども、本当はマンガを読むことはいいことだということを知っている人は少ない。1997年にライフデザイン研究所が行ったアンケートによると、マンガを読まない人の54%は他の本も読まないが、マンガを読むが他の本は読まない人は14%しかいなかった。つまり、マンガを読む人のほとんどがマンガではないものも読んでいるのである。マンガを読む人が増えたからだとは言えないかもしれないが、1975年から1995年の

20 年間に図書館の数は 2.2 倍に、図書館から本を借りる人の数は 5 倍にも増えている。最近の日本人はテレビばかり見て、本を読まないと言われるが、そうではない。マンガという大衆文化は、日本人のリテラシーに大きく貢献しているのである。

読んだ後で

A. 上の文章 (text) の各段落 (each paragraph) の 一番大事なポイントを書いて下さい。

　　一段落目 (paragraph 1)

　　二段落目 (paragraph 2)

　　三段落目 (paragraph 3)

B. 下の質問に日本語で答えて下さい。

1. この文章 (text) を書いた人はマンガはいいものだと思っていますか。よくないものだと思っていますか。
2. 日本ではどんな人がマンガを読みますか。
3. 日本のアニメやマンガにはどんな物がありますか。
4. マンガはどうして「絵のついた小説のようなもの」なのですか。
5. 「マンガ大国」とはどういう意味ですか。
6. どうして人前ではマンガを読まない人がいるのですか。
7. マンガを読む人と読まない人では何が違いますか。
8. この文章を書いた人はマンガと図書館の数とはどんな関係 (relationship) があると思っていますか。

C. 日本のマンガを読んでみて、次のことを考えて下さい。

1. どうして日本人はマンガが好きなのだと思いますか。
2. マンガのどんなところがやさしいと思いますか。どんなところが難しいと思いますか。
3. 日本語を勉強する人にとって、マンガを読むのはいいことだと思いますか。

総合練習
そうごう

A. 世界の習慣
かん

1. Work with a partner. Discuss what other people do for you and what you are allowed to do in the following situations, and make a short presentation about your culture. The example dialogue below is based on the speaker's experience.

Example:　A:　〜さんは大学生になった時、何かしてもらいましたか。

　　　　　　B:　ええ、両親に新しい車を買ってもらいました。

　　　　　　A:　わあ、いいですね。

　　　　　　B:　〜さんは、何かしてもらいましたか。

　　　　　　A:　一緒にアパートをさがしてもらいました。
　　　　　　　　　しょ

　　　　　　B:　そうですか。大学生になる前と後ではどう生活が変わりましたか。
　　　　　　　　　　　　　　　　　　　　　　　　　　　　　　　　かつ

　　　　　　A:　そうですね。今は色々なことをさせてもらえますよ。
　　　　　　　　たとえば、高校生の間はたいてい両親と一緒に住まなければなら
　　　　　　　　ないけれど、今は、一人で住まわせてくれますね。
　　　　　　　　　　　　　　　　　　　　　　　しょ

　　　　　　B:　そうですね。

	してもらうこと	させてもらうこと
大学生になる		
成人 (legal adult) になる せいじん		
結婚する		

2. Interview Japanese students or students from other countries about the items you discussed in Exercise 1, and make a presentation about the differences and similarities in cultural practices in your country and theirs.

B. 私の国の習慣
かん

1. The following chart shows some customs in Japan. Look at each custom and place a check in the column した方がいいこと if you think Japanese people would expect other Japanese to follow that custom. Check よくすること if you think Japanese people would often follow the custom even though they may not be expected to do so. Check あまりしないこと if you think Japanese people would rarely follow the custom even if there is no prohibition against it. Check してはいけないこと if this is not an acceptable thing to do in Japan.

	した方が いい	よくする	あまり しない	しては いけない
家の中に入る時、くつをぬぐ				
家の中ではスリッパ (slippers) をはく				
たたみの部屋でスリッパ をはく				
トイレではトイレのスリッパ をはく				
トイレのドアはいつもしめておく				
部屋のドアはいつもしめておく				
だれかの部屋に入る時はノックをする				
朝御飯にサラダを食べる				
朝御飯にあまい物を食べる				
朝御飯は和食だけだ				
食事をする時、お客さんはドアから一番 遠いところにすわる				
食べ物を口に入れて話す				
食事が終わったら、たばこをすう				
お風呂はお父さんが一番はじめに入る				
ゆぶね (bath tub) の中で体を洗う				
人の家に行く時、電話をしてから行く				
近所に引っ越してきた人の所にあいさつ に行く				
人に何かもらったら、何かをかえす				
カラオケではみんながうたう				

2. Work in groups of four. Discuss what checkmarks you assigned to each item in Exercise 1. Use casual speech. List the items that everyone agrees or disagrees with and why. Report the results to the class using polite speech.

Example:　A:　日本の家ではくつをぬぐことになってるよね。

B:　今でもそうかな？ 今は、もうぬがなくてもいいんじゃない？

C:　いや、そんなことないと思うよ。

D:　うん、ぼくの日本人の友達もくつをぬぐから。くつはぬがなきゃ
いけないんじゃない？

私達のグループでは日本の家ではくつをぬぐことになっていると思う人が多
いですが、今はぬがなくてもいいという人もいます。

3. Work with a partner. Create a similar list about customs in your country. Make copies for your classmates and ask them to mark them. Tally the results and check if your list accurately reflects what you thought would be the most likely outcome.

ロールプレイ

1. You are about to visit a Japanese friend's house. You are in front of the house. Ring the bell, greet your friend's mother, and go into the house.

2. You are visiting a Japanese friend's house. It is close to dinner time, so you should leave. Initiate the conversation to take your leave in an appropriate manner.

3. You are leaving school to help out your parents. Your friends are having a farewell party for you. Describe the memories of what you have experienced here, and express your nostalgic feelings.

4. Your Japanese friend has been invited to a wedding ceremony, and he does not know what to wear, what kind of present to give, etc. Make suggestions to your friend about customs for wedding ceremonies and receptions in your country.

5. You are in Japan. Your Japanese friends want to know what you like or don't like about Japanese culture. Express your opinions by comparing Japanese culture with your culture.

6. Your Japanese friend does not know much about religion and asks about religions in your country. Describe them to him or her.

Chapter 10

第十課
<ruby>第<rt>だい</rt></ruby><ruby>十<rt></rt></ruby><ruby>課<rt>か</rt></ruby>

MIXA/Getty Images

文句と謝罪
もんく　しゃざい
Complaints and Apologies

Objectives	Expressing complaints, requesting a change of behavior, expressing the intention to make a change
Vocabulary	Relationships among people, annoying things, expressing complaints and annoyance, things you don't want to be forced to do
Dialogue	静かにするように言って下さい。 *Please tell him to be quieter.* しず
Japanese Culture	Neighborhood relations, trash collection
Grammar	I. Expressing complaints using the causative-passive form
	II. Expressing or requesting efforts to change behavior using the plain present form of verbs + ように
	III. Expressing unchanged conditions using 〜まま
	IV. Using the conditional 〜ても and question word 〜ても
	V. Using the plain form + のに, *despite ~*, *although ~*
Listening	Annoying things
Communication	Expressing complaints or anger, making apologies
Kanji	Structure of **kanji** compounds
	相 談 貸 借 返 開 閉 伝 覚 歌 声 静 夜 直 置 記 注 句 合 忙 然 号 村
Reading	Understanding the characteristics of expository writing, いじめ

単語
<ruby>たん</ruby>

Nouns

あいて	相手	companion, conversation partner, the other party
あかちゃん	赤ちゃん	baby
おおや	大家	landlord, landlady
おと	音	sound
おとな	大人	adult
かぎ	鍵	key, かぎをかける to lock
かべ	壁	wall
こ	子	child. こ is usually preceded by a modifier. としうえのこ older child, いいこ good child
ごみ／ゴミ		trash, garbage (ごみ can be written either in **hiragana** or in **katakana**)
しりあい	知り合い	acquaintance
としうえ	年上	older
としした	年下	younger
なか	仲	relationship (among people), なかがいい to have a good relationship, なかが悪い to have a bad relationship
にっき	日記	diary, にっきをつける to keep a diary
ひ	日	day
ピアノ		piano
ほんとう	本当	truth, ほんとうに indeed, really
めいわく	迷惑	trouble, めいわくをかける to give (someone) problems
よなか	夜中	late at night, the middle of the night
もんく	文句	complaint, もんくをいう to complain
らくがき	落書き	graffiti, らくがきをする to write graffiti

Verbal nouns

ちゅうい	注意	attention, warning, ちゅういする to warn, to call attention to, ちゅういをする to warn, to call attention to
そうだん	相談	consultation, そうだんする to consult with

い -adjectives

うるさい		noisy, Shut up! (when used as a phrase by itself)
きたない	汚い	dirty
たまらない		cannot stand, unbearable
ひくい	低い	low

な -adjectives

しあわせ（な）	幸せ（な）	happy
しょうじき（な）	正直（な）	honest
めいわく（な）	迷惑（な）	troublesome, annoying, めいわくをかける to give (someone) trouble, to inconvenience (someone)

う -verbs

おこる	怒る	to get angry
からかう		to tease
さわぐ	騒ぐ	to make noise
たたく		to hit, to slap
ひく	弾く	to play (the piano/guitar, other stringed instrument), ピアノをひく to play the piano
ゆるす	許す	to forgive

る -verbs

おくれる	遅れる	to be late
かける	掛ける	to hang, hook, かぎをかける to lock
かたづける	片付ける	to clean up, to organize
たてる	立てる	to stand something up, おとをたてる to make noise
つける	付ける	to write (in a diary), にっきをつける to keep a diary

Expressions

いいかげんにしてよ。	いい加減にしてよ。	Give me a break! (female speech)
いいかげんにしろよ。	いい加減にしろよ。	Give me a break! (male speech)
おとをたてる	音を立てる	to make noise
きがつかなくて	気がつかなくて	I didn't realize (it).
きをつける	気をつける	to take care, to pay attention
ごめいわくおかけして もうしわけありません。	ご迷惑おかけして 申しわけありません。	I'm sorry to cause you problems.
しかたがない	仕方がない	Nothing can be done about it, there's no use.

じょうだんじゃないよ。	冗談じゃないよ。	You've got to be kidding.
ほっといてくれよ。		Leave me alone. (male speech)
ほっといてよ。		Leave me alone. (female speech)
やめろ。		Cut it out. (male speech)
もうしわけありません。	申し訳ありません。	I'm sorry. (polite and formal)
もうしわけございません。	申し訳ございません。	I'm sorry. (very polite and formal)

単語の練習
たん

A. 人と人とのかんけい　Relationships among people

知り合い し　あ	acquaintance		年下の子 としした	younger child
年上の子 としうえ	older child		大家（さん） おお や	landlord, landlady
赤ちゃん あか	baby		相手 あい て	conversation partner, the other party
大人 お と な	adult		なかがいい	to get along with someone
なかが悪い	to not get along with someone			

覚えていますか。
おぼ

年を取る　家族　祖父　祖母　両親　父　母　兄弟　兄　姉　弟　妹　主人　つま　ご家族
おじいさん　おばあさん　ご両親　お父さん　お母さん　お兄さん　お姉さん　弟さん
妹さん　ご主人　おくさん　近所の人

Activity 1　Which words fit the following descriptions?

1. お父さんやお母さん
2. 自分よりわかい人
3. その人を好きじゃなかったりよくけんかすること
4. 友達じゃないけど知っている人
5. ０さいの子供
6. その人といい友達でいること
7. 自分より年を取っている相手
あい て
8. アパートや家を貸す人
か
9. 自分の話を聞いている人
10. 子供じゃない人

Activity 2   質問に答えて下さい。

1. なかがいい人とはどんなことをしますか。知り合いとはどうですか。
2. アパートを借りるなら、どんな大家さんがいいですか。
3. 年上の兄弟と年下の兄弟とどちらの方がいいと思いますか。
4. 赤ちゃんが好きですか。きらいですか。どうしてですか。

B. めいわくなこと   Annoying things

授業におくれる
to come late
for class

夜中にさわぐ
to be noisy
late at night

音をたてる
to make noise

ピアノをひく
to play the piano

たたく
to hit

かべに落書きをする
to write graffiti
on the wall

からかう
to tease

くつがよごれる
for shoes to get dirty

めいわくをかける
to give (someone) trouble, to
inconvenience (someone)

覚えていますか。
<small>おぼ</small>

どろぼう　はんざい　ひがい　足をふむ　いじめる　歌を歌う　うそをつく
<small>うた　うた</small>
うわさをする　お金を引き出す　お金をぬすむ　おそう　終わる　車が止まる
車を家の前に止める　車をぶつける　けがをする　けんかをする　交通事故にあう
さいふを落とす　しぬ　宿題を忘れる　　すてる　たばこをすう　名前を間違える
にげる　バイトをやめる　人をだます　間違う　物をこわす　指を切る
洋服をよごす　雪がふる　わかれる　笑う　悪口を言う　きらい　遠い　弱い
<small>よう</small>
悪い

Activity 3　下の文に適当な (appropriate) 言葉を書いて下さい。
<small>てきとう</small>

1. ぼくは彼女が好きだから、＿＿＿＿＿＿てしまうんです。
<small>かの</small>

2. 知り合いのおじさんは車をかべに＿＿＿＿＿＿、こわしてしまった。
<small>し　あ</small>

3. 年上の子が年下の子を＿＿＿＿＿＿＿、泣かせてしまった。
<small>としうえ　　としした</small>

4. 赤ちゃんが寝ているので、大きい＿＿＿＿＿＿を＿＿＿＿＿＿＿下さい。
<small>あか</small>

5. 教室のかべに＿＿＿＿＿をして、先生にしかられてしまった。
<small>しつ</small>

6. となりの人が夜中にパーティをして＿＿＿＿＿＿のて、寝られない。
<small>よなか</small>

7. 雨の日に道を歩いていたら、車に服を＿＿＿＿＿＿＿。

8. 電車の中で、女の人に足を＿＿＿＿＿＿、とても痛かった。

9. 寝られないので、夜ピアノを＿＿＿＿＿＿＿＿＿。

10. ＿＿＿＿＿＿＿くつをはいて、家の中に入ってはいけません。

11. あの子は毎日＿＿＿＿＿＿に＿＿＿＿＿＿のて、先生が困っている。

12. 人に＿＿＿＿＿＿をかけたら、あやまらなければならない。

Activity 4　質問に答えて下さい。

1. 子供がよくすることは、どんなことですか。
2. 大学生がよくすることは、どんなことですか。
3. あなたが今までにやったことは、どんなことですか。
4. やってはいけないけれど、やってみたいことは、どんなことですか。
5. どんなことで人にめいわくをかけたことがありますか。

C. 文句を言う   Expressing complaints and annoyance
もん く

おこる	to get angry
（〜に）気をつける	to be careful about
注意する ちゅうい	to warn, to call attention to, to watch out for
相談する そうだん	to consult with
ゆるす	to forgive
めいわく（な）	to be annoyed, annoying
たまらない	cannot stand, unbearable
きたない	dirty
うるさい	noisy
仕方がない しかた	there is nothing one can do about it, there is no use
本当だ	true
ひくい	low

覚えていますか。
おぼ

ごめん　ごめんなさい　無理　無理をする　あやまる　困る　しかる　心配する
む　　　む
止める　ええっと／すみません　失礼ですが　それはちょっと　いや（な）
残念（な）　大変（な）　気分が悪い　こわい　ひどい
ねん

Activity 5   下の文に適当な (*appropriate*) 言葉を書いて下さい。
てきとう

1. 授業におくれたので、先生に＿＿＿＿＿れた。

2. その話はうそじゃなくて＿＿＿＿＿です。

3. 友達は、変なうわさをたてられて＿＿＿＿＿＿＿から、先生に＿＿＿＿＿した。

4. 友達が変なことを言ったので、＿＿＿＿＿＿、文句を言った。
   もん く

5. となりの家のピアノの音が＿＿＿＿＿、たまらない。

6. そのシャツは＿＿＿＿＿から、洗いました。

7. 私はせが＿＿＿＿＿から、前にせが高い人がいると、とても困るんです。

8. 道をわたる時は、右と左に＿＿＿＿＿を＿＿＿＿＿下さい。

9. 雪で私の飛行機がキャンセルになりました。＿＿＿＿＿が＿＿＿＿＿ので、
   き
   今日は家に帰って、明日出るつもりです。

Activity 6   質問に答えて下さい。

1. どんな時に両親に文句を言いますか。どんな時に両親に注意されますか。
2. どんなことについて友達に相談しますか。
3. どんな時に人にあやまりますか。どんな時にはあやまりませんか。

D. させられたくないこと   Things you don't want to be forced to do

日記をつける	to keep a diary
かたづける	to organize, to clean up
犬の散歩をする	to walk the dog
ごみを出す	to take trash out, to discard trash
引っ越す	to move (residence)
かぎをかける	to lock (the door, the window, etc.)
ピアノを習う	to learn piano

覚えていますか。

説明する　洗濯をする　そうじする　単語を覚える　はたらく　勉強する
むかえに行く　休む

Activity 7   Work with a group of four. One person should act out one of the actions
in the list or the 覚えていますか section above. The rest of the group
should guess what is being done. Anyone who makes a correct guess
receives one point.

Activity 8   質問に答えて下さい。

1. よくすることは、どれですか。
2. 全然しないことは、どれですか。
3. どんなことをしてみたいですか。
4. よく人にどんなことをしてもらいますか。
5. よく人にどんなことをしてあげますか。

ダイアローグ

はじめに

下の質問に日本語で答えて下さい。

1. 近所では、何か問題がありますか。
2. となりの人がうるさい時、どうしますか。
3. 近所のめいわくにならないように、どんなことに気をつけていますか。
4. どんな時に大家さんと話をしますか。
　　　　　おおや

🔊 **静かにするように言って下さい。** *Please tell him to be quieter.*
　　しず

The following **manga** frames are scrambled, so they are not in the order described by the dialogue. Read the dialogue and unscramble the frames by writing the correct number in the box in each frame.

a

b

c

d

e

f

リーさんはアルバイトの広告 (*advertisements*) を見ています。そこに、上田さんが
　　　　　　　　　　　　こうこく
来ました。

上田：　リーさん、何、見てるの？

リー：　新しいバイト、さがしてるんだ。

上田：　え、どうして？　前のアルバイトやめちゃったの？

リー：　いや、やめさせられちゃったんだよ。最近寝られなくて、何度も仕事に
　　　　おくれちゃったから。

上田：　寝られないって？　どこか悪いの？

リー：　いや、そうじゃないんだ。となりの人がうるさくてね。

上田：　となりの人？　先月引っ越してきた？

リー：　うん、毎晩おそくまで大きな音でテレビを見たり、音楽聞いたり。それに、よく友達が来て夜中までさわぐんだから、たまらないよ。

上田：　本当？　ひどいね。文句言ったの？

リー：　うん、何度静かにするように言ってもだめなんだ。

上田：　そう、大家さんに言って注意してもらうようにたのんでみたら？

リー：　うん、そうだね。このままだと、病気になりそうだから、仕方ないかな。

リーさんは大家さんに電話をかけました。

リー：　もしもし、あの、さくらアパートの 201 号室に住んでいるリーなんですけれども。

大家：　あ、リーさん、どうしたんですか。

リー：　あのう、ちょっと おねがいしたいことがあるんですが。

大家：　何ですか。

リー：　すみませんが、となりの青木さんに夜静かにするように言っていただけないでしょうか。

大家：　そんなにうるさいんですか。

リー：　ええ。よく夜中に、テレビやステレオの音を大きくしてさわぐので、寝られないんです。何度もたのんだんですが、聞いてくれないんです。

大家：　そう、困りましたね。じゃあ、私の方から言っておきますよ。

リー：　ごめいわくをおかけしてもうしわけありませんが、よろしくおねがいします。

DIALOGUE PHRASE NOTES

- 何度も means *many times.*
- そんなに means *so, that much, that many.*
- ～号室 is a suffix for a room number.

ダイアローグの後で

A. 質問に答えて下さい。

1. リーさんは、どうしてアルバイトをさがしているのですか。
2. リーさんは、どうして寝られないのですか。
3. リーさんのとなりのアパートには、だれが住んでいますか。その人はどんな人だと思いますか。どうしてそう思いますか。
4. 上田さんは、リーさんにどうしたらいいと言いましたか。
5. 大家さんは、リーさんのためにどんなことをしてあげるつもりですか。
   おお や

B. 下の文章 (paragraph) は青木さんが書いたものです。自分を青木さんだと思って
   ぶんしょう   あお き   あお き
   下線 (underline) のところに適当な言葉を入れて下さい。
   か せん   てきとう

今日大家さんから電話があって、夜＿＿＿＿＿＿＿＿＿＿＿＿ように言われた。
   おお や
となりの人が、＿＿＿＿＿＿＿＿＿そうだ。ぼくはテレビやステレオの音が
＿＿＿＿＿＿＿＿＿とは思わなかったが、このアパートはかべがうすい (thin) のかもしれない。

C. Underline the phrases that express Li-san's annoyance and complaints.

日本の文化

近所の人とつきあう

Neighborhood relations are important in any country but are probably more complicated in Japan due to its high population density. To comprehend the amount of living space available to the Japanese people, first imagine the state of California, which has roughly the same geographical area as Japan. Now remove 80 percent of that since that much space in Japan is taken up by mountains and is not habitable. Finally, put one-half the entire U.S. population into the remaining 20 percent of California. This is the population density of Japan. A complicating factor is that the highly populated metro areas, which take up just 1 percent of the habitable land, house one half of Japan's population. Therefore, 1m² of living space in Tokyo costs several times more than it would in New York City. Also, many people live in high-rise apartment buildings rather than houses. Even so, the average living space per person is 30.9m² in Japan, which is less than half of that in the United States (64.0m²). In other words, many Japanese families live in very crowded areas.

One of the most common problems is noise. There is not much distance between houses, and thin walls separate apartments, so sound travels easily. Things that would not bother your neighbor in the United States can be a big nuisance in Japan. The sound of a chair being pulled out or someone taking a shower can be just as annoying as the sound of children running in the room. Noise prevention is thus very important. For example, it is a good idea not to take a bath or shower or do laundry early in the morning or late at night if you live in an apartment. Also, placing a stereo and musical instruments away from the wall and on a carpet can prevent sounds from traveling to your neighbors. Department stores and do-it-yourself stores sell a variety of gadgets to prevent noise.

ゴミを集める

Another common problem is the collection of trash and recyclables. Garbage collection is very efficient but also somewhat complicated in Japan. Garbage is classified according to type, and the classification and frequency of collection can vary from region to region. In Tokyo, for example, you first need to distinguish among combustible garbage (燃えるごみ／可燃ごみ), non-combustible garbage (燃えないごみ／不燃ごみ), recyclables (リサイクル), and large trash (粗大ごみ) such as furniture and appliances.

Combustible garbage is burned, and non-combustible garbage is broken into small pieces and taken to the dump site directly. Which items are placed in which category may differ slightly depending on local laws. Garbage can be placed in trash buckets or

in special plastic bags that have been approved by local authorities. Garbage placed in an unapproved container may not be collected.

Also, it is necessary to take garbage to the designated collection location on the day it will be collected. The collection days for each type of garbage are posted at every waste collection area. Waste must not be left overnight. Leaving uncollected

Kenneth Hamm / Photo Japan

garbage for a prolonged period of time in the collection area is a nuisance for people who live close to the area.

In the Tokyo metro area, combustible garbage is usually collected three times a week and non-combustible garbage is collected once a week. Recyclables (cans and bottles) are also collected once a week. These services are free for residential waste. In many cases, large waste items are collected by the department of waste management by special arrangement for a fee. In some districts, you can also take large garbage to a designated site by yourself.

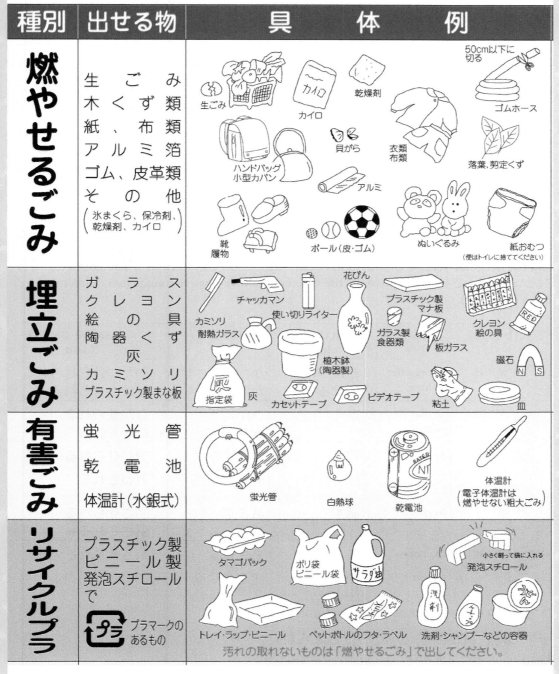

Types of trash. This circular from Hiroshima identifies several types of trash, including (from top) combustible trash, landfill trash, toxic trash, and recyclable plastics.

文法

I. Expressing complaints using the causative-passive form

A causative-passive sentence is a direct passive where the causee of an action is the subject and the causer is the agent of the action. Such sentences convey the viewpoint of the causee. In a causative-passive sentence, the subject (the causee) is always forced to do something by the agent (the causer).

Subject (Causee)		Agent (Causer)		Action		
Noun	Particle	Noun	Particle	Noun	Particle	Verb (causative-passive)
私	は	先生	に	本	を	読まされた。

I was made to read the book by the teacher.

When the causer is understood from the context, it can be omitted.

子供の時、毎朝運動させられた。
I was forced to do exercise every morning when I was a child.

The formation of the causative-passive is identical to the formation of the passive. However, う-verbs have two causative-passive forms, （さ）せられる and （さ）される, while る-verbs and the irregular verb する tend to have only （さ）せられる. In cases where both （さ）せられる and （さ）される are possible, the shorter causative-passive sounds more direct and more colloquial.

Verb types	Meaning	Dictionary form	Causative form	Causative-passive form
る -verbs	to organize to lock	かたづける かける	かたづけさせる かけさせる	かたづけさせられる かけさせられる
う -verbs	to play (the piano)	ひく	ひかせる or ひかす	ひかせられる ひかされる
	to learn	習う	習わせる or 習わす	習わせられる 習わされる
	to speak	話す	話さす	話させられる 話さされる＊
Irregular verbs	to come	来る	来させる	来させられる
	to warn	注意する	注意させる	注意させられる

＊う-verbs ending in す normally do not use the short form.

子供の時、毎日部屋をかたづけさせられた。
I was made to clean up my room every day when I was a child.
家の子供には、いつも心配させられる。
My child makes me worry all the time. (lit.: *I am made to worry about my child all the time.*)

小学校の時、先生に日記をつけさせられました。

I was made to write a diary by my teacher when I was in elementary school.

NOTE

- Use the て+もらう／いただく if the subject is being allowed to do something by the causer.

  私は両親にピアノを習わせてもらった。

  My parents let me learn piano. (lit.: I was allowed to learn piano by my parents.)

話してみましょう

Activity 1　A mother is talking about what she has had her child do. You are the child and you don't like doing any of these things, but you are forced to do them anyway. Change the following statements of the mother to conform to your perspective using the causative-passive construction.

Example:　私は子供に毎朝牛乳を飲ませます。
　　　　　私は母に毎朝牛乳を飲まされるんです。

1. 私は子供に毎日運動をさせます。
2. 私は子供にごみを出させます。
3. 私は子供に時々近所のスーパーに買い物に行かせます。
4. 私は子供にそうじを手伝わせるんです。
5. 私は子供に自分の部屋をかたづけさせます。
6. 私は子供に毎日日記をつけさせるんです。
7. 私は子供にピアノを習わすんです。
8. 私は子供に犬の散歩をさせるんです。

Activity 2　Work with the class. Ask your classmates what kind of things they were made to do by their parents when they were children.

Example:　A:　子供の時、親にどんなことをさせられましたか。
　　　　　B:　おさらを洗わせられました／洗わされました。

Activity 3 — Your boss asked you to do the following things. You could not refuse his requests, so you have done them. Express your negative feelings about what you were asked to do using the causative-passive.

Example:　明日大阪に行ってくれないか。

　　　　　大阪に行かせられました／行かされました。

1. コピーを 100 まい取っておいてくれないか。
2. 空港まで知り合いの子供をむかえに行ってもらいたいんだ。
3. 明日までにこのプロジェクトのレポートを出してほしいんだが。
4. ちょっとお茶をいれてもらえないか。
5. この荷物を持ってくれないか。
6. 今日は忙しいから、五時まで待ってくれないか。
7. 今週の日曜日は会社に来てもらいたいんだ。

Activity 4 — Work with a partner. Each of you should write the things you want the people listed under 私 in the following chart to let you do (させてもらいたいこと) and the things you don't want other people to make you do (させられたくないこと). Then compare and discuss your responses with your partner.

Example:　A: 先生にどんなことをさせていただきたいと思いますか。

　　　　　B: そうですね。英語で話させていただきたいですね。

　　　　　A: 私もそう思います。

　　　　　B: じゃあ、先生にどんなことをさせられたくないですか。

　　　　　A: そうですね。作文を書かされたくないですね。

　　　　　B: そうですか。私は毎日テストを受けさせられたくないですね。

私

〜に	させてもらいたいこと	させられたくないこと
先生		
両親		
ルームメート		
主人 or つま (current or future spouse)		

パートナー

〜に	させてもらいたいこと	させられたくないこと
先生		
両親		
ルームメート		
主人 or つま (current or future spouse)		

II. Expressing or requesting efforts to change behavior using the plain present form of verbs + ように

A. Requesting efforts to change behavior using ～ように言う／たのむ／おねがいする／注意する

The plain present form of the verb + 言う／たのむ／おねがいする／注意する is used to request or tell someone to make the behavior change expressed by the verb phrase. The meaning is *to tell/ask (someone) to make an effort to ～* or *to make an effort not to ～*. It is an alternative to the quotation form ～と＋言う／たのむ／おねがいする／注意する.

かぎをかけるように言った。	*I told (someone) to lock the door.*
「かぎをかけて下さい。」と言う。	*I said "please lock the door."*
からかわないように言った／注意した。	*I told/warned (someone) not to tease.*
からかってはいけないと言った／注意した。	*I told/warned (someone) that they must not tease.*
「からかわないで下さい。」と言った。	*I said, "Don't tease."*
「からかってはいけませんよ。」と言った。	*I said, "You must not tease."*
先生は、時間におくれないように言った。	*The teacher told us not to be late.*
大家さんは私に早く引っ越すように言った。	*The landlord told me to move soon.*

弟は字がきたないので、母は弟に習字を習うように言った。
My brother has poor handwriting, so my mother told him to learn calligraphy.

スミスさんにパーティでピアノをひくようにおねがいした。
Mr. Smith was asked to play the piano at the party.

B. Expressing efforts to change behavior using ～ように

The plain present form of the verb + ように is used when such changes are expressed with a verb phrase. The meaning is *to make an effort to do ～*. The difference between a simple statement such as 早く来ます and 早く来るようにします is that the latter implies that the speaker will try to change his behavior for a prolonged period of time, but the former describes one occasion only.

交通事故に気をつけるようにします。	*I will try to be careful about traffic accidents.*
かぎをかけるようにします。	*I will try (to remember) to lock the door.*
あまり遊ばないようにします。	*I will try not to goof off much.*

夜中にさわがないようにしてくれませんか。
Please try to not make noise in the middle of the night.

きたない部屋ね。少しはかたづけるようにしたらどう？
What a messy room. Why don't you make an effort to tidy it up a bit?

赤ちゃんが寝ているから、大きい声を出さないようにして下さい。
Please try to not raise your voice because the baby is sleeping.

火曜日の朝ゴミを出すようにした方がいいですよ。
You should try to take the trash out every Tuesday morning.

ここは、横断歩道じゃないんだから、わたらないようにして下さい。

Please don't cross the street here because it is not a crosswalk.

NOTES

- ようにする can be used to request a change of behavior and it is often used to make a complaint.
- The plain present form of verbs + ようにします implies that the speaker intends to make an effort. The plain present form of verbs + ようにしています indicates that the speaker is making such efforts, and means *I make it a rule to ~.*

  一週間に一度部屋をかたづけるようにします。
  I will make an effort to clean up the room once a week.

  一週間に一度部屋をかたづけるようにしています。
  I make it a rule to clean up the room once a week.

  めいわくをかけないようにします。
  I will make an effort to not give you any trouble.

  めいわくをかけないようにしています。
  I make it a rule to not give you any trouble.

- The phrases 〜ようにして下さい／くれませんか／いただけませんか, etc., are less direct than 〜て下さい／くれませんか／いただけませんか, etc., and imply that the speaker wants the listener to make a prolonged effort to change behavior. These expressions are often used for complaints.

話してみましょう

| **Activity 1** | Describe what each person asked or told his or her conversational partner, using 〜ように＋言う／たのむ／おねがいする／注意する. |

Example: 先生は私に授業におくれないように言いました／注意しました。

	〜は	〜に	
Ex.	先生	学生	授業におくれてはいけませんよ。
1	先生	その子	となりの子をたたいてはだめ。
2	先生	となりの子	その子をゆるしてあげてね。
3	大家さん	私	夜中にさわいではいけませんよ。
4	大家さん	私	出かける時はかぎをかけて下さい。
5	お医者さん	母	この薬を全部飲まなければなりませんよ。
6	お医者さん	母	一週間ぐらい運動はしないで下さい。
7	ルームメート	私	ゴミを出しておいてくれない？

Activity 2　Work with a partner. Imagine that you are the supervising R.A. of a dormitory. You are writing a set of rules to maintain order. Based on a discussion with your partner, use 〜ように to write six regulations you want the students in the dorm to follow.

Example:　A:　りょうの学生にどんなことをするように言ったらいいでしょうか。

　　　　　　B:　そうですね。十時までに、りょうに帰るように言ったらどうでしょうか。

You write:　十時までにりょうに帰るようにすること

Activity 3　Work with a group of four, and create two teams of two people each. One member of each team ("A1" and "B1") should get together and decide on a location, such as a restaurant. They then return to their partners and one of them (A1) begins the game by giving his or her partner a clue to the identity of the location, using the 〜ようにして下さい expression. If the partner can figure out what the location is, that team gets a point. If not, the other partner gets a guess. If it is correct, that team gets a point; if not, then "B1" must provide a clue for his or her partner, and the guessing game starts over again.

Example:　A1: たばこをすわないようにして下さい。

　　　　　　A2: 病院ですか。

　　　　　　A1: いいえ。

　　　　　　B2: 銀行ですか。

　　　　　　A1: いいえ。

　　　　　　B1: ジャケットを着るようにして下さい。

　　　　　　B2: レストランですか。

　　　　　　B1: はい、そうです。

Activity 4　Work with a partner. Imagine that the two of you are neighbors, and you are having some problems with one another. Each of you should write five things the other has been doing that you find annoying, and then ask the other to stop doing these things.

Example:　A:　あのう、すみませんが。

　　　　　　B:　はい、何でしょうか。

　　　　　　A:　家の前に止めてある白い車、〜さんのですか。

　　　　　　B:　あ、そうですが。

　　　　　　A:　出られなくなるから、止めないようにしていただけませんか。

　　　　　　B:　あ、すみません。これからは止めないようにします。

III. Expressing unchanged conditions using 〜まま

まま is a noun that expresses a lack of change in something. Literally it means *as it is, leave ~ as it is*, or *remain unchanged*. However, it is often difficult to translate a sentence with まま literally because it can be expressed in a variety of ways in English.

In the following example, まどを開けたまま、寝てしまった , the speaker opened the window, and it was left open when he or she went to bed. The sentence そのまま来て下さい indicates that the speaker wishes the listener to come without making any change to his/her appearance or physical state.

まどを開けたまま、寝てしまった。　*I slept with the window open.*

そのまま、来て下さい。　*Please come as you are.*

Grammatically まま works like a regular noun and it can be modified by a noun, an adjective or a verb.

Type	Formation	Example
Verbs	(plain past affirmative) + まま (plain present negative) + まま	おこったまま *stay angry* かたづけないまま *left unorganized*
い -Adjectives	〜い + まま	きたないまま *left dirty*
な -Adjectives	〜な + まま	きれいなまま *stay nice* 正直なまま *stay honest*
Nouns	〜の + まま	知り合いのまま *remain an acquaintance* このまま *stay as things are now*

このままお待ち下さい。　*Wait (just as you are), please.*

いつまでも、子供のままではいられない。　*You can't stay a child forever.*

この家は今のままでは売れないと思う。　*I don't think this house will sell as it is.*

父は横になったまま、ずっと寝ている。　*My father has been sleeping in the same position he was in when he lay down.*

大人になっても、せがひくいまま変わらない。　*Even though I've become an adult, I'm still as short as I always was.*

このトマト、青いままで、全然赤くならない。　*This tomato has just stayed green, without getting red at all.*

好きなまま、何も言わなければ、何も起きないよ。　*Nothing will happen if you keep your feelings of love to yourself and never say anything.*

何が起きたか分からないまま、ここに来た。　*I came here without having any idea of what had happened.*

話してみましょう

Activity 1　　Express the following situations using まま.

Example:　手紙を書きましたが、その後、出していません。

　　　　　　<u>手紙を書いたまま、出していません。／手紙を書いたままです。</u>

1.　まどを開けましたが、その後、閉めていません。
2　車をぬすまれました。その後、見つかって (to be found) いません。
3.　落書きをしましたが、その後、けしていません。
4.　洋服がよごれましたが、その後、洗っていません。
5.　友達から手紙をもらいましたが、その後何もしていません。
6　子供の時、せがひくかったです。今もひくいです。
7.　その部屋は昨日もきたなかったです。今も、きたないです。

Activity 2　　Explain the situations described in the pictures using まま.

Example:　まどを開けたまま、<u>出かけてしまった。</u>

Example　　　　　　1　　　　　　2　　　　　　3

4　　　　　　　　5　　　　　　　　6

Activity 3

Work with a partner. Create a short conversation using the pictures and the sentences with まま that you composed in Activity 2.

Example:　A:　どうしたの、この部屋は？

　　　　　B:　どろぼうに入られちゃった。

　　　　　A:　え、なんで？

　　　　　B:　あー、出かける時、まどを開けたままだった。

　　　　　A:　え、本当！

Example　　　　　　　　　　1　　　　　　　　　　2

3　　　　　　　　　　4　　　　　　　　　　5

6　　　　　　　　　　7

IV. Using the conditional ～ても and question word ～ても

Chapter 1 of this book introduced ～てもいい, which expresses permission. This expression literally means *it is OK even if ~*, and it consists of the conditional ても and いい. This chapter introduces a more general use of this conditional phrase.

A. ～ても , even if, even though.

The conditional ても expresses future and hypothetical conditions.

好きな人なら、お金がなくても、結婚します。
If I loved a person, I would marry him even if he didn't have any money.

好きな人なら、お金がなくても、結婚していたと思う。
I think that if I had loved him I would have married him even if he didn't have any money.

〜ても can also be used with a factual situation. In this case, 〜ても may be replaced by 〜けれど or 〜が, but 〜ても implies a stronger affective involvement of the speaker than 〜けれど or 〜が.

お金がなくても、しあわせです。   *I am happy even though I don't have any money.*

お金がないけれど、しあわせです。   *I am happy though I don't have any money*

お金がありませんが、しあわせです。   *I don't have any money, but I am happy.*

This in turn means that けれど or が cannot be replaced with ても if the speaker is not expressing a strong emotion or when けれど or が has been used to introduce a topic.

日本語は話せないけれど、日本の映画を見に行きました。
I don't speak Japanese but I went to see a Japanese movie.
日本語は話せませんが、日本の映画を見に行きました。
I don't speak Japanese but I went to see a Japanese movie.
~~日本語は話せなくても、日本の映画を見に行きました。~~
~~I went to see a Japanese movie even though I did not speak Japanese.~~

宿題ですけど、明日出してもいいですか。   *Regarding the homework, can I turn it in tomorrow?*

宿題ですが、明日出してもいいですか。   *Regarding the homework, can I turn it in tomorrow?*

~~宿題でも、明日出してもいいですか。~~   *~~Even if it is homework, I turn it in tomorrow?~~*

The て-form of a verb, adjective, or copular verb can be used in the ても conditional.

安くても、きたない所には泊まりたくない。   *Even if it is cheap, I don't want to stay in a dirty place.*

うるさくても、こわいから、何も言えない。   *Even though he is noisy, I can't say anything because I'm afraid of him.*

せがひくくても、足は長いんです。   *Even though I'm short, I have long legs.*

それが本当でも、言わない方がいいと思う。   *Even if it is true, I don't think you should say it.*

なかのいい友達でも、ゆるせなかった。   *I couldn't forgive him even though he was a good friend of mine.*

引っ越しても、私のことを忘れないで下さいね。   *Please don't forget me even after you move.*

相手にたたかれても、おこってはいけない。   *You should not get angry even if you were hit by the other party.*

スミスさんがゆるしても、私がゆるさない。   *Even if Mr. Smith forgives you, I won't.*

NOTE

- To explicitly state that a condition is open, add the adverb たとえ, which also means *even if*.

たとえしんでも、あなたのことは忘れない。
I won't forget you even if I die.

たとえ大人でも、泣きたい時は泣くんだ。
Even an adult will cry when he/she wants to.

B. Question word 〜ても , no matter (who/what/when/where/etc.) ~

When a question word is used with the conditional ても, it means *no matter (who/what/when/where/etc.) ~*.

最近何を食べても、おいしい。
No matter what I eat recently, it all tastes good.

赤ちゃんが何をこわしても、お母さんはおこらない。
No matter what the baby breaks, the mother does not get angry.

どんな悪口を言っても、相手はいやな顔をしなかった。
No matter how many insults I made, he/she did not appear to be affected.

この料理はだれが食べても、おいしくないと言うと思う。
No matter who might eat this, I think he/she will say that it's no good.

林さんはだれといても、よく話す。
No matter whom she is with, Ms. Hayashi talks a lot.

私の大家さんはいつ会っても、気持ちのいい人だ。
No matter when I meet him/her, my landlord/landlady is a pleasant person to be around.

この店は何曜日に来ても、閉まっている。
No matter which day I come, this store is closed.

いい物なら、いくら高くても、買いますよ。
No matter how expensive it is, I will buy it if it is a quality item.

このクッキーは、いくつやいても、すぐ売れてしまう。
These cookies sell very quickly no matter how many of them I bake.

何歳になっても、好きな人は好きです。
I'll love the person I love no matter how old he gets.

このマンガは何度読んでも、おもしろい。
No matter how many times I read it, this cartoon is still funny.

この子は何回しかっても、またいたずらをする。
No matter how many times I scold him, this child still gets into mischief.

いくら文句を言っても、だれも助けてくれない。
No matter how much I complain, no one will help me.

いくら泣いても、だめなものはだめ。
No matter how much you cry, no is no.

いくら勉強しても、漢字が覚えられないんです。
No matter how hard I study, I cannot learn kanji.

どんなになかが悪くても、悪口を言ったり、たたいたりしてはいけない。
No matter how bad your relationship with him is, you must not speak ill of him or hit him.

どんなにしかられても、その子はあやまらなかった。
No matter how much he was scolded, the child did not apologize.

どんなにめいわくをかけても、お母さんはゆるしてくれる。
My mother forgives me no matter how much trouble I give her.

子供がどんなにほしがっても、今はお金がないから、買ってあげられない。
No matter how much the child wants it, I can't buy it for him now because I don't have any money.

話してみましょう

| Activity 1 | Mr. Jack Sprat and Mrs. Jane Sprat are a couple, and they have opposite traits. Based on the statements being made about Jack, use 〜ても to explain Jane's characteristics. |

Example:　ジャックさんは食べたらすぐふとります。

でも、ジェーンさんは食べてもふとりません。

1. ジャックさんは、運動すると、すぐつかれます。
2. ジャックさんは、かなしい映画を見ると、すごく泣きます。
3. ジャックさんは、お金があると、すぐ使ってしまいます。
4. ジャックさんは、病気になると、すぐ病院に行きます。
5. ジャックさんは、新しい服を買うと、すぐ着てみたくなります。
6. ジャックさんは、新しい所に引っ越すと、すぐ近所の人にあいさつに行きます。

Activity 2   Work with the class. Ask your classmates what they could do if the statements in the table below were true, and what they could not do even if they were true, and complete the table with at least two answers in each cell. Make sure to write the name of the respondents as well.

Example: A: 日本語が上手になったら、どんなことが出来ますか。

B: 日本語で小説が読めます。

A: そうですか。じゃあ、日本語が上手になっても、出来ないことがありますか。

B: そうですね。通訳 (interpreter) にはなれないでしょうね。

	〜たらできること	〜てもできないこと
日本語が上手になる		
たくさん勉強する		
大学を卒業する		
日本に行く		

Activity 3   Ms. Suzuki seems to have some problems. Pretend that you are Ms. Suzuki and answer the questions using the form question word 〜ても, and then write a description of the restaurant based on your answers.

Example: A: あまり食べませんね。どうしたんですか。

B: 何を食べても、おいしくないんです。

Example   1   2

3   4   5

1. この店、閉まっていますね。どうしたんですか。

2. 鈴木さんは、何度も電話していますが、どうしたんですか。

3. 鈴木さんは、ダイエットしているそうですが、どうですか。

4. 鈴木さんは、英語を習っているそうですが、どうですか。

5. となりの人がよくさわぐそうですが、注意しましたか。

Activity 4   Work with a partner. A person who has recently moved into an upstairs apartment has been causing a lot of problems. Imagine that you are a tenant and your partner is the manager of the apartment. Create a dialogue using a question word + ても.

Example: A: あのう、すみませんが。

B: はい、何でしょうか。

A: 私のアパートのとなりの人がとてもうるさいんです。注意していただけませんか。

B: その人と話したことはありますか。

A: ええ、昨日も一昨日も静かにするように言ったんですが、全然だめなんです。

B: そうですか。分かりました。じゃあ、私が注意しておきます。

1. となりの人が夜中にピアノをひく。

2. となりの人がゴミを出してはいけない日に、ゴミを出す。

3. となりの人のペットがにわ (garden) の花をふむ。

4. となりの人のペットが家の前をよごす。

V. Using the plain form + のに , despite ~, although ~

The conjunction のに (although, despite) indicates a strong contrast between two clauses. Its meaning is the exact opposite of ～ので (because). The のに construction is used to express a result which was not expected. In this sense, のに expresses the speaker's disbelief, surprise, regret, sorrow, frustration, or opposition to a situation that is the opposite of his/her expectations.

年上の子が年下の子をたたいているのに、先生は何も言わない。
Although the elder child is hitting the younger child, the teacher does not say anything.

赤ちゃんが泣いているのに、お母さんは何もしない。
Although the baby is crying, the mother does not do anything.

たくさんめいわくをかけたのに、両親はゆるしてくれました。
Although I caused my parents a lot of trouble, they forgave me.

うそをついたのに、みんな本当だと思っています。
Although I lied, everyone thinks I was telling the truth.

その子は大事にしていたおもちゃをこわされたのに、全然おこっていません。
<small>ぜんぜん</small>

Although that child got his precious toy broken, he is not angry at all.

落書きをしないように言ったのに、また落書きをしている。
<small>らくが</small> <small>らくが</small>

Although I told him not to, he is writing graffiti again.

〜のに is preceded by the same forms that come before 〜ので or 〜のです. な is used for the present affirmative tense of な-adjectives and the copula verb, and plain forms are used for all other adjectives, copulas, and verbs.

Verbs	い -adjective	な -adjectives	Copula verb
かぎをかける	こわい	しあわせ	本当
かぎをかけるのに	こわいのに	しあわせなのに	本当なのに
かぎをかけないのに	こわくないのに	しあわせじゃないのに	本当じゃないのに
かぎをかけたのに	こわかったのに	しあわせだったのに	本当だったのに
かぎをかけなかったのに	こわくなかったのに	しあわせじゃなかったのに	本当じゃなかったのに

As was the case with 〜ので, the main clause can express only a statement or a question. For requests, commands, suggestions, offers, invitations, or other expressions which indicate strong feelings from the speaker, use 〜け(れ)ど or 〜が.

ちょっと重いですが、持ってくれませんか。 *It's a little heavy, but could you hold it?*

ちょっと重いけど、持ってくれませんか。 *It's a little heavy, but could you hold it?*

~~ちょっと重いのに、持ってくれませんか。~~ ~~*Although it's a little heavy, but could you hold it?*~~

その人とは、あまりなかはよくないけど、うそは言いたくありません。
Although I don't get along with him very well, I don't want to lie to him.

~~その人とは、あまりなかはよくないのに、うそは言いたくありません。~~
~~*Although I don't get along with him very well, I don't want to lie to him.*~~

If the main clause has been omitted, the 〜のに clause is translated as *should* or *should have*. This usage is very common in conversation.

電話をかければよかったのに。 *You should have called.*

うるさいならうるさいと言えばいいのに。 *He should say so if he thinks it is noisy.*

The following compares the functions of 〜が／〜けれど, 〜ても, and 〜のに.

		が・けれども	ても	のに
1	Can be applied to a future situation	○	○	
2	Use for a current or past situation	○	○	○
3	Expresses a hypothetical situation		○	
4	Main clause can contain a phrase that expresses the speaker's feelings and opinions	○	○	
5	Expresses the speaker's surprise or critical feeling			○
6	Introducing a topic, weak "but"	○		
7	Can end the sentence without a main clause	○		○

Examples:

1 and 4　大変だけど、がんばって下さい。　*It's tough, but please do your best.*

　　　　　大変でも、がんばって下さい。　*Even if it may be tough, please do your best.*

　　　　　~~大変なのに、がんばって下さい。~~　*~~Although it's tough, please do your best.~~*

2　　　　スミスさんに聞いたけど、分からなかった。
　　　　　I asked Mr. Smith, but I didn't get the answer.
　　　　　スミスさんに聞いても、分からなかった。
　　　　　Even though I asked Mr. Smith, I didn't get the answer.
　　　　　スミスさんに聞いたのに、分からなかった。
　　　　　Even though I asked Mr. Smith, I didn't get the answer.

3　　　　~~スミスさんに聞いたけど、分からなかっただろう。~~
　　　　　~~I asked Mr. Smith, but he probably would not have known the answer.~~
　　　　　スミスさんに聞いても、分からなかっただろう。
　　　　　Even if I asked Mr. Smith, he probably would not have known the answer.
　　　　　~~スミスさんに聞くのに、分からないだろう。~~
　　　　　~~Even though I ask Mr. Smith, he probably would not know the answer.~~

5　　　　たのんだけど、キムさんはしなかった。(no feeling of surprise)

　　　　　たのんでも、キムさんはしなかった。 (no feeling of surprise)

　　　　　たのんだのに、キムさんはしなかった。(feeling of surprise)

6　　　　かべの落書きのことですが、もうけしましたか。
　　　　　About the grafitti, have you gotten rid of it yet?
　　　　　~~かべの落書きのことでも、もうけしましたか。~~
　　　　　~~Although about the grafitti, have you gotten rid of it yet?~~
　　　　　~~かべの落書きのことなのに、もうけしましたか。~~
　　　　　~~Even though about the grafitti, have you gotten rid of it yet?~~

7   私はよく知りませんが。   *I don't know much about it, but . . .*
       ~~私はよく知らなくても。~~   ~~*Although I don't know much about it . . .*~~
       私はよく知らないのに。   *Even though I don't know much about it . . .*

話してみましょう

Activity 1   Make a sentence by adding のに to the cue sentence.

Example: 日本に十年住んでいました。
            日本に十年住んでいたのに、日本語が話せません。

1. 今日はゴミを出してはいけません。
2. そのうわさは本当じゃありません。
3. 私は落書きをしていません。
     らく が
4. ピアノを習いたくありません。
5. どろぼうにお金をぬすまれました。
6. 洋服をよごされました。
     よう
7. 足をふまれました。
8. 引っ越しました。
     こ
9. めいわくはかけていません。
10. 正直に話しています。
     しょうじき

Activity 2   Work with a partner. Look at the following pictures and say what is odd about them.

Example: A: この絵、変 (*strange*) ですね。

B: そうですね。天気がいいのに、かさをさしています。(*~has an umbrella open*)

Example   1   2

3   4   5

6   7   8

Activity 3   Work with a partner. One person should describe a problem listed in 1 through 6 by using のに, and the other person should give advice.

Example: 昨日となりの人に文句を言いましたが、今日もとなりの人は、
私の家の前に車を止めています。

A: どうしたんですか。

B: となりの人が家の前に車を止めるので、困ってるんですよ。

A: そうなんですか。となりの人と話はしたんですか。

B: ええ、昨日も注意したのに、全然だめなんです。

A: そうですか。じゃあ、家の前に〜さんの車を止めておいたらどうですか。

B: ああ、それはいいかもしれませんね。

1.   友達はむかえに来るといいましたが、まだ来ていません。

2.   となりの人に夜中にさわがないようにたのみましたが、全然静かにして
くれません。

3.   主人は友達をむかえに行くと言いましたが、ゴルフに行ってしまいました。

4.   いじめられたり、からかわれたりしていますが、先生は助けてくれません。

5.   どろぼうにかぎをこわされたんですが、大家さんはかぎを直してくれません。

6.   うそをついたと正直に話しましたが、相手はまだおこっていてゆるして
くれません。

聞く練習

めいわくなこと   Annoying things

聞く前に

Work with a partner. Discuss what kinds of annoying things people in the situations described in 1 through 5 below might tend to experience.

1.   一人で住んでいる女の人
2.   りょうに住んでいる学生
3.   外国人
4.   アルバイトをしている学生
5.   きびしい (strict) 先生の授業を取っている学生

聞いてみましょう

 次の会話を聞いて、だれについて話をしているのか書いて下さい。そして、どんな問題があるのか書いて下さい。

Example: You hear: 男の人：どうしたの。何かあったの？

女の人：家のかべに車、ぶつけられたの。

男の人：えっ？　だれに？

女の人：ほら、あの、さくらアパートに住んでいる大学生。

男の人：ああ、あの、かみの長い。

女の人：そうよ。

You write: だれについて：　さくらアパートに住んでいる大学生

問題：　女の人の家のかべに車をぶつけました。

ケース１　だれについて：＿＿＿＿＿＿＿＿＿＿＿＿＿＿＿＿＿＿＿＿＿

問題：＿＿＿＿＿＿＿＿＿＿＿＿＿＿＿＿＿＿＿＿＿

ケース２　だれについて：＿＿＿＿＿＿＿＿＿＿＿＿＿＿＿＿＿＿＿＿＿

問題：＿＿＿＿＿＿＿＿＿＿＿＿＿＿＿＿＿＿＿＿＿

ケース３　だれについて：＿＿＿＿＿＿＿＿＿＿＿＿＿＿＿＿＿＿＿＿＿

問題：＿＿＿＿＿＿＿＿＿＿＿＿＿＿＿＿＿＿＿＿＿

聞いた後で

A. Work with a partner. Write two possible solutions for each of the above problems.

B. Listen to the follow-up conversations for each of the cases above and write down the suggestions that have been given to the person.

C. Work with the same partner you had in Exercise A. Compare the suggestions given in Exercise B with your own suggestions. Say which suggestion you think is best and explain.

聞き上手話し上手

文句を言う、おこる、あやまる
もんく
Expressing complaints or anger, and making apologies

Complaining about people or their actions is a sensitive topic. Japanese people feel that complaints threaten the "face" of the person being complained about and can make that person feel uneasy, which is not conducive to future harmonious relationships. Therefore, it is important to make complaints carefully so as not to create an uneasy atmosphere afterwards. This is especially true if you are complaining about someone you know very well.

One way to make complaints non-threatening is to talk around the problem, stating it but not admitting to being actually bothered by it. This is often achieved by just mentioning the topic of conversation and leaving out the verbal phrase which might follow, as shown in the following example:

大木： あのう、すみませんが。	*Excuse me, but . . .*
石川： ええ、何でしょうか。	*Yes, what is it?*
大木： あのう、ちょっとテレビの音が …。	*Well it's just the sound from your TV is . . .*
石川： あ、すみません、大きすぎましたか。	*Oh, I'm sorry. Was it too loud?*
大木： ええ、おねがいします。	*Yes, please.*

If the person does not realize what you are talking about, you can complain more explicitly.

大木： あのう、すみませんが。	*Excuse me, but . . .*
石川： ええ、何でしょうか。	*Yes, what is it?*
大木： あのう、ちょっとテレビの音が …。	*Well it's just the sound from your TV is . . .*
石川： え？　テレビの音がどうかしましたか。	*What about the sound from my TV?*
大木： あのう、少し小さくしていただけませんか。もう 11 時になりますので。	
	Could you turn it down a bit? It's already 11:00 p.m.
石川： あ、すみませんでした。気がつかなくて。これから気をつけるようにします。	
	Oh, you're right. I'm sorry. I didn't realize—I'll be more careful from now on.
大木： おねがいします。	*Yes, please do.*

In the above example, expressions such as 気がつかなくて, and これから気をつけます are useful when apologizing. The phrase 気がつかなくて expresses the absence of any ill will, and これから気をつけます indicates his intention to correct his mistake. Although what deserves apology differs from culture to culture, the Japanese apologize frequently. This is because apologies do not just mean the admittance of one's failure or guilt. Rather, apologies indicate that a person recognizes the failure to meet the expectations of others is his or her responsibility. This in turn removes blame from others and therefore shows thoughtfulness and kindness towards them. Apologies also indicate admittance of one's weakness, which invites understanding and sympathy. Therefore, the Japanese tend to be more willing to accept apologies and more eager to apologize. The common apologies are:

ごめん。	*Sorry, Excuse me.*	(casual)
ごめんなさい。	*Sorry, Please forgive me.*	
すみません。	*I'm sorry.*	
もうしわけありません。	*I'm sorry.*	
もうしわけございません。	*I'm sorry.*	(polite and formal)

もうしわけありません and すみません can also used to express gratitude, as when receiving a gift. It is customary to bow when apologizing in Japan. The more sorrow you feel, the more slowly and deeply you bow.

In general, the Japanese consider showing anger in public to be childish. When two people fall out over something, they make every effort to settle the dispute amicably through discussion and sometimes by going out for drinks. However, expressions of anger are sometimes necessary, even toward strangers, to protect oneself from harassing phone calls, stalkers, etc. The following are common expressions used in such cases.

やめて（下さい）。(male/female)／やめろ。(male)   *Cut it out.*

何するのよ。(female)／何するんだよ。(male)   *What are you doing?*

いいかげんにしてよ。(female)／いいかげんにしろよ。(male)   *Give me a break./
Cut it out.*

ほっといてよ。(female)／ほっといてくれよ。(male)   *Leave me alone.*

じょうだんじゃないよ。(male, female)   *You've got to be kidding.*

1. Work with a partner. Listen to the two versions of a conversation between Mr. Ishikawa and Mr. Oki on page 484 and practice and act out the dialogue. Pay attention to the tone of voice.

2. Work with a partner. Imagine that your partner is your neighbor. Complain to him/her about trash, parking, noise, etc. Your partner should apologize. Before starting the conversation, listen to the model dialogue.

3. Work with a partner. One person plays the role of teacher and the other person plays the role of student. The teacher should complain to the student about forgotten homework, tardiness, etc. The student should apologize for the behavior.

4. Listen to the expressions of anger on the recording and repeat them. Pay particular attention to the intonation and the tone of voice.

5. Work with a partner. Imagine that your partner is a very persistent salesperson who makes frequent phone calls and visits to your house. Express your anger and tell him/her not to contact you anymore.

漢字

Structure of kanji compounds

As you have seen, two or more kanji are often combined to form a new word, known as a **kanji** compound. Different types of relationships can be found among the individual kanji in a compound, and a study of these relationships will help you better guess and learn the meanings of unknown compounds, thus increasing your vocabulary. Some of the most common relationships in compounds are described below.

1. The same **kanji** is repeated.
   人々 (*many people*)   国々 (*many countries*)   (See Chapter 2 for 々.)

2. Two **kanji** with similar meanings are put together.
   教授 (*teach + give= professor*)   研究 (*study + pursue = research*)

3. Two **kanji** with opposite meanings are combined.
   男女 (*man and woman*)   朝晩 (*morning and night*)   兄弟 (*older and younger brothers = siblings*)

4. The first **kanji** is the subject of the second one, which is a verb/adjective.
   新聞 (*new + hear = newspaper*)   音楽 (*sound + joyful = music*)

5. The first **kanji** modifies the second one.
   大学 (*big + school/study = university*)   住所 (*residing + place = address*)

6. The first **kanji** is a verb and the second one is the subject, object, or indirect object of the first.
   有名 (*exist/have + name = famous*)   入学 (*enter + school = entering school*)

7. The first **kanji** is a prefix or the second kanji is a suffix.
   不利 (*no + profit = disadvantage*)   毎朝 (*every + morning = every morning*)

Try to classify the following **kanji** compounds into these categories. Guess the meaning of each compound.

大小　新車　入国　毎日　通行　色々　飲食　白黒　朝食　乗車　急行　父母
家族　受験　生物

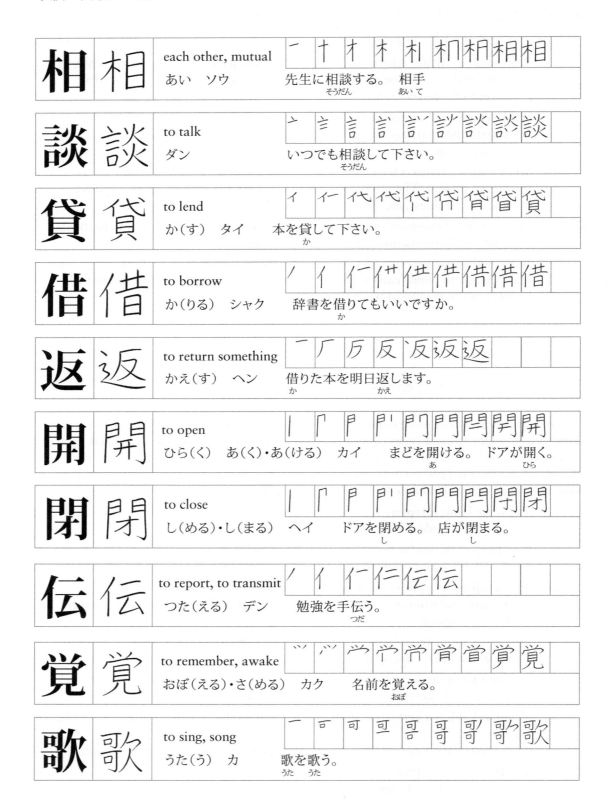

声 声　voice
　　こえ　セイ　　大きい声で歌う。
　　　　　　　　　こえ　　うた

静 静　quiet, calm
　　しず（か）　セイ　　先生の家がある所はとても静かです。
　　　　　　　　　　　　　　　　　　　　　　　しず

夜 夜　night, evening
　　よる　ヤ　　夜は寒くなりますよ。
　　　　　　　　よる

直 直　to mend, to correct
　　なお（す）　チョク・ジキ　　コンピュータを直せます。　正直な人
　　　　　　　　　　　　　　　　　　　　　　なお　　　　　しょうじき

置 置　to put, to place
　　お（く）　チ　　つくえの上に置いて下さい。
　　　　　　　　　　　　　　　　　お

記 記　chronicle
　　キ　　ここに名前を記入して下さい。　日記
　　　　　　　　　　　　き にゅう　　　　　　　にっき

注 注　to pour
　　そそ（ぐ）　チュウ　　ラーメンを注文する。　注意
　　　　　　　　　　　　　　ちゅうもん　　　　ちゅうい

句 句　phrase
　　ク　　あまり文句を言わないで下さい。
　　　　　　　　　もん く

合 合　to fit
　　あ（う）　ゴウ　　知り合いの赤ちゃん　服が合わない。　都合が悪い
　　　　　　　　　　　し　あ　　　　　　　　あ　　　　　　つごう

忙 忙　busy
　　いそが（しい）　ボウ　　試験があるので、とても忙しい。
　　　　　　　　　　　　　　　　　　　　　　　　いそが

然 然　so, yes
　　ゼン・ネン　　病気が全然よくならない。　自然 (nature)
　　　　　　　　　ぜんぜん　　　　　しぜん

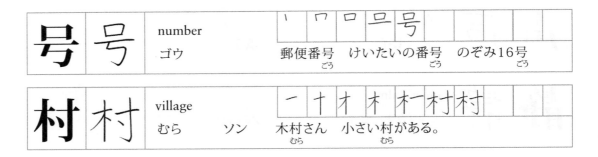

号 号　number　ゴウ　　郵便番号　けいたいの番号　のぞみ16号
村 村　village　むら　ソン　　木村さん　小さい村がある。

読めるようになった漢字

全然　注意　注文する　意味　知り合い　都合が悪い　覚える　歌　歌う　文句
俳句　番号　信号　直る　直す　正直　貸す　借りる　返す　置く　声　開く
開ける　閉める　閉まる　手伝う　日記をつける　相手　相談　日記　夜　夜中
静か　赤ちゃん　大人　大家　仕方　音

日本人の名前：木村　青木

練習

1. 日本語の勉強のために、毎日日記をつけて、漢字を二十覚えています。
2. 昨日の夜友達とカラオケで大きい声で歌を歌って、のどが痛くなりました。
3. この問題について大家さんに相談するつもりですか。
4. 借りた本を返す時は、そのテーブルの上に置いて下さい。
5. 知り合いが貸したお金を全然返してくれないので、文句を言いました。
6. 近所の知り合いが夜中にさわぐので、静かにしてほしいと言ったら、相手はとてもおこった。
7. となりの人は何度注意しても、いつも大きな音で音楽を聞くので困る。
8. 私のアパートの郵便番号は 384-1205 です。
9. 木村さんはとても正直な人なので、ぜったいにうそはつきません。
10. 広い部屋ですね。まどを閉めて、ドアを開けて下さい。
11. 忙しそうですね。その仕事、手伝いましょうか。

読む練習

上手な読み方

Understanding the characteristics of expository writing

In English, expository text tends to have a clear structure, with a topic statement, support and conclusion. However, Japanese expository text is not always as organized as English. For example, one of the rhetorical organizations of Japanese expository writing, the Ki-Sho-Ten-

Ketsu organization, presents a difficult obstacle for learners, as it is fundamentally different from the western style rhetorical organization. Expository text in Japanese frequently does not have any thesis statement, and paragraph development is often not as straightforward as it is in English. Text based on the Ki-Sho-Ten model consists of four parts: the opening; the development; the shift of a topic to an unrelated element of the previous paragraph; and the conclusion. The third section, the topic shift, creates a more esthetic flare rather than a logical development, which is a very difficult concept for western learners to grasp.

Also, pronouns are rarely used to create cohesion in Japanese. Instead, repetitions and deletion of nouns are heavily used as cohesive devices. Learning to use these devices tends to be very difficult, as neither deletion nor repetition is commonly used in English.

練習

Go to the Japanese or English website of the *Asahi Shinbun* newspaper and look for an editorial column either in English or in Japanese. Check to see how the rhetorical organization is different from English.

いじめ

読む前に

質問に日本語で答えて下さい。

1. いじめにあったり、いじめを見たことがありますか。どんないじめがありましたか。
2. 学校ではどんな人がよくいじめられると思いますか。
3. どんな人が人をいじめると思いますか。
4. だれかがいじめられていたら、どうしますか。

読んでみましょう

言葉のリスト

自殺 (じさつ)	国際 (こくさい)	行う (おこなう)	場合 (ばあい)	生徒 (せいと)
suicide	international	conduct	the case	junior and senior high school students

　日本では、1990年代からいじめが問題になっている。特に最近はインターネットのブログや携帯メールに悪口を書いたりするいじめが増えている。ネット上では、誰がいじめをしているか分かりにくいので、誰かがいじめを始めると、おもしろがって他の子もいじめをしてしまう。いじめられた子は、学校に行かなくなったりするだけではなく、自殺してしまうこともある。いじめは日本だけの問題ではなく、アメリカ、イギリス、ノルウェー、オーストラリアなどでも増え

た。そのため、日本で「いじめ問題国際シンポジウム」が開かれたが、このシンポジウムの前に、いじめについて、一万人の小学生、中学生、高校生にアンケートが行われた。

　そのアンケートによると、日本ではいじめをする生徒はいじめられる生徒のクラスメートであるケースが70%にもなることが分かった。また、いじめをした生徒にどんな生徒をいじめたかと聞くと、普通の友達をいじめた場合が一番多く、その次に、仲がいい友達やあまりよく知らないクラスメートをいじめたケースが多かった。そして、「前から仲が悪かった」生徒をいじめたと答えた生徒は一番少なかった。つまり、いじめをした子供はそのクラスメートがきらいだから、いじめたのではない。

　では、どうして子供達はきらいでもないクラスメートや仲がいい友達をいじめるのだろうか。この質問については、「いじめがおもしろいから、いじめてみたいから、いじめをするのだ。」という答えが多くみられた。いじめをした後、「おもしろかった」、「よかった」と思う子供は小学生で20%ぐらいだが、中学生では38%、高校生では41%ぐらいになる。これにたいして、いじめをした後、悪いことをしたと思う子供は、小学生の場合は、80%ぐらいいるが、中学生では70%、高校生になると、50%ぐらいにしかならない。

　それでは、いじめられている子供はどうするのだろうか。いじめられた子供が小学生の場合、80%の子供がだれかに相談したり、いじめる子供に止めるように言ったりするが、中学生や高校生になると、50%の学生がだれにも言わないし、30%ぐらいの生徒はいじめられても何もしない。そして、先生に相談する子供は小学生では30%ぐらいだが、中学生では20%、高校生になると、8%ぐらいしかいない。

　また、いじめを見ているクラスメートや友達もたいてい何もしないし、先生にも相談しない。これはどうしてだろうか。

　アンケートによると、小学生の場合、先生に言ったことがいじめている子供に分かるともっといじめられるという答えが多い。中学生や高校生では、先生は何も出来ないという答えが30%ぐらいで、いじめは自分達の問題だから先生には言わない方がいいという答えが30%ぐらいになる。

読んだ後で

A. Circle はい if the statement is true according to the text you have just read and いいえ if it is not.

1. はい　　いいえ　　いじめの問題は日本だけの問題である。

2. はい　　いいえ　　いじめはクラスでよく起こる。

3. はい　　いいえ　　日本ではクラスメートをいじめることが多い。

4. はい　　いいえ　　日本では、いじめをする生徒（せいと）はたいてい自分がきらいな生徒（せいと）をいじめる。

5. はい　　いいえ　　中学生の方が高校生よりいじめをした後、悪いことをしたと思っている。

6. はい　　いいえ　　高校生はいじめられた時、あまり先生に言わない。

7. はい　　いいえ　　いじめを見ている生徒（せいと）は、いじめられたくないから何もしない。

8. はい　　いいえ　　小学生は先生がいじめをやめさせることは出来ないと思っている。

B. 下の質問に答えて下さい。

1. どうして、「いじめ国際（こくさい）シンポジウム」が開かれたのですか。

2. 日本人の子供はどうしていじめをすると言っていますか。

3. 小学生と中学生と高校生のいじめはどこがにています (similar) か。どこが違いますか。

4. どうして年が上になると、いじめが悪いと思わなくなるのでしょうか。

5. いじめられている子供は、どうしてほかの人に相談しないのですか。

C. Work in pairs or groups of four. Discuss the following situations in your country, and report your findings to the class.

1. あなたの国でも、いじめは大きい問題だと思いますか。

2. あなたの国では、どんな子供がどんな子供をいじめるケースが多いと思いますか。日本とは、どんなことが同じですか。どんなことが違いますか。

3. いじめはどうすればなくなると思いますか。学校はいじめをやめさせるために、どんなことをしたらいいでしょうか。大人はどうすればいいでしょうか。先生や友達はどうしたらいいと思いますか。

総合練習
そうごう

A. 学生生活を楽しくしましょう　Let's make college life enjoyable

Work with the class. Interview three classmates about things that make their school life difficult, based on the following categories. Ask them how they cope with these problems.

Example:　A:　〜さんはりょうに住んでいて、どんなことがいやですか。

　　　　　　B:　そうですね。同じ部屋に住んでいる学生に部屋をよごされるので困ります。

　　　　　　A:　そうですか。それで、その学生に何か言いましたか。

　　　　　　B:　ええ、一週間に一度そうじをするように言いました。

B. 大変な経験

1. Work on the following dictgloss task:

   (a) Listen to the short story and try to understand the meaning.
   (b) Listen to the story again, and try to write down as much of what is being said as you can.
   (c) Work with a partner and try to reconstruct the text of the story as accurately as you can.
   (d) Work with your partner. Listen to the story again to check the accuracy of the story you and your partner have reconstructed.

2. Write a short story based on your own experience in which you encountered a problem and resolved the issue. Make it as interesting as you can, and share it with your classmates.

ロールプレイ

1. Your boss makes you do a lot of things that are not part of your job. Describe things you are forced to do and complain to your co-workers.
2. Your house has been burglarized. Call the police station, describe the condition of the house, and tell the police what has been stolen.
3. Your classmate makes fun of you all the time. Tell your instructor about the situation, describe how the classmate makes fun of you, and ask for help.
4. Your neighbor's son has been making a lot of noise. Complain to your neighbor.
5. You are a representative of a labor union, and you don't like the working conditions at the company. Complain to the management.

Chapter 11

第
<ruby>十<rt>だい</rt></ruby>
一
<ruby>課<rt>か</rt></ruby>

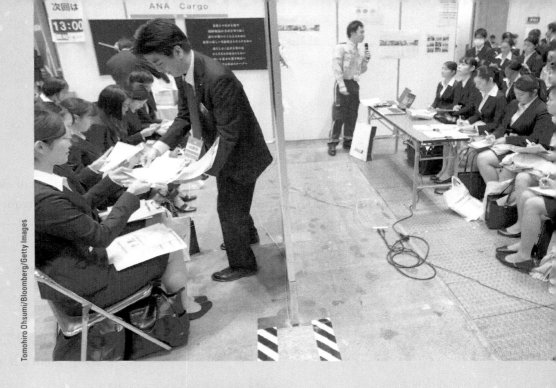

Tomohiro Ohsumi/Bloomberg/Getty Images

就職相談
<ruby>しゅうしょく<rt></rt></ruby>

Talking about Employment

単語
<small>たん</small>

Nouns

エントリー		entry (the process of expressing interest in employment opportunities by requesting information from a company), エントリー・シート a form required for entry
かいぎ	会議	meeting, conference
かつどう	活動	activity
きかい	機会	opportunity
きにゅう	記入	filling out, きにゅうする to fill out, 申込用紙にきにゅうする to fill out an application form <small>もうしこみ</small>
きゅうりょう	給料	wages
けっか	結果	result, outcome
こうこく	広告	advertisement
じこ	自己	self, a formal version of 自分, often used with another word such as じこしょうかい self introduction, じこ PR self promotion, じこうんどう self-motion, じこ中 selfishness <small>ちゅう</small>
じこ PR	自己 PR	self promotion
しめきり	締め切り	deadline
しゅうしょくかつどう	就職活動	job hunting (abbreviated as しゅうかつ（就活）in casual conversation)
しょうかい	紹介	introduction, 〜に〜をしょうかいする to introduce ~ to ~, じこしょうかい self introduction
じょうほう	情報	information
しょるい	書類	document
すいせんじょう	推薦状	letter of reference, recommendation
せつめいかい	説明会	a briefing session, an explanatory meeting
せんもん	専門	field of specialty
そら	空	sky
てつづき	手続き	procedure
どうき	動機	a motive, しぼうどうき a motive for applying to a company, a school, etc.
どりょく	努力	effort, どりょくする to make an effort
ひっきしけん	筆記試験	a written test
プロジェクト		project

やりがい	やり甲斐	worth doing, やりがいがある it is worth doing
めんせつ	面接	interview, めんせつしけん an oral exam, interview
りれきしょ／りれきしょ	履歴書	CV (curriculum vitae), resume

Verbal nouns

おうぼ	応募	entry, application (for a program, recruitment, subscription, offer, etc.), おうぼする to enter, to apply for (a contest, recruitment, subscription, offer, etc.) c.f. もうしこむ to apply (for a bank account, phone service, etc.)
しぼう	志望	a wish, a desire, an ambition, しぼうする to desire
しゅっちょう	出張	business trip, しゅっちょうする to go on a business trip
へんじ	返事	response, へんじ（を）する to respond
れんらく	連絡	contact, 〜にれんらくする to make contact with, to get in touch with

い-adjectives

よろしい		good (polite)

な-adjectives

ひつよう（な）	必要（な）	necessary (similar to 〜がいる [to need])

う-verbs

いたす	致す	to do (humble)
いただく	頂く	to eat, to drink (humble)
いらっしゃる		to go, to come, to return, to be (honorific)
うかがう	伺う	to visit, to ask (humble)
おいでになる		to come in, to show up (honorific)
おっしゃる		to say (honorific)
おめにかかる	お目にかかる	to meet (humble)
おやすみになる	お休みになる	to sleep (honorific)
おる		to exist, to be (humble)
ござる		to exist (polite verb for ある and いる)
ごらんになる	ご覧になる	to look at (honorific)
ぞんじております	存じておる	to know, to think (humble)
でござる		to be (polite verb for です)
なさる		to do (honorific)

まいる	参る	to go, to come (humble)
めしあがる／めしあがる	召し上がる	to eat, to drink (honorific)
もうす	申す	to say (humble)
やとう	雇う	to employ

る -verbs

おめにかける	お目にかける	to show (humble)
しらせる	知らせる	to notify
ぞんじる／ぞんじる	存じる	to know (humble)
たずねる	訪ねる	to visit
もうしあげる／もうしあげる	申し上げる	to say (humble)

Irregular verbs

| はいけんする | 拝見する | to look at (humble) |

Prefixes

| じこ〜 | 自己〜 | self, じこしょうかい self introduction, じこ PR self promotion |

Expressions

おせわになっております。	お世話になって おります。	I thank you for your assistance.
こんごともよろしく おねがいいたします	今後ともよろしく お願いいたします。	I ask for your continued assistance.
そういってもらえると、 うれしいです。	そう言ってもらえると、 嬉しいです。	I'm glad that you said so.
そうでもありません。／そうでもございません。		No, not really.
そうなんですよ。		That's right.
そんなことないですよ。／ そんなことはありませんよ。		No, that is not the case.
まあまあです。		So-so.
まだまだです。		I still have a lot to learn.
ごぶさたしております。	ご無沙汰して おります。	I'm sorry to have stayed out of touch for so long.
おかげさまで	お陰様で	because of your help (common phrase when you thank for somebody for their assistance)
ざんねんながら、 わたしのちからぶそくで	残念ながら、 私の力不足で	Regrettably, due to the lack of my ability . . . (unfortunately I was unable to . . .)

単語の練習
たん

A. そんけい語とけんじょう語　Honorific and humble expressions

Honorific expressions are used for actions performed by people with higher social status than the speaker. Study the following special honorific verbs. Humble expressions are used for actions performed by you or a member of your in-group when these actions affect or are related to a social superior. You will learn more about these in the grammar section.

Meaning	Regular form	Honorific verbs	Humble verbs
to go	行く	いらっしゃる／おいでになる	まいる
to come	来る	いらっしゃる／おいでになる	まいる
to exist/to be	いる	いらっしゃる／おいでになる	おる
to do	する	なさる	いたす
to see/to look at	見る	ごらんになる	拝見する はいけん
to say	言う	おっしゃる	申す / 申し上げる もう　　　もう
to know	知っている	ご存じだ ぞん	存じておる ぞん
to eat	食べる	めし上がる	いただく
to drink	飲む	めし上がる	いただく
to sleep	寝る	お休みになる	N/A
to meet	会う	N/A	お目にかかる
to inquire	聞く	N/A	うかがう
to visit	たずねる	N/A	うかがう
to think	思う	N/A	存じる ぞん
to be (copula)	だ	でいらっしゃる	N/A

- いただく is also a humble expression for もらう as introduced in Chapter 6.

覚えていますか。

いただく　下さる　差し上げる
　　　　　　　　　　さ

Activity 1   下の文をそんけい語かけんじょう語を使って、書いて下さい。

1. 鈴木先生はおすしを食べました。石田先生はビールを飲みました。
   すず
2. 山田先生はこの映画をもう見ましたか。
3. 木村先生は来年オーストラリアに行きます。そして、スミス先生がオーストラリアから来ます。
4. 川上先生はゴルフをします。
5. 山下先生、先生は日本語の先生ですか。
6. 私は中村と言います。
7. 昨日、先生の家でビールを飲んで、おいしい料理を食べました。
8. 明日、大学で田中先生に会います。
9. 山田先生に聞いてみます。
10. 先週、先生の絵を美術館で見ました。
    びじゅつ

Activity 2   Work with a partner. Say an honorific verb, and your partner should respond with the corresponding regular verb. Once you get used to it, try it with the book closed.

Activity 3   Work with a group of three. One person should say a regular verb, and the rest of the group should respond with the corresponding honorific verb. The first person to correctly name the honorific verb gets a point.

Activity 4   Work with a partner. Imagine you are a teacher and your partner is a student. Make a simple request or ask a question using the regular form of a verb. Your partner will respond using the corresponding humble form. Once your partner gets used to it, try it with the book closed.

Example: A: ここに来て下さい。

　　　　　　B: はい、まいります。

Activity 5   Work with a group of three. One person should play the role of teacher and make requests or ask questions. The other members of the group are students who try to respond to the teacher as quickly as possible using humble expressions. The first person to respond correctly gets a point.

B. ていねい語　Polite expressions

Meaning	Regular expression	ていねい語 (Polite expression)
to be	だ	でござる（ございます）／です
to exist	ある	ござる（ございます）
to exist	いる	おる（おります）
good	いい	よろしい
Mr./Mrs./Ms.	〜さん（お客さん、山田さん）	〜さま（お客さま、山田さま）
that way	そっち	そちら
that way over there	あっち	あちら
Polite prefix for nouns or adjectives		お + word (Japanese origin)
sushi	すし	おすし
customer, visitor	客	お客
gentle	やさしい	おやさしい
beautiful, pretty	きれい	おきれい
		ご + word (Chinese origin)*
sickness	病気	ご病気
kind	親切	ご親切
splendid	立派 りっぱ	ご立派 りっぱ

*An exception is the word お電話 (*telephone*), a Chinese origin word using お and not ご.

Notes

- Polite expressions are used in any formal situation.
- そちら and あちら can be used as a polite equivalent of その人 and あの人, respectively.
- Not all adjectives or nouns take polite prefixes. For example, the following words do not take either お or ご.

  大きい　多い　黄色い　新しい　四角い　すてきな　だめな
  　　　　　　き　　　　　　　かく
  大丈夫な　大好きな　春　夏　秋　冬　研究室
  じょうぶ　　　　　　　　　　　　　けんきゅうしつ

- Some words are almost always used with the particle お or ご.

  おなか　（お）茶　（お）食事　（お）すし　ご飯　（ご）主人
  （ご）質問　　　　　　　　　　　　　　　　　　　　しゅ

覚えていますか。　**What are their less polite equivalents?**

こちら　どちら　この方　その方　あの方　お辞儀　お茶　お見舞（い）
　　　　　　　　　　　　　　　　　　　　　　　　　　　　　　　ぎ　　　　ま
お土産　お礼　有り難うございます　色々お世話になりました　おかげさまで
みやげ
お気を使わせてしまいまして　お気を使わないで下さい　お好きだとよろしいの
ですが　お早うございます　これからもどうぞよろしくおねがいします　おめで
とうございます　失礼します　どうもご馳走様でした　申し訳ございません
　　　　　　　　　　　　　　　　　　ち そうさま　　　　　もう　わけ

Activity 6   Change the verbs in the following sentences into ていねい語.

Example: 山田さんの家は立派ですね。
　　　　　山田さんのおたく（a polite form of 家）はご立派ですね。

1. 電話はかいだんの下にあります。
2. 婦人服売り場は三がいです。
3. 先生の子供はとても元気だそうです。
4. 今日は休みです。
5. 気分が悪いそうです。
6. 先生の家族は何人家族ですか。
7. 向かい側に交番がある。
8. 小さくてもいいですか。
9. そっちは博物館で、あっちは図書館だ。

C. 就職活動と会社で使う言葉
Expressions used in job hunting and business environments

手続き	procedure
広告	advertisement
じょうほう	information
エントリー	a process to express your interest to a company and request information from that company
記入する	to fill out
給料	wages
しぼう動機	employment objective
自己しょうかい	self introduction
自己PR	self promotion
履歴書	resume
すいせんじょう	letter of reference

説明会	a briefing session by a company
おうぼ（する）	application (to apply)
返事（する） へんじ	response (to respond)
書類 しょるい	documents
筆記試験 ひっき	written test
面接（試験） めんせつ	interview
結果 けっか	result, outcome
知らせる し	to notify
プロジェクト	project
会議 かいぎ	meeting
出張（する） しゅっちょう	business trip (to go)
やとう	to employ, to hire
やりがいがある	to be worth doing
努力（する） どりょく	effort (to make an effort)

覚えていますか。

相手　海外　〜会　会場　計画（する）　研究（する）　社長　就職（する）上司
けんきゅう　　　　　　しゅうしょく　じょうし
説明（する）　相談（する）　同僚　年　べんごし　普通　バイト　部下
りょう
ぼうえき会社　マネージャー　用紙　理由　集める　えらぶ　がんばる　決まる
決める　ことわる　さがす　じゅんびする　調べる　続ける　手伝う　働く
き　　　　　　　　　　　　　　　　　　つづ　　　　　　はたら
申し込む
もう　こ

Supplementary Vocabulary: 会社に関する言葉
かん
Other expressions related to businesses

きぎょう	企業	a firm, a corporation
きゅうじん	求人	help-wanted, job offer, きゅうじん広告 こうこく help-wanted ad
しゃいん	社員	a company employee
しょるいせんこう	書類選考	document screening
しりょう	資料	material, data
せいきゅう（する）	請求（する）	request, しりょうをせいきゅうする to request materials
せんこう（する）	選考（する）	to screen
つうち	通知	notification
ないてい	内定	an unofficial decision

Activity 7　次の説明に合う言葉を下線 (*underline*) に書いて下さい。
かせん

1. 仕事のために行く旅行です。　　　　　　　　　　　　＿＿＿＿＿＿＿＿＿＿
2. 仕事をした時にもらうお金です。　　　　　　　　　　＿＿＿＿＿＿＿＿＿＿
3. 質問や招待に答えることです。　　　　　　　　　　　＿＿＿＿＿＿＿＿＿＿
4. 奨学金がほしい時に先生に書いていただくものです。　＿＿＿＿＿＿＿＿＿＿
   しょう
5. 会社で働いてもらうと決めることです。　　　　　　　＿＿＿＿＿＿＿＿＿＿
   はたら
6. その人に会って色々質問をすることです。　　　　　　＿＿＿＿＿＿＿＿＿＿
7. 自分の住所や学校や仕事について書くものです。　　　＿＿＿＿＿＿＿＿＿＿
8. 色々な人が相談するために集まってすることです。　　＿＿＿＿＿＿＿＿＿＿
9. 知らない人に自分のことを知ってもらうために話す
   ことです。　　　　　　　　　　　　　　　　　　　　＿＿＿＿＿＿＿＿＿＿
10. 自分のいいところを知ってもらうためにする
    ことです。　　　　　　　　　　　　　　　　　　　　＿＿＿＿＿＿＿＿＿＿
11. その会社について知りたいとき集めるものです。　　　＿＿＿＿＿＿＿＿＿＿
12. 会社がおうぼする人のために開く会です。　　　　　　＿＿＿＿＿＿＿＿＿＿
13. 書いて受けるテストのことです。　　　　　　　　　　＿＿＿＿＿＿＿＿＿＿
14. どうしてその会社で働きたいかということです。　　　＿＿＿＿＿＿＿＿＿＿
    はたら
15. 勉強や仕事をがんばってすることです。　　　　　　　＿＿＿＿＿＿＿＿＿＿

Activity 8　Complete the following sentences with the appropriate words.

1. 仕事をさがす時には、まず会社について＿＿＿＿＿＿をたくさん集めること
   が大事だ。そして、行きたい会社を＿＿＿＿＿＿ら、エントリーする。
2. エントリー・シートには、＿＿＿＿＿＿や＿＿＿＿＿＿を＿＿＿＿＿＿く。
3. エントリーしたら、会社から＿＿＿＿＿＿について、＿＿＿＿＿＿があるはずだ。
4. 会社説明会には、＿＿＿＿＿＿を持って行った方がいい。
5. 書類せんこうで＿＿＿＿＿＿人達は、筆記試験を受けることが出来る。
   しょるい　　　　　　　　　　　　ひっき
6. 筆記試験に＿＿＿＿＿＿ら、面接がある。面接では＿＿＿＿＿＿がとても
   ひっき　　　　　　　　　めんせつ　　　　めんせつ
   大事だそうだ。
7. ＿＿＿＿＿＿が多くても、＿＿＿＿＿＿がある仕事がしたい。
8. 面接の＿＿＿＿＿＿について、早く＿＿＿＿＿＿ほしい。
   めんせつ

Activity 9   下の質問に答えて下さい。

1. 仕事におうぼする前に、どんなことをしなければなりませんか。

2. 会社におうぼする時に、どんな書類がひつようですか。
    しょるい

3. あなたが就職したい所では、どんな経験が大事ですか。
    しゅうしょく

4. 卒業したら、どんな専門の仕事をしてみたいですか。
    せんもん

5. そこで、どんなプロジェクトをやってみたいですか。

6. やりがいのある仕事って、どんな仕事ですか。やりがいのない仕事は？

7. 機会があれば、どんな仕事をしてみたいと思いますか。
    き かい

ダイアローグ

はじめに

下の質問に日本語で答えて下さい。

1. どんな仕事をしたことがありますか。
2. 仕事をさがす時、会社に何を送りますか。
3. 仕事をさがす時、だれかに相談しますか。どんなものを見たり読んだり
    しますか。
4. 大学を卒業したら、どんな仕事をしたいですか。

リーさんの相談   *Mr. Li's consultation with Professor Motoyama*

The following **manga** frames are scrambled, so they are not in the order described by the dialogue. Read the dialogue and unscramble the frames by writing the correct number in the box in each frame.

a

b

c

d

e

f

リーさんと本山先生が話しています。
　　　　　もとやま

　　　リー：　あのう、本山先生、就職のことでちょっとご相談したいことがある
　　　　　　　　　　　もとやま　　しゅうしょく
　　　　　　　のですが、研究室にうかがってもよろしいでしょうか。
　　　　　　　　　　　けんきゅうしつ
　本山先生：　ええ、いいですよ。今日は終わらせなければならない仕事があるか
　もとやま
　　　　　　　ら無理ですが、明日なら大丈夫ですよ。
　　　　　　　　　む　　　　　　　　　　　じょうぶ
　　　リー：　では、明日の何時ごろ研究室にうかがったらよろしいでしょうか。
　　　　　　　　　　　　　　　　　けんきゅうしつ
　本山先生：　一時ごろには来ていますが、来られますか。
　もとやま
　　　リー：　はい、大丈夫です。では、一時ごろまいります。よろしくおねがい
　　　　　　　　　じょうぶ
　　　　　　　します。

次の日、リーさんは本山先生の研究室に来ました。
　　　　　　　　　　もとやま　　けんきゅうしつ

　本山先生：　あ、どうぞ。
　もとやま
　　　リー：　失礼します。

　本山先生：　そこにすわって下さい。
　もとやま
　　　リー：　はい。

　本山先生：　相談したいことって何ですか。
　もとやま
　　　リー：　はい。再来年卒業する予定なんですが、出来たら日本で就職したい
　　　　　　　　　　　　さ　　　　　　　　　　　　　　　　　しゅうしょく
　　　　　　　と思っています。

　本山先生：　へえ、そうなんですか。
　もとやま
　　　リー：　ええ。それで、就職活動について教えていただけないかと思って。
　　　　　　　　　　　しゅうしょくかつどう
　本山先生：　いいですよ。まず、三年生の秋ごろから、会社のじょうほうを集め
　もとやま
　　　　　　　はじめるんですね。そして、三年の三月ごろまでにおうぼしたい会
　　　　　　　社を決めて、その会社にエントリーします。
　　　　　　　　　き
　　　リー：　あのう、エントリーって何でしょうか。

　本山先生：　エントリーは、自分がその会社に興味があることを知らせて、資料
　もとやま　　　　　　　　　　　　　　　　　　　　　　　　　　　　　しりょう
　　　　　　　をせいきゅうする手続きのことです。エントリーをしないと、会社の
　　　　　　　　　　　　てつづ
　　　　　　　説明会や会社のじょうほうが送られてこないことがありますから、気
　　　　　　　をつけて下さい。

　　　リー：　そうですか。それは知りませんでした。

本山先生：　その後、会社説明会に行って、その会社に就職したいと思ったら、
もとやま

　　　　　　　おうぼします。その時は履歴書を持って行って下さい。そして、書類
りれきしょ　　　　　　　　　　　　　　　しょるい

　　　　　　　でえらばれたら、筆記試験と面接があります。内定すれば、四年生
ひっき　　　めんせつ　　　　　　ないてい

　　　　　　　の八月か九月ごろに会社かられんらくが来ます。

　　リー：　すいせんじょうはいらないんでしょうか。

本山先生：　そうですね。筆記試験の後、すいせんじょうを送るように言ってく
もとやま　　　　　　　ひっき

　　　　　　　る会社もありますが、ないところも多いですね。

　　リー：　そうですか。じゃあ、もしすいせんじょうがひつようになったら、

　　　　　　　先生におねがいしてもよろしいでしょうか。

本山先生：　もちろんいいですよ。でも、ご両親はいいんですか、リーさんがた
もとやま

　　　　　　　いわんに帰らなくても。

　　リー：　ええ、両親は私の自由にしていいと言ってくれています。10 年も日

　　　　　　　本語を勉強してきたから、日本で働ける機会がありそうなら、さが
はたら　きかい

　　　　　　　してみたいと言ったら、いいよと言ってくれたんです。ですから、

　　　　　　　日本で仕事をさがすことにしたんです。

本山先生：　分かりました。じゃあ、がんばって下さい。
もとやま

　　リー：　はい、有り難うございます。

読んだ後で

A. Mr. Li is describing his discussion with Professor Motoyama. Complete the following
description using the appropriate expressions.

ぼくは＿＿＿＿＿＿＿＿たら、日本で＿＿＿＿＿＿＿＿したいと思っています。それで、
本山先生に、仕事のさがし方について＿＿＿＿＿＿＿と思って、先生の＿＿＿＿＿＿＿＿
もとやま
に＿＿＿＿＿＿＿に行きました。本山先生によると、日本ではまず＿＿＿＿＿＿＿＿＿＿。
もとやま
そして、会社説明会に行って、＿＿＿＿＿＿＿＿＿。会社かられんらくが来たら、筆記
ひっき
試験や面接を＿＿＿＿＿＿＿＿ことになります。でも、＿＿＿＿＿＿＿＿はあまりひつよう
めんせつ
ではないようです。

B. 質問に答えて下さい。

1. 本山先生はいつリーさんに会うのですか。どうして今日はだめなのですか。
もとやま

2. 日本では仕事をさがす時、どうしますか。

3. リーさんのご両親はリーさんが日本で就職することについてどう思って
しゅうしょく
　いますか。

C. Underline the honorific and humble expressions used by Mr. Li. Then paraphrase
them using regular polite speech.

日本の文化

雇用状況
こようじょうきょう
Employment trends

Major Japanese companies have followed the so-called lifetime employment（終身雇用）
しゅうしん こ
よう
policy since Japan's first economic success in the 1920s. In this system, companies
recruit new graduates from college, train them, and guarantee them employment for
life. This provides job security and promotes company loyalty. The collapse of the
Japanese asset price bubble in 1991 and the subsequent economic recession did not
change this practice much, although economic reform in 2003 encouraged companies to
discontinue or weaken the practice of lifetime employment and hire 派遣社員
は けんしゃいん
(*temporary workers*) or 契約社員 (*contract workers*). Although new graduates are still
けいやくしゃいん
recruited for full-fledged (regular) employment positions, the proportion of temporary
workers has been increasing.

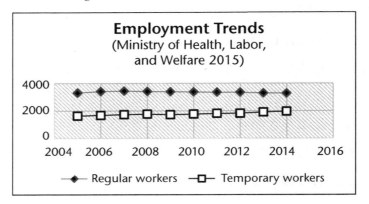

As in other countries, Japanese female workers face problems with inequality in
employment practices. Although the number of female workers and their net income
has increased, the average income of female workers is 70% of that of male workers.
This is because a majority of female workers are temporary and the proportion of
female executives is small compared to Western countries.

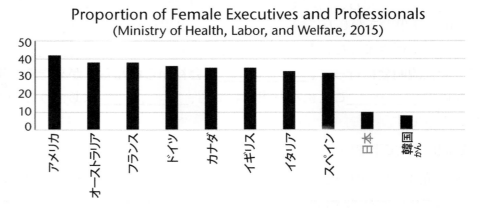

Despite the passage of legislation known as 男女雇用機会均等法 (employment
だんじょ こ よう き かいきんとうほう
equality between sexes) in the late 1980s, gender inequality in Japan remains greater
than in other developed countries. The recent change in the traditional employment

system may provide an opportunity for female workers, for whom the traditional system has offered few advantages.

More non-Japanese nationals are being hired for full-time positions than was once the case, although this is still not as common as in the United States. The facts show that (1) science majors do better at getting jobs than non-science majors, (2) people with graduate degrees do better than those without, and (3) a high proficiency in the Japanese language is required in most cases.

日本で就職する　Getting a job in Japan

As in many other countries, Japanese college students start looking for a job once they become juniors. They request information about companies, attend information sessions organized by company personnel, and send applications. This is called 会社回り, which means making the rounds of companies. There are some companies that give applicants written tests. All of them have interviews called 面接試験 or simply 面接. The applicants typically have freshly-cut hair and wear suits that are navy blue or some other dark color.

Although hiring practices have started changing recently, there are two features which still characterize Japanese recruiting and job-hunting practices: (1) the overwhelming majority of people entering the job market in a given year do so at the same time, and (2) new recruits have little significant work experience prior to graduation. The regular employment practice is to hire college graduates in April of every year, since the academic year ends in March. Japanese universities do not have intern programs or other systems that enable their students to interact with the outside world. Also, virtually all college students maintain full-time student status throughout college. It is still rare (and difficult) for students to take, for example, a year off from college to take a job and then come back to finish school. This means that companies must rely on extensive on-the-job training (研修) for their new recruits (新入社員).

For this reason, the companies generally look for graduates from the more famous schools, because they see these graduates as being more promising "raw material" for development into full-fledged employees. This is changing, however, as Japanese companies venture further into the international world and begin to value diversity and individuality in their own workforces. Some companies even mask the names of recruits' colleges during the recruiting process. Further, there is no longer the stigma that was once attached to changing jobs, so some people in the job market may have had prior work experience.

Students fill out job application forms

People working for Japanese companies are paid a monthly salary (給料). In addition, most companies pay a bonus (ボーナス) twice a year. The amount of the bonuses is determined by the financial state of the company, but usually amounts to the equivalent of two months' salary. Promotions are traditionally made by seniority; however, use of the merit system to determine both promotions and salary raises is getting increasingly more attention.

文法

I. Using honorific expressions to show respect

A. Using honorific verbs to describe actions by a social superior

So far, we have learned two forms of speech: the polite form (です, with the ます form of verbs) and the plain form (だ, with the dictionary form of verbs). These forms are used to express levels of formality and politeness toward a listener. The polite forms are used in more formal situations, often when the listener is not socially close to the speaker, and the plain form is used in more casual situations (e.g. among friends).

In this section, we will learn honorific and humble expressions, which introduce a new concept to the discussion: that of showing respect toward the topic of conversation or a socially superior listener. The topic of the conversation can be the person you are speaking with, or it can be a third person, who is not even present. This means that it is not uncommon in a Japanese conversational context for two friends talking about a teacher to use honorific and humble expressions while at the same time using the plain form of verbs. In the following example, two friends, Mr. Kimura and Mr. Li, are having a casual conversation; thus, they use the plain form of verbs, but still use the honorific お帰りになる to express the actions of Professor Yamada.

木村：　リーさん、山田先生、もうお帰りになった？
Mr. Li, has Prof. Yamada gone home?

リー：　うん、もうお帰りになったよ。
Yes, he is already gone.

Social superiority may be measured by age, social status, experience, or the benefactor-recipient relationship. For example, a recipient of a favor usually uses honorific forms toward the giver. Furthermore, honorific forms are often used in situations where the speaker knows little or nothing about the listener. It is very common to hear telephone operators, hotel clerks, and restaurant clerks using honorific forms with their customers.

学生：　山田先生は、まだいらっしゃいますか。
Is Prof. Yamada still here?

受付の人：　いいえ、もうお帰りになりました。
(*receptionist*)　*No, he has already gone home.*

学生：　先生は何をめし上がりますか。
What would you like to eat? (honorific)

先生：　天ぷらにします。
I'd like to have tempura.

それは先生がお書きになった本です。
That is the book the professor wrote.

山田：　先輩は明日の会議のことをご存じですか。
Senpai, do you know there is a meeting tomorrow? (honorific)

鈴木先輩：　ああ、知ってるよ。
Yes, I know.

今日、なかま銀行の方がおいでになって、その書類を持っていらっしゃいました。

A representative from Nakama Bank came today and brought that document. (honorific)

In general, honorific verbs are formed by お + the stem of the verb + に + なる. Honorific verbs with verbal nouns are formed by (お／ご) + verbal noun + なさる. There are many irregular honorific verbs shown in the vocabulary section of this chapter.

Verb types	Dictionary form	Honorific verbs
る -verbs and う -verbs		お +verb (stem) + に + なる
	やとう (*to hire*) 待つ (*to wait*) 見せる (*to show*)	おやといになる お待ちになる お見せになる
Verbal noun + する		お／ご + verbal noun + なさる
	電話する (*to telephone*) れんらくする (*to get in touch with*)	お電話なさる ごれんらくなさる

NOTES

- なさる, いらっしゃる, and おっしゃる are う-verbs. Their polite forms are なさいます, いらっしゃいます, and おっしゃいます, respectively.

- When a verb is combined with an auxiliary verb such as 〜ている or 〜てくれる, you only need to change the auxiliary verb into its honorific form.

  読んでいる　　→　　読んでいらっしゃる
  　している　　→　　していらっしゃる
  貸してくれる　→　　貸して下さる
  起こしてくれる　→　　起こして下さる

- In the case of 〜ている, there are some exceptions to this rule.

  行っている／来ている　　→　おいでだ or いらっしゃっている
  言っている　　　　　　　→　おっしゃっている
  食べている／飲んでいる　→　めし上がっている／
  　　　　　　　　　　　　　　　食べていらっしゃる／
  　　　　　　　　　　　　　　　飲んでいらっしゃる
  寝ている　　　　　　　　→　お休みだ（お休みになっている）
  着ている　　　　　　　　→　おめしだ（おめしになっている）

- For some verbs, you can use お + the verb stem + です instead of 〜ていらっしゃる.

  書いている　→　お書きだ／書いていらっしゃる
  待っている　→　お待ちだ／待っていらっしゃる

B. Making requests with honorifics

Honorific forms can be used in requests. In general, an honorific request is formed by お +
verb (stem) + 下さい. It is customary to use honorific requests when speaking to customers in
locations such as restaurants, hotels, banks, and stores. Use 下さいませんか or いただけま
せんか to make the request even more polite.

ここでお待ち下さい。	*Please wait here.*
おうぼ用紙をお使い下さい。	*Please use an application form.*
この履歴書をごらん下さい。	*Please look at this resume.*
明日おいで下さいませんか／ 明日おいでいただけませんか。	*Could you please come here tomorrow?*
こちらでお待ち下さいませんか／ お待ちいただけませんか。	*Could you please wait here?*

An honorific request with a verbal noun is formed by お／ご + Verbal noun + 下さい.

Verb types	Dictionary form	Honorific verbs
る -verbs and う -verbs		お + verb (stem) + 下さい
	えらぶ (*to select*) 知らせる (*to notify*) 待つ (*to wait*)	おえらび下さい お知らせ下さい お待ち下さい
Verbal noun + する		お／ご + verbal noun + 下さい
	電話する (*to call*) れんらくする (*to get in touch with*)	お電話下さい ごれんらく下さい

An honorific request using irregular honorific verbs ending with 〜になる can be formed by
replacing 〜になる with 下さい.

Verbs (dictionary form)	Honorific (dictionary form)	Honorific request
行く／来る／いる 見る 寝る 着る	おいでになる ごらんになる お休みになる おめしになる	おいで下さい ごらん下さい お休み下さい おめし下さい

Honorific requests made from other irregular honorific verbs are formed by using the て-form
of the verb + 下さい.

Verbs (dictionary form)	Honorific (dictionary form)	Honorific request
行く／来る／いる する 言う 食べる／飲む	いらっしゃる なさる おっしゃる めし上がる	いらっしゃって下さい なさって下さい おっしゃって下さい めし上がって下さい

C. Using the honorific forms of adjectives

Honorific adjectives are made by adding the prefix お to the adjective. Some な-adjectives such as 立派 take the prefix ご instead（ご立派）.

社長のおくさまはおきれいな方だ。
The company president's wife is a beautiful person.

社長は、ゴルフがお上手です。
The company president is good at golf. (honorific)

社長はむすめさんが結婚なさったので、毎日おさびしそうです。
The company president looks sad all the time because his daughter got married. (honorific)

あの先生は、とてもご立派な方です。
That professor is a very outstanding person. (honorific)

今日は、ご病気でいらっしゃれません。
(He/She) is ill and cannot come today. (honorific)

Some adjectives do not have honorific forms. For example, おもしろい, 大きい, and 有名な do not have honorific forms.

話してみましょう

Activity 1　　Change 私 to 先生 and rewrite the sentences using the appropriate honorific forms.

Example: 明日から東京に行きます。

先生は明日から東京にいらっしゃいます。

1. 私は九時ごろ帰ります。
2. 私はそのプロジェクトについてよく知っています。
3. 私は会議に出るつもりです。
4. 私は昨日十二時ごろ寝ました。
5. 私はここに来ています。
6. 私はやりがいのあるプロジェクトをしています。
7. 私はとても元気です。
8. 私はテニスが上手です。

Activity 2   Work with a group of four. You are a company president. Write five sentences you can act out. The rest of the group will try to describe what you are doing, using honorific forms. Anyone who correctly describes the action gets a point.

Example: A: *pretends to read a newspaper*

B: 社長は本を読んでいらっしゃいます。

A: いいえ、そうじゃありません。

C: 社長は新聞を読んでいらっしゃいます。

A: はい、そうです。

Activity 3   Work with a partner. You are working in the locations cited in 1–6 below and need to make various requests to the customer, as described. Your partner is the customer. Make a request using the honorific request form.

Example: レストラン／ここで少し待ってほしい

A: お客さま、こちらでお待ち下さい。

B: はい。

1.   レストラン／ここにすわってほしい
2.   レストラン／ジャケットを着てほしい
3.   旅行会社／クレジットカードの番号を教えてほしい
4.   旅行会社／明日までにお金を払ってほしい
5.   ホテル／この用紙に記入してほしい
6.   ホテル／十一時までにロビーに来てほしい

Activity 4   Work with a partner. Imagine that you are an editor of a school newspaper. Your partner is a famous Japanese person who has come to the campus to give a lecture. (Decide on the topic.) Interview the person politely so that you can write an interesting article. Your instructor will give you a table containing the information you should obtain.

Example: 学生：　はじめまして、スミスと申します。よろしくおねがいします。
　　　　　　お名前を教えていただけませんか。

田中：　はじめまして。東京大学の田中です。

学生：　田中さまのお仕事／ご専門は何ですか。

田中：　ロボットの研究です。

学生：　そうですか。いつこちらにおいでになりましたか。／
　　　　　　いつこちらにいらっしゃいましたか。

田中：　一昨日の晩に着きました。

II. Using humble expressions to show respect

Like honorifics, humble verbs and their equivalents are used to express respect for the subject of the conversation, who may or may not be the listener. While honorifics are used to describe the actions of the person who is the object of respect, humble verbs are used to describe the actions of the speaker and his/her in-group. Their intent is to show that the speaker considers himself/herself socially inferior to the person being discussed.

Humble verbs are not used unless the speaker's actions are related to or in some way affect the social superior who is the subject of the conversation. For this reason, they are often used when the speaker does a favor for the social superior.

先生： だれか、この荷物を持ってくれませんか。
  Would someone hold/pick up this bag?

田中： 私がお持ちします。
  Yes, I will hold it (for you).

学生： 先生にお話ししたいことがあるのですが、研究室にうかがっても
     （けんきゅうしつ）
  よろしいでしょうか。
  I have something I would like to talk with you about. May I come to your office?

先生： ええ、いいですよ。
  Yes, that is fine.

先生： ちょっと待ってくれますか。
  Sorry, could you wait a little bit?

学生： はい、ここでお待ちします。
  Yes, I will wait here.

Remember that in these situations, the て -form of the verb + 差し上げる as in「はい、持って差し上げます。」and「はい、ここで待って差し上げます。」can be used, but this form is not preferred because it sounds rather arrogant.

In general, humble verbs are formed with お + the verb stem of the verb + する. Humble verbs with a verbal noun are formed with お／ご + verbal noun + する.

Verb types	Dictionary form	Humble verbs
る -verbs and う -verbs		お + verb (stem) + する
	知らせる (*to notify*) 見せる (*to show*) 送る (*to send*)	お知らせする お見せする お送りする
Verbal noun + する		お／ご + verbal noun + する
	電話する (*to call*) 説明する (*to explain*)	お電話する ご説明する

There are many irregular humble verbs included in the vocabulary section. Here are other examples of the special humble form.

つれて行く／つれて来る　→　おつれする

持って行く／持って来る　→　お持ちする

The following humble forms are also used as polite forms. That is, they are used in formal situations and the action does not have to be related to the listener or a third party. The action must be the speaker's own.

まいる (*to go*)	山田：	どちらへいらっしゃるんですか。
	川口：	東京へまいります。
おる (*to be/to have*)	山田：	お子さんはいらっしゃいますか。
	川口：	ええ、一人おります。
申す (*to say*) もう	山田：	はじめまして。山田と申します。 もう
	川口：	はじめまして。川口と申します。 もう
いたす (*to do*)	山田：	いつも何時までお仕事なさいますか。
	川口：	十時までいたします。
努力する (*to make an effort*) どりょく	山田：	明日までにおねがいできますか。
	川口：	ちょっと難しいと思いますが、努力 いたします。　　　　　　　　　どりょく

話してみましょう

Activity 1　　Your teacher has expressed the following requests and questions. Respond to him/her using the humble form of the verb.

Example:　いつ私の本を持ってきてくれますか。

　　　　　　<u>明日お持ちします。</u>

1. 何時に研究室に来られますか。
   けんきゅうしつ
2. 研究室に来る前にれんらくして下さい。
   けんきゅうしつ
3. 研究室に来る時に送別会の写真を持ってきて下さい。
   けんきゅうしつ　　　　　べつ
4. それから、私の本はもう読みましたか。
5. その会社のじょうほうをもらってきて下さい。
6. 会社の人に私のことを話しましたか。
7. 少しおそくなるかもしれませんが、何時ごろまで待ってくれますか。
8. じゃあ、後でまた会いましょう。

Activity 2　　Work with a group of four. Each person should think of five requests, imagining that he/she is the president of a company and the other members are employees. Make a request. The rest of the group must respond to the request using humble forms. The person who responds appropriately to the request first scores a point.

Example:　社長：　来週の会議で使う書類を持って来てくれませんか。
　　　　　　　　　かいぎ　　　　しょるい

　　　　　　部下：　はい、今、お持ちします。

Activity 3 Work with a partner. You are preparing for a job interview. Introduce and sell yourself within one minute.

Example: はじめまして。～と申します。～からまいりました。大学では～を専攻して、日本語は大学の一年生の時から勉強しております。でも、まだあまり上手じゃないので、これからも努力いたします。私はチャレンジが好きですから、どんな仕事でもがんばってするつもりでおります。どうぞよろしくおねがいいたします。

Activity 4 Work with a partner. Imagine that one person is a prospective employer and the other person is a student. The employer should interview the student. The student should respond to questions using humble verbs and polite speech.

Example: A: はじめまして。山田です。

B: はじめまして。スミスと申します。どうぞよろしくおねがいいたします。

A: スミスさんの専攻は何ですか。

B: 経営学です／経営学を専攻しております。

1. 専攻は何ですか。
2. この会社にしぼうした動機は何ですか。
3. 日本語で書いたものがあれば、後で会社に送ってくれますか。
4. 出張が多い仕事は大丈夫ですか。
5. どんな仕事がしたいですか。
6. 日本語はどのぐらい勉強しましたか。

III. Expressing directionality in time using 〜ていく and 〜てくる

In Chapter 4, you learned that the て-form of the verb + いく or くる indicates an action or event which moves away from or toward the speaker. For example, 持っていく, which consists of the verb 持つ (to hold) and 行く (to go) means to take, but 持ってくる means to bring. The same construction can be used to indicate movement along a time line.

A. Expressing the continuation of a currently on-going action (or situation) into the future using 〜ていく and the process of change to an event or an action experienced by others using 〜ていく

The following example sentences illustrate a situation where the current location is temporal, not spatial. For example, in the first sentence, the speaker is expressing his/her intention of continuing to look for a job.

これからも日本での就職活動を続けていくつもりです。
しゅうしょくかつどう つづ

I intend to continue to look for a job in Japan.

これからは夜が長くなっていくよ。

Nights will start getting longer now.

これからも先輩の下で仕事をしていきたいと思います。
ぱい

I would like to continue working under my senior.

In the next example sentences, the auxiliary verb いく indicates the process of change of state but does not express spatial or temporal movement. Rather, it indicates that the speaker views this process as something psychologically distant from himself. Therefore, this use of 〜ていく describes an objective or impersonal situation and is often used for a change of process that does not involve the speaker or someone close to the speaker.

その人は、お金を少しずつ返していった。

He returned the money little by little.

その時から、会社は少しずつ大きくなっていきました。

From that time, the company gradually began to grow larger.

いく is considered an auxiliary verb because it no longer retains the meaning *to go*. For this reason, いく is written in **hiragana** in this usage.

B. Expressing continuation of an action or event that began in the past and continues to the present day using 〜てくる and expressing the beginning of a process experienced by the speaker or someone close to the speaker using 〜てくる

The following examples indicate that the action or event started in the past and has continued to the point where it has reached the present. In this usage, the auxiliary verb くる is usually in the past tense.

日本語を十年間勉強してきました。

I have been studying Japanese for 10 years now.

今までがんばって働いてきたんだから、これからも続けていこうと思う。
はたら   つづ

I have worked hard until now, so I think I will continue to do so.

The following sentences indicate the beginning of a process.

元気が出てきた。	*I have begun to feel better.*
あっ、雨がふってきたよ。	*Oh, it has begun to rain.*
仕事がおもしろくなってきました。	*My job is starting to get more interesting.*
手続きが分かってきた。	*I have begun to understand the procedure.*
てつづ	
風がふいてきた。	*The wind has just begun to blow.*

In these cases, the verb くる no longer has the meaning of coming, but instead acts as an auxiliary verb. Therefore, it is often written in hiragana.

NOTE

● When the て-form of the verb + くる indicates a change of process, the subject must be the speaker or someone close to the speaker. This therefore expresses the speaker's psychological involvement or subjectivity. In the following sentences, やせてきた indicates that the speaker began to lose weight. One the other hand やせていった indicates someone else's process of losing weight and does not indicate the beginning of a process or that the process involves the speaker or someone close to him/her.

やせてきた。 *I have begun to lose weight.*

高木さんは、やせていった。 *Mr. Takagi lost weight* (over time).

話してみましょう

◆ **Activity 1**   Look at the following pictures and describe what is beginning to take place.

Example: あ、空が晴れてきましたよ。
そら

| Example | 1 | 2 | 3 |

| 4 | 5 | 6 | 7 |

◆ **Activity 2**   Work with the class. Ask your classmates if there is some activity they began a long time ago and are still doing to this day. If so, ask them what it is and how long they have been doing it.

Example: A: 何か今まで続けてきたことがありますか。
つづ
            B: ええ、ゴルフをしてきました。
            A: どのぐらいしてきたんですか。
            B: 小学校一年の時からです。
            A: それはすごいですね。

名前	してきたこと	どのぐらい

◆ **Activity 3**   Using 〜ていく write what the following famous people would say when they are interviewed about their future plans.

Example: イチロー

これからもヒットをたくさんうって (*to hit*) いこうと思っています。

イチロー　　バラク・オバマ (Barack Obama)　　トヨタの社長
バットマン　　ブラッド・ピット (Brad Pitt)　　あらし
アウンサンスーチー　　　(Aung San Suu Kyi)　　ビル・ゲイツ (Bill Gates)

◆ **Activity 4**   Work as a class. Ask your classmates what they want to accomplish in the future, what they have been doing to achieve their goals, and whether they think they will continue to do so. Note that そのために means *for that purpose*.

Example: A:　将来何をしたいと思いますか。
　　　　　　　　しょう
　　　　　　B:　日本語の先生になりたいと思います。

　　　　　　A:　そのために、どんなことをしてきましたか。

　　　　　　B:　日本語を勉強してきました。

　　　　　　A:　これからも日本語を勉強していくつもりですか。

　　　　　　B:　ええ、勉強していくつもりです。

IV. Pronoun の, the noun こと, and ことになる／ことにする

The particle の as in 大きいの (*large one*) and the word こと as in 仕事のこと (*thing about my job*) were introduced in *Nakama 1*. Here we will introduce the extended use of の and こと with clauses.

A. の as an indefinite pronoun

The pronoun の was introduced as an indefinite pronoun in Chapter 5 of *Nakama 1* as in 大きいの (*large one*). It can be used when the object it refers to is clear from the context.

このペンはちょっと小さいですね。もっと大きいのはありませんか。
This pen is a bit small. Is there a bigger one?

Strictly speaking, this の is not an indefinite pronoun. It is instead a particle connecting two nouns. The noun following の is omitted in this usage because it can be inferred from the context.

それは田中さんのプロジェクトですが、これは山田さんのです。
That is Ms. Tanaka's project but this is Mr. Yamada's.

However, the indefinite pronoun の does exist in Japanese. It occurs with a clause, and is translated as one, thing, or what (as in *what I want to do*).

私が先生に書いていただきたいのはすいせんじょうです。
What I want you to write is a letter of reference.
就職活動で一番大切なのは自己PRだ。
The most important thing in job hunting is self-promotion.
筆記試験に受かったのはトムだけだった。
The only person who passed the written exam was Tom.
面接で聞かれたのはしぼう動機と大学の専門についてだった。
What I was asked in the interview was why I applied for the job and questions about my major.
五年前サラリーマンだったのは中村先生です。
The person who was a salaried businessman five years ago is Professor Nakamura.

The pronoun の can be modified by nouns, adjectives, and verbs. Use な for the present affirmative form of both な-adjectives and nouns with the copula verb. Otherwise, use the plain form.

	Verbs	い -adjective	な -adjectives	Noun+ copula verb
	やとう (to hire)	いい (good)	ひつようだ (necessary)	締め切りだ (deadline)
Present affirmative	やとうの	いいの	ひつようなの	締め切りなの
Present negative	やとわないの	よくないの	ひつようじゃないの	締め切りじゃないの
Past affirmative	やとったの	よかったの	ひつようだったの	締め切りだったの
Past negative	やとわなかったの	よくなかったの	ひつようじゃなかったの	締め切りじゃなかったの

The particle の cannot be used by itself. It has to be preceded by an adjective, a verb, a phrase, or a clause, but not by demonstrative expressions such as この, その, あの, or どの.

きれいなの *clean one*
きれいじゃないの *the one that is not clean*
聞こえるの *the one I hear / what I hear*

聞こえないの	*the one I can't hear / what I can't hear*
山田さんが昨日読んだの	*The one that Ms. Yamada read yesterday / What Ms. Yamada read yesterday*

The particle の can refer to either tangible or intangible things.

社長がえらんだのは、このおうぼ書類です。
しょるい

What the company president has selected is this application document.

社長がえらんだのは、山田さんのアイデアです。

What the company president has selected is Ms. Yamada's idea.

B. こと as a noun

The word こと is a noun that refers to an intangible thing and can be translated as *thing* or *matter*. Just like any other noun, こと is used in noun modifying clauses.

先生がおっしゃったことを覚えていますか。	*Do you remember what the teacher said?*
私が言わなかったことを言っていた。	*He was saying things that I hadn't said.*
社長がご存じないことは何もありません。 ぞん	*There is nothing that the company president does not know.*

こと can be modified by nouns, adjectives and verbs, and the formation is identical to の, except that the particle の is used to modify こと with a noun, as in 履歴書のこと.
りれきしょ

大事なことは忘れません。

I don't forget important things.

石田さんはこの手続きのことをよく知っている。
てつづ

Mr. Ishida knows a lot (of things) about this procedure.

来年就職するために、今からしておかなければならないことは、どんなこと
しゅうしょく
でしょうか。

What kind of things should we do now to find employment next year?

先生がすいせんじょうにお書きになったことは本当のことなんでしょうか。

Is what the professor wrote in the recommendation letter true?

Unlike の, which cannot stand alone, こと can be used by itself and can also co-occur with demonstrative words such as この, その, and あの.

ことが大きくなってしまうと、みんなが困る。

If the situation gets blown up, it will be a big hassle for all of us.

そのことは、だれにも言わないで下さい。

Please do not tell anyone about that matter.

The construction noun のこと is often translated as *about ~* when it is used with verbs such as 話す, 知っている, 言う, and 読む.

山田さんは、その活動のことをよく知っていた。
かつどう

Mr. Yamada knew about all about that activity.

広告の締め切りのことを話す。
こうこく　　し　き

I will talk about the deadline for the advertisement.

C. Expressing personal decisions using 〜ことにする

The expression noun + にする, *to decide on* 〜, to indicate the speaker's decision is introduced in Chapter 9 of *Nakama 1*. You learned in Chapter 11 of *Nakama 1* that the adverbial form of the adjective + する, as in はやくする, indicates that the speaker has caused a change of state to occur. The plain present form of the verb +ことにする is related to these expressions, except that 〜ことにする expresses the speaker's decision to do something. It follows a clause that ends with a plain present affirmative or a plain present negative form.

Plain present affirmative form of verbs	行くことにする
Plain present negative form of verb	行かないことにする

筆記試験を受けることにしました。
ひっき
I have decided to take a written exam.

その会社に興味があるので、エントリーすることにした。
I am interested in the job, so I've decided to submit an entry form.

返事をもらったので、説明会に行くことにした。
へんじ
I received a response, so I've decided to go to the briefing session.

他の会社におうぼしないで、面接の結果を待つことにしました。
めんせつ　けっか
I've decided to wait for the results of the interview and not apply for jobs at other companies.

新聞の広告に出ていた仕事におうぼすることにしました。
こうこく
I've decided to apply for a job that was advertised in the newspaper.

今晩上田さんとカラオケに行くことにしたんだけど、一緒に行かない？
しょ
We've decided to go out for karaoke with Ms. Ueda this evening; would you like to come with us?

NOTES

- The expression 〜ことにしている expresses a habit or routine activity that has evolved as a result of a personal decision. It is translated as *I have decided to do ~* or *I have made it a rule to do~*. It is similar to 〜ようにしている (Chapter 10), but ようにしている implies that the speaker is making an effort do something rather than that he or she has made a decision to something.
- 返事はすぐすることにしている。　*I make it a rule to reply promptly.*
  へんじ
- 返事はすぐするようにしている。　*I make an effort to reply promptly.*
  へんじ

D. Expressing something that has been decided or come about using 〜ことになる, *it has been decided that* 〜

While 〜ことにする expresses the speaker's own decision, 〜ことになる expresses the idea that something has been decided or has happened due to circumstances beyond the speaker's control. The use of する implies the existence of an actor responsible for the action of the verb, whereas なる describes an action where the actor is unknown or where a change of state has come about naturally. The clause preceding 〜ことになる must end with the plain present form of the verb.

今度東京に引っ越すことになりました。

It has been decided that I will move to Tokyo.

このプロジェクトについては、私が説明することになりました。

It has been decided that I will explain this project.

悪い結果を知らせることになった。

It's been decided that I will be the one to notify people of the bad results.

会議に山本先生をご招待することになりました。

It's been decided that we will invite Professor Yamamoto to the conference.

If the speaker cannot be involved in the decision-making process, 〜ことになる must be used. But in some cases 〜ことになる is used even though the decision was in fact made by the speaker. This use of ことになる is more humble and polite than 〜ことにする.

新しい人をやとうことにしました。   *We've decided to hire a new person.*

新しい人をやとうことになりました。 *It's been decided that we will hire a new person.*

NOTES

- The phrase 〜ことになっている indicates a decision was made at some point in the past and the result of the decision is still in effect. It is often used to express customs, regulations, rules, regularly scheduled events, and expectations.

  アメリカでは二十一さい以上じゃないと、おさけを飲んではいけないことになっている。

  It's long been the case that you cannot drink alcohol in the United States unless you are over 21 years old.

- The expression 〜ことになっている can also be used to avoid responsibility by obscuring who made the decision.

  明日の九時にれんらくすることになっている。

  It's been decided that I am to contact him/her at nine o'clock tomorrow.

話してみましょう

Activity 1　Read the statements and make questions that fit the answer using の.

Example:　山田さんは昨日手紙を書きました。

A:　　手紙です。
　　　山田さんが昨日書いたのは何ですか。

1. 鈴木さんは会社の説明会で自己しょうかいをさせられました。
   A: 自己しょうかいです。

2. 山田さんは日本語の研究に興味があります。
   A: 日本語の研究です。

3. スミスさんは面接の結果を待っています。
   A: 面接の結果です。

4. ジョンソンさんは履歴書を送らなければなりません。
   A: 履歴書です。

5. 鈴木さんは出張で東京に出かけました。
   A: 東京です。

6. 木村さんは自己 PR が上手じゃありません。
   A: 自己 PR です。

Activity 2　Work with a partner. Ask each other about things that you might often do on the following occasions, and complete the chart. Use casual speech.

Example:　A:　友達によく話すことって、どんなこと？
　　　　　B:　そうだね、好きな人のことかな。

	パートナーの答え
友達に話します	
ブログに書きます	
新聞で読みます	
インターネットで見ます	
学校で聞きます	

Activity 3   Imagine that the following offers and suggestions have been made to you. Respond using 〜ことにする.

Example: この車は 7,000 ドルの車ですが、1,000 ドル安くしますから、買いませんか。

この車を買うことにします。 or この車は買わないことにします。

1. 田中さんが日本に帰るそうですから、一緒に見送（しょ）りに行きませんか。

2. そんなに大変なら、がんばらなければいいんですよ。

3. しぼう動機（どうき）を説明してくれませんか。

4. お父さんには相談しなくてもいいんじゃない？

5. 履歴書（りれきしょ）がひつようかどうかれんらくしてみたらどうですか。

6. ご飯を食べる時には新聞を読まない方がいいんじゃないですか。

Activity 4   The people at your workplace and your parents have made the following requests that you could not refuse, so you will be doing them favors. Express what's been decided using 〜ことになる.

Example: 今度の休みに家に帰って来てもらいたいんだ。

今度の休みに家に帰ることになりました。

1. 明日からニューヨークに出張（しゅっちょう）してもらいたいんだが、いいね？

2. 来週までに今度のプロジェクトのじょうほうを集めてほしいんだが、いいね？

3. 明日締め切（し き）りだから、今日書類（しょるい）を作っておいてくれないか？

4. 国に帰って、お父さんの仕事を手伝ってほしいんだけど。

5. お母さんが病気だから、家に帰って、弟の世話をしてほしいんだ。

6. お金がないから、悪いけど、大学には行かないでほしい。

7. 田中さんの就職（しゅうしょく）祝いのプレゼントをえらんでほしいんだけど。

8. むかえに行く時間がないから地下鉄に乗ってきて。

V. Expressing quantity-related emphasis using quantity expression + も

Quantity expressions such as 一度も and 何度も are used to either emphasize a large quantity or the lack of quantity, depending on the quantity preceding も. Here we will see how the construction quantity expression + も works in sentences.

A. Expressing zero quantity or frequency using 1 + counter + も ~negative

Expressions of quantity or frequency where the number one is followed by も and a negative ending indicate zero quantity or frequency. These are translated as *not even one/once*.

山田さんは 一度も 車をぶつけたことが ありません 。

Mr. Yamada has never hit anything with his car. (lit.: not even once)

昨日のパーティには知り合いは 一人も 来なかった 。

Not even a single acquaintance (of mine) *came to the party yesterday.*

中村先生はビールを 一本も めし上がりませんでした 。

Professor Nakamura did not drink any beer at all. (honorific)

今年はおうぼが 一つも ないですね。

There are no applicants this year.

B. Emphasizing large quantity or high frequency using number/ question word + counter + も～ affirmative

When も follows a quantity or frequency expression in an affirmative sentence, it emphasizes the speaker's feeling that the quantity or frequencies are abnormally large.

就職活動のために 二十回も 会社説明会へ 行った 。
しゅうしょくかつどう

I went to TWENTY orientation sessions as part of my efforts to find a job.

トムはステーキを 四まいも 食べた 。

Tom ate FOUR steaks.

その面接は 三時間も かかった 。
めんせつ

The interview lasted THREE HOURS!

In the following example, the difference between 電話で二時間話した and 電話で二時間も話した is that, in the first sentence, the speaker does not think a two-hour telephone conversation is long, while in the second sentence, the speaker thinks two hours are very long.

大木： 昨日何度も電話したんですが。

　　　　I called you MANY TIMES yesterday.

道子： ああ、ごめんなさい。知り合いから電話がかかってきて、二時間ぐらい
　　　　話していたんです。

　　　　Oh, I'm sorry. I got a phone call from an acquaintance and talked to him for two hours.

大木： え、二時間も話してたんですか。

　　　　Really? You talked for TWO HOURS?

If a quantity or frequency expression with も contains a question word instead of a number, it means many, much or a lot of and is used to emphasize a large quantity or high frequency. The sentence must end with an affirmative verb form.

このプロジェクトについては何回も会議<ruby>会議<rt>かい ぎ</rt></ruby>をした。
We had meetings MANY TIMES regarding this project.

さとるには今まで何度もからかわれたから、おこってるんだ。
I've been teased by Satoru MANY TIMES before, so I am mad at him.

<ruby>書類<rt>しょるい</rt></ruby>を作るため、何さつも本を読まなければならない。
I must read MANY BOOKS in order to compile the document.

話してみましょう

Activity 1   The following chart illustrates what Mr. Aoki and Mr. Chung did or did not do last week. Answer the questions about them, using quantity or frequency expressions and も.

Example: A: 青木さんは先週ご両親に電話をかけましたか。チョンさんはどうですか。

B: 青木さんは一度もかけませんでした。チョンさんは四回もかけました。

	青木	チョン
両親に電話をかける	0回	四回
テレビを見る	二十時間	0時間
本を読む	五さつ	0さつ
犬の<ruby>散歩<rt>さん</rt></ruby>に行く	0回	十回
アルバイトをする	十時間	二十時間
ピアノをひく	0時間	0時間
部屋をそうじする	三度	一度
作文を書く	1ページ	10ページ
大家さんに注意される	六回	0回

1. 青木さんはテレビを見ましたか。チョンさんはどうですか。
2. チョンさんは本を読みましたか。青木さんはどうですか。
3. チョンさんは犬の<ruby>散歩<rt>さん</rt></ruby>に行きましたか。青木さんはどうですか。
4. チョンさんはアルバイトをしましたか。青木さんはどうですか。
5. 青木さんはピアノをひきましたか。チョンさんはどうですか。
6. 青木さんは部屋をそうじしましたか。チョンさんはどうですか。
7. チョンさんは作文を書きましたか。青木さんはどうですか。
8. 青木さんは大家さんに注意されましたか。チョンさんはどうですか。

◀ **Activity 2** ▶ Work with the class. Ask your classmates about other people's repetitive, annoying actions.

Example: A: 〜さんはいやなことをたくさんされたことがありますか。

B: ええ、あります。小学校の時、同じクラスにいた男の子に何度も
からかわれたことがあります。

◀ **Activity 3** ▶ Work with the class. Ask your classmates whether they have done the things listed. If they have, ask them how frequently. Find out who in the class has performed each of the actions most frequently.

Example: A: 日本に行ったことがありますか。

B: いいえ、一度もありません。
or
はい、あります。

A: 何度ぐらい行ったことがありますか。

B: 三度ぐらいあります。

A: 三度も行ったんですか。いいですね。

	名前	〜度／〜かい／〜か月／〜年 , etc.
日本に行く		
日本に住んでいる		
何かぬすまれる		
面接を受ける めんせつ		
変な (strange) うわさを される		
筆記試験に落ちる ひっき		
先生にしかられる		

聞く練習

面接試験　A job interview
めんせつ

聞く前に

1. Work with a partner. Discuss and create at least five questions in Japanese that a potential employer might ask an applicant.

2. Politely answer the questions you created in Exercise A as though you were applying for a job.

聞いてみましょう

 Listen to the three interviews between applicants and a representative of IACE Travel. Take notes about each applicant and complete the following table. Then rank them.

	◀》1	◀》2	◀》3
名前			
おうぼした理由			
専攻 _{せんこう}			
英語			
コンピュータ			
外国に住む			

聞いた後で

Work with a group of four. Discuss your information and decide which person is the best candidate and why.

聞き上手話し上手

Responding to compliments and expressing politeness and modesty in formal situations

Compliments are often used to start a conversation. In the United States, compliments on clothing, hairstyles, or other visual features such as "you have a nice ring," express friendliness. In Japan, however, complimenting visual features as a means of breaking the ice is not as common as it is in the US. Close friends may compliment clothing if it is related to the topic of the conversation. The Japanese are more likely to compliment a person's skill or intelligence, especially in formal situations.

Compliment responses can be classified into three types: acceptance, denial, and avoidance. Studies in compliment responses show that English speakers tend to use the acceptance strategies more than Japanese and rarely use the denial strategy. Japanese speakers use the denial strategy more than English speakers, but they still use the avoidance strategy or the acceptance strategy more often than the denial strategy.

The avoidance strategy may be expressed in an explanation of why the speaker obtained the item being complimented (前からほしかったんで、買ったんです。 *I wanted it for a long time, so I bought it*), when he/she get it (前に買ったんですけど。 *I bought it a while ago*), or who gave it to him/her (父にもらったんです。) Another way to avoid responding to the compliments is to return the question (そうですか。), offer the item to the person who complimented it (あげましょうか。), or simply keeping silent or shifting the topic.

To accept the compliment, you may express your gratitude (ありがとうございます。), agreement (そうなんですよ。*That's right*), your happiness at receiving the compliment

(そういってもらえうると、うれしいです。　*I'm glad to hear you say so*) or return the same compliments to your coversational partner.

In formal situations the Japanese may use denial to respond to compliments. This is because stating something negative about yourself indicates that you are lowering your own social status and raising the listener's status, thereby showing respect and politeness. This type of denial is common for compliments directed to you personally or to your family members. Instead of saying "Thank you," you can express regret (すみません) or disagree by saying:

そんなことないですよ。／そんなことはありませんよ。　*No, that is not the case.*

そうでもありません。／そうでもございません。　　　*No, not really.*

まあまあです。　　　　　　　　　　　　　　　　　*I am just so-so./ It's just so-so.*

These expressions can be followed by a negative or positive statement. For example, when you say something in Japanese, you may be complimented immediately on your proficiency in Japanese, no matter how rudimentary it is. If you receive such a compliment, you can respond by saying まだまだです。(*I still have a lot to learn*).

青木：　日本語がお上手ですね。
　　　　Your Japanese is very good.

山田：　いいえ、まだまだです。
　　　　No, I still have a lot to learn.
　　　　or
　　　　有り難うございます。でも、まだまだなんです。
　　　　Thank you very much. But I still have a lot to learn.

A.　Write the appropriate responses to the following compliments.

1.　日本語がお上手ですね。
2.　よく仕事が出来るんですね。
3.　〜さんの会社はとても立派ですね。
　　　　　　　　　　　りっぱ
4.　〜さんは頭がいいんですね。
5.　いい車をお持ちですね。
6.　テニスがお上手なんですね。

B.　Listen to the dialogue. Assuming that you are Mr. Smith in the dialogue, respond to the compliment.

Example:　You hear:　A:　はじめまして、スミスと申します。どうぞよろしくおねが
　　　　　　　　　　　　　　　　　　　　　もう
　　　　　　　　　　　　　　いします。

　　　　　　　　　　　B:　山本です。こちらこそ。スミスさんは日本語がお上手
　　　　　　　　　　　　　　ですね。

　　　　　You write:　いいえ、まだまだです。

1.　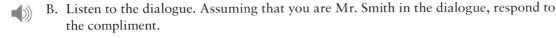_____

2.　_____

3.　_____

4.　_____

5.　_____

C. Work with a group of four. Three of you will be interviewers from a human resources department and one of you will be a job seeker. The group should decide on the type of company and the type of employees being sought. Read the job interview manners your instructor will supply you and role-play a job interview situation.

Example: A: 〜さん。

B: はい。（ノック、ノック）

A: どうぞお入り下さい。

B: 失礼します。

漢字

Electronic tools for reading and writing Japanese

In addition to electronic dictionaries (電子辞書) mentioned in the **kanji** section in Chapter 8, there is a wide range of electronic tools available to help you read Japanese text in general, including **kanji**.

Online help with reading Japanese text

Rikai.com is one of the most popular online tools available. It embeds a bilingual dictionary in any Web page so that it opens pop-up windows containing vocabulary information when you touch words with the mouse. Pop Jisyo is another site that works similarly to rikai.com.

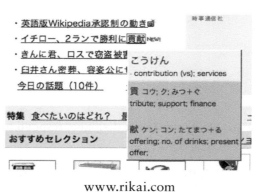

www.rikai.com

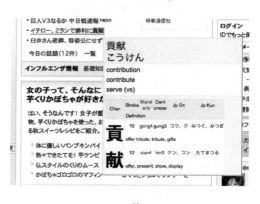

www.popjisyo.com

Reading Tutor (リーディング チュウ太) requires you to copy and paste Japanese text to process it; however, it provides more comprehensive information about vocabulary for the entire Japanese text.

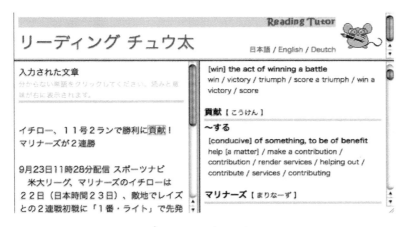

language.tiu.ac.jp

Goo 辞書 (dictionary.goo.ne.jp) and Yahoo! 辞書 (dic.yahoo.co.jp) are good examples of free online dictionaries.

Writing Japanese with a computer

With the wide-spread use of the internet and electronic communication has become the main channel of information exchange. This, in turn, is changing the mode of writing in Japanese, and virtually all newer PCs can handle Japanese text without additional software. There are some steps you have to go through to enable Japanese characters for your computer. Once you enable Japanese support on your PC, you will type Japanese text through romanization. The computer will automatically convert romanization to **hiragana**, and then to **kanji**, **kanji** and **kana** combinations, or **katakana**. One thing you have to be careful about is that you cannot make spelling errors when you type. A series of **kana** that contains a spelling error will not be converted to the correct **kanji** or **kanji** compounds. For example, がくせい must be typed as *gakusei* to be converted to 学生. Another caution is that you may end up producing sentences that you may not be able to read because the conversion dictionary can convert words into **kanji** you do not know yet. We recommend you do not over-convert words into **kanji** so that the text you type reflects your current ability.

We recommend that you practice writing **kanji** by hand until you learn about 500 **kanji** because this will provide you with a good knowledge of the basic structure of **kanji** components. At the same time, however, you should not be hesitant to take advantage of available tools.

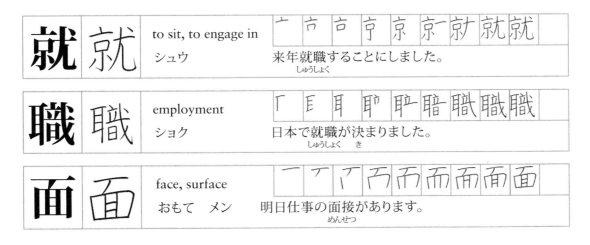

接	接	to come into contact	一	扌	扌	扩	护	拉	按	接	接
		セツ・セッ			面接は九時からです。						
					めんせつ						

広	広	wide, spacious	`	一	广	広	広				
		ひろ(い) コウ			広い家ですね。 広い公園 広告						
					ひろ ひろ こうこく						

告	告	to announce, inform	ノ	一	牛	生	告	告			
		つ(げる) コク			広告会社に就職したいです。						
					こうこくがいしゃ しゅうしょく						

立	立	to stand	`	一	宀	立	立				
		た(てる)・た(つ) リツ・リッ			立って下さい。 立派なホテル						
					た りっぱ						

派	派	group, party, school	`	`	シ	シ	シ	汿	沅	派	派
		ハ・パ			立派な病院ですね。						
					りっぱ						

研	研	to study, research	一	丆	丆	石	石	石一	石一	矴	研
		ケン			日本語を研究しています。						
					けんきゅう						

究	究	to study	'	'	宀	宀	空	空	究		
		キュウ			研究は楽しいです。						
					けんきゅう						

室	室	room	'	'	宀	宀	宏	宏	宓	窣	室
		シツ			先生の研究室はどちらですか。						
					けんきゅうしつ						

専	専	exclusive	一	一	戸	戸	百	車	車	専	専
		セン			専門は経済学です。 専攻はビジネスです。						
					せんもん ざい せんこう						

門	門	gate	l	厂	門	門	門	門	門	門	
		モン			先生のご専門は何ですか。						
					せんもん						

働	働	to work	イ	イ	仁	伯	俥	偅	偅	衝	働
		はたら(く) ドウ			会社で働いています。						
					はたら						

給	給	to supply	幺	幺	糸	糸	刹	糾	給	給	給
		キュウ			この仕事は給料が安いんですよ。						
					きゅうりょう						

申	申	to say (humble) もう（す）　シン	丨 丨 冂 冃 日 申	田中と申します。　申し込む 　　　もう　　　　　もう　こ
努	努	effort, endeavor, try つと（める）　ド	乀 夕 女 如 奴 妈 努	努力する。 どりょく
力	力	power, strength ちから　リキ・リョク	刀 力	力がある。　力が強い。　努力 ちから　　　ちから　　　どりょく
続	続	to continue つづ（ける）・つづ（く）　ゾク	乚 纟 纟 糸 糸 結 結 続 続	面接の手続きをする。　雨が続く。 めんせつ　てつづ　　　　　つづ
活	活	life, activity カツ	丶 冫 氵 汁 汗 活 活 活	生活が楽しい。　活動 せいかつ　　　かつどう
決	決	to decide き（める）　き（まる）　ケツ	丶 冫 氵 沪 沪 決 決	日本に行くことに決めました。 　　　　　　き
機	機	machine, opportunity キ	木 杉 杉 杉 機 機 機 機 機	動機は文化的な興味です。　機械工学　飛行機 どうき　　　　　　　　　きかいこうがく　　き
向	向	to face, to turn む（く）・む（かい）　コウ	′ 亻 冂 向 向 向	銀行の向かい側 　　む　がわ
存	存	to know (humble) ソン・ゾン	一 ナ 才 右 右 存	存じております。 ぞん

読めるようになった漢字

就職　面接　広い　広告　立派な　立つ　研究　研究室　専門　専攻　働く　給料
こう
申す　申し込む　申込用紙　努力する　力　続く　続ける　手続き　生活　活動
こ　　　こみ
決める　決まる　動機　飛行機　機械　向かい側　存じる　記入する　返事
かい　　　がわ
締め切り　今後
し

日本人の名前：本山　中村

練習

下の文を読んで下さい。

1. 最近就職活動をしていますが、毎日面接試験が続いて、とても忙しいです。
2. 木村さんの専門は何かご存じですか。
3. いい機会ですから、どこに留学するか決めたら、この申込用紙を持って来て下さい。
4. この仕事は給料が安すぎて生活できないので、もう働きたくありません。
5. 山田先生の研究室はとても広くて立派な部屋です。
6. もうすぐ飛行機に乗る時間だから、用事があるなら、早くして下さい。
7. 向かいの店の広告が新聞に出ていた。
8. 政治の仕事は人々の生活がよくなるように努力することです。

読む練習

仕事さがし　Job hunting

読む前に

下の質問に答えて下さい。

1. 求人広告 (help-wanted ads) にはどんなことが書いてあるか考えて下さい。
2. 求人広告にはどんな単語が使ってありますか。それを日本語では何と言いますか。知らない言葉を先生に聞いて下さい。

読んでみましょう

A. 下はジャパントラベルという会社の求人広告です。知らない単語がたくさんありますが、どういう意味か考えながら、質問に答えて下さい。

> ジャパントラベル
>
> 正社員・パート募集
> ・マーケティングアナリスト
> ・ツアーガイド
> 経験者、バイリンガル優遇
> 詳細は山本まで
> 電話 (03) 3331-1234
> ファックス (03) 3331-1235

1. ジャパントラベルは何の会社だと思いますか。
2. この会社は何が出来る人がほしいと思いますか。
3. この会社に就職したいと思う人は、だれに電話をしたらいいですか。

B. 下の二つの履歴書はジャパントラベルに来たものです。一人は日本人で、もう
   一人はアメリカ人です。二人の履歴書を見て、質問に答えて下さい。

1. 日本の履歴書にあって、アメリカの履歴書にないものがありますか。

2. アメリカの履歴書にあって、日本の履歴書にないものがありますか。

3. どんなことが日本の履歴書にもアメリカの履歴書にも書いてありますか。

4. この二人のどちらの方がジャパントラベルに就職できると思いますか。どうし
   てですか。

Jeff McGlone

Current Address
1-1- Kakomachi
Naka-ku, Hiroshima
Hiroshima 730-0812

phone: (082) 123-4567

Permanent address
316 Hamilton Street
Lafayette, Indiana 47906

phone: (765) 123-4567

Education

Bachelor of Arts in Japanese	
Purdue University	2012
Nanzan Exchange program	2010
Westside Senior High School	2008

Work Experience

Japanese Exchange and Teaching (JET) Program (worked as a JET assistant in Hiroshima)	2012–present

Certificates and Awards

Japanese Proficiency Test (Level 2)	2016

履　歴　書

平成 28 年　9 月　1 日 現在

ふりがな	さとう　　かずひろ		性別
氏　名	佐藤　和広　㊞		※　⦿男・女

生年月日　　平成 3 年　4 月　10 日生（満　25　才）

ふりがな	とうきょうと　おおたく　ちゅうおう	
現住所　〒　143-0024		
	東京都　大田区　中央 4-5-6	
TEL　（03）1234-5678	携帯電話　（090）1234-5678	
FAX	E-mail ksato@abc.efg.jp	

ふりがな		TEL
連絡先　〒	（現住所以外に連絡を希望する場合のみ記入） 方	

年	月	学歴・職歴など（項目別にまとめて記入）
平成 9	4	大田区立大森第三小学校　入学
平成 15	3	同校卒業
平成 15	4	大田区立大森第二中学校　入学
平成 18	3	同校卒業
平成 18	4	東京都立富士高等学校入学
平成 21	3	同校卒業
平成 21	4	早稲田大学商学部入学
平成 25	3	同校卒業
		職歴
平成 25	4	JR 東日本株式会社　入社
		賞罰
		なし

記入上の注意　　1．鉛筆以外の黒又は青の筆記具で記入。　　2．数字はアラビア数字で、文字はくずさず正確に書く。
　　　　　　　　3．※印のところは、該当するものを○で囲む。

年	月	免許・資格
平成 21	8	普通自動車免許
平成 23	6	英語検定一級合格

免許・資格に関する特記事項（取得に至った経緯・取得予定の資格など）

趣味	特技
旅行　スキー　テニス　スポーツ	英語

長所・短所	健康状態
	良好

志望動機

旅行・観光に関連した職種を希望

自己PR

通勤時間	扶養家族数	配偶者の有無	配偶者の扶養義務
約　　　分	人	※有・無	※有・無

本人希望記入欄（特に給料・職種・勤務時間・勤務地・その他についての希望などがあれば記入）

C. 下はマグローンさんの履歴書を日本語で書いたものです。これを見ながら
　　自分の履歴書_{りれき}を日本語で書いて下さい。

履 歴 書　　　　　　　　　平成 28 年 10 月 8 日 現在

ふりがな		
氏　名	マグローン　ジェフ	

生年月日　平成 2 年　　3 月　3 日生（満 26 才）　　※ ⑲ ・ 女

ふりがな　　ひろしまけん　ひろしまし　なかく　かこまち	電話
現住所　〒730-0812　　広島県広島市中区加古町 1-1	(082) 123-4567

ふりがな	電話
連絡先　〒　　　　　　　　　（現住所以外に連絡を希望する場合のみ記入）　316 Hamilton ST, Lafayette, Indiana 47906　　　　　　方	+1 (765) 123-4567

年	月	学 歴 ・ 職 歴　（項目別にまとめて記入）
平成 8	8	Hamilton Elementary School 入学
平成 13	5	同校卒業
平成 13	8	Hamilton Middle School 入学
平成 17	5	同校卒業
平成 17	8	Westside Senior High School 入学
平成 20	5	同校卒業
平成 20	8	パデュー大学入学
平成 22	8	南山大学交換留学プログラム参加
平成 23	5	同プログラム修了
平成 24	5	パデュー大学言語・文化学科　卒業
		職歴
平成 24	8	JET 日本語プログラム講師
		賞罰
		なし

記入上の注意　　1．鉛筆以外の黒又は青の筆記具で記入。　2．数字はアラビア数字で、文字はくずさず正確に書く。
　　　　　　　　3．※印のところは、該当するものを○で囲む。

年	月	免　許　・　資　格
平成 24	8	普通自動車免許
平成 26	12	日本語能力試験　一級取得

志望の動機、特技、好きな学科、アピールポイントなど	通勤時間
志望の動機：日本語が使える仕事につきたい 特技：日本語　コンピュータ 得意な学科：日本語 趣味：映画鑑賞　旅行	約　　　　時間　　　　分

通勤時間
約　　　時間　　　分

扶養家族（配偶者を除く） 　　　　　　　　人

配偶者	配偶者の扶養義務
※ 有 ・ 無	※ 有 ・ 無

本人希望記入欄（特に給料・職種・勤務時間・勤務地・その他についての希望などがあれば記入

D. Write a letter to your professor/instructor requesting a recommendation. Use the templates which follow.

Written requests

In general, this type of letter does not have to be long or overly polite, but the proper honorific language should be used. You should give ample time for a writer to finish the letter. One month will usually be sufficient. Since e-mail has become a convenient and common mode of communication, sending a request letter by e-mail is not considered rude.

The basic structure of a request letter along with some common phrasings is as follows:

① Opening

- ご無沙汰しておりますが、いかがお過ごしですか。
  It's been a while since we met, how have you been?

- いつもお世話になっております。
  I thank you for your assistance. (This is a common phrase when you are in constant contact with the person.)

② Reason for the request
- 来年卒業するので、就職活動をしています。
  I have begun job hunting since I am graduating next year.
- 日本で働きたいと思っております。
  I want to work in Japan.

③ Request
- 推薦状を書いていただけないでしょうか。
  すいせんじょう
  Would you mind writing a letter of recommendation?
- 先生に推薦状を書いていただきたいのですが、お願い
  すいせんじょう　　　　　　　　　　　　　　　　　　　ねが
  出来ませんでしょうか。
  I would very much like you to write a letter of recommendation. May I ask you to write one? (polite)

④ Closing:
- お忙しいところ、申し訳ありませんがよろしくお願いいたします。
  わけ　　　　　　　　　　　　　　ねが
  I am sorry to bother you at a busy time, but please assist me.

Sample request letter for a recommendation

山田先生

　いつもお世話になっております。私は来年卒業する予定ですので、就職活動を始めました。専攻は日本語とアジア研究ですから、日本語を使える仕事がしたいと考えております。新聞にジャパントラベルという日本の旅行会社の求人広告がありましたので、応募しようと思っております。そこで、先生に推薦状を書いていただきたいのですが、お願い出来ませんでしょうか。応募の締め切りは11月30日です。お忙しいところ、申し訳ありませんがよろしくお願いいたします。

ジェフ・マグローン

Students often forget to send a thank-you letter. You should inform the writer of the outcome of your application whether it is successful or not. The letter does not have to be long, but sending a letter is important and considered to be good manners. It ensures the continuation of your relationship with the writer so that you can feel more comfortable asking him/her to write another one if the occasion arises.

Thank-you letters

① Thanking
- この間は、お忙しいところ推薦状を書いて下さいまして、どうも
  すいせんじょう
  有り難うございました。
  I thank you very much for writing a letter of recommendation for me at a time when you were so busy.

② Reporting the result

Successful case
- おかげさまで就職出来ました。
  Because of your support, I was able to get the job.

Unsuccessful case

- 残念ながら、私の力不足で、就職は出来ませんでした。

  Regrettably, due to my lack of ability, I was not able to get the job.

③ Closing:

- 今後ともよろしくお願いいたします。

  I ask for your continued assistance.

Sample thank-you letter for a successful result

山田先生

　この間は、お忙しいところ推薦状を書いて下さいまして、どうも有り難うございました。<u>おかげさまで、ジャパントラベルに就職出来ることになりました。</u>会社の仕事は大変かもしれませんが、がんばろうと思っています。今後ともよろしくお願いいたします。本当に有り難うございました。

　ジェフ・マグローン

Sample thank-you letter for an unsuccessful result

山田先生

　この間は、お忙しいところ推薦状を書いて下さいまして、どうも有り難うございました。<u>残念ながら、私の力が足りず、就職することは出来ませんでした。せっかく先生に推薦状を書いていただいたのに、申し訳ありません。</u>またお願いすることもあるかと思います。今後ともよろしくお願いいたします。

　ジェフ・マグローン

総合練習

新しい仕事

1. Work with a group of four. Imagine that you are staff at a company and you need to hire someone, either for a full-time or a part-time position. Discuss what kind of company you work at and the position you wish to offer, and fill out the following chart. Then make a help wanted ad for the position and post it on the blackboard, along with a box or envelope to collect applications.

   Example:　A：どんな会社にしましょうか。

   　　　　　B：コンピュータの会社はどうですか。

   　　　　　C：おもしろそうですね。

   　　　　　D：私は、旅行会社はどうかと思うんですが。

   　　　　　A：それもよさそうですね。どうしましょうか。

会社について	
名前	
どんな会社か	
仕事について	
正社員 (*full time*) かパートか せいしゃいん	
どんな仕事か	
どんな人がやといたいか	
休み	
ボーナス (*bonus*)	
給料	

2. Using the forms provided by your instructor, each person in the class should now prepare a resume and make a few copies of it. Each person is looking for a job. Look at the ads on the blackboard, and apply for two jobs by placing your resume in the box provided by the companies. You are not allowed to apply for the job you have helped draft.

3. Go back to your original groups. Read the resumes and choose at least three candidates. Write a short message to invite them for an interview. Discuss with your group what questions need to be asked.

4. Interview the candidates. Take notes during each interview. After all interviews are completed, go back to your company group and negotiate with each other to decide who will get the job offer. Report to your instructor who has been selected and why you selected that person.

ロールプレイ

1. You are a secretary to the president of your company. He has several meetings today. Make a schedule and report to him using honorific forms.

2. Imagine that you are talking with a consultant at an employment agency. Tell the person your educational background, other qualifications, and what kinds of jobs you would like to do. Use polite expressions.

3. Your boss is assigned a project you are interested in, so you would like him/her to consider including you on the project team. Tell him/her why he/she should choose you. Use humble forms.

LIST OF PARTICLES

Particle	Meaning	Use	Text Reference
か	1. Question	ジョンさんはアメリカ人ですか。 *Are you an American, John?* 何時に寝ますか。 *What time do you go to bed?*	1-50
	2. Indirect question	どこでその人に会ったかおぼえていません。 *I don't remember where I met that person.* その人に会ったかどうかおぼえていません。 *I don't remember whether I met that person.*	2-188
が	1. Subject marker A subject is also marked by が in a noun-modifying clause or a subordinate clause with conjunctions such as とき, のに, ので, or から.	だれが来ますか。 *Who is coming?* 山田さんと中山さんが来ます。 *Yamada-san and Nakayama-san are coming.* 私が先週買った本はこれです。 *The book I bought last week is this one.*	1-103, 1-193, 1-448, 1-503
	2. Object with potential form When the verb is in the potential form, the direct object of the verb takes either が or を, except for できる, which takes only が.	にくが／を食べられます。 *I can eat meat.* テニスができます。 *I can play tennis.*	2-48
	3. but	こうちゃは好きですが、コーヒーはあまり好きじゃありません。 *I like black tea, but do not like coffee very much.*	1-272
から	from	日本語の授業は十時から十一時までです。 *The Japanese class is from 10 o'clock to 11 o'clock.*	1-190
しか	nothing/nobody/no~ but~ only ~ negative	ジョンは英語しか分かりません。 *John can only understand English.* これは日本でしか食べられません。 *You can't eat this anywhere but in Japan.*	2-382
だけ	only ~ affirmative	山田さんだけ（が）きました。 *Only Yamada-san came.* 山田さんにだけ話した。 *I told only Yamada-san.*	2-382

で	1. among ~	世界で一番高い山はヒマラヤです。 *The Himalayas are the highest mountains in the world.*	1-275
	2. at; in; on (Location of action)	図書館で勉強します。 *I study at the library.* 日本で日本語を勉強しました。 *I studied Japanese in Japan.*	1-101
	3. Means	バスで大学に行きます。 *I go to the university by bus.* 日本語で話して下さい。 *Please speak in Japanese.*	1-190
	4. Scope and limit	あと一週間で休みです。 *Vacation starts in a week.* そのみかんは五つで 300 円です。 *Those oranges are 300 yen for five.*	2-236
と	1. and	ニューヨークとシカゴで仕事をしました。 *I worked in New York and Chicago.*	1-222
	2. Name or quote	私は山田と申します。 *I am called Yamada.* 「タイタニック」という映画を見ました。 *I saw a movie called "Titanic."*	2-297, 2-514
に	1. to (Destination)	明日家に帰ります。 *I am going back home tomorrow.* 両親に手紙を書きました。 *I wrote a letter to my parents.*	1-100, 1-223
	2. Extent of action	一週間に一度映画を見ます。 *I watch a movie once a week.*	1-497
	3. at, in , on (Location of existence)	いすの上にねこがいます。 *There is a cat on the chair.* 山田さんはどこにいますか。 *Where is Yamada-san?*	1-142, 1-151
	4. Agent in a passive or caus- ative sentence (the agent is the doer of an action.)	私は先生にほめられました。 *I was praised by my teacher.* 上司は山田さんに東京へ行かせた。 *My boss made Yamada-san go to Tokyo.*	2-370, 2-421
	5. by, from (Source with receiving verb)	私は姉にゆびわをもらいました。 *I received a ring from my sister.* 田中さんは山田さんに花をもらいました。 *Tanaka-san received a flower from Yamada-san.* 弟は父にコンピュータを買ってもらった。 *My brother got my father to buy him a computer.* 私は先生に本を貸していただいた。 *I had the teacher lend me the book.*	2-418

	6. at, in, on (Time)	何時に起きますか。 *What time do you get up?* 日本語の授業は水曜日にあります。 *The Japanese class is held on Wednesday.*	1-106
	7. Purpose	本を読みに図書館に行きます。 *I go to the library to read books.*	1-224
ね	Seeking agreement	おすしはおいしいですね。 *Sushi is good, isn't it?*	1-95, 1-155
の	1. it is that ~ (casual speech) -- (This is a contracted form of 〜のです. It is often used by female speakers.)	どうして食べないの。 *Why are you not eating?* おなかがいたいの。 *It is because my stomach hurts.*	1-311
	2. ~ing, that ~ (Nominalizer)	私は本を読むのが好きです。 *I like reading books.* 日本語で映画を見るのはおもしろいです。 *Watching movies in Japanese is interesting.*	1-268
	3. of, 's, in, from	山田さんは私の友達です。 *Yamada-san is my friend.* 山田さんはイリノイ大学の学生です。 *Yamada-san is a student of University of Illinois.* これは山田さんのペンです。あれは私の (ペン) です。 *This is Yamada's pen. That is mine (my pen).*	1-53
	4. one (Pronoun). This の is classfied as a pronoun, not as a particle.	私は黒いのが好きです。 *I like the black one.* 去年買ったのはあまりよくありませんでした。 *The one I bought last year was not very good.*	2-518
は	topic and contrast marker	きのうは何も食べませんでした。 *I did not eat anything yesterday.* (topic) 東京は人が多い。 *There are a lot of people in Tokyo.* (topic) 新聞をよく読みますが、雑誌はあまり読みま せん。 *I often read newspaper, but I don't read magazines very often.* (contrast)	1-46, 1-116, 1-271
まで	until	きのう二時まで勉強しました。 *I studied until two o'clock yesterday.*	1-190
までに	by (Time limit)	明日までに宿題をします。 *I will do the homework by tomorrow.*	2-202

も	1. also	山田さんも文学部の学生です。 *Yamada-san is also a student in the school of liberal arts.* ディズニーランドはフロリダにあります。東京にもあります。 *Disneyland is in Florida. It is also in Tokyo.*	1-61, 1-193
	2. both ~ and ~ (Lack of preference)	東京も京都もおもしろい所です。 *Both Tokyo and Kyoto are interesting places.*	1-278
	3. as many as ~, not even one ~ (Emphasis on quantity)	ジョンはステーキを三まいも食べられる。 *John can eat as many as three steaks.* 日本に一度も行ったことがありません。 *I have not been to Japan even once. (I have never been to Japan.)*	2-525
	4. any ~ (question word + でも), no ~ (question word + も)	私は何でも食べられます。 *I can eat anything.* 病気で今は何も食べられません。 *Due to my sickness, I can eat nothing.*	2-342
や	~ and ~ and so on (Inexhaustive listing)	山田さんや田中さんがゴルフをしている。 *Yamada-san and Tanaka-san and others are playing golf.*	1-264
よ	Giving information	これはおいしいですよ。 *This is good, you know.*	1-42, 1-155
より	than	大阪の方が京都より大きいです。 *Osaka is bigger than Kyoto.*	1-276
を	1. Direct object	山田さんは水をたくさん飲みます。 *Yamada-san drinks a lot of water.* 七時にごはんを食べます。 *I eat at seven.*	1-99
	2. out of ~ , from (Point of detachment)	新宿で電車をおります。 *I get off the train at Shinjuku.* 朝七時に家を出ます。 *I leave home at seven in the morning.*	2-236
	3. in, on, across, through (Route)	私はこの道を通って、大学に行きます。 *I take this road to the university.* 公園を通ります。 *I go through the park.*	2-236

KANJI LIST

No.	Kanji	Ch.	Kun-reading	On-reading	Examples
1	大	1-4	おお(きい)	ダイ	大学生　大きいビル
2	学	1-4	まな(ぶ)	ガク・ガッ	学校　大学
3	校	1-4		コウ	学校
4	先	1-4	さき	セン	先生
5	生	1-4	なま・う(まれる)	セイ	学生　先生　一年生
6	山	1-5	やま	サン・ザン	山川さん　富士山　山の上
7	川	1-5	かわ・がわ	セン	小川さん　川中さん　ミシシッピ川
8	田	1-5	た・だ	デン	上田さん　田中さん
9	人	1-5	ひと	ジン・ニン	日本人　あの人
10	上	1-5	うえ・かみ・あ(がる)	ジョウ	テーブルの上　上がって下さい。
11	中	1-5	なか	チュウ	へやの中　中国
12	下	1-5	した・くだ(さい)	カ・ゲ	まどの下　いって下さい
13	小	1-5	ちい(さい)	ショウ	小さいへや
14	日	1-5	ひ・び	ニチ・ニ・ジツ・カ	日本　昨日　今日　明日
15	本	1-5	もと	ホン・ボン・ポン	山田さんの本　日本
16	今	1-6	いま	コン	今、何時ですか。今週　今日
17	私	1-6	わたし・わたくし	シ	私は日本人です。
18	月	1-6	つき	ゲツ・ガツ	月曜日
19	火	1-6	ひ	カ	火曜日
20	水	1-6	みず	スイ	水曜日
21	木	1-6	き	モク	大きい木　木曜日
22	金	1-6	かね	キン	金曜日
23	土	1-6	つち	ト・ド	土曜日
24	曜	1-6		ヨウ	月曜日　火曜日　水曜日　木曜日　金曜日　土曜日
25	何	1-6	なに・なん		何曜日　何ですか。何をしますか。
26	週	1-6		シュウ	今週の週末　先週
27	末	1-6	すえ	マツ	週末に何をしますか。
28	休	1-6	やす(む)	キュウ	休みの日に何をしますか。
29	時	1-7	とき	ジ	一時　二時半　五時間べんきょうします。その時　時計
30	間	1-7	あいだ	カン	時間がありません。
31	分	1-7	わ(ける)・わ(かる)	フン・ブン・プン	二十分　分かりました。
32	半	1-7		ハン	毎日六時半におきます。
33	毎	1-7		マイ	毎週シカゴにいきます。毎日　毎月
34	年	1-7	とし	ネン	三年生　毎年
35	好	1-7	す(き)	コウ	テニスが好きです。大好き
36	語	1-7	かた(る)	ゴ	日本語　フランス語ではなします。
37	高	1-7	たか(い)	コウ	古い高校　高い山
38	番	1-7		バン	やさいが一番好きです。

No.	Kanji	Ch.	Kun-reading	On-reading	Examples
39	方	1-7	かた	ホウ	サッカーの方がフットボールより好きです。
40	新	1-7	あたら(しい)	シン	新しいレストラン　新聞
41	古	1-7	ふる(い)	コ	カラオケで古いうたをうたいます。
42	安	1-7	やす(い)	アン	今日はやさいが安いです。
43	友	1-7	とも	ユウ	友達とかいものにいくのが好きです。
44	一	1-8	ひと(つ)	イチ	一つ　一本　いぬが一匹います。
45	二	1-8	ふた(つ)	ニ	りんごが二つあります。二さつ　二本
46	三	1-8	みっ(つ)	サン	けしゴムを三つ買いました。三本
47	四	1-8	よ・よん・よっ(つ)	シ	四つ　四時　ビールが四本あります。
48	五	1-8	いつ(つ)	ゴ	五つ　ベルトが五本あります。
49	六	1-8	むっ(つ)	ロク・ロッ	六つ　六時　えんぴつが六本あります。
50	七	1-8	なな(つ)	シチ	七時　七本　オレンジが七つあります。
51	八	1-8	やっ(つ)	ハチ・ハッ	八つ　八時　ペンが八本あります。
52	九	1-8	ここの(つ)	キュウ・ク	九つ　九時　バナナが九本あります。
53	十	1-8	とお	ジュウ・ジュッ	ぼうしが十あります。十本　十時
54	百	1-8		ヒャク・ビャク・ピャク	二百　三百　六百
55	千	1-8		セン・ゼン	二千　三千　八千　千円
56	万	1-8		マン	一万円　百万円
57	円	1-8		エン	五十円　このセーターは七千八百円です。
58	店	1-8	みせ	テン	大きい店　店の人　喫茶店
59	行	1-9	い(く)	コウ	来年日本に行きます。銀行
60	来	1-9	く(る)	ライ	いつアメリカに来ますか。来週は来ない
61	帰	1-9	かえ(る)	キ	たいてい七時にうちに帰ります。
62	食	1-9	た(べる)	ショク	あさごはんを食べてください。学食
63	飲	1-9	の(む)	イン	ビールを二本飲みました。
64	見	1-9	み(る)	ケン	えいがを見に行きませんか。
65	聞	1-9	き(く)	ブン	インターネットでラジオを聞く　新聞
66	読	1-9	よ(む)	ドク	本を読むのが好きです。
67	書	1-9	か(く)	ショ	てがみをあまり書きません。図書館　辞書
68	話	1-9	はな(す)	ワ	友達と電話で話すのが好きです。会話
69	出	1-9	で(る)・で(かける)・だ(す)	シュツ	出かけます。
70	会	1-9	あ(う)	カイ	人と会って、カフェで話します。会話 学生会館
71	買	1-9	か(う)	バイ	買い物が好きです。
72	起	1-9	お(きる)	キ	毎朝六時に起きます。
73	寝	1-9	ね(る)	シン	十二時ごろ寝ます。
74	作	1-9	つく(る)	サク	ばんごはんはカレーを作りましょう。
75	入	1-9	はい(る)・い(れる)	ニュウ	はこに入れます。店に入ります。

No.	Kanji	Ch.	Kun-reading	On-reading	Examples
76	男	1-10	おとこ	ダン	女の人と男の子がいます。
77	女	1-10	おんな	ジョ	山本さんは帽子をかぶった女の人です。
78	目	1-10	め	モク	目がわるいです。上から二番目です。
79	口	1-10	くち・ぐち	コウ	口が小さいです。川口
80	耳	1-10	みみ	ジ	私は耳があまりよくありません。
81	足	1-10	あし	ソク	ジョンはせが高くて、足がながいです。
82	手	1-10	て	シュ	手がきれいですね。テニスが上手です。
83	父	1-10	ちち・とう	フ	父のなまえはジョンです。お父さん
84	母	1-10	はは・かあ	ボ・モ	母のしごとは高校の先生です。お母さん
85	姉	1-10	あね・ねえ	シ	姉は私より三さい上です。お姉さん
86	兄	1-10	あに・にい	ケイ・キョウ	兄が一人います。お兄さん　兄弟
87	妹	1-10	いもうと	マイ	妹はいません。
88	弟	1-10	おとうと	ダイ	弟は四時にアルバイトに行きます。兄弟
89	家	1-10	いえ・(うち)	カ	父は七時ごろ家に帰ります。新しい家
90	族	1-10		ゾク	私の家は四人家族です。
91	両	1-10		リョウ	両親はニューヨークにすんでいます。
92	親	1-10	おや	シン	両親はアメリカが好きです。親切な人
93	子	1-10	こ	シ	男の子が三人います。母のなまえは 「よし子」です。
94	天	1-11		テン	明日の天気はいいでしょう。
95	気	1-11		キ	昨日は天気がよくありませんでした。元気
96	雨	1-11	あめ	ウ	雨がしずかにふっています。
97	雪	1-11	ゆき	セツ	明日は大雪です。
98	風	1-11	かぜ	フウ	風がつよいです。台風が来ます。
99	晴	1-11	は(れる)	セイ	ずっと晴れていて、雨がふりません。
100	温	1-11	あたた(かい)	オン	先週は気温が35度まで上がりました。
101	度	1-11		ド	おふろの温度は42度ぐらいです。
102	東	1-11	ひがし	トウ	まちの東の方にこうえんがあります。
103	西	1-11	にし	セイ	きょうとは東京の西にあります。
104	南	1-11	みなみ	ナン	南のうみはとてもきれいで温かいです。
105	北	1-11	きた	ホク	ほっかいどうは日本の北の方にあります。
106	寒	1-11	さむ(い)	カン	カナダのふゆは寒いです。
107	暑	1-11	あつ(い)	ショ	東京のなつはむし暑いです。
108	多	1-11	おお(い)	タ	シンガポールは雨が多いです。
109	少	1-11	すく(ない)・すこ(し)	ショウ	このまちは人が少ないです。
110	冷	1-11	つめ(たい)	レイ	暑いから冷たいものを飲みましょう。
111	春	1-12	はる	シュン	春は雨が多いです。春休み
112	夏	1-12	なつ	カ	日本の夏は暑いです。夏休み
113	秋	1-12	あき	シュウ	秋の山はとてもきれいです。
114	冬	1-12	ふゆ	トウ	冬は寒いから、時々雪がふります。冬休み
115	朝	1-12	あさ	チョウ	日曜日の朝、おそくまで寝るのが好きです。今朝
116	昼	1-12	ひる	チュウ	母が昼御飯を作りました。
117	晩	1-12		バン	明日の晩御飯は天ぷらです。今晩

No.	Kanji	Ch.	Kun-reading	On-reading	Examples
118	午	1-12		ゴ	午前　月曜日の午後、両親と家族が来ます。
119	前	1-12	まえ	ゼン	午前九時ごろに電話をかけます。中学の前　名前
120	後	1-12	あと・うし(ろ)・のち	ゴ	午後は暑かったです。一か月ぐらい後　つくえの後ろ
121	去	1-12	さ(る)	キョ	去年、南アメリカに行きました。
122	昨	1-12		サク	一昨年日本に行きました。昨日
123	供	1-12	とも・ども	キョウ	子供が二人います。
124	元	1-12	もと	ゲン	父は元気です。元気なお母さん
125	思	1-12	おも(う)	シ	昨日の朝は風がつよかったと思います。
126	明	1-12	あか(るい)	メイ	明るいへや　明日　明るい人
127	回	1-12	まわ(る)	カイ	私の弟は一か月に十回ぐらいラーメンを食べます。

No.	Kanji	Ch.	Kun-reading	On-reading	Examples
1	病	2-1	やま(い)	ビョウ	病気になる。病院に行く。
2	院	2-1		イン	入院する。大学院生
3	医	2-1		イ	医者になる。
4	者	2-1	もの	シャ	今日は歯医者に行きます。
5	体	2-1	からだ	タイ・テイ	体が大きい。体をうごかす。
6	歯	2-1	は	シ	歯が痛い。歯医者に行く。
7	変	2-1	か(わる)	ヘン	大変です。
8	熱	2-1	あつ(い)	ネツ	熱がある。熱いコーヒー
9	薬	2-1	くすり	ヤク	これはいい薬です。
10	顔	2-1	かお	ガン	顔色がわるい。
11	色	2-1	いろ	ショク・シキ	顔の色がくろい。色々な人
12	指	2-1	ゆび	シ	指がながいですね。親指は *thumb* です。
13	切	2-1	き(る)	セツ	あっ、痛い、指を切った。親切な人
14	歩	2-1	ある(く)	ホ	家まで歩いて帰る。公園を散歩する。
15	走	2-1	はし(る)	ソウ	毎日10キロ走っています。
16	勉	2-1	つと(める)	ベン	日本語を勉強する。
17	強	2-1	つよ(い)	キョウ	この薬は強いです。勉強はたのしい。
18	忘	2-1	わす(れる)	ボウ	走って、ストレスを忘れます。
19	早	2-1	はや(い)	ソウ	朝早く起きる。
20	持	2-1	も(つ)	ジ	指を切ったので、かばんが持てません。気持ち
21	痛	2-1	いた(い)	ツウ	昨日走りすぎて、足が痛い。
22	頭	2-1	あたま	ズ	頭が痛い。山田さんは頭がいい。
23	横	2-1	よこ	オウ	テーブルの横
24	海	2-2	うみ	カイ	海が好きです。海外旅行　北海道
25	外	2-2	そと	ガイ	家の外　外国人
26	国	2-2	くに	コク・ゴク	小さい国　中国　国内　韓国
27	旅	2-2	たび	リョ	旅行が好きです。
28	館	2-2		カン	旅館　図書館　学生会館
29	予	2-2	あらかじ(め)	ヨ	予定があります。ホテルの予約
30	定	2-2	さだ(める)	テイ	明日は病院に行く予定です。
31	約	2-2		ヤク	旅館を予約した。
32	計	2-2	はか(る)	ケイ	旅行の計画をたてる。高い時計ですね。
33	画	2-2	カク	ガ	来年の計画はまだありません。映画
34	荷	2-2		ニ・カ	大きい荷物を持って行く。
35	物	2-2	もの	ブツ・モツ	荷物　食べ物　飲み物　動物園　買い物
36	答	2-2	こた(える)	トウ	しつもんに答える。
37	知	2-2	し(る)	チ	名前を知っています。知らない人
38	泊	2-2	と(まる)	ハク・パク	二泊三日の旅行　ホテルに泊まる。
39	乗	2-2	の(る)	ジョウ	でんしゃに乗る。ふねに乗る。
40	着	2-2	つ(く)・き(る)	チャク	日本に着く。シャツを着る。
41	名	2-2	な	メイ・ミョウ	お名前は何ですか。有名なばしょ
42	空	2-2	そら	クウ	成田空港に行きます。空がきれいです。

No.	Kanji	Ch.	Kun-reading	On-reading	Examples
43	港	2-2	みなと	コウ	羽田空港はべんりです。港 に着く。
44	森	2-2	もり	シン	これは森田先生の荷物です。
45	林	2-2	はやし	リン	林さんは旅館に泊まりました。
46	々	2-2	N/A	N/A	色々な人　時々
47	言	2-3	い(う)・こと	ゲン・ゴン	もう一度言って下さい。言葉
48	葉	2-3	は	ヨウ	韓国の言葉は日本語と違います。
49	漢	2-3		カン	中西さんは漢字がたくさん書けます。
50	字	2-3		ジ	漢字を読むのは大変です。
51	質	2-3		シツ・シチ・チ	旅行の計画について質問する。
52	問	2-3	と(う)・と(い)	モン	漢字の質問はありますか。
53	卒	2-3		ソツ	大学を来年の五月に卒業する予定です。
54	業	2-3	わざ	ギョウ・ゴウ	大学の卒業式　日本語の授業
55	授	2-3	さず(ける)	ジュ	授業を三つとっています。
56	仕	2-3	つか(える)	シ・ジ	新しい仕事を中国ではじめる。
57	事	2-3	こと	ジ	来年の仕事　大事なテストがある。食事に行く。
58	結	2-3	むす(ぶ)	ケツ・ケッ	来年、結婚する。
59	婚	2-3		コン	結婚式の予約をとりました。
60	式	2-3		シキ	友達の卒業式に行く。
61	社	2-3	やしろ	シャ	会社の社長の仕事は大変です。会社員　神社
62	同	2-3	おな(じ)	ドウ	同じ本を読んだ。高校の同窓会がある。
63	違	2-3	ちが(う)・ちが(い)	イ	答えが間違っている。毎日天気が違う。
64	留	2-3	と(める)・と(まる)	リュウ・ル	留学生センター　日本に留学する。
65	達	2-3		タツ・ダチ	昨日、子供の時の友達と会った。
66	電	2-3		デン	携帯電話の番号を知りません。電気をつける。電車
67	英	2-3		エイ	会社の仕事は英語でしています。
68	客	2-3		キャク	お客さんがたくさん来ました。
69	残	2-3	のこ(る)・のこ(す)	ザン	仕事が残っています。残念
70	郵	2-4		ユウ	この葉書に郵便番号を書いて下さい。
71	便	2-4	たよ(り)	ベン・ビン	郵便ポスト　宅配便　便利な
72	局	2-4		キョク	郵便局に行きます。
73	銀	2-4		ギン	銀行に行きます。きれいな銀のネックレスですね。
74	送	2-4	おく(る)	ソウ	メールを送る。送別会
75	紙	2-4	かみ	シ	手紙を書きます。コピー用紙を下さい。
76	住	2-4	す(む)	ジュウ	東京に住んでいます。住所が分かりません。
77	所	2-4	ところ	ショ	住む所がない人をホームレスといいます。
78	引	2-4	ひ(く)	イン	銀行からお金を引き出す。
79	練	2-4	ね(る)	レン	会話の練習をする。
80	習	2-4	なら(う)	シュウ	テニスを練習する。
81	宿	2-4	やど	シュク	宿題を出すのを忘れてしまった。
82	題	2-4		ダイ	今晩、宿題をしなければなりませんか。
83	試	2-4	こころ(みる)・ため(す)	シ	日本の入学試験は二月にあります。
84	験	2-4		ケン	明日の日本語の会話試験は大変です。

No.	Kanji	Ch.	Kun-reading	On-reading	Examples
85	受	2-4	う(ける)	ジュ	試験を受ける。受験する。
86	教	2-4	おし(える)	キョウ	作り方を教えて下さい。教科書　教室
87	文	2-4	ふみ	ブン・モン	作文　文法　文房具　文学
88	法	2-4		ホウ	この文法の使い方を教えて下さい。
89	意	2-4		イ	言葉の意味が分かりません。
90	味	2-4	あじ	ミ	この文の意味を説明して下さい。
91	取	2-4	と(る)	シュ	日本語の授業を取りたいと思っています。
92	用	2-4	もち(いる)	ヨウ	用事があります。用紙
93	場	2-5	ば	ジョウ	駐車場　売り場　場所　会場
94	寺	2-5	てら	ジ	大きいお寺　東大寺　清水寺
95	橋	2-5	はし	キョウ	橋をわたります。橋本さん　大橋さん
96	町	2-5	まち	チョウ	大きい町に住んでいます。
97	映	2-5	うつ(る)・うつ(す)	エイ	映画　映画館
98	公	2-5	おおやけ	コウ	公園
99	園	2-5	その	エン	動物園じゃなくて遊園地に行きたい。
100	図	2-5	はか(る)	ズ・ト	図書館の近くの地図をみる。
101	地	2-5		チ・ジ	デパートの地下　地下鉄の地図
102	鉄	2-5		テツ	地下鉄
103	駅	2-5		エキ	地下鉄の駅　電車の駅
104	育	2-5	そだ(てる)・そだ(つ)	イク	体育館であそぶ。
105	道	2-5	みち	ドウ	道なり　横断歩道を歩く　道路
106	部	2-5		ブ	部屋　全部で学部は十あります。
107	屋	2-5		ヤ・オク	駅のそばの本屋　私の部屋はきれいです。
108	車	2-5	くるま	シャ	車　自転車　電車　各駅停車
109	右	2-5	みぎ	ウ	道の右側　右手　右足
110	左	2-5	ひだり	サ	駅の左側　左耳
111	近	2-5	ちか(い)	キン	大学の近く　最近　遊園地に近い
112	遠	2-5	とお(い)	エン	公園から遠い。
113	通	2-5	とお(る)	ツウ	小さい町を通って行きました。普通
114	飛	2-5	と(ぶ)	ヒ	飛行機で行きます。
115	京	2-5		キョウ・ケイ	東京駅　京都行きの電車　京成線
116	犬	2-6	いぬ	ケン	家に犬がいます。かわいい子犬です。
117	花	2-6	はな	カ	母の日の花はカーネーションです。生け花
118	形	2-6	かたち	ケイ・ギョウ	日本人形
119	服	2-6		フク	洋服　紳士服　婦人服
120	辞	2-6	や(める)	ジ	お礼に辞書をあげました。
121	礼	2-6		レイ	お礼にと思いまして。
122	祝	2-6	いわ(う)	シュク	これはお祝いです。
123	誕	2-6		タン	誕生日のお祝い
124	自	2-6	みずか(ら)	ジ・シ	自転車　自分　自由な生活　自己PRをする。
125	転	2-6	ころ(がる)・ころ(ぶ)	テン	自転車に乗る。
126	運	2-6	はこ(ぶ)	ウン	毎日運動します。運転免許証

No.	Kanji	Ch.	Kun-reading	On-reading	Examples
127	動	2-6	うご(く)	ドウ	手の運動　動物園　足が動かない。
128	使	2-6	つか(う)	シ	大使館　気を使う。車を使う。
129	写	2-6	うつ(す)	シャ	古い写真がたくさんあります。
130	真	2-6	ま	シン	写真　真っすぐ　真ん中
131	絵	2-6		エ・カイ	ピカソの絵を買いました。
132	雑	2-6		ザツ	これは日本の雑誌みたいですね。
133	誌	2-6		シ	この雑誌はおもしろいですよ。
134	音	2-6	おと	オン	日本の音楽
135	楽	2-6	たの(しむ)	ガク・ラク	音楽は楽しいです。
136	世	2-6		セ・セイ	お世話になります。
137	石	2-6	いし	セキ	石田さん　石川さん　川の石
138	説	2-6		セツ	小説　説明する
139	料	2-7		リョウ	日本料理を作る。料理の材料　授業料
140	理	2-7		リ	フランス料理が好きです。無理です。
141	飯	2-7	めし	ハン	ご飯を食べる。炊飯器　朝御飯　昼御飯
142	野	2-7	の	ヤ	野球が好きです。野菜を食べます。
143	菜	2-7		サイ	この野菜サラダはおいしいです。
144	果	2-7	くだ	カ	果物を食べる。結果
145	魚	2-7	さかな	ギョ	魚をつる。魚料理
146	鳥	2-7	とり	チョウ	木に鳥が止まっています。
147	肉	2-7	にく		肉を食べる。肉料理
148	油	2-7	あぶら	ユ	サラダ油　石油　油を足す。
149	止	2-7	と(まる)・や(める)	シ	車が止まる。タバコを止める。
150	始	2-7	はじ(まる・める)	シ	まず始めに　学校が始まる。
151	終	2-7	お(わる)・お(える)	シュウ	宿題が終わる。
152	洗	2-7	あら(う)	セン	手を洗う。洗濯をする。
153	悪	2-7	わる(い)	アク	つごうが悪い。
154	黒	2-7	くろ(い)	コク	黒い犬がいます。黒板に書いて下さい。
155	白	2-7	しろ(い)	ハク	白いねこ　雪は白いです。
156	青	2-7	あお(い)	セイ	青い海　空が青い。
157	赤	2-7	あか(い)	セキ	赤いりんご
158	茶	2-7		チャ・サ	茶色いかばん　お茶を飲む。喫茶店
159	短	2-7	みじか(い)	タン	このスカートは短いです。
160	長	2-7	なが(い)	チョウ	長い　会社の社長
161	焼	2-7	や(く)・や(ける)	ショウ	ケーキを焼く。火事で家が焼ける。
162	心	2-8	こころ	シン	母の病気のことが心配です。
163	配	2-8	くば(る)	ハイ・パイ	心配しないで下さい。
164	困	2-8	こま(る)	コン	となりの人がうるさくて困っています。
165	難	2-8	むずか(しい)	ナン	説明が難しかった。
166	弱	2-8	よわ(い)	ジャク	体が弱い。
167	招	2-8	まね(く)	ショウ	食事に招待されました。
168	待	2-8	ま(つ)	タイ	パーティに招待されました。待って下さい。

No.	Kanji	Ch.	Kun-reading	On-reading	Examples
169	呼	2-8	よ(ぶ)	コ	タクシーを呼んで下さい。
170	遊	2-8	あそ(ぶ)	ユウ	友達と遊園地で遊びました。
171	泳	2-8	およ(ぐ)	エイ	魚みたいに泳ぎます。
172	建	2-8	たて(る)・た(つ)	ケン・コン	建物　建設
173	経	2-8		ケイ・キョウ	日本の経済　経済学　経験
174	売	2-8	う(る)	バイ	ネットでギターを売りました。
175	交	2-8	まじ(わる)	コウ	交通事故にあう。
176	落	2-8	お(ちる)・お(とす)	ラク	試験に落ちました。
177	暗	2-8	くら(い)	アン	暗いから気をつけて下さい。
178	洪	2-8		コウ	洪水
179	利	2-8		リ	電車を利用する。便利
180	全	2-8	まった(く)	ゼン	全然悪くありません。全部　安全
181	急	2-8	いそ(ぐ)	キュウ	急に家に帰った。急行　特急
182	故	2-8		コ	交通事故
183	台	2-8		ダイ・タイ	車が三台ある。台風
184	不	2-8		フ	ここは不便です。
185	笑	2-9	わら(う)	ショウ	友達に笑われました。
186	泣	2-9	な(く)	キュウ	子どもに泣かれて、困りました。
187	助	2-9	たす(かる)・たす(ける)	ジョ	とても助かります。
188	考	2-9	かんが(える)	コウ	よく考えてから、話す。
189	払	2-9	はら(う)	フツ	レストランでお金を払わなかった。
190	化	2-9	ば(ける)	カ	日本の文化　インド文化
191	調	2-9	しら(べる)	チョウ	図書館で調べる。
192	集	2-9	あつ(める)・あつ(まる)	シュウ	九時に集まって下さい。
193	的	2-9	まと	テキ	日本的な建物
194	失	2-9		シツ	失礼します。
195	当	2-9	あ(たる)	トウ	本当ですか。
196	期	2-9		キ	秋学期と春学期　期末試験
197	和	2-9		ワ	和食　平和　和風
198	重	2-9	おも(い)	ジュウ	重い荷物
199	界	2-9		カイ	世界で一番高い山　世界旅行
200	正	2-9	ただ(しい)	セイ・ショウ	正しい答えは何ですか。正座　正月
201	由	2-9		ユウ	理由がわかりません。自由
202	宗	2-9		シュウ・ソウ	宗教
203	治	2-9	おさ(める)・なお(す)	ジ・チ	病気を治す。政治
204	次	2-9	つぎ	ジ	次の問題は難しいです。
205	有	2-9	あ(る)	ユウ	有名な先生です。有り難う
206	最	2-9	もっと(も)	サイ	最近
207	興	2-9	おこ(す)	キョウ・コウ	日本の文化に興味があります。
208	相	2-10	あい	ソウ	先生に相談する。相手
209	談	2-10		ダン	いつでも相談して下さい。
210	貸	2-10	か(す)	タイ	本を貸して下さい。
211	借	2-10	か(りる)	シャク	辞書を借りてもいいですか。

No.	Kanji	Ch.	Kun-reading	On-reading	Examples
212	返	2-10	かえ(す)	ヘン	借りた本を明日返します。
213	開	2-10	ひら(く) あ(く)・あ(ける)	カイ	まどを開ける。ドアが開く。
214	閉	2-10	し(める)・し(まる)	ヘイ	ドアを閉める。店が閉まる。
215	伝	2-10	つた(える)	デン	勉強を手伝う。
216	覚	2-10	おぼ(える)・さ(める)	カク	名前を覚える。
217	歌	2-10	うた(う)	カ	歌を歌う。
218	声	2-10	こえ	セイ	大きい声で歌う。
219	静	2-10	しず(か)	セイ	先生の家がある所はとても静かです。
220	夜	2-10	よる	ヤ	夜は寒くなりますよ。
221	直	2-10	なお(す)	チョク・ジキ	コンピュータを直せます。正直な人
222	置	2-10	お(く)	チ	つくえの上に置いて下さい。
223	記	2-10		キ	ここに名前を記入して下さい。日記
224	注	2-10	そそ(ぐ)	チュウ	ラーメンを注文する。注意
225	句	2-10		ク	あまり文句を言わないで下さい。
226	合	2-10	あ(う)	ゴウ	知り合いの赤ちゃん　服が合わない。 都合が悪い
227	忙	2-10	いそが(しい)	ボウ	試験があるので、とても忙しい。
228	然	2-10		ゼン・ネン	病気が全然よくならない。自然
229	号	2-10		ゴウ	郵便番号　けいたいの番号　のぞみ16号
230	村	2-10	むら	ソン	木村さん　小さい村がある。
231	就	2-11		シュウ	来年就職することにしました。
232	職	2-11		ショク	日本で就職が決まりました。
233	面	2-11	おもて	メン	明日仕事の面接があります。
234	接	2-11		セツ・セッ	面接は九時からです。
235	広	2-11	ひろ(い)	コウ	広い家ですね。広い公園　広告
236	告	2-11	つ(げる)	コク	広告会社に就職したいです。
237	立	2-11	た(てる)・た(つ)	リツ・リッ	立って下さい。立派なホテル
238	派	2-11		ハ・パ	立派な病院ですね。
239	研	2-11		ケン	日本語を研究しています。
240	究	2-11		キュウ	研究は楽しいです。
241	室	2-11		シツ	先生の研究室はどちらですか。
242	専	2-11		セン	専門は経済学です。専攻はビジネスです。
243	門	2-11		モン	先生のご専門は何ですか。
244	働	2-11	はたら(く)	ドウ	会社で働いています。
245	給	2-11		キュウ	この仕事は給料が安いんですよ。
246	申	2-11	もう(す)	シン	田中と申します。申し込む
247	努	2-11	つと(める)	ド	努力する。
248	力	2-11	ちから	リキ・リョク	力がある。力が強い。努力
249	続	2-11	つづ(ける)・つづ(く)	ゾク	面接の手続きをする。雨が続く。
250	活	2-11		カツ	生活が楽しい。活動
251	決	2-11	き(める)・き(まる)	ケツ	日本に行くことに決めました。
252	機	2-11		キ	動機は文化的な興味です。機械工学　飛行機
253	向	2-11	む(く)・む(かい)	コウ	銀行の向かい側
254	存	2-11		ソン・ゾン	存じております。

JAPANESE-ENGLISH GLOSSARY

This glossary contains all Japanese words that appear in the main vocabulary list for each chapter in both *Nakama 1* and 2. They are listed according to *gojuuon-jun* (Japanese alphabetical order). Each entry follows this format: word written in **kana**, word written in **kanji**, part of speech, English translation, Nakama book number, and *chapter number* where the word first appears. In general, notations are identical to the labels used in each chapter's vocabulary list.

adv.	adverb	*conj.*	conjunction	*q. word*	question word
い*-adj.*	い-adjective	*inter.*	interjection	*pref.*	prefix
な*-adj.*	な-adjective	*count.*	counter	*suf.*	suffix
う*-v.*	う-verb	*n.*	noun	*part.*	particle
る*-v.*	る-verb	*exp.*	expression	*cop. v.*	copula verb
irr. v.	irregular verb	*demo.*	demonstrative	*number*	number

A - あ

ATM　*n.* automatic teller machine 2-*4*

CD/DVD うりば (CD/DVD 売り場)　*n.* CD/DVD section 1-*8*

DVD(ディーヴィーディー)　*n.* DVD 2-*6*

J R　*n.* Japan Railway, pronounced as ジェイアール . Formerly government owned but now privatized railway system 2-*5*

T シャツ　*n.* T-shirt 1-*8*

あいさつ (挨拶)　*n.* greeting, ～にあいさつ (を) する to greet with (someone) ～ . 2-*9*

アイスクリーム　*n.* ice cream 1-*9*

あいだ (間)　*n.* between 2-*5*

あいて (相手)　*n.* companion, conversation partner, the other party 2-*10*

あいます (会います)　う *-v.* (to) meet. The dictionary form is あう . 1-*6*

あう (遭う・遇う)　う *-v.* to encounter 2-*8*

あおい (青い)　い *-adj.* blue 1-*4*

あかい (赤い)　い *-adj.* red 1-*4*

あかちゃん (赤ちゃん)　*n.* baby 2-*10*

あがってください (上がって下さい)　*exp.* Please come in. 1-*5*

あがる (上がる)　う *-v.* to rise; to go up 1-*11*

あかるい (明るい)　い *-adj.* bright 1-*5*

あかるい (明るい)　い *-adj.* cheerful 1-*10*

あき (秋)　*n.* fall, autumn 1-*11*

あく (開く)　う *-v.* (for something) to open 2-*3*

アクセサリー　*n.* accessories 1-*8*

アクセサリーうりば (アクセサリー売り場)　*n.* accessories department 1-*8*

あけましておめでとうございます。(明けましておめでとうございます。)　*exp.* Happy New Year! 1-*12*

あける (開ける)　る *-v.* to open 2-*1*

あける (開ける)　る *-v.* to open (something) 2-*3*

あげる (上げる)　る *-v.* to raise (something) c.f. あがる to rise 2-*1*

あげる　る *-v.* to give (to a socially equal person) 2-*6*

あげる (揚げる)　る *-v.* to deep-fry 2-*7*

あさ (朝)　*n.* morning 1-*3*

あさごはん (朝御飯)　*n.* breakfast 1-*3*

あさって (明後日)　*n.* the day after tomorrow 1-*3*

あし (足)　*n.* leg, foot 1-*10*

あじ (味)　*n.* taste 2-*7*

アジアけんきゅう (アジア研究)　*n.* Asian studies 1-*2*

あした (明日)　*n.* tomorrow 1-*3*

あそこ　*demo.* over there; that place (far away from both speaker and listener) 1-*4*

あそびます (遊びます)　う *-v.* (to) play. The dictionary form is あそぶ . 1-*6*

あたたかい (温かい)　い *-adj.* warm 1-*9*

あたたかい (暖かい／温かい) い -*adj.* warm, 暖かい (air temperature) 温かい (other objects such as water, food, heart, etc.) 1-*11*

あたためる (温める) る -*v.* to heat up 2-*7*

あたま (頭) *n.* head, あたまがいい smart, intelligent 1-*10*

あたらしい (新しい) い -*adj.* new 1-*4*

あつい (熱い) い -*adj.* hot 1-*9*

あつい (暑い／熱い) い -*adj.* hot, 暑い (air temperature) 熱い (other objects such as water, food, heart, etc.) 1-*11*

あつまる (集まる) う -*v.* to get together, to gather, (in one place) にあつまる 2-*3*

あつめる (集める) る -*v.* to collect (something/someone), to gather together 2-*3*

アドバイス *n.* advice, アドバイスをする to advise 2-*9*

あに (兄) *n.* older brother (the speaker's) 1-*10*

アニメ *n.* animation 2-*9*

あね (姉) *n.* older sister (the speaker's) 1-*10*

あの *demo.* that [+noun] over there 1-*5*

あのう *inter.* uh, well... 1-*2*

アパート *n.* apartment 1-*4*

あびます (浴びます) る -*v.* (to) take (a shower), シャワーをあびます take a shower. The dictionary form is あびる . 1-*3*

あぶら (油 (oil) ／脂 (fat)) *n.* oil, あぶらがおおい fatty, oily 1-*9*

あまい (甘い) い -*adj.* sweet 1-*9*

あまり *adv.* not very often (used with negative verb forms) 1-*3*

あまりきをつかわないで下さい。(あまり気を使わないで下さい。) *exp.* Please don't put yourself out for me. 2-*6*

あめ (雨) *n.* rain 1-*11*

アメリカ *n.* America; the United States 1-*2*

あやまる (謝る) う -*v.* to apologize 2-*9*

あらう (洗う) う -*v.* to wash 2-*7*

ありがとうございます。 *exp.* Thank you. 1-*1*

ありがとう。たすかります。(有り難う。助かります。) *exp.* Thank you. That helps me a lot. 2-*4*

あります う -*v.* (to) be held, (to) have. The dictionary form is ある . 1-*3*

あるいて (歩いて) *exp.* on foot 1-*5*

あるきます (歩きます) う -*v.* (to) walk, 〜まであるきます (to) walk up to 〜 . The dictionary form is あるく . 1-*6*

アルバイト *n.* part time job 1-*6*

あれ *demo.* that object over there; that 1-*4*

あれはにほんごでなんといいますか。 *exp.* What do you call that (over there) in Japanese? How do you say that (over there) in Japanese? (cf p29) 1-*1*

アレルギー *n.* allergy 2-*1*

あんしん (安心) *n.* a sense of relief, あんしんする to feel relieved 2-*8*

あんぜん (な)(安全 (な)) な -*adj.* safe 2-*8*

い

いい い -*adj.* good 1-*4*

いいえ *inter.* no, don't mention it, you're welcome 1-*2*

いいえ、そうじゃありません／そうじゃないです。 *exp.* No, that's not so. 1-*2*

いいえ、そんなことはありません。 *exp.* No, that's not the case. 1-*10*

いいえ、ちがいます (よ)。(いいえ、違います (よ)。) *exp.* No, you have the wrong number (literally: No, it's not correct.) 2-*2*

いいえ、どうぞおかまいなく。 *exp.* Please do not bother/worry about it. 1-*9*

いいえ、まだまだです。 *exp.* No, I still have a long way to go. 1-*10*

いいえ、わかりません。 *exp.* No, I don't understand (it). 1-*1*

いいかげんにしてよ。(いい加減にしてよ。) *exp.* Give me a break! (female speech) 2-*10*

いいかげんにしろよ。(いい加減にしろよ。) *exp.* Give me a break! (male speech) 2-*10*

いいます（言います）　う -v. (to) say. The dictionary form is いう . 1-6

いかが　q. word how (polite form of どう) 1-8

いき（息）　n. breath, いきをする to breathe, いきができない to be out of breath 2-1

〜いき・〜ゆき（〜行き）　suf. bound for 〜 , 東京行き（とうきょういき）bound for Tokyo, 京都行き（きょうといき）bound for Kyoto 2-5

いきます（行きます）　う -v. (to) go. The dictionary form is いく . 1-3

イギリス　n. England; UK 1-2

いくつ　q. word how many 1-8

いくつ　q. word How old 〜 ? おいくつ (polite form) 1-10

いくら　q. word how much (money) 1-8

いけばな（生け花）　n. flower arrangement 2-9

いじめ　n. bullying, いじめにあう being bullied 2-8

いじめる（苛める）　る -v. to bully 2-8

いしゃ（医者）　n. medical doctor, doctor お医者さん 2-1

いす（椅子）　n. chair 1-5

イスラムきょう（イスラム教）　n. Islam 2-9

いそがしい（忙しい）　い -adj. busy 1-6

いたい（痛い）　い -adj. hurt, painful 2-1

いたす（致す）　う -v. to do (humble) 2-11

いただく（頂く）　う -v. to receive 2-6

いただく（頂く）　う -v. to eat; to drink (humble) 2-11

いためる（炒める）　る -v. to stir-fry, to saute (cooking) 2-7

イタリア　n. Italy, イタリアりょうり Italian cuisine 1-9

いち（一）　number one 1-3

いちご（苺）　n. strawberry 2-7

いちじ（一時）　time exp. one o'clock 1-2

いちねんせい（一年生）　n. freshman; first-year student (The suffix せい may be dropped.) 1-2

いつ　q. word when 1-3

いっしょに（一緒に）　adv. together 1-6

いってください。　exp. Please say it. / Repeat after me. 1-1

いつも　adv. always 1-3

いぬ（犬）　n. dog 1-5

いのり（祈り）　n. prayer, おいのりをする to offer a prayer 2-9

いま（今）　n. now 1-2

います　る -v. to be; to exist (used for animate beings). The dictionary form is いる . 1-4

いみ（意味）　n. meaning 2-4

いもうと（妹）　n. younger sister (the speaker's) 1-10

いもうとさん（妹さん）　n. younger sister (someone else's) 1-10

いや（な）　な -adj. unpleasant, yuck 1-11

イヤリング　n. earring 1-8

いらっしゃい。　exp. Welcome. Come in. 1-5

いらっしゃいませ。　exp. Welcome. 1-8

いらっしゃる　う -v. to go; to come; to return; to be (honorific) 2-11

いりぐち（入り口／入口）　n. entrance 2-5

いる（要る）　う -v. to need something, ソースがいる。 It needs sauce. おかねがいる（お金が要る）to need money 1-9, 2-4

いれる（入れる）　る -v. to put, はこに入れる to put in a box 1-8

いろいろおせわになりました。（色々お世話になりました。）　exp. You've taken very good care of me. Thank you for everything. 2-9

いろいろ（な）（色々（な））　な -adj. various 2-1

〜いわい（祝い）　suf. congratulatory gift, 結婚祝い（けっこんいわい）wedding gift, 就職祝い（しゅうしょくいわい）gift for getting a new job, 卒業祝い（そつぎょういわい）graduation gift 2-6

いわう（祝う）　う -v. to celebrate 2-9

〜いん（〜員）　suf. member, 会社員（かいしゃいん）businessman,　銀行員（ぎんこういん）banker,　ゆうびんきょくいん postal employee,　店員（てんいん）store clerk, 会員（かいいん）membership, member (of an association, a society) 2-3

インターネット　n. internet, it can be abbreviated as ネット 2-9

う

うえ（上）　loc. n. on; above; over 1-5

うかがう（伺う）　う -v. to visit; to ask (humble) 2-11

うける（受ける）　る -v. to receive, to get, しけんをうける to take an exam. 2-4

うごかす（動かす）　う -v. to move (something) (transitive verb) 2-1

うさぎ（兎）　n. rabbit 2-8

うしろ（後ろ）　loc. n. behind; back of 1-5

うすい（薄い）　い -adj. thin, あじがうすい to have very little taste 2-7

うそ（嘘）　n. lie, falsehood 2-8

うた（歌）　n. song 1-7

うたう（歌う）　う -v. to sing 1-7

うち（家）　n. home 1-3

うっそー　exp. No way! (very casual) 2-8

うでどけい（腕時計）　n. wristwatch 1-8

うどん　n. Japanese wheat noodles 1-9

うまれる（生まれる）　る -v. (for someone/something) to be born 2-3

うみ（海）　n. ocean, sea 1-12

うりば（売り場）　n. department, section (of a store), CD/DVD 売り場 CD/DVD section 1-8

うる（売る）　う -v. to sell 2-8

うるさい　い -adj. noisy; shut up! (when used as a phrase by itself) 2-10

うれしい（嬉しい）　い -adj. happy 1-6

うわさ　n. rumor 2-8

うんてんめんきょしょう（運転免許証）　n. driver's license 2-4

うんどう（運動）　n. exercise (physical), うんどう（を）します (to) exercise（を is commonly deleted.) 1-6

え

え（絵）　n. picture 1-5

えいが（映画）　n. movie 1-3

えいがかん（映画館）　n. movie theater 2-5

えいご（英語）　n. English 1-2

ええ、ええ　exp. uh, huh 2-8

ええっと／すみません、それは　ちょっと（こまるんですが）。　exp. Well, uh, I'm sorry but...(that presents some problems). 2-1

えーと　exp. Well, Let's see... 1-12

えき（駅）　n. station 1-4

えさ（餌）　n. food (for animal, fish) 2-6

えび／エビ（海老）　n. shrimp, えびだんご（海老団子）shrimp dumplings 2-7

えらぶ（選ぶ）　う -v. to choose 2-6

〜えん（〜円）　count. Yen, counter for Japanese currency 1-8

エンジニア　n. engineer (as in electrical engineer) 2-3

エントリー　n. entry (the process of expressing interest in employment opportunities by requesting informantion from a company), エントリー・シート a form required for entry 2-11

えんぴつ（鉛筆）　n. pencil 1-4

お

お〜　pref. polite prefix, おなまえ polite form of なまえ (name) 1-2

（お）さしみ（御刺身）　n. sashimi (fillet of fresh raw fish, usually used with お) 1-9

（お）すし（御寿司／鮨）　*n.* sushi (usually preceded by お) 1-9

おいしい　い-*adj.* delicious, good, tasty 1-7

おいでになる　う-*v.* to come in; to show up (honorific) 2-11

おいわい（お祝い）　*n.* congratulatory gift 2-6

おうだんほどう（横断歩道）　*n.* pedestrian crossing 2-5

おうぼ（応募）　*n.* entry, application (for a program, recruitment, subscription, offer, etc.), おうぼする to enter, to apply for (a contest, recuritment, subscritpion, offer, etc.) c.f. もうしこむ to apply (for a bank account, phone service, etc.) 2-11

おえる（終える）　る-*v.* to end (something) , to finish (something) 2-3

おお～（大～）　*pref.* heavy, big, 大雨 heavy rain, 大雪 heavy snow, 大かじ big fire, 大じしん big earthquake 2-8

おおい（多い）　い-*adj.* a lot, much 1-9

おおきい（大きい）　い-*adj.* big 1-4

おおきいこえでいってください。　*exp.* Please speak loudly. (Teacher's request) 1-1

おおきいこえでおねがいします。　*exp.* Please speak loudly. (Student's request) 1-1

おおさじ（大さじ）　*n.* tablespoon 2-7

オーストラリア　*n.* Australia 1-2

オーブン　*n.* oven 2-7

おおや（大家）　*n.* landlord; landlady 2-10

おかあさん（お母さん）　*n.* mother (someone else's) 1-10

おかえし（お返し）　*n.* thank-you gift 2-6

おかげ（さま）で（お陰（様）で）　*exp.* thanks to ～ 2-9

おかげさまで（おかげさまで）　*exp.* Because of your help (common phrase when you thank for somebody for their assistance) 2-11

おかし（お菓子）　*n.* confectionary, sweets 2-6

おかね（お金）　*n.* money 2-2

おきます（起きます）　る-*v.* (to) get up, (to) wake up. The dictionary form is おきる. 1-3

おきもの（置物）　*n.* ornament placed in an alcove, cabinet, etc., such as figurines, clocks, pottery and other art pieces 2-6

おきゃくさん（お客さん）　*n.* customer, guest 1-8

おきる（起きる）　る-*v.* to happen, to take place 2-8

おきをつかわせてしまいまして。（お気を使わせてしまいまして。）　*exp.* You shouldn't have gone to so much trouble for me/us. 2-6

おきをつかわないで下さい。（お気を使わないで下さい。）　*exp.* Please don't go to so much trouble. 2-6

おくさん（奥さん）　*n.* wife (someone else's) 1-10

おくりもの（贈り物）　*n.* gift 2-6

おくる（送る）　う-*v.* to send 2-4

おくれる（遅れる）　う-*v.* to be late 2-10

おこさん（お子さん）　*n.* child (someone else's) 1-10

おこす（起こす）　う-*v.* to wake up (someone) 2-3

おこす（起こす）　う-*v.* to cause (something) to happen 2-8

おこる（怒る）　う-*v.* to get angry 2-10

おじいさん（お祖父さん）　*n.* grandfather (someone else's) 1-10

おじいさん　*n.* elderly man 2-6

おしいれ（押し入れ）　*n.* Japanese-style closet; storage space 1-5

おしえる（教える）　る-*v.* to tell, to teach 2-4

おじぎ（お辞儀）　*n.* bowing, おじぎをする to bow 2-9

おじさん　*n.* middle-aged man; someone else's uncle, also used when speaking to one's own uncle 2-6

おじゃまします。（お邪魔します。）　*exp.* Thank you. (literally, I will intrude on you.)　(said before going inside someone's house or apartment) 1-5

おすきだとよろしいのですが。（お好きだとよろしいのですが。）　*exp.* I hope this will be to your liking. 2-6

おせいぼ（お歳暮）　*n.* end-of-year gift exchange 2-6

おせわになっております。　*exp.* I thank you for your assistance. 2-11

おそう（襲う）　う-*v.* to attack 2-8

おだいじに（お大事に）　*exp.* Please take care of yourself. 2-1

おちゃ（お茶）　*n.* tea, green tea 1-7

おちゅうげん（お中元）　*n.* mid-year gift exchange 2-6

おちる（落ちる）　る -*v.* (for something) to fall 2-3

おっしゃる　う -*v.* to say (honorific) 2-11

おと（音）　*n.* sound 2-10

おとうさん（お父さん）　*n.* father (someone else's) 1-10

おとうと（弟）　*n.* younger brother (the speaker's) 1-10

おとうとさん（弟さん）　*n.* younger brother (someone else's) 1-10

おとこ（男）　*n.* male おとこの人 man 1-10

おとす（落とす）　う -*v.* to drop (something) 2-3

おととい（一昨日）　*n.* the day before yesterday 1-3

おととし（一昨年）　*n.* year before last 1-12

おとな（大人）　*n.* adult 2-10

おどろく（驚く）　う -*v.* to be surprised, ～におどろく to be surprised at ～ 2-8

おとをたてる（音を立てる）　*exp.* to make noise 2-10

おなか（お腹）　*n.* stomach 2-1

おなじ（同じ）　な -*adj.* same, AとBはおなじ A and B are the same. AはBとおなじ A is the same as B.
　（な must be deleted before a noun as in おなじ人）2-3

おにいさん（お兄さん）　*n.* elder brother (someone else's) 1-10

おねえさん（お姉さん）　*n.* elder sister (someone else's) 1-10

おばあさん（お祖母さん）　*n.* grandmother (someone else's) 1-10

おばあさん　*n.* elderly woman 2-6

おばさん　*n.* middle-aged woman; someone else's aunt; also used when speaking to one's own aunt 2-6

おはようございます。　*exp.* Good morning. / Hello. 1-1

おはよう。　*exp.* Good morning. / Hello. (casual) 1-1

おふろ（お風呂）　*n.* bath 1-3

おぼえる（覚える）　る -*v.* to memorize, おぼえている to remember, to recall 2-4

おみまい（お見舞い）　*n.* sympathy gift 2-6

おみやげ（お土産）　*n.* souvenir 2-2

おめでとうございます。　*exp.* congratulations! 2-6

おめにかかる（お目にかかる）　う -*v.* to meet (humble) 2-11

おめにかける（お目にかける）　る -*v.* to show (humble) 2-11

おもい（重い）　い -*adj.* heavy 2-6

おもいで（思い出）　*n.* memories 1-12

おもう（思う）　う -*v.* to think 1-10

おもしろい（面白い）　い -*adj.* interesting 1-6

おもちゃ　*n.* toy 2-6

おやすみになる（お休みになる）　う -*v.* to sleep (honorific) 2-11

およぎます（泳ぎます）　う -*v.* (to) swim. The dictionary form is およぐ. 1-6

おりる（降りる）　る -*v.* to get off 2-5

おる　う -*v.* to exist; to be (humble) 2-11

おれい（お礼）　*n.* thank-you gift 2-6

おれいにとおもいまして。（お礼にと思いまして。）　*exp.* I thought I would make this a token of my
　appreciation. 2-6

オレンジ　*n.* orange 1-7

おわる（終わる）　う -*v.* (for something) to end, えいががおわる the movie ends 1-7

おわる（終わる）　う -*v.* (for something) to end 2-3

おんがく（音楽）　*n.* music 1-6

おんせん（温泉）　*n.* hot spring 2-2

おんど（温度）　*n.* temperature 1-11

おんな（女）　*n.* female おんなの人 woman 1-10

か

か　*part.* question marker 1-2

か　*part.* or, either or 2-3

カード　*n.* card 2-4

カーネーション　*n.* carnation 2-6

〜かい（〜階）　*count.* counter for floors of a building 1-8

〜かい（〜回）　*suf.* 〜 times 1-12

〜かい（〜会）　*suf.* party, 同窓会（どうそうかい）reunion, 送別会（そうべつかい）farewell party, 誕生日会（たんじょうびかい）birthday party 2-3

かいがい（海外）　*n.* overseas, かいがいりょこう overseas travel 2-2

かいぎ（会議）　*n.* meeting; conference 2-11

がいこく（外国）　*n.* foreign countries 1-12

かいさつ（ぐち）（改札（口））　*n.* ticket gate 2-5

かいしゃ（会社）　*n.* company, かいしゃいん businessman, ぼうえきがいしゃ trading company 2-3

かいしゃいん（会社員）　*n.* businesssperson 1-10

かいだん（階段）　*n.* stairs 2-5

かいて ください。　*exp.* Please write. 1-1

ガイドブック　*n.* guidebook 2-2

かいもの（買い物）　*n.* shopping, かいもの（を）します (to) go shopping 1-6

かいわ（会話）　*n.* conversation 2-4

かう（買う）　う -*v.* to buy 1-7

かう（飼う）　う -*v.* to raise, keep (an animal) 2-6

かえす（返す）　う -*v.* to return something 2-4

かえります（帰ります）　う -*v.* (to) return, (to) go home. The dictionary form is かえる. 1-3

かえる（替える／変える）　る -*v.* to change; セクションをかえる（セクションを替える）to change a section 2-4

かお（顔）　*n.* face 1-10

かおいろ（顔色）　*n.* facial tone, complexion 2-1

かかります　う -*v.* (to) take (time), it costs. The dictionary form is かかる. 1-5

かかる　う -*v.* (for a telephone) to ring 2-3

かぎ（鍵）　*n.* key, かぎをかける to lock 2-10

かきます（書きます）　う -*v.* (to) write. The dictionary form is かく. 1-6

かくえきていしゃ（各駅停車）　*n.* local train (literally: train that stops at every station) 2-5

がくしゃ（学者）　*n.* scholar 2-3

がくしょく（学食）　*n.* school cafeteria (a shortened form of 学生しょくどう) 1-5

がくせい（学生）　*n.* student 1-2

がくせいかいかん（学生会館）　*n.* Student union 1-5

〜かげつ（〜か月）　*suf.* counter for months 1-12

かけます　る -*v.* (to) make (a phone call). The dictionary form is かける. でんわをかけます to make a phone call 1-6

かける　る -*v.* to put on (glasses) 1-10

かける（掛ける）　る -*v.* to hang, hook, かぎをかける to lock 2-10

かける　る -*v.* to pour 2-7

かさ（傘）　*n.* umbrella 1-8

かじ（火事）　*n.* a fire 2-8

かす（貸す）　う -*v.* to lend 2-4

かぜ（風）　*n.* wind 1-11

かぜ（風邪）　*n.* (a) cold, かぜをひく to catch a cold 2-1

かぞく（家族）　*n.* family, the speaker's family 1-10

ガソリンスタンド　*n.* gas station 2-5

〜かた（〜方）　*suf.* person (polite form), いいかた (nice person) 1-10

かた（肩）　*n.* shoulders, 肩がこる to have stiff shoulders 2-1

〜かた（〜方）　*suf.* how to, way of 〜ing 2-4

かたい（固い）　い -*adj.* hard, tough 1-9

かたづける（片付ける）　る -*v.* to clean up; to organize 2-10

〜がつ（〜月）　*suf.* month 1-*11*

がっき（学期）　*n.* semester, quarter, いちがっき one semester, はるがっき spring semester/quarter 1-*12*

かっこいい　い *-adj.* good-looking, cool, neat 1-*10*

がっこう（学校）　*n.* school 1-*3*

かつどう（活動）　*n.* activity 2-*11*

カップ　*n.* cup, けいりょうカップ measuring cup 2-*7*

かど（角）　*n.* corner 2-*5*

かなしい（悲しい）　い *-adj.* sad 1-*6*

カナダ　*n.* Canada 1-*2*

かに／カニ（蟹）　*n.* crab 2-*7*

かのじょ（彼女）　*n.* girlfriend, she 2-*8*

かばん（鞄）　*n.* luggage, bag 1-*4*

カフェ　*n.* coffee shop, café (recent term) 1-*4*

かぶき（歌舞伎）　*n.* kabuki (Japanese traditional performing art) 1-*12*

かぶる　う *-v.* to put on (a hat or cap) 1-*10*

かべ（壁）　*n.* wall 2-*10*

かみ（髪）　*n.* hair（かみのけ is commonly used as well）1-*10*

かみなり（雷）　*n.* lightning, かみなりがおちる lightning strikes 2-*8*

かめ（亀）　*n.* turtle, tortoise 2-*8*

かゆい（痒い）　い *-adj.* itchy 2-*1*

かようび（火曜日）　*n.* Tuesday 1-*3*

から　*part.* from 1-*5*

〜からきました。　*exp.* came from 〜 [casual] 1-*2*

からい（辛い）　い *-adj.* spicy 1-*9*

カラオケ　*n.* Karaoke, sing along 1-*7*

からかう　う *-v.* to tease 2-*10*

からだ（体）　*n.* body 2-*1*

かりる（借りる）　る *-v.* to borrow, to rent (a house, apartment) 2-*4*

かるい（軽い）　い *-adj.* light 2-*6*

かれ（し）（彼（氏））　*n.* boyfriend, he 2-*8*

カレーライス　*n.* Japanese curry and rice dish. (abbreviation: カレー) 1-*9*

カロリー　*n.* calorie 1-*9*

かわ（川）　*n.* river 1-*5*

〜がわ（〜側）　*suf.* side, こちらがわ this side, むかいがわ the other side, the opposite side, みぎがわ（右側）right-hand side, ひだりがわ（左側）left-hand side 2-*5*

かわいい（可愛い）　い *-adj.* cute, adorable 1-*10*

かわる（変わる／替わる）　う *-v.* (for something) to change 2-*3*

〜かん（〜館）　*suf.* mansion, building　図書館（としょかん）library, 体育館（たいいくかん）gym, 水族館 aquarium, 博物館（はくぶつかん）museum, 美術館（びじゅつかん）art museum, 旅館 Japanese style inn, 映画館（えいがかん）movie theater, 大使館（たいしかん）embassy 2-*5*

かんがえる（考える）　る *-v.* to think intellectually, to take (something) into consideration 2-*3*

かんこう（観光）　*n.* sightseeing, かんこうする to go sightseeing, かんこうバス chartered bus for sightseeing, かんこうりょこう sightseeing trip, かんこうち tourist attraction, sightseeing spot 2-*2*

かんこく（韓国）　*n.* South Korea 1-*2*

がんばる（頑張る）　う *-v.* to try to do one's best, to hang on 2-*3*

き

き（木）　*n.* tree 1-*5*

きいてください。　*exp.* Please listen. 1-*1*

きいろい（黄色い）　い *-adj.* yellow 1-*4*

きえる（消える）　る *-v.* (for something) to go out, to go off 2-*3*

きおん（気温）　*n.* air temperature 1-*11*

きかい（機会）　*n.* opportunity 2-*11*

きがつかなくて。(気が付かなくて)   *exp.* I did not realize (it). 2-*10*

ききます (聞きます／聴きます)   う -*v.* (to) ask (聞きます); (to) listen to (聴きます). The dictionary form is きく . 1-*6*

きこう (気候)   *n.* climate 1-*11*

キス   *n.* kiss, キスをする to kiss 2-*9*

きせつ (季節)   *n.* season 1-*11*

きた (北)   *n.* north 1-*11*

きたない (汚い)   い -*adj.* dirty 2-*10*

きっさてん (喫茶店)   *n.* coffee shop (traditional term) 1-*4*

きって (切手)   *n.* postage stamp 2-*4*

きっぷ (切符)   *n.* ticket, でんしゃのきっぷ train ticket 2-*2*

きにゅう (記入)   *n.* filling out, きにゅうする to fill out, 申込用紙 (もうしこみようし) にきにゅうする to fill out an application form 2-*11*

きのう (昨日)   *n.* yesterday 1-*3*

きぶん (気分)   *n.* feeling, spirits, mood, きぶんがわるい to feel annoyed, feel sick/ill/unwell 2-*1*

きます (来ます)   *irr. v.* (to) come. The dictionary form is くる . 1-*3*

きまる (決まる)   う -*v.* (for something) to be decided 2-*3*

きめる (決める)   う -*v.* to decide, 〜に きめる to decide on, 〜を きめる to decide something 2-*2*

きもち (気持ち)   *n.* feeling, sensation, きもちがわるい to feel nausea, (nausia,) feel unpleasant, feel weird, feel revolted 2-*1*

きもの (着物)   *n.* traditional Japanese clothes, kimono 1-*12*

きゃく (客)   *n.* customer, guest, かんこうきゃく tourist 2-*2*

キャベツ   *n.* cabbage 2-*7*

キャンディ   *n.* candy 2-*6*

キャンプ   *n.* camping 1-*12*

きゅう (な)(急 (な))   な -*adj.* sudden きゅうに suddenly 1-*11*

きゅう、く (九)   *number* nine 1-*3*

きゅうこう (れっしゃ)(急行 (列車))   *n.* express train 2-*5*

ぎゅうにく (牛肉)   *n.* beef 2-*7*

ぎゅうにゅう (牛乳)   *n.* cow's milk 1-*7*

きゅうり   *n.* cucumber 2-*7*

きゅうりょう (給料)   *n.* wages 2-*11*

きょう (今日)   *n.* today 1-*3*

きょういく (教育)   *n.* education 2-*9*

きょうかい (教会)   *n.* church 1-*12*

きょうかしょ (教科書)   *n.* textbook 1-*4*

きょうしつ (教室)   *n.* classroom 1-*5*

きょうだい (兄弟)   *n.* sibling(s) 1-*10*

きょうみ (興味)   *n.* interest, 〜にきょうみがある interested in 〜 2-*9*

きょねん (去年)   *n.* last year 1-*11*

きらい (な)(嫌い (な))   な -*adj.* dislike, hate 1-*7*

キリストきょう (キリスト教)   *n.* Christianity 2-*9*

きる (着る)   る -*v.* to put on (sweater, shirt, jacket) 1-*10*

きる (切る)   う -*v.* to cut 2-*1*

きれい (な)   な -*adj.* clean; pretty; neat 1-*4*

きをつける (気を付ける)   *exp.* to take care, to pay attention 2-*10*

ぎんこう (銀行)   *n.* bank 1-*4*

きんじょ (近所)   *n.* neighborhood, 近所の人 neighbor 2-*6*

きんようび (金曜日)   *n.* Friday 1-*3*

く

くうこう (空港)   *n.* airport 2-*2*

くじ (九時)   *time exp.* nine o'clock 1-*2*

クジラ　*n.* whale 2-8

くすり（薬）　*n.* medicine, drug, ointment 2-1

くださる（下さる）　う -*v.* to give (from a social superior to me or a person in my in-group) 2-6

くだもの（果物）　*n.* fruit 1-7

くち（口）　*n.* mouth 1-10

〜くち・ぐち（〜口）　*suf.* 〜 entrance/exit, にしぐち（西口）west exit 2-5

くつ（靴）　*n.* shoes 1-8

クッキー　*n.* cookie 1-9

くつした（靴下）　*n.* socks 1-8

くに（国）　*n.* country 2-2

くび（首）　*n.* neck 2-1

くま（熊）　*n.* bear 2-8

くも（雲）　*n.* cloud 1-11

くもり（曇り）　*n.* cloudy 1-11

くもる（曇る）　う -*v.* to become cloudy 1-11

くらい（暗い）　い -*adj.* dark 1-5

〜ぐらい・くらい　*suf.* about 〜 ; approximately (duration or quantity) 1-5

クラシック　*n.* classical music 1-7

クラス　*n.* class 1-3

グラム　*n.* gram 2-7

クリスマス　*n.* Christmas 1-12

くるま（車）　*n.* car 1-5

クレジットカード　*n.* credit card 2-2

くれる　る -*v.* to give (to a socially equal or subordinate in-group person) 2-6

くろい（黒い）　い -*adj.* black 1-4

くわえる（加える）　る -*v.* to add (an ingredient) 2-7

け

けいえいがく（経営学）　*n.* management/business administration 1-2

けいかく（計画）　*n.* plan 2-2

けいけん（経験）　*n.* experience, 経験する to have an experience 2-8

けいざい（経済）　*n.* economy 2-9

げいじゅつ（芸術）　*n.* art 2-9

けいたい（でんわ）（携帯（電話））　*n.* cellular phone, mobile phone (c.f. スマホ smart phone) 1-5

ケーキ　*n.* cake 1-7

ゲーム　*n.* (computer) game 1-6

けが（怪我）　*n.* injury 2-1

けさ（今朝）　*n.* this morning 1-11

けしゴム（消しゴム）　*n.* eraser 1-4

けしょうひん（化粧品）　*n.* cosmetics, also use コスメ 2-6

けす（消す）　う -*v.* to turn off 2-3

けっか（結果）　*n.* result; outcome 2-11

けっこん（結婚）　*n.* marriage, 〜とけっこんする to marry 〜 , けっこんしている to be married 1-10

げつようび（月曜日）　*n.* Monday 1-3

けれども　*conj.* however 2-2

けんか　*n.* fight, quarrel, けんかをする to fight 1-12

けんか（喧嘩）　*n.* a fight 2-8

げんき（な）（元気（な））　な -*adj.* healthy, cheerful, lively (person) 1-6

けんきゅう（研究）　*n.* research, けんきゅう（を）する to do research 2-3

けんこう（な）（健康）　な -*adj.* healthy, けんこうな人 healthy person, (can be used as a noun) けんこうのため for the sake of health 2-1

こ

こ（子）　*n.* child, おとこのこ boy, おんなのこ girl 1-10

こ（子）　*n.* child, こ is usually preceded by a modifier. としうえのこ（年上の子）older child, いいこ（いい子）good child 2-10

〜ご（〜語）　*suf.* language, にほんご Japanese language 1-2

ご（五）　*number* five 1-3

〜ご（〜後）　*suf.* from 〜, after 〜 (3年ご three years from now) 1-12

コーヒー　*n.* coffee 1-3

こ〜（子〜）　*pref.* baby 〜, こいぬ（子犬）puppy, こねこ（子猫）kitten 2-6

ご〜（御〜）　*pref.* polite prefix, ごちゅうもん polite form of ちゅうもん (order) 1-9

こい（濃い）　*い -adj.* thick, あじがこい to have a strong taste 2-7

こうえん（公園）　*n.* park 1-4

こうがく（工学）　*n.* engineering 1-2

こうこう（高校）　*n.* high school 1-2

こうこく（広告）　*n.* advertisement 2-11

こうざ（口座）　*n.* bank account 2-4

こうさてん（交差点）　*n.* intersection 2-5

こうずい（洪水）　*n.* flood 2-8

こうちゃ（紅茶）　*n.* black tea 1-7

こうつう（交通）　*n.* traffic, こうつうじこ traffic accident 2-8

こうはい（後輩）　*n.* one's junior at a school, university etc. 2-6

こうばん（交番）　*n.* police box 1-4

コート　*n.* coat 1-8

コーヒーカップ　*n.* coffee cup, mug 2-6

コーラ　*n.* cola 1-7

コーンスターチ　*n.* cornstarch 2-7

ごかぞく（ご家族）　*n.* family (someone else's) 1-10

ごきょうだい（ご兄弟）　*n.* siblings (someone else's) 1-10

こくない（国内）　*n.* domestic, こくないりょこう domestic travel 2-2

こくばん（黒板）　*n.* blackboard 1-5

ここ　*demo.* here; this place 1-4

ごご（午後）　*n.* p.m.; afternoon, 1-2

こころぼそい（心細い）　*い -adj.* lonely, helpless 2-9

こさじ（小さじ）　*n.* teaspoon 2-7

ござる　*う -v.* to exist (polite verb for ある and いる) 2-11

こし（腰）　*n.* lower back 2-1

ごじ（五時）　*time exp.* five o'clock 1-2

ごしゅじん（ご主人）　*n.* husband (someone else's) 1-10

こしょう　*n.* pepper (spice) 2-7

ごぜん（午前）　*n.* a.m.; morning, 1-2

こたえる（答える）　*る -v.* to answer, しつもんにこたえる to answer a question 2-2

こちら　*n.* this person; this way 1-2

こちらがわ（こちら側）　*n.* this side 2-5

こちらこそ。　*exp.* It is I who should be saying that. Thank YOU. Same here. 1-2

こづつみ（小包）　*n.* parcel post 2-4

こと　*n.* thing (intangible) 1-7

ことし（今年）　*n.* this year 1-11

ことば（言葉）　*n.* language, words, expressions 2-2

こども（子供）　*n.* child 1-10

ことわる（断る）　*う -v.* to refuse, to decline, たのみをことわる to decline a request, 招待をことわる to decline an invitation 2-9

この *demo.* this [+noun] 1-5

このへん（この辺） *n.* this area 1-4

ごはん（御飯） *n.* meal, cooked rice 1-3

ごぶさたしております（ご無沙汰しております） *exp.* I'm sorry to have stayed out of touch for so long. 2-11

こまる（困る） う -*v.* to be in trouble 2-8

ごみ／ゴミ *n.* trash, garbage（ごみ can be written either in **hiragana** or in **katakana**.) 2-10

こむ（混む） う -*v.* to become crowded 2-5

こむぎこ（小麦粉） *n.* flour 2-7

こめ／おこめ（米／お米） *n.* uncooked rice 2-7

ごめいわくおかけしてもうしわけありません。（ご迷惑おかけして申しわけありません。） *exp.* I'm sorry to cause you problems. 2-10

ごめん（なさい）（ご免（なさい）） *exp.* I'm sorry. (used only for an apology, more colloquial than すみません) 2-4

ごめんください（御免下さい） *exp.* Excuse me. Anyone home? 1-5

ごらんになる（ご覧になる） う -*v.* to look at (honorific) 2-11

こる（凝る） う -*v.* to be stiff, かたがこる (to) have stiff shoulders 2-1

ゴルフ *n.* golf 1-7

これ *demo.* this object, this 1-4

これからもどうぞよろしく（おねがいします）。（これからもどうぞよろしく（お願いします）。） *exp.* Please stay in touch (with me) in the future, too. 2-9

これはにほんごでなんといいますか。 *exp.* What do you call this in Japanese? 1-1

〜ごろ *suf.* about 〜 (used only with a time expression) 1-3

こわい（怖い） い -*adj.* frightening, scary 2-8

こわす（壊す） う -*v.* to destroy 2-8

こん〜（今〜） *pref.* this, こんしゅう this week, こんばん tonight 1-3

こんげつ（今月） *n.* this month 1-12

こんごともよろしくおねがいいたします。（今後ともよろしくお願いいたします。） *exp.* I ask for your continued assisstance. 2-11

コンサート *n.* concert 1-6

こんしゅう（今週） *n.* this week 1-3

こんど（今度） *n.* next time 1-6

こんにちは。 *exp.* Good afternoon. / Hello. 1-1

こんばん（今晩） *n.* tonight 1-3

こんばんは *exp.* Good evening. / Hello. 1-1

コンビニ *n.* convenience store 1-4

コンピュータ *n.* computer 1-5

さ

〜さ *suf.* suffix to convert an adjective to a noun for measurement, 大きさ (size), 高さ (height), ながさ (length), おもさ (weight) 2-6

〜さい（〜歳／才） *suf.* 〜 years old 1-10

さいがい（災害） *n.* disaster, calamity 2-8

さいきん（最近） *n.* recent, recently 1-11

さいごに（最後に） *conj.* lastly, at last, finally 2-7

さいふ（財布） *n.* wallet, purse 2-3

ざいりゅうカード（在留カード） *n.* residence card 2-4

ざいりょう（材料） *n.* materials, ingredients 2-7

サイン *n.* signature, サインをする to sign 2-4

さがす（探す／捜す） う -*v.* to look for. Use 捜す to look for something that has been lost. Otherwise, use 探す 2-2

さかな（魚） *n.* fish 1-7

さがる（下がる） う -*v.* to fall; to go down 1-11

さき（先） *n.* beyond, further ahead 2-5

さくぶん（作文） *n.* composition 2-4

さけ (酒)　*n.* rice wine, alcoholic beverage (おさけ is also common.) *1-7*

さげる (下げる)　る *-v.* to lower (something) c.f. さがる to go down *2-1*

さしあげる (差し上げる)　る *-v.* to give (to a socially superior out-group person) *2-6*

〜さつ (〜冊)　*count.* counter for bound objects (e.g. books, magazines) *1-8*

ざっし (雑誌)　*n.* magazine *1-6*

さとう (砂糖)　*n.* sugar *2-7*

さどう (茶道)　*n.* tea ceremony *2-9*

さびしい (寂しい)　い *-adj.* lonely *1-6*

さます (冷ます)　う *-v.* to let something cool down, おゆを冷 (さ) ます to let hot water cool down *2-7*

さむい (寒い)　い *-adj.* cold *1-11*

さようなら。／さよなら。　*exp.* Good-bye. *1-1*

さら／おさら (皿／お皿)　*n.* plate *2-7*

サラダ　*n.* salad *1-9*

サラダゆ／サラダあぶら (サラダ油)　*n.* vegetable oil (lit. salad oil) *2-7*

さる (猿)　*n.* monkey *2-8*

さわぐ (騒ぐ)　う *-v.* to make noise *2-10*

〜さん　*suf.* Mr./Mrs./Miss/Ms. 〜 *1-1*

さん (三)　*number* three *1-3*

さんじ (三時)　*time exp.* three o'clock *1-2*

サンドイッチ　*n.* sandwich *1-9*

ざんねん (な)(残念 (な))　な *-adj.* sorry, regrettable *1-6*

さんねんせい (三年生)　*n.* junior, third-year student (The suffix せい may be dropped.) *1-2*

ざんねんながらわたしのちからぶそくで (残念ながら私の力不足で)　*exp.* Regrettably, due to the lack of my ability…(unfortunately I was unable to…) *2-11*

さんぽ (散歩)　*n.* walk; stroll, さんぽ (を) します (to) take a walk *1-6*

し

し (詩)　*n.* poetry *2-9*

〜じ (〜時)　*suf.* 〜 o'clock *1-2*

ジーンズ　*n.* jeans *1-8*

しあわせ (な)(幸せ (な))　な *-adj.* happy *2-10*

しお (塩)　*n.* salt *2-7*

しかくい (四角い)　い *-adj.* square *1-10*

しかたがない (仕方がない)　*exp.* Nothing can be done about it, there is no use. *2-10*

しかる　う *-v.* to scold *2-8*

〜じかん　*suf.* 〜 hours *1-5*

じかん (時間)　*n.* time, じかんがある to have time, じかんがない to not have time *2-2*

しき (式)　*n.* ceremony *2-3*

〜しき (〜式)　*suf.* ceremony, 卒業式 (そつぎょうしき) graduation ceremony, 入学式 (にゅうがくしき) matriculation ceremony, 結婚式 (けっこんしき) wedding ceremony *2-3*

しけん (試験)　*n.* examination, test *2-4*

じこ (事故)　*n.* accident, こうつうじこ traffic accident *2-8*

じこ (自己)　*n.* self, a formal version of 自分 , often used with another word such as じこしょうかい self introduction, じこ PR self-promotion *2-11*

じこ〜 (自己〜)　*pref.* self, じこしょうかい self introduction, じこ PR self-promotion *2-11*

じこ PR(自己 PR)　*n.* self-promotion *2-11*

しごと (仕事)　*n.* job; work *1-6*

じしょ (辞書)　*n.* dictionary *1-4*

じしん (地震)　*n.* earthquake *2-8*

しずか (な)(静か (な))　な *-adj.* quiet *1-5*

した (下)　*loc. n.* under; beneath *1-5*

しちじ (七時)　*time exp.* seven o'clock *1-2*

しっている (知っている) る -v. to know. Use しらない to express do not know. しる means come to know, and it is an う -verb. 2-2

しつど (湿度) *n.* humidity 1-11

じつは (実は) *exp.* Actually 2-4

しつもん (質問) *n.* question, しつもん (を) します (to) ask a question 1-6

しつれい (な)(失礼 (な)) な -adj. rude 2-9

しつれいします。 *exp.* Good-bye. / Excuse me. 1-1

しつれんする (失恋する) *irr.-v.* to be disappointed in love 1-12

じてんしゃ (自転車) *n.* bicycle 1-5

しぬ (死ぬ) う -v. to die 2-3

じぶん (自分) *n.* self, oneself, I 2-3

しぼう (志望) *n.* a wish; a desire; an ambition, しぼうする to desire 2-11

します *irr.-v.* (to) do. The dictionary form is する . 1-3

しまる (閉まる) う -v. (for something) to close 2-3

しめきり (締め切り) *n.* deadline 2-11

しめる (閉める) る -v. to close (something) 2-3

～しゃ (～者) *suf.* person of, 学者 scholar, 研究者 (けんきゅうしゃ) researcher, 医者 doctor 2-3

じゃあ、また。 *exp.* See you later. (literally: Well then, again.) 1-1

しゃかい (社会) *n.* society 2-9

じゃがいも *n.* potato 2-7

しやくしょ (市役所) *n.* city hall 2-5

ジャケット *n.* jacket 1-8

しゃしん (写真) *n.* photograph 1-5

ジャズ *n.* jazz 1-7

しゃちょう (社長) *n.* company president 2-3

シャツ *n.* shirt 1-8

ジャム *n.* jam 2-7

シャワー *n.* shower 1-3

じゅう (十) *number* ten 1-3

じゆう (自由) *n.* freedom, じゆう (な) is a な -adjective meaning free. 2-3

じゆう (な)(自由 (な)) な -adj. free, じゆうな生活 free (independent) lifestyle 2-3

じゅういちじ (十一時) *time exp.* eleven o'clock 1-2

～しゅうかん (～週間) *suf.* for ～ weeks 1-12

しゅうかん (習慣) *n.* custom 2-9

しゅうきょう (宗教) *n.* religion 2-9

しゅうじ (習字) *n.* calligraphy 2-9

じゅうじ (十時) *time exp.* ten o'clock 1-2

じゅうしょ (住所) *n.* address 2-4

しゅうしょく (就職) *n.* getting a job, ～にしゅうしょくする to get a job at ～ 2-3

しゅうしょくかつどう (就職活動) *n.* job hunting (abbreviated as しゅうかつ (就活)in casual conversation) 2-11

ジュース *n.* juice 1-7

じゅうにじ (十二時) *time exp.* twelve o'clock 1-2

しゅうまつ (週末) *n.* weekend 1-3

じゅぎょう (授業) *n.* class, course 1-3

じゅぎょうりょう (授業料) *n.* tuition 2-4

しゅくだい (宿題) *n.* homework 1-3

しゅじん (主人) *n.* husband (the speaker's) 1-10

しゅっちょう (出張) *n.* business trip, しゅっちょうする to go on a business trip 2-11

しゅみ (趣味) *n.* hobby 1-7

じゅんび (準備) *n.* preparation, じゅんびする to prepare, じゅんびができる Preparations are complete. 2-2

～しょう (～証) *suf.* card (for identification), 学生証 (しょう) student identification 2-4

～じょう (～状) *suf.* letter of, しょうたいじょう letter of invitation 2-3

しょう～ (小～) *pref.* elementary, 小学生 elementary school student, 小学校 elementary school 1-10

しょうかい (紹介)　*n.* introduction, 〜に〜をしょうかいする to introduce 〜 to 〜, 自己 (こ) しょうかい self introduction 2-*11*

しょうがつ (正月)　*n.* the New Year (often used as おしょうがつ) 1-*12*

じょうし (上司)　*n.* boss 2-*6*

しょうじき (な)(正直 (な))　な -*adj.* honest 2-*10*

しょうじょう (症状)　*n.* symptom 2-*1*

じょうず (な)(上手 (な))　な -*adj.* good at, skillful 1-*10*

しょうせつ (小説)　*n.* novel 2-*6*

しょうたい (招待)　*n.* invitation, しょうたいする to invite 2-*3*

じょうだんじゃないよ。(冗談じゃないよ。)　*exp.* You've got to be kidding. 2-*10*

じょうほう (情報)　*n.* information 2-*11*

しょうゆ (しょう油)　*n.* soy sauce 2-*7*

しょうらい (将来)　*n.* future 2-*3*

ジョギング　*n.* jogging 1-*6*

しょくじ (食事)　*n.* dining, しょくじする to dine 1-*7*

しょくひん (食品)　*n.* a food item 1-*8*

しょくひんうりば (食品売り場)　*n.* food department 1-*8*

しょっき (食器)　*n.* dishes 2-*6*

しょっぱい／しおからい (塩辛い)　い -*adj.* salty 1-*9*

しょるい (書類)　*n.* document 2-*11*

しらせる (知らせる)　る -*v.* to notify 2-*11*

しらべる (調べる)　る -*v.* to check, investigate, explore 2-*2*

しりあい (知り合い)　*n.* acquaintance 2-*10*

しる (知る)　う -*v.* to come to know, しっている to know, しらない don't know 1-*11*

しろい (白い)　い -*adj.* white 1-*4*

〜じん (〜人)　*suf.* 〜 nationality, アメリカじん American 1-*2*

しんごう (信号)　*n.* traffic signal 2-*5*

しんしふく (紳士服)　*n.* men's wear 1-*8*

しんしふくうりば (紳士服売り場)　*n.* menswear department 1-*8*

じんじゃ (神社)　*n.* Shinto shrine 1-*12*

しんじる (信じる)　る -*v.* to believe 2-*9*

しんせつ (な)(親切 (な))　な -*adj.* kind 1-*10*

しんとう (神道)　*n.* Shinto religion 2-*9*

しんぱい (心配)　*n.* anxiety, anxious, 心配する to be worried 2-*8*

(そんな) しんぱいしないでください。((そんな) 心配しないで下さい。)　*exp.* Please do not worry about me. 2-*6*

しんぶん (新聞)　*n.* newspaper 1-*6*

す

す (酢)　*n.* vinegar 2-*7*

スイーツ　*n.* sweets 2-*6*

すいせん (推薦)　*n.* recommendation, すいせんする to recommend, すいせんじょう recommendation (letter) 2-*4*

すいせんじょう (推薦状)　*n.* letter of reference; recommendation 2-*11*

すいぞくかん (水族館)　*n.* aquarium 1-*12*

すいはんき (炊飯器)　*n.* rice cooker 2-*7*

すいようび (水曜日)　*n.* Wednesday 1-*3*

すう (吸う)　う -*v.* to inhale, たばこをすう to smoke 2-*1*

スーツ　*n.* suit 1-*8*

スーツケース　*n.* suitcase 2-*2*

スーパー　*n.* supermarket 1-*4*

スープ　*n.* soup 1-*9*

スカート　*n.* skirt 1-*8*

すき (な)(好き (な))　な -*adj.* like 1-*7*

スキー　*n.* skiing, ski 1-7

すきでもきらいでもありません。（好きでも嫌いでもありません。）　*exp.* I neither like nor dislike it. 1-7

すぐ　*adv.* immediately, right away 2-1

すぐ　*adv.* soon, shortly 2-5

すくない（少ない）　い-*adj.* little (in number), few 1-9

すごい（凄い）　い-*adj.* amazing, awesome, terrible, すごい先生 amazing teacher, すごい雨 terrible rain 2-4

すこし（少し）　*adv.* a little, a few 1-8

すこしずつ（少しずつ）　*adv.* little by little 2-7

すずしい（涼しい）　い-*adj.* cool 1-11

すっぱい（酸っぱい）　い-*adj.* sour 1-9

ステーキ　*n.* steak 1-9

すてる（捨てる）　る-*v.* to throw away, to discard 2-8

ストッキング　*n.* stockings, pantyhose 1-8

ストレス　*n.* stress 2-1

スパゲティ　*n.* spaghetti 1-9

スプーン　*n.* spoon 2-7

スペイン　*n.* Spain 1-2

スポーツ　*n.* sports 1-7

（あのう、）すみません。　*exp.* (Eh,/Um) Excuse me. 1-1

すみません。　*exp.* I am sorry. / Excuse me. 1-1

すむ（住む）　う-*v.* to reside, 〜にすんでいる to live in 〜 1-10

する　*irr-v.* to put on (accessories) 1-10

すわる（座る）　う-*v.* to sit down 2-9

せ

せ（背）　*n.* back (part of the body); height (of a person) 1-10

〜せい（〜生）　*suf.* 〜 student だいがくせい college student, いちねんせい freshman 1-2

せいかく（性格）　*n.* personality 1-10

せいかつ（生活）　*n.* life, living 1-3

せいざ（正座）　*n.* formal Japanese-style sitting posture, せいざをする to sit in a formal Japanese style 2-9

せいじ（政治）　*n.* politics 2-9

セーター　*n.* sweater 1-8

セール　*n.* sale 1-8

せかい（世界）　*n.* world 2-9

せき（咳）　*n.* cough 2-1

せっけん（石けん）　*n.* soap 2-6

ぜったい（に）（絶対（に））　*adv.* definitely 2-9

セット　*n.* Western-style fixed menu, ハンバーガーセット hamburger set 1-9

せつめい（説明）　*n.* explanation, せつめいする to explain 2-4

せつめいかい（説明会）　*n.* a briefing session, an explanatory meeting 2-11

せなか（背中）　*n.* back, upper back 2-1

ぜひ（是非）　*adv.* I'd love to. by all means 1-6

せまい（狭い）　い-*adj.* cramped; narrow 1-5

ゼロ（ゼロ）　*number* zero 1-3

せわになる／おせわになる（世話になる）　*exp.* to be cared for or helped by somebody 2-6

せん（千）　*number* thousand 1-8

〜せん（〜線）　*suf.* line (train line), 山手線（やまのてせん）the Yamanote Line, 中央線（ちゅうおうせん）the Chuo Line 2-5

せんげつ（先月）　*n.* last month 1-12

せんこう（専攻）　*n.* major (field of study in college) 1-2

せんしゅう（先週）　*n.* last week 1-3

せんせい　*n.* teacher 1-1

〜せんせい　*suf.* Professor 〜 *1-1*
ぜんぜん（全然）　*adv.* not at all (used with negative verb forms) *1-3*
せんたく（洗濯）　*n.* laundry, 〜のせんたくをします or 〜をせんたくします (to) wash/ do laundry *1-6*
せんぱい（先輩）　*n.* one's senior at a school, university, office, etc. *2-6*
ぜんぶで（全部で）　*exp.* all together *1-8*
せんもん（専門）　*n.* field of specialty *2-11*

そ

ぞう（象）　*n.* elephant *2-8*
そういってもらえると、うれしいです。　*exp.* I'm glad that you said so. *2-11*
そうじ（掃除）　*n.* cleaning, 〜のそうじをします or 〜をそうじします (to) clean up *1-6*
そうだん（相談）　*n.* consultation, そうだんする（相談する）to consult with *2-10*
そうですか。　*exp.* Is that so? I see. *1-2*
そうでもありません。／そうでもございません。　*exp.* No, not really. *2-11*
そうなんですよ。　*exp.* That's right. *2-11*
そうべつかい（送別会）　*n.* farewell party *2-3*
ソース　*n.* sauce *2-7*
そこ　*demo.* there; that place (close to the listener or slightly removed from both speaker and listener) *1-4*
そして　*conj.* and *1-6*
そつぎょう（卒業）　*n.* graduation, 〜をそつぎょうする to graduate from 〜 *2-3*
そと（外）　*loc. n.* outside *1-5*
その　*demo.* that [+noun] *1-5*
そのあいだ（に）（その間）　*conj.* during that time *2-2*
そのあと（で）（その後で）　*conj.* after that *2-2*
そのとき（に）（その時に）　*conj.* at that time *2-2*
そのまえ（に）（その前に）　*conj.* before that *2-2*
そば（蕎麦）　*n.* Japanese buckwheat noodles *1-9*
そふ（祖父）　*n.* grandfather (the speaker's) *1-10*
ソファ　*n.* sofa *1-5*
そぼ（祖母）　*n.* grandmother (the speaker's) *1-10*
そら（空）　*n.* sky *2-11*
それ　*demo.* that object; that (close to the listener or slightly removed from both speaker and listener) *1-4*
それから　*conj.* and, in addition, then *1-7*
それで　*conj.* then, so *2-2*
それで…そのあと、どうなったんですか。（それで…その後、どうなったんですか。）　*exp.* Well then..., what
　　happened after that? *2-8*
それに　*conj.* in addition *1-10*
それはにほんごでなんといいますか。　*exp.* What do you call that in Japanese? *1-1*
それはおきのどくでしたね。（それはお気の毒でしたね。）　*exp.* I am sorry to hear that. *2-8*
そろそろしつれいします。（そろそろ失礼します。）　*exp.* I should be going. *2-9*
ぞんじておる（存じておる）　う -*v.* to know, to think (humble) *2-11*
ぞんじる（存じる）　る -*v.* to know (humble) *2-11*
そんなことないですよ。／そんなことはありませんよ。　*exp.* No, that is not the case. *2-11*

た

ターミナル　*n.* terminal, バスターミナル bus depot *2-5*
だい〜（大〜）　*pref.* very much; 大すき like very much *1-7*
たいいくかん（体育館）　*n.* gym *1-5*
ダイエット　*n.* diet *2-1*
だいがく（大学）　*n.* college, university *1-2*
だいがくいんせい（大学院生）　*n.* graduate student *1-2*
だいがくせい（大学生）　*n.* college student *1-2*

だいじ (な) (大事 (な))　　な -*adj.* important 2-3

たいしかん (大使館)　　*n.* embassy, 大使 (たいし) ambassador 2-5

たいしたものじゃありませんから。(たいした物じゃありませんから。)　　*exp.*　It is of little value. 2-6

だいじょうぶ (な) (大丈夫 (な))　　な -*adj.* all right, no problem 1-6

たいせつ (な) (大切 (な))　　な -*adj.* precious, important 2-6

たいそう (体操)　　*n.* physical exercise, calisthenics 1-7

たいてい　　*adv.* usually 1-3

たいふう (台風)　　*n.* typhoon 1-*11*

たいへん (な) (大変 (な))　　な -*adj.* tough 1-6

たいわん (台湾)　　*n.* Taiwan 1-2

タオル　　*n.* towel 2-6

たかい (高い)　　い -*adj.* tall, high 1-4

たかい (高い)　　い -*adj.* expensive (Chapter 4: high, tall) 1-7

だから　　*conj.* so 2-2

たく (炊く)　　う -*v.* to cook, ごはんをたく to cook rice 2-7

たくさん　　*adv.* a lot, many, much 1-8

タクシー　　*n.* taxi 2-5

たくはいびん (宅配便)　　*n.* parcel delivery service. Also called 宅急便 (たっきゅうびん), a registered company trademark commonly used instead of 宅配便 (たくはいびん) 2-4

だけど　　*conj.* but 2-2

だし　　*n.* broth 2-7

たす (足す)　　う -*v.* to add, to make up (for the deficit) 2-7

だす (出す)　　う -*v.* to take out, to prescribe, to submit, くすりをだす to prescribe medicine, しゅくだいをだす to submit homework 2-*1*

たすかります。(助かります)　　*exp.* That will be helpful. 2-4

たすける (助ける)　　る -*v.* to save, to help 2-9

たずねる (訪ねる)　　る -*v.* to visit 2-*11*

たたく　　う -*v.* to hit; to slap 2-*10*

たつまき (竜巻)　　*n.* tornado 2-8

たてもの (建物)　　*n.* building, structure 1-4

たてる (建てる／立てる)　　る -*v.* to build, establish, make. Use 建てる to build something. Otherwise, use 立てる 2-2

たてる (立てる)　　る -*v.* to make something stand up, おとをたてる to make noise 2-*10*

たとえば (例えば)　　*conj.* for example 1-7

たのしい (楽しい)　　い -*adj.* fun 1-6

〜のをたのしみにしています (〜のを楽しみにしています)　　*exp.* to be looking forward to 〜 , お会い出来るのをたのしみにしています。I am looking forward to seeing you. 2-5

たのみ (頼み)　　*n.* request 2-9

たのみ／ねがいをきく (頼み／願いを聞く)　　*exp.* to grant a request 2-9

たのむ (頼む)　　う -*v.* to order, to ask (someone to do 〜) 1-9

たばこ・タバコ (煙草)　　*n.* cigarette 2-*1*

タブレット　　*n.* tablet computer 2-6

たべます (食べます)　　る -*v.* (to) eat. The dictionary form is たべる . 1-3

たべもの (食べ物)　　*n.* food 1-7

たまご (卵／玉子)　　*n.* egg 1-7

だます (騙す)　　う -*v.* to deceive 2-8

たまねぎ (玉ねぎ)　　*n.* onion 2-7

たまらない　　い -*adj.* cannot stand; unbearable 2-*10*

だめ (な) (駄目 (な))　　な -*adj.* no good, impossible, hopeless, not useful, not acceptable 2-4

ためる (貯める)　　る -*v.* to save (money) 2-4

だれ　　*q. word* who 1-4

たんご (単語)　　*n.* vocabulary 2-4

たんじょうび (誕生日) *n.* birthday 1-*8*

たんす (箪笥) *n.* chest; drawers 1-*5*

ち

ちいさい (小さい) い *-adj.* small 1-*4*

チーズ *n.* cheese 1-*9*

ちか (地下) *n.* basement, ちかいっかい B1 1-*8*

ちかい (近い) い *-adj.* close to, near, こうえんにちかい close to the park 2-*5*

ちがう (違う) う *-v.* to be different, AとBはちがう A and B are different. AはBとちがう A is different from B. 2-*3*

ちかく (近く) *loc. n.* near; vicinity 1-*5*

ちかてつ (地下鉄) *n.* subway 2-*5*

チキン *n.* (cooked) chicken 1-*9*

チケット *n.* ticket for entertainment such as movies, theaters, and concerts 2-*6*

ちず (地図) *n.* map 2-*5*

ちち (父) *n.* father (the speaker's) 1-*10*

ちちのひ (父の日) *n.* Father's day 2-*6*

チップ *n.* tip, gratuity 2-*9*

チャーハン *n.* Chinese-style fried rice 1-*9*

ちゃいろい (茶色い) い *-adj.* brown 1-*4*

ちゃわん (茶碗) *n.* rice bowl, (お) ちゃわん (polite) 2-*7*

ちゅう〜 (中〜) *pref.* middle, 中学生 middle school student, 中学校 middle school/junior high school 1-*10*

ちゅうい (注意) *n.* attention; warning, ちゅういする (注意する) to warn; to call attention to, ちゅういをする (注意をする) to warn; to call attention to 2-*10*

ちゅうがく (中学) *n.* junior high school (shortened form of 中学校) 1-*12*

ちゅうかりょうり (中華料理) *n.* Chinese cuisine 1-*9*

ちゅうごく (中国) *n.* China 1-*2*

ちゅうしゃじょう (駐車場) *n.* parking lot 2-*5*

ちゅうもん (注文) *n.* order, ちゅうもんする to order 1-*9*

チョコレート *n.* chocolate 1-*9*

〜 (は) ちょっと *exp.* 〜 in a bit 1-*7*

ちょっと *adv.* a little, a few (more casual than すこし) 1-*8*

ちょっとつごうがわるくて (ちょっと都合が悪くて) *exp.* I'm a little busy. (literally, Sorry, it's a little inconvenient.) 1-*6*

ちょっとようじがあって (ちょっと用事があって) *exp.* Sorry, I have some errands/business to attend to. 1-*6*

ちょっとおねがいがあるんですけど (ちょっとお願いがあるんですけど) *exp.* I have a small favor to ask. 2-*4*

つ

〜つ *count.* general counter (Japanese-origin number) 1-*8*

ツアー *n.* tour 2-*2*

つかう (使う) う *-v.* to use 2-*2*

つかれる (疲れる) る *-v.* to grow tired, つかれている to be tired 2-*1*

つぎ (次) *n.* next 2-*5*

つきあい *n.* keeping company with someone, associating with someone 2-*9*

つきあう う *-v.* to go out with, to keep company with, to have a steady relationship 2-*9*

つきあたり (突き当たり) *n.* at the end of the street, T-road 2-*5*

つぎに (次に) *conj.* next 2-*2*

つく (着く) う *-v.* to arrive, (place) につく to arrive at (a place) 2-*2*

つく (付く) う *-v.* (for something) to turn on 2-*3*

つくえ (机) *n.* desk 1-*5*

つくる (作る) う *-v.* to make 1-*7*

つける (付ける) る *-v.* to attach, apply (medicine) 2-*1*

つける (漬ける・浸ける) 　る -*v.* to dip, to soak, to pickle 2-7

つける (付ける) 　る -*v.* to write (in a diary), にっきをつける (日記を付ける) to keep a diary 2-10

つづく (続く) 　う -*v.* to continue 1-11

つづける (続ける) 　る -*v.* to continue (something) 2-3

つつむ (包む) 　う -*v.* to wrap 2-6

～っていいます。　*exp.* You say ～ . You call it ～ . colloqual version of ～といいます。1-2

～ってなんですか。　*exp.* What does ～ mean? 1-1

つとめる (勤める) 　る -*v.* to become employed, ～につとめている to be employed at, work for 1-10

つま (妻) 　*n.* wife (the speaker's) 1-10

つまらない　い -*adj.* boring 1-6

つまる (詰まる) 　う -*v.* to be clogged 2-1

～つめ (～つ目) 　*suf.* ordinal numbers, ひとつめ (一つ目) first 2-5

つめたい (冷たい) 　い -*adj.* cold 1-9

つもる (積もる) 　う -*v.* to accumulate, ゆきがつもる snow accumulates 1-11

つゆ (梅雨) 　*n.* rainy season 1-11

つよい (強い) 　い -*adj.* strong 1-11

つり (釣り) 　*n.* fishing 1-7

つれていく (連れて行く) 　う -*v.* to take (someone to somewhere) 2-4

つれてくる (連れてくる) 　*irr. v.* to bring (someone) 2-4

て

て (手) 　*n.* hand, arm 1-10

で　*part.* at; in; on; etc. (location of action or event), としょかんでべんきょうします。1-3

で　*part.* by means of; by; with 1-5

で　*part.* limit 2-5

ていしょく (定食) 　*n.* Japanese or Asian-style dish set, set meal さしみていしょく sashimi set 1-9

ていねい (な)(丁寧 (な)) 　な -*adj.* polite 2-9

～ている　*aux. v.* resultant state 1-10

デート　*n.* dating, デートする go out on a date 1-12

テーブル　*n.* table 1-5

でかけます (出かけます) 　る -*v.* (to) go out. The dictionary form is でかける . 1-6

てがみ (手紙) 　*n.* letter 1-6

～てき (な)(～的 (な)) 　*suf.* suffix that converts **kanji** compound nouns to な -adjectives meaning pertaining
　　to ～ , e.g. でんとうてき traditional, せいじてき political, けいざいてき economical or pertaining to economics,
　　しゃかいてき social, ぶんかてき cultural 2-9

てきとう (な)(適当 (な)) 　な -*adj.* appropriate 2-7

でぐち (出口) 　*n.* exit 2-5

でござる　う -*v.* to be (polite verb for です) 2-11

デザート　*n.* dessert 1-9

デジカメ　*n.* digital camera デジタルカメラ 2-2

です　*cop. v.* (to) be 1-2

ですから　*conj.* therefore, so 2-2

テスト　*n.* test 1-4

てつだう (手伝う) 　う -*v.* to assist, to help 2-4

てつづき (手続き) 　*n.* procedure 2-11

テニス　*n.* tennis, テニスをします (to) play tennis 1-6

デパート　*n.* department store 1-4

てまえ (手前) 　*n.* just before 2-5

でも　*conj.* but 1-5

～てもいいですか。*exp.* May I ～ ?, Is it OK to ～ ? 2-1

てら (寺) 　*n.* Buddhist temple, (often used as おてら) 1-12

でる (出る) 　る -*v.* to come out, せきがでる to cough, ねつがでる to run a fever 2-1

でる (出る) 　る -*v.* to leave, うちをでる (家を出る) to leave home, ねつがでる to have a fever 2-2

でる（出る）　る -*v*. to attend, しきに出る to attend a ceremony 2-3
テレビ　*n*. television, TV 1-3
（お）てんき（天気）　*n*. weather 1-11
でんき（電気）　*n*. electricity, electric lamp 2-3
てんきよほう（天気予報）　*n*. weather forecast 1-11
でんしゃ（電車）　*n*. train 2-2, 2-5
でんしレンジ（電子レンジ）　*n*. microwave oven 2-7
でんとうてき（な）（伝統的（な））　な -*adj*. traditional 2-9
てんぷら（天麩羅／天ぷら）　*n*. tempura (fish, shrimp, and vegetables battered and deep-fried) 1-9
でんわ（電話）　*n*. telephone 1-5
でんわばんごう（電話番号）　*n*. telephone number 1-3

と

と　*part*. with, together with (association) 1-6
と　*part*. and (exhaustive listing) 1-6
〜ど（〜度）　*suf*. degree, temperature 1-11
〜ど（〜度）　*suf*. times 1-12
〜と　いいます。／〜って　いいます。　*exp*. It is called 〜 . You say 〜 . 1-1
ドア　*n*. door 1-5
〜という　*exp*. 〜 called 2-5
というのは　*conj*. it's because 2-2
トイレ　*n*. toilet; restroom 1-5
どう　*q. word* how 1-6
どういたしまして。　*exp*. You are welcome. 1-1
どうき（動機）　*n*. a motive, しぼうどうき（志望動機）a motive for applying to a company school, etc. 2-11
〜たらいいですか。　*exp*. Should I do 〜 ?　どうしたらいいですか。What should I do?, 飲んだらいいですか。Should I drink? 2-1
どうして　*q. word* why 1-8
どうしましたか。／どうしたんですか。　*exp*. What's wrong? 2-1
どうそうかい（同窓会）　*n*. reunion party 2-3
〜（は）どうですか。　*exp*. How about 〜 ? 1-7
どうぶつ（動物）　*n*. animal 2-6
どうぶつえん（動物園）　*n*. zoo 1-12
どうも　*adv*. very 1-4
どうもありがとうございます。　*exp*. Thank you very much. 1-2
どうもごちそうさま（でした）。（どうもご馳走様（でした）。）　*exp*. Thank you very much for the meal/drinks. 2-9
どうりょう（同僚）　*n*. co-worker; colleague 2-6
どうろ（道路）　*n*. road, street 2-5
とおい（遠い）　い -*adj*. far from, こうえんからとおい far away from the park 2-5
トースト　*n*. toast 1-9
とおる（通る）　う -*v*. to go through, to pass 2-5
とき（時）　*n*. when, at the time of 〜 , 子供の時 when I was a child 1-12
ときどき（時々）　*adv*. sometimes 1-3
とくに（特に）　*adv*. especially, in particular 2-2
とけい（時計）　*n*. clock; watch 1-5
どこ　*q. word* where 1-2
どこからきましたか。　*exp*. Where are you from? (casual style) 1-2
ところ（所）　*n*. place 1-5
ところで　*conj*. by the way 2-2
とし（年）　*n*. age, としうえ elder, older, としした younger 1-10
とし（年）　*n*. year, age, 年をとる to grow old, 年が上 older 2-3
としうえ（年上）　*n*. older 2-10
としした（年下）　*n*. younger 2-10

としょかん（図書館）　*n.* library 1-3

どちら　*q. word* where (more polite than どこ), which way 1-2

どちらからいらっしゃいましたか。　*exp.* Where are you from? (polite way) 1-2

とっきゅう（れっしゃ）（特急（列車））　*n.* limited express train 2-5

とても　*adv.* very (always used with an affirmative form) 1-4

とどく（届く）　う *-v.* (for something) to arrive, to be delivered 2-4

とどける（届ける）　る *-v.* to deliver, to send 2-4

となり（隣）　*loc. n.* next to 1-5

どの　*demo.* which [+noun] 1-5

どのぐらい・どのくらい　*exp.* how long, how much, how many 1-5

トマト　*n.* tomato 1-7

とまる（泊まる）　う *-v.* to stay, (place) にとまる to stay in (a place) 2-2

とまる（止まる）　う *-v.* (for someone or something) to stop [intransitive verb] 2-5

とめる（止める）　る *-v.* to stop (something) [transitive veb] 2-5

ともだち（友達）　*n.* friend 1-6

どようび（土曜日）　*n.* Saturday 1-3

ドライブ　*n.* driving (for pleasure) 1-7

とり（鳥）　*n.* bird 2-8

とりにく（鶏肉／鳥肉）　*n.* chicken (meat) 2-7

どりょく（努力）　*n.* effort, 努力する to make an effort 2-11

とる（撮る）　う *-v.* to take (a photograph), しゃしんをとる 1-7

とる（取る）　う *-v.* to take 1-8

ドル　*n.* dollar 2-4

どれ　*q. word* which one 1-4

ドレス　*n.* dress 1-8

ドレッシング　*n.* (salad) dressing 2-7

どろぼう（泥棒）　*n.* thief 2-8

どんな　*q. word* what kind of 1-4

な

なあ　*part.* A particle of exclamation to express desires or feelings without addressing anyone in particular. Used in casual speech. 1-12

ナイフ　*n.* knife 2-7

なおす（治す／直す）　う *-v.* to cure, to fix, to repair (something) 2-3

なおる（治る／直る）　う *-v.* (for something) to heal, to be fixed 2-3

なか（中）　*loc. n.* in; inside 1-5

なか（仲）　*n.* relationship (among people), なかがいい（仲がいい）to have a good relationship, なかがわるい（仲が悪い）to have a bad relationship 2-10

ながい（長い）　い *-adj.* long 1-10

なく（泣く）　う *-v.* to cry 1-12

なくなる（亡くなる／無くなる）　う *-v.* to pass away, to die; to disappear, to get lost, to run out of 2-3

なさる　う *-v.* to do (honorific) 2-11

なつ（夏）　*n.* summer 1-11

なつやすみ（夏休み）　*n.* summer holidays, summer break, はるやすみ spring break, ふゆやすみ winter break 1-12

なな、しち（七）　*number* seven 1-3

なに／なん（何）　*q. word* what 1-2

なべ（鍋）　*n.* pot 2-7

なまえ（名前）　*n.* name 1-2

ならう（習う）　う *-v.* to learn 2-9

なんせい（南西）　*n.* southwest 1-11

なんとう（南東）　*n.* southeast 1-11

なんのおかまいもしませんで。（何のおかまいもしませんで。）　*exp.* We did not offer much (by way of treats). 2-9

に

に (二) *number* two 1-3

に *part.* at; on; in (point in time) 10じにねます。1-3

に *part.* to, (goal, activity + に) クラスにいきます。1-3

に *part.* in order to; for (purpose) 1-6

に *part.* to (goal, receiver) 1-6

に *part.* from 〜にもらう (〜からもらう) to receive something from 〜 2-6

〜にします *exp.* to decide on 〜 . 1-9

にがい (苦い) い -*adj.* bitter 1-9

にぎやか (な)(賑やか (な)) な -*adj.* lively (place or event) 1-6

にく (肉) *n.* meat 1-7

にげる (逃げる) る -*v.* to run away, to escape 2-8

にし (西) *n.* west 1-*11*

にじ (二時) *time exp.* two o'clock 1-2

〜にち (〜日) *suf.* day 1-*12*

にちようび (日曜日) *n.* Sunday 1-3

〜について *exp.* about 〜 , そのりょこうについて about the trip 2-2

にっき (日記) *n.* diary, にっきをつける (日記を付ける) to keep a diary 2-10

にねんせい (二年生) *n.* sophomore; second-year student (The suffix せい may be dropped.) 1-2

にほん (日本) *n.* Japan 1-2

にもつ (荷物) *n.* one's belongings, luggage 2-2

にゅういんする (入院する) *irr. v.* to be hospitalized 2-1

にゅうがく (入学) *n.* entering a school 〜ににゅうがくする to enter 〜 2-3

にる (煮る) る -*v.* to boil, to stew 2-7

にわかあめ (にわか雨) *n.* shower (rain) 1-*11*

〜にん (〜人) *suf.* 〜 people 1-*10*

にんぎょう (人形) *n.* doll 2-6

にんじん *n.* carrot 1-7

ぬ

ぬいぐるみ *n.* stuffed animal 2-6

ぬぐ (脱ぐ) う -*v.* to take off (shoes, clothes) 2-2

ぬすむ (盗む) う -*v.* to steal 2-8

ね

ねぎ *n.* green onion 2-7

ネクタイ *n.* tie 1-8

ねこ (猫) *n.* cat 1-5

ねつ (熱) *n.* fever, (high) temperature 2-1

ネックレス *n.* necklace 1-8

ねます (寝ます) る -*v.* (to) go to bed. The dictionary form is ねる . 1-3

〜ねん (〜年) *suf.* year, いちねん first year 1-2

〜ねん (〜年) *suf.* specific year (2008 年), counter for year (十年) 1-*12*

の

の *part.* noun modifier marker (of), ('s) 1-2

ノート *n.* notebook 1-*4*

のこす (残す) う -*v.* to leave (something) 2-3

のこる (残る) う -*v.* (for something) to be left, to remain 2-3

のせる (乗せる) る -*v.* to give a ride (to someone) 2-3

のせる (乗せる) る -*v.* to put on, ごはんにのりをのせる to put seaweed on the rice. Does not apply to clothing. 2-7

〜のち〜　*exp.* after, あめのちはれ clear skies after rain 1-*11*

のど（咽）　*n.* throat 2-*1*

のみます（飲みます）　う -*v.* (to) drink. The dictionary form is のむ. 1-*3*

のみもの（飲み物）　*n.* beverage, drink 1-*7*

のり（海苔）　*n.* seaweed 2-*7*

のりかえる（乗り換える）　る -*v.* to transfer, to change transportation 2-*5*

のる（乗る）　う -*v.* to get on, to ride, ひこうきにのる to get on a plane 1-*12*

は

は　*part.* topic marker 1-2

は（歯）　*n.* tooth 2-*1*

〜はありませんか。　*exp.* Do you have 〜 ? / Do you carry 〜 ? (lit., Isn't there 〜 ?) 1-*8*

〜はにほんごでなんといいますか。　*exp.* How do you say 〜 in Japanese? 1-*1*

パーティ　*n.* party, パーティをします (to) host a party 1-*6*

はい、わかりました。　*exp.* Yes, I understand it. 1-*1*

ええ／はい、そうです。　*exp.* Yes, that's so. 1-*2*

はい／ええ　*inter.* yes 1-*2*

はい／ええ、かまいません。　*exp.* I don't mind. (=yes, please) 2-*1*

はい／ええ、どうぞ。　*exp.* Yes, please. 2-*1*

はい／ええ、もちろん。　*exp.* Yes, of course, sure. 2-*1*

ハイキング　*n.* hiking 1-*7*

はいく（俳句）　*n.* Japanese verse form that consists of three lines, containing five, seven and five syllables respectively. 2-*9*

はいけんする（拝見する）　*irr.v.* to look at (humble) 2-*11*

はいります（入ります）　う -*v.* (to) take (a bath), (to) enter. The dictionary form is はいる. おふろにはいります take a bath 1-*3*

はがき（葉書）　*n.* postcard 2-*4*

はかる（計る）　う -*v.* to measure 2-*1*

はく（吐く）　う -*v.* to exhale, to throw up 2-*1*

〜はく（ぱく）（〜泊）　*suf.* 〜 nights 〜はく（ぱく）〜日 nights and days 2-*2*

ハグ　*n.* hug ハグをする to hug 2-*9*

はく　う -*v.* to put on (skirt, pants, socks, shoes) 1-*10*

はくぶつかん（博物館）　*n.* museum 1-*12*

はこ（箱）　*n.* box 1-*8*

はし（橋）　*n.* bridge 2-*5*

はし（箸）　*n.* chopstick(s) 2-*7*

はじまる（始まる）　う -*v.* (for something) to begin, じゅぎょうがはじまる the class begins 1-*7*, 2-*3*

はじめて（初めて）　*adv.* for the first time 1-*12*

はじめてなんですが。（初めてなんですが。）　*exp.* This is my first time... 2-*1*

はじめまして。〜です。どうぞよろしく。　*exp.* How do you do? I am 〜 . Pleased to meet you. 1-*1*

はじめる（始める）　る -*v.* to begin (something) 2-*3*

ばしょ（場所）　*n.* location 2-*2*

はしる（走る）　う -*v.* to run 2-*1*

バス　*n.* bus 1-*5*

バスケットボール　*n.* basketball (abbreviated as バスケット or バスケ) 1-*7*

バスてい（バス停）　*n.* bus stop 2-*5*

パスポート　*n.* passport 2-*2*

パソコン　*n.* personal computer 2-*6*

バター　*n.* butter 2-*7*

はたらく（働く）　う -*v.* to work 2-*3*

はち（八）　*number* eight 1-*3*

はちうえ（鉢植え）　*n.* potted plant; house plant 2-*6*

はちじ (八時)　*time exp.* eight o'clock 1-*2*

はっきり　*adv.* explicitly 2-*9*

はっけん (発見)　*n.* discovery, 発見する to discover 2-*8*

はな (鼻)　*n.* nose 1-*10*

はな (花)　*n.* flower 2-*6*

はなします (話します)　う -*v.* (to) talk. The dictionary form is はなす. 1-*6*

バナナ　*n.* banana 1-*7*

はは (母)　*n.* mother (the speaker's) 1-*10*

ははのひ (母の日)　*n.* Mother's Day 2-*6*

はやい (速い)　い -*adj.* fast; quick 1-*5*

はやい (早い)　い -*adj.* early 1-*11*

ばら／バラ (薔薇)　*n.* rose 2-*6*

はらう (払う)　う -*v.* to pay 2-*2*

はる (春)　*n.* spring 1-*11*

はれ (晴れ)　*n.* clear skies 1-*11*

はれる (晴れる)　る -*v.* to become sunny 1-*11*

バレンタインデー　*n.* St. Valentine's Day 1-*12*, 2-*6*

ハロウィン　*n.* Halloween 1-*12*

はん (半)　*time exp.* half past いちじはん 1:30 1-*2*

ばん (晩)　*n.* night, evening 1-*3*

パン　*n.* bread 1-*9*

〜ばん (め)(〜番 (目))　*suf.* 〜 th (ordinal suffix) 1-*10*

はんこ (判子)　*n.* seal 2-*4*

ばんごはん (晩御飯)　*n.* supper, dinner (meal eaten in the evening) 1-*3*

はんざい (犯罪)　*n.* crime 2-*8*

〜ばんせん (〜番線)　*suf.* track number (train), 三番線 (さんばんせん) Track 3 2-*5*

パンツ　*n.* trousers, shorts 1-*8*

はんとし (半年)　*n.* a half year 1-*12*

ハンドバッグ　*n.* handbag 1-*8*

ハンバーガー　*n.* hamburger 1-*9*

ひ

ひ (火)　*n.* fire 2-*7*

ひ (日)　*n.* day 2-*10*

ピアノ　*n.* piano 2-*10*

ビーフ　*n.* beef 1-*9*

ビール　*n.* beer 1-*7*

ひえる (冷える)　る -*v.* (for something) to cool down 2-*3*

ひがい (被害)　*n.* damage, loss 2-*8*

ひがえり (日帰り)　*n.* day trip 2-*2*

ひがし (東)　*n.* east 1-*11*

〜ひき (〜匹)　*count.* counter for fish and small four-legged animals 1-*8*

ひきだす (引き出す)　う -*v.* to withdraw (money) 2-*4*

ひく　う -*v.* to catch, かぜをひく to catch a cold 2-*1*

ひく (弾く)　う -*v.* to play (the piano, guitar, other stringed instrument), ピアノをひく to play the piano 2-*10*

ひくい (低い)　い -*adj.* low, カロリーがひくい low in calories 1-*9*

ひくい (低い)　い -*adj.* low 2-*10*

ピクニック　*n.* picnic 1-*6*

ひこうき (飛行機)　*n.* airplane 1-*12*

ピザ　*n.* pizza 1-*9*

ビジネス　*n.* business 1-*2*

びじゅつかん (美術館)　*n.* art museum 1-*12*

ひだり（左）　*loc. n.* to the left; left side 1-5

ひっきしけん（筆記試験）　*n.* a written test 2-11

ひっこし（引っ越し）　*n.* moving (house, residence, etc.) , ひっこし（を）する to move (house, residence) 2-3

ひっこす（引っ越す）　*う -v.* to move (house, etc.), to relocate 2-3

ヒップホップ　*n.* hip-hop music 1-7

ひつよう（な）（必要（な））　*な -adj.* necessary (similar to ～がいる (to need)) 2-11

ビデオ　*n.* video 1-5

ひと（人）　*n.* person; people; human being 1-5

ひどい　*い -adj.* serious (injury) , ひどいけが serious injury 2-1

ひとりっこ（一人っ子）　*n.* an only child 1-10

ひま（な）（暇（な））　*な -adj.* free, idle, unscheduled 1-6

ひゃく（百）　*number* hundred 1-8

ひやす（冷やす）　*う -v.* to chill, to let (something) cool down 2-3

びょういん（病院）　*n.* hospital 1-4

びょうき（病気）　*n.* sickness 2-1

ひらく（開く）　*う -v.* to open, こうざをひらく to open an account 2-4

ひる（昼）　*n.* afternoon 1-3

ビル　*n.* building 1-4

ひるごはん（昼御飯）　*n.* lunch 1-3

ひろい（広い）　*い -adj.* spacious; wide 1-5

ふ

ふうとう（封筒）　*n.* envelope 2-4

プール　*n.* pool 1-6

ふえる（増える）　*る -v.* to increase 2-8

フォーク　*n.* fork 2-7

ぶか（部下）　*n.* junior employee; subordinate 2-6

ふく（服）　*n.* clothing 1-8

ふく（吹く）　*う -v.* to blow 1-11

ふじんふく（婦人服）　*n.* women's clothing 1-8

ふじんふくうりば（婦人服売り場）　*n.* women's clothing section 1-8

ぶたにく（豚肉）　*n.* pork 2-7

ふつう（普通）　*n.* ordinary, regular 2-3

ふつう（れっしゃ）（普通（列車））　*n.* local train, same as かくえきていしゃ（各駅停車）2-5

ふつうよきん（普通預金）　*n.* regular bank acount 2-4

ぶっきょう（仏教）　*n.* Buddhism 2-9

ぶつける　*る -v.* to hit (with a car), to crash into 2-8

フットボール　*n.* (American) football (アメフト is also common.) 1-7

ふとる（太る）　*う -v.* to gain weight, ふとっている to be fat 1-10

ふとん（布団）　*n.* futon 1-5

ふね（船）　*n.* ship, boat 2-2

ふべん（な）（不便（な））　*な -adj.* inconvenient 2-8

ふむ（踏む）　*う -v.* to step on, 足をふむ to step on somebody's foot 2-8

ふゆ（冬）　*n.* winter 1-11

フライドチキン　*n.* fried chicken 1-9

フライパン　*n.* frying pan, skillet 2-7

ブラウス　*n.* blouse 1-8

フランス　*n.* France 1-2

ふる（降る）　*う -v.* to fall (as in rain or snow) 1-11

ふるい（古い）　*い -adj.* old 1-4

フルーツ　*n.* fruit 2-6

プレゼント　*n.* present, gift 1-12

ブログ　*n.* blog 2-9

プロジェクト　*n.* project 2-*11*
ブロンド (ブロンド)　*n.* blond 1-*10*
〜ふん (〜分)　*count.* 〜 minute(s) , (for) 〜 minute(s) 1-*3*
ぶんか (文化)　*n.* culture 2-*9*
ぶんがく (文学)　*n.* literature 1-*2*
ぶんぽう (文法)　*n.* grammar 2-*4*
ぶんぼうぐ (文房具)　*n.* stationery 1-*8*
ぶんぼうぐうりば (文房具売り場)　*n.* stationery section 1-*8*

へ

へ　*part.* to (direction)　がっこうへいきます。To go to school 1-*3*
へえ、そうですか。　*exp.* Oh, I see. 2-*8*
ベッド　*n.* bed 1-*5*
ペット　*n.* pet 2-*6*
へび (蛇)　*n.* snake 2-*8*
へや (部屋)　*n.* room 1-*5*
ベルト　*n.* belt 1-*8*
へん (辺)　*n.* area, このへん (この辺) this area 2-*5*
ペン　*n.* pen 1-*4*
べんきょう (勉強)　*n.* study 1-*3*
べんきょうします (勉強します)　*irr.v.* (to) study. The dictionary form is べんきょうする . 1-*3*
べんごし (弁護士)　*n.* lawyer 2-*3*
へんじ (返事)　*n.* response, reply, へんじをする to respond 2-*3*
へんじ (返事)　*n.* response, へんじ (を) する to respond 2-*11*
べんり (な)(便利 (な))　な -*adj.* convenient 2-*2*

ほ

ほう (方)　*n.* direction 1-*11*
ぼうえき (貿易)　*n.* trading, ぼうえきがいしゃ trading company 2-*3*
ぼうし (帽子)　*n.* hat, cap 1-*8*
ほうちょう (包丁)　*n.* kitchen knife, butcher knife 2-*7*
ボウル　*n.* mixing bowl 2-*7*
ほうれんそう (ほうれん草)　*n.* spinach 2-*7*
ポーク　*n.* pork 1-*9*
ボール　*n.* ball 2-*6*
ボールペン　*n.* ballpoint pen 1-*4*
ほか (他)　*n.* other, ほかの人 other people, ほかの学生 other students 2-*9*
ぼく (僕)　*pron.* I (normally used by males) 1-*2*
ほくせい (北西)　*n.* northwest 1-*11*
ほくとう (北東)　*n.* northeast 1-*11*
ポスト (ポスト)　*n.* public mail collection box 2-*4*
ほそながい (細長い)　い -*adj.* long/elongated 1-*10*
ほっといてくれよ。　*exp.* Leave me alone. (male speech) 2-*10*
ほっといてよ。　*exp.* Leave me alone. (female speech) 2-*10*
ポップス　*n.* pop music 1-*7*
ほめる (誉める)　る -*v.* to praise 2-*8*
ほん (本)　*n.* book 1-*3*
〜ほん (〜本)　*count.* counter for long, cylindrical objects (e.g. bottles, films, pens, pencils) 1-*8*
ほんだな (本棚)　*n.* bookshelf 1-*5*
ほんとう (本当)　*n.* truth, ほんとうに (本当に) indeed; really 2-*10*
ほんとうに／ほんとに (本当に)　*adv.* truly, really, indeed. ほんと (に) is more conversational than
　　ほんとう (に). 1-*11*
ほんとうにいいんですか。(本当にいいんですか。)　*exp.* Are you sure you are OK with it? 2-*4*

ほんのきもちですから。（ほんの気持ちですから。） *exp.* Just a token of my appreciation. 2-6
ほんのすこしですから。（ほんの少しですから。） *exp.* It's not such a big deal., Just a little bit. . . 2-6
ほんや（本屋） *n.* bookstore 1-4

ま

まあまあです。 *exp.* So-so. 2-11
〜まい（〜枚） *count.* counter for thin objects (e.g. film, paper, plates, shirts) 1-8
まい〜（毎〜） *pref.* every　まいしゅう every week, まいあさ every morning, まいばん every night, まいにち every day 1-3
まいあさ（毎朝） *n.* every morning 1-3
まいしゅう（毎週） *n.* every week 1-3
マイナス　*n.* minus 1-11
まいにち（毎日） *n.* every day 1-3
まいばん（毎晩） *n.* every night 1-3
まいる（参る）　う *-v.* to go; to come (humble) 2-11
まえ（前） *loc. n.* in front of; in the front 1-5
〜まえ（〜前） *suf.* 〜 ago, 一年まえ one year ago 1-12
まがる（曲がる）　う *-v.* (for someone or something) to turn [intransitive verb] 2-5
まさか。 *exp.* You're kidding 2-8
まじー *exp.* Are you serious? (very casual) 2-8
まずはじめに（まず始めに） *conj.* first (of all) 2-2
まぜる（混ぜる）　る *-v.* to mix 2-7
まだ　*adv.* still, yet 2-2
また　*conj.* also 2-2
まだまだです。 *exp.* I still have a lot to learn. 2-11
まち（町） *n.* town 1-4
まちがう（間違う）　う *-v.* (for someone) to be mistaken, commonly used as まちがえている 2-3
まちがえる（間違える）　る *-v.* to miss (something); to make a mistake 2-3
まちます（待ちます）　う *-v.* (to) wait. The dictionary form is まつ. 1-6
マッサージ　*n.* massage 2-1
まっすぐ（真っ直ぐ） *adv.* straight 2-5
まつり（祭り） *n.* festival (often used as おまつり) 1-12
まで　*part.* until; to 1-5
までに　*part.* by, 五時までにかえる。 I will come back by 5 o'clock. 2-3
まど（窓） *n.* window 1-5
マヨネーズ　*n.* mayonnaise 2-7
まるい（丸い）　い *-adj.* round 1-10
まん（万） *number* ten thousand 1-8
マンガ（漫画） *n.* cartoon, graphic novel, manga 2-9
まんなか（真ん中） *n.* center, middle, middle child 1-10

み

み（ん）な（皆） *n.* all, everyone, みなさん（皆さん） everyone 2-9
みえる（見える）　る *-v.* can see 〜 (literally: something is visible) 2-5
みおくり（見送り） *n.* farewell, leave taking 2-9
みぎ（右） *loc. n.* to the right 1-5
ミキサー　*n.* (electric) mixer 2-7
みじかい（短い）　い *-adj.* short (length) 1-10
みず（水） *n.* water（おみず is also common.） 1-7
みずうみ（湖） *n.* lake 2-2
みずをきる（水を切る） *exp.* to drain 2-8

みせ（店）　*n.* store, shop 1-*8*
みせる（見せる）　る -*v.* to show 1-*8*
みそ（味噌）　*n.* soybean paste 2-*7*
みち（道）　*n.* road, street, way 2-*5*
みちなりに（道なりに）　*exp.* following the road 2-*5*
みてください。　*exp.* Please look at it. 1-*1*
みなみ（南）　*n.* south 1-*11*
みます（見ます）　る -*v.* (to) see, (to) watch. The dictionary form is みる . 1-*3*
みみ（耳）　*n.* ear 1-*10*
ミュージカル　*n.* musical 1-*12*
ミルク　*n.* milk (for babies), creamer (for coffee etc.) 1-*7*

む

むかいがわ（向かい側）　*n.* the other side, the opposite side 2-*5*
むかえ（迎え）　*n.* meeting, greeting, むかえに行く／来る to go/come to pick up (someone) 2-*9*
むしあつい（蒸し暑い）　い -*adj.* humid 1-*11*
むす（蒸す）　う -*v.* to steam 2-*7*
むずかしい（難しい）　い -*adj.* difficult 1-*6*
むだ（な）（無駄（な））　な -*adj.* useless, wasteful 2-*8*
むね（胸）　*n.* chest, breast 2-*1*
むり（無理）　*n.* overwork, overstrain, むりをする to overwork, to overdo it 2-*1*
むりをする（無理をする）　*exp.* to push oneself too hard, to overwork 2-*1*

め

め（目）　*n.* eye 1-*10*
めいわく（迷惑）　*n.* trouble, めいわくをかける（迷惑をかける) to give (someone) problems 2-*10*
めいわく（な）（迷惑（な））　な -*adj.* めいわくをかける to give (someone) trouble, to inconvenience (someone) 2-*10*
〜メートル　*suf.* meter (distance measurement), 10 メートル ten meters 2-*5*
メール　*n.* email 1-*6*
めがね（眼鏡）　*n.* eyeglasses 1-*10*
メキシコ　*n.* Mexico 1-*2*
めしあがる（召し上がる）　う -*v.* to eat; to drink (honorific) 2-*11*
めんせつ（面接）　*n.* interview, めんせつしけん an oral exam, interview 2-*11*

も

も　*part.* similarity marker (also, too) 1-*2*
もう　*adv.* 〜 more, another 〜 1-*8*
もう　*adv.* already, yet, any more 2-*2*
もういちどいってください。　*exp.* Please say it again. (Teacher's request) 1-*1*
もういちどおねがいします。　*exp.* Please say it again. (Student's request) 1-*1*
もうすこし（もう少し）　*adv.* a little more 1-*8*
もうすこしゆっくりおねがいします。　*exp.* Please say it slowly. 1-*1*
もうちょっと　*adv.* a little more 1-*8*
もうしあげる（申し上げる）　る -*v.* to say (humble) 2-*11*
もうしこむ（申し込む）　う -*v.* to apply, もうしこみようし application form 2-*4*
もうしわけありません。（申し訳ありません）　*exp.* I'm sorry. (polite and formal) 2-*10*
もうしわけございません。（申し訳ございません。）　*exp.* I'm sorry. (very polite and formal) 2-*10*
もうす（申す）　う -*v.* to say (humble) 2-*11*
もくようび（木曜日）　*n.* Thursday 1-*3*
もしもし　*exp.* Hello (on the phone) 2-*2*
もつ（持つ）　う -*v.* to hold, もっている to be holding, to own 2-*2*
もっていく（持って行く）　う -*v.* to take something 2-*2*

もってくる（持って来る）　*irr. v.* to bring (something) 2-4

もっと　*adv.* more 1-7

もどる（戻る）　う -*v.* (for someone) to return 2-2

もの（物）　*n.* (tangible) thing 1-5

もらう　う -*v.* to receive, to get 1-12

もんく（文句）　*n.* complaint, もんくをいう（文句を言う）to complain 2-10

もんだい（問題）　*n.* problem 2-9

や

〜や（〜屋）　*suf.* retail store, owner of the retail store, さかなや fish market, にくや butcher, はなや flower shop, 本屋 bookstore 1-4, 2-3

や　*part.* and (when listing examples), おちゃやコーヒー tea, coffee, and so on 1-7

やきゅう（野球）　*n.* baseball 1-7

やく（焼く）　う -*v.* to bake, to fry, to grill 2-7

やくにたつ（役に立つ）　*exp.* useful 2-6

やける（焼ける）　る -*v.* to burn 2-8

やさい（野菜）　*n.* vegetable 1-7

やさしい（易しい／優しい）　い -*adj.* easy（易しい）, kind（優しい）1-6

やさしい　ことばで　いってください。（やさしい言葉で言って下さい。）　*exp.* Please say it in easier words. 1-8

やすい（安い）　い -*adj.* inexpensive 1-7

やすみ（休み）　*n.* rest; absence, a day off 1-6

やすみのひ（休みの日）　*n.* a day off; holiday 1-6

やすむ（休む）　う -*v.* to rest 2-1

やせる　る -*v.* to lose weight, やせている to be thin 1-10

やとう（雇う）　う -*v.* to employ 2-11

やま（山）　*n.* mountain 1-5

やまのぼり（山登り）　*n.* mountain climbing 1-12

やむ（止む）　う -*v.* to stop, 雨がやむ the rain stops 1-11

やめる（止める）　る -*v.* to quit doing (something) 2-1

やめろ。　*exp.* Cut it out. (male speech) 2-10

やりがい（やり甲斐）　*n.* worth doing, やりがいがある it is worth doing 2-11

やる　う -*v.* to give (to socially subordinate person) 2-6

やる　う -*v.* to do 2-7

やわらかい（柔らかい）　い -*adj.* soft 1-9

ゆ

ゆ（湯）　*n.* warm water, hot water 2-3

ゆうえんち（遊園地）　*n.* amusement park 1-12

ゆうがた（夕方）　*n.* evening 1-11

ゆうびんうけ（郵便受け）　*n.* mailbox to receive mail 2-4

ゆうびんきょく（郵便局）　*n.* post office 1-4

ゆうびんばんごう（郵便番号）　*n.* postal code 2-4

ゆうめい（な）（有名（な））　な -*adj.* famous 1-4

ゆか（床）　*n.* floor 2-9

ゆき（雪）　*n.* snow 1-11

ユダヤきょう（ユダヤ教）　*n.* Judaism 2-9

ゆっくり　*adv.* slowly, ゆっくりします to relax; (to) take it easy 1-6

ゆでる（茹でる）　る -*v.* (to) boil, (to) poach 2-7

ゆび（指）　*n.* finger 2-1

ゆびわ（指輪）　*n.* ring 1-8

ゆるす（許す）　う -*v.* to forgive 2-10

ゆれる（揺れる）　る -*v.* to shake 2-8

よ

ようし（用紙）　*n.* form 2-4

ようしょく（洋食）　*n.* western style cuisine 1-9

～ようび（～曜日）　*suf.* days of the week 1-3

ようふく（洋服）　*n.* western style clothes (not traditional Japanese attire) 2-6

よきん（預金）　*n.* bank account, よきんする to deposit money, よきんがある to have money in the bank 2-4

よく　　*adv.* often, well 1-3

よこ（横）　*loc. n.* next to; at the side of 1-5

よごす（汚す）　う -*v.* to make (something) dirty 2-3

よこになる（横になる）　*exp.* to lie down 2-1

よごれる（汚れる）　る -*v.* (for something) to become dirty 2-3

よじ（四時）　*time exp.* four o'clock 1-2

よてい（予定）　*n.* schedule, plan, よていをたてる to make plans 2-2

よなか（夜中）　*n.* late at night, the middle of the night 2-10

よねんせい（四年生）　*n.* senior; fourth-year student (The suffix せい may be dropped.) 1-2

よびます（呼びます）　う -*v.* (to) call (someone); (to) invite. The dictionary form is よぶ. 1-6

よみます（読みます）　う -*v.* (to) read. The dictionary form is よむ. 1-3

よやく（予約）　*n.* reservation, きっぷのよやくをする／きっぷをよやくする to reserve a ticket 2-2

よる（夜）　*n.* night 1-11

よる（寄る）　う -*v.* to drop by 2-5

よるおそくまで（夜遅くまで）　*exp.* until late at night 2-1

よろこぶ（喜ぶ）　う -*v.* to be pleased 2-6

よろしい　い -*adj.* good (polite) 2-11

よわい（弱い）　い -*adj.* weak 1-11

よん、し（四）　*number* four 1-3

よんで ください。　*exp.* Please read. 1-1

ら

ラーメン　*n.* Chinese-style noodle soup 1-9

らい～（来～）　*pref.* next, 来（らい）学期 next semester/quarter/term、来週 next week, 来月 next month, 来年 next year 2-4

ライオン　*n.* lion 2-8

らいげつ（来月）　*n.* next month 1-12

ライス　*n.* rice 1-9

らいねん（来年）　*n.* next year 1-2

らくがき（落書き）　*n.* graffiti, らくがきをする（落書きをする）to write graffiti 2-10

らくご（落語）　*n.* rakugo, traditional storytelling performance 2-9

ラップ　*n.* rap music 1-7

ランチ　*n.* lunch, A ランチ Lunch set A 1-9

り

りっぱ（な）（立派（な））　な -*adj.* fine; splendid; nice 1-4

リボン　*n.* ribbon, リボンをかける to put on a ribbon 2-6

りゆう（理由）　*n.* reason (for doing something) 2-9

りゅうがく（留学）　*n.* study abroad, りゅうがく（を）する to study abroad, りゅうがくせい international student 2-3

りゅうがくせい（留学生）　*n.* foreign/international student 1-2

りょう　*n.* dormitory 1-4

りょうしん（両親）　*n.* parents 1-6

りょうり（料理）　*n.* cooking; cuisine, りょうりをします (to) fix a meal 1-6

りょかん（旅館）　*n.* Japanese-style inn 2-2

りょこう（旅行）   *n.* traveling, りょこうする (to) travel 1-7
りれきしょ（履歴書）   *n.* CV (curriculum vitae) 2-*11*
りんご   *n.* apple 1-7

る

ルーム   *n.* room, コンピュータ・ルーム computer room, computer lab 1-5

れ

れい（零）   *number* zero 1-3
れきし（歴史）   *n.* history 1-2
レストラン   *n.* restaurant 1-4
レタス   *n.* lettuce 1-7
レポート   *n.* report, term paper, term project 2-4
れんしゅう（練習）   *n.* practice, れんしゅうする to practice 2-4
れんらく（連絡）   *n.* contact, 〜にれんらくする to make contact with ; to get in touch with 2-*11*

ろ

ろく（六）   *number* six 1-3
ろくじ（六時）   *time exp.* six o'clock 1-2
ロック   *n.* rock and roll 1-7

わ

ワイン   *n.* wine 1-7
ワイングラス   *n.* wine glass 2-6
わかい（若い）   い-*adj.* young, わかい is used to describe teenagers and young people older than teenagers, but not small children. 2-3
わかす（沸かす）   う-*v.* to bring (water, bath) to boil 2-3
わかりましたか。   *exp.* Do you understand (it)? 1-*1*
わかる（分かる）   う-*v.* to understand, 〜がわかる 1-*10*
わかれる（別れる）   る-*v.* to leave, to break up 2-8
わく（沸く）   う-*v.* (for water, bath) to be boiled 2-3
わしょく（和食）   *n.* Japanese cuisine（にほんりょうり）1-9
わすれる（忘れる）   る-*v.* to forget 2-*1*
わたし（私）   *pron.* I (used by both males and females) 1-2
わたる（渡る）   う-*v.* to cross (bridge, road, etc.) 2-5
わるい（悪い）   い-*adj.* bad 1-*11*
わるい（悪い）   い-*adj.* bad, かおいろがわるい look pale 2-*1*
わるくち（悪口）   *n.* bad-mouthing, speaking ill of a person 2-8
ワンピース   *n.* dress (worn on informal occasions) 1-8

を

を   *part.* direct object marker, ほんをよみます。1-3
を   *part.* from, じゅぎょうを休む be absent from a class 2-*1*
を   *part.* place in which movement occurs 2-5
を   *part.* out of 〜, from 〜 2-5
〜をおねがいします（〜をお願いします）   *exp.* I would like to have 〜. 1-9
〜をください（〜を下さい）   *exp.* Please give me 〜. 1-8

INDEX

日本地図
に ほん ち ず

韓国
かんこく

N
W E
S

0   100   200 Km.
0   100   200 Mi.

松江
まつえ

福岡
ふくおか

山口
やまぐち

広島
ひろしま

⑥

鳥取
とっとり

金沢
かなざわ

福井
ふくい

富山
と

長崎
ながさき

大分
おおいた

松山
まつやま

岡山
おかやま

⑤

神戸
こう

京都
きょうと

岐阜
ぎ ふ

④

熊本
くまもと

⑧

高松
たかまつ

⑦

高知
こうち

徳島
とくしま

大阪
おおさか

奈良
な ら

名古屋
なごや

甲府
こう ふ

鹿児島
かごしま

宮崎
みやざき

和歌山
わ か やま

静岡
しずおか

沖縄
おきなわ

那覇
な は

0   10   20 Km.
0   10   20 Mi.

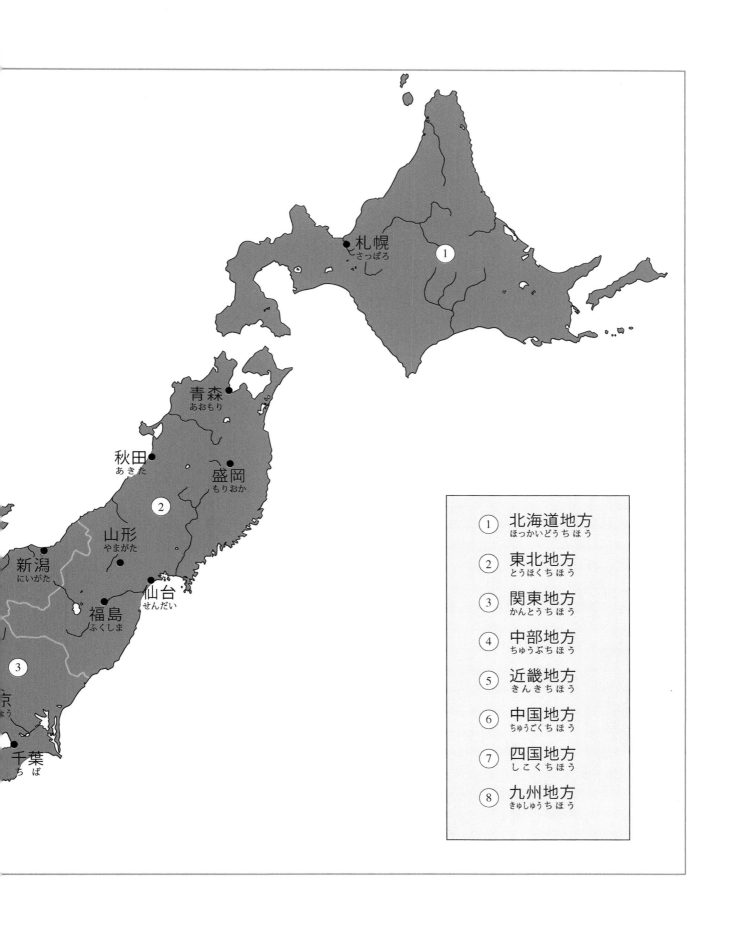

① 北海道地方
　ほっかいどうちほう

② 東北地方
　とうほくちほう

③ 関東地方
　かんとうちほう

④ 中部地方
　ちゅうぶちほう

⑤ 近畿地方
　きんきちほう

⑥ 中国地方
　ちゅうごくちほう

⑦ 四国地方
　しこくちほう

⑧ 九州地方
　きゅうしゅうちほう

札幌
さっぽろ

青森
あおもり

秋田
あきた

盛岡
もりおか

山形
やまがた

新潟
にいがた

仙台
せんだい

福島
ふくしま

京
ょう

千葉
ば

ち